INTERNATIONAL ECONOMIC PROBLEMS AND POLICIES

INTERNATIONAL ECONOMIC PROBLEMS AND POLICIES

H. Peter Gray
Rutgers University

ST. MARTIN'S PRESS, INC.
New York

cover design: Darby Downey
text design: Helen Granger/Levavi & Levavi

ISBN: 0–312–42088–9

Acknowledgments

Mark Drabenstott, "U.S. Agriculture: The International
Dimension," *Economic Review,* November 1985, pp. 3–8.
Reprinted by permission of the Federal Reserve Bank
of Kansas City.

Joseph G. Kvasnicka, "Mexico's Stop-and-Go Road to
Economic Prosperity," International Letter No. 548,
July 1985. Reprinted by permission of the Federal
Reserve Bank of Chicago.

Ingo Walter, "Crisis in Trade Policy," *NYU Business,* 1
(Fall 1981/Winter 1982), pp. 17–20. Reprinted by
permission.

Preface

Any textbook author makes three basic decisions: the level at which to explore the material, the range of material to be included, and the sequence in which to present it. Let me address these points directly so that readers will have a good understanding of what this book aims to accomplish; it is for them to judge the success of the venture.

LEVEL OF MATERIAL Determining the level of rigor for a text involves first defining the target group of students for whom it is intended and then deciding the degree to which the complexities of reality can be countenanced.

This book is aimed primarily at students taking a one-semester survey course in international economics for which the only prerequisite is two semesters of introductory economics. With some additional reading assignments, the text could be used in a two-semester course as well. The purpose of the book is to provide students with a feeling for—a grasp of—international economics. The goal is not to lay the first foundations in developing international economists; that requires a two-semester course of greater range and rigor in all areas of coverage. Keeping that in mind, I have used as my representative introductory text the eighth edition of McConnell's *Economics;* any analytical device not found there is fully explained when it first appears in this text.

The study of any branch of economics involves two difficulties: those inherent in the subject itself and those relating to the abstract tools of analysis which are to be used. Clearly, these overlap. To portray complex phenomena with precision we need highly sophisticated, specialized tools of analysis, and even then some concepts defy precise analysis. In attempting to convey the niceties of certain international economic relationships, however, our discipline often postulates a static world, to the detriment of conveying reality in much of our analyses. Some recognition of change is needed, for international economics entails complex interrelationships that undergo rapid change on occasion. Some of these dynamics can be explained, if not precisely modeled, in nondifficult terms. Yet neither the difficulties of subject nor those of techniques can be reduced beyond a certain point, for the vital cogs in international economic relationships must be understood if students are to obtain a minimal grasp of the material. This book, then, seeks to countenance the complexities of our subject while keeping the reliance on abstruse analytical devices to the minimum.

RANGE OF MATERIAL   Consensus exists concerning the core material for a survey of international economics as well as for various interests and preferences that might be termed "second level." This book offers both and allows a choice of emphasis (although the choices are still restricted by limited space and time). It includes more material than most instructors will want to cover in a one-semester course, unless the secondary material is covered lightly. Multinational corporations—though not central—have been included because they are quantitatively important. Similarly, the European Economic Community is covered, even though its star seems to be fading currently; it provides a useful consideration of intra-industry trade and also is quantitatively important. Commercial policy and balance-of-payments problems are continuing sources of international economic strain and negotiation. And the international financial system and the trade patterns of developing countries both have their fascination.

Some material (Chapters 8, 10, and 12, for example), can be left to students for individual study and need not be covered in class. The chapter-ending supplements also may be handled independently: Some contain technical information, and others present examples of cases and issues that are deemed interesting and the stuff of which lively class discussions are made.

SEQUENCE OF MATERIAL   The text has been organized so that instructors may begin either by covering trade and commercial policy—and anticipating balance-of-payments problems—or by initiating the survey via financial problems and then moving to resource allocation. Instructors who prefer to begin with balance-of-payments aspects of international economics might consider the following sequence:

Introductory material—Chapters 1 and 2
International payments—Chapters 12 through 15
International financial system—Chapters 16 through 18
International trade—Chapters 3 through 5
International trade policy—Chapters 6 through 11
Multinational corporations—Chapters 19 through 21

Contents

INTERNATIONAL
ECONOMIC
PROBLEMS
AND POLICIES

BACKGROUND

The growth of international trade has been spectacular since World War II ended in 1945, and nations have benefited from this growth. A concomitant feature of that growth is a world in which no nation is as immune to events that take place abroad as it once was. The technical term for this state is "interdependence." The new high level of interdependence has resulted from technological innovations, and it encompasses both trade in goods and services and investments in assets. The international world is more complex than the simple world of a closed economy, which has no "external interaction," and shocks or disturbances that occur abroad impinge on the domestic economy. Sometimes governments erect barriers against international trade (imports of foreign goods) to try to isolate themselves from these developments, but they do so at a cost. While some changes take place in the supply and demand for a single good or group of closely related goods, other changes intrude because of macroeconomic developments. The latter make themselves felt mainly through changes in the rate of exchange between two national currencies.

1

1

Growing International Economic Involvement

 $\mathbf{W}$ hether we like it or not, the United States is becoming steadily more closely linked to the rest of the world. This growing interdependence exists in both the economic and the political dimensions. Indeed, the two dimensions cannot be kept separate. International economic policy is now recognized as impinging on the "high politics" of intergovernmental relationships: conflicts on economic matters have tended to escalate into factors that affect the tone of political relationships, and vice versa.[1] Public awareness of this fact is tending to lag behind reality. Foreigners' actions can and do affect the prosperity and resilience of the American economy, the profits of American firms, and the wage rates of American workers.

Examples of our growing interdependence are commonplace. Our vulnerability to political unrest in the Persian Gulf is shared with oil-importing nations in Europe and Asia. The American banking system has been made less robust by excessive lending to foreigners, including loans of more than $55 billion to Argentina, Brazil, and Mexico. In Africa, the United States walks a political tightrope between black African nations and the Republic of South Africa. Both blocs supply raw materials that are essential to the smooth running of the world economy. American multinational corporations have substantial assets in South Africa. Pressures of imports of manufactured goods from Japan, Korea, and Taiwan

---

[1]See Richard N. Cooper, "Trade Policy Is Foreign Policy," *Foreign Policy*, (Winter 1973), pp. 18–76, for the classic argument.

are disrupting employment in their counterpart industries in North America.

The need for an understanding of international economic relations applies to voters, politicians, business persons, and economists. This book provides a practical approach. Alfred Marshall, a famous English economist, described economics in the following terms:

> Economic science is but the working of common sense aided by the appliances of organized analysis and general reasoning, which facilitate the task of collecting, arranging, and drawing inferences from particular facts. Though its scope is always limited, though its work without the aid of common sense is vain, yet it enables common sense to go further in difficult problems than would otherwise be possible.[2]

It is in this spirit that this book is written. Practical considerations that affect economic policies are to be stressed, and theory is introduced as a means to an end. The book emphasizes the interrelationship between political and economic aspects of foreign relations and identifies three important subareas: the exchange of goods among nations (international trade) and impediments placed in the way of such trade (commercial policy), the acquisition of foreign assets (including investments by multinational corporations), and the problems of international finance (the balance of payments).

International trade (including trade in services as well as trade in basic commodities and manufactured products) is carried out among residents of different nations because they can gain by exchanging goods that they produce for goods made by foreigners. The gain is mutual. In this context a good can be a barrel of oil from the Middle East or a haircut bought in France by an American in Paris. Trade covers a wide range of transactions that involve goods produced for sale. The traditional interest in this subject is the forces that determine which goods a nation will export (sell to foreigners) and which it will import (buy from foreigners). A closely related area of interest is commercial policy. Commercial policy is any tax or regulation imposed by a government in order to affect the pattern and composition of international trade. Usually commercial policy is designed to benefit the economy of the country imposing the measure; even more commonly in democracies, commercial policy is instituted to protect the interests of a vocal pressure group—to benefit one segment of the economy. On occasion the role of commercial policy is more political than economic, and its intent is to damage a foreign economy. On these occasions it is called "trade warfare" and has, as its purpose, to inflict damage on an antagonist even though the home economy

[2]Alfred Marshall, *The Principles of Economics,* 8th ed. (London: Macmillan, 1920), p. 38.

may also be damaged. These two topics will be of considerable interest to Americans for the remainder of the twentieth century.

International investment involves the acquisition of an asset located abroad by an American or of an asset located in the United States by a foreigner. There are two distinct types of investment—the acquisition of physical assets and the acquisition of financial assets. Of these, the former is more interesting in terms of current policy issues because it involves multinational corporations (MNCs). A multinational corporation is a large (usually privately owned) corporation that operates profit-seeking units in two or more countries. The growth of multinational corporations has been phenomenal. The value of assets owned abroad by American MNCs increased from $56.6 billion in 1967 to $168.1 billion in 1978. The amount of investment in the United States by foreign multinationals grew from a book value of $14 billion in 1972 to $68.4 billion in 1980.[3] These foreign corporations can become important influences in the operation of national economies and impinge upon the sovereignty (or economic independence) of the host nation. Though MNCs indisputably provide benefits, they also raise policy problems and can create international political strains.

The balance of payments of a nation is a record of the dealings by residents of one country with residents of the rest of the world. Just as a single individual has to ensure that he or she has cash available to cover his or her spending, so too does a nation—this is the problem of balance-of-payments policy. How does a nation correct a situation in which its residents are spending more abroad than they obtain from abroad? Is there an automatic mechanism that will ensure the needed correction? What is of interest here is the macroeconomic repercussions on employment and prosperity of a tendency to spend more abroad than is being obtained from abroad.

These three areas of interest are examined separately in this book, although the interrelationship of the sectors will be referred to from time to time. The concluding chapter will put the three subareas into a joint focus.

Nothing in economics is completely separate. International trade and commercial policy do have macroeconomic implications but are essentially microeconomic. Problems in trade and "protection" (as commercial policy is frequently called) deal with the behavior of a firm or industry and the allocation of economic resources in a country and in the world. Except when macroeconomic considerations are explicitly introduced (as when the argument for a tariff is that it will reduce domestic unemployment), the underlying assumption is always that the country is fully employed or will attain full employment quite quickly once the repercussions of

[3]Data are taken from Neil Hood and Stephen Young, *The Economics of Multinational Corporations* (London: Longman, 1978), and Jane Sneddon Little, "Recent Trends in Foreign Direct Investment in the United States," in H. Peter Gray, ed., *Uncle Sam as Host* (Greenwich, Conn.: JAI Press, 1986).

some change in conditions or in policy work themselves out. Foreign investment by MNCs is also mainly microeconomic. The problems here are the problems of an individual firm and its ability to earn a larger profit by establishing production and sales units in foreign countries. There are macroeconomic aspects to the behavior of MNCs—for employment in the country of origin and for its balance of payments—but the primary questions are, how does the individual MNC fare, and what makes it possible for it to earn a larger profit by establishing foreign subsidiary firms? Balance-of-payments analysis is, in contrast, almost purely macroeconomic. The policy approach to the elimination of a deficit in balance of payments (spending more abroad than foreigners spend at home) is conducted in almost exactly the same analytic framework as attaining full employment in macroeconomic principles. Monetary policy, fiscal policy, and levels of employment all affect the balance of payments, and to these familiar instruments must be added exchange-rate policy. Finally, the operation of the international financial system and its strength are closely analogous to the commercial banking system's ability to withstand some traumatic event in a closed, national economy. This, too, is essentially macroeconomic, because the analyst is concerned with the interaction of sectors of the economy and is only peripherally concerned with the behavior of an individual economic unit.

The organization of the book is such that the reader can approach the problems of international economic policy in either of two ways. The subject matter lends itself to studying the macroeconomic aspects first and then concentrating on the microeconomic phenomena; the subject matter can equally as well be studied by examining the causation of international trade, commercial policy, and MNC behavior first and then continuing on to examine the macroeconomic aspects of the international economic system. At the instructor's behest, the macroeconomic aspects may precede or follow the microeconomic topics. As the book is written, the international trade and protection problems come first and are followed by the macroeconomic problems of the balance of payments in Part IV. But Parts IV and V can precede Parts II and III without any loss of clarity.

Part I provides the background. After the introductory chapter, a short chapter describes the monetary setting in which international transactions take place. This background chapter is vital if the microeconomic aspects of international trade are to precede the macroeconomic problems of balance of payments. But it is also useful as a stage setter if the monetary and balance-of-payments aspects are to be studied first. Monetary considerations are important because buyers and sellers use different currencies, so international transactions always involve two kinds of money. Perhaps more than any other, the problem of reconciling two different monetary units distinguishes international economic phenomena from their national equivalents. Because one party to the transactions must incur costs denominated in one currency and receipts in a second currency, another degree of risk is introduced into all trade and investment. The student must therefore develop a familiarity with the rate of exchange between two currencies and with the way in which the foreign exchange market works.

People in smaller nations with more proximate foreign countries (and currencies) develop a much greater familiarity with the conversion of units of one currency into another and how this will affect trade and investment patterns. With much greater proportions of consumption goods imported or containing imported ingredients and with much more frequent travel abroad, people in European and Asian countries tend to be much more aware of the variability of exchange rates over time than are American students. Until recently, foreign goods affected the U.S. economy relatively less (because of the broad resource base of the United States), and few students travel abroad enough to develop a sense of the peculiarities of foreign currencies in terms of dollars. Excepting those who live near our borders, American students tend to be at a disadvantage in their understanding of exchange rates. Yet such is the growth of MNCs that roughly one student in five who graduate from college in the United States will work for a firm with an international involvement. It is not an exaggeration to say that an understanding of foreign exchange markets and exchange rates should be as much a part of the arsenal of every student as the knowledge of how to make a computer do simple, straightforward things.

Part II deals with the pattern and the quantity of international trade. Why do nations exchange goods? What are the benefits that derive from these exchanges? Do these benefits vary according to the type of good traded? How do money prices guide the buyer, and how are these money prices arrived at? What of goods that a nation cannot produce at home? These are called "noncompetitive" imports because they do not compete with domestic production. They prove to be very important elements in the gains from international trade and crucial to trade warfare—(sanctions) a deliberate attempt by one country to damage the economy of an antagonist nation.

Chapter 3 sets out the first rudimentary theory of international trade. Chapter 4 is concerned with the basic modern theory (based on factor proportions) and demonstrates that a very simple version is not adequate to explain the modern world. Chapter 5 introduces some of the complications necessary for an understanding of modern patterns of international trade.

Part III concerns commercial policy. The most common weapon in commercial policy is the tariff—a tax levied on foreign-made but not on domestically made goods. Chapter 6 begins by setting down the traditional argument for the nonexistence of tariffs and similar instruments of commercial policy. This is the argument for free trade. It is a powerful argument. Chapter 7 deals with the mechanics of tariffs and similar measures, the ways in which they are used, and the ways in which they affect the pattern of international trade. This chapter also assesses individual arguments for protection. But all measures of commercial policy are imposed by political decision, so the student must understand the political aspects of commercial policy, both within the nation that imposes tariffs and in the international arena, where nations conspire to set up organizations that will blunt the pressure of domestic industries and keep the world economy moving toward free trade. Chapter 9 considers the problems of an advanced nation when world trading conditions change quickly— the problem of adjustment. Chapters 10 and 11 are devoted to two special matters. Chapter 10 considers the problems of developing nations, in many of which the argument for free trade is rejected firmly. This chapter considers the problems of commercial policy from the point of view of this very important group of nations and their "dialogue" with the developed world. Chapter 11 deals with the success story of the post–World War II world, the European Economic Community (EEC). The EEC is a special problem in commercial policy because the member nations combined to establish free trade among themselves and a common set of tariffs to outsiders. This is the phenomenon of *economic integration*. It also requires that a new approach to international trade be formulated to analyze the transactions among the member nations (and, to a lesser degree, among all developed manufacturing nations). The EEC was blessed with great economic success, at least until the global recession of the late 1970s and early 1980s.

Part IV tackles the macroeconomic problem of balance-of-payments adjustment. The automatic cure, the policy-invoked cure, and the impact of either cure on the welfare of people at home and abroad are the main aspects of the problem. Here it is important to distinguish between causes of imbalance. For example, the imbalance that derives from high prices for imported oil gives rise to a different kind of policy reaction than an imbalance caused by cost-push inflation in one country but not in others.

It may be useful here to distinguish three kinds of shocks or disturbances to the international economic system that will induce change and may require action by policymakers. A *cyclical* shock takes place when a country lapses into a recession and its trading partner does not. The trading partner loses some demand for exports and finds that it is spending more abroad than it is taking in from foreigners. There is a tendency for the government in the trading partner to try to preserve its (foreign exchange) reserves under such circumstances, and this could induce a recession in the trading partner and aggravate the situation. Correct policy, then, is for the trading partner to resist any temptation to fall into recession, while the country in recession tries to reestablish a satisfactory rate of capacity utilization and is not constrained by an international payments deficit. A *price-level* disturbance takes place when two trading-partner nations are suffering from inflation at different rates so that one country's goods become relatively more expensive under a system of fixed rates of exchange. If the exchange rate is allowed to change in sympathy with the two rates of inflation ($\Delta\epsilon = \Delta p_1 - \Delta p_2$) (where Δ represents a small change),[4] the disparity in rates of inflation does *not* cause an international disturbance. In terms developed in Chapter 12, the real rate of exchange will remain constant. This should occur when the world operates under a system of flexible exchange rates (as now). Finally, there is a *real* disturbance, which features a change in the underlying conditions of supply and demand in major countries or in major commodities. The most obvious recent example is the two huge increases in the price of oil in 1974 and 1979 and the weakening of oil prices in 1983 through 1985 and their spectacular decline in early 1986.

Part V describes the development of the world's financial system. This is the setting in which balance-of-payments adjustments have to take place. It is also the source of discipline for a national government faced with the problem that its international reserves are declining rapidly because foreigners are spending less in the home country than home-country citizens are spending abroad. The chapters look briefly at the gold standard in its heyday in the period between the defeat of Napoleon at Waterloo and the outbreak of World War I in 1914, the financial chaos that took place between the two world wars, and how that debacle contributed to the depth of the Depression in the 1930s. Finally, the material looks at the present system and the strains to which it is subjected.

Part VI addresses the benefits and problems that result from having factors of production (capital, technology, and skilled workers) migrate among nations. The main emphasis in this part is on the role and contribution of multinational corporations: how an MNC functions and its costs and benefits for the global economy—including, of course, the political costs and benefits faced by both home (parent) and host countries.

Chapter 22 concludes the book by examining the interrelationships among the three blocks of subject matter treated more or less separately: trade and commercial policy, international financial problems, and multinational corporations.

A familiarity with the material presented in this book will provide business executives with a better background in international economic facts and relationships. In a recent study of the importance of international expertise in the major corporations of the United States, Professor Stephen J. Kobrin of New York University found strong agreement that international involvement by managers had increased strongly since the mid-1970s and was expected to increase into the 1990s.[5] This greater involvement took place in the face of a reduction of numbers of Americans

---

[4] The changes should be seen as percentages, so Δp_1 is the percentage inflation in country 1 per year.
[5] Stephen J. Kobrin, *International Expertise in American Business* (Washington, D.C.: Institution for International Education, 1985).

working abroad. A familiarity with this material will also lead to better-informed voters who have a broader awareness of the effects of foreign events on the home economy and the limits of the power of the home government to offset them.[6] The material is also of value to economists who might become less willing to bury themselves in ivory-tower models of closed economies.

International economics is a living subject. As time passes, some problems grow less urgent and others take their place. The political strains and realities of the world wax and wane. The final fifteen years of the twentieth century are likely to be dominated by several international problems. As in all things international, matters of war and peace and political relationships take precedence over the achievement of narrow economic goals. If détente and peace are the biggest issues, what will economics and economic know-how contribute to these problems and their solution? One force to be considered is directly international—trade warfare, whereby a nation tries to weaken the military and economic capability of its adversary. A second is the degree to which voters in the industrial democracies will vote for larger military budgets (on the presumption that greater military strength is a tension-reducing, peace-enhancing force). Larger military budgets exert an impact on trade patterns as they change expenditure patterns within nations. On the international economic front (more narrowly defined), there are currently three pressing problems. The growth of manufacturing capacity in developing countries is creating severe dislocation in labor markets in industrial countries and causes great political pressures for protectionism. These pressures, in turn, lead to political strains between the rich and the poor nations. Does the world need to regulate the actions of multinationals in fear that they are capable of exerting too much economic power, or can the problem safely be left to national control and discipline? Finally, will the international financial system prove capable of adapting to the strains imposed on it by changes in international (political) relationships and sudden changes in the distribution of gains from trade?

The future in international economic relations will not be dull.

Bibliography

Bergsten, C. Fred, and Lawrence B. Krause, eds. *World Politics and International Economics*. Washington, D.C.: The Brookings Institution, 1975.

Kobrin, Stephen J. *International Expertise in American Business*. Washington, D.C.: Institute for International Education, 1985.

Spero, Joan Edelman. *The Politics of International Economic Relations*. 2nd ed. New York: St. Martin's, 1981.

[6]Richard N. Cooper (formerly under-secretary of state for economic affairs) argued in a Washington conference that a serious current problem is the public's excessively high level of expectation of government's power to curb the impact of international events; see W. R. Cline, ed., *Trade Policy in the 1980s* (Cambridge: M.I.T. Press, 1983), pp. 735–737.

2

Monetary Arrangements In International Trade

Before one can usefully study the causes and practice of international trade (the exchange of goods among nations), it is valuable to have at least a first acquaintance with the monetary dimension in international economics. The reason that international trade takes place is because goods can be bought more cheaply from abroad than they can be made at home. In a nation with no international trade, all transactions are settled in a single currency. In international dealings, the exporter (seller) must pay for the costs of production in the local or home currency (dollars), and the importer (foreign buyer) will use the goods to generate money denominated in the currency of the foreign country (pesos). This is true whether the importer simply resells the goods to local business people or uses the goods for products destined for the market in the importing country. The pesos realized by the exported product must be converted to dollars. This is done by having the importer buy dollars with pesos in the foreign exchange market. The cost of the imported goods will depend not only on the price quoted in dollars but also on the number of pesos needed to buy a dollar when the conversion is made. A more detailed treatment of international finance is contained in Parts IV and V of the book; the purpose of this chapter is to provide that "first acquaintance" needed to facilitate an understanding of problems in international trade. The chapter has three topics: the actual mechanics of international payments, the determination of the rate of exchange and the features of the market for foreign exchange, and the way in which a nation will make sure that its payments to foreigners are equal to (not more than) the amount of foreign money earned by its exporters.

The exposition of international economic phenomena is made easier when international transactions (exporting, importing, investing, etc.) are spoken of as taking place between nation-states. This is a simplification. In Western decentralized economies such as the countries in Europe and North America (and Japan), the dominant role in international trade is played by profit-seeking corporations. Constant repetition of the role of individual firms in international transactions would be tedious, and it is legitimate to refer to nations actually conducting the trade and investment. Two reasons warrant this simplification: It is the *nation* that must ensure that its monetary expenditures to foreigners do not exceed its monetary inflow (receipts from exports plus borrowings)—this is the problem of the balance of payments; and the solution to the very basic problem in international economics of which goods will be exported and which imported depends on *national* economic characteristics (resources and tastes). In importing and exporting on their own account, individuals and firms serve merely as agents through which is generated the pattern of international trade that fits the economic characteristics of the countries involved.

THE MECHANICS OF PAYMENT

It is axiomatic in business that a sale is not made (and certainly not completed) until the goods have been delivered *and paid for*. For a salesman to get the order is good, but that is only the first step in a transaction. When goods are sold to a foreign firm, the costs of doing business are higher than for domestic transactions. In addition to the obvious aspect of (probably) higher shipping costs, there are the problems of separate legal jurisdictions if there is a dispute, the costs of clearing national customs, and the risk of nonpayment by the buyer.[1] This last risk has been effectively eliminated by a system of financial procedures that govern international trade. These procedures have developed over the years to minimize credit risk in international dealings. The trick is for the seller to retain legal title to the goods shipped until the buyer makes a binding commitment to pay.

When goods are shipped, they are itemized on a *bill of lading*, which, when signed by the carrier (the transportation company), acknowledges receipt of the goods. A second copy of the bill of lading is sent to the exporter's agent in the foreign port of arrival. The agent will endorse the bill of lading to the importer, thereby transferring ownership and

[1]Harry L. Sharp, "Controlling Risk in Global Trade," *Financial Executive*, April 1980, pp. 14–17, defines *export risk* as that "additional commercial risk when goods and services are purchased by a foreign party." It includes such things as credit risks; risks of damages for nonperformance of product, particularly when the problem is not within the control of the seller; and insurance fees. Excluding transportation costs, these costs might amount to as much as 11 percent of the cost of the goods.

authorizing access to the goods once payment has been assured. Payment can be made in cash in the importer's currency, but this is unlikely. Usually payment will be denominated in the exporter's currency and will be made by issuing a *bill of exchange*. This is a formal acknowledgment of the debt and is in many ways equivalent to writing a check. The bill of exchange instructs someone (the drawee) to make payment to the exporter (the payee) and to charge the payment to the credit of the importer (the maker of the bill). Usually, but not always, the drawee is the importer's bank, in which event the bill is virtually identical to a check—especially since it does not guarantee that there is money in the bank to cover the check. If the bill of exchange is due when presented (a so-called sight draft), the bank pays the funds to the exporter, and the transaction is completed. The risk to the exporter has been minimized since the exporter retains legal title to the goods until the moment that the buyer undertakes to make payment (thereby acknowledging the debt). If the buyer had gone bankrupt while the goods were being shipped, the seller retains title and could, at worst, sell the goods at auction or find another buyer.

Frequently, large orders are not paid for by sight drafts: The importer is given a period of grace. Suppose that the exporter extends the importer credit for ninety days so that the payment is due ninety days after the bill of exchange has been issued. This arrangement is made when the order is placed and will be sensitive to such things as the eagerness of the buyer to buy and of the exporter to sell as well as to traditional practice within the industry.[2] The bill then becomes, in effect, a postdated check, and the exporter runs the risk of the importer's going bankrupt in the interim. To avoid such a risk, the seller may require that the importer have its bank "accept" the bill so that the bill becomes a *banker's acceptance*. This process shifts the risk of bankruptcy from the exporter to the importer's bank (who should have much better knowledge of the firm's strength). The bank charges a fee to the importer for this service. Note that the invoice (bill of exchange) is denominated in dollars (foreign currency), and the importer is thus running the risk that the peso (local currency) will weaken and the cost of the imports will increase during the period of credit. There are ways of sheltering oneself from such a risk, for a small fee. This possibility is considered in Chapter 12.

RATE-OF-EXCHANGE DETERMINATION

Trade between residents of two different nations must expose one of the firms to rate-of-exchange risk. The rate of exchange is merely the price of one currency in terms of another, and, confusingly, it can be

---

[2]For greater detail, see David K. Eiteman and Arthur I. Stonehill, *Multinational Business Finance*, 3rd ed. (Reading, Mass.: Addison-Wesley, 1982), pp. 517–544.

quoted in two ways: There are, say, 200 pesos per dollar, or a peso is worth half a cent. The two prices are, naturally, reciprocals, and either way is correct. The problem arises when a firm places an order for goods to be delivered substantially later. The buyer can compute the cost by using the rate of exchange at the time the order is placed, but if the rate of exchange changes in the interim, the goods can cost more or less than originally estimated. It is essential, then, for managers indulging in international trade to have a firm understanding of the way in which exchange rates are likely to behave.[3]

Like any other price, a rate of exchange is determined by the supply of foreign currency and the demand for that same foreign currency by people offering the home-country currency. For an examination of the foreign exchange market, it is better to work in terms of two substantial world currencies, the U.S. dollar and the German mark (deutsche mark, abbreviated D-mark or DM). Figure 2-1 shows the quantity of foreign exchange (D-marks) offered and demanded in terms of U.S. dollars. The price of the mark (the rate of exchange) is measured vertically, and the quantity of foreign exchange traded is measured horizontally. The supply curve (of people selling marks and seeking dollars) is shown as upward-sloping so that as the mark becomes more expensive, people want to supply more of them. The demand curve for deutsche marks is downward-sloping, showing that the cheaper the mark, the more willing people are to buy them. (This is not very surprising.) For the most part, the slopes of the two curves can be explained in terms of the relative costs of German-made and American-made goods. If the D-mark is very expensive, say 70 cents, German goods with costs determined in marks will be expensive in the United States, so Americans will want to buy fewer German-made goods and will need fewer dollars to pay for imports from Germany. But when the 70-cent price holds, American-made goods are very cheap in Germany, and Germans will be eager to buy American-made goods and will therefore have a strong demand for dollars. As shown, more marks are supplied than demanded at 70 cents, and the price of the D-mark must fall. The rate of exchange will decline in the face of an excess supply of foreign exchange (marks) or, what amounts to the same thing, in response to a shortage of dollars.[4] Equilibrium is shown to exist at a rate of exchange of 50 cents, at which price the quantity of marks supplied is equal to the quantity demanded.

---

[3]For an idea of the dangers involved, especially when economic policy is inept, consider the plight of a Mexican importer who placed an order in August 1976 when the rate of exchange was 12.50 pesos to the dollar and had the goods delivered in October of the same year when the rate of exchange was 25.49 pesos to the dollar. The peso had lost half its value (in foreign currency) in two months. The months of July and August 1982 saw a similar decline in the value of the peso in terms of dollars. Data are taken from International Monetary Fund, *International Financial Statistics* (Washington, D.C., 1977 and 1983).

[4]For simplicity we assume that there are no capital movements (that is, no trading in assets at this time).

Figure 2-1

THE DOLLAR–DEUTSCHE MARK EXCHANGE MARKET

The D-mark (West German currency) is used here as foreign exchange. It is only one of many markets in which the U.S. dollar is traded against foreign currencies. Since the market is dealing in two currencies, the demand for D-marks is really a measure of the supply of dollars seeking D-marks, and the supply of D-marks is the demand for dollars.

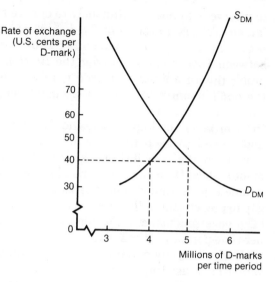

Figure 2-1 really shows a freely operating foreign exchange market in which the demand and supply schedules are determined only by economic units seeking dollars and marks for their own sakes. The role of governments in such markets is, presumably, negligible. This is an interesting analytic case, but governments are never very far away from the foreign exchange market of their currency. There are three ways in which a foreign exchange market can operate. The first of these allows the rate of exchange to be determined by free play of market forces without any government participation (except for any international transactions undertaken by the government for its own purposes). This arrangement is called a "clean float" because the rate of exchange finds its own level depending on the supply and demand schedules; the mechanism is not "dirtied" by government interference seeking to affect the rate of exchange for some tactical reason. The second way allows for the free play of market forces to determine the rate of exchange most of the time unless the market becomes erratic, at which time the government would intervene and buy or sell foreign exchange in order to stabilize the price. Government intervention under a "dirty float" is supposed not to stop underlying movements in the forces determining the equilibrium value of the exchange rate from making themselves felt and is supposed to allow the rate of exchange to settle at its equilibrium rate. The purpose of intervention is to prevent too much day-to-day fluctuation in the exchange rate. Wide daily fluctuations will inhibit international trade by causing unnecessary uncertainty and could inflict unwarranted costs and benefits randomly on exporters and importers. The third mechanism is for the rate of exchange to be predetermined by government fiat and for governments to intervene almost continuously to ensure that the official rate is maintained. This is a system of fixed rates of exchange or fixed parities, as prevailed during the nineteenth century under the gold standard and between 1946 and 1971 under the Bretton Woods system. There is no problem with a system of fixed parities if each agreed-to parity is also the equilibrium rate over a reasonably long period of time. But if the equilibrium rate diverges from the parity rate, there is trouble. Suppose that, in terms of Figure 2-1, the American and German governments had agreed to keep the price of the D-mark at 40 cents (which may have been the equilibrium value when the original arrangement was made). More D-marks are demanded by Americans than dollars are demanded by Germans, and the two governments would have to fill the gap to prevent the dollar from weakening or the mark from strengthening. (The government action would have to amount to about DM 1 million per time period.) Ultimately, the United States would run out of D-marks with which to buy dollars in order to maintain its price (at 40 cents). It would have used up its reserves of gold, its reserves of marks, and its other convertible currencies and would have borrowed to its limit, and then it would no longer be possible to retain the 40-cent rate of exchange.

With one important difference, the problem facing the United States in supporting the dollar at 2.5 marks is exactly the same as supporting the price of wheat. If the government fixes the price of wheat at a level in excess of what supply and demand will generate, the government must add to the demand for wheat; similarly, if the price of wheat is set too low, the government must have wheat in its granary to sell. When the government has to buy wheat to maintain the announced price, it must either store the wheat or give it away so that it does not affect the price on the home market. Storing costs money (in addition to the funds spent buying the wheat). The big difference between the two price supports is that the government needs only dollars to support the price of wheat, and it can borrow dollars and even print them. To support the dollar in the foreign exchange market, Uncle Sam needs marks, and Uncle Sam may not print marks any more than the German government can print dollars.

If a fixed system of exchange rates is to be maintained, policymakers may hope that the agreed-on parity will survive because nothing happens to change the underlying equilibrium, or they can discipline the domestic economy to force it into a position in which the existing parity dominates domestic policy concerns. Suppose, for example, under fixed rates, a nation (the United States) suffered a small burst of inflation and all prices rose by 5 percent. Its goods would become more expensive in international markets—and both the supply and the demand schedules in Figure 2-2 would shift—supply of marks would shift to the left and demand to the right. The only way in which the parity could be maintained is for the government to force domestic price levels down. This could require a

Figure 2-2

INFLATION AND EXCHANGE RATES

The inflation of prices by 5 percent in the United States decreases German demand for U.S. goods and services and, because they are now relatively cheaper, increases American demand for German goods (the demand for DM). The new equilibrium rate is established when real factors remain unchanged and the rate of exchange has adapted to the price-level disturbance to adjust by 5 percent (from 50 to 52.5 cents). For the U.S. government to try to sustain the old parity of 50 cents would require sales of marks equal to the horizontal distance between the two dashed schedules at 50 cents.

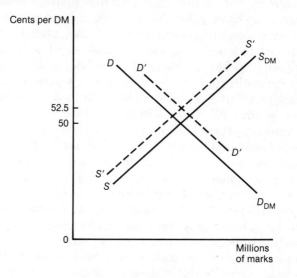

severe and prolonged recession. Impossible as it may have seemed after World War II, the United States did find itself eventually unable to support the dollar at the agreed-on parity in the foreign exchange market. The decision to relinquish the fixed parity was made on August 15, 1971, by President Nixon and ended a quarter of a century of fixed rates of exchange.[5]

Either rates of exchange must reflect market conditions at all times—a clean float—or fixed parities must yield to market conditions in the very long run. The rate of exchange risk faced by an importer is sensitive to the mechanism in force in foreign exchange markets. If conditions are fairly stable (meaning the absence of disturbances—cyclical, price-level, or real), rates of exchange will not be subject to much pressure, and no serious risk is incurred when short-term exposures are permitted. But when the world is subject to serious disruptions or when a nation is experiencing rapid inflation, exchange rates cannot be expected to

[5]For further details, see Chapter 17.

hold. When fixed rates of exchange prevail, governments can be relied on to do their best to maintain the official parity, but when international reserves are exhausted, the importer faces a much bigger change in the exchange rate than would ever be incurred under flexible rates.

BALANCE OF PAYMENTS

Like an individual, a nation must find the money needed to pay its bills to foreigners. For an individual, all that matters is that he or she have the necessary money, but for a nation, it is necessary that it have foreign exchange acceptable to its creditors. In fact, there is a close similarity between the balance-of-payments problems of a country and the straightforward cash flow problems of an individual or a family. A deficit exists when expenditures exceed revenues over a period of time. To meet such a deficit, an individual can sell assets, draw down balances in bank accounts, or borrow: All three actions generate a cash inflow, but all three face limits. Actions of this kind can go on until their potential has been exhausted, and then the deficit becomes binding—expenditures can no longer exceed income. A nation facing a deficit in its balance of payments has the same options: For a time it can run down (sell off) its holdings of financial assets (including stocks of gold) and can borrow from foreign banks and governments. But as for an individual, such policies can be pursued only for a specified amount of time. Sooner or later, expenditures must be cut or revenues increased.

A nation's international payments are in balance when its government does not have to borrow or sell off assets in order to make up any deficiencies in foreign exchange revenues as a result of "spontaneous actions"— actions undertaken for their own sake in response to income levels, relative prices, and so on. Deliberately selling off assets to finance a deficit on spontaneous transactions may be called achieving an artificial balance. The problem of an international payments imbalance is nowhere near so urgent for a nation faced with a surplus: A surplus can result simply in the accumulation of financial assets forever, and although this may not be the best policy, there is no outside economic pressure to cause the nation to change its policy. The pressure to make some change in its spending and earning pattern (to adjust to the imbalance) is all on the deficit nation, and eliminating a deficit, for an individual or a nation, almost inevitably means lowering the standard of living. For an individual, the cure would be fairly self-evident and direct if not enjoyable: An individual reduces the quality or quantity of wine or pizza, goes out less frequently, walks instead of taking transportation, and so on. For a nation, the problem is more complex—it has to reduce the national standard of living by consuming fewer imports and by devoting more of its productive capacity to supplying exports, and both of these actions imply fewer goods available at home, with the result that the standard of living goes down. The problem is that the government cannot simply ask all citizens to reduce their standard of living by, say, 2 percent; it must enforce such a joint decision through tight monetary policy or tight fiscal policy (the same cure that was used in introductory economics when the nation tried to live beyond its income by trying to buy more than it could produce—so-called demand-pull inflation). In addition to the macroeconomic policy measures described, the nation has to tempt foreigners to buy locally made goods and dissuade its citizens from buying imported goods. The way in which this is done is to change the relative costs: imports are made more expensive at home and exports made cheaper abroad. This can be achieved in two ways: having the price level fall in the home country so that an export costs fewer units of foreign currency at a constant rate of exchange or by allowing the home currency to weaken in foreign exchange markets so that domestic prices are constant but translate into lower foreign prices.

If the value of the home currency is allowed to fall in the foreign exchange markets (the exchange rate in Figure 2-1 goes from 40 cents to 50 cents to the mark), the price in Germany of goods costing $10 will drop from DM 25 to DM 20, and more units of those goods should be sold in Germany. At the same time, foreign goods costing DM 1,000 would have cost $400 but will now cost $500. The change in relative prices will motivate a switch from German- to American-made goods, and the deficit will be reduced if not eliminated. But the standard of living of the deficit nation will have had to be reduced in order to reduce the deficit: More exports will have to be given up to buy fewer imports.[6] This is the simple way in which flexible exchange rates are supposed to work to eliminate a deficit. There are complications, which are considered in detail in Chapters 14 and 15.

The alternative corrective mechanism also involves a reduction in the standard of living if a deficit is to be removed and takes place under a system of fixed rates of exchange. The idea is compatible with the working of the full gold standard and can be described simply. Consider two countries in which the money supply is determined by the amount of gold in circulation. If one country spends more on imports than it earns from the sale of its exports, foreign creditors will demand payment in money that they can use—gold is the international money par excellence. A deficit, then, is automatically accompanied by an outflow of gold, the money supply decreases, and the only way in which the smaller money stock can support the rate of production compatible with full employment is for the national price level to fall. In the time needed for the mechanism to work itself out and for domestic price levels to fall, there will be unem-

---

[6]The equivalent for the individual is having to work longer hours to buy fewer goods because the wage rate has been reduced to make possible the longer workweek. The assumption here is that only transactions in goods take place between nations.

ployment in the deficit nation: In fact, unemployment is a strong causal
factor in the lowering of the price level. When domestic prices are lower,
foreigners find domestic goods more attractive and buy more of them,
while domestic firms and consumers will want less from foreign sources.
A similar, inflationary pattern of adjustment will take place in the surplus
nation. The deficit-eliminating mechanism under fixed rates works in
much the same way as under flexible rates: Both require that the deficit
nation accept a reduction in living standards. This mechanism was first
understood by a Scottish philosopher-economist, David Hume.[7] The system worked well during the nineteenth century when the world lived
under a gold standard and, given a constant amount of gold in each
unit of each national currency, exchange rates were fixed.

Only when spontaneous international transactions lead to balanced
payments will it be possible to conceive of a system without ongoing
changes caused by adjustment to payments imbalances. For this reason,
analyses of international trade flows always assume that international
payments do, in fact, balance, and in this way analysts are able to focus
exclusively on the pattern of international trade and its underlying causes.
However, this approach omits some real-world complexities. Nations do
run imbalances on the exchange of goods for very long periods of time
(especially when a nation is receiving a steady inflow of capital by means
of loans and investments by multinational corporations). The implications
of an imbalance in trade are considered in Chapter 5.

What is assumed in Parts II, III, and VI (on international trade, commercial policy, and multinational corporations, respectively) is that international trade is balanced. Let us spell out the implications of this assumption in fairly precise terms.

$$P_x \cdot X = P_m \cdot \epsilon \cdot M \tag{1}$$

where P_x is the average price of exports in home currency and X is the
quantity of exports, so the left-hand side of equation (1) identifies receipts
measured in domestic currency. P_m and M are the equivalent measures
for imports, but P_m is measured in foreign currency: ϵ identifies the rate
of exchange measured as cents per unit of foreign currency. When trade
is balanced, equation (1) holds, and expenditures ($P_m \cdot \epsilon \cdot M$) equal revenues ($P_x \cdot X$), it follows that

$$\frac{P_x}{P_m \cdot \epsilon} = \frac{M}{X} \tag{2}$$

Putting aside the problems in measuring such a wide range of goods as
are exchanged among nations, equation (2) shows that if a nation can

[7]David Hume, "On the Balance of Trade," in *Essays: Moral, Political and Literary,* vol. 1 (Oxford:
Oxford University Press, 1973). The gold standard is considered in Chapter 16.

get a high price for its exports relative to that paid for its imports, it will receive a large quantity of imports per unit of export. Thus if foreign demand for exports were to increase and the price of exports were to rise, the country would experience a favorable change, which would be identifiable in $P_x/(P_m \cdot \epsilon)$. A change in $P_x/(P_m \cdot \epsilon)$ is an important happening for a national economy since it effectively allows the country to increase its standard of living by earning more imports with the same quantity of exports. The ratio $P_x/(P_m \cdot \epsilon)$ is referred to as the *terms of trade*. In Part II, it is also called the *ratio of interchange*. The actual value of the terms of trade is not so important as a change in its value. If events cause the ratio to increase (there is a favorable real disturbance), foreign trade is helping gross national product (GNP) to increase (over and above the benefits received from international trade by trading at the original terms of trade). The terms of trade prove to be an important concept in the theory of international trade and in balance-of-payments analysis. In the latter, the concept is changed slightly, and it is useful to speak of the *real rate of exchange*—the value of ϵ adjusted for inflation in the two countries (if inflation rates are equal, the nominal rate of exchange, ϵ, is equal to the real rate). In both concepts, there is the problem of dealing with aggregates and with all of the potential errors in measurement that such aggregation makes possible.

SUMMARY

International trade takes place because goods can be bought from abroad more cheaply than they can be obtained (produced) at home. The international dimension of trade requires that the rate of exchange be introduced into the costing comparison. Ideally, rates of exchange will be "neutral," that is, they will not distort the pattern of trade. The best way of defining neutrality is that the rate of exchange shall be that which will balance trade flows at full employment, and this is the value of the rate of exchange that underlies nearly all of Parts II and III of this book. If the rate of exchange is not neutral, the pattern of trade will be affected. In the real world, rates of exchange are seldom neutral because of the existence of other kinds of transactions that affect the rate of exchange (international lending, for example). But as Chapter 5 shows, the effect of such transactions and the attendant nonneutrality of the exchange rate can easily be incorporated into the theory of international trade conceptually, and some rough-and-ready estimates of its effects can be diagnosed for different industries.

International trade (and lending) takes place in a different, more complex economic environment than straightforward domestic trade. Some extra degree of uncertainty exists. This will reduce the volume of international trade below that which would take place in a world of perfect certainty and perfect information. However, we neglect these possibilities in the analysis of international trade patterns because they are relatively small and because they are virtually impossible to quantify exactly. Most international trade is conducted on a continuing basis, and there are very few isolated transactions between "new sellers" and "unfamiliar buyers," so risk is not as important as it may seem at first.

The purpose of this book is to allow the reader to develop a basic understanding of the real world in which international economic transactions take place.. The real world works in money terms. Money is introduced explicitly in Chapters 4 and 5, and this chapter has sought to provide enough background so that the necessary complication of a "bridge" between two currencies (the rate of exchange) does not cause problems. Rates of exchange can and do change because of events that occur in the international economy, and when the rate changes, the relative desirability of imports and home-produced goods changes in both the home and the foreign market. The causes of change in a rate of exchange can be identified in terms of three kinds of disturbances: cyclical, price-level, and real. In the theory of international trade, some analysis of real disturbances takes place, but the assumption of full employment in the basic analysis means that cyclical disturbances are not considered until the topic of unbalanced trade is dealt with in Chapter 5. Price-level disturbances are also neglected because they do not affect the fundamentals and contribute only to balance-of-payments problems. In Parts II and III, the nominal and inflation-adjusted or real exchange rates can be taken as identical.

Bibliography

Eng, Maximo. "Trade Financing." In Ingo Walter and T. Murray, eds. *Handbook of International Business*. New York: Wiley, 1982, ch. 13.

Frenkel, Jacob A. "Efficiency and Volatility of Exchange Rates and Prices in the 1970s." *Columbia Journal of World Business*, Vol. no. 14 (Winter 1979), 15–27.

Walter, Ingo, and Kaj Areskoug. *International Economics*. 3rd ed. New York: Wiley, 1981.

II

INTERNATIONAL TRADE

The essence of international trade is the benefits that it generates. To conceive of these benefits it is vital to understand the mechanism by which a freely operating system of international markets will allow an increase in global GNP. "Comparative advantage" is the expression coined in the nineteenth century for the forces that determine which goods will be imported and which exported. To understand why a nation has a comparative advantage in a particular good, economists have developed the *factor-proportions theory*. These two theories have been combined into a body of theory that sets out a detailed description of the processes that generate international trade. These theories are severely restricted by assumptions intended to make the underlying relationships stand out quite starkly. When those assumptions are dropped, the analysis is less clear-cut, but it is also more satisfying and more relevant. The less tidy and more pragmatic analysis can serve as a basis for policy prescription.

The benefit of approaching any subject by means of a body of theory is that theory makes the fundamental relationships stand out starkly. The problem to be confronted by the theorist is how many fundamental relationships are to be included: too few, and you omit an important dimension; too many, and the apparatus becomes unwieldy and disguises the salient features.

3

Comparative Advantage

The fundamental reason for international trade taking place between a pair of nations is that both nations will benefit from the transaction. If prices are good guides to the alternative uses of factors of production (and in a market economy they are), a nation will benefit from international trade when it buys a good from abroad more cheaply than it can buy the same good from domestic sources. The benefit, which may be thought of as an increase in real GNP compared with a situation of no trade, is referred to as the "gain from trade." The simplest way to conceive of this gain is to think of a country importing a good that it is physically incapable of producing in the home economy. If the country cannot produce the good, it must either import the good or do without. Importing from abroad requires that some product be given up in exchange, since nations do not, under ordinary circumstances, make gifts to foreigners. The import is acquired from the foreign source by selling to the foreign nation a good of equal value produced at home. This good is renounced from domestic consumption because it is exported, so the gain from trade consists of the value of the import minus the value of the export. If the good imported cannot be produced at home, it can have very high value to the home economy; in contrast, giving up a few units of a good produced at home is unlikely to constitute a sacrifice of great importance. If the need for the imported good is very strong (oil in Japan, for example) and if, in a two-country world, each country exports a good that the other is incapable of producing, both nations increase material welfare from the exchange of goods. The process is one of barter, lubricated, as it were, with money. In practice, the two-country assumption is highly simplifying, since nations trade with several other nations at the same time (multilateral trade), and trade will not be balanced (value of exports equaling value of imports) with each country.

Trade between two nations in goods that cannot be produced in the importing country can only increase the total well-being of the nations involved. This class of goods (noncompetitive goods) must require for their production a specific input (factor of production) that is not universally available. Examples of such inputs are mineral deposits, climatic conditions, and, possibly, very advanced technology. Noncompetitive goods imported by the United States include bauxite from the Caribbean nations, platinum from South Africa, tea from India, Sri Lanka, and China, bananas from Central America, and emeralds from Colombia. Other developed nations import similar products, while poorer nations will tend to import goods whose production requires a technology that is more advanced than that available domestically.

But trade also takes place among nations in other classes of goods. The United States imports cars, radios, and television sets, despite the fact that the country is quite capable of producing huge quantities of all three goods. The clear-cut advantage that exists in noncompetitive goods is not adequate to explain the pattern of international trade. A satisfactory theory of international trade should be able to provide answers to five questions; the first two are major, the three others minor.

1. What advantage do nations reap from the international exchange of goods, and what facts create that advantage or gain?
2. If a nation is to trade with other countries, which of the goods that it can produce will it export, and which will it import?
3. How will the global or world gain from trade be divided among the participant nations?
4. What determines the terms of trade (the price of imports reckoned in terms of exports)?
5. Will everyone in each nation share in the gain from trade?

This chapter deals with the basic answer to questions 1, 3, and 4: What is the source of the benefit or advantage from trade? How will the global gain from trade be divided? and What determines the terms of trade? The other questions are answered in succeeding chapters. Chapter 3 deals only with trade in goods that can be made in both countries. Noncompetitive goods are introduced in Chapter 5, and brand-name consumer durables and consumer goods are discussed briefly in Chapter 5 and dealt with more thoroughly in Chapter 11.

In fact, the question of gain from trade has already been somewhat simplified. There are in practice four ways through which a nation can gain from international trade. The first and most obvious method, touched on briefly earlier, is through the exchange of noncompetitive goods. This is intuitively obvious.

The second kind of gain from trade is the one that occupies most of this chapter, the exchange of goods that the importing nation could produce if it were advantageous to do so. Nations gain from specialization in producing goods that they produce relatively efficiently.

The third kind of gain deals with relatively sophisticated manufactured goods (although the argument can be extended to different kinds of food). Any firm will limit the number of different types of goods it makes (although counting the models and available sets of options in the Chevrolet or Ford line of cars might make one question the assertion). When international trade in these goods takes place, the consumer has available a wider range of designs and options, those produced by foreign firms as well as those produced by domestic corporations. The individual consumer is better off because of the availability of a wider choice. It is also possible that domestic firms will not be producing the type of product that consumers want and need to lose sales to foreign firms in order to be made aware of this fact. The old Volkswagen "Beetle" was solely responsible for American automakers' thinking in terms of producing a smaller car in the late 1950s.

Fourth, there is the question of domestic monopoly or oligopoly. Monopolists in a country can charge high prices and make large profits. But if foreign competition can provide an alternative source of supply, the monopoly power of the domestic monopolist is reduced, and prices come down, to the benefit of the consumer. What is different about this kind of gain from trade is that the threat of competition may be enough, and actual physical trade may not be necessary for the gain to be generated.

The main concern of this chapter is to determine the cause of the second gain from trade. For this it is necessary to address the principle of comparative advantage.

COMPARATIVE ADVANTAGE

The basic work in determining the principle of comparative advantage as the basis for international trade (and the accompanying benefits) was done by David Ricardo in the early nineteenth century.[1] He was answering and correcting a theory put forward by Adam Smith, who in his campaign for reliance on market forces (and no interference by government in the domestic economy or in international trade) had argued for allowing trade to take place without hindrance on the simple grounds that some goods were produced abroad more efficiently than in Great Britain.

---

[1]David Ricardo, *The Principles of Political Economy and Taxation* (1817), ch. 7.

If a foreign country can supply us with a commodity cheaper than we ourselves can make it, better buy it of them with some part of the produce of our own industry, employed in a way in which we have some advantage. The general industry of the country, being always in proportion to the capital which employs it, will not thereby be diminished, . . . but only left to find out the way in which it can be employed with the greatest advantage. It is certainly not employed to the greatest advantage, when it is thus directed towards an object which it can buy cheaper than it can make. The value of its annual produce is certainly more or less diminished, when it is thus turned away from producing commodities evidently of more value than the commodity which it is directed to produce. According to the supposition, that commodity could be purchased from foreign countries cheaper than it can be made at home. It could, therefore, have been purchased with a part only of the commodities, or, what is the same thing, with a part only of the price of the commodities, which the industry employed by an equal capital would have produced at home, had it been left to follow its natural course. The industry of the country, therefore, is thus turned away from a more to a less advantageous employment, and the exchangeable value of its annual produce, instead of being increased, according to the intention of the lawgiver, must necessarily be diminished by every such regulation. . . .

The natural advantages which one country has over another in producing particular commodities are sometimes so great, that it is acknowledged by all the world to be in vain to struggle with them. By means of glasses, hot-beds, and hot-walls, very good grapes can be raised in Scotland, and very good wine too can be made of them, at about thirty times the expense for which at least equally good can be brought from foreign countries. Would it be a reasonable law to prohibit the importation of all foreign wines, merely to encourage the making of claret and burgundy in Scotland? But if there would be a manifest absurdity in turning towards any employment thirty times more of the capital and industry of the country than would be necessary to purchase from foreign countries an equal quantity of the commodities wanted, there must be an absurdity, though not altogether so glaring, yet exactly of the same kind, in turning towards any such employment a thirtieth or even a three-hundredth part more of either. Whether the advantages which one country has over another be natural or acquired, is in this respect of no consequence. As long as the one country has those advantages and the other wants them, it will always be more advantageous for the latter rather to buy of the former than to make. It is an acquired advantage only which one [manufacturer] has over his neighbor who exercises another trade; and yet they both find it more advantageous to buy of one another than to make what does not belong to their particular trades.[2]

Absolute Advantage

Smith's explanation of the advantages of allowing individual initiative and market forces to determine the volume of international trade is a descriptive, rather than a precise, piece of thinking, which gives the appearance of resting on a mechanism quite similar to the argument in favor of trade in noncompetitive imports. Smith argues in terms of *absolute advantage,* whereby imports consist of goods made more efficiently abroad and exports consist of goods made more efficiently at home. In essence, the proposition runs almost entirely in terms of both foreign and domestic industry having areas in which each is more efficient. Therefore, through international trade, a nation would benefit because the exports needed to pay for the imports would cost less to produce in real terms than the provisions for domestic production of replacements for the potential imports. This is the essence of *opportunity cost.* The opportunity cost of importing goods from abroad is the quantity of real sources devoted to the production of the requisite exports. If the exports cost less in terms of resources than the domestic manufacture of the import substitutes, an advantage in international trade exists in the amount of goods that can be produced with the resources saved.

Smith's contribution can be seen in another way. Before Smith, international trade was seen, in modern parlance, as a zero-sum game—if one country gained something through trade, the other country lost an equal amount. There was no gain from trade worldwide, but trade did allow one country to reap a gain at the expense of its trading partner. By his example of absolute advantage, Smith showed that there was a potential global gain from trade and that both countries could be better off—a positive-sum game.

Smith's Argument Refined

Ricardo felt that for all the emphasis on opportunity costs, Smith failed to appreciate the fundamental cause of the benefits of international trade. Ricardo wanted to show that trade could take place between two nations to the advantage of each when one nation was absolutely more efficient in the production of both goods. He argued that it was the comparative advantage of a nation in producing a good relative to the second nation that determined international trade flows. In his system, absolute efficiency was not a vital condition. To prove the theory of comparative

[2]Adam Smith, *An Inquiry into the Nature and Causes of the Wealth of Nations,* Book IV (Oxford: Clarendon Press, 1869), pp. 29–31.

advantage, Ricardo used a very simple model that has many limitations. But the model does provide considerable insight into the international trading mechanism. In particular, it answers the following question: What creates the gain from international trade?

Ricardian theory made several assumptions:

1. Two countries, England and Portugal, made up the world, and two goods, wine and cloth, were all that were produced.
2. Costs did not vary with the level of production and were proportional to the amount of labor used in each.
3. Quality of goods did not vary among nations. (To anyone who has drunk wine made from British grapes, this is obviously a brave assumption.)
4. One country was more efficient in the production of both goods (and with a modesty becoming in an Englishman at the time of the industrial revolution, Ricardo attributed the greater efficiency to Portugal).
5. Transportation cost nothing.
6. Labor was of one quality in both countries.
7. The value of exports equaled the value of imports.
8. Labor (factors of production) could move freely within a country but was incapable of moving between two countries. This theoretical simplification does not hold in the real world. But it does not seriously affect the results if, as seems reasonable, it is considerably easier for a factor to move within a nation than from one nation to another.

England was deemed able to produce a unit of cloth with 100 labor years and a unit of wine with 120 labor years (and cooperating factors of production). Portugal was supposed to require only 80 labor years per unit of wine and 90 labor years per unit of cloth. As a consequence, Portugal enjoyed an absolute advantage in the production of both goods. The task was to show that Portugal and England could each benefit from trade between the two nations. In the absence of any international trade, the relative prices of cloth and wine would be determined in the two countries by their relative costs of production (because, in modern terms, elasticities of supply of both goods were infinite because of the assumption of constant costs). Thus, in a no-trade situation called *autarky*, a unit of wine in Portugal would be exchanged for $8/9$ of a unit of cloth, while in England a unit of wine would cost $6/5$ of a unit of cloth. The real income per employed person is shown by the productivity data.

	Cloth	Wine
Portugal	1/90	1/80
England	1/100	1/120

Portugal has a higher national income per employed worker no matter whether cloth or wine is used as the basis for measurement. However, the influence of tastes is already apparent. If both countries consumed nothing but wine, Portuguese national income per employed worker would be 50 percent greater than the English equivalent. If tastes were such that cloth was the only item consumed, national income per employed worker would differ by only 11 percent.

Ricardo did not allow for tastes (national patterns of demand) to be an overt feature of his theory of comparative advantage; he did not need to do so to establish his point. The crux of the matter lies in the difference in the relative costs (and therefore in the relative prices) of wine and cloth in Portugal and in England when no trade takes place. If trade were opened between the two nations, it would be possible for a Portuguese merchant to buy wine in Lisbon, take it to London, and sell it for cloth at the English price (1 unit wine = $\frac{6}{5}$ cloth), take the cloth back to Portugal (at assumed zero transportation cost), and sell the cloth at the local prices of 1 unit cloth = $\frac{9}{8}$ wine. The profit on the transaction is spectacular; investing enough money to buy one unit of wine, the merchant would reap a profit of

$$\left[\frac{6}{5} \cdot \frac{9}{8}\right] - 1 = \frac{14}{40}$$

or 35 percent on invested capital per round trip. Similarly, English merchants would make a profit by taking English cloth to Lisbon and carrying out the equivalent transaction there. If the money prices represent costs accurately (as assumed), there is a gain from international trade brought about by having the English produce more cloth and sell it to the Portuguese and the Portuguese produce more wine to exchange for the English cloth. In the example just given, the merchants acquire the whole of the gain from trade.

But the merchants' profit rate will not last. The creation of international trade will make wine cheaper (relative to cloth) in England and cloth cheaper (relative to wine) in Portugal. No longer will English wine producers and Portuguese cloth makers manage to charge the same old pretrade prices: Their industries will be depressed as a result of cheap foreign imports, and land and labor will have to be transferred out of the declining industries into the expanding industries. (How else is Portugal to produce enough additional wine to supply the English and England enough additional cloth to supply the Portuguese?) With zero transport costs, trade will expand until the prices of cloth in terms of wine in the two countries have reached equilibrium—if not, there will always be an incentive for more trade to depress further the price of wine in England and of cloth in Portugal. Once the relative prices of the two goods are the same in the two countries, merchants will make only a normal rate of profit, and the gain from trade will be experienced by wine consumers in England and cloth buyers in Portugal. It is only in the initial stage that the merchant makes the spectacular profit, and the forces of competition among merchants will erode the profitability of such ventures and pass the benefits on to users.[3]

If the exchange of goods (Portuguese wine for English cloth) is to be able to continue at a constant rate, the value of cloth exports from England must be equal to the value of wine exports from Portugal. If they are not equal, money will be leaving one country, and there will be repercussions in the money supply and on the price levels in both countries. This is how David Hume's equilibrating mechanism works.

The crux of the mechanism that generates international trade between Portugal and England is that Portugal produces wine comparatively or relatively better than England produces cloth. This relationship can best be seen by computing the costs of production from the productivity data provided. If 80 labor years are required to produce a barrel of wine in Portugal, how much cloth could those labor years have produced? The answer (the opportunity cost) is $8/9$ of a unit of cloth. In the same way, 120 labor years in England will produce 1 unit of wine or $6/5$ units of cloth. By using Portuguese workers to produce wine, the world is giving up $1/90$ of a unit of cloth per labor year. By using English workers to produce cloth, the world is giving up $1/120$ of a unit of wine per labor year. Consider the gain to the world if 80 Portuguese workers are set to produce wine for export and produce one unit to be shipped to England. World production of cloth has decreased by $8/9$ of a unit. If England makes an additional $8/9$ of a unit of cloth for export, roughly 88 labor years will be required, equivalent to about $3/4$ of a unit of wine. World output has grown by $1/4$ unit of wine as a result of the international redistribution of production. There is a gain from trade to be reaped from redistributing international production in line with comparative advantage.

International trade will take place as long as the world price of wine in terms of cloth is sufficient to tempt both nations to trade and to rearrange their domestic production to suit the volume of trade. In autarky, the price of a unit of cloth in England will be $5/6$ of a unit of wine, and England will trade only if it can get a higher price for its cloth. Similarly, Portugal will trade only if it can sell its wine for better than $8/9$ of a unit of cloth. The comparative efficiency (productivity or cost) data set the limits at which international trade will take place. This is shown in Figure 3-1: A straight line extending from the origin shows a price. The line is a series of points connecting quantities of wine, measured horizontally, and quantities of cloth, measured vertically, that have the

---

[3]Remember that in a pure market system excess profit is the motive power that triggers the expansion of one industry and the decline of another and leads to reallocation of economic resources. When the reallocation is complete, normal profit levels return to the firms in both industries.

Figure 3-1

RICARDO'S PRODUCTION
DATA

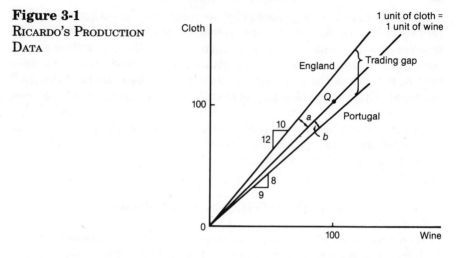

same monetary value (Ricardo's seventh assumption, that trade was balanced). The steeper line shows the limits of English willingness to export cloth, and the flatter line shows the limiting willingness of Portugal to sell wine. Any price between the limits—the trading gap—will result in a gain for both countries as a result of the redistribution of production between the two nations in line with comparative advantage.

Ricardo's system is not fully determinate in that it provides no way of computing the world price of cloth in terms of wine. This ratio is the ratio of interchange or the terms of trade considered in Chapter 2. The terms of trade are usually measured as the ratio of the price of exports to the price of imports: Anything that causes the value of this ratio to increase, given the fulfillment in reality of the assumptions of the analysis, will mean that the country gets more imports for the same quantity of exports and will therefore be better off—its trading partner must necessarily suffer a reduction in the gain from trade as its terms of trade deteriorate. Ricardo's analysis merely sets limits to the world price of cloth in terms of wine—it defines the trading range.

Although Ricardo's system is hemmed in by many assumptions, it can be used to show four relationships that derive from the existence of international trade. Even if some of the simplifying assumptions are dropped, making the analysis more complicated (more accurately reflecting the complexity of the real world), these four basic relationships are still valid and can be recognized for what they are. This groundwork will make it easier to grasp more complex models. The examples provided give the answer to the first major question, What causes gain from trade to be enjoyed by the participating countries? and to the first minor question, How will the gain from trade be divided among the participating nations?

The root of the benefit accorded by the international exchange of goods is always the reallocation (compared with autarky, a situation of no trade or complete isolation) of production in line with comparative advantage. Ricardo assumed constant opportunity costs of production of a good—that is, the cost of the good did not change with the amount of the good produced. This assumption means that the more international trade that takes place, the greater the amount of efficiency-promoting reallocation of production will be allowed. It also means that the greater the difference in the autarkic cost ratios, the greater the gain from trade per unit quantity of trade that takes place.

FOUR HYPOTHESES ABOUT TRADE

Hypothesis 1: Gains from international trade can be achieved when different opportunity-cost ratios exist in autarky. The existence of gains does not depend on relative levels of absolute efficiency.

Hypothesis 2: The larger the trading gap, the greater the global gain from trade. Thus, to the extent that both countries have an absolute advantage in one good and that this condition will widen the trading gap, absolute advantage is just a special (and more favorable) case of Ricardo's model.

Hypothesis 3: The greater the volume of trade at any given terms of trade, the greater the global gain from trade.

Hypothesis 4: The further the equilibrium or final terms of trade from a country's autarkic cost ratio and the nearer to the other country's autarkic cost ratio, the larger the share of the given global gain from trade accruing to the first country.

It is important to develop a feel for these hypotheses because they are basic to international trade. For this reason, the hypotheses are dealt with arithmetically in the text in terms of establishing a gain from the creation of some (arbitrarily defined) amount of international trade. These arithmetic examples are designed to enable the reader to identify the mechanism by which changes in global production are created through international trade and divided between the participating nations. The examples are indicative only and do not constitute "proof."

Hypothesis 1

The existence of gains from trade depends on differences in autarkic opportunity-cost ratios and not on absolute efficiency. This hypothesis can be supported by showing that England and Portugal will both gain from international trade despite Portugal's lower real costs of production (greater absolute efficiency) in *both* goods.

This statement has already been supported by showing that world output will increase when Portugal produces 1 extra unit of wine and sells it to England for 8/9 of a unit of cloth. But in that example, England made all the gain, so the argument does need to be taken one step further to show that the increase in world output will be shared by the two nations. Then Portugal as well as England will have gained from trade.

Let Portugal transfer 7,200 workers from cloth to wine production: Portuguese cloth production will decline by 80 units and wine production will increase by 90 units. Let Portugal sell this additional wine to England at a price between the two limits set out in Figure 3-1—for simplicity, let that price be 1 unit of cloth exchanges for 1 unit of wine. England must be ready to provide Portugal with 90 units of cloth (in exchange for the wine) and will transfer 9,000 workers out of English vineyards and into cloth production. Portugal is better off: Cloth production was cut by 80 units, but 90 units of English cloth were obtained in exchange. England is better off than before trade: Wine production fell by 75 units (9,000 ÷ 120), but 90 units of wine were received from abroad. The difference between the example given earlier and this example (in addition to the volume of trade) is that in this example the world terms of trade are assumed to settle at $1W = 1C$ and not at the English cost ratio. As noted, there is nothing in Ricardo that determines the final terms of trade. This will be shown to depend on the intensity of desire of each country for the other's imports. But between the limits, any terms of trade are feasible.

Hypothesis 2

If the trading gap gets wider, the gain from trade gets bigger.

Change the cost data for cloth in England from 100 labor years to 80 labor years per unit of cloth; leave all other costs the same. The English autarkic ratio is now 3 cloth exchange for 2 wine:

	Cloth	Wine
Portugal	90	80
England	80	120

and England is now absolutely more efficient in cloth production than Portugal. By changing the English cost data for cloth, the model has been transformed from one in which a country is more efficient in both kinds of goods to one of absolute advantage (each country is more efficient in one kind of goods). England still has a comparative advantage in cloth but also has an absolute advantage as well. Repeat the same exercise as for Hypothesis 1. Portugal transfers 7,200 workers from cloth to wine and increases wine output by 90 units. These 90 units are sold to England for 90 units of cloth. (Nothing different so far.) To produce these 90 units of cloth for export, England now need only transfer 7,200 workers out of wine and into cloth production. England has a larger gain because local wine production now falls by only 60 units. Thus the hypothesis is supported: World gain from trade increases with the size of the trading gap.

Hypothesis 3

The greater the volume of trade, the greater the global gain from trade at any given terms of trade.

This follows self-evidently from the numbers given in support of Hypothesis 1. If the quantity of trade is doubled, the gain will be doubled. But this anticipates the issue of how tastes affect the volume of international trade. Suppose that the quantity of trade described in Hypothesis 1 satisfies the desires of the two nations so that total potential gain from trade is 10 units of cloth for Portugal and 15 units of wine for England. The reason for this limit is that England simply does not want any more Portuguese wine at a cost of giving up a unit of cloth for every unit of wine imported, and Portugal would prefer to retain wine than to provide England with any more at a price of $1W = 1C$. But now let the Portuguese suddenly have an urge to become fancy dressers and have a desire for much more English cloth at a price of $1W = 1C$ while, at the same time, the English decide that wine is the elixir of life and that clothing is much less important. The changes in tastes will lead to a larger volume of international trade, and the gain from trade will increase. (Under the conditions specified, doubling the volume of trade will generate twice the gain.)[4]

Hypothesis 4

As the terms of trade move closer to England's autarkic cost ratio, Portugal's share of global gain from trade increases.

Revert to the original data and the example given in Hypothesis 1. Portugal transfers 7,200 workers and produces 90 more units of wine (at the expense of 80 units of domestic cloth production). Now let the terms of trade be 1 unit of wine exchanges for 1.05 units of cloth. Wine has become more expensive—perhaps because the English have become

---

[4]This argument, like those of the other hypotheses, is developed more exactly in H. Peter Gray, *International Trade, Investment, and Payments* (Boston: Houghton Mifflin, 1979), ch. 2.

thirstier. Now Portugal exchanges the extra 90 units of wine for 94.5 units of cloth, and its gain from trade has increased from 10 units of cloth to 14.5 units. England must now produce 94.5 units of cloth in addition to that needed for domestic purposes and must transfer 9,450 workers out of wine production, causing a reduction in domestic wine output of 78.75 units. England's gain from trade is reduced by the change in domestic wine output and falls from 15 units of wine to 11.25. As the terms of trade change, the division of the gain from trade between the participating nations changes. When the terms of trade get bigger (the price of exports in terms of imports increases), the share of global gain from trade increases.

The four hypotheses show that the gain from international trade derives from the reallocation of international production in accordance with comparative advantage (the second kind of gain among the four listed at the beginning of the chapter). The gain exists because nations have different *relative* or *comparative* efficiencies of production in different goods in autarky—goods have different opportunity costs in different countries. The larger the difference in opportunity costs, the larger the global gain from trade tends to be (suggesting that international trade in noncompetitive imports can give rise to very large gains from trade). The distribution of the gain from trade depends on the ratio of the price received for exports to the price paid for imports (the terms of trade). In terms of Figure 3-1, the global gain from trade is determined by the size of $a + b$ and the distribution by a/b. The results are summarized in Table 3-1.

Table 3-1
RESULTS OF THE FOUR HYPOTHESES

Condition Tested	Portuguese Gain from Trade	English Gain from Trade
Original autarkic costs; open trade at terms of trade of $1W = 1C$.	10 units of cloth*	15 units of wine
Wider disparity in autarkic costs: England has absolute advantage in cloth. Terms of trade remain $1W = 1C$.	10 units of cloth*	30 units of wine
Increased tastes for imports by both countries. Terms of trade remain at $1W = 1C$. Original autarkic costs.	20 units of cloth	30 units of wine
Original autarkic costs. Changed terms of trade: $1W = 1.05C$. Terms of trade change in favor of wine (Portugal).	14.5 units of cloth	11.25 units of wine

* The gain is the difference between the amount of cloth imported and the reduction in the production of cloth caused by transferring out of cloth production the workers needed to generate the necessary wine exports.

A MONETARY APPROACH TO COMPARATIVE ADVANTAGE

Ricardo's example is abstract and does not recognize that the motive force behind international trade is that a person will import when he or she can get something from abroad more cheaply than from a domestic source. Money prices serve to indicate comparative advantage. Prices are the signals that must influence buying patterns. People, even those who have studied the theory of international trade, do not worry about which nation has the comparative advantage when buying something. A person in a wine shop does not look at the price of a bottle of California red and a bottle of Bordeaux and then say, "I wonder whether France or the United States has a comparative advantage in wine production." The buyer relies on price (after allowing for quality differences) to tell which country has the comparative advantage. It is useful, therefore, to show how the comparative-advantage mechanism works in terms of money prices.

Let Ricardo's original cost data hold, and let the value of an English pound sterling and a Portuguese escudo be equal. Let the exchange rate be fixed.[5] Let the wage rate be $\frac{1}{10}$ of a pound (£) in England and $\frac{1}{10}$ of an escudo (Esc) in Portugal. Wage rates have the same monetary value in both countries in autarky. The autarkic costs of the goods (on the assumption that labor is the only input) will be

	Cloth	Wine
Portugal	Esc9	Esc8
England	£10	£12

The Portuguese standard of living is higher because equal wages face lower prices in Portugal.

When trade begins, both Portuguese goods will be cheaper than their English counterparts. This state of affairs exists because wage rates are the same and Portuguese efficiency is greater in both goods. England will therefore tend to buy cheaper Portuguese wine and give up English wine and to buy cheaper Portuguese cloth and give up English cloth. Ships will sail from Lisbon loaded down with full cargo holds. They will return from England empty except for gold coins used in payment. Now see how David Hume's mechanism works to bring trade into balance and to establish comparative advantage. England will face a reduction in the amount of money circulating in the English economy; the rate of interest will rise, and a recession will ensue. The recession will also be

---

[5]As under a gold standard (see Chapter 14). Note that wage rates are assumed to be flexible downward in what follows and that productivity data have been changed to worker-hours rather than worker-years.

attributable to the lack of output in the cloth and wine industries, which
will be decimated by cheap Portuguese imports. Unemployment and recession will force down the price of English goods and English wage rates.
In Portugal there will be a boom—a demand-pull inflation fed by the
money received from England—and prices will rise. Let the wage in
England fall to $\frac{1}{11}$ of a pound, and the wage in Portugal rise to $\frac{1}{9}$ of an
escudo. Prices (costs) will change as follows:

	Cloth	Wine
Portugal	Esc10	Esc8.9
England	£9.1	£10.9

As a result of the change in wage rates, English cloth is now cheaper
than Portuguese cloth, and England can export cloth to Portugal in exchange for imported wine. Balanced trade is now possible (though some
further adjustment of wage rates may be needed) because both Portugal
and England are exporting one good. The English export is the one that
first became competitive with Portuguese competition and is the one in
which England has a comparative advantage.

Note that the differences in wage rates reflect the differences in the
standard of living in the two countries and that this in turn reflects
the difference in the productivity of the workers. The same mechanism
could be shown using fixed wage rates and a flexible rate of exchange
so that the pound would depreciate (weaken) against the escudo and
make English goods relatively cheaper.

Setting the Ricardian model out in money terms provides exactly the
same result: Trade will take place even though Portugal is more efficient
in the production of both goods and England will export the one in which
it has a comparative advantage (it is this good that first becomes cheaper
and competitive with its Portuguese counterpart when the price levels
are adjusting in the face of balance-of-payments imbalances). Ricardo's
assumption of balanced trade is necessary if Hume's mechanism is not
to be activated.

DETERMINATION OF THE TERMS
OF TRADE

Hypothesis 4 showed that the distribution of the global gain from trade
between England and Portugal is sensitive to the equilibrium price of
wine in terms of cloth—that is, to the terms of trade. To identify the
way in which the terms of trade are determined, it is necessary to develop
a concept known as an *offer curve*. Since this is a new analytic device,
it is developed from scratch here, together with the introduction of tastes

Table 3-2

ENGLISH AND PORTUGUESE TRADING SCHEDULES

Portugal		Terms of Trade	England	
Exports (Wine)	Imports (Cloth)		Exports (Cloth)	Imports (Wine)
30	10	$3W = 1C$	135	405
70	35	$2W = 1C$	130	260
90	60	$1\frac{1}{2}W = 1C$	110	165
100	100	$1W = 1C$	100	100
110	165	$1W = 1\frac{1}{2}C$	90	60
130	260	$1W = 2C$	70	35
135	405	$1W = 3C$	30	10

and increasing (rather than constant) opportunity costs. Offer curves tie together the cost conditions in the nations and their tastes; they show how involvement in international trade depends on these two basic sets of forces. The device is useful in consideration of tariffs and commercial policy as well as in the theory of international trade.

The willingness of a country to trade with foreign nations depends on the terms of trade it faces. Imports may be assumed to have the familiar downward-sloping demand curve so that as the price of imports is reduced (by the terms of trade becoming more favorable), the volume of imports will increase and the volume of exports offered in recompense will also increase if the demand for imports is price-elastic. In a state of perfect knowledge, it would be possible to determine the quantity of imports sought and the quantity of exports given up at different terms of trade. These data would provide a "trading schedule" (see Table 3-2). The pictorial representation of the trading schedule is the offer curve. It is drawn on the assumptions of full employment and the absence of impediments to international trade. Each position on the offer curve shows a potential trading equilibrium on the part of the country whose offer curve is being drawn. Offer curves appear in Figures 3-2 and 3-4.

The development of the offer curve given here relies on a commonsense approach. A more formal and elaborate means of deriving an offer curve was developed originally by Professor James E. Meade.[6]

In Figure 3-1, the two straight lines showing the autarkic production cost ratios in Portugal and England delimit the terms of trade. Any point within the area encompassed by those two lines shows a combination of English exports of cloth and Portuguese exports of wine potentially acceptable to both countries. For example, the point Q shows England exporting 100 units of cloth in return for 100 units of Portuguese wine, and the terms of trade of $1C = 1W$. But there is nothing to suggest

---

[6]For a summary presentation, see Gray, *International Trade,* pp. 43–51. In reverting to a "commonsense" or more intuitive approach, the text follows Meade's predecessors.

Figure 3-2
ENGLAND'S OFFER CURVE

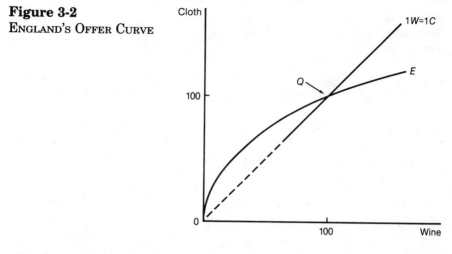

that this is the actual volume of trade that England wants to conduct at those terms of trade.

Now let us introduce tastes into the analysis and with them the familiar principle of diminishing marginal utility. This principle asserts that if the first 10 units of wine consumed by an individual provide a certain amount of satisfaction, a second (additional) 10 units of wine provide less additional satisfaction. The more a person consumes of a good per unit time, the less additional satisfaction an additional unit of consumption generates and the less desirable an additional unit of that good becomes. But the principle of diminishing marginal utility works in two ways in international trade: The more a nation imports, the less desirable an additional unit of imports becomes *and* the more exports must be given up in exchange. Exports become more desirable as larger quantities are surrendered and fewer remain for home consumption. This double relationship is identified in the curvature of an indifference curve.[7]

Given the principle of diminishing marginal utility, it is possible to recognize that there will be a maximum amount of trade that England will be willing to undertake at terms of trade $1C = 1W$. How much wine will be imported at that price depends on the (marginal) intensity of demand for wine and the marginal disutility of giving up cloth in return. One thing is clear: If England were prepared to offer 100 units of cloth for 100 units of wine at terms of trade $1C = 1W$, England would be willing to accept more wine imports only if wine became cheaper. A trading schedule for England would show a willingness to export 100 units of cloth for 100 units of wine at the ratio $1C = 1W$, and other points on the schedule would show up as a curved line through Q in Figure 3-1. This is shown in Figure 3-2: If point Q lies on England's

[7]Indifference curves are developed in Campbell R. McConnell, *Economics*, 8th ed. (New York: McGraw-Hill, 1981), pp. 481–485. See the supplement following this chapter.

Figure 3-3
INCREASING OPPORTU-
NITY COST

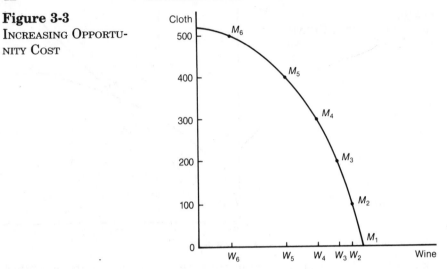

offer curve, the offer curve (OE) will pass through Q and would slope
outward (denoting a willingness to import ever larger amounts of wine
at ever more favorable terms of trade). (Recall that the terms of trade
can be shown as any straight line radiating from the origin.) It is the
effect of diminishing marginal utility of import (and the counterpart increased marginal utility of the retained exports) that imparts the curvature to the offer curve.

It is now time to dispense with the unreasonably simple assumption
that the (relative) costs of production (opportunity costs) do not vary
with the mix of output. Increasing opportunity costs are associated
with "bulging" production possibility curves—more formally, such curves
are described as "concave to the origin." As more wine is produced in
Portugal, factors of production less well suited to wine production will
be transferred from cloth production, and the opportunity cost of wine
in terms of cloth production increases. Figure 3-3 shows the production
possibilities curve of a country producing wine and cloth under conditions
of increasing opportunity cost. These production data can be used to
show how a country's willingness to trade internationally depends on
production data as well as on demand data. Fortunately, both production
and demand features impart the same kind of curvature to the offer
curve: To induce a nation to take additional imports (with diminishing
marginal utility) by renouncing increased quantities of exports (with
increasing opportunity costs) requires that imports become progressively
cheaper in terms of exports.

The production effects can be shown with reference to Figure 3-3, which
identifies equal (absolute) increases in cloth production in terms of wine
production renounced. Starting at point M_1, where the country produces

only wine, increase production of cloth to 100 units. The nation must renounce only a very small quantity of wine (M_1W_2). To produce a second 100 units of cloth (200 units in all), the nation must move along its production possibilities curve to M_3 and reduce wine production by a *further* $W_2W_3(M_1W_2)$. This process continues as ever increasing amounts of cloth are produced until, finally, to raise cloth production from 400 to 500 units requires very important amounts of wine to be given up (W_5W_6). To induce the country to give up domestic production of wine to buy it from abroad by exporting cloth requires ever cheaper wine because the cost of cloth production (in terms of wine production renounced) is forever increasing. The curvature of the offer curve (OE) in Figure 3-2 depends, then, on the rate at which exports to foreigners run into increasing opportunity costs and on the rate at which the desirability of imports diminishes. International trade requires that a country export goods in return for imports, and to trade internationally therefore requires that production of the good in which it has a comparative advantage be increased (to supply foreigners). The more goods supplied to foreigners, the greater the per-unit cost of the additional import because of the increasing opportunity costs of producing exports. At the same time, additional imports yield progressively less satisfaction. These two basic forces combine to determine the terms of trade that will ultimately reconcile the trading desires of both countries. International trade can only settle at a rate at which the willingness of Portugal to buy English cloth and to ship wine is compatible with the English willingness to ship cloth and to acquire Portuguese wine. Assuming full employment, the only variable that can reconcile the two sets of desires is price (the terms of trade). Figure 3-4 pictures the data provided in Table 3-2. The curve OP is the Portuguese offer curve, showing a whole series of possible trading combinations acceptable to Portugal. The curve OE shows the English equivalent. At point Q, the desires of the two countries are in equilibrium, and the value of exports equals the value of imports (as it does for all points on either offer curve). The shape of the curves follows from the existence of increasing opportunity cost of exports and the diminishing marginal utility of imports. An intersection (equilibrium) must occur when the two curves have this particular shape. Imports gradually become less and less desirable at the margin (OP becomes steeper throughout and OE becomes flatter).[8]

The gain from trade (from the reallocation of production among nations) can be thought of as proportional to the size of the "football" enclosed by the two offer curves. Each nation's individual gain can be reckoned in terms of the part of the "football" between its own offer curve and the terms-of-trade line. More precisely, the gain from trade is measured

---

[8]It is possible for the offer curve to bend back, but this possibility need not concern the reader in an introductory treatment of the subject.

Figure 3-4

Portuguese and English Offer Curves

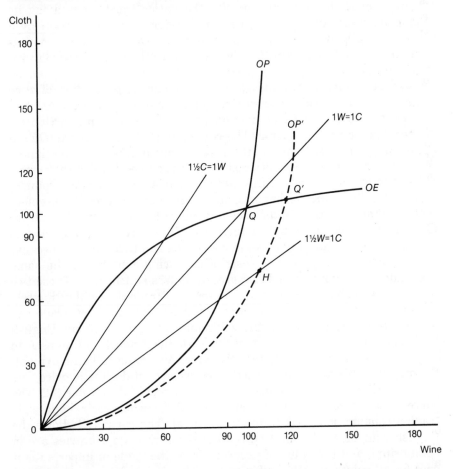

by the angle of divergence of the two offer curves (or, for a nation, the offer curve and the terms-of-trade line) so that the gain from trade falls off rapidly as the volume of trade increases when the offer curves are converging.[9] This is fairly straightforward. A nation importing a vital noncompetitive import will have a very flat (or steep) offer curve near the origin because it will be willing to offer lots of exports for the particularly good. As the urgent need for noncompetitive imports is satisfied, nations import goods in which they have a pronounced comparative disadvantage, and the degree of disadvantage declines as more and more trade takes place. There is an almost negligible gain from trade from the last units imported. There is a tendency (as in Figure 3-4) to draw offer curves as symmetrical. That need not be so. One country could have

---

[9]The standard reference for this analysis is Jacob Viner, *Studies in the Theory of International Trade* (New York: Harper Bros., 1937), pp. 570–575.

the ability to export a noncompetitive good as well as ordinary goods and would have perhaps only a relatively small gain from trade because its imports could be produced at home at only slightly higher cost. A second country importing the noncompetitive import might have a very large gain from trade.

To sum up, an offer curve is merely a pictorial representation showing the willingness of a country to trade at various terms of trade. The offer curve is always drawn on the presumption of full employment and balanced trade. Its shape is determined by the two self-reinforcing relationships of increasing opportunity costs of exports and diminishing marginal utility of imports. Two countries (or one country and the rest of the world) will have an intersection that will determine the equilibrium terms of trade. The stronger the demand for imports, given the production possibility curve, the farther to the right the Portuguese offer curve (and the higher the English), will be and the less favorable the terms of trade.

Changes in Demand

Offer curves are drawn on the basis of certain underlying conditions: tastes and production facilities. When the underlying conditions change, the offer curve shifts. This is shown in Figure 3-4 by the dotted offer curve, OP', representing Portugal's new offer curve after a change in its taste patterns. Suppose that Portuguese people suddenly increase their desires for cloth and that wine falls into relative disfavor. English tastes are unchanged. Portugal will want more imports and is willing to offer more exports for more imports at each price. Consider the price, $1C = 1\frac{1}{2}W$: Portugal was originally prepared to buy 60 units of cloth in exchange for 90 units of wine. Now with demand for cloth more intense, Portugal is prepared to buy 70 units of cloth at that price for 105 units of wine. The combination is shown at point H. H is on the new offer curve, OP'. The English offer curve is unchanged, and the new equilibrium at Q' will be determined by the intersection of the (constant) English offer curve with Portugal's new offer curve. The terms of trade have shifted adversely to Portugal to Q'. England's gain from trade has increased in accordance with Hypotheses 3 and 4. It is not possible to determine whether Portugal has gained or lost because its tastes have changed and there is no basis for comparison. Certainly Portugal would be worse off at Q' with its old tastes.

Changes in Supply

Let Portugal experience a sudden increase in productivity in the export industry, wine, perhaps due to the development of a new strain of grape that increases the yield of each vine or the disappearance of a grape-damaging insect. Portugal's production possibilities curve will have elongated somewhat in favor of more wine production, and Portuguese income will have increased. Unless the Portuguese are willing to use all of their increase in income (from the higher productivity) for the purchase of wine (the home good whose production has increased), they will try to buy more cloth and will offer more wine in exchange. But the only way to tempt the English to offer the extra cloth is for the Portuguese to accept a lower price for wine (a deterioration of the terms of trade). The Portuguese offer curve will shift outward just as when Portugal experienced the change in tastes and increased its desire for imports.

Note that both changes in underlying conditions show Portugal suffering a deterioration in the terms of trade because the Portuguese wanted more imports or were prepared to offer more exports in the international market. There is no reason for underlying changes always to be adverse. Portugal might suddenly desire more wine and less cloth or experience an increase in productivity in cloth production. In either event, the dotted offer curve, *OP'*, would move inward, and Portuguese terms of trade would improve.

Supply-side changes give an insight into the relationship between economic growth and the terms of trade. If growth takes place, the country has more income. The change in the terms of trade will depend on the increases in production of the two goods that will take place at the existing relative prices and also on the increases in consumption of the two goods. Suppose that Portugal experiences a 10 percent increase in productivity in both goods and therefore a 10 percent increase in income. Cloth production will increase by 10 percent, and so will wine production (this is called *neutral growth*). Suppose Portugal is prepared to increase its consumption of both goods equally (neutral demand); Portugal will have excess wine and a shortage of cloth at the existing relative price levels. This is so because Portugal was exporting wine and importing cloth originally, and it will want to increase both wine exports and cloth imports by 10 percent each. Then wine will become cheaper. Neutral growth turns the terms of trade against the growing country. This does not mean that growth is undesirable. What it means is that the trading partner gets some of the benefits of growth as the growth process spills over through a shift in the terms of trade that is adverse to Portugal. England will see the Portuguese offer curve shift and will enjoy the greater gains from trade that come from a new equilibrium at *Q'*.

Tacitly, we have assumed that Portugal grew while England was stagnant. This is unlikely; both countries will probably be growing at different rates. In that event, neutral growth in both countries will shift the terms of trade against the faster-growing country.

SUMMARY

The theory of comparative advantage is essentially a supply-side theory of international trade; tastes come into the Ricardian construct only secondarily. The theory of comparative advantage explains how it is possible for a country that is more efficient in the production of both goods to gain from international trade. It determines which goods will be exported and which imported, but only in terms of the raw productivity and cost data supplied. There is no underlying theory of what causes Portugal to have a comparative advantage in the production of wine. Unless the simple theory is elaborated on by the addition of diminishing marginal utility of imports and increasing opportunity cost of exports, the theory cannot provide a determinate value for the terms of trade.

When international trade takes place according to comparative advantage, there is a gain from trade brought about by the redistribution of production among nations in line with comparative advantage. The gain from trade of a country is determined not only by the terms of trade but also by the curvature of the offer curve (the intensity of demand for imports). When the original conditions change, the offer curves shift, and the global gain from trade can either be increased or reduced.

The theory compares a situation of international trade with one of autarky or no trade. In reality, it is changes in conditions in the world that can affect the gains from trade that a country enjoys and that require changes in the mix of output and consumption.

The theory of comparative advantage has answered three of the five questions posed at the beginning of the chapter. The identification of which goods will be exported and which imported remains, as does the question of the effect of international trade on income distribution within the trading nations.

Bibliography

Allen, William R. *International Trade Theory: Hume to Ohlin.* New York: Random House, 1965.

Haberler, Gottfried. *A Survey of International Trade Theory.* Princeton, N.J.: International Finance Section, Princeton University, 1961.

Meade, James Edward. *A Geometry of International Trade.* London: George Allen & Unwin, 1952.

Ohlin, Bertil. *Interregional and International Trade.* Cambridge, Mass.: Harvard University Press, 1933, chs. 1–3.

Walter, Ingo, and Kaj Areskoug. *International Economics,* 3rd ed. New York: Wiley, 1981.

Questions and Problems

Questions
1. Distinguish between comparative advantage and absolute advantage.
2. Absolute advantage is just a special case of comparative advantage. Show this to be true.

3. What makes an offer curve curve?
4. The impersonal market will determine for a nation which product has a comparative advantage. Explain how this will be accomplished.
5. The larger the trading gap, the greater the gain from trade in the Ricardian model. Explain.
6. It is unfortunate to develop tastes that lead to larger imports. Criticize this statement.

Problems

1. Portugal produces 150 units of wine and 50 units of cloth and consumes 100 units of each. England has no growth while Portugal grows to be able to produce 110 units of wine and 55 units of cloth. What will happen to the terms of trade? Explain the answer.
2. The following data provide the trading schedules of Germany and Argentina. What are the equilibrium terms of trade?

| GERMANY | | | ARGENTINA | |
Machinery Exports	Agricultural Imports	Terms of Trade	Machinery Imports	Agricultural Exports
12	6	2M = 1A	8	4
10	7½	2M = 1½ A	9	6
8	7	1M = 1A	6	6
6	9	1M = 1½ A	6	9
7	10	1M = 2A	5	10

Indifference Curves

A set (or map) of indifference curves[1] shows how the tastes of an individual determine the response to a change in price (or income). A single consumer indifference curve shows how different combinations of two goods, cloth and wine, can yield the same amount of satisfaction. The consumer has predetermined tastes, and these tastes obey the law of diminishing marginal utility. This enables us to identify the general shape of an indifference curve (see Figure 3-A). The position and curvature of the indifference curve depend on the tastes of the individual. Starting at point Q, the person has reached the level of satisfaction I. The same level of satisfaction can be attained by any other point on the indifference curve I, such as R or T. Point R involves the consumption of more wine and less cloth than Q. How much more wine will be required to offset a decline in cloth depends on tastes and is a measure of substitutability. Because of the law of diminishing marginal utility, we do know that the amount of additional wine needed to substitute for the loss of cloth in moving from Q to R (QP) will be less than the amount of wine needed to substitute for an equal loss of cloth going from R to T. If QP equals RS, then ST must exceed PR. This point determines the shape of an indifference curve, but its degree of curvature depends on the rate at which the taste for wine (in terms of cloth) diminishes as wine consumption increases.

A person is indifferent to the combination of the two goods represented by any point on the same indifference curve. A higher curve yields more satisfaction because one can have more of *both* goods (point U with reference to point Q or point R).

An individual will maximize satisfaction (spend income most wisely) when expenditures are allocated between the two goods according to the relative costs of the goods and the relative amounts of satisfaction yielded by both goods *at the margin* (that is, for the last dollar spent

---

[1]This construct is necessary for an understanding of Chapter 4. It is introduced in McConnell, *Economics,* pp. 481–485. The subject is introduced here because many students might have missed it.

Figure 3-A
INDIFFERENCE CURVES

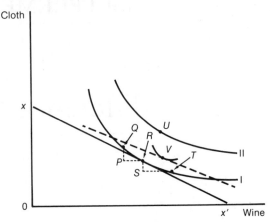

on each good). Let the person have $100 to spend. Relative prices are such that if all of the $100 is spent on cloth, it will buy OX units (if cloth costs $20 per unit, $OX = 5$). If wine is $10 per unit, it will buy 10 units of wine, and $OX' = 10$. The slope of the line XX' represents the relative prices of wine and cloth, and the individual will do as well as possible when he or she attains the highest indifference curve possible. Point R is the best pattern of expenditure given the person's tastes and income ($100) and relative costs. Now suppose that wine becomes cheaper and money income remains the same. Cheaper wine flattens the slope of XX' to the dotted line; the person can now reach a higher indifference curve, indicating an increase in satisfaction and shown by point V. More of both goods is consumed. This behavior is compatible with the price of wine falling to $8 per unit: The individual could buy the combination at R (say 2½ cloth and 5 wine) with $90 and have $10 left over to spend on more of each. An increase in income with prices remaining constant would shift the XX' line outward and enable the individual to attain higher levels of satisfaction.

The movement to point V is what happens when the terms of trade become more favorable, as at point Q' in Figure 3-4 for England.

Indifference curves can be used for countries as well as for people, but the assumptions become braver. Community indifference curves have the same qualities as individual curves, but the economist must assume that the tastes of the country are not affected (through changes in income distribution) by any change in the prices of goods. If changes in relative prices and income distribution are small, this presents no serious problem.

4

Causes of Comparative Advantage

What Ricardo and his followers provided was an analytic system that explains why trade takes place (differences in opportunity costs allow exchange to generate gains from trade) without explaining how the differences in opportunity costs actually came about. Another problem with Ricardo's theory is that it does not tie in to the performance of either national economy—the analysis floats in some undefined space between two countries. Self-evidently, the effect of international trade on a domestic economy can be important, particularly in affecting income distribution between profits and wages and the prosperity of different sectors. Some additional explanation is needed to answer the question, Will everyone in the nation gain from international trade or will some people actually lose?

The answer to this question and the other outstanding question (Which goods will be exported and which imported?) is provided by the factor-proportions theory developed by two Swedish economists, Eli Heckscher and Bertil Ohlin. This theory depends on differences in resource endowments between the two countries (the availability of factors of production). It is often referred to as the Heckscher-Ohlin (H-O) theory, and Ohlin was awarded the 1977 Nobel Prize in economics for his contribution to the theory of international trade.

The factor-proportions theory argues that different national endowments of factors of production (adjusted for the size of the country) will generate different prices for those factors when each country is in isolation (i.e., in autarky). When trade is permitted between the two countries, the difference in autarkic factor prices will generate different (opportunity and money) costs of production for different goods. The product that the home country makes relatively cheaply will be exported and the one that the country makes expensively will be imported. The basic proposition is that a factor that is relatively plentiful in a country will be cheaper than in a foreign country where it is relatively scarce. It follows that a product that uses large amounts of the plentiful and cheap factor will be relatively cheap in world markets and one that needs relatively large amounts of the factor that is scarce and expensive in autarky will be expensive in world markets. What matter are the relative costs of factors of production. The easiest way to understand the concept of relative factor endowments is to compare national data to global averages. Suppose that the world (the sum of the two countries) has ten workers for every unit of capital. This average is made up of five workers per machine (unit of capital) in Country I and fifteen workers per machine in Country II (the two countries have the same number of machines). Country I is relatively short of labor, and in autarky, labor will be expensive there relative to the cost of capital. Thus, according to the H-O theory, Country I will export goods that use lots of capital and import labor-intensive goods. Country II will have relatively low wages and will have a cost advantage in goods that need lots of labor. The H-O theory, then, is a theory of differing supply capabilities, and the pattern of demand plays a relatively minor role. Demand patterns (tastes) are allowed for, but countries are likely to differ more in their comparative resource endowments (and supply capabilities) than in their tastes.

Once the relative autarkic money costs of production have been determined (either by fluctuations in the exchange rate between the two currencies or by variations in price levels in the two countries), the H-O theory can be fitted into the Ricardian framework of comparative advantage. Except for Ricardo's exclusive emphasis on labor as a factor of production, virtually all of the Ricardian assumptions hold.

THE FORMAL FACTOR-PROPORTIONS THEORY

Consider two nations, I and II, each with given endowments of two factors of production. To begin with, they can be identified as capital and labor. Each country is capable of producing two goods, A and B. Good A is capital-intensive and good B is (inevitably) labor-intensive because, for any given ratio of the cost of capital to the cost of labor, good A will use a higher proportion of capital in its production than good B. Note that capital intensity and labor intensity are relative concepts that say nothing about absolute amounts—the H-O theory has as many relatives as a family gathering. If a nation has a great deal of capital and relatively little labor, it will be capable of producing a lot of the capital-intensive good when all of its resources are devoted to the production of A and significantly fewer units of the labor-intensive good (B) when all of its resources are devoted to producing good B. In contrast, the other country will be able to produce more of the labor-intensive good and less of the capital-intensive good. The difference in the factor endowments will affect the shape of the countries' production possibility curves. The capital-plentiful country (Country I) will have a curve with a bulge in the direction of the capital-intensive good; Country II will have its production possibility curve bulge in the direction of the labor-intensive good. Assume that tastes are the same in both countries, and let this fact be denoted by both countries having a common set of indifference curves to represent national preferences between goods A and B. This situation is illustrated in Figure 4-1. In autarky in Country I, the relative cost and relative price line, αα, shows a large amount of the capital-intensive good, A, exchanging for a relatively small amount of the labor-intensive good, B. To work this out, extend the line αα to the horizontal and vertical axes. Then regard the line αα as a budget constraint showing the quantity of each good that can be purchased with a given sum of money. This gives relative quantities with the same value and, therefore, relative prices. Production in Country I is at point Q, and consumption shows the same mix of goods (as must be in autarky). The price line at the production possibility curve (PP) shows relative

Figure 4-1

COMPARATIVE AUTARKIC POSITIONS

Note that the slopes of αα and ββ are different. This derives from the shapes of the production possibility curves and not from the positions or shapes of the community indifference curves (1C), which are drawn identically. The different shapes of the production possibility curves derive from the different endowments of productive factors in the two countries.

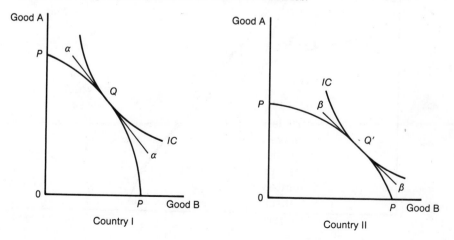

marginal costs of production, and the price line at the indifference curve (*IC*) shows relative marginal utilities of the two goods. In Country II, the production point is *Q'*. The price or cost line, ββ, is much flatter, showing that good A (capital-intensive) is relatively more expensive there and the labor-intensive good is relatively cheap. Country I has a comparative advantage in the good (A) that uses its relatively plentiful factor relatively intensively. Country II's comparative advantage lies in good B. The factor-proportions theory has explained the pattern of international trade.

Figure 4-2 shows the equilibrium situation when trade has been instituted (with zero transportation costs). The two individual country figures in Figure 4-1 have been combined, with the indifference curve being common to both. Points *Q* and *Q'* are no longer positions of production

Figure 4-2

INTERNATIONAL TRADE EQUILIBRIUM

Country I exports *OF* of good A and imports *FC* of good B. Country II, the trading partner, exports *GO'* (= *FC*) of good B and imports *GC* (= *OF*) of good A. The terms of trade are those compatible with *PP*.

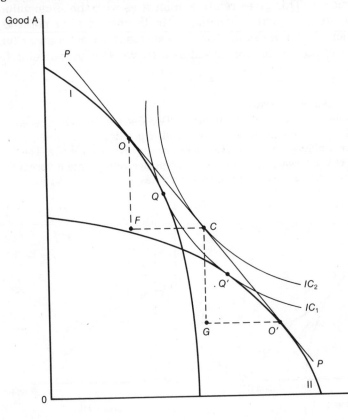

or consumption. Prices of the two goods must be the same, or there will be an incentive to increase the volume of trade, and therefore the trading equilibrium can be shown by a straight price line (*PP*) tangent to the two production blocks. Each country will produce more of the good in which it has a comparative advantage and consume more of the good that it imports than in autarky. The new consumption point, *C,* is the same for both countries and *C* is on a higher indifference curve than either *Q* or *Q'*, the autarkic consumption points. This shows a gain from international trade for both countries. Country I produces at point *O,* and the difference between its output mix at *O* and its consumption mix at *C* shows the pattern of international trade. Consumption of good B in excess of production is imported (*FC*) and production of good A in excess of consumption is exported (*OF*). The same kind of adjustment has taken place in Country II. Note that the equilibrium shown in Figure 4-2 is vastly simplified to make the figure clear. The two countries are the same size and have the same pretrade standard of living (shown by indifference curve 1); tastes are identical; and the countries divide the global gain from trade equally since each country improves its standard of living from indifference curve 1 to indifference curve 2.

It is useful at this juncture to relate Figure 4-2 to the offer curve diagram (Figure 3-4 in Chapter 3). The line *PP'* (or *OO'*) corresponds to the (net barter) terms of trade *OQ* where one wine exchanges for one cloth. The two autarkic price lines, and αα and ββ in Figure 4-1, may be seen as equivalent to Ricardo's autarkic price ratios as shown in Figure 3-1 in Chapter 3.

Figure 4-3 shows the same equilibrium using the separate subfigures given in Figure 4-1. The important requirement in any two-country exposition of international trade is to recognize that the trade of each country must exactly match the trade of the other.

In practice, the assumption of identical tastes is necessary only to

Figure 4-3
INTERNATIONAL TRADE EQUILIBRIUM

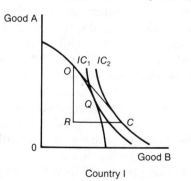

Country I

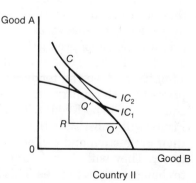

Country II

simplify the exposition. The same argument follows exactly as long as the difference in tastes is less than the difference in factor endowments so that good A is, in fact, relatively cheap in autarky in Country I. As long as Country I's indifference curves (tastes) touch its production possibility curve in autarky below *O*, Country I produces good A relatively cheaply.

Perverse tastes exist if Country I's indifference curves are so oriented toward good A that Country I imports good A. This will occur when Country I's indifference map touches the autarkic production possibility curve between *O* and the vertical axis. The demand for the capital-intensive good is so intense that good A will be relatively expensive in autarky. In that event, intuitively, the factor of production that is relatively plentiful in a physical sense is going to be relatively expensive. It is going to be the scarce factor in an economic sense. Capital in Country I will be the expensive factor of production.

Income Distribution and International Trade

According to Figures 4-2 and 4-3, international trade leads to increased production of the good using the relatively plentiful (and therefore relatively cheap) factor of production intensively. Necessarily, this implies reduced output of the other good. For Country I, trade implies increased production of good A and reduced production of good B. Trade implies the transfer of factors of production from industry B to industry A in Country I. At the autarkic ratio of factor prices, good B uses more labor per unit of capital than good A. When industry B declines, it will release factors of production in the proportion of, say, two units of labor per unit of capital, and industry A will require the factors in the ratio, say, of one capital for one labor. Either there will be a surplus of labor or a shortage of capital when output of good B decreases. The price of capital would tend to go up and that of labor to go down. Exactly the opposite pattern of behavior is taking place in Country II. Good B is expanding there and trying to absorb more labor per unit of capital than Country II's industry A is releasing: The price of labor is tending upward and that of capital downward. The cheap factor in both countries is tending to get more expensive as a result of international trade, and *relative* prices of factors of production are tending toward equality. This tendency is about all that can be established without resorting to unrealistic assumptions. Even the tendency toward an equalization of relative factor prices in each country assumes that full employment exists in the trade equilibrium in both countries. How will full employment be reestablished? Firms will substitute the now cheaper scarce factor of production in their production and will economize on the now more expensive plentiful factor. They will alter the mix of factors used in production in response to changed relative prices. This is a slow-working process. Thus in Country

I, when full employment and international trade coexist, industry A will use, say, 1¼ units of labor (now cheaper) per unit of capital and industry B will use 2¼ units of labor per unit of capital. Because of international trade, labor has become less scarce in Country I. Put in the simplest terms, this is because the need for labor in Country I is being met in part by the use of foreign labor (Country II's labor), which is embodied in imports. With imports available, the home supply of labor can be used more productively by transferring some of it to industry A. The reverse takes place in Country II.

This allows us to answer the fifth question: Does everyone gain from the inauguration of international trade? The plentiful factor clearly gains because its relative return increases (the demand for the factor shifts to the right as production of the good in which it is used intensively increases as a result of export demand). The plentiful factor also enjoys some share of the efficiency gains from trade. The case for the scarce factor is less clear. It must balance its share of the gain from trade against a loss in its relative return due to its suffering from competition from imports. Whether labor in Country I is better or worse off as a consequence of international trade is simply not determinable without many specific assumptions being made. Each nation gains because the benefits achieved by the plentiful factor must exceed the losses of the scarce factor (if any) by the gains from trade. In practice, many factors of production are specific to an industry and would suffer the loss of return of any industry-specific characteristics. For example, a textile engineer would suffer if international trade resulted in smaller production of textiles and the engineer in question had to return to college to retrain as a civil engineer or an electronics engineer or was forced to accept a less well-paid position. Not everyone gains from international trade when factors of production are disaggregated from the two all-embracing labels of capital and labor.

In practice question 5 is rather remote. No country has the choice between autarky and full trade—if only because of the vital need for noncompetitive imports and the huge gain from trade that they generate. The question of income distribution relates to how certain groups within a country favor full, uninhibited international trade as compared with some limitations being placed on imports (so that a smaller volume of exchange takes place). This aspect of the problem is considered in Part III, where the question of protection is analyzed.

The Factor-Proportions Theory in Money Terms

International trade always takes place in response to differences in money costs and prices prevailing in the market, and it is money prices that transmit to the buyer which country has a comparative advantage in which good.[1] Of course, if the discrepancy in comparative advantage is large, the good will only be made and produced in one country, and the signaling mechanism will, inevitably, work accurately. What follows is a simple development of the factor-proportions theory in terms of money prices. It is assumed that all four industries have constant returns to scale but that money costs of production vary as factor prices vary. Country I is well endowed with capital and Country II with labor, so the following autarkic set of factor prices is reasonable.

	Cost of One Unit	
	Capital	Labor
Country I	$2.00	$1.00
Country II	P 8 (= $2.67)	P 1 (= $0.33)

The exchange rate that balances international trade is one dollar exchanges for three pesos, so labor is absolutely more expensive in Country I and capital is absolutely cheaper there. Assume that good A uses six units of capital ($6K$) and four units of labor ($4L$) in both countries; good B uses $2K$ and $4L$ in both countries. (An important simplification is made here to simplify the arithmetic. In practice, we might expect that the mix of factors would be more labor-intensive in both industries in Country II because labor is relatively cheaper there.) The money costs of the goods in autarky are:

	Good A	Good B
Country I	$16.00	$8.00
Country II	P 52 ($17.33)	P 20 ($6.67)

Country I produces good A relatively cheaply in money terms, and Country II produces good B relatively cheaply. The pattern of trade in a world using money is the same as that identified by the formal theory. (Note also that the fact that each country produces one good relatively cheaply in money terms shows that the rate of exchange—P 3 = $1.00—is a feasible one for balanced trade.)

---

[1]As noted, even specialists in international trade theory do not bother to work out which country has a comparative advantage in a good. They simply rely on the price mechanism. The appearance of foreign and domestically produced goods side by side on a supermarket shelf usually indicates a relatively small difference in comparative advantage that reflects variations in taste and quality. One sees Norwegian sardines next to American sardines because the sardines are not identical. One does not see imported detergent on the shelf next to American-made detergent because there is too little distinction in detergents to warrant trying to set up a distribution outlet for Norwegian detergent.

Recall that the assumption is always that the value of exports equals the value of imports. If that were not so (if the exchange rate was distorted from its "true" value for some reason), it might be that a nation would have a competitive advantage in a good in which it had a comparative disadvantage. This possibility makes more sense when multiple goods are being traded and produced and the distortion in the exchange rate is substantial.

If desired, comparative advantage can be computed from the money costs in the standard way: Relative costs in Country I are 16/8 and in Country II are 52/20.

The analysis becomes more realistic if the existence of several (say, six) goods is assumed. These goods can be ranked by comparative advantage in terms of their comparative difference in autarkic money costs. Table 4-1 shows production and cost data for the six goods under the original set of tastes in columns 1 through 7. Good A is now identified as good 3 and good B as good 4. Columns 2 and 3 give the input requirements and are ranked in decreasing order of capital intensity. Columns 4 and 5 give money costs of production in domestic currency, and column 6 applies the rate of exchange to Country II's peso costs to bring the two sets of cost data into a common measure of value. Column 7 computes the proportionate difference in money costs of production (D) where

$$D = \frac{C^I - C^{II}}{C^I}$$

and C is the dollar cost of producing each good in autarky in the country denoted by the superscript. Good 1, for example, has a negative value of D of 22 percent, showing that it is cheaper to manufacture good 1 in Country I. Country I exports that good. Note that Country I enjoys a large gain from trade from the export of this good, even if the corresponding import were something it could produce for almost the same money cost as it pays for the import: In that event it would be exchanging something that it makes 22 percent more cheaply for something that it could make about as cheaply as the foreign country can. To make the same point in a different way, the exchange of good 1 for good 5 brings a larger gain from trade than exchanging good 3 for good 4. In terms of the offer curve diagram, Figure 4-4, the exchange of good 1 for good 5 constitutes the wide part of the football and the large per-unit gain from trade.[2]

Now it is possible to reexamine the impact of a demand-based disturbance to the system (compare the last part of Chapter 3).

Let Country II suddenly experience a significant increase in its demand for good 1, an import. In terms of Figure 4-4, its offer curve will shift upward and to the left, indicating a more intense desire for imports at all terms of trade. Country I will enjoy improved terms of trade, and this will show itself in a strengthening of Country I's currency ($). Let the new exchange rate be $1 = P 3.33—a 10 percent appreciation of the dollar. The values of D change for all six goods, as shown in column 8. The effect of the change is striking. The increase in demand for good 1 by Country II has affected the competitive position (D) for all the other

---

[2]Of course, imports of good 5 would generate diminishing material utility, so the argument in the text applies only to the first few units of good 5 imported.

Table 4-1
COMPARATIVE ADVANTAGE OF TERMS OF MONEY COSTS

(1) Good	(2) Capital Content	(3) Labor Content	(4) Cost in I ($)	(5) Cost in II (P)	(6) Cost in II ($)	(7) Value of D ($1 = P 3)	(8) Value of D ($1 = P 3.3)	(9) Cost in I ($)	(10) Cost in II (P)	(11) Cost in II ($)	(12) Value of D ($1 = P 3.3)
1	8	2	18	66	22.0	−22%	−11%	22	81.2	24.6	−11.8%
2	6	2	14	50	16.7	−19%	−8%	17	61.4	18.6	−9.4%
3	6	4	16	52	17.3	−8%	+1.5%	19	63.4	19.2	0
4	2	4	8	20	6.7	+16%	+24%	9	23.8	7.2	+20.0%
5	2	6	10	22	7.3	+27%	+33%	11	25.8	7.8	+29.0%
6	2	8	12	24	8.0	+33%	+39%	13	27.8	8.4	+35.4%

Factors prices for Columns 1 through 8 are P_K = $2 and P 8 and P_L = $1 and P 1.
Factors prices for columns 9 through 11 are P_K = $2.5 and P 9.9 and P_L = $1 and P 1.
Values of D are approximate. To preserve the arithmetic simplicity of the model, factor proportions do not change, and factor productivity does not change without output. Dotted lines indicate that some price change has occurred.

Figure 4-4

SHIFT IN FOREIGN
DEMAND

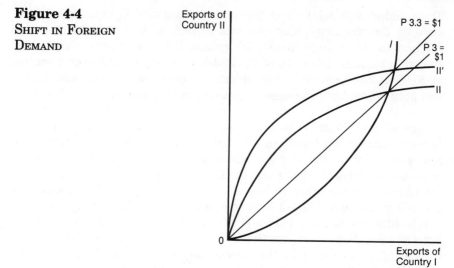

goods. The industry in Country I producing good 2 now finds that its prices have gone up as far as foreigners are concerned, and export sales will probably fall off. Industry 1 gains, of course, from the increase in demand for its products. The most severe impact is on good 3: Here Country I's industry is all set to be eliminated since Country II's industry can now make the good more cheaply (D has switched from −8% to +1.5%). Industries 4, 5, and 6 are all likely to experience an increase in foreign demand and to have greater prosperity in Country II.

The change in demand conditions in industry 1 has reacted upon the prosperity of all industries through the change in the rate of exchange (the terms of trade). Country I is undoubtedly better off—has a larger gain from trade—because of its improved terms of trade. It is, strictly, not possible to say that Country II is worse off because its tastes have changed and a comparison of "after" with "before" cannot be made. But the position indicated in Column 8 is unlikely to be the final equilibrium. The increase in world demand for good 1 will have increased the demand for the factor of production capital (K) in both countries: in Country I because it is producing more of good 1 and less of good 3 and in Country II because its production of good 3 will have increased. Capital will become more expensive relative to labor in both countries, and new money prices for factors will come about. Assume that the new money prices of K and L are as follows:

	Capital	Labor
Country I	$2.50	$1.00
Country II	P 9.9	P 1.0

These induced changes affect the international trading equilibrium. Assuming, for simplicity, that the mix of factors in each good does *not* respond to the change in relative prices, the new domestic costs are shown in columns 9 and 10 of Table 4-1. The rate of exchange remains at $1 = P 3.3. Column 1 now shows the comparative cost advantage, and good 3 now costs the same to produce in both countries and becomes a good that is not traded between the two countries. Note that owners of capital are better off in both countries and laborers are worse off. Income distribution has been affected by the change in the pattern of tastes and in the terms of trade. There is also a short-run impact (called the costs of adjustment) whereby the factors are relocated out of declining industries into expanding industries. People will be laid off in industries 2 and 3 in Country I because their export markets have declined. They will be hired in industry 1. People in industries 2 and 3 experience problems of relocation, short-run (frictional) unemployment, and feelings of insecurity. Any change in the composition or pattern of international trade has short-run repercussions on the domestic economy and permanent effects on relative earnings of factors of production.

THE FACTOR-PROPORTIONS
THEORY: REVIEW

The Heckscher-Ohlin or factor-proportions theory is a theory of international trade that relies on the relative endowments of different factors of production to explain differences in relative supply capabilities. The theory recognizes that the differences in factor endowments between two nations can be reduced or magnified by differences in patterns of demand but generally assumes that supply differences are larger than demand differences. Under these conditions, a factor in plentiful supply in some physical sense is also the plentiful (or cheap) factor in an economic sense. By recognizing the tie-in between the use of factors of production for exports and their disemployment in import-competing industries, the H-O theory allows the pattern of international trade and the performance of the domestic economy to be interrelated.

The H-O theory says that a country will export (have a comparative advantage in) goods that use relatively intensively its relatively plentiful factors of production. What this means in money terms is that a country will be able to produce relatively cheaply (and will export) the goods that use relatively intensively its relatively cheap factors of production. Nearly always this theory is expressed in terms of two factors of production (capital and labor), two goods, and two countries. Under such assumptions, the results are clear-cut because, inevitably, the goods in which one country has a comparative advantage are easily identifiable. Provided that the number of factors is restricted to two, the theory can readily be seen to hold in a multigood, two-country framework as shown in Table 4-1. This framework is most easily understood when expressed in terms of money costs, but it could be identified without reference to money costs simply by ranking goods in terms of their factor intensities.

It is useful at this juncture to recall the five basic questions and the four possible types of gain from international trade in Chapter 3 to see which have been explained and which still need to be explained.

1. The advantage of trade to a nation is explained by the H-O theory in much the same way as by the Ricardian theory. Countries exchange goods that they make relatively efficiently in terms of opportunity cost for goods that they make relatively inefficiently. The theory of comparative advantage has been given depth by explaining its cause—differences in factor endowments.
2. Exported goods will be those that use relatively intensively the factors of production that are relatively plentiful and, therefore, cheap.
3. The global gain from trade will be distributed according to the intensity of the demand for imports and the willingness to supply exports. With multiple goods (Table 4-1), this depends on the mix of demand as well as on the terms of trade; the gain from trade depends on the curvature of the offer curve as well as the terms of trade.
4. The price of exports in terms of imports (the terms of trade) is determined by the intersection of the countries' offer curves—that is, by their joint willingness to buy and to supply goods in the international marketplace.
5. It cannot be guaranteed that everyone in the nation will benefit from international trade because scarce factors could be worse off under trade than under autarky. The pattern of trade affects relative factor prices within each country. If a scarce factor's loss in relative income is not made up for by the country's gain from trade, the scarce factor could be absolutely worse off as a result of the introduction of international trade. Such a result is extremely unlikely when noncompetitive imports are allowed for, because the gain from trade from such imports is or can be tremendous. Certainly, the scarce factor will gain less than the plentiful factor from international trade. However, in reality, the question should be set in terms of small changes in the volume of international trade and impediments to it: Under these conditions, some factors can lose as a result of freer international trade or can gain from the imposition of impediments to trade even in terms of a model based on large groups of homogeneous factors. When industry-specific skills are allowed for (and industry-specific machinery), people with skills in declining industries can lose income (senile industry protection will be discussed in Chapter 7).

How does the H-O theory apply to the four basic types of gain from trade?

1. The gain from trade achieved by the exchange of noncompetitive goods has not been explained by the standard version of the H-O theory, which limits its field of analysis to standard factors of production such as labor and capital. These are "generally applicable" factors of production, and all goods are assumed to require only these factors; consequently, all (both) goods can be made in both countries.
2. The gain from trade through the global redistribution of production in line with national comparative advantage is the type of gain from trade to which the H-O theory addresses itself. The H-O theory is, then, a refinement of the theory of comparative advantage.
3. Trade in differentiated goods is not addressed by the H-O theory.
4. The gain from trade achieved by limiting the power of domestic monopolists has not been explained by the H-O theory.

TESTING THE SIMPLE FACTOR-PROPORTIONS THEORY

Any economic theory is so much supposition, albeit logical supposition, until it has been tested empirically. Unfortunately, many economic models are very difficult to test because the data are less than fully suitable and because real-world conditions do not lend themselves to an exact interpretation of the analysis. The primary test of the factor-proportions theory of international trade was made by Professor Wassily Leontief in the early 1950s. He used his own invention of an input-output table to determine the factor proportions of each good exported and imported. One of the difficulties in testing the factor-proportions theory of international trade is that internationally traded goods use many different kinds of products in their production; for example, a car uses steel, paint, rubber, textiles and aluminum as well as the value added by the automobile industry. A test of the capital and labor intensity of a car must therefore allow for the different capital and labor intensities of all the other industries contributing to the construction of cars as well as the capital-to-labor in the automobile industry itself. Virtually every unit produced relies on all other industries, and the achievement of input-output analysis is that it allows this complex interrelationship to be taken into account.[3]

Leontief was not so naive as to believe that there were only two factors of production, capital and labor, but he wanted to find out if the role of the relative proportions of capital to labor was so dominant in international trade that economists could legitimately concentrate on the simplified two-factor version of the H-O theory. Similarly, the use of the input-

---

[3]Leontief won the Nobel Prize in economics in 1973 for developing the means of reconciling the input-output feedback mechanisms. For a nonmathematical description, see Paul R. Gregory and Robert C. Stuart, *Comparative Economic Systems*, 2nd ed. (Boston: Houghton Mifflin, 1985), pp. 173–177.

output mechanism acknowledged the fact that all goods are not final goods and that the economy is more complex than a simple two-good assumption allows. (Even in the analysis of Table 4-1, it was implicit that each good is produced wholly by its own industry, without feedbacks.)

In practice, the task of confronting an empirical test of something as complex as the international trading system was useful because it made people think hard about the real world. The input-output approach solved the feedback problem, and Leontief did allow for the existence of goods that could not be produced in the United States—although his list was surprisingly short, comprising only bananas, jute, tea, and coffee, which indicates how difficult it is to call to mind Hawaii from Cambridge, Massachusetts. Despite Leontief's efforts to eliminate the more obvious problems, the test was less than ideal: It did not allow for land, and it assumed that the production methods in the United States were identical to those used abroad (because Leontief had capital and labor data only for U.S. industries). However, the big news was that Leontief came out with results that refuted the simple H-O theory: American exports were expected to contain more capital and less labor than U.S. imports because the United States was the richest country in the world in the 1950s, but American exports were shown to contain *less capital and more labor than imports*. In other words, a reduction in the volume of international trade would reduce exports and imports equally and would release more labor from export industries than would be absorbed into the (expanding) import-competing industries. Given the postwar dominance of the U.S. economy, no more favorable time could have been found to support the two-factor H-O theory: Europe and Japan were both devastated by the war, and the only rich economy not seriously damaged was Canada's.

Some economists were quick to attribute the failure of the test (or of the theory) to imperfections in the test itself. Obviously, land should have been included. Some imports (like copper) are produced at home in a very capital-intensive way. A test conducted on goods with a natural-resource content showed that the paradox, as Leontief's findings were called, could be explained by eliminating goods with a natural-resource content. Other people argued that 1947 was a bad year because Europe and Japan were still recovering from the war and therefore the test was not appropriate to the theory's assumptions. Running the numbers again for 1954 did not solve the paradox. Leontief himself pointed out one feature that he had neglected but that might begin to help explain the paradox. The United States exported goods with great amounts of skilled labor and relatively little unskilled labor. So if skills were regarded as human capital (as opposed to physical capital), the paradox would disappear.

What followed Leontief's findings was a surge of rethinking. The criticism of Leontief's test concerning the omission of goods with a large natural-resource content was accepted quite easily. The United States

Table 4-2

LABOR REQUIREMENTS BY SKILL MIX

Country	Percent Distribution of Labor Requirements by Skill Class									
	Exports					Imports				
	I	II	III	V	VIII	I	II	III	V	VIII
United States	5.0	2.9	2.7	8.4	45.4	2.8	1.7	2.0	3.9	57.4
Canada	4.2	2.3	2.4	5.4	49.8	4.1	2.4	2.6	7.1	49.1
United Kingdom	3.8	2.3	2.4	7.2	49.7	3.2	2.0	2.1	5.3	54.0
Austria	2.8	1.8	1.9	5.7	54.9	3.4	2.2	2.3	7.1	51.6
Belgium	2.8	1.7	2.0	4.7	54.9	3.7	2.3	2.3	6.1	51.5
France	3.2	1.9	2.2	5.3	53.2	3.6	2.2	2.3	6.6	48.9
Germany	3.9	2.5	2.3	8.4	47.8	3.0	1.9	2.0	5.3	55.2
Italy	2.8	1.8	2.0	4.3	58.9	4.2	2.5	2.5	7.9	47.7
Netherlands	3.6	2.4	2.3	5.0	51.9	3.9	2.4	2.3	6.2	52.0
Sweden	3.5	2.3	2.2	8.9	46.0	3.6	2.3	2.3	6.3	52.1
Switzerland	3.5	2.4	2.2	7.8	50.6	3.5	2.1	2.3	6.4	51.5
Japan	2.5	1.7	1.8	4.6	58.4	5.1	3.1	2.7	9.5	42.6
India	0.7	0.6	1.1	1.3	72.1	4.3	2.6	2.5	7.1	46.7
Hong Kong	0.7	0.5	1.1	1.3	—	—	—	—	—	—

Notes: These data show the combination of the U.S. skill-mix distribution for 1960 with the 1962 pattern of international trade in 46 industries for the individual countries. Thus differences in the data reflect only the differences in the mix of international trade. Classes I, II, and III represented highly skilled technicians, Class V comprised skilled blue-collar workers, and Class VIII was "unskilled workers."

Source: Donald B. Keesing, "Labor Skills and Comparative Advantage," *American Economic Review,* vol. no. 56 (May 1966), pp. 249–258.

exports agricultural products because it has great amounts of agricultural land and imports copper ore because it has no large, rich copper deposits. In fact, this argument was carried back almost to the Ricardian framework in which a country exported the primary products that it could produce relatively cheaply because of natural-resource endowments. Capital and labor were much less important in such goods. Thus Portugal exported wine and, because England had few natural resources, England exported manufactured goods.

But the main thrust of the new wave of thinking was toward the introduction of technology and trade in manufactures. Donald B. Keesing did some thorough (if necessarily rough) work on the question of skilled labor in exports and imports.[4] Table 4-2 shows his results. The more advanced the country (measured in GNP per capita), the larger the concentration of skilled workers in exports and the more unskilled labor contained in imports.

Keesing defined skilled workers as consisting of "scientists and engineers," "technicians and draftspeople," "other professionals," and "ma-

---

[4]Donald B. Keesing, "Labor Skills and Comparative Advantage," *American Economic Review*, vol. no. 56 (May 1966), 249–258.

chinists, electricians, and tool and die-makers." Keesing did not include managers on the grounds that the managerial function is equally necessary for export and import-substitute industries. The idea of skilled workers or human capital being used relatively intensively in the exports of developed countries, however appealing, seems to imply that exporting firms used Ph.D.'s in physics and chemistry in ways that affect the actual costs of producing the goods. This almost suggests that Du Pont, for example, has its scientists working on the production line. Though not impossible, this is somewhat unlikely. Another economist, Raymond Vernon, together with two coauthors, developed the idea that developed nations exported goods made in industries that used lots of skilled personnel in research and development (R&D). In other words, a large usage of skilled personnel implied relatively large expenditures on R&D and therefore exports of new, technologically advanced products. This is the important innovation. Everyone knew that you could not analyze international trade without considering land and natural resources, but introducing technology was original. It is fundamental to modern explanations of international trade but also to an understanding of the modern phenomenon, the multinational corporation. For this pattern to evolve it is necessary to consider not only the work of Vernon and his coauthors but also that of another Swedish economist, Staffan Burenstamm Linder.

Table 4-3 shows the results of an empirical test by Gruber, Mehta, and Vernon.[5] The huge endowment of skilled persons in the United States did not mean only that human capital was cheaper and that the United States had a comparative advantage in goods using skilled labor but also that the United States had a comparative advantage in the generation of technological know-how. Therefore, the United States would export goods in which the R&D component was used intensively. Table 4-3 shows that whether technology is measured by R&D expenditure or by scientists and engineers employed in R&D as a percentage of the total labor force, sales of R&D-intensive goods are export-oriented. The discrepancy between the five industries with a high research effort and fourteen other industries is clear. The United States' comparative advantage in manufacturing lies in goods with a high technological component. This conclusion is confirmed in later data, presented in Table 4-4, which shows the trend of the trade balance in different categories of goods. When international trade data are collected in a highly inclusive way, in this table, they will include both exports and imports, and the best indication of comparative advantage or disadvantage is the value of exports less the value of imports. It is clear that the United States not only has a comparative disadvantage in goods in which the technological

[5]William Gruber, Dileep Mehta, and Raymond Vernon, "The R&D Factor in International Trade and International Investment of United States Industries," *Journal of Political Economy*, 75 (February 1967), 20–37.

Table 4-3

R&D Commitment and Export Performance

	Research Effort		Export Performance	
	R&D Expenditures	Category I in R&D*	Exports	Exports-Imports
Industry	% Sales	% Total Employment	% Sales	% Sales
Transportation	10.0	3.4	5.5	4.1
Aircraft	27.2	6.9	8.4	7.6
Other	2.8	1.0	4.2	2.6
Electrical machinery	7.3	3.6	4.1	2.9
Instruments	7.1	3.4	6.7	3.2
Chemicals	3.9	4.1	6.2	4.5
Machinery (nonelectrical)	3.2	1.4	13.3	11.4
Five industries with highest research effort	6.3	3.2	7.2	5.2
Fourteen other industries	0.5	0.4	1.8	−1.1

* Category I is taken from Keesing's terminology—scientists and engineers.

Source: William Gruber, Dileep Mehta, and Raymond Vernon, "The R&D Factor in International Trade and Investment of United States Industries," *Journal of Political Economy,* 75 (February 1967), 20–37, table 1. Copyright © 1967 by University of Chicago. Reprinted by permission.

component is small but also that for industries in which technology has been becoming less important (automobiles, for example), the advantage has turned into a disadvantage. Note that trade in manufactures is by no means always balanced—partly because total trade is not balanced but also because of changes in the net balances of other categories of goods, such as agricultural produce and industrial supplies.

What matters next is how this resource endowment of technology can be translated into comparative advantage, and the crucial ingredient is the proprietary or private quality of the technology. It belongs to a single firm. It either helps make a new product or it reduces the cost of manufacture of an existing product. Usually, the role of technology is conceived in terms of a new product and derives from Vernon's product cycle.[6] The product cycle suggests that R&D will be spent on the solution to a problem perceived in the country in which the R&D is carried out. Probably, since R&D expenditures are likely to be greatest in the most advanced countries, the technological breakthrough will respond to conditions in that country. The need for a new product or machine is perceived when one branch of industry gets ahead of another and generates "catch-up" problems or, alternatively, when a new piece of quite fundamental research lays bare a new principle that can be put to commercial use. In advanced countries where problems exist and the receptivity of the econ-

[6]The authoritative reference to the product cycle is Raymond Vernon, "International Investment and International Trade in the Product Cycle," *Quarterly Journal of Economics,* 80 (May 1966), 190–207.

Table 4-4
U.S. TRADE BALANCE BY PRODUCT GROUPING (BILLIONS OF DOLLARS)

	1960	1965	1970	1975	1976	1977	1978	1979	1980	1981	1982
Chemicals	1.0	1.6	2.4	5.0	5.2	5.4	10.0	14.2	17.3	17.5	16.5
Nonelectrical machinery	3.0	4.1	5.6	14.6	14.8	13.6	17.6	21.5	28.6	31.0	26.7
Electrical machinery	0.8	1.0	0.7	2.7	1.8	1.8	2.3	1.9	2.3	3.0	2.4
Aircraft	1.0	1.0	2.4	5.6	5.7	5.2	6.2	8.9	10.9	9.1	5.6
Professional and scientific instruments	0.2	0.4	0.7	1.5	1.4	1.5	0.5	0.7	0.8	0.9	0.9
All R&D-intensive manufacturing	5.9	8.1	11.7	29.3	29.0	27.6	36.6	47.2	59.9	61.5	52.1
All non-R&D-intensive manufacturing	-0.2	-2.0	-8.3	-9.5	-16.5	-24.4	-86.8	-105.7	-128.4	-76.0	-119.5
Foods, feeds, beverages	-0.1	0.9	-0.3	9.6	8.2	5.7	9.7	12.2	17.2	19.8	14.2
Industrial supplies and materials	0.0	-2.1	-1.6	-19.3	-32.3	-42.1	-42.8	-48.0	-56.5	-66.9	-50.3
Petroleum and products	-1.1	-1.6	-2.4	-26.0	-33.5	-43.6	-38.0	-55.0	-72.1	-7.3	-54.6
Automotive vehicles, engines, parts	0.6	1.0	-1.7	-1.2	-4.3	-5.8	-9.9	-9.1	-11.2	-11.7	-17.6
Textiles, clothing, footwear	-0.4	-0.8	-2.2	-3.0	-3.7	-5.2	-4.5	-4.5	-5.0	-6.2	-7.2
Steel products	0.2	-0.5	-0.8	-1.7	-1.5	-3.7	-1.3	-1.3	-0.8	-3.7	-4.0
Total merchandise trade	4.9	5.0	2.6	9.0	-9.4	-31.1	-28.4	-24.5	-0.2	-27.6	-31.7

Source: Data for 1960–1977 from Rachel McCulloch, "U.S. Trade Performance: The Role of Technology," *Eastern Economic Journal*, vol. no. 6 (January 1980), pp. 33–38. Reproduced by kind permission of the Eastern Economic Association and the author. Data for remaining years from *Highlights of Export and Import Trade*.

omy to new products is high (the human capital is there to be used with the new product), new products will be born. Then the corporation that owns the new technology (usually under patent protection) will begin to manufacture it and to market it. While the product is still in the formative stages, it is vital that there be a close link between the manufacturing and design activity and the marketing organization. The product is still subject to being tested by customers (users), and design changes can be made as information is relayed to the factory by sales personnel. While the good is in this stage (stage 1 of the product cycle), international cost comparisons are irrelevant. What matters is geographic proximity between place of use and place of manufacture. In stage 2, the product has become standardized, and some sales are made to foreign markets. Stage 3 involves the replacement of export sales by foreign production if foreign nations have a comparative advantage in manufacturing the good, provided that the technology is transplanted into their economies. This is, of course, a crucial step. It implies that privately owned technology will be transplanted to a foreign economy by its owner if, by so doing, the firm can reduce the costs of manufacture. By this time, of course, there is no need for a close geographic link between sales and manufacture—the product is now standardized. Stage 4 occurs when foreign-produced goods are imported into the country in which the R&D was originally developed.

How does the technology get abroad? There are two main channels. First is through the multinational corporation, which builds a foreign manufacturing facility and uses the firm's proprietary technology in the foreign plant as well as in the home plant. Second, the technological know-how can be rented (licensed) to a foreign company that will use the knowledge and pay a royalty for the privilege of using it.

The introduction of technology as a factor of production requiring explicit recognition is a major advance, but it also weakens the idea that international trade can be analyzed in some timeless equilibrium. The reason now is that the transfer of an input from one country to another has been recognized as fundamental to the determination of the pattern of international trade. Of course, what matters is the *net* technological advantage of one country vis-à-vis the rest of the world, and the product cycle does not necessarily involve changes in the relative factor endowments. The product cycle conceived of a continuous stream of new technology slowly being absorbed into new products and slowly being shifted to other nations. Thus the composition of U.S. exports changes over time without any apparent change in the underlying factor endowments—as one piece of technology is transferred abroad, another is created to take its place and to preserve the "technological lead." Of course, this has the advantage of allowing timeless analysis but, as Table 4-4 shows, a technological lead can wane. The best way of solving this problem is to conceive of the pattern of trade as being determined at any given time by the existing distribution of resources and explicitly recognizing the possibility of change over time. Some analysts attribute the weakening of the competitiveness of the U.S. economy to this transfer of technology and to changes in the U.S. technological lead—partly due to the transfer of technology abroad and partly due to large increases in R&D outlays (as a percentage of GNP) by Japan and the European nations.

The effects of a failure to maintain a technological lead is obvious in the figures for the automotive and steel industries in Table 4-4. Of course, if relative wage costs in money terms had adjusted to match changes in technological advantage (or productivity), the U.S. industries might have been able to avoid the heavy inroads into the domestic market made by foreign firms. Other industries experienced similar effects.[7]

The final criticism of the factor-proportions theory is assiciated with the name S. B. Linder.[8] He saw that international trade among developed, manufacturing nations was much larger than could reasonably be explained by the H-O theory. For example, in 1971, ten continental European nations (not including the United Kingdom) conducted more than 78 percent of their trade with other manufacturing nations.[9] This relationship tends to contradict the H-O theory, which would have large amounts of trade take place between blocs of countries with the most significant disparities in capital and labor endowments, and we would therefore expect most trade to take place between the industrialized countries and the labor-plentiful developing countries. Linder argued that the H-O theory really only explained trade in agricultural goods and primary products (with natural-resource or land content). Linder argued that trade took place among manufacturing countries because countries with similar levels of development (per capita incomes) would have similar tastes and that goods produced for the home market in one country would find ready acceptance in another manufacturing country. The potential for international trade among industrialized nations is, therefore, very great.

Linder's argument is important because it provides an explanation for the very high volume of trade among nations with comparable (but not identical) factor endowments. Linder asserted that trade in manufactured goods will take place among rich nations with similar per capita incomes because such nations will produce goods with a very similar degree of sophistication and reliability. If these nations are geographically close so that transportation costs are small and if barriers to trade among these nations are low, the nations will specialize in different versions of what is essentially the same product, and there will be a large amount of international trade. The important thing that facilitates trade in goods

---

[7]See, for example, the plight of workers in the television industry in H. Peter Gray, *The Economics of Business Investment Abroad* (London: Macmillan, 1972), pp. 201–207. Also see the source of Table 4-4.
[8]S. B. Linder, *An Essay on Trade and Transformation* (New York: Wiley, 1961).
[9]Calculated from data in International Monetary Fund, *Direction of Trade Annual, 1969–75* (Washington, D.C., 1976), pp. 2–8. Note that this kind of international trade has flourished in the European Common Market and is discussed in greater detail in Chapter 11.

of this kind (mainly consumer durables) is that because per capita incomes are approximately equal, factor costs will also be approximately equal, and there will be approximately equal costs of production. In the absence of important impediments to trade in the form of transportation costs and duties on imports (tariffs), costs of production of similar items will be about equal in the importing country, and consumers will choose among the goods according to their preference in terms of the version in question. This can most easily seen in terms of automobiles. In Europe a traveler will see Fiats (Italian) and Renaults (French) in Germany, Volkswagens in France and England, and British-made Fords in Italy. Because the transportation costs are so small, the distinguishing features (even the desire to be different and to own a foreign-made car) will make it possible for people in one country to choose between a foreign car and a domestic car with almost no influence on the part of cost, so that a country will export cars and import cars of quite similar specifications. Such trade could, in theory, take place between Germany and the United States, but transport costs are very high, and the United States exports very few cars to Europe because German costs are lower.

Other factors leading to high levels of trade among industrialized countries in manufactured goods are economies of scale in specialist lines of production, specialization in different parts of a single industry in different countries, and trade in intermediate goods among subsidiaries of multinational corporations. For example, consider two companies, one in France and one in Germany, producing different types of what is essentially the same product. If economies of scale are obtainable, it will be advantageous for the French firm to specialize in one of the two items and for the German firm to specialize in the other. For such a trade pattern to come about, all that is necessary is that the economies of scale exceed the costs of transportation. Trade among subsidiaries of multinational corporations probably resembles the example of the benefits of exploiting scale economies quite closely except that multinationals are likely to plan their production according to some least-cost formula and may be able to take advantage of small differences in input costs as well.

This pattern of international trade—particularly in differentiated consumer durables—explains the gains from trade that derive from giving consumers a wider choice than could be expected in autarky. It runs counter to the simple theory of comparative advantage and the H-O theory in the usual way in which those theories are presented.

SUMMARY

The factor-proportions theory represents a decided step forward over the Ricardian-type theory because it identifies the source of comparative advantage and allows the effects of international trade to be tied into the pattern of production of national economies. The latter attribute connects the pattern and volume of international trade with the socially sensitive problem of income distribution. However, in its simple two-factor, two-commodity approach, the H-O theory has proved inadequate to explain observed patterns of international trade. The surge of rethinking that followed Leontief's bombshell produced three additional strands of analysis that need to be taken into account explicitly if international trade is to be understood: natural resources, human capital, and privately owned technology. The emphasis on natural resources and the recognition that not all resources are available in each country serve as the basis for identification of the role of noncompetitive imports and the potentially huge gain from trade that they offer (for example, Japan is almost wholly dependent on foreign oil and coal). The identification of the role of skilled workers and of privately owned technology also complicates the issue by allowing for the possibility that not all technology is available everywhere and therefore some less developed countries may find that some high-technology goods are also noncompetitive imports.[10] The emphasis on technology and its transferability between nations by multinational corporations confounds one of the basic assumptions of both Ricardo and Heckscher-Ohlin: that factors of production are not internationally mobile. Factor proportions (in the wider sense) can change as technology is transferred, and this change can occur at a much greater speed than can capital-to-labor ratios as a result of investment and population growth.

To explain reality, a theory of international trade must be more complex than a simple capital-to-labor factor-proportions theory. But the underlying truth remains: International trade takes place because goods can be bought more cheaply from abroad than they can be produced at home. In this sense, the factor-proportions theory continues to hold as long as factor scarcity is reflected in factor prices and, through that, in the cost of goods produced. Even trade in manufactured goods among industrialized nations can be made compatible with the factor-proportions theory by identifying the underlying need for basic equality in the costs of major factors of production so that minor differences in detail and taste can be allowed to show themselves in the marketplace.

Bibliography

On Factors Proportion
Ohlin, Bertil. *Interregional and International Trade.* Cambridge, Mass.: Harvard University Press, 1933, chs. 1–3.
Caves, R. E. *Trade and Economic Structure.* Cambridge, Mass.: Harvard University Press, 1960, pp. 23–30.

[10]This fact is extremely important in analyses of the trade patterns of developing countries and explains their sense of urgency to be allowed to sell goods to the industrialized nations.

On the Leontief Paradox

Caves, R. E. *Trade and Economic Structure,* pp. 273–274.

Gray, H. Peter. "Factor Proportions in International Trade with Noncompetitive Imports Redefined." *Weltwirtschaftliches Archiv,* 95 (1965), 156–163.

On Broadening the Theory

Gray, H. Peter. "The Theory of International Trade among Industrialized Nations." *Weltwirtschaftliches Archiv,* 116 (1980), 447–470.

Linder, S. B. *An Essay on Trade and Transformation.* New York: Wiley, 1961.

Vernon, Raymond. "International Investment and International Trade in the Product Cycle." *Quarterly Journal of Economics,* 80 (May 1966), 190–207.

Questions and Problems

Questions

1. Explain in words why the pattern of trade shown in Table 4-4 has evolved as it did.
2. Why is the factor-proportions theory able to address things such as income distribution?
3. Why would people expect the United States to be well endowed with capital in the early 1950s?
4. Why do noncompetitive imports provide large gains from trade on average? Explain in terms of the data in Table 4-1.
5. A nation well endowed with capital can be said to acquire additional labor by sending out (exporting) some of its capital through international trade. Explain.
6. What are the four ways in which international trade can benefit the trading nation? Which of these gains is likely to be the most important?
7. How do nations gain from having the ability to import goods that are similar to those produced at home at, roughly, the same price as home-produced goods?
8. Why does the H-O theory lead an economist to expect large volumes of trade between rich and poor nations and very little trade between nations of the same income level?

Problems

1. Recompute Table 4-1 (columns 8, 9, 10, and 12) when there is an increase in demand for good 6 by Country I and the rate of exchanges to $1.00 = P 2.75 and when the price of capital sinks to $1.75 and P 7.00 (with the price of labor holding steady at $1.00 and P 1.00).
2. Add a new good to Table 4-1 (a new invention that is highly capital-intensive using 11 units of K to 2 units of L). At what rate of exchange will good 3 have a value of $D = 0$ in column 7?

5

Toward Greater Realism

The great lesson that came out of Leontief's work, despite its approximations, was that the real world was infinitely more complex than could be adequately represented by a static, two-factor analysis. The simple distinction between capital and labor was not enough. The follow-up work by Linder, Keesing, and Vernon (among others) showed that international trade patterns and relationships cannot be understood unless natural resources, skilled labor (human capital), and proprietary technology are added to the list of inputs: A five-factor approach is a minimum. Economic analysis can then begin to represent the conditions in which real-world problems exist and policies are made. These policies are determined in the hurly-burly of domestic political infighting and compromise as well as in the tedium of international conferences. They are determined by grass-roots impressions, newspaper headlines, and careful analytic presentations made to congressional committees.

This chapter presents a straightforward, five-factor theory of international trade that recognizes the changes inherent in the passage of time by assuming a short-term horizon. Change can be introduced by allowing factor prices and availabilities to change quite rapidly as technology is transferred among nations. The theory is a simplified representation of the real world, but it will allow the causalities to stand out more clearly than a model based on all-encompassing generic factors of production.

THE FACTOR-PRICE THEORY OF INTERNATIONAL TRADE

At a minimum, a real-world explanation of the pattern of international trade among nations needs to encompass five classes of factors of production. This will still only provide a basic analytic framework because it might be necessary to subdivide some of the factors of production. For example, in a five-factor model, land must encompass all natural resources and must therefore include variations in climate for agriculture, different mineral deposits for ore extraction, and, ultimately, different locations. To the two traditional factors of production—physical capital (machinery) and labor (unskilled)—must be added natural resources (land), human capital, and proprietary technology.[1] The existence of product-requisite inputs (such as copper ore for copper) exceeds the scope of an introductory text but must be allowed for if the existence of noncompetitive imports is to be recognized.

Differing endowments of natural resources and technology explain the existence of noncompetitive imports. A nation can make ICBMs only if its defense firms have or can rent the appropriate technology. A nation can produce rubber only if it has a suitable climate. (Adam Smith's idea of grapes in Scotland is sufficiently farfetched that most analysts would count grapes as a noncompetitive import in Scotland.) This kind of good is important in international trade and has to be explicitly included in any real-world theory. The theories developed in Chapters 3 and 4 are based on the assumption that the goods traded can be produced in either country. Of course, the fact that a country can make a good does not mean that it will: Sewing machines are no longer made in the United States. Once the existence of noncompetitive imports is recognized, the gains from international trade become considerably larger. The football becomes much wider. The exchange of noncompetitive imports can be termed "super absolute advantage" and is an extreme case of Hypothesis 2 in Chapter 3.

It is worth distinguishing three kinds of noncompetitive imports.

1. *Absolutely noncompetitive imports* are goods that rely for their production on a natural resource not available in the importing country. Examples of such goods are relatively scarce in the United States because of the richness of its natural resources and the wide range of climates it enjoys. Platinum is an absolutely noncompetitive import. Tea is absolutely noncompetitive. Small countries such as Belgium and Taiwan would have much longer lists of absolutely noncompetitive imports. A country will never be able to produce its own absolutely noncompetitive imports (except by finding a mineral deposit).

2. *Gap-filling noncompetitive imports* are goods in which the importing

---

[1] For special analyses, it often is necessary to consider economies of scale in the production of manufactured goods as well. Recall that noncompetitive imports are products that the country cannot produce.

country has some of the necessary resources but nowhere near enough to be self-sufficient at the going world price. Oil in the United States is a perfect example. Wheat and animal-feed grains in many small food-importing countries are also gap-filling imports. Usually, domestic production is pushed to the maximum possible, and imports of the good do not compete with domestic output in the sense that fewer imports means more domestic output. Frequently, domestic industries such as these are supported by their governments through subsidy or some similar scheme.

3. *Technological noncompetitive imports* are goods for which the needed technology is not available in the importing country. Third-generation computers cannot be produced in India because the know-how is not available in that country. The reason for the technology's unavailability is usually that it is privately owned (by IBM, for example) and cannot be used by an Indian corporation without IBM's permission. Thus, even if some engineer in India knew what the technology was, the Indian computer industry still could not use the technology. The important distinction between absolutely noncompetitive imports and technological noncompetitive imports is that technology can be transferred. Climate and natural-resource deposits cannot move. Technology can be made available, in our example, by IBM's opening a factory in India and using the technological know-how or by IBM's licensing an Indian corporation to use the technology for a fee (a royalty). Finally, the patent guarding the specific knowledge can lapse, and the knowledge can become freely available to all corporations everywhere.

Reliance on noncompetitive imports that are central to the production system makes the economy quite vulnerable to interruptions in the flow of international trade. This is particularly true if the existing ways of operation in the country would be unsustainable in the absence of the noncompetitive imports. Many developed nations would face undreamed-of economic disruption if oil imports were to be completely interrupted for any protracted period of time. This is a second source of the importance of international trade in this kind of good in addition to the huge gains from trade that it can engender. Economic warfare really consists of attempts to close off the supply of vital noncompetitive imports to an antagonist nation.[2]

The factor-proportions theory of international trade, reduced to its simplest form, stated that a nation had a comparative advantage in and would export goods that used intensively the factors of production with which the nation was relatively well endowed. This statement had to be qualified to exclude the possibility that tastes were so markedly different in the two countries as to be perverse. But the factor-proportions

---

[2] See the supplement following Chapter 7.

theory implies that the relatively plentiful factor is also the relatively cheap factor of production. Therefore any good whose production relied heavily on the use of the (relatively) cheap factor would be cheaper to make in the home country than abroad and would be exported. Tastes (perverse or normal) can be put aside when the factor-proportions theory is expressed in factor prices instead of factor quantities because factor prices subsume both tastes (demand for factors) and endowments (supply). A nation, then, has a comparative advantage in the goods it makes relatively cheaply, and it will make relatively cheaply goods that use the (relatively) cheap factors of production heavily (relatively intensively). Note that in the two-factor cost comparison of Chapter 4, comparative costs are merely weighted averages of the prices of factors, the weights being the factor intensities.

The use of money costs of production of goods in different countries to determine the way in which a good will be expected to perform in the international market is useful because it allows the analysis to incorporate more than two factors of production quite easily. The money costs of production can be computed from given factor prices for all five factors and given factor intensities. So much capital is multiplied by the cost of capital,[3] so much labor by the money wage rate, so much land by the cost of land, so much technology by the rental cost of technology, and so much human capital by the higher pay needed by a skilled worker. Goods that use labor intensively will apply a heavy weight to the cost of (unskilled) labor. The cost of all goods can then be calculated in domestic (home) currency. A similar set of costs can be computed for the foreign country in its currency, and the costs can be compared by converting one currency's prices into the other's by means of the rate of exchange. For simplicity, assume that the rate of exchange that prevails and is used is the one that will equalize the value of exports and imports when full employment holds. What follows is simply a multifactor version of the money cost comparison presented in Chapter 4, and it serves exactly the same purpose: to establish the ranking of goods by the relative difference in costs (D) and therefore by comparative cost advantage.[4]

Let the autarkic factor prices be as follows:

Factor	Country I	Country II
Physical capital (K)	$2	P 18
Human capital (H)	$3	P 14
Unskilled labor (L)	$3	P 4
Land (R)	$4	P 14
Technology (T)	$1	P 8

---

[3] The cost of capital is a tricky concept. It comprises the amount of capital invested multiplied by the rate of interest and the amount of capital used up (depreciation of capital) valued, presumably, by the cost of replacing the machine that is being worn out in production.

[4] $D = \dfrac{C^I - C^{II}}{C^I}$

Because land varies considerably, the concept of setting a simple price for its use is a major simplification. Similarly, the complexities of the measurement of the cost of capital are ignored, and it is assumed that there exists a single price of capital for each industry. A skilled worker receives $6 or P 18 per hour—a combination of the return to unskilled labor ($3 and P 4) and to the human capital attached to the body ($3 and P 14). These prices are assumed to be unaffected by the opening up of trade.

The rate of exchange is $1 = P 4. Good A uses inputs in the following proportions: $5K + 3H + 4L + 1R + 2T$ in both countries (the same simplifying assumption as used in Chapter 4). Good B uses $1K + 1H + 6L + 2R + 1T$. Here are the costs for good A:

Country I: $\$(5 \times 2) + (3 \times 3) + (4 \times 3) + (1 \times 4) + (2 \times 1) = \$37 \, (= P \, 148)$

Country II: $P \, (5 \times 18) + (3 \times 14) + (4 \times 4) + (1 \times 14) + (2 \times 8) = P \, 178$

Here are the costs for good B:

Country I: $\$(1 \times 2) + (1 \times 3) + (6 \times 3) + (2 \times 4) + (1 \times 1) = \$32 \, (= P \, 128)$

Country II: $P \, (1 \times 18) + (1 \times 14) + (6 \times 4) + (2 \times 14) + (1 \times 8) = P \, 92$

It is evident that Country I is a rich manufacturing country in which technology, physical capital, and skilled labor are relatively cheap and that Country II is a poor nation with a large unskilled population. Equally, good A is intensive in the use of technology and both kinds of capital, and good B uses unimproved (unskilled) labor intensively. The relative costs of production in Country I are 37/32 and in II are 178/92: Clearly, Country II has a comparative advantage in good B, and this accords with the actual money costs computed. It is possible for factors other than physical capital and labor to be the determining influence in relative cheapness; for example, wheat production will be heavily influenced by the cost of land and computers by the cost of technology.[5]

In exactly the same way as in Chapter 4, we can use the concept of the proportionate difference in money cost of production to develop the ranking by comparative advantage. This in turn provides a more realistic

[5] It is difficult to attribute a price to privately owned technology. This can be done for illustrative purposes by conceiving of the price that the owner would charge a licensee (a user paying a royalty) in the two countries. Generally, the more plentiful historic expenditure on R&D, the cheaper the cost of technological know-how.

Note that it is necessary to distinguish between the cost of technology seen as a fair rate of return on invested capital and the rate that market conditions allow the company to charge. Strictly, R&D expenditures are "sunk costs" and, if conditions so require, can be costed at zero. Such a situation will not encourage the corporation to invest further in R&D. It is still useful, as an aid to understanding the theory, to consider "normal times" and to conceive of the firm charging a fair rate of return on inputs of technology.

Table 5-1

COMPETITIVE RANKING OF GOODS

	Good	Type
Country I	1	Absolutely noncompetitive
Imports	2	Absolutely noncompetitive
	3	Gap-filling noncompetitive
	4	Gap-filling noncompetitive
	5	Ordinary
	6	Ordinary
	7	Ordinary
Country II	8	Ordinary
Imports	9	Ordinary
	10	Ordinary
	11	Gap-filling noncompetitive
	12	Gap-filling noncompetitive
	13	Technological noncompetitive
	14	Technological noncompetitive

basis for determining how trade patterns are established and how they respond to changes in the underlying conditions. Table 5-1 ranks fourteen goods listed by the negative values of D. Country II will export the goods at the top of the list to Country I, and vice versa. Because the specific input needed for their production is not available in the importing country (and must therefore be seen as having an infinitely high price), noncompetitive imports are at the extreme ends of the list.

There is no way of distinguishing degrees of comparative advantage for absolutely noncompetitive goods, so the distinctions between goods 1 and 2 and 13 and 14 are spurious. If the United States is Country I, good 1 might be bauxite (the raw material for aluminum) and good 2 might be tea or jute. Good 3 would clearly be oil and good 4 copper. The middle range of goods are so-called ordinary goods that can conceivably be made in both countries. Goods 13 and 14 might be highly sophisticated computers and highly sophisticated military aircraft. Goods 11 and 12 would be human grains (wheat and rice) and feed grains for livestock (soybeans and corn). (Note that the United States is an important exporter of these agricultural products due to an extremely efficient agricultural system that combines large amounts of technology with large amounts of available agricultural land.)

A realistic version of international trade theory can best be assembled by developing a distribution of representative values of D (the percentage difference in production costs) for the fourteen goods in Table 5-2 and using those (fictitious) data to examine the three following relationships:

1. The relationship between the value of D and the per-unit gain from trade

Table 5-2
DEGREES OF COMPARATIVE ADVANTAGE

Imports		Exports	
Good	Value of D	Good	Value of D
1	$+\infty$	8	-0.1
2	$+\infty$	9	-0.25
3	$+0.8$	10	-0.33
4	$+0.65$	11	-0.8
5	$+0.5$	12	-0.9
6	$+0.25$	13	$-\infty$
7	$+0.125$	14	$-\infty$

Positive values of D show higher costs in Country I. Absolutely noncompetitive goods cannot be produced in the importing country, so the value of D is infinite.

2. The relationship between the value of D and the volume of trade for any good
3. The forces that determine the position of the dividing line that separates exports from imports

Table 5-2 presents the values of D for fourteen goods. D is infinite for goods 1, 2, 13, and 14 because they are absolutely and technological noncompetitive goods. The absolute value of D then decreases as the dividing line is approached.

1. The average or per-unit gain from trade is clearly related to the value of D. The bigger the value of D for the import, the greater the efficiency gain of exchanging for it a good made at home in which the country has some small comparative advantage. In Table 5-2, Country I is shown as having a comparative disadvantage in good 3 of 0.8 and a comparative advantage in the production of good 12 of 0.9. To export good 12 provides a large gain from trade, even if the import is something that could be made at home as cheaply as it could be bought from abroad ($D = 0$). If, instead of some marginal import, the money earned is spent on something that could be made at home only at an exorbitant cost ($D = 0.8$), the gain from trade is so much greater. This is why the exchange of noncompetitive imports yields such great gains from international trade. To exchange good 8 for good 7 yields little per-unit gain from trade because the disadvantage in making good 7 is quite small. The exchange of noncompetitive imports explains why the football spreads out and becomes wide and the ultimate exchange of goods with low absolute values of D are indulged in only near the equilibrium point.

Put another way, only a small adverse shift in the terms of trade would make the country internationally competitive in good 7.

2. The volume of trade in a particular good is not necessarily and is certainly not reliably determined by the value of D. In Figure 5-1, the domestic demand and supply schedules are drawn in the left-hand panel.

Figure 5-1
DOMESTIC/INTERNATIONAL INTERACTION

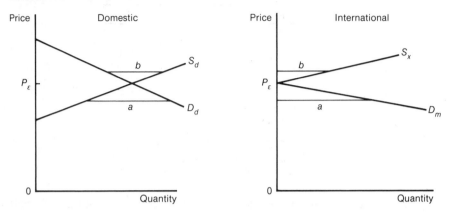

In autarky, the market clears at price P_ϵ. If the world price is different, the good will be traded internationally, and the right-hand panel shows the international demand and supply schedules, according to the international price, of the product. If the world price is higher than P_ϵ, the good will be exported, and the slope of the supply schedule is equal to the sum of the supply and demand curves shown in the left-hand panel. If the price is less than P_ϵ, there is net international demand, and the good is imported. Note that the volume of trade is determined by the value of D—the difference between the international or world price and P_ϵ—*given the slopes of the domestic demand and supply curves* (and, of course, foreign schedules). Figure 5-2 shows the domestic schedules for a primary and manufactured product in order to illustrate the unreliability of the relationship between D and the volume of trade. The primary product is shown as having less elastic schedules than the manufactured good so that a greater value of D for the primary product coexists with a smaller volume of trade.

3. The separation of exports from imports in the ranking (in Table 5-2) is determined by the costs of production in local currencies and the rate of exchange. The relative intensities of the five factors and their local prices determine the cost per unit in domestic currency, and the rate of exchange makes direct cost comparisons possible. When the rate of exchange changes, due, for example, to a real disturbance and a change in the terms of trade, the dividing line ($D = 0$) also changes. For simplicity, the exposition has assumed that the rate of exchange in force is the one that brings the value of exports and the value of imports into equality.

Given tastes, production relationships (functions), and factor endowments, costs of all goods in domestic currency are determined. The terms of trade determine which goods will be exported and which imported, and the rate of exchange is the monetary equivalent of the terms of

Figure 5-2

VARIABILITY OF TRADE
VOLUME, GIVEN COST
DIFFERENCES
P identifies a primary
product and *M* a
manufactured good.

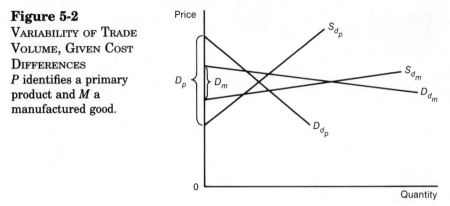

trade. In the absence of other international transactions, the two are conceptually identical. A change in the terms of trade bespeaks a change in the exchange rate. Figure 5-3 can be used to confirm the identity of the two concepts when international trade in goods and services are the only international transactions. Figure 5-3 has its nonmonetary counterpart in Figure 3-4 in Chapter 3. The vertical axis in Figure 5-3 measures the rate of exchange in pesos per dollar (so an upward movement represents a strengthening of the dollar). The horizontal axis measures the quantity of dollars that flows through the foreign exchange market in each time period and, therefore, the value of international trade. The demand curve is the demand of Country II's residents for Country I's goods—it is the demand curve for dollars—and the stronger the peso or the cheaper the dollar, the larger the demand. The supply curve of dollars is the volume of money that Country I's residents are willing to spend on goods whose prices are denominated in pesos (imports into Country I). As the dollar gets stronger, the demand gets larger. The rate of exchange is determined when the demand for dollars and the supply of dollars are equal—shown at \$1 = P3. This is the rate of exchange—the monetary equivalent to the terms of trade—which separates goods that are exports from those that are subject to import competition. Figure 5-3 also shows a change in the demand for imports by Country II: This shift in tastes is similar in effect to that analyzed in reference to Table 4-1 in Chapter 4. Country II desires more of Country I's exports, and the demand for dollars shifts to the right. The dollar strengthens to 3.3 pesos to the dollar, the terms of trade have moved in favor of Country I, and the value of *D* for each individual good in Table 5-2 is changed. The exchange rate diagram does not yield as much information as the offer curve diagram since the former gives no indication as to the division of the increase in the demand for imports by Country II among ordinary and noncompetitive goods. Conceptually, this change would be featured in an offer curve diagram.

Figure 5-3
RATE-OF-EXCHANGE
DETERMINATION

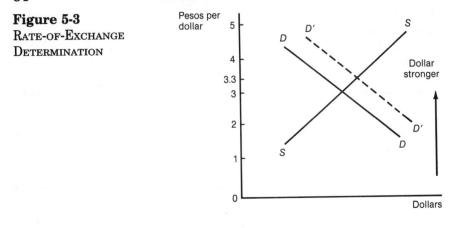

When a country experiences a change in the pattern of foreign demand, it adjusts internally to produce a different mix of goods (in very simple terms, it moves along its production possibility curve). This causes the relative prices of factors of production to change. This was demonstrated in Table 4-1 but must now involve change in the prices of all five factors of production, depending on the factor intensities of the goods whose outputs have increased and decreased.

This is a practical model of international trade. When it is embellished to allow for industry-specific factors of production, changes in international tastes or cost conditions can wreak quite violent changes on the mix of output and on income distribution. An industry-specific factor of production can best be conceived of in terms of training (human capital) that is useful only in a particular industry: Such a factor could have most of its human capital wiped out by a change in demand patterns or foreign supply capabilities. This is why the transfer of privately owned technology by a multinational corporation (see Chapter 20) can be so devastating to workers. Of course, not all human capital is lost; some is generally applicable. But a great deal of a person's income can be eliminated when industry know-how is made useless. The model relies on money costs of production to identify comparative cost advantage and disadvantage, but it also identifies the underlying causes of comparative advantage and disadvantage in terms of factor availability and endowments and tastes. A nation will export goods that use relatively intensively its relatively cheap factors of production. The cheap factors are those in plentiful supply relative to the demand for them and relative to the mix of factor availability and demand in trading-partner countries. Changes in the terms of trade will manifest themselves through the rate of exchange (terms of trade) and will have broad effects on the prosperity of different industries.[6] Changes in conditions (domestic or

---

[6] It is changes in *real* exchange rates that bring about changes in the terms of trade.

foreign) can have widespread repercussions. All of the interactions follow the basic pattern laid down in the discussion of the simple version of the factor-proportions theory in Chapter 4. The crucial distinction is the incorporation of tastes (by specifying the model in money terms) and the recognition that not all of the different varieties of the individual factors are available in every country. This leads to the inclusion of noncompetitive imports.

TRANSPORTATION COSTS

Despite the usefulness of the simplifying assumption about the absence of transportation costs made to this point, transportation costs really cannot be neglected. Once the causative mechanism of international trade is understood, the effects of transport costs can be added on fairly easily.

Figure 5-4 shows, schematically, the different types of invoicing terms relating to transportation of goods. Any good must be transported from its place of production to its place of use, and there exists a fair degree of latitude as to how the bill for transportation is paid. Usually an importer will agree on a price with an exporter, and the exporter will include in that price the cost of transporting the goods from the factory to the dockside in the exporting country. This method of billing is called *f.a.s.* (free alongside ship). The importer then pays for the actual loading (through an agent). More usual is for the exporter to bill the customer *f.o.b.* (free on board) so that the importer pays for the actual transportation costs directly but only indirectly for the costs of loading. If the exporter agrees to prepay the costs of shipping, the goods are quoted on a *c.i.f.* (cost, insurance, and freight) basis. The unloading in the importer's home port and the domestic transportation and the costs of clearing customs

Figure 5-4

INTERNATIONAL TRANSPORTATION

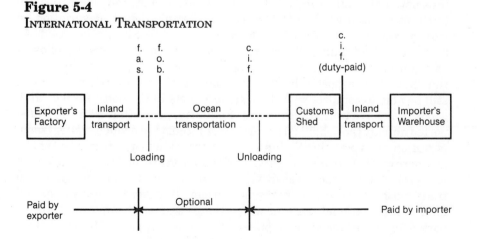

are all paid by the importer. The different arrangements depend to some degree on tradition in the particular industry, and any costs incurred by the exporter are passed on to the buyer. If there is a buyer's market, the exporter may use payment of transportation costs as a means of shaving the quoted price.

Transportation costs will reduce the volume of international trade (in comparison with a world of no transport costs). The extent to which transport costs affect the volume of trade and the mix of goods traded depends on the proportionate costs of transportation. Some goods are cheaper to ship than others, and trade in these goods will be impeded less than trade in goods that are expensive to transport. The impediment is going to depend not on the costs of transportation per ton but on the costs of transportation relative to the f.o.b. cost of the good. Cement is very heavy and therefore expensive to transport, but it is nowhere near as costly to ship as diamonds, which require large outlays for insurance and security. A ton of cement will be shipped for far less than a ton of diamonds. Yet diamonds are traded internationally a great deal and cement hardly at all. Why? Because the transportation costs as a *percent of value* are high for cement and low for diamonds. A difference in domestic costs of production of 10 percent or less will be sufficient to preclude international trade in cement but not in diamonds. Suppose that Country I can produce cement for $100 per ton and Country II can produce it for P 270 ($1 = P3); Country II has a comparative advantage. But if it costs $15 to ship a ton of cement from Country II to Country I, no international trade in cement will take place. Cement will be a nontraded good or a domestic good.

The costs of transportation depend on the weight-to-value ratio of goods and on the type of transportation used and the distance the goods must travel. It is the total effect of these three forces that determines the proportionate transportation costs and, therefore, the degree to which international trade is impeded. Distance and weight-to-value ratios are fairly straightforward concepts. There is a great deal of variation in transportation costs according to the means of transportation used. As a general rule of thumb, air transportation is the most expensive, followed by train and truck, with sea transport being the cheapest. Thus goods that can be transported by sea can come from much farther away and still be able to compete with domestic products in the home market than goods that have to travel overland. Similarly, goods that must be transported quickly (perishables) or very urgent items have much higher transportation costs per mile. Bananas, which travel in fast, refrigerated ships, are more costly to transport per pound than iron ore, and trade in bananas is therefore much more sensitive to distance. The form of international trade most sensitive to distance is tourism. Tourism is merely a special form of international trade in which the consumer or importer is transported to the exporter or supplier of tourism services. Human beings usually place a high premium on time and go by air, and they insist on careful and comfortable travel conditions. What is more, they have to travel both ways, whereas commodities make a one-way journey.

Ocean shipping costs vary significantly according to the type of shipping used. Raw materials tend to be transported more cheaply than finished goods because of the standardization of port facilities, the avoidance of high-cost commercial ports such as New York and San Francisco, and lower shipping costs. Machinery and other finished goods are usually shipped on cargo liners that run a scheduled service from one port to a group of other ports (say, New York to London, Rotterdam, and Hamburg and back again). These ships charge high prices for transportation because they leave on schedule whether fully loaded or not, their price schedules are fixed by monopolies (shipping conferences), they charge according to bulk rather than weight, and they use high-cost facilities in commercial ports.

Figure 5-5 shows how transportation costs will diminish the volume of trade in a particular good. Panel A shows the demand and supply curves for the good in two countries and the two autarkic prices, m and k. When transportation costs are zero, international trade can exist only at price p, at which the volume of exports supplied by Country I equals the volume of imports demanded by Country II. The volume of trade is equal to the horizontal difference between the demand and supply curves at price p. When there are transportation costs, the two prices in the two countries have to differ by the costs of transportation, f, and the volume of exports must equal the volume of imports. These conditions are met by prices p_{II} and p_I (panel B).

Figure 5-5
TRADE WITH TRANSPORTATION COSTS

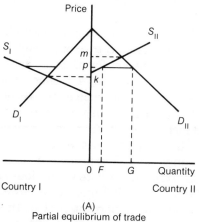

(A)
Partial equilibrium of trade
with zero transportation costs

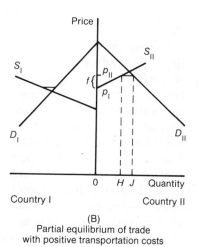

(B)
Partial equilibrium of trade
with positive transportation costs

Now consider what would happen if the distance f in panel B were greater than the difference in autarkic prices in panel A. Country I's comparative advantage in the good would be less than the costs of transportation. The good would not be traded, and autarkic prices would exist. Therefore, the ranking developed in Table 5-2 is oversimplified in terms of the real world. There should be three divisions, not two: imports on top of one dividing line and a number of domestic or nontraded goods and exports under a lower dividing line. The domestic goods will affect the comparative costs of all the goods by affecting the prices of factors and the pattern of demand. Their influence on international competitiveness is indirect.

The final concern with transportation costs is what happens when they change. Suppose all transportation costs were reduced equiproportionately—say, by 10 percent. The volume of trade in each good would increase. Some domestic goods would become vulnerable to competition from abroad, and some domestic goods would find that they could now compete in foreign markets. Costs of ocean shipping change quite frequently because of forces of supply and demand. In 1967 the Suez Canal was closed and trade between Europe and Asia was diverted around South Africa. The result was a substantial loss of competitiveness in Asian markets for European firms and a significant gain for Japanese firms. Similarly, the cost of shipping oil from the Persian Gulf to Europe increased substantially until the development of supertankers brought the costs of transportation down again. When the costs of transportation fall, both countries gain (unless one has a monopoly in international transportation), but the terms of trade between the two nations are also likely to change. This change will depend on the pattern of demand and the elasticity of supply of traded goods to lower transport costs.

IMPERFECT COMPETITION

The expression "imperfect competition" covers a whole range of possibilities, from monopoly (a single seller) at one extreme to monopsony (a single buyer) at the other. In between are such market forms as oligopoly (a few sellers who are likely to get together to act as a monopoly if they can agree) and competition in differentiated goods such as television sets and automobiles. Equally, imperfect competition can exist in a product market and, in most of its forms, in a factor market. A union stranglehold on the supply of labor to an industry is as much a monopoly as control over the cigarette industry by a single manufacturer.

In Chapter 3, four types of gains from trade were listed. The fourth of these—the gain from competition by foreign firms in limiting the power of domestic monopolists and oligopolists—is an important part of this section. But imperfect competition will also affect the pattern of trade, and the reader needs to understand how the existence of an imperfectly competitive industry in one country will impinge on the pattern of international trade—with its consequent repercussions on factor prices in the exporting country.

The effect of the existence of imperfect competition in its various forms on the theory of international trade can be considered under three separate aspects. How will imperfect competition affect the mix of exports and imports of a nation? Will the existence of imperfect markets require fundamental changes in the theory of international trade and the distribution of income? And will the gains from trade be affected by the existence of imperfect markets? Some aspects of imperfect competition, such as dumping and the protection of a monopoly position by commercial policy measures, are better considered in the chapters dealing with commercial policy (Part III). This section limits its scope to the three basic questions just raised and to the one form of imperfect competition that is peculiarly international—the cartel.

Imperfect Competition and the Mix of Trade

With the exception of cartels and global natural monopolies, imperfect competition usually exists only in a national market. Thus the existence of imperfect competition can affect the willingness of an industry to supply exports or its ability to compete with foreign firms. This two-dimensional quality applies whether the imperfection exists in the product market or in a relevant factor market, since any effects caused by the factor-market imperfections will be passed on in the product market. Monopolistic competition is best considered in the context of differentiated goods in Chapter 11. This section, therefore, can confine its attention to monopoly or oligopoly structures. Because monopolies are an extreme version of imperfect competition, they represent a less complex analytic task, and the majority of the argument will be carried on in terms of monopoly.[7] The analysis will be conducted first in terms of imperfections in goods markets and then in markets for factors of production.

A *monopoly* exists when a firm has command over the whole market for a product, say, aluminum sheets, because it is the only seller. Usually this entails control over some natural resource, some proprietary knowledge, or, possibly, a position of preeminence achieved by being first in the market and by exploiting financial strength and economies of scale to exclude competitors. The standard closed-economy monopoly diagram appears in Figure 5-6. It shows that a monopolist has the power in autarky to determine the quantity supplied so that it can set the price in the market to its own greatest advantage. This achievement is effected by

---

[7] Chapter 19 considers the possibility that oligopolistic markets provide a reason for the existence of multinational corporations.

Figure 5-6
MONOPOLY SELLING
POLICY
Note that when a demand
curve is flat, the price
charged is both the
average and the marginal
revenue. Thus when the
import price is P_2, the
monopolist will produce at
Q_2.

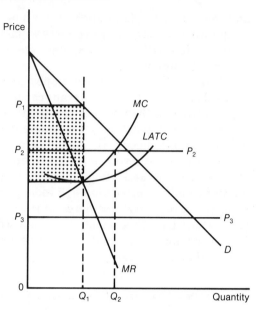

setting marginal cost equal to marginal revenue and determining the
quantity to be produced in that way. The quantity is then priced at the
rate at which demand allows it to be sold. In Figure 5-6, $MC = MR$ at
Q_1. This quantity can be thought of as constituting a perfectly inelastic
(vertical) short-run supply curve, and the price, P_1, is determined by
the intersection of supply and demand. Monopoly profits amount to the
shaded area, showing the product of the quantity sold and the difference
between the price P_1 and the average total cost for Q_1. It is always possible
that the monopolist will sell at a price below P_1 if that price would be
likely to attract entrants into the industry or bring about antitrust pro-
ceedings. What matters in international trade theory is how the existence
of foreign suppliers and foreign consumers will affect the price P_1 as
the monopolist's selling price. Will the monopolist be able to maintain
the profit rate at home, and will it choose to sell abroad at a price different
from that at which exports would be made if the industry were perfectly
competitive? The solution depends on the comparative advantage enjoyed
by the home country. If the good involved is one in which the nation
has a sizable comparative advantage, the question of export price is
important. If the nation has a comparative disadvantage or only a very
small comparative advantage, the question of import competition is important.

Assume that there exists a foreign industry that is perfectly competitive
and prices its product at marginal cost. If the foreign industry can sell
to the home country at a price of less than P_1, the monopolist will be
forced to meet the foreign competition, and the power of the monopoly
will be reduced. If the foreign industry has a comparative advantage

such that it can sell to the home country at a c.i.f. price of P_3, there is no point in having a monopoly position in production in the home country. It is possible that a monopolist would be able to generate congressional approval for a protective tariff that would shift the foreign supplier's price up to P_2 from P_3. In that case, substantial monopoly profits would still be obtained, but the consumer in the importing country would be substantially better off because per-unit profit would be reduced as a result of the foreign competition. If the foreign supplier were also a monopolist, it is probable that some cartel-like agreement would be worked out so that both firms would earn and share monopoly profits. If the foreign nation does not have a comparative advantage but does have a competitive industry, it can still export the product. The existence of a monopoly in the home country may allow foreign suppliers to penetrate the domestic market. In Figure 5-6, suppose that foreign suppliers had a perfectly elastic supply curve of exports to the home country at the c.i.f. price of P_2 and that there was no tax on imports. Despite the comparative advantage of the home industry, imports might still occur. The home-country monopolist would have the power to eliminate imports by pricing its product at a fraction less than P_2 and would still enjoy substantial monopoly profits. This analysis shows clearly, albeit in a simple framework, that international trade will reduce the effect of the market imperfections in the importing nation to the benefit of consumers.

If the monopolist's nation has a comparative advantage, the question then concerns the price at which it will sell in foreign markets. Assume that foreign markets are supplied by a competitive (but disadvantaged) foreign industry, so that the monopolist faces a perfectly elastic foreign demand curve at some given price. The monopolist may be able to discriminate between the home and foreign markets by charging a different price in each. Such pricing policy relies on the fact that no export sales can be reintroduced into the home market at less than monopoly price because of tariffs, control by the monopolist, or transport costs. The two markets are fully separated. The general assumption is that competition will be more severe abroad and, therefore, the monopolist will charge a lower price abroad than at home. But there is a problem with such a policy. This pricing policy involves *dumping*—selling at a lower price abroad than at home—and governments will not tolerate such a practice. They will prefer to levy countervailing import duties against dumped products. (Dumping is analyzed in Chapter 8). By the same token, a monopolist cannot hope to sell abroad, in a more competitive market and hindered by freight costs, at the same price that is enjoyed at home. If exports are to be made and if the monopolist is using its full market power at home, there is no choice but to discriminate between the two markets. Theoretically, the prohibition against dumping and possible retaliatory action mean that a country may not sell abroad goods in which it has a comparative advantage simply because the monopolist wishes to reap the full benefits of its domestic market power.

A national monopoly can be curbed by international trade, but the existence of monopoly can result in goods flowing in directions other than those prescribed by true comparative advantage (that is, what would have occurred had both industries been perfectly competitive).

Factor-market imperfections are likely to have any power only in industries in which the industry's structure in the product market is also imperfect. In other words, a labor monopoly can generate a wage greater than that justified by its productivity only if the producers can pass the increased costs on to the consumer. The alternative is for the labor union to eat into the firms' profits and for the firm eventually to die because the rate of profit is not sufficient to generate reinvestment in the industry. This possibility becomes particularly important in reference to tariff theory and protection because, frequently, important industries have the political muscle needed to generate tariff protection to preserve the unnecessarily high average costs.

The introduction of imperfect competition—that is, the explicit recognition of its existence—does not require a complete change in the theory of international trade. What it does mean is that the ranking of goods (as in Table 5-2) can no longer be set up and determined independent of market structure (the degree of imperfection in competition). Instead, goods must be ranked by a comparison of prices actually charged in different countries (as opposed to costs of production). The underlying cost structure is still important: It determines the potential degree of foreign competition. But the ranking can no longer be built up in an abstract way from an identification of demand schedules, production functions, and factor supplies (including available technology). Comparative advantage should still depend on the relative costs of goods as they would be determined in perfectly competitive industries. Imperfections in competition can neutralize comparative advantage and lead to a less than ideal allocation of production in the world economy.[8] Nor is it true that a country necessarily has a comparative disadvantage in goods that are imported.

The effect of market imperfections, then, is to cloud the apparatus developed in Chapters 3 and 4 and so far in this chapter. It will probably affect the quantity of trade and the price of goods sold at home more than it will cause a reversal in the direction of trade against comparative advantage. It can have important effects for income distribution, but these effects will be concentrated in favor of groups that have some leverage from the market imperfections—stockholders of monopolizing corporations and managers and workers in the same industries. People with industry-specific skills can expect to benefit greatly from imperfect competition. People engaged in competitive industries will suffer in comparison.

---

[8] The existence of firm-specific proprietary knowledge raises questions about the possibility of perfect competition in its formal sense.

These effects are, fundamentally, no different from the effects of market imperfections in a closed economy: If anything, the effects will be weaker in an international economy.

The most virulent form of imperfect competition in international markets is a *cartel*. A cartel is an agreement among business corporations to cooperate in their joint interest. It is a move to create a single monopoly instead of competing large firms (which are likely to have erratic fits of competitive zeal). On occasion, the cartel divides markets among its members so that each has a monopoly in a different regional market. It is the international quality (agreement among firms of different nationalities) that distinguishes this phenomenon from a collusive oligopoly in a single country. Frequently, the agreement (which may be written and explicit) conceives of global profit maximization with some profit sharing in order to stop weaker (higher-cost) firms from trying to cut cartel prices in order to increase their market share.

Currently, the existence of cartels—particularly in primary products—is made more complex by the fact that nationally owned firms are major actors in the cartel. Nearly all of the members of the Organization of Petroleum Exporting Countries (OPEC) are nationally owned corporations in which the parent governments play an active role. This feature of cartels introduces a very political element into their operation, and simple joint profit maximization is no longer an adequate framework for analysis of cartels.

What cartels do to international trade may be considered under two headings. A straightforward joint monopoly restricts the quantity produced so that the combined membership receives a large profit analogous to that of the domestic monopolist shown in Figure 5-6. The danger is always that less profitable members of the group will attempt to act independently and to increase their own profits by cutting their prices. In terms of the existing petroleum market, the basic problem for OPEC is that the reserves commanded by nonmembers have grown substantially since the heyday of oil profits in 1974, and therefore the cartel is merely one large joint supplier: It no longer has a monopoly or close to one. This does not mean that OPEC is not an important force in the global economy, but it does mean that the cartel itself is not strong enough to warrant the use of monopoly analysis. The second effect of a cartel is to reduce the gains that might otherwise be achieved from international trade. Consider an arrangement among a group of national monopolists. If governments did not interfere to help their national corporations (the monopolists), the national industries would compete in each others' markets, and some international trade would take place. There would be a gain from trade in the usual sense of the term, although it might not be as clearly defined or as identifiable as the analysis just presented. Nonetheless, some gain from trade in the particular product will exist. If the cartel divides the national markets through an agreement not to compete in foreign markets, each individual nation will have its own autarkic monopoly, and there will be no international trade in the product in question and no gain from trade.

DROPPING THE BASIC ASSUMPTIONS

Fundamental to the whole theory of international trade and specialization in production, as the subject has been developed to this point, are the two assumptions that all economies are fully employed and that the value of exports of goods is equal to the value of imports (trade is balanced). These assumptions underlie the theories of Ricardo and of Heckscher and Ohlin as well as the multifactor pragmatic theory developed at the start of this chapter. These assumptions, though valuable for expositional purposes, do not hold in the real world. The industrialized nations maintained high levels of employment and capacity utilization prior to the deep recession that began in the aftermath of the first oil-price shock in 1974. Large imbalances of trade account have occurred from time to time, and this is likely to indicate that the rate of exchange is not correctly reflecting national price levels and the underlying conditions of supply and demand. In 1984 the United States had a deficit in trade of approximately $150 billion at the same time that the rate of unemployment hovered around 7.5 percent (more than 8 million people). The implications of the release of these assumptions must be considered.[9]

The theories assumed balanced trade so that they could consider the problem of international resource allocation in a timeless framework and so that Hume's payments-adjustment mechanism (Chapter 2) would not be disturbing the situation. In fact, the monetary conditions require only that the balance on current account be zero so that exports of goods and services and receipts of investment income equal the value of their counterparts (imports of goods and services and payments of investment income). Because the United States receives large sums from investment income (from the subsidiaries of American multinational corporations), the nation would run a deficit on goods and services even when balanced current account existed.[10] Therefore, the first scenario to be investigated must be the one that allows the current account to be balanced but the balance of goods and services to be in deficit (for practical purposes, the balance of goods and services is the equivalent of the trade balance used in the exposition of trade theory). The second problem occurs when the rate of exchange is "wrong" and the balance of goods and services is unbalanced by more than net receipts from investment income. Finally, the implications of unemployment must be considered.

[9] Data on the U.S. balance of payments are given in Table 13-2; the reason for the large U.S. deficits in 1983–1985 is given in the second part of Chapter 15.

[10] A schematic table (on p. 306) shows the distinction schematically.

Net Receipts of Investment Income

When a country or its residents have invested abroad (acquired foreign assets) in years gone by, the country will receive annual payments of interest and dividends. Because, in a free enterprise system, foreigners will also have invested in the home country, it is net amounts that are of immediate concern. Thus if payments on current transactions are balanced and there are no further transactions in capital markets, the existence of investment income must imply a deficit in international trade in goods and services. In 1984 U.S. net receipts of investment income amounted to roughly $19 billion. This figure is an approximation of the value by which imports will exceed exports. The rate of exchange is therefore different from the one that would establish balanced trade, and the value of ϵ that gives $D = 0$ in Table 5-2 will be changed in consequence. Under a dirty float (a system of flexible exchange rates with some government interference), the rate of exchange of the dollar will be stronger than the rate that would generate balanced trade. The benefits from the foreign investment in earlier years is the improvement in the terms of trade that the investment income now makes possible.[11]

The strengthening of the dollar will have caused some industries to lose their competitiveness (D will change from negative to positive), and the mix of output will be altered (similarly to the change shown in Table 4-1). Industries in which the United States had a comparative advantage with balanced trade will now be less profitable because they will either have lost their comparative advantage or have smaller foreign markets. Nontradable-goods industries will benefit but not import-competing industries. It is important to note that this difference between balanced trade and balanced current account is likely to change only slowly over time, so the effects will have been gradually assimilated by the home economy. There is no need to expect the dislocation that would come with a sudden change. In fact, the change may come at a sufficiently slow pace that the normal adaptive powers of the economy (through economic growth and depreciation of capital and retirement of workers) may be able to absorb the change without any dislocation.

There is no need to attribute an imbalance in trade uniquely to the net receipts of investment income. Any transaction that goes through the foreign exchange market and that does not result from trade in goods or services will affect the rate of exchange and generate similar repercussions. The United States, until quite recently, has traditionally been a net exporter of capital by more than its receipts of investment income (this is not surprising for a rich and technologically advanced country). Therefore, the exchange rate of the dollar was relatively weak, and the United States ran a surplus in international trade—the outflow of capital

---

[11] It is shown in Chapter 14 that the improvement in the terms of trade also allows an increase in the rate of spending.

has made the terms of trade less favorable, and exporting and import-competing industries flourished.

The "Wrong" Exchange Rate

Contrast the scenario of the preceding section in which the imbalance in current account does not change violently from year to year with what happens when the exchange rate goes wrong for a relatively short period of time. Consider what happens when a flood of money rushes into the country in search of temporarily higher interest rates. The rate of exchange suddenly appreciates, and the value of D of all home industries increases. This state of affairs is not permanent and will be reversed at some time in the future when the home interest rate subsides. Tradable-goods industries will find their markets eroded as their goods become less competitive abroad or face heavier competition from foreign suppliers. Consumers enjoy far more favorable terms of trade than "should" exist and flock to foreign resorts and other destinations to enjoy the strong dollar. Ultimately, things will reverse and the industries that have suffered during the period of the dollar's strength will have to rebuild to accommodate normal demand.

The behavior of the U.S. dollar in 1983–1985 is testimony that this scenario can be played out under flexible exchange rates. The problem was more common under a system of fixed rates of exchange and typifies the plight of the United States in 1969–1971 and of Great Britain at several times in recent history. The overvaluation of a currency (its rate of exchange is stronger than conditions warrant) under a fixed-rate system could derive from real change or from too great a rate of inflation in the home country (or a combination of the two). In the case of the United States, the dollar could not be devalued without recasting the whole international financial system (see Chapter 17). Although this ultimately proved to be unavoidable, it is easy to see why the U.S. government was slow to initiate the change. The classic example of the overvaluation of the British pound took place in 1966–1967, and the government did not devalue because they thought, mistakenly, that they could increase the competitiveness of the economy by domestic policies alone. The pound was devalued in 1968. In both instances, tradable-goods industries were squeezed by low profits and severe competitive pressures so that they emerged from the period of overvaluation in a weakened state.[12]

The problem here is that industries receive the "wrong" signals about their ability to compete in markets in the long run. The heavy foreign competition is a transitory phenomenon, but industry cannot know this (and certainly cannot act on it without a great deal of courage because one never knows when the temporary state of affairs will end). The divid-

---

[12] The classic diagnosis of the problem under a system of fixed rates of exchange is the study of the British economy by Nicholas Kaldor, "Conflicts in National Economic Objectives," *Economic Journal*, vol. no. 81 (March 1971), 1–16. Also see Chapter 15.

ing line shifts—either because the rate of exchange has changed when it should not have (flexible rates) or because the rate of exchange has not changed when it should have (fixed rates)—and all tradable-goods industries are affected. As these industries adapt to short-run indicators, the mix of plant capacity in the country is changed only to have to change back when conditions revert to their true long-run state.

Unemployment

The theory of international trade assumes that full employment exists in all countries. There are two possible ways to consider the existence of unemployment. First, consider what happens when all countries lapse into a recession simultaneously and by roughly the same amount. The volume of international trade will fall as imports fall with GNP, but this will hold for all countries, and it seems unlikely that there will be any substantial change in the terms of trade. The lost sales of exports will be those of income-sensitive goods and, if the exports are raw materials or intermediate goods, those used in income-sensitive goods. The terms of trade might shift if one country were a supplier of income-sensitive goods and the other a supplier of basic goods, but such a clear-cut distinction is improbable.

When one country suffers from a recession and the other countries in the world maintain high levels of output, there will be an effect on the terms of trade. In terms of Figure 5-3, if Country I suffers from a recession, the supply curve of dollars shifts to the left (not drawn), and the dollar strengthens. The ramifications of such a shift for the competitiveness of national tradable-goods industries follows the normal path except that firms will have spare capacity and may therefore be willing to shave profit margins on exports by maintaining the price of exports in pesos. (This policy implies some room for maneuver on pricing policy). Any strengthening of the dollar will impede the recovery from the recession, which is likely to deepen as the output of tradable goods diminishes. If the rates of exchange are fixed (either by government intervention in a dirty float or by a fixed-rate regime), the country suffering from the recession will accumulate reserves, and the strengthening of its currency will not add to the recession. This policy has some obvious benefits when a single country is in recession, but in a general depression it could involve all countries and be counterproductive (see Chapter 17).

SUMMARY

Chapter 3 began the consideration of international trade with a highly simplified analysis based on comparative advantage that did not really explain the underlying causation. Chapter 4 developed the factor-proportions theory to explain that causation. Chapter 5 has tried to push the theory toward reality. Such real-world complexities as land (natural resources), skilled workers (human capital), and proprietary technology not being freely available are absolutely vital if real-world patterns of trade are to be explained and understood. Then the role of transportation costs and monopoly must be taken into account and the possibility of a relaxation of the basic assumptions of balanced trade and full employment dropped. A working acquaintance with this material allows the student to identify the causes of international trade (and to understand why some goods are not traded internationally), and it sketches in the various factors that interrelate in the real world to bring about the pattern of trade. Real-world events can be fitted to this framework and their implications for the pattern of trade worked out in principle. It would be impossible to start from a position of autarky and compute who would trade what with whom; no model can permit such a complex task. The model presented here does provide a framework for incorporating real-world changes into an existing pattern of international trade and for analyzing the repercussions of these changes.

Bibliography

Crandall, Robert W. "Import Quotas and the Automobile Industry: The Costs of Protectionism." In Robert E. Baldwin and J. David Richardson, ed. *International Trade and Finance,* 3rd ed., pp. 62–74. Boston: Little, Brown, 1986.

Gray, H. Peter. *A Generalized Theory of International Trade.* London: Macmillan, 1974.

Hogendorn, Jan S., and **Wilson B. Brown.** *The New International Economics.* Reading, Mass.: Addison Wesley, 1979, chs. 10 and 11.

Krugman, Paul. "New Theories of Trade among Industrialized Countries," *American Economic Review,* 73 (May 1983), 343–347.

Lawrence, Robert Z. "Changes in U.S. Industrial Structure: The Role of Global Forces, Secular Trends, and Transitory Cycles," in *International Trade and Finance,* 3rd ed., ed. Robert E. Baldwin and J. David Richardson, pp. 3–18. Boston: Little, Brown, 1986.

Questions

1. Why are industry-requisite inputs necessary for the existence of noncompetitive imports, and why are such imports likely to generate large per-unit gains from trade relative to "ordinary goods"?
2. Why is a gap-filling import an important class of noncompetitive goods?
3. Technologically noncompetitive goods can be produced in the importing country. Explain.
4. The volume of trade in a good is determined not by the difference between the autarkic and with-trade equilibrium prices but by the elasticities of supply and demand. Explain.
5. Diamonds cost more to transport than coal, and diamonds cost less to transport than coal. Explain.

6. Some goods are not traded internationally. Explain the factors likely to contribute to this state of affairs.
7. International trade can have only good effects on the level of competition in a country. Explain.
8. Cartels are evil. Discuss.
9. Unbalanced trade affects the value of D through the value of the exchange rate. This affects the competitiveness of certain industries so that they (and their factors of production) are damaged. Describe the mechanism by which a steady flow of capital or dividends and interest from Country I to Country II will enhance the competitiveness of Country I's industries.
10. Unemployment in Country I may contribute to unemployment in Country II. Explain.
11. A recession in Country I will strengthen its currency in the foreign exchange market if a system of freely flexible rates of exchange are in force. Using a partial-analytic framework, show this to be true. How will it affect the pattern of international trade?

SUPPLEMENT

International Trade in Services

The exchange of products between nations is not limited to exporting and importing tangible goods (commodities and manufactures) but also includes a group of activities known as "services." This group has a "residual" flavor because it comprises anything that is not a commodity or a manufactured product. The group includes such varied activities as "data processing," international travel and tourism, transportation, management advisory services, and renting proprietary (privately owned) technology. Sometimes service transactions do include tangible items such as the costs of fuel and food in a foreign port when a ship calls to unload cargo or a plane lands to unleash tourists; in the same way, tourists frequently bring back tangible souvenirs of the places they have visited. The important distinction is that the tangible items are not the reason for the activity and are merely a minor or secondary item.

International trade in services is important for two reasons. First, services are quantitatively important. In the United States in 1984, services exports and imports amounted to $267 billion (49 percent of the value of trade in tangible goods).[1] Quantitative data on the importance of individual services are given in Table 13-3. Second, the Reagan administration has taken a strong stand on the issue of greater freedom of trade in services by pushing hard for international negotiations under the auspices of the General Agreement on Tariffs and Trade. Whether the Reagan administration will succeed in this matter is open to doubt because trade in services often infringes in areas that nations regard as of purely national concern—such as domestic banking and insurance. These industries are regulated by governments in nearly all countries, and governments argue against international trade because they feel they can have adequate control over such firms only when the firms are locally owned and operated.

---

[1] These numbers include the profits of multinational corporations and interest and dividend payments on foreign financial assets. This is the customary definition, but, as will be explained shortly, the inclusion of payments of this kind in "services trade" is questionable.

The data were taken from *Survey of Current Business* (April 1985), p. 33.

100

In terms of the mix of factors of production required in their output, services are a very heterogeneous group. Lodging (hotels) will need proportionately large amounts of low-skilled labor, medical professional services must have a very heavy reliance on very highly skilled workers, and passenger transportation uses very expensive and highly sophisticated capital. It is thus not possible to consider services as a single entity and for a country to think of itself as having a competitive advantage in all services any more than it can have a cost advantage in all manufactured goods.

When asked quickly what sort of activity constitutes a service, most people think quickly of cashing a check at their local bank, having their hair cut or styled, and eating a meal in a restaurant. These activities do not easily lend themselves to international trade because they require that the supplier and the user be in close contact. International trade in services between a country in Europe and a country in North America seems, at first blush, to be something of a contradiction in terms. This contradiction is reinforced by the Ricardian assumption of the international immobility of factors of production. In fact, something has to move internationally if services are to be traded between two nations. The clearest example here is the service industry of *tourism,* in which the consumer moves temporarily to the country that is supplying the service.

It is possible to identify five categories of services that are traded internationally (though no such categorization can be completely exclusive):

1. Services that are derivative from international trade in tangible goods. This category includes freight transportation of all kinds, insurance, and the related financial services.
2. Services in which location-specific attributes (natural and created) are the dominant inputs. Tourism is the preeminent example here, but proprietary technology is, in practice, specific to the country in which its owner is located.
3. Services that are location-joining. These include passenger transportation and international communications.
4. Services that are usually provided in all nations. They can be consumed anywhere and by anyone and provided anywhere and by any firm. These services include such financial services as insurance and banking, internal communication services, and professional services.
5. Services that derive from intrafirm relationships—usually between two units of a multinational corporation.

This supplement considers the argument that gains from trade in services exist in the same way that the exchange of goods creates gains from trade. Some of the more important services are considered separately. The supplement concludes with an assessment of obstacles to trade in services.

GAINS FROM TRADE IN SERVICES

Four distinct kinds of gains from international trade were listed in Chapter 3, and trade in services can be expected to provide gains of each type. The greatest gains from trade per unit of exchange derive from the importation of noncompetitive imports. Services generate this kind of gain from trade mostly through goods of category 2. It is impossible to appreciate the glories of the Taj Mahal, the pyramids, or the Great Wall of China without traveling to India, Egypt, and China and "importing" tourism services from those countries. Similarly, an important kind of trade in services is the leasing of technological know-how to foreign enterprises. When such technology is vital to the production of a particular product, the international trade in services gives rise to noncompetitive imports since the technology is simply not available in the importing country.

Traditional gains from trade (the type emphasized by Ricardo) derive from the reallocation of production in line with comparative advantage, that is, according to the relative factor endowments and factor costs. Ideally, one might expect developing (labor-plentiful) countries to hold a competitive edge in resort tourism and in maritime shipping. In fact, resort tourism also needs certain natural resources, and maritime transportation requires a seafaring tradition. However, certain poor nations have a tradition by which men will serve as seamen on foreign ships for a period of years and then return home with some substantial capital sum.

Trade in differentiated products exists in tourism when Europeans choose to weekend in Paris or Amsterdam or London. The idea of spending a weekend in one of these cities is different only in terms of the ambience one can experience in the different cities—the basic attributes of hotels, meals, museums, and entertainment remain the same. Equally, some financial firms have specialty activities that are differentiated from the standard service, and these can be introduced into foreign countries.

Pressure from outside suppliers will always weaken the market power of a home industry. This may take the form of forcing innovations on a domestic industry in order to keep out foreign suppliers of services (such as special banking or financial services or alternative transportation services). European nations tend to keep their intracontinental air fare structure relatively high but are forced by international competition to offer significantly lower rates on routes in which foreign carriers participate. Air France and British Airways have steadfastly preserved their monopoly on the rich London-Paris market and can only do this through a government-generated monopoly.

The obstacle to international trade in services is the difficulty of delivering the service generated in one place to a person resident in another country. Location-joining activities such as maritime and passenger transportation have the service provided by having local factors of production (ships and aircraft as well as crew) move internationally. When a resident of one country buys foreign services, the consumer moves internationally. Some services are provided by electronic communication—this is particularly relevant for the processing of data generated in one country by computers in a second country. The data are transmitted in off-peak hours, they are processed, and the results are returned in the same way. Engineering services may be delivered in the form of blueprints, but to consider this an example of trade in goods would be unsuitable. Even so, international trade in services must incorporate some "delivery system," and if that system is very costly, the volume of trade in the relevant service activity will be very small. International trade in haircuts, for example, except as an offshoot of tourism, is not carried out because it is not worth the time and expense needed to take advantage of a substantial difference in the price of haircuts.

Because of the difficulties and potential costs of delivery systems, many services remain as nontraded goods.

DIFFERENT TYPES OF TRANSACTION
IN SERVICES

Tourism expenditures are probably, when taken together with international passenger transportation fares, one of the single most important categories of world trade in value terms. But tourism itself comprises several kinds of activities: pleasure travel, business travel, medical travel, and travel for study abroad all have different motivations and different sensitivities to costs. Pleasure travel, the largest category, can be broken down into "wanderlust" tourism and resort tourism ("sunlust" tourism). Wanderlust comprises travels to enjoy the sights and experiences of a foreign country; because much of this is noncompetitive trade, wanderlust travel is likely to be less sensitive to transportation costs than resort tourism. In contrast, resort tourism tries not to stress the locale of the resort so much as its ability to provide the needed comforts and activities. Resort tourism is more competitive with local tourism resorts. Hawaii (if it can be called local for people on the mainland of the United States) competes with Jamaica, Curaçao, and Bermuda, as does Florida. Mazatlán and Acapulco (Mexico) both cater to American visitors and deemphasize the Mexican ambience except insofar as it enables them to add a little product differentiation to the resort. This degree of direct competition far exceeds that between New Orleans or San Francisco and Paris, Rome, or London.

Because of these distinctions in competition, the costs of transportation are far more important in determining the volume of business for resort tourism than for the other kinds. This feature is reflected in the fare structures of international airlines. Competition from New York and other major East Coast cities in the United States to Caribbean resorts is fiercely competitive. Business travelers are recognized as usually having little flexibility in their schedules and, for this reason, are presumed to have inelastic demand for air travel. The intercontinental air routes distinguish between travelers who can reserve their flights well in advance (wanderlust tourists) and those who travel at short notice. The latter are deemed to have very inelastic demand and are charged relatively high fares. In contrast, airlines compete fiercely to attract price-sensitive travelers who can make their plans sixty days ahead of time and who can travel on the less crowded midweek flights.

Air transportation is controlled by governments. This arrangement was agreed to at the 1944 Chicago Conference. Governments approve the exchange of routes between "designated carriers." When the foreign government also owns the airline, it is natural to expect that airline to be the designated carrier on most important routes. Thus Air France is the French designated carrier on most routes. In the United States, where privately owned airlines are established, the government designates a carrier or two to service individual routes. The negotiations are conducted by the State Department of the United States with technical support from the Department of Transportation. All route exchanges are agreed upon bilaterally. These bilateral agreements are usually called "Bermudas" after the first bilateral agreement, signed between the United Kingdom and the United States, which set the standard for others. The crucial problem in any industry in which the cost of carrying one more person is less than the average cost is to prevent competitors from undertaking price wars, which weaken the industry financially. Fares always require government approval, even though they may be negotiated between airlines or among groups of airlines that service a region. The industry body that oversees these negotiations and generally represents the industry in negotiations with governments on such matters as safety measures and airport requirements is the International Air Transport Association (IATA). In recent years airlines have been given greater flexibility in setting prices, but this freedom is approved only as a range around some base fare level.

Maritime transportation is necessary if international trade in goods is to take place. Clearly, it would be inefficient for, say, American ships to carry all U.S. imports and to ride empty (in ballast) from the ports of the United States while other countries' ships were coming to the United States empty and returning home loaded. Generally speaking, cargoes can be carried by a ship of any nationality. One way in which nations try to help their own merchant marines is through so-called cargo preference. The United States aids its merchant fleet in this way by reserving cargoes for U.S.-flag ships. All military cargoes are carried by American ships, and 50 percent of agricultural aid is shipped in "U.S.

bottoms." As may be expected, the United States is notoriously uncompetitive in merchant shipping because ships compete on the open ocean, and U.S. wages are much higher than those of European countries and higher still than those of poor countries. The United States provides ships in its merchant marine with a subsidy that offsets the differences in operating costs (and this subsidy is in excess of 100 percent of foreign operating costs). The ostensible reason for this subsidy of the merchant marine is that ships are needed in time of war. Another such device is reserving local shipping to U.S.-flag vessels. All transportation along and between the individual coasts of the *fifty* states and Puerto Rico is carried in high-cost U.S.-flag ships. The high costs of transportation (under the Jones Act) impede domestic trade between different American coasts. The high transportation costs give a competitive edge to foreign suppliers, which can escape the "penalty" transportation costs.

The renting of proprietary technology to foreign firms and giving them consulting advice are important kinds of international trade. In these services, the factor of production moves to the country of the user. Much of this kind of international trade takes place between units of multinational corporations (see Part VI). Parent corporations permit foreign units to use their technology for a royalty fee and send teams of engineers to the foreign country to train local workers in the necessary skills. Some trade of this kind takes place between unrelated firms and constitutes "bona fide" international trade.[2]

The remaining major category of internationally traded services is category 4. Many services that are primarily domestic (because of difficulties in arranging delivery services) can be supplied from abroad under special circumstances. These services are provided and consumed in all nations, and international trade in such services is likely to result in increased efficiency of the home industry because foreign firms will be able to compete successfully only if they have specialist know-how to counter the difficulty of operating in an alien environment. What this suggests is mainly the provision of services by firms based in developed countries in which new techniques and new products have evolved, to users in poorer nations. In poorer nations, the local industry will be less sophisticated in its product line and less up-to-date in its methods of doing business. Financial and communication services are preeminent here, and financial firms, in particular, are likely to derive a competitive edge from their access to the financial markets in the rich, developed countries in Europe, Japan, and North America. In most instances, the provision of services from firms in rich countries to users in poorer countries requires

---

[2] The theory of international trade assumes that the two parties are not part of the same organization. Intrafirm trade (between two units of the same organization) is quantitatively important. This kind of trade facilitates international coordination of production and is also important because many firms have foreign subsidiaries devoted exclusively to the sale of their goods in foreign countries.

the presence of a local subsidiary. This subsidiary will be almost exclusively a base for local operations (a marketing outlet).

Engineering firms will generate international trade in services through local subsidiaries with contacts in the local business community and a knowledge of local regulations. Advertising and accounting, by contrast, consist mainly of loosely related partnerships that are largely autonomous, and these firms tend to generate very little international trade in services.

One very large component included in services in the international accounts ought to be considered separately. Dividends sent home by foreign subsidiaries out of their profits and interest earned on foreign bonds is included in transactions in services. A country exports a service when resident factors of production are embodied in an intangible asset to be sold to a foreigner or are themselves made available to a foreigner for a rental charge. The factors of production used must be available to the exporting economy when the service is produced. Dividends and interest on illiquid assets held abroad should, by this definition, not count toward international trade in services.[3]

BARRIERS TO INTERNATIONAL TRADE IN SERVICES[4]

Despite the apparently obvious advantages of unimpeded international trade, nations do "protect" their home firms from the stress of foreign competition. The Reagan administration has urged greater access to foreign services markets for U.S. firms and greater openness of U.S. markets to foreign firms, but this is meeting with serious opposition from both European countries and, more vociferously, from developing countries such as Brazil and India.

Tourism is seldom impeded. The only way in which tourists' expenditures abroad can be impeded is by denying would-be tourists access to foreign currency. This is commonplace in Europe in times of balance-of-payments stress. But tourists' expenditures are also one of the categories of international trade that is most sensitive to changes in relative prices and exchange rates. It is also very sensitive to levels of unemployment (recessions). Most European nations have legislation on the books that will allow them to curtail the availability of foreign exchange to pleasure travelers and invoke it in times of crisis. This measure is less effective now than in the past because people have now acquired assets denominated in foreign currencies as a defense against such measures. The

---

[3] Net flows of dividends and interest do not contribute to aggregate demand in the same way as net exports.

[4] This section anticipates Part III of the book. For that reason, the language of the discussion has been kept atechnical. Rereading the section after having read Part III would also be valuable.

United States did toy with this possibility in the late 1960s, but the proposal also involved limitations on the ability of servicemen stationed abroad to have their dependents accompany them, and this invoked furious opposition from the Department of Defense.

Other than subsidization of merchant ships and cargo preference rules, the freedom of a shipper to choose a ship according to need has never been seriously interfered with. The same independence from barriers to trade has also blessed international passenger transportation. Even when tourists' access to foreign exchange was being limited, there was no barrier to flying (or sailing) to anywhere and no discrimination between home-country and foreign airlines. Of course, governments tend to have their people fly the national airline.

It is in the services in category 4 that impediments to international trade exist. Recall that this category is very dependent on the existence of a foreign unit in the country in which the service is to be supplied. Impediments to the establishment of such subsidiary units can effectively block international trade in those services.

Sometimes the reason underlying the obstacles placed in the way of foreign suppliers of services is the desire to keep the local market in the hands of local firms, even if the latter are not technologically up-to-date. The feeling here is that the country will never be able to have its own indigenous industry. Another reason, and one that even an advocate of free trade in services, Professor Brian Hindley, admits to have some validity,[5] is that if corporations have, by the nature of the business, a high ratio of debt to equity (own funds) in certain industries, some regulation of those industries is desirable. This argument applies mainly to financial industries such as banking and insurance. If a foreign subsidiary operates in such a market, it is difficult to define its "capital adequacy," and there is always the fear that in the event of crisis, the regulators would find themselves holding a mere shell and the parent corporation would be beyond their reach.[6]

SUMMARY

Services are the fastest-growing sectors and sources of employment in many mature, industrialized countries. This fact alone would be sufficient to ensure that service industries will remain in the public eye in the coming years. The initiative of the Reagan administration in pushing for freer international trade in services will also prove to be a source of

---

[5] See Brian Hindley, "Economic Analysis and Insurance Policy in the Third World," *Thames Essay*, 32 (London: Trade Policy Research Centre, 1982).

[6] Ronald S. Shelp, *Beyond Industrialization* (New York: Praeger, 1981), pp. 136–7, describes the reception of the European Community to greater freedom in the insurance industry. The answer was a definite no.

attention given to these industries. In fact, the industries with great potential for growth in international trade will be the focus of the Reagan initiative and the source of any spectacular gains that may develop.

Bibliography

"The Economics of International Tourism." *Annals of Tourism Research,* 9 (Spring 1982). Special issue.

Gray, H. Peter. "A Negotiating Strategy for Trade in Services." *Journal of World Trade Law,* 17 (September-October 1983), 377–388.

Hindley, Brian. "Economic Analysis and Insurance Policy in the Third World." *Thames Essays,* 32 (London: Trade Policy Research Centre, 1982).

Shelp, Ronald K. *Beyond Industrialization.* New York: Praeger, 1981.

Walter, Ingo, and Tracy Murray, eds. *Handbook of International Business.* New York: Wiley, 1982, chs. 11 and 14.

SUMMARY OF PART II

The theory of international trade has answered the five questions that underlie the advantages that countries reap from indulging in international trade. These gains comprise the (very large) gains from trade in noncompetitive goods, the gains from specialization in production according to comparative advantage, the wider availability of different types of consumer goods, and the probable reduction in the domestic power of monopolies by competition from abroad. The causation of trade lies in differences in economic conditions (resource availability, tastes, and industry structure) in different countries. Of these conditions, differences in resource endowments or availability is the single most important.

The original theory, which emphasized a two-factor or two-input approach, was shown to be inadequate by Leontief's empirical research. At a minimum, a practical theory requires that five factors of production be identified: capital, human capital, proprietary technology, land or natural resources, and (unskilled) labor. The United States, which is well endowed with technology, skilled labor, and land, finds its main exports in high-tech goods that have heavy expenditures on R&D and use highly skilled labor and in agricultural products wherein the abundance of land is accompanied by a very high level of applied agricultural technology. (In agriculture, the importance of technology is not so much that the know-how is unique to the United States but that the agricultural system employs highly technical workers so that known technology is in fact used.) Even in this less clear-cut theory, the importance of the factor-proportions theory of Heckscher and Ohlin is still apparent, and it contributes importantly to the modern understanding of comparative advantage.

The introduction of multiple goods (as well as multiple factors) indicates that not all goods have the same degree of comparative advantage. Goods can be ranked according to their comparative advantage, and those at the extreme ends of the ranking will generate the largest per-unit gains from trade. Usually these will be noncompetitive goods, which rely on the availability in the exporting country of a product-requisite input that is not available in the importing country. Gains are made from trade in goods that can be produced in both countries, but these are less spectacular.

The standard model of international trade neglects the costs of transportation as an unnecessary complication. But transportation costs are important because their existence creates a class of nontradable goods for which the value of D is less than the costs of transportation. Transportation costs constitute a "natural barrier to trade" (in contrast to artificial barriers such as tariffs), and they reduce the potential gains from trade. Their effect is less important for countries in close proximity to each other than for distant partners. Trade between countries that are close to each other and have similar endowments allows the exchange of consumer durables and, in this way, widens the range of choice available to consumers.

The power of foreign competitors to moderate the strength of any domestic monopoly also leads to benefits from international trade that are not captured in the simple offer curve depiction of gains from trade.

Because international trade takes place in response to money prices, the rate of exchange between currencies plays an important role. Departures of the rate of exchange from the value prescribed by the underlying conditions of supply and demand can result in distortions of world trade flows with potentially serious implications for the long-run viability of tradable-goods industries in the country with the overly strong (overvalued) currency. This problem is particularly important when the cause of the overvaluation is temporary and will lapse at some unknown time in the future.

The gains from trade reach their potential only when international trade is unimpeded by artificial barriers—that is, when the volume of trade that is beneficial is as great as possible. This fact is the basis for the argument for a hands-off attitude toward international trade, prescribed as a basic economic policy stance. We now turn our attention to the temptations to put obstacles in the way of international trade to curry favor with a pressure group—the economics and politics of protection.

III

INTERNATIONAL TRADE POLICY

Policymakers are perennially torn between the appeal of greater global GNP (efficiency) that can be generated by free trade and the need to respond to the needs of their constituents, whose main desires are to preserve their immediate (short-run) interests. The elimination of protective measures (or the failure to institute such measures) will inevitably damage the interests of the few much more severely than free trade will benefit the per capita income of the many: Nondiscriminatory international trade among firms of different nations will allow production to be organized globally in the most efficient way in the *long run*. When spontaneous change takes place in the world economy, some industries in some countries will be damaged (possibly eliminated), and important groups can have their own narrow interests damaged. They will attempt to exert political pressure to neutralize the change. The problem of rapid adjustment is a severe one because it can dislocate the economy. The benefits of free trade are long-run, equilibrium benefits that may take years to attain, and the costs are immediate.

111

Traditional consideration of commercial policy measures is conducted in terms of rich, industrialized nations. But since independence, the poor nations have learned quickly. This group of nations has particularly severe problems of commercial policy, since their need for noncompetitive imports is so great as to make free trade impractical because of the simple inadequacy of foreign exchange.

6

The Case for Free Trade

P_{art} III deals with the practice of nations of putting obstacles in the way of foreign exporters and interfering with the free passage of goods and services in international trade. This is an important arena in international politics as well as in international economics. Impediments placed in the way of imports usually follow from the exertion of domestic political influence. In attempts to work out the damage done to each other's national economies by this practice, a great deal of international consultation and negotiation takes place.[1]

Free trade is a state of affairs that exists when nations make no distinction in demand or supply between foreign goods and markets and domestic goods and markets. The most common reason for a country's imposing some impediment against a foreign source of supply is the domestic political pressure exerted by a domestic industry that is adversely affected by the foreign source of supply. This is why international trade policy or commercial policy is often called "protection"—the government is protecting the profitability of one of its own industries against foreign competition.

The theory of international trade enunciated in Part II suggests that maximum gains from international trade will be achieved when governments do not discriminate against foreign sources of supply—when free trade exists. Chapter 3 identified four kinds of gain from trade, and the

---

[1] International economic policy is virtually always subservient to a nation's international political (war-and-peace) policy; see Chapter 8.

argument for free trade can be couched in terms of these four gains from international trade.

1. Unimpeded international trade will result in noncompetitive imports' being purchased from abroad to the point at which their contribution to the economic welfare of the nation is exactly equal to the welfare cost of giving up domestic products in exchange. The greater the volume of such imports brought in, the less favorable the terms of trade and the more exports that will have to be given up. Arbitrarily to limit imports of noncompetitive goods would mean that imports of such goods were stopped at a point (volume of imports) at which the benefits from the importation of another unit of noncompetitive imports would exceed the opportunity cost of the marginal exports shipped abroad—not an optimal solution. Absolutely noncompetitive imports are not usually interfered with in this way, although some European nations levy a very high tax on coffee imports because this is a valuable means of raising revenues for the government (to the great dismay of Brazil). Sometimes imports of technological noncompetitive imports are limited by developing countries that face serious shortages of foreign exchange. Gap-filling noncompetitive imports are frequently impeded to benefit the domestic producers. In the United States this policy might either involve the continued existence of an industry that would otherwise disappear in the face of foreign competition (such as cane sugar in Louisiana and Florida or beet sugar in the Midwest), or it might involve higher profit rates for a resource-extractive industry such as oil or copper mining.

2. Given the emphasis of traditional thinking in international trade on goods that can be produced either at home or abroad, it will come as no surprise to find the main burden of the case for free trade resting on the reallocation of production among nations. This second type of gain from international trade (increased efficiency in the international allocation of production) is part and parcel of the Ricardian and factor-proportions theories. The greater the volume of world trade, the greater the gain from trade. Any artificial (political) impediment to international specialization will reduce the degree to which world production is distributed among different countries according to their comparative-cost advantage. For example, the production of clothing in the United States because of restrictions placed on imports from Hong Kong and Korea and even from Sri Lanka is inefficient according to the theory. Sri Lanka, where low-skilled labor is abundant and cheap, should be employed in making clothing for the developed world, allowing workers in the industrialized countries to make sophisticated goods for Sri Lanka.[2] Similarly,

---

[2] As will be shown in Chapter 9, reservations must be made about this example. The theory of international trade assumes full employment. It is not clear that the United States would be able to find jobs for all the (relatively) low-skilled workers displaced if it were to open its markets unrestrainedly to imports from the developing nations. At a minimum, a long period of adjustment would be required.

it is not appropriate for the Philippines to be making steel and aluminum given the high capital intensity of such products and the relative abundance of labor in the Philippines.

3. If imports of consumer durables were to be impeded, it is likely that consumers would face a narrower range of choice. Consider what would have happened in the United States if there had been very high, prohibitive impediments placed in the way of importation of foreign cars. The absence of the old VW Beetle in the late 1950s would have prevented consumers from signaling their desire for a small, high-mileage automobile or would have prevented the Big Three from taking any notice of any signals sent. Similarly, in the 1970s, the absence of Japanese cars with their record of high reliability would have limited the ability of American consumers to indicate their dissatisfaction with the quality of the products of U.S. automotive factories (see Table 9.3 and the related discussion in Chapter 9).

4. Finally, the absence of foreign competition would allow any American firm with some degree of monopoly or oligopoly power to exercise that power. Imports from foreign companies reduce the degree to which a firm can exercise its monopoly power and reduce the profit rate of such a firm. Some experts argue that foreign competition is a more effective means of antitrust enforcement than the U.S. Department of Justice.[3]

The case for free trade, then, is simply one of global efficiency (defined to mean that more is being produced). But if the cause of impediments to imports is usually a yielding by politicians to domestic pressure groups, the question of income distribution (who gains and who loses) must be closely intertwined. In terms of the strict factor-proportions theory, an impediment to international trade will benefit the factor of production used relatively intensively in the import-substitute good. In the simple two-factor model, labor would gain in a capital-plentiful country, and vice versa. But in the more complex real world, impediments are not placed equally on all imports. Some imports are taxed or otherwise impeded while others are left to trade freely. People who are employed in or own firms in protected industries will benefit because they will be able to produce more and, possibly, charge a higher price. Thus to impede automotive imports is to benefit the shareholders of General Motors, Ford, and Chrysler and the United Automobile Workers at the expense of the buyers of cars. The steel industry would also benefit from the prosperity of its important customers. But in addition to American car buyers, workers employed in foreign auto industries would suffer.

The idea that by impeding trade with foreigners a nation can improve the welfare of people at home while penalizing foreigners is the essence

---

[3] See J. Fred Weston, "International Competition, Industrial Structure, and Economic Policy," in Irving Leveson and J. W. Wheeler, eds., *Western Economies in Transition* (Boulder, Colo.: Westview, 1980).

of mercantilism. Adam Smith and the theory of the value of free markets vanquished mercantilism in the nineteenth century, but mercantilist practices have recently been creeping back into international economic policies.

The theory of international trade suggests that a nation's gain from trade will be bigger, the bigger its volume of imports and the better its (net barter) terms of trade. In other words, a nation's gain from trade is greater, the farther out along its offer curve it trades.[4] But the two sources of gain (volume and the terms of trade) work against each other: The imposition of an impediment to trade will, by itself, simultaneously reduce the volume of imports and improve the terms of trade. (In the context of Figure 3-4 in Chapter 3, an impediment to imports by Portugal would make cloth imports less attractive at all terms of trade and cause Portugal's offer curve to shift in generating an intersection on OE to the left of Q.) The notion is possible, then, that a nation might, by judicious imposition of impediments to trade, affect the distribution of gains from trade at the expense of foreigners by reducing the volume of trade. This gives rise to the idea of optimum rate of impediment (usually referred to as the "optimum tariff"), which might be said to be a mercantilist's idea of bliss. The optimum tariff would be levied in such a way that the gain from the improvement in the terms of trade would reap the maximum net benefit in terms-of-trade gains and volume loss. Self-evidently, it is possible to levy too high a tariff, since a prohibitive tariff on all imports would result in no trade at all, and that would be a suboptimal state.

There are two snags with this idea. It would be impossible to work out in the real world the appropriate rates of tariffs for many kinds of goods with widespread interdependencies in production. More important, perhaps, is the idea that the foreign nation would not sit passively by and be subjected to one-sided mercantilist policies but would also institute some of its own; it would retaliate. Then the world faces a definitely suboptimal solution in which both countries have moved their offer curves inward so that neither side gains better terms of trade and both countries lose out because of a smaller volume of imports. Figure 6-1 shows how successive rounds of retaliation might reduce gains from international trade despite the fact that each nation strives to improve its own national benefit. From an original, free trade position indicated by the intersection of the two offer curves, 0-I and 0-II, Country I imposes an impediment to trade groping toward its optimum tariff. This shifts 0-I in toward the origin to 0-I′, garnering Country I a larger gain from its improved terms of trade at the expense of a small loss of gain from trade due to a reduction in volume. Country II's retaliation shifts its offer curve down-

[4] For analytic support of this proposition, see H. Peter Gray, *International Trade, Investment, and Payments* (Boston: Houghton Mifflin, 1979), pp. 46–49.

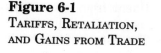

Figure 6-1

TARIFFS, RETALIATION,
AND GAINS FROM TRADE

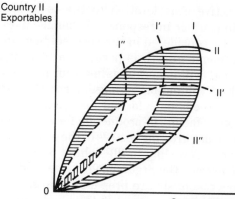

ward to 0-II', restoring (more or less) the original terms of trade and causing a total loss in the global gain from trade that can be represented by the horizontally striped area.[5] A further effort by Country I to exploit its mercantilistic potential shifts its offer curve inward again to 0-I", providing an improvement in the terms of trade over both the original position and the terms of trade prevailing when both countries had shifted their offer curves once. But Country II retaliates again, restoring (more or less) the original terms of trade and leaving as representative of the gain from trade only the small vertically striped area. There is no reason to suppose that nations would move all the way back to autarky—ultimately common sense would prevail, and no nation would think seriously of taxing absolutely noncompetitive imports or technological noncompetitive imports. However, cutthroat commercial policy and retaliation did take place during the 1930s when the world was in a very deep recession and all nations tried either to export unemployment to others or to prevent others from exporting their unemployment by running bigger balance-of-trade surpluses so that (in macroeconomic terms), $\Delta(X - M)$ became positive and larger.

The case for free trade relies, in its basic form, on the interaction between free international trade and global efficiency in production allocation. It rests on the assumptions of the theory from which the argument derives. This means that it will be vulnerable if free trade is in some way not compatible with full employment. The argument is strengthened considerably by the addition of the gains from a wider range of consumer choice and the gains from international competition that weakens national monopolies and oligopolies. But the analytic framework is static—no increase in GNP over time is countenanced. This means that the impact of free trade on economic growth must be argued without reference to static international trade theory, and the free trade argument does not

---

[5] As noted earlier, the change in the gain from trade can be usefully approximated by the change in the size of the "football" enclosed by the two offer curves.

give active consideration to the costs of adjustment from one output mix to another in response to changes in foreign economies. Adjustment costs are considered in the succeeding chapters. The impact of free trade on economic growth is positive in two ways: Freedom to specialize and to export will generate gains from international trade and increase the absolute volume of savings, if not the rate of saving; and freedom to import weeds out old and decaying domestic sectors, releasing capital and other factors of production for employment in new, more vital industries. If fast-growing sectors of the economy are starved for inputs because old industries cling to life behind protective devices, growth is impeded.

Sometimes the argument for free trade takes on normative overtones. Many economists are prepared to argue that the developed countries of the world have a moral duty to help poorer countries in the process of economic development. Since developing nations are chronically short of foreign exchange, any measures by developed countries that inhibit the exports of developing countries are morally wrong. The United Nations conference on Trade and Development (UNCTAD) takes this argument one stage further and reasons that the developed countries should give preferential access to exports from developing countries over those of other developed, manufacturing nations.

Once the free trade argument is put into a normative framework, it encounters the familiar stricture that economists have no monopoly on wisdom as to the desirabilities of different distributions of income and wealth. Arguments in favor of the poorer countries, however appealing, also tend to gloss over the income-distributional effects of such policies in the developed countries. Imports from developing countries are likely to place the greatest burdens on the poor and unskilled or low-skilled workers in the developed economies. Since these people have the fewest employment options and probably have the smallest capabilities to avail themselves of opportunities in other parts of their country, the simple, straightforward argument of free trade for imports of developing countries cannot be accepted without giving serious consideration to the pattern of adjustment in the developed nations.

SUMMARY

This brief chapter has laid out the background within which the mechanics and politics of international trade or commercial policy should be considered. Virtually every argument for impeding international trade can be assessed by examining its benefits in terms of efficiency and its costs in terms of income-distributive effects (who gains and who loses). Sometimes such computations are confined to individual industries, sometimes they are based on national standpoints, and, as here, sometimes they are confronted in terms of developed versus developing nations. What is of particular interest is to notice how the means by which protection is achieved are becoming more sophisticated (less obvious) and more closely tailored to the economic target. The subtlety of protectionism is limited only by the imagination of the bureaucrats (and of those in the industries seeking protection). It is this recent increase in sophistication that has given rise to the expression "neomercantilism" to describe present-day practices.[6]

---

[6] For an example of neomercantilism in steel, see Ingo Walter, "Protection of Industries in Trouble: The Case of Iron and Steel," *World Economy*, 2 (May 1979), 155–187.

7

Commercial Policy

There are many ways of interfering with the free flow of goods and services in international trade. It is a good idea, therefore, to define *commercial policy* as any governmental measure that discriminates against foreign suppliers. This could, theoretically, and does involve the idea that a nation can damage a foreign supplier by subsidizing exports as well as by the more obvious means of treating imports differently from home-produced goods. The most common device used for discriminating against foreign suppliers is the tariff. In fact, tariffs have been the mainstay of commercial policy to such an extent that discriminatory measures are divided quite simply into "tariffs" and "nontariff barriers to international trade."

THE MECHANISM OF TARIFFS

A tariff is a tax and, as such, must have both a rate and a base. Most tariffs are computed as a stated percentage (the rate) of the cost of imports c.i.f. (the base).[1] This method is known as ad valorem. Another method is the specific tariff, in which the rate is a sum of money and the base is a physical unit. Thus an ad valorem tariff is stated as "30 percent" and a specific tariff as "$5 per ton." For a given value of any commodity, a specific tariff has an exact ad valorem equivalent. However, in a period of inflation, a specific tariff is eroded as a barrier to imports,

---

[1] The c.i.f. (cost, insurance, and freight) value of a good is its value at the port of entry.

while an ad valorem tariff retains its degree of protectiveness. For the rest of this book, all unqualified references will imply ad valorem tariffs. It is possible to refer to the *level* of tariffs imposed by a country as some measure of the average rate of duty levied on imports. In contrast, the *structure* of tariffs refers to any systematic variation in tariff rates on different categories of goods.

A Tariff in Partial Equilibrium

A tariff raises the price of foreign-made goods to domestic users of those goods. Consequently, the imposition of a tariff will result in larger domestic production of import substitutes. The level of consumer satisfaction, the volume of imports, the global gains from trade, and the international terms of trade are all subject to change. Some of these effects can be analyzed with Figure 7-1, which shows how a tariff affects the market for a single good. The line DD is the domestic demand curve for the good. The supply schedule, $S_d S_d$, shows the willingness of domestic producers to supply the good at different prices. It is drawn as a solid line where it is fully applicable and as a dotted line where it denotes rates of production that are not achieved. The horizontal line S_f shows that foreign suppliers are willing to supply ample amounts at price p_1. The horizontal line $S_f + t$ shows the foreign supply schedule as affected by the tariff $(p_2 - p_1)/p_1$ percent. Under free trade, domestic production is $0A$, imports are AD, and total consumption is $0D$ at price p_1. When a tariff is imposed, the foreign supply schedule shifts so that $S_f + t$ exceeds S_f by the amount of the tariff. When the tariff is in force, domestic consumption is reduced to $0C$, imports are reduced to BC, and domestic production has increased to $0B$.

Figure 7-1
The Effects of a
Tariff in a Single
Market

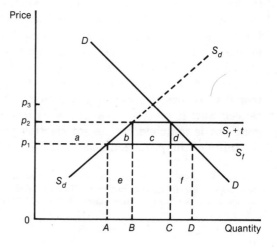

The loss of consumer satisfaction in the importing country can be identified by the decrease in the area under the demand curve between the price existing with free trade (p_1) and the price existing with protection (p_2). This loss is identified by the sum of the four areas a, b, c, and d. The logic of this device is that the demand curve represents consumers' marginal utility derived from consuming the import; therefore, the total area under the demand curve represents total utility, and the total area under the supply curve represents total cost. The area under the demand curve and above the supply curve represents a surplus enjoyed by consumers from being able to obtain the good at the equilibrium price. A change in the price indicates a change in the surplus: Increasing the price from p_1 to p_2 reduces the surplus by $a + b + c + d$. When consumption is reduced by the tariff from $0D$ to $0C$, consumers lose utility in the amount of d plus the area f, but since area f represents the opportunity cost of exports sold to facilitate the imports CD, the net loss to consumers is simply the triangle d. Consumers' net benefits are reduced by $p_2 - p_1$ for imports of $0C$ (the three areas $a + b + c$). Area a represents a straightforward increase in net income for domestic suppliers of the import substitute. This is the reason that producers (management and labor) will expend great efforts in convincing politicians that a tariff is desirable. Area a is a surplus for the industry and can be divided among shareholders, managers, workers, and inefficiency. If as a result of protection the industry is allowed to continue to be inefficient or to become inefficient, some or all of area a is used up, and less is left over to be shared among people in the industry.[2] But area a is "gravy"—meaning more income or less work—for the industry. Government revenues increase by c, the value of imports multiplied by the tariff rate. This is a loss to consumers but could be refunded by diminishing taxes on a general basis. The triangle d is a net loss of consumer satisfaction that is not acquired by anyone else in the home economy (or, for that matter, in the world). Similarly, the triangle b is a net loss to society because it represents higher marginal costs of producing the import substitute. (These two triangles represent the cost of protection excluding problems of redistribution.) When output is increased from $0A$ to $0B$, the marginal costs of production go up (as shown by the industry supply curve). Costs of production for AB units comprise the areas b and e—these are the opportunity costs of the factors transferred into the industry producing the import substitute. Area e cancels out: It represents a loss of satisfaction in giving up the "other" good but is matched by the satisfaction yielded by the consumption of AB units of the protected good. Area b is left over and represents a net

---

[2] The question of efficiency is something that economics handles badly. Management may simply not be capable of generating least-cost inputs. Harvey Leibenstein calls this possibility "X-inefficiency"; see his article "X-Efficiency: From Concept to Theory," *Challenge*, September-October 1979, pp. 13–22.

cost to the nation caused by using factors to produce an import substitute when they could have been more efficiently used in export industries (to be exchanged for imports).

The tariff, then, has transferred revenue from foreign producers to domestic producers and to the government treasury. Consumers are less well off as a result of the tariff. Their total loss is mainly transferred to the government and to domestic producers, but there are also total or deadweight losses in national welfare, corresponding to the triangles *b* and *d*.

The redistributive, revenue, and deadweight loss effects of a tariff depend on the slopes of the two supply schedules and on the demand schedule. The steeper the domestic supply schedule, the greater the proportion of the increase in the total revenue of domestic producers that is clear gain. The flatter the two curves, the greater the reduction in imports for a given tariff and, therefore, the greater the sensitivity of government revenues to the tariff rate. Clearly, in Figure 7-1 if the tariff is raised to $(p_3 - p_1)/p_1$ percent, there are *no* imports and *no* governmental revenues. Tariff revenue can be very sensitive to the tariff rate and the volume of trade.

Given the description of the effects of a tariff so far, protection seems to be nothing but a "power play" by a greedy industry. Usually tariffs are introduced under slightly different circumstances that affect what may be called the "morality" of the situation without affecting the mechanics.

Figure 7-2 is almost identical to Figure 7-1 except that it incorporates some change in international conditions that results in a strengthening

Figure 7-2

A "DEFENSIVE" TARIFF Foreign supply shifts downward because of an appreciation of the home currency.

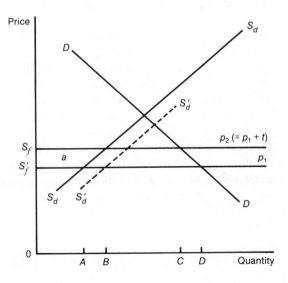

(appreciation) of the home country's currency. This can come about by a sudden increase in foreign demand for the home country's "noncompetitive" export and resembles the analysis of the effect on good 3 in Table 4-1 when the dollar appreciated from P 3 to P 3.33. Now p_2 is the original domestic price, and the change in international trading conditions reduces the foreign price to p_1. Workers will be thrown out of work in the amount equivalent to AB (and the flatter the domestic supply schedule, the larger AB for any given change in foreign price).[3] A tariff is required not to increase the welfare of people in the industry but to preserve jobs and maintain the earlier standard of living. Workers in the industry at price $p_1 + t$ ($= p_2$) are still better off by area a (as in Figure 7-1), but their standard of living has not improved. They are fighting to hold on to their jobs in the industry they know. If the labor market is working perfectly, the defensive actions are unnecessary because workers will find reemployment elsewhere, although there will be a short period of unemployment. If labor markets are not working well, the workers face protracted periods of unemployment, and their behavior is more understandable. The problem is that workers and management seem to think that labor markets do not work well, and their first reaction to foreign competition is to seek protection. All of the mechanisms from Figure 7-1 still apply. If labor markets are working well, it is wasteful to continue to employ people in industries that cannot compete unaided with foreign competition. Two of the more valid arguments for protection considered in this chapter depend on imperfect labor markets. If the workers and managers in the afflicted industry do not want to leave it, they have the option of reducing costs to meet foreign competition. Such a tactic would be perfectly efficient, although it is not very appealing to the people in the industry because it means lower wages and salaries and, if new machinery is brought into production, fewer jobs. This course of action would shift the supply curve down to the dotted position ($S_d{'}$), and domestic output would not be changed by the appreciation of the national currency. This course of action is not feasible if the original wage provides only subsistence income (as is almost the case in apparel and shoes in the United States) but could be effected when an industry pays particularly high wage rates (as in automobile production and steel). If other jobs were readily available at (more or less) the original wage rate, workers would leave the industry voluntarily rather than take a pay cut to shift the domestic supply schedule down to $S_d{'}$, and resources would be allocated efficiently. Imposing a tariff would prevent such an exodus from the threatened industry.

---

[3] Manufacturing industries are likely to have very flat supply schedules because the costs of production do not vary with output up to full capacity. They are therefore very vulnerable.

THE THEORY OF EFFECTIVE PROTECTION

The straightforward approach to the analysis of the impact of a tariff suggests that its degree of protectivity and the benefits it accords to domestic producers depend directly on the tariff rate *(t)* and the slopes of the three schedules. But an additional factor must be taken into account: differences in the cost of raw materials or inputs. The question of the *effective rate of protection* is important for developing countries exporting primary products and for industries in manufacturing countries that use as an input a raw material that is protected from foreign competition. Just as a tax on consumer goods penalizes the consumer, a tax on inputs penalizes the industry using them. Table 7-1 provides a relatively straightforward numerical example of the way in which quite high rates of protection can be afforded to activities by seemingly small tariff rates. A good must involve more than a single activity or process, and the table shows a good requiring raw material, an intermediate process, and a finishing process. The raw material can only be produced in Country B. Country A has three options: to import the raw material and carry out the second- and the third-stage processes, to import the semifinished good and to carry out the finishing stage at home, and to import the finished good. Table 7-1 provides imaginary cost data for the production of such a good in Country B and computes how much protection the tariff structure affords firms that consider performing the second- and third-stage activities in Country A. Note—and this the key to the problem—that Country A imposes higher tariffs as the good nears completion. This is a very common kind of tariff *structure* in manufacturing nations, called "cascad-

Table 7-1

EFFECTIVE PROTECTION: AN EXAMPLE

	Value of Import c.i.f. ($)	Nominal Tariff (%)	Value of Import (Tariff Paid) ($)	Effective Tariff (%)
Raw material	.50	0	.50	0
Cost of second stage in Country B	.20			
Semifinished good	.70	10	.77	
Potential cost of second stage in Country A			.27	$\dfrac{.27 - .20}{.20} = 35$
Cost of third stage in Country B	.30			
Finished good	1.00	20	1.20	
Potential cost of third stage in Country A			$1.20 - .77 = .43$	$\dfrac{.43 - .30}{.30} = 43.3$

ing tariffs."[4] Business in Country A can import the raw material free of duty for 50 cents per unit, and they can import the semifinished product for 77 cents (70 cents cost and 7 cents tax or duty). The domestic firm carrying out the processing of the raw material into the semifinished good can compete with foreign costs if it can perform the operation for 27 cents (77 − 50). The degree of protection afforded is determined by computing the difference between what the domestic firm can perform the operation for (its cost of the second-stage process) and the actual costs in Country B and expressing it as a percentage of the costs in Country B. The effective rate of protection is (.27 − .20)/.20 percent, or 35 percent. This is in contrast to a nominal rate of tariff protection (as listed in Country A's tariff code) of 10 percent. The same computation can be made for the choice between importing the semifinished good and conducting the third stage in Country A or of importing the finished good from Country B. The effective rate of protection for the third stage is 43.3 percent—substantially higher than the nominal rate of 20 percent.

The nub of the problem is that, in the second stage, the raw material is being taxed at 10 percent when incorporated in the semifinished import but not at all when imported as a raw material and processed in Country A. Recompute the effective rate of protection on the second-stage process when the duty is levied on the semifinished import at 10 percent on the value added in the second stage abroad. The nominal and effective rates are now equal. The magnification effect (the ratio of the effective to the nominal rate) depends on how important the raw material is relative to the second-stage processing cost. If the damage done to a national economy by a tariff is positively related to the rate of the tariff, it is the effective and not the nominal rate which is important.

Several aspects of effective protection can be considered.

1. Because tariff rates and transportation costs have analytically equivalent effects, it is clear that transportation costs that vary with the stage of processing can magnify the degree of protection of transportation costs to as great an extent as can cascading tariffs. Given the relatively low costs of shipping raw materials and the higher rates imposed on manufactures by cargo liners, transportation costs can afford significant amounts of protection to home manufacturing industries.

2. When a request for protection by an industry is being considered by the government, the government should, in its consideration of the merits of the argument, take into account the magnification effect on the potential user of the product. (In the United States, the government

---

[4] Recall that the tariff level is an average of tariff rates (in a two-good context, it is the tariff rate on the import). The structure is the distribution of tariff rates across various goods and activities or processes. Thus the practice of raising the rate as the good nears completion is a particular kind of tariff *structure*.

body is the International Trade Commission, which judges whether or not an industry is entitled to "import relief" according to a fairly precise set of criteria given to it by Congress.)

3. High rates of effective protection on intermediate goods can impose severe handicaps on attempts by raw-material-producing countries to increase their manufacturing base. The natural avenue for industrialization is likely to involve the processing of raw materials in which the country has a comparative advantage (probably an absolute advantage), and this can be closed by high effective rates of duty levied on exports of semifinished goods.

4. When pollution controls are imposed on an industry and increase costs of production, they encourage imports of substitutes. If the costs of pollution controls (environmental protection) increase as goods near the final stages of production, pollution controls will result in high *negative* rates of protection in the importing country and will provide large advantages to foreign industries where pollution is seen as less important.

The idea that the structure of tariffs can lead to negative protection for home industries is not a simple theoretical nicety—negative protection has been identified, although that result is not usually what the government of the importing country had in mind. It was simply due to a lack of understanding of effective protection. To see this, work out the effective rate of protection at stage 3 in Table 7-1 when the nominal tariff on imports of the finished good is 5 percent. The landed cost of the import is $1.05, and the effective rate of protection is negative: $(28 - 30)/30 = -.07$. Clearly, the structure of protection attributable to pollution controls will depend on the spread of pollution generation in the different stages of production. There is no simple a priori way of specifying the pattern of effective protection.[5]

5. In simple tariff analysis, the consumer is shown as bearing the cost of the tariff and, indeed, to the extent that the structure of tariffs affects the final price of goods, the consumer of the goods is still the main "target." But the structure of protection allows much more useful insights into the economics of protection. The existence of a tariff on an imported semifinished product will raise the cost of inputs to "downstream industries" and reduce the ability to compete with foreign competition. Steel users, for example, are damaged by any inefficiency in or protection of the steel industry. The final goods industry is hurt by taxes on intermediate products, given the level of protection it enjoys against foreign-made final goods.

These interactions are, obviously, extremely complex and would prove difficult to analyze in practical terms—especially when the effects of trans-

---

[5] For examples of quite extravagant rates of effective protection, see H. G. Johnson and P. B. Kenen, *Trade and Development* (Geneva: Librairie Droz, 1965), pp. 16, 22, and 23. For an analysis of pollution controls, see Ingo Walter, ed., *Studies in Environmental Economics* (New York: Wiley, 1976), ch. 9.

portation costs, X-inefficiency, and environmental controls all have to be factored into the analysis. Certainly, another strand of the argument for free trade is that governments have imposed tariff structures in ignorance and in the distant past and have little idea of their effect on the output mix in the home country.

ARGUMENTS FOR TARIFFS

Arguments in favor of the imposition of tariffs are frequently advanced in the following areas.

1. National defense
2. Infant industry
3. Employment
4. Protection of domestic labor's income
5. Retaliation
6. Making adjustment more gradual
7. Differences in working conditions
8. Protecting the jobs of the unskilled

National Defense

Some industries need protection because they are necessary in a time of war. As a consequence, it is desirable to keep these domestic industries alive and viable in peacetime even though they operate at a comparative disadvantage. In such cases, potential national defense considerations outweigh sheer (peacetime) economic efficiency considerations.

Since national defense is unquestionably important, it is worth paying a price to reduce a nation's vulnerability in time of wars. This argument favors a defense establishment of any kind, and the efficiency loss that results from tariffs on vital goods is probably a small fraction of the total cost of national defense (including a standing army).

For absolutely noncompetitive imports (and, possibly, for the other two kinds as well—see Chapter 5) the answer lies not so much with tariff protection as with stockpiling (amassing inventory) of strategic materials.

Despite its essential validity, the argument can be misapplied, and in many instances a subsidy would be a more efficient approach, even when protection is needed. It is certainly possible for industries with a remote connection to national defense to attempt to use this argument to protect their own interests. The crucial question, of course, involves the extent of the present cost (to the consumer) relative to the potential benefit. Would it be possible to achieve the same amount of defense strength by a cheaper alternative, such as a stockpile of parts, or by governmental purchase and storage of the machinery needed for the production of the goods? Clearly, the benefits depend on the importance of the goods to a war effort, the ease with which their manufacture can be started when hostilities commence, and whether they can be stockpiled in realistic quantities.

A substantial argument can be based on the fact that a subsidy to the industry will be less costly to the nation than a tax on imports. The following example serves as a good illustration of this point. Consider a good that will be required in far smaller amounts in wartime than in peacetime. Therefore, there is no defense argument for keeping more than a small domestic industry alive. But what if the production of that good is subject either to constant costs or to economies of scale in production? In terms of Figure 7-1, constant costs (or perfectly elastic supply) imply that the domestic supply schedule will be flat, but above the (flat) foreign supply schedule. The imposition of a tariff large enough to create a small domestic industry would, at the same time, ensure that the nation became self-sufficient in the good. A subsidy of the amount (per unit) of the national disadvantage could be given to some domestic firms so that only an adequate amount of domestic capacity was kept in production. The subsidy has the further advantage that the volume of output, on which the subsidy is paid, could be varied with the computed defense needs for the particular good.

The merchant marine obviously warrants protection for defense purposes. However, the merchant marine operates in international waters and cannot be protected by a tariff. Subsidy is the only possibility. For nations, such as the United States, whose merchant marines are not internationally competitive, subsidies are given and are based on the difference in operating costs between U.S. and foreign vessels. In practice, this subsidy is limited mainly to the more prosperous segments of the international marine transportation industry—the cargo liner segment that operates under a cartel-like structure. For the other segments of the industry in which gross margins are slimmer and the United States' comparative disadvantage is greater, there exists the device of *flags of convenience*. Under this arrangement, ships that are politically loyal to the United States can be registered in Liberia, Panama, and Honduras and sail under their flags. In peacetime, these ships enjoy the benefits of labor at the lower rates prevailing in these countries, but the ships can be recalled to the United States if hostilities should break out.[6]

The defense argument for a tariff, then, has some essential validity. It is important that this argument not be overused for spurious reasons. Since practically all industries have some connection to national defense,

---

[6] For a good summary of the history and details of maritime subsidies in the United States, see Samuel A. Lawrence, *United States Merchant Shipping Policies and Politics* (Washington, D.C.: Brookings Institution, 1966), chs. 3 and 6.

the most important reservation about the argument is whether the number of industries that can be described as defense industries for the purpose of protection can be kept to a minimum. Moreover, once the decision to grant an industry some degree of help has been made, the possibility of a tariff is only one course among many. The choice among the various measures to help the industry must be carefully screened so that the most efficient means will be selected.

Infant Industry

The infant-industry argument dates back to the late eighteenth and early nineteenth centuries, when it was formulated by Alexander Hamilton in the United States and by Friedrich List in Germany. Both men were concerned with industrializing their nations and saw the possibility for British industries to frustrate the industrializations. In its present widespread form, the argument refers to nations in the process of industrialization and, therefore, primarily to developing nations. However, it could be applied to any industry that enjoys significant economies of scale in any country.

The basic argument for infant-industry protection states that the nation considering protection does not have a comparative disadvantage in the production of the good in question in long-run equilibrium. But in the immediate short run, no firm can start up. This inability stems from the fact that maturation of a firm or industry does not occur spontaneously. The industry must start up on a relatively small scale and grow by increasing its capacity. However, the small or infant firm would not be able to survive to grow to maturity because its costs would be too high and foreign firms would undersell it in its domestic market. The industry would be stillborn. For this reason, the industry is deemed to need temporary tariff protection until it develops sufficiently. A second reason for the lack of ability of a new firm or industry to achieve the economies of scale that are technologically available is the relatively small size of the domestic market. Domestic demand will grow with economic development, and ultimately the industry will be capable of reaping all of the economies of scale that technology permits.

Two basic features are always present in arguments for infant-industry tariff protection: the assumption of future viability in the domestic market and the availability of economies of scale. In principle, the argument can be strengthened by the contention that the industry has a potential comparative advantage—so that exports are quite feasible once the industry has grown to full maturity. In fact, all that is necessary is for the industry to attain viability in the domestic market, given the degree of protection afforded by the average tariff rate and by transportation costs. The logic of the argument is clear. Infant-industry protection is a temporary device designed to permit a domestic industry to achieve its proper place in the country's industrial sector. Since the industry will become efficient, the economic growth of the nation will eventually be enhanced by the tariff protection.

This mechanism is shown in Figure 7-3. Let the establishment of an industry proceed by stages so that Q_1 is the first size at which output can be generated. At a cost denoted by the long-run average cost curve (*LATC*) equal to p_1, the industry would be undercut in a free trade situation by foreign suppliers selling at p_2. However, as soon as the rate of domestic output exceeds Q_2, the firms comprising the industry are able to sell at less than the foreign price. During the same time required to bring industry output up to Q_2, a tariff would be required. Initially, the tariff could be levied at a rate of $(p_1 - p_2)/p_2$. This rate could be gradually reduced when output expanded and costs decreased as economies of scale were realized.

This argument is valid for certain industries in certain countries in certain stages of development. However, there is a real, and possibly important, short-run cost to this kind of protection as well as a potential long-run cost. The short-run cost exists for the period during which the protected industry is supplying the domestic economy at a price in excess of the cost of imports c.i.f. If the good is a final good, the cost is simply a loss of consumer surplus, and except for any effect on the flow of saving from the household sector the effect of the tariff is much the same as for any other tariff. But if the good is an intermediate good that is used in other industries, the costs of infant-industry protection can be high in that the tariff would retard industrialization in these other industries. The cause of such retardation is the problem of effective protection. If

Figure 7-3

INFANT-INDUSTRY TARIFF

Price is measured in constant value units of foreign exchange. For expositional ease, it is assumed in this figure and in the text that the product is sold at long-run average total costs (*LATC*). Of course, for firms with decreasing per-unit costs (usually due to economies of scale), marginal cost pricing may lead to ruinous interfirm competition.

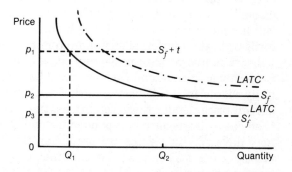

an intermediate good has a high rate of protection, foreign manufacture and imports of the finished good may actually be subsidized. A tax on an input is a tax on the uses of the input! It is possible that a subsidy might be preferable to an infant-industry tariff in some cases. Unfortunately, industrializing nations rarely have such efficient systems of taxation and record keeping that they can realistically make subsidy payments to infant industries.

The potential long-run cost is fairly obvious. To argue for protection now on the grounds of efficiency later requires some ability to foresee the future. In terms of Figure 7-3, it requires the ability to determine the flat part of the $LATC$ schedule from a knowledge of the part of the curve in the neighborhood of Q_1. Forecasts of this kind are notoriously inaccurate and may contain more wishful thinking than hard fact. Thus there exists the possibility that the infant industry will never mature to the point at which it can slough off tariff protection and meet foreign competition on an equal basis. In Figure 7-3, the mature industry might be more expensive than foreign supplies as shown by S_f' at price p_3. If the forecast were mistaken, the short-run protection cost and the actual investment in the industry will have both been incurred unsatisfactorily. The assets corresponding to those costs—capacity in the infant industry—represent an inefficient industry that has yielded a low rate of return on the invested capital. If the forecast of costs when full economies of scale are achieved is wrong and $LATC$ is always above the foreign supply schedule, S_f', the industry may be protected forever for no better reason than the fact that it exists. This policy may be necessary to bolster national pride and save political face. Alternatively, the industry can be left to die by being stripped of its protection. If the industry is to die, no further long-run cost is incurred; but the question remains as to how best to phase out such an industry. (The question of phasing out an industry will be considered shortly.) If the industry is to be maintained behind a tariff wall, the burden of such an industry is potentially infinite.

There is one further possibility. It is quite possible that the original forecast was correct and the nation did have an industry that was potentially viable in its domestic market with average total costs less than foreign price. Under these conditions, the tariff protection may not have been cut away as output expanded beyond Q_1 (Figure 7-3). The industry may have retained excessive protection (at the original tariff rate and price p_1) and may develop internal inefficiencies. Managers may not be as cost-conscious or as hardworking as they should be. Labor may be provided unduly benevolent working conditions and higher wages than are justified by the supply of labor. A labor union could introduce an imperfection in the national labor market so that the chosen few employed in the industry are treated as privileged workers and command a premium over excluded workers. Under such circumstances, the $LATC$ schedule of the industry would slowly shift upward from the solid line to the dashed line, *LATC'*. Thus the industry lacks viability not because of any lack of comparative advantage in real terms but because the protected position of the industry has allowed insiders to reap the benefits that were destined for the economy as a whole. Under such circumstances, tariff elimination may never be possible if the insiders have enough political muscle. Finally, the estimation of the flat part of the *LATC* schedule may not be able to make allowances for changes in relative factor prices as development takes place during the time needed to increase capacity from Q_1 to Q_2 or for foreign technological gains (especially those that introduce further economies of scale to extremely large foreign industries).

Both the defense and the infant-industry arguments are reasonably valid for tariff protection or subsidy. The problem facing authorities is to distinguish between the truly deserving and the undeserving—in the face of vociferous and emotional appeals from both types of industry. The best single criterion is probably to exert extreme caution and require the presentation of very strong cases before a tariff is granted on either ground. Such a procedure would put a major burden of proof on the advocates of protection. Another means of safeguarding against the possible risks of inefficiency is to award infant-industry protection as a special kind of tariff in which the nominal rate is predetermined and decreases at a specified rate each year until it disappears completely at some time in the future. The infant industry would receive a tariff or a subsidy of so many percent ad valorem for, say, five years. After that time, the nominal rate would decline by 10 percent of the original rate in each of the next ten years. Such an approach would give the industry protection that was finite in duration, and the gradually decreasing nominal rate would help to prevent internal inefficiencies from being generated within the industry as scale economies are achieved and would provide a margin of safety. The fact that the protection afforded declines to zero does not prevent the industry from seeking and obtaining a change in the protection formula. However, the seeking of such a change would constitute an admission of the industry's failure to establish itself in accordance with its original potential. This would at least inaugurate some review of the industry's future prospects.

Employment

The use of a tariff to expand employment traces its antecedents back to the thinking of mercantilists, who saw a positive balance of trade in goods and services as a means of assuring domestic prosperity. This practice revived between the two world wars when the purpose was to increase the volume of aggregate demand within a nation by a judicious mixture of undervalued exchange rates and tariffs. The French franc was particularly undervalued in this era, and the cheapness of living in France at that time on an income specified in dollars attracted Ernest

Hemingway and other American writers and artists to Paris in the 1920s.

If employment levels are a matter of serious concern, there is a shortage of aggregate demand in the home country. An increase in the trade balance $(X - M)$ can expand employment. This argument should *not* be used for legislating tariff protection. If trading partner nations are also suffering from a shortage of aggregate demand, an increase in $X - M$ for the home country means a decrease for trading partner nations and a decrease in employment there. A retaliatory tariff is almost inevitable, and the world will be no better off. If the trading partner nations are fully employed, a devaluation or depreciation of the currency that both protects imports and subsidizes exports is more effective (see Chapter 14).

Protection of Domestic Labor's Income

This argument clearly favors income redistribution for its own sake or constitutes a power play by a segment of society to improve its own share of the national income.

The argument has three subcategories: the cheap foreign labor argument, the so-called scientific tariff, and the redistribution of income from one factor to another.

The American worker can easily make a superficial comparison of the wage earned with the wage paid to foreign workers converted at the going rate of exchange. Foreign labor will seem to be much cheaper and, in developing countries, will command only a small fraction of the American wage. The presence of an army of cheap labor available in foreign nations could cause sleepless nights for a nervous American worker. European and Japanese workers can suffer from the same fear, although their argument is less clear-cut because their money wages are likely to be smaller than those of their American counterparts. The worker in a rich nation can visualize goods being made with this cheap foreign labor and hence costing much less than the domestically made equivalent. The worker in the rich country envisions a life under the continuous threat of unemployment as a result of an upsurge in imports in the industry that provides work. This is the rationale for a tariff to protect the continued existence of an import substitute industry.

There is no reason for couching this argument exclusively in terms of cheap foreign labor. In some countries, industries ask for protection against cheap foreign capital. Any industry that is hard-pressed by foreign competition can always spot the source of the foreign rival's cost advantage and ask for protection against it.

The reasoning that uses the availability of cheap foreign labor as a basis for argument is false. Labor is not the only factor of production, and prices depend on many things. Wages represent a single item in production costs and may or may not dominate the cost structure and determine an industry's competitiveness. What matters is not the wage rate but the labor cost per unit of output, which, in turn, is determined by both marginal productivity and the wage rate. American workers can attribute their high wages to their productivity, which derives from their embodied human capital, the large amount of cooperating capital at their disposal, their unions' negotiating power, and the productive organization of American industry. In contrast, the low wages of foreign competitors can be traced to their lack of skill and training, the small amount of productive capital at their disposal, the less productive economic and social structure in many foreign countries, and the large army of surplus labor in many poor, developing countries. There is no guarantee that American workers will not suffer as a result of the availability of cheap foreign labor and that the differential may not be reduced in time. If capital and know-how flow from rich countries and are adapted to suit the low-wage labor available in developing nations, U.S. labor can be hurt. The outcome for U.S. labor is more likely to be adverse if the market to be served by the combination of advanced capital, know-how, and cheap foreign labor is the domestic U.S. market. This particular problem may call for a tariff to ease the adjustment, but whether it would extend to permanent protection of an industry is questionable.

The argument to protect domestic factors against cheap foreign factors is carried to its logical extreme by the so-called scientific tariff argument. In this guise, the absurdity of the argument becomes obvious. The scientific tariff states that a tariff should be levied on all imported goods that foreigners can produce more cheaply than domestic industry at an ad valorem rate that is scientifically determined to bring the cost of foreign goods into exact equality with their domestic counterparts. Universal application of such a principle would eliminate any cost advantage that foreigners have in certain goods, comparative advantage would be frustrated, and international trade in competitive goods would cease. If trade ceases, the gain from trade is sacrificed, and autarky reigns.

It may be that such a tariff would not be levied on goods that cannot be produced in the importing nation—that is, noncompetitive goods. In this way, some international trade would still take place. Such trade would be limited to a special case of absolute advantage. Gains from trade would be very great per unit volume of such trade, but large gains might still be sacrificed.

The third argument is the Stolper-Samuelson question of using a tariff to redistribute national income among the various factors of production. If income shares are to be changed, domestic measures that directly affect income shares will probably prove to be more efficient in achieving some socially desired income reallocation than a tax on foreign goods. The greater desirability of domestic measures will be enhanced if the onset of tariffs leads to foreign retaliation.

Retaliation

The basic argument for retaliatory tariff action is that it is the only way to prevent foreign governments from actually imposing tariffs on the exports of the focus nation. A retaliatory tariff will match, or more than offset, a tariff imposed on an export. Since a single nation is likely to take the lead in imposing tariffs on focus-country exports, the retaliatory tariff would be imposed on a commodity that was supplied by the country that imposed the original tariff. The net result of tariff and countertariff would be the unhappy one depicted in Chapter 6 in Figure 6-1. However, the idea of retaliation as a rationale for tariffs is preventive. By letting it be widely known both by word of mouth and by deed that foreign tariffs will be matched by a tariff on exports, the focus nation makes the foreign nation fully aware that tariff imposition will yield no net advantage.

Another kind of foreign commercial policy can call for retaliation and has an important place in the history of tariffs. The process of dumping involves the sale of goods to foreign customers at lower prices (f.o.b.) than the same goods are sold to domestic wholesalers. A corporation can engage in the process of dumping only if it is a monopolist or oligopolist at home and if a sale to foreigners cannot be profitably returned to the country of origin. The incentive to a firm to sell the same good at two different prices is the increase in profits that can be realized by charging different prices to different users.

Is there anything undesirable about receiving goods from a foreign nation for less than the going price in that foreign nation? At first blush, the idea that the foreign firm treats its foreign customers more benignly than its domestic customers would seem to be grounds for applause rather than for retaliatory tariff action. Provided that the foreign firm can be relied on to continue this practice for a very long time, there is no sensible argument for retaliation against dumping—particularly if the importing nation is a developed nation that is not concerned with the possible prevention of the creation of a domestic industry. If the prevention of the creation of a domestic industry were the motivation for dumping, the resulting retaliatory tariff would be as much an infant-industry tariff as a tariff imposed in retaliation against dumping. The danger to the importing country comes when the foreign firm will dump only for a short period of time. Its purpose may be to reduce excessive inventories without disrupting its pricing policy in the domestic market, to use excess capacity, or to attempt to eliminate competition in the importing nation. Reduction of inventories or using excess capacity can be termed *sporadic dumping* since the actions are short-lived. The danger from this type of dumping is the disruption it will cause in the domestic industry. Domestic firms will not expand at the socially desirable long-term growth rate, and if excess capacity exists in one country, there is a good chance that the capacity of the domestic industry is also less than fully utilized and the action of dumping is an employment-creating action conducted on an industry, rather than a national, level. When the purpose of dumping is to destroy competition in the importing nation, the action is termed *predatory*. The long-term aim in such a case is to be able, first, to cease dumping at some future time and then to charge prices that contain an element of monopoly rent abroad in much the same way that a monopoly rent is earned at home. The disadvantages to the importing nation of this kind of dumping are obvious. Tariffs can be imposed for predatory or sporadic dumping.

It is possible for a national government to encourage exports in a particular industry to bolster that industry's level of capacity utilization in order to remedy national balance-of-payments difficulties. One way a country may attempt to do this is to impose an export subsidy so that even if markets were reasonably perfect, exports could be sold at below the domestic selling price and, probably, below domestic money costs of production. This policy should always be conducted under the provision that such exports cannot be reimported and used to undersell unsubsidized goods in the home market. This commercial policy measure does discriminate among industries and can unwarrantably damage the import substitute industry in the importing nation. If this subsidy is temporary and will be removed when the excess capacity or balance-of-payments problem has disappeared, the disruption to the industry in the importing country is not to be tolerated. The subsidy will be offset by a countervailing import duty or tariff that should exactly match the export subsidy. Note that the use of an export subsidy to solve a balance-of-payments deficit is different from a depreciation of the national currency, which reduces the price to foreigners of all domestically made goods equiproportionately.

Making Adjustment More Gradual

The argument for free trade (and the maximization of gains from trade due to the distribution of production in line with comparative advantage) omits any consideration of the passage of time. Once the concepts of change and of adjustment to change are introduced, the free trade case needs qualification: Adjustment costs can reduce the gains from free trade and warrant government intervention. The costs can take two forms, and both may warrant government imposition of protection on a temporary basis; because the problems of adjustment are transitional and temporary, the protection is also temporary. What is argued, then, is that if the *rate* of adjustment exceeds that which the economy can handle without difficulty, the life of the threatened industry should be extended so that the rate of adjustment can be slowed. The adjustment process is not eliminated.

It is in the natural way of things that some industries in developed, manufacturing nations will lose their (price) competitiveness over time as industries in developing countries acquire technology. The technology transfer may come about through the action of multinational corporations (as in television manufacture)[7] or through the acquisition by developing nations of managerial and marketing techniques. Developing countries, as a rule, are much more plentifully endowed with labor, and toward the bottom end of the range of skills, human capital is also cheaper. Therefore, if the developed country loses the technological advantage, its industry is prey to heavy import competition.[8] This process will be aided by changes in the rate of exchange as the developed countries introduce new advanced goods at the top of the ranking by competitiveness. Under these dynamic conditions, a domestic industry may find itself confronted with devastating import competition quite quickly. The free trade argument would have the vulnerable industry in the developed country disappear and that nation's resources reallocated into other industries not outcompeted by foreign firms. This solution ignores the question of the rate at which the resources should be reallocated—that is, the rate at which the declining industry should be allowed to die. An industry such as this can be termed *senile* or *moribund*.

The life of the threatened industry can be extended so as to reduce the rate at which change is inflicted on the economy. A tariff is one means of achieving this result. Generally, there is an argument for achieving any prolonging of life of a senile industry by subsidizing the industry instead of putting a tariff on imports because the interests of the consumer of the good are more fairly treated by this means.

There are two reasons for slowing down the elimination of a senile industry. First is the argument that a sudden elimination of an industry will cause any industry-specific capital goods (machinery) to become worthless almost instantaneously and, in the same way, any industry-specific skills possessed by workers and managers to be wasted. These losses are both private (to the shareholders of the firms and to the employees) and social (to the nation). By slowing down the rate of decline of the industry, this waste of industry-specific capital is reduced. Machines are worn out through use, and the human capital is used up as people retire voluntarily. The industry will continue to produce (and to use up the industry-specific capital) only if protected by some means for a period of time. By the same reasoning, government policy should not be so

---

[7] See, for example, the testimony of Mr. Paul Jennings, president of the International Union of Electrical, Radio, and Machine Workers, in H. Peter Gray, *The Economics of Business Investment Abroad* (London: Macmillan, 1972), pp. 201–204.

[8] Foreign workers in developing countries earn lower wages because of the country's endowment of labor in a straightforward factor-proportions sense, but they also earn lower money wages because their consumption consists largely of nontradable goods that are priced on the basis of very cheap labor. A worker in New York (or anywhere else in the United States) could not live on $1.00 an hour, but this would provide a highly sought-after income in many parts of Asia, Africa, and South America.

generous that the industry does not decline and ultimately disappear. Therefore, the protection should have a predetermined life and, possibly, be scaled down as time passes and people have retired and machinery been assigned to scrap. Needless to say, this is necessarily a rough-and-ready rather than an exact measurement process.

The second argument relates to workers displaced from the declining industry and the difficulty they will have in finding alternative employment. This aspect of the problem ignores the question of industry-specific skills and considers the problems of workers with general, transferable skills: The social and private losses from adjustment are directly and positively related to the duration of unemployment. This is the problem of "labor market congestion." It has three dimensions. When an industry is in decline, it tends to lay off workers with similar levels of skill. If the positions available in other industries do not exactly fit this skill, workers will have difficulty in finding jobs. They are likely to have to downgrade themselves to occupations requiring lower levels of skill (and, consequently, to lower wages). Very clearly, if displaced workers all have the same characteristics, the likelihood of finding a set of job vacancies that matches the skills available is quite small. If similar skills are being laid off from other industries, as competition from developing nations may make likely, it is possible that displaced workers will have extended periods of unemployment. For this reason, the U.S. government provides workers who can "prove" that import competition was the cause of their being laid off with "trade adjustment assistance." This program entitles workers to have longer (and higher) periods of unemployment compensation. The program has been scaled down in the period of budget deficits of the Reagan administration and is now incorporated in the Job Training Partnership Act of 1981. The problem here is not so much that the displaced workers themselves cannot find work when they have finally come to terms with the fact that they will not be rehired in their original industry but that they take lower-skilled jobs and displace a worker who is less skilled. This process of "bumping" goes on until the residual workers are the least skilled.

The second dimension, a related one, considers congestion of labor markets in terms of geography rather than skills. Many industries are concentrated geographically, and a serious decline in the industry will lead to workers' being displaced in a region that is awash with unemployed. By slowing down the rate of change, time is allowed for workers to relocate and for new industries to come into the area. The repercussions of the decline of a locally concentrated industry are most graphically portrayed by the fate of Detroit and the state of Michigan, which rely heavily on the prosperity of the automobile industry. Had Chrysler declared bankruptcy, Detroit would have been threatened with financial collapse.

The third dimension is national in scope but probably reflects both

Figure 7-4
RELEASING SENILE
INDUSTRY PROTECTION

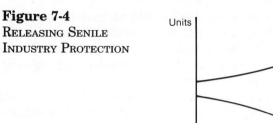

other aspects. When workers are laid off during a recession, they remain
unemployed for longer periods of time than in periods of prosperity. It
can therefore be argued that governments should consider protecting
senile industries during recessions and allow the protection to lapse quite
quickly when the economy is again prosperous.

All of these arguments make very good sense but present significant
practical problems. The greatest danger is, perhaps, that the government,
having instituted protection for legitimate reasons, will be lobbied into
maintaining it forever (or for much longer than could be justified). This
is certainly a powerful argument against governments' imposing protection in any form at any time. But it suggests pretty incompetent government. Government must be able to impose protection for finite periods
of time, if adjustment costs are to be reduced, and to see the protection
lapse. One study suggests that the administration will not be able to
gain congressional authorization to conduct negotiations to reduce tariffs
multilaterally if some provision is not made for workers harmed by
changes in the international trade situation.[9]

Figure 7-4 shows how a phaseout policy might be enacted. The upper
line shows domestic consumption of the good growing steadily, and the
lower line shows the steady decrease in domestic output as industry-
specific assets are fully depreciated. Imports are allowed in according
to the vertical distance between consumption and domestic production,
and the country becomes fully dependent on imports after N years. The
ideal length of the phaseout period would vary from industry to industry
and would be, in part, dependent on the effort and resources that government was willing to put into retraining and relocation programs. The
figure shows the rate of domestic production decreasing relatively slowly

[9] See C. Michael Aho and Thomas A. Bayard, "American Trade Adjustment Assistance after Five Years,"
World Economy, 3 (November 1980), 359–376, esp. 364–367. Also see Chapter 9 of this book.

at first, but the rapid reduction in output in the later years would encourage younger workers to adjust into other industries given the certain knowledge that their industry will die in a specified number of years. Other workers can make a conscious change in their life-style and plan on early retirement.

Differences in Working Conditions

The idea that all countries share equal concern for the health and safety of their workers is not tenable. The greater the population pressures, the more eagerly will workers seek employment and the less attention will be paid to productivity-decreasing health regulations and safety measures. Even if wage rates were the same throughout the world, it is possible that some countries could export labor-intensive goods thanks to what seems to developed countries to be a callous disregard for workers.

A failure to concern the economy with problems of the environment is a similar means of achieving a competitive advantage that may not be warranted by the underlying factor proportions.

In practice, cheap labor and a lack of concern for safety will go together, and both will tend to displace workers with low skills from industries in industrialized countries. As labor becomes scarcer (with growth), concerns for labor safety begin to creep into the economic conscience. Workers are likely to form bargaining groups that can insist on some health care even at the expense of wage increases.

Protecting the Jobs of the Unskilled

The free trade argument tacitly assumes that all people are employable at better than subsistence income. Thus the elimination of an industry by foreign competition will merely cause the displaced factors of production to find new jobs in other industries at, perhaps, lower rates of return or wages. Developed nations in the late twentieth century may well find this assumption invalid. When the competition for domestic production springs from developing nations with large amounts of cheap, low-skilled labor, it is industries that use low-skilled labor intensively that will be vulnerable. Unskilled or low-skilled labor (with skills measured in terms of the transferability of skills to other industries) will be laid off. The export industries will not require them in the same amount (per unit value added) as they are laid off, and they may not be able to find work. Table 7-2 shows the difference in the characteristics of the labor force of export industries and import-competing industries in the United States: Older workers, women, and minority workers with low education predominate in the import-competing industries. Unskilled workers, once displaced, may not be employable in other industries because they may

Table 7-2
CHARACTERISTICS OF THE INDUSTRIES IN WHICH TRADE HAD THE LARGEST POSITIVE AND NEGATIVE IMPACT ON JOB OPPORTUNITIES, 1964–1975

	Average of the Twenty Industries in Which Trade Had the Most Favorable Impact on Job Opportunities	Overall Manufacturing Average	Average of the Twenty Industries in Which Trade Had the Least Favorable Impact on Job Opportunities
Demographic Characteristics of the Labor Force (%)			
Female	21.50	29.40	41.10
Minority	7.40	10.10	11.50
Under 25 years old	15.40	16.40	15.80
Over 50 years old	24.40	26.50	28.00
Family income below the poverty level	5.80	7.00	9.80
Annual earnings under $10,000	72.10	77.40	81.70
Annual earnings under $12,000	83.50	87.20	89.70
High school education (4 years)	39.10	36.60	34.00
College education (4 years)	6.90	5.10	3.10

Occupational Breakdowns and Industry Characteristics

Unionized workers as a percentage of the labor force	40.00	51.30
Skill measured as a percentage of the average wage in manufacturing (1973)	104.00	49.00
	100.00	97.80
Skilled workers as a percentage of the labor force	55.80	50.00
		38.80
White-collar workers as a percentage of the labor force	36.30	30.30
Technical intensity (scientists and engineers as a percentage of the labor force)	6.87	3.20
		21.10
Technical intensity (R&D as a percentage of sales)	5.90	2.36
		2.29
Foreign direct investment proxy (foreign dividends plus tax credits as a percentage of firm's assets)	0.53	0.34 (median)
		1.39
		0.52

Source: C. Michael Aho and James A. Orr, "Demographic and Occupational Characteristics of Workers in Trade Sensitive Industries," *Economic Discussion Paper 2* (Washington, D.C.: International Labor Affairs Bureau, Department of Labor, 1979).

not be able to obtain or absorb the training needed for the jobs that are available.

Not everyone has the same ability to absorb training. Natural or genetic differences are likely to be compounded by social inefficiencies. Parents with low skill levels are unlikely to create a home atmosphere that puts a heavy emphasis on skill acquisition at school or through self-application. Nor are the school districts in which such families reside likely to be efficient or affluent. Habits formed in childhood may well last a lifetime and prevent a segment of the population from being able to absorb training when it is offered. If foreign competition causes widespread layoffs of people in industries that rely heavily on low-skilled labor, the result may be a permanent increase in the national rate of unemployment. Protection of industries with heavy reliance on low-skilled workers may, therefore, be justifiable. This argument becomes even stronger if there already exists a "reserve army of unskilled or low-skilled unemployed" because there are not enough low-skilled jobs to go around. (A low-skilled job is the easiest to replace by a machine!)[10] Under these conditions, protection of industries that use unskilled labor intensively must be considered pending the development of programs designed to upgrade low-skilled workers (when possible) and to recognize the possibility that there may be an inevitable tendency for the society, as currently structured, to create excess numbers of low-skilled or unskilled workers. The problem could become even more severe when semiskilled production workers are vulnerable to foreign competition in automobiles, steel, and similar industries. Table 7-3 summarizes some common arguments for protecting industries.

NONTARIFF BARRIERS

The imposition of a tax on imports as they enter the nation is not the only means by which national governments can attempt to distort the pattern of world trade, ostensibly to gain general advantages for their citizenry or to benefit a small pressure group. Tariffs have been an extremely important measure of commercial policy and have attracted considerable attention because their nominal rates are both defined and fully visible. Thus any change in tariff rates can be clearly reported even if the change in the effective rate of protection varies substantially from the change in the nominal rate. However, many other types of discrimination against foreign suppliers and even against foreign buyers

[10] The rate of unemployment of unskilled workers in the United States is usually between 12 and 20 percent, depending on how *skill* is defined, even when the aggregate rate of unemployment is about 5 percent. See George E. Johnson, "Structural Unemployment Consequences of Job Creation Policies," in *Creating Jobs*, ed. John L. Palmer (Washington: Brookings Institution, 1978), p. 125.

Table 7-3

The Validity of Arguments for Protection

Argument	Validity	Probability of Abuse
National defense	Valid	High: coverage too broad
Infant industry	Can be rational-ized	High: no built-in phaseout features and misapplied
Employment	None (see Low-skilled workers)	Yes
Protecting labor's share	None	Yes
Retaliation	Valid if used preventively	Yes
Senile industry	Valid	High: phaseout aspects not fulfilled
Differences in working conditions	Not valid (see Low-skilled workers)	Yes
Low-skilled workers	Possibly valid—better countered by adjustment support	Yes

Note the potential for abuse for all arguments for tariffs and protection. This is really a strong dimension of the argument for a complete hands-off policy by government and explains the fervor with which some economists view free trade as part of a professional credo.

exist. As with tariffs, some of these protective measures are instituted for defensible and even valid reasons, and others represent merely a response to the special interests of small groups. These other means of discrimination against foreigners take on many different forms and are referred to under the generic name of *nontariff barriers to trade* (NTBs).

The success of nations since World War II in reducing tariffs multilaterally has two implications. If tariffs are reduced and NTBs are left untouched, existing NTBs must become more important. If international rules and commitments preclude nations from imposing tariffs to achieve commercial policy goals, alternative measures (NTBs) will be imposed where possible. Both of these phenomena have occurred to the point that the Tokyo round of multilateral bargaining to reduce impediments to international trade explicitly included NTBs as a target for reduction.[11]

Nontariff barriers include many different measures. The diversity of

[11] The success of the developed nations of the world in reducing the level of tariffs is described in Chapter 8. The importance of NTBs is now such that the latest round of negotiations to reduce protection (the Tokyo round) *explicitly* included the barriers imposed by NTBs. The negotiations enjoyed only limited success in this endeavor.

the category must often provide an NTB that will be more effective for a particular type of protection than a tariff. Frequently, NTBs provide more flexibility with less difficulty than tariffs. The most important single NTB is a quota.

Quotas

A quota on imports of a particular commodity merely limits the number of units of the good that can be imported per year. No price effect is involved directly, as with the imposition of a tax. A quota is a declaration with legal force. Its enforcement requires that permits be issued to privileged importers, and imports can only be brought into the country legally when validated by a permit. The imposition of a quota necessarily involves an economy in a partial abandonment of the price mechanism and in a move toward direct controls.

To be effective, any quota must reduce the inflow of imports to a lesser degree than would have occurred in its absence. For example, if ongoing imports are, say, 10,000 units, there is no point in instituting a quota of 12,000 in the absence of perceived growth in demand. Once a quota is effective and restricts the supply of imports, it reduces overall supply and makes the good scarcer. Therefore, the quota acts to raise the domestic price of the import. Since a tariff will have the same effect, the similarity between the two measures is clear and suggests the possibility of conceiving of the nominal tariff equivalent of a quota. The tariff equivalent of a quota of 10,000 units of good X would be the ad valorem rate on good X that would limit imports to exactly 10,000 units.

The first task is to examine the similarities and differences between a tariff and a quota. Figure 7-5 is the quota equivalent of the tariff diagram (Figure 7-1). In the figure, S_dS_d is the domestic supply schedule and DD the demand schedule. The horizontal line S_f indicates a perfectly

Figure 7-5

THE EFFECTS OF A QUOTA

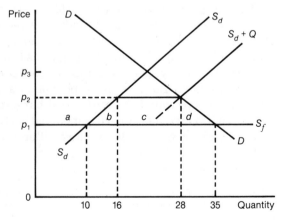

elastic supply of imports to be available at c.i.f. price p_1. In the absence of any impediment to trade, the price will be p_1, and domestic industry will supply 10,000 units out of total consumption of 35,000. Now impose a quota limiting imports to 12,000 units per annum. Domestic production increases to the point at which the new price, p_2, is equal to the marginal costs of domestic production. The price p_2 is determined by the intersection of the demand curve with the total available supply. Total supply is equal to the output of domestic industry plus the quota of 12,000 units, and this supply curve is shown as $S_d + Q$. At the new higher price, domestic demand is only 28,000 units. The tariff equivalent of the quota is $(p_2 - p_2)/p_1$. If imports were prohibited (a quota equal to zero), the domestic price would be p_3. While a tariff can be more than prohibitive—greater than $(p_3 - p_1)/p_1$—a quota cannot. However, a tariff must have some effect if there are any imports at all but a quota (in excess of 25,000 in the figure) would be ineffective. The effects of the quota can be analyzed in terms of the four areas, a, b, c, and d. The effect of the quota on the profitability of domestic industry (area a) is exactly the same as that of its equivalent tariff. Similarly, the two deadweight losses in efficiency (areas b and d) are the same as the equivalent tariff. The area c is not the same. The major difference between a quota and its equivalent tariff lies in the allocation of the funds corresponding to area c. With a tariff, c represents governmental revenues. With a quota, the funds can be acquired by the government, the importers, or the exporters. Assume that the government allocates the import licenses by giving each importer 12/25 of the preceding year's imports. If the foreign suppliers are perfectly competitive, importers will be able to buy the commodity in foreign markets at the price p_1 and sell it to domestic consumer at the price p_2. Importers will receive a windfall profit, which will, in all likelihood, more than make up for the restriction on the quantity of goods that they may import. However, it is possible that importers will be numerous and sellers will be few and organized. In this case, the sellers will realize that they can sell 12,000 units at a higher price than p_1 and will work in collusion to fix the price at p_2 so that the exporters will reap windfall profits.

Government can gain the revenues by the simple, but untried, expedient of auctioning the import licenses to importers. If the auction works well, the importers will bid $(p_2 - p_1)$ dollars per unit covered by the import license, and the government will acquire the proceeds. Note that the net barter terms of trade that result from the imposition of a quota are not as precisely determined even at the present level of abstraction as they are with a tariff. A tariff shifts an offer curve inside the free trade offer curve throughout its length because it is known that the proceeds of the tariff will accrue to the government in the importing nation. When a quota is imposed, the terms of trade could conceivably move against the quota-imposing country if foreign exporters raise their prices to the full limit and if the elasticities of demand and domestic supply are compatible.

The advantages of a quota over a tariff are that the measure has greater flexibility, which is a valuable asset in countering short-run disturbances. In addition, a quota is a more certain measure than a tariff and works when a tariff would be ineffectual. The quota's administrative flexibility derives from the fact that quotas can be imposed by a single unilateral action. In contrast, tariff increases need to be cleared in advance with members of trading blocs and are liable to retaliation in certain cases according to the regulations of the GATT. This administrative flexibility makes a quota much more suitable for dealing with short-run disturbances when a policy reversal eliminating the quota can be expected within two or three years once the need for it has disappeared. Quotas, then, are useful for sudden changes in the market for individual commodities or temporary balance-of-payments problems. Tariffs are generally considered to be more permanent measures.[12]

Other NTBs[13]

It is almost instinctive to think of commercial policy in the context of protecting domestic industries from foreign competition in the home market. In this way, a nation can shift its offer curve inside the free trade offer curve and improve its own net barter terms of trade. However, an offer curve contains both demand and supply factors and can be shifted under certain circumstances by restricting or stimulating exports, as well as by restricting imports. Thus commercial policy can be both import-directed and export-directed. Somewhat illogically, a subsidy on exports (or a negative export tariff, which amounts to the same thing) is usually categorized as an NTB rather than the tariff variant that it really is. Once the dual role of NTBs is recognized, the next task is to be able to distinguish among them to acquire some idea of their importance. To this end, it is desirable to categorize them by their intent with regard to international trade. Some NTBs impinge on international trade unintentionally, and it would be straining the meaning of the term to conceive of these as commercial policy measures.

1. *Pure NTBs.* Pure NTBs are measures designed primarily to serve the purpose of commercial policy. They strengthen domestic industry in competition with foreign suppliers both at home and abroad. Those that affect foreign competitiveness in domestic markets are import-directed, and those that affect the competitiveness of domestic firms

---

[12] Always assuming that government intervention is warranted.
[13] This section draws heavily on Ingo Walter, "Non-tariff Barriers and the Free Trade Option," *Banca Nazionale del Lavoro Quarterly Review*, March 1969, pp. 16–45.

in foreign markets are export-directed. Such measures may be clearly visible or covert.

2. *Quasi-NTBs.* Quasi-NTBs are trade-distorting practices whose primary purpose is to deal with problems that do not involve international trade but whose side effects can affect international markets. These measures can, on occasion, be imposed for commercial-policy purposes. Their advantage is that the imposing nation can claim them to be instituted only for domestic purposes. Their potential disadvantage is that when used for commercial-policy purposes, they have sizable domestic repercussions.

3. Accidental NTBs. Accidental NTBs are policies and practices with a purely domestic intent that have repercussions in international markets.

In any analysis of commercial policy, pure NTBs can be considered straightforward alternatives to tariffs. Quasi-NTBs are possible commercial-policy measures, and trading partners must be alert to whether they are, by intent, pure NTBs in disguise. Accidental NTBs can be disregarded.

There are probably five major categories of pure import-directed NTBs. Quantitative restrictions on imports (quotas) are the most visible and the most frequently used NTB. On occasion, governments will negotiate to resolve the problems of an industry damaged by foreign competition, and the exporting government will agree to impose a *voluntary export quota*. In reality, this quota represents an import-directed NTB by the importing nation.

Variable levies take many forms. They can be either ad valorem or specific charges on imports, or they can comprise quantitative restrictions having much the same effect. These NTBs are variable because they are changed according to prevailing conditions in the home market. If domestic supply is large, the levies are high. If domestic supply is low, the levies are low and imports are encouraged. Usually, this NTB is applied to agricultural imports—particularly type B (gap-filling—see Chapter 5) noncompetitive imports. A variant on the system of variable levies is the so-called *import calendar* whereby import restrictions vary seasonally throughout the year. The import calendar also applies predominantly to agricultural goods, and, frequently, the time of year can transform the status of a good from noncompetitive to competitive. The exporting of tomatoes to the United States from Mexico is the subject of much pressure by Floridian tomato growers. Mexican tomatoes are an absolutely noncompetitive import for about two months a year and a competitive good (or gap filler) for another two or three months when the Floridian crop is being harvested. In the warmer months they compete with domestic growers in many states. Austria uses an import calendar to restrict imports of carrots in the growing and storage season and to restrict imports of strawberries in the short growing season from June 1 to July 13.

Another kind of NTB serving the same purpose as the variable levy is a *minimum import price*. This NTB is really a quota that requires foreign suppliers to reap the revenues that correspond to rectangle c in Figure 7-5. Obviously, the intent of the measure is directed more toward protection of the domestic industry than toward exploitation of foreigners.

Discriminatory government purchasing practices are very important. First, they can apply both domestically and internationally. Second, they can be overt or covert. Third, they create uncertainty in the mind of the foreign supplier about the terms under which competition will take place and in that way reduce both the attractiveness of and the foreign interest in some domestic markets. In modern mixed economies, governments are spenders of a considerable fraction of national income. Therefore, if governments bias their purchases in favor of domestic suppliers, the protective effect can be substantial. The degree of bias can be formalized or can vary at the discretion of the government, taking into account prevailing conditions in both the nation and the industry concerned. As with all aspects of commercial policy, the consumer pays more. When governments pay more to high-cost domestic suppliers, the taxpayer becomes the consumer. These measures, like all commercial policy, may have a nationwide purpose, or they may represent a specific effort to help a particular industry. Frequently, overt governmental bias is initiated in response to national policy needs (balance-of-payments deficits). One such costly example took place during the Kennedy-Johnson administration in the early sixties. The Department of Defense enforced a general tariff rate of 50 percent (in some cases, up to 100 percent) in favor of domestic suppliers on articles of military use by requiring that foreign firms bidding on contracts be low bidder by a given percentage. Simultaneously, attempts were made to reduce the foreign-exchange burden of the overseas contingents of the U.S. military forces. The Department of Defense directed that goods and services for use overseas be procured in the United States whenever the cost of U.S. supplies or services (including transportation) did not exceed the cost of foreign supplies or services by more than 50 percent.[14] Frequently, discrimination in governmental purchases is absolute and not announced. In fact, it is possible for governmental purchases not only to be directed away from low-cost foreign suppliers but also to exclude low-cost domestic branches of multinational corporations. Such covert discrimination cannot be made the subject of negotiations because it is unannounced and unmeasurable; also, agreements to prohibit it would be unenforceable. Governmental discrimination becomes international when the government acts as the purchasing agent for certain needed imports. The theory here is that the government, by

[14] See Harry G. Johnson, "An Overview of Price Levels, Employment, and the Balance of Payments," *Journal of Business*, July 1963, pp. 279–289. Johnson was citing evidence given by an assistant secretary of defense before a congressional committee.

acting as a single buyer, can obtain better terms than can a series of individual firms that must compete among themselves in the foreign market. This practice is known as *state trading* and was popular after World War II but has since fallen into disuse. It gave the greatest benefit to the purchaser when a single buyer was faced with a bunch of competing suppliers from a single country. When one state agency dealt with another, little gain could be achieved.

The government can also be the chief exponent of a "buy home goods" campaign, instilling in the population a belief that self-interest, patriotism, and sheer quality considerations are all indulged if home goods are given a decided preference over foreign goods.

Subsidies to import substitute firms are self-explanatory. Export-directed NTBs mainly reflect their import-directed counterparts.

Subsidies are self-explanatory but can be covert by means of subsidization of export shipping costs in ships of the national flag. Subsidies run the risk of encountering countervailing duties because they can be considered the equivalent of dumping. Export credit insurance schemes and subsidy of extensions of long-term credit allow private firms to sell at prices that are lower than would be possible if all aspects of the transactions were conducted in free markets. The subsidization of credit conditions by an arm of the government has become particularly common. Quotas and charges applied to exports imply that the nation has a monopoly element in the market for a particular good. In this way, Sri Lanka attempts to increase its earnings from tea exports. The United Kingdom attempted a similar practice after the 42 percent devaluation of the pound sterling in 1949. Rather than have individual firms compete in the North American markets, the government encouraged distillers to maintain the price of Scotch whisky in dollars rather than in devalued sterling. The government also tried to achieve the same effect with automobile firms, without success. At that time, a worldwide shortage of mature Scotch whisky existed but only a mild shortage of automobiles in North America.

Quasi-NTBs can operate on both the import and the export side simultaneously. These impediments to international trade are side effects of domestic procedures that are undertaken for their inherent desirability for internal purposes. The various measures are merely listed here:

1. Arbitary customs valuation procedures
2. Variable customs classification procedures
3. Border-tax adjustments involving rebates of indirect tax payments on exported goods and the levying of similar or equivalent taxes on imports
4. Marketing regulations that can require certain ingredients, impose packaging requirements, and require mark-of-origin identification

5. Special regulations that can discriminate against foreign suppliers, such as health standards imposing sanitary requirements on food imports that increase foreign costs unnecessarily or impose long delays in shipment at the frontier, and safety and pollution-emission requirements for automobiles that can be used to handicap foreign suppliers
6. Foreign exchange restrictions that limit the availability of foreign currencies for imports. (These can apply generally but are often used discriminatingly. They are a favorite means for controlling tourist expenditures and are instituted for balance-of-payments purposes in most cases.)[15]

All these measures have potential for use either as an impediment to the importation of foreign goods or to promote exports. Like pure NTBs, they are difficult to quantify, and it would be a hard task to argue that quasi-NTBs constitute a deliberately imposed barrier to protect home industry. Therefore, they present almost insuperable difficulties for any attempts to eliminate all impediments to international trade by multilateral tariff negotiations.

Accidental NTBs are numerous. Practically every governmental measure can be shown to have some small effect on an international market. Walter listed thirteen separate categories of accidental NTBs. He also examined the degree of reliance on NTBs by commodity group and by nation for members of the Organization for Economic Cooperation and Development, a group of manufacturing nations.[16] The use of NTBs was concentrated in agricultural goods and goods using natural resources, suggesting that NTBs found their greatest applicability for noncompetitive goods: 44 percent of all food and live animals were subject to NTBs, 41 percent of beverages and tobacco, 23 percent of mineral fuels, and 11 percent of animal and vegetable oils and fats. The nation most reliant on NTBs was Japan, imposing them on 34 percent of import categories. European Economic Community (EEC) members depend extensively on NTBs because of their participation in the community's Common Agricultural Program. This program is designed to give maximum protection to the community's farm sectors. To achieve this purpose, variable levies are imposed on imports of competitive goods, the proceeds of which are applied to the provision of export subsidies designed to engender export sales for the otherwise high-cost agricultural surpluses.[17] Walter noted relatively little reliance on NTBs in manufactured products except for Japan and, to an indeterminate degree, Portugal and New Zealand. These

---

[15] This practice was more prevalent when the international financial system was based on a series of fixed exchange rates between national currencies. Nowadays exchange rates are flexible, so there is less need for measures to protect currencies. (See Chapter 12.)

[16] Walter, "Non-tariff Barriers," p. 35.

[17] See Lawrence B. Krause, *European Economic Integration and the United States* (Washington, D.C.: Brookings Institution, 1968), ch. 3.

latter two nations automatically require licenses for the importation of industrial goods and are therefore marked as heavy users of NTBs. This control might merely represent a safeguard that can be imposed when balance-of-payments problems arise and that in ordinary circumstances has no discriminatory effect.

SUMMARY

Both tariffs and NTBs can serve legitimate purposes as instruments of national economic policy, but they are more generally instituted in response to domestic political pressures and breed inefficiency.[18] These topics are considered in the next two chapters. The national defense argument aside, arguments for tariffs seem to be strongest when they involve a dynamic setting and are used to slow down or bring about change over time. The three strongest arguments are the infant industry, senile industry, and retaliation arguments. All three require sophisticated knowledge and analysis on the part of government policymakers if they are to be used correctly. The problem with low-skilled labor is considered in greater detail in Chapter 9, where it too becomes a dynamic argument.

Unfortunately, tariffs and NTBs tend to be instigated to preserve the original position and to oppose change. This is a very different argument from that of controlling the speed of change because the latter ensures that change does in fact take place. Preservation of the original position merely allows industries to preserve more privileged positions and individuals in those industries to enjoy higher incomes than are warranted by global market forces.

Bibliography

Aho, C. Michael, and J. D. Aronson. *Trade Talks.* New York: Council on Foreign Relations, 1985.

Culbertson, John M. *International Trade and the Future of the West.* Madison, Wisc.: 21st Century Press, 1984.

Gray, H. Peter. "Senile Industry Protection: A Proposal." *Southern Economic Journal,* 39 (April 1973), 569–574.

Grubel, Herbert G. "Effective Tariff Protection." In *Effective Trade Protection,* ed. H. G. Grubel and H. G. Johnson, pp. 1–15. Geneva: General Agreement on Tariffs and Trade and the Graduate Institute of International Studies, 1971.

---

[18] One outrageous argument for the institution of tariffs is that put forward in England by the Cambridge Economic Policy Group, which argues that Great Britain needs a once-and-for-all increase in tariffs without retaliation simply because the British people have gotten used to the better terms of trade. For a rebuttal, see H. Peter Gray, "The Case against General Import Restrictions: Another Perspective," *Bulletin of Economic Research* May 1982, pp. 71–76, and other references cited there.

Schlosstein, Steven. *Trade War*. New York: Congden and Weed, 1984.
Walter, Ingo. "Non-tariff Barriers and the Free Trade Option." *Banca Nazionale del Lavoro Quarterly Review,* March 1969, pp. 16–45.

Questions and Problems

Questions

1. An infant-industry tariff is likely to be unwarranted because no economist could correctly assess the cost of production when full economies of scale have been attained. Is this a strong argument against infant-industry protection? Is it the strongest available argument?
2. Which is the most valid argument for a tariff, in your opinion? What are its weaknesses and costs?
3. Retaliatory tariffs will eliminate all trade. Argue the case for or against this assertion.
4. NTBs allow governments to protect home industries without seeming to want to. Explain.
5. The problem with quotas is that they do not raise revenues for governments. This is particularly true when the foreign supplier can collude to extract the quasi-rent. Consider this argument in light of the quota on imports of Japanese cars in the United States in the early 1980s (see Robert W. Crandall, "Import Quotas and the Automobile Industry: The Costs of Protectionism," *Brookings Review,* 2 (Summer 1984), 8–16, reprinted in *International Trade and Finance: Readings,* 3rd ed., ed. R. E. Baldwin and J. D. Richardson (Boston: Little, Brown, 1986).

Problems

1. From Table 7-1, compute the effective rates of protection for the second- and third-stage processes in the following situations:
   a. Nominal tariff rates are 20 percent on the semifinished good and 20 percent on the finished good.
   b. Nominal tariff rates are 30 percent on the semifinished good and 10 percent on the finished good.
   c. With the original tariff rates, set the cost of the raw material at $1.00 (instead of 50 cents).
2. The original (free trade) price is $4.00 per unit, original domestic production is 200 units, and original consumption is 800 units. The slope of the domestic supply curve is +1, the foreign supply curve is flat, and the demand curve has a slope of −1. The government imposes a quota of 300 units. What is the new price in the home market, and what is the (ad valorem) tariff equivalent of the quota?

SUPPLEMENT

Trade Warfare

Trade warfare is becoming an increasingly common arm of international politics. Both Presidents Carter and Reagan have invoked economic warfare measures against the Soviet Union in order to penalize that nation for its interference in Afghanistan and its support for repressive policies in Poland. The United States and the European Economic Community imposed sanctions against Argentina as a result of that country's use of armed force in the seizure of the Falkland Islands. It is true that President Reagan revoked the main measure of Carter's trade warfare early in his presidency, but the reason for lifting the grain embargo to the Soviet Union was more a gesture toward Republican farmers than any sign that the Soviet Union had changed its behavior pattern. In fact, Argentina had largely replaced the United States at small net cost to the Soviets.

Nations may impose trade warfare for two reasons: They hope to change the behavior pattern of their antagonist, or they merely wish to punish the antagonist for some action without much hope that the antagonist will change. In either case, trade warfare will be effective only if it causes economic damage in the antagonist nation. This supplement considers the problems of invoking trade warfare and the mechanics of the process.[1]

Trade warfare can be defined as an extreme form of interference with the free flow of goods and services instituted by an offensive nation against an antagonist nation. Commercial policy is instituted to improve the welfare of the country exercising that policy, and any deterioration of the real income of (erstwhile) trading partners is an unsought consequence.[2] Trade warfare, in contradistinction, is a deliberate attempt to damage the antagonist nation and its economy. Some damage will be inflicted on the economy of the offensive nation; these costs are undesir-

---

[1] For a treatment that emphasizes the political as well as the economic dimension of trade warfare, see H. Peter Gray and Roy Licklider, "International Trade Warfare: Economic and Political Strategic Considerations," *European Journal of Political Economy*, 1 (1985), 563–583.

[2] Except under mercantilist assumptions, when the damage inflicted on the enemy economy was perceived to be directly beneficial to the domestic economy.

able but deliberately incurred consequences. Trade warfare is almost inevitably instituted by the imposition of nontariff barriers (in the form of zero quotas).

Three types of trade warfare can be distinguished:

1. An offensive country restricts the sale of exports to an antagonist country. The restrictions can cover all exports or can cover only the export of certain goods. The restrictions on trade with communist-bloc countries by the United States is this type of trade warfare. In recent years, the intensity of this trade warfare has varied inversely with the level of détente. In 1980, President Jimmy Carter escalated trade warfare significantly after the invasion of Afghanistan by the USSR by imposing an embargo on grain sales (in excess of amounts under written contract).
2. An offensive country blockades a foreign country so that the ability of the antagonist country to import goods from any source is restricted. This is a broader version of type 1.
3. An offensive country or bloc restricts imports from an antagonist country. This form of trade warfare is frequently employed by a group of nations acting in unison against a nation that has a large dependence on a single product. Modern examples of this form of trade warfare are the renunciation of imports from Rhodesia (now Zimbabwe) by Great Britain and associated nations during the intransigence of the Smith regime and from Uganda during the rule of Idi Amin.

Trade warfare is defined as effective if the level of income or output of the antagonist nation is reduced. The "net effectiveness" of trade warfare is defined as any loss in income on the part of the antagonist nation minus any loss of income by the offensive nation. Income losses will normally be measured in relative terms.

Distinguish between trade warfare that imposes on the antagonist only a reduction in its real income (a quantitative change) and measures that actually cause a major change in the way in which the antagonist economy can operate (a qualitative change).[3] Only the ability to withhold noncompetitive imports from an antagonist can bring about a qualitative change. For a nation to impose trade warfare measures that have positive net effectiveness, to damage the antagonist economy more than its own,

---

[3] In the simplest terms, a quantitative change merely causes the economy to choose a new point on an unchanging production possibility surface. A qualitative change involves a reduction in the level of output—the production possibility surface shrinks inward toward the origin as noncompetitive imports cease to be available. The relationship between trade warfare and a qualitative change was identified in Donald K. Losman, *International Economic Sanctions* (Albuquerque: University of New Mexico Press, 1979), p. 11, where he argues that as a result of a shortage of "intermediate goods for which domestic production is difficult or impossible, some production (and factories) may have to be abandoned."

it must be able to withhold noncompetitive goods. Trade warfare does not make practical sense in terms of general goods.

If trade warfare is to be conducted in a world without noncompetitive goods (with general goods only), both the antagonist and the offensive (warfare-invoking) nation will suffer two kinds of costs: the adjustment costs from the original, prewar situation to the new mix of output and the loss of gain from trade caused by the reversion toward autarky. The first of these is a transitional cost; the second is to be endured for the duration of the trade war. (Of course, some transitional cost has to be undergone for a second time when or if trade warfare lapses.)

Let us assume that the world is divided into only two nations or blocs, so the imports proscribed by the offensive bloc cannot be traded through third countries. Under these conditions, the warfare measures are not weakened in any way. The damage inflicted on the antagonist nation will be merely quantitative, and this degree of damage may be matched by the costs borne by the offensive country. Only if the two blocs are of markedly unequal size—the members of the United Nations imposing restrictions on a single country, for example—is the net effectiveness of trade warfare likely to be substantial. Under these conditions, the small antagonist country will have to submit to a much larger proportionate change in its output mix and will suffer a much larger percentage loss of gain from trade.

The effectiveness of trade warfare will also be reduced by any *slippage* that may weaken the embargo on exports (or imports). If the world consists of three blocs—the offensive and antagonist nations and their allies and a neutral bloc comprising the rest of the world—it is quite possible that the antagonist will be able to avoid the effects of the embargo by obtaining the proscribed goods from the neutral bloc. The replacement of embargoed imports will probably involve reliance on a higher-cost supplier and will therefore result in an adverse shift in the terms of trade to the antagonist nation, but this is preferable to autarky. A second kind of slippage can occur when shipments of proscribed goods are purchased by the antagonist country or bloc after having been transshipped in the neutral bloc—"laundered," in modern parlance.[4] Evasions of this kind weaken trade warfare in exactly the same way that smuggling weakens prohibitions of imports instituted for reasons of commercial policy. Slippage of both kinds effectively changes the relative size of the offensive and antagonist blocs. If the antagonist can obtain the embargoed goods from a third country, that country becomes a member of the antagonist bloc, and the size of the neutral bloc is reduced. If the export restrictions are completely circumvented by a rearrangement of trade patterns, the effectiveness of trade warfare is reduced to the effect of any induced adverse shift in

[4] "Soviets May Make Up for Lost U.S. Grain but Embargo Exacts Toll in Other Ways," *Wall Street Journal,* April 11, 1980, p. 35, provides an indication of the importance of slippage of this kind.

the terms of trade. Net effectiveness could easily be negative. Much the same possibility of slippage applies to type 3 warfare: It may be possible to export the proscribed goods to the neutral bloc or even to "smuggle" them into the offensive bloc, but the antagonist nation will still experience an adverse shift in its terms of trade.

At best, this analysis rings only partly true. It explains action by the UN, but it does not satisfactorily explain trade warfare being instituted by a single nation or by a group of small nations. Nor does it satisfactorily explain trade warfare measures being instituted by one bloc against another of approximately equal size. It may indeed be possible for a bloc of nations to proscribe exports to another large bloc and for the sets of elasticities of substitution and transformation to be such that the antagonist nation will be more seriously damaged than the offensive bloc so that the warfare would have positive net effectiveness. Such an outcome is unlikely. Even more important, it is extremely unlikely that the offensive bloc will be able to estimate the elasticities with sufficient certainty to warrant instituting warfare measures.

Trade warfare is much more likely to be perceived to have positive net effectiveness when the existence of noncompetitive imports is allowed for.[5] With the possible exception of agricultural goods, which are gap fillers in many countries, type 1 and type 2 warfare depends on the existence of goods that cannot be produced domestically in the antagonist bloc. If warfare is to be worthwhile (that is, if it is to have positive net effectiveness), it must involve more than a movement over the production possibility surface of the antagonist; it must cause the surface to shrink inward. The intent of trade warfare is to create bottlenecks of such severity that qualitative change is enforced and the behavior of the antagonist altered. Type 3 warfare takes effect in two ways: First, the antagonist or target is deprived of foreign exchange because it cannot sell its exports and, second, it must be able to find gainful employment for workers displaced from the traditional export industries. Type 3 warfare is likely to be effective against developing nations with exports concentrated in one or two products. Such nations lack the flexibility required for a smooth reallocation and have an urgent need for foreign exchange because of their intense need for noncompetitive imports.

Historically, though, trade warfare has never been very successful in changing the political stance of the antagonist. It may be that trade warfare unites the antagonist country behind its government and steels its resolve, or it may be that antagonist nations can always escape the worst effects at a price (through slippage).

Let us now assume three countries or blocs, as in Figure 7-A: the

[5] This additional dimension also adds realism to analysis of smuggling. Smugglers will respond to the highest perceived profit, and this will most likely be obtainable on goods whose domestic production and import are prohibited on grounds of social welfare. See H. Peter Gray and Ingo Walter, "Smuggling and Economic Welfare: A Comment," *Quarterly Journal of Economics,* 89 (1975), 643–650.

Figure 7-A

PREWARFARE TRADING
PATTERNS

G identifies general goods,
and NC_1, NC_2, and NC_3
are different kinds of
noncompetitive imports.

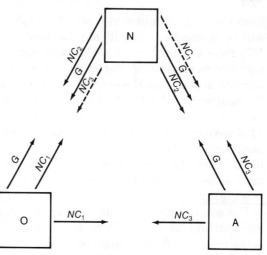

offensive country and its allies (O); the antagonist country and its allies
(A); and a neutral bloc (N). As soon as the analysis is considered in
terms of blocs, the meaning of noncompetitive imports has to be adapted
to mean imports that cannot be produced within the bloc. Country O
can only expect to impose trade warfare that has positive net effectiveness
if it can withhold a noncompetitive import from Country A *and* if it can
replace any noncompetitive imports that it obtains from Country A. Let
trade be balanced multilaterally and goods flows exist in accordance
with Figure 7-A. Because of political strain, no trade in general goods
takes place between Countries O and A, but each supplies the other
with a noncompetitive import. Country O institutes warfare against Country A by withholding supplies of noncompetitive import 1. The success
(positive net effectiveness) of the move will depend on any difference
between the intensity of desire for or need of NC_1 in Country A and the
desire for or need of NC_3 in Country O *or* on the ability of the individual
countries or blocs to acquire the good from the neutral bloc. Not all
noncompetitive imports are needed with the same degree of intensity:
Coca-Cola is not a vital noncompetitive import, but oil imports into Japan
would be absolutely vital. Identifying the United States as Country O
and Russia and the Eastern bloc as Country A, NC_1 might be wheat
and NC_3 might be platinum, which is important in refining oil. (Countries
A and O exchange no ordinary goods because they are politically estranged
and do not grant each other favored trading status.)

As indicated, the effectiveness of trade warfare (in purely economic
terms) depends on the degree to which Country O's action will prevent
Country A from obtaining NC_1, and this depends on whether or not
that good can be obtained from the neutral bloc. If the good is obtainable

from Country N, albeit at a slightly higher price, Country O's measure will be ineffectual. It will also be ineffectual if Country O cannot get NC_3 from Country N or if shipping companies are able to bypass the regulations instituting trade warfare. Slippage aside, the success of trade warfare depends on the existence of the two dashed lines radiating from the neutral bloc (N). If NC_1 does not exist and NC_3 is a solid line (indicating availability), trade warfare can, in the absence of slippage, be effective. This asymmetry points out the importance of the neutral bloc and the need for Country O to win over other nations to its point of view and induce them to transfer from the N bloc to the O bloc. This will not be easy since the transfer requires renunciation of good prices for their exports.

The second possible source of effectiveness is for NC_3 to be relatively unimportant and for NC_1 to be vital. The likelihood of trade warfare being effective (in economic terms) will be greater (1) the more important the O bloc is as a source of noncompetitive imports (and the larger the O bloc), (2) the greater the absolute importance of the noncompetitive imports withheld, and (3) the smaller the scope for slippage. If the N bloc is a poor source of NC_1 either because it has little in the way of surplus production over domestic needs or because the quality is poor, warfare should be successful. If the O bloc is very large relative to the A bloc, warfare will be successful. If the opportunity for slippage can be restrained (through a type 2 blockade) and if NC_1 is essential, trade warfare should be economically effective.

But it is impossible to estimate accurately, ahead of time, how great net effectiveness will be. In a democratic country, it is essential to have the support of the electorate; otherwise, support for the project will be withdrawn. Technological noncompetitive imports, which are likely to be the key vital noncompetitive imports available from industrialized countries, are unlikely to have an immediate effect since there is a lag in introducing technology into an economy. However, some technological noncompetitive imports may be important when they are sophisticated manufactured parts for equipment previously sold to the A bloc. This equipment might include both high-tech machinery and high-performance military and civilian aircraft.

Although the size component is important, in most instances, such as the United Nations versus Zimbabwe or Rhodesia, it is overshadowed by the importance of vital noncompetitive imports. The proof of this was the ability of the Arab oil-exporting nations to inflict severe hardship on the industrialized world in 1973 by instituting a boycott of oil shipments. Strangely enough, this boycott did not succeed in its original objective, which was to separate Israel from its supporters and to reestablish the rights of the Palestinians to the territory lost in the 1967 war. The oil-exporting nations suddenly realized the extent of their market power and learned that they could control supply enough to increase the world price of oil by 400 percent to $12 per barrel. Once the financial implications of their policy had dawned on them, the net effectiveness became negative—the cost of withholding oil at $12 per barrel was tremendous, and they renounced trade warfare in the interests of profit. But here is a classic example that the size of the offensive bloc was much less important than the degree of control exercised over a vital noncompetitive import.

8

The Politics
of Commercial Policy

Commercial policy is formulated and enacted by politicians. It is administered by the civil service. The legislators frame the policy in terms of their own beliefs and under the influence of political pressures. These political pressures exist at two different levels—national and international. National pressures derive from expressions of self-interest that emanate from within the community. Internationally, commercial policy is an exercise in bargaining and diplomacy carried out in a setting that is simultaneously both extant and evolving. Two separate kinds of national pressures exist: pressures designed to exploit the foreigner to the ostensible benefit of the nation as a whole and pressures whose primary motivation is to improve the well-being of a particular sector of the economy at the expense of the foreigner and of other domestic sectors. These two types of pressure are represented, respectively, by the average *level* of tariffs and the *structure* of tariffs on different commodities. International pressures are the reactions, actual or potential, of other nations to the expression of nationalist positions—what might be called the countervailing power of foreigners. A nation's international position on commercial policy is an arm of foreign political policy as a composite unit and cannot be seen as a purely commercial endeavor responding only to the material interests of the nation and its constituent pressure groups. One example of the interrelationship between commercial policy and political policy is the U.S. encouragement in the 1950s of the formation of the European Economic Community. The political gains that derived from the establishment of an alliance based on economic interdependence were deemed to outweigh the recognized adverse shift in the U.S. net barter terms of trade that would inevitably follow from the integration. Another example of placing political interests above narrow commercial concerns is the generally placatory attitude taken by the manufacturing nations toward developing countries and the consequent creation of a system of preferential tariffs.[1]

This chapter will not develop the concept of interdependency between international political and economic policies. Instead, it will elaborate on the way in which commercial policy is formed in response to domestic pressure, describe briefly the institutional setting in which commercial-policy negotiations are conducted, and examine the progress made since World War II in reducing the general level of barriers to trade through multilateral bargaining.

DOMESTIC PRESSURES

The idea of exploiting the foreigner and allowing the consequent gain (increased gain from trade) to fall randomly on the economy is the essence of mercantilism, the sixteenth- and seventeenth-century idea that the way to domestic growth was to prevent imports as much as possible. This type of policy pays little attention to which sectors of the domestic economy benefit. The policy would be achieved by equal increases in tariffs on all imports to improve the terms of trade, to foster economic growth, and to export any unemployment that might afflict the country. In contrast, a national defense argument might have selective implications for different industries. Similarly, narrow sectoral pressures represent the interests of individual industries, so they are likely to affect the level of tariffs (and the benefits of any tariff increases) quite unequally. Domestic pressures emanating from individual sectors will affect the structure of tariffs directly and the level of tariffs only indirectly. Industries faced with potential reductions in profit rates or actual losses as a result of competition from foreigners will exert pressure on their political representatives to protect the interests of their own industry. Inevitably, tariffs or other protection granted to a single industry will decrease the prosperity of other groups within the economy (especially users of the protected good) and will damage foreign suppliers.

In the sectoral strife implicit in the pressures of forming commercial policy, many sectors are neutral and of little direct concern. The others can be divided into the protection-biased sector and the trade-biased sector.[2] Analysis of the components of these two groups and their behavior

---

[1] The question of the generalized system of preferences is considered in Chapter 10.

[2] This discussion relies heavily on Ingo Walter, "How Trade Policy Is Made; A Politico-economic Decision System," in *The United States and International Markets*, ed. Robert G. Hawkins and Ingo Walter (Lexington, Mass.: Lexington Books, 1972), pp. 23–34. Used by permission of the publisher.

will provide insights into the way in which an operating commercial policy evolves out of the domestic pressures. The interests of these two groups are not reconcilable, so there is always pressure for a policy change. In times of overall prosperity, the forces for protectionism will be less strident, and in recessions they will be stronger.

The protection-biased sector is composed of import-competing firms, suppliers of those firms and industries, and the interests of the labor unions and professional associations predominantly represented in those industries. The gains that accrue to import-competing firms from the imposition of a tariff or a quota have been shown to be significant in Figures 7-1 and 7-5 in Chapter 7. Firms that favor protection may be established firms in old industries in which inefficiencies have grown up through time. Such inefficiencies might comprise archaic work rules, outmoded managerial procedures, or a general lack of modern technology. But a tariff-seeking firm may also be a member of a senile industry as defined in Chapter 7—a firm that is efficient in terms of the domestic economy but has suddenly lost its comparative advantage. In this age of multinational corporations (MNCs), import-competing firms cannot always be relied on to fight for protection of a threatened activity. Instead, an MNC will close down the factory and transfer production to a factory located in another country that enjoys a comparative advantage in the activity. Such actions heavily burden the labor union representing the workers. The labor union is likely to receive support from industries that supply the import-competing firm and from local politicians. The effectiveness of the protection-biased sector will depend on its ability to strike responsive political chords in legislatures. As noted in Chapter 7, industries tend to be well organized for such action through either trade associations or labor unions, both of which will maintain political action wings.

Generally, the trade-biased sector favors low barriers to domestic markets. Firms and associated parties in this sector desire access to foreign markets, rely on the availability in the domestic nation of imported goods and services, and fear foreign retaliation to the institution of domestic barriers to imports. The trade-biased sector consists of firms with an interest in international trade: exporters themselves, as well as the wholesale and retail merchants that market imported goods. Less obvious as a group in this sector are firms that use large amounts of imported goods in the production of goods for the home market. Domestic barriers impede exports in two ways: through a reduction in the amount of foreign exchange earned by trading partners and through retaliatory action. Large retail chains, especially those large enough to purchase goods directly from foreign suppliers, are, effectively, a combination of the wholesale importer and the retail distribution outlet. As such, they can be relied on to campaign for free, or freer, trade. In this effort, they also represent the interest of their customers—consumers. Consumers represent the largest single group that has an interest in lower barriers to imports but they were, prior to the advent of Ralph Nader as their Washington spokesman, badly organized to oppose the erection of barriers to trade favored by "injured industries." In the United States, some important segments of the agricultural sector are strong voices in favor of free trade. In the early 1980s, these exporters (of grains) strongly opposed trade warfare against the USSR because of its adverse effect on agricultural prices. Until roughly 1973, American farmers required government help to export, but since then the highly productive American farm sector has become able to export on a straightforward cost basis, and the emphasis on free trade in this sector has grown. One of the problems of the trade-biased sector is that most of its gains from freer international trade come on top of existing prosperity. These industries have safe home markets and a comparative advantage in foreign markets. The protection-biased sector is usually able to plead distress, if not poverty; trade-biased industries do not ordinarily have evidence of damage to show a legislature in support of their arguments. Multinational corporations tend to be trade-biased. Frequently, these corporations combine the roles of foreign manufacturer, importer, and domestic distributor. They are also likely to be sensitive to the exposed position of their assets in some foreign countries and are not, therefore, in favor of having their home country exclude exports and antagonize foreign governments.

The transformation of these postures and pressures into political action is a more complex process. Too many independent forces are at work on a legislature for the role of a single kind of pressure group or the effect of a single issue to be clearly identified. By and large, the effectiveness of domestic pressure groups in the formulation of trade policy will depend on the degree to which they are supported by the leanings of the neutral bloc and on the degree to which the desires of the domestic groups coincide with the atmosphere that exists at the international level. For example, protectionist measures are less likely to receive a sympathetic hearing when the nation's representatives are in the middle or final stages of an extended series of multilateral negotiations on the lowering of tariffs and NTBs.[3] Similarly, the receptivity of politicians will reflect the state of the economy, which will probably coincide with the position of the neutral bloc. Changes in underlying conditions may be needed as catalysts to effect significant change in the balance of power in the protrade or antitrade positions. In the United States, there has been a historic tendency for "swings toward liberalization . . . to occur over relatively extended periods of time, while swings toward protection tend to be much more abrupt and short-term in character, often occurring in an atmosphere of crisis."[4]

[3]Robert E. Baldwin, *The Multilateral Trade Negotiations* (Washington, D.C.: American Enterprise Institute, 1979) pp. 5–7, qualifies this point.
[4]Walter, "How Trade Policy Is Made," p. 33.

The process of forming national policy toward international trade has another interesting aspect. The factor proportions theory argues that freer trade will tend to benefit the plentiful factor and that greater protection will enhance the real income of the scarce factor. As a consequence, then, it is to be expected that labor would be protectionist and capital would favor international trade in the United States. A study of the positions taken by representatives of industry associations and unions testifying before the Committee on Ways and Means in the U.S. Congress in 1973 on what became the Trade Reform Act of 1974 tested this hypothesis.[5] Some unions and industry associations took mixed positions with regard to the question of freer trade—doubtless in response to internal conflicts of interest on the subject. However, the testimony yielded twenty-one industries for which a stance could be identified with management (capital) and unions (labor). If the H-O theory is correct, unions and trade associations will take opposing views. But if labor and capital conceive of themselves as factors specific to the industries in which they are currently employed and negate the possibility that they can be transferred easily and without serious cost into a new industry, both will take the same political stance toward freer trade. Magee constructed a 2×2 contingency table showing the stances taken by labor and capital in the same industry. There are four possible outcomes: Both will support freer trade, both will be protectionist, labor will be protectionist and management will support freer trade, and labor will support freer trade and management will be protectionist. If the H-O theory is correct, all observations will lie on the upward-sloping diagonal. If the theorem is correct and labor is the scarce factor, all twenty-one entries will be in the bottom left-hand cell. If the theorem does not apply to the formulation of trade policy by industry groups, the entries will be in the cells on the downward-sloping diagonal. Magee's results were:

	Position of Labor	
Position of Capital	Protectionist	Freer Trade
Protectionist	14	1
Freer trade	1	5

Clearly, the H-O theory fails as an explanation of the way in which pressure groups formulate their positions toward proposed changes in international trade policy. These results mean that factors of production formulate attitudes toward commercial policy on the basis of their expected incomes as members of the industry in which they are currently employed. Furthermore, they attach little benefit to the possibility of

[5]Stephen P. Magee, "Three Simple Tests of the Stolper-Samuelson Theorem," in Peter Oppenheimer (ed.) *Current Issues in World Trade and Payments* (London: Routledge and Kegan Paul, 1979).

employment in and income from other industries to which they might relocate. They attach zero weight to the possibility of such earnings in the computation of their future income. However, the results do not disprove the theory as it applies to international trade in the long run but rather show that industry and labor take a short-run view of the world in determining their own interests and refuse to recognize the possibility of jobs in other industries.[6] Presumably, the position that is taken can be held with varying degrees of intensity according to the realism of the nontransferability postulate. Thus the textile and footwear industries, in which low-skilled people would have great difficulties relocating, may well be more adamant than industries that recognize some possibility of moving but refuse to allow it to affect their stance.

Another study has attempted to measure the total protection afforded to different industries (both tariffs and NTBs) according to the labor intensity of the industry, the level of skill (human capital) used in the work force, and the average size of the manufacturing establishment.[7] In the study, the manufacturing industries were divided into quartiles by the height of protective tariffs, and the labor intensity results were found to be complex. As expected, the quartile with the lowest degree of protection was the least labor-intensive. The most highly protected quartile was the next least labor-intensive, and protection decreased and labor intensity increased in the second and third quartiles. Measuring human capital by the average income per worker, the analyst found that the level of protection decreased almost consistently with the importance of skills in the labor force. This crucial finding is consistent with the human-capital explanation of the Leontief paradox. Finally, levels of protection decreased as the average size of the establishment grew, indicating the value of scale economies.

The formulation of domestic trade policy is a complex affair that is subject to many influences: rational self-interest, international atmosphere, ideological beliefs. Not only are the pressures hard to identify and not really reliable, varying with economic conditions as they do, but the attitudes of pressure groups do not exactly correspond to the reactions of legislatures. Signals can be lost en route. The observation of slow but general progress toward freer trade may depend on the success of such efforts since World War II, but the reversion to protectionism as an aftermath of economic crisis is well documented and is probably the most reliable relationship that can be substantiated.

---

[6]This attitude is compatible with the need for a short-run theory of international trade. If individuals and pressure groups make their policy decisions on a short-run basis, the theory of international trade must be able to adapt to a similar time horizon.

[7]See Richard E. Caves and Ronald W. Jones, *World Trade and Payments: An Introduction* (Boston: Little, Brown, 1973), pp. 285–286. The data refer to protection after the reductions implemented in the Kennedy round.

INTERNATIONAL INSTITUTIONS

As shown in Figure 6-1, there is a clear danger that each nation will impose higher impediments to imports from its trading partners either in seeking its own self-interest or by yielding to an industry's cry for help. An apparent gain can always be achieved by the exercise of commercial policy. Unilateral action of this kind breeds retaliation, and the greater part of the global gain from trade may be sacrificed. The limit for this movement toward protectionism applies only to competitive and differentiated goods and probably will not affect trade in noncompetitive goods. As a general rule, most progress toward a reduction in impediments to trade since the eclipse of narrow mercantilism in the early nineteenth century has come about as a result of *joint international initiatives*.

Before World War I, Great Britain, then the leading industrial nation in the world, was a strong advocate of free trade. However, it is likely that this espousal of free trade was as much in the self-interest of the leading manufacturer as protectionism was in countries trying to catch up. During this era, the concept of "most favoured nation" (MFN) status was the main vehicle for the spread of both freer trade and multilateral trade. The issue became prominent again in the early 1970s because of the desire of the USSR to achieve MFN status with the United States.[8] The principle is still important because it remains operative and affects the current conduct of international trade. Originally, there were two versions of the MFN clause. The conditional version was used mainly by the United States and was relinquished only in 1922; the unconditional clause was accepted in Europe as early as the first half of the nineteenth century and became the modern standard.[9] The general principle underlying MFN status was that a nation guaranteed all nations holding this status equal treatment of imports on more favorable terms than the treatment that was accorded the imports from other nations. In other words, MFN status was a simple form of discrimination. If a nation reduced its duties on import X from France, the rate of duty charged on X from all other nations with MFN status was also reduced. However, there were two ways of interpreting the clause. The conditional interpretation stated that a nation receives a concession made to another MFN country only in return for a concession of equal magnitude made to the nation granting the original concession. The unconditional interpretation is obvious: that the extension of the concession to other MFNs was automatic and required no counterpart concession. It is arguable that the insistence on the conditional clause was a minor, though noteworthy, factor in earning the United States the reputation of a high-tariff nation—

---

[8]See Franklyn Holzman, *International Trade under Communism* (New York: Basic Books, 1976), pp. 165–170.

[9]This is why the European, or British, spelling of *favoured* has been used in the text. This section draws heavily on Gottfried Haberler, *International Trade* (New York: Macmillan, 1936), pp. 360–371.

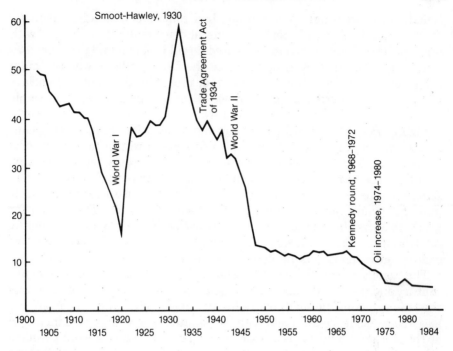

Figure 8-1

AVERAGE TARIFF RATES ON DUTIABLE IMPORTS, 1900–1984

The peak tariff rate in 1930 was the infamous Smoot-Hawley tariff. Tariff rates fell during the wars because of the effect of inflation on specific duties and because of sharp decreases in imports of luxuries. The effect of the Kennedy round can be seen between 1967 and 1972. The reduction in the average rate of duty since 1974 is due to the very large increase in the value of oil imports with a very low tariff duty.

Source: *Historical Abstract of the United States.*

a reputation the United States has not entirely lived down even though it ceases to be true. In fact, the United States tended to be a high-tariff nation, relative to Europe, until the 1930s.[10] Average tariff rates are shown in Figure 8-1.

The conditional form failed because it was a source of diplomatic disputes. It was not possible to provide an operational definition for the phrase "same or equal value" that described the requirement of the matching concession and was incorporated into the commercial treaties. Measurement of the protectivity of a tariff is hardly feasible, and the whole concept of the scientific approach to such measurement was unknown in the nineteenth century. The second reason for eliminating the condi-

[10]For a brief history of U.S. tariff policy, see Peter B. Kenen, *International Economics* (Englewood Cliffs, N.J.: Prentice-Hall, 1964), pp. 24–26.

tional clause was that some nations had commercial treaties involving conditional clauses with some nations and unconditional clauses with other nations. This variation presented a real problem and some obvious scope for unfair interpretations. Since the United States was the main proponent of the conditional clause and, probably, the main beneficiary of any unfairness from the coexistence of the two principles, an example of how the United States might profit from such an arrangement is worth reporting. Haberler provides the following illustration. Suppose that Germany granted a reduction of duties to Austria in return for a reciprocal concession. France, which has an unconditional treaty with Germany, would get the same concession without making any reciprocal concession. Since the United States has conditional treaties with France and Germany, it would receive the concession for nothing, too. The reason for this is that the United States could cite the French treatment by Germany (and exclude the Austrian negotiations) as the basis for claiming the concession without making any reciprocal gesture.

The historical coincidence of the lowering of tariffs in the nineteenth century and the expansion of the application of the MFN principle suggests that the principle did lead to a reduction in global tariff levels. Nonetheless, the coincidence argument can be disputed. The widespread inclusion of the unconditional MFN clause in commercial treaties would lead to an irrefutable reduction in global tariff levels if (and only if) the following condition was satisfied: the existence of the MFN clause might deter a nation from granting a concession in a bilateral commercial negotiation with a single trading partner. Probably, the additional costs of the inevitably greater breadth of coverage of the concession would deter the making of the concession.

During the Depression, tariff levels soared in all nations, and this increase, coupled with competitive depreciations of national currencies, signaled a return to mercantilist concerns. Even the British, who had been the champions of free trade, formed the Commonwealth preferential tariff in 1932 by raising tariffs on goods imported from countries outside the British Commonwealth. They escaped the MFN clause by claiming that MFN clauses referred only to foreigners and that members of the Commonwealth were, by definition, not foreign.

After World War II, the collective minds of the victorious allies were raised above petty nationalism in the euphoria of victory, and a whole array of international cooperative bodies was created by international agreement. The United Nations was the political manifestation of this spirit. The International Monetary Fund (IMF), the International Bank for Reconstruction and Development (the World Bank), and the International Trade Organization (ITO) were to be the three main economic institutions. The IMF was to assure balance-of-payments cooperation and sanity in international financial matters (see Chapter 19). The World

THE POLITICS OF COMMERCIAL POLICY

Bank was to assist in channeling capital funds from rich to poor nations. The ITO, whose purpose was to promote international cooperation in international trade, was the product of the UN Conference on Trade and Employment in Havana in 1947–1948. The conference report became known as the Havana Charter. It concerned itself with the need for economic growth, the transfer of economic resources to poor nations, high employment, commercial policies and restrictive practices with reference to international trade in finished and semifinished products, and steps to promote price stabilization schemes for primary products. The Havana Charter never became fact. It was too idealistic for the governments of developed nations to accept, even in their postwar euphoria. One major barrier was that every nation had an equal vote, so Uruguay and the United States, for example, would carry equal weight in the councils. This policy was in obvious contrast not only with the UN, where so-called Great Powers dominated the Security Council, which, in turn, dominated the General Assembly, but also with the IMF, in which nations voted according to the value of their subscription, which was, in turn, fixed by the importance of the nations as traders. In fairness to the developed, manufacturing nations, they were still unsure, in the late 1940s, of how they could control their own economies; their thinking was still dominated by the evils of the Depression. In any event, the treaty failed in its attempt for ratification by the U.S. Senate and died there.

While the ITO was going through the ritual of creation, the General Agreement on Tariffs and Trade (GATT) was instituted as a temporary substitute. With the failure of the Havana Charter, the GATT became the vehicle by which developed nations could hope to achieve some of the goals of the ITO.[11] In practice, the adoption of the GATT meant the renunciation of the aspects of international trade that most reflected the interests of the developing nations: price stabilization schemes for primary products, transfer of economic resources to poor nations, concern with the need for economic growth, and concern with restrictive practices in finished and semifinished products. Perhaps the United Nations Committee on Trade and Development (UNCTAD) would not have been necessary as a bargaining forum by the third world if the ITO had been ratified.[12]

The GATT is a framework of rules (a set of rules of the game) under which nations will manage their commercial policy in a socially acceptable

---

[11]The GATT did not have the status of a treaty in the United States and, therefore, did not need Senate approval. For a detailed analysis, see Kenneth W. Dam, *The GATT: Law and International Economic Organization* (Chicago: University of Chicago Press, 1970).

[12]UNCTAD was formed in the 1960s as a vehicle to represent the developing nations as a bloc in a dialogue with the manufacturing nations. It is considered in greater detail in Chapter 10. The third world comprises all developing or underdeveloped countries outside the orbit of the Soviet Union.

way. It also has a secretariat that sets the stage for international negotiation on any of the four areas of concern to the GATT:

1. Multilateral negotiations designed to bring about a lowering of barriers to international trade
2. Nondiscrimination in international trade
3. The undesirability of quantitative restrictions and other NTBs
4. The provision of a forum for the settlement of disputes arising out of commercial-policy practices

The achievements of the GATT in multilateral negotiations have been substantial, are still ongoing, and are dealt with in the next section. Nondiscrimination, however desirable, has not been achieved with any great degree of success. Trading blocs (giving preferential treatment to members) have been formed all over the world. The formation of trade blocs escapes GATT regulations. The European Economic Community is the most successful (and is considered in detail in Chapter 11), but there have been blocs formed between Europe and Africa (the Lomé Convention), within Latin America, and in Asia. It was probably idealistic even to suggest that the GATT would be able to prevent the formation of trade blocs, and except in a world where no barriers to trade exist, trade blocs may well be productive innovations. Control over quantitative restrictions has come under the "heading" of multilateral negotiations in the sense that the Tokyo round, the most recent set of multilateral negotiations designed to lower impediments to trade, expressly addressed itself to NTBs. Even prior to that, the GATT did serve as an arbitrator for quantitative restrictions as well as for disputes arising out of other commercial-policy practices. The settlement of any such disputes is by negotiation among trading partners (usually bilaterally). Consultations are open to any members who may have an interest in the outcome of the dispute. If no resolution is achieved bilaterally, the GATT forms a reconciliation committee that will offer possible solutions to the conflict. The offender can offer a substitute tariff concession on another good to offset the damage done by the protective measure at the bottom of the dispute. If no settlement is reached, the damaged party is entitled under GATT rules to retaliate by raising a tariff (or imposing an NTB) of its own. Often, the damaged party will use the occasion to raise a tariff on a very sensitive import and end up with a "mercantilist gain." The GATT's role as a mediator of disputes is a very valuable one.

In much the same vein, the GATT recognizes subsidies paid on exports as contravening its rules, and nations are allowed to levy offsetting countervailing duties as soon as export subsidies have been identified. One of the problems with this process is that a nation may subsidize a domestic industry for domestic reasons, which means that the subsidy on exports is an accidental NTB.

BARGAINING BARRIERS DOWN

The whole theory of the general advantages to be derived from mutual reductions of tariffs and other impediments to international trade is based on the argument implicit in Figure 6-1. Mutual reductions of tariffs will cause trade volume to increase, and the terms of trade will not change unduly in favor of any participant. Presumably, the bargaining process, which involves inputs that reflect the domestic pressures, will be sufficiently broad to ensure that any change in the terms of trade will be small. Domestic pressures will lead to the protection of very sensitive industries, and broad coverage will ensure that errors average out to the advantage of no individual participant.

There were five principal rounds of trade negotiations prior to the Kennedy round. These took place in 1947, 1949, 1951, 1956, and 1960–1961. They accomplished significant reductions in tariffs, many of which were paper reductions—in terms of Figure 7-1, they still left a tariff rate in excess of $(p_3 - p_1)/p_1$, a prohibitive tariff—or concessions that had little impact on domestic industries. Nonetheless, an impressive increase in the volume of international trade took place in the 1950s and 1960s, and the role of the GATT negotiation was not without significance as a contributory factor. The negotiations for the Kennedy round lasted from 1964 to 1967. The name was a tribute to the assassinated John F. Kennedy because the negotiations were made possible by the Trade Reform Act of 1962, which was submitted to the U.S. Congress by the Kennedy administration. The Kennedy round was by far the most ambitious and complex of all negotiations conducted under the auspices of the GATT. It is not possible to assess its accomplishments with any reliability; the task is too complex. However, tariffs were cut on goods that accounted for 75 percent of world trade.[13] The main achievements of the Kennedy round were concentrated in industrial products traded among developed nations. Tariff reductions averaged about 35 percent on industrial products for all the major participants. Tariff reductions were made on 70 percent of their dutiable imports by industrialized countries (agricultural imports excepted). Two-thirds of the cuts were in excess of 50 percent of the prenegotiation tariff rates. But the Kennedy round had less success with agricultural trade than with trade in industrial goods; one of the stumbling blocks here was the Common Agricultural Policy of the EEC (see Chapter 11).

The Kennedy round introduced a new method of approaching the problem of negotiating the reduction of tariffs. Prior to the Kennedy round, nations bargained on an item-by-item basis. The bargaining process for

---

[13]One reason the Kennedy round was regarded as so successful was that its achievements surpassed expected achievements by a wide margin. Its success can be seen in Figure 8-1 by the decrease in protection between 1968 and 1973.

multilateral tariffs involved a huge series of simultaneous bilateral negotiations. Pairs of countries bargained in search of "balanced exchanges of concessions," and each country would bring to the bargaining table a list of products on which it felt it could reduce protection. Once a series of bilateral agreements had been attained, the far more complex process began of generalizing them into an acceptable package so that the sum of the parts was also a "balanced exchange of concessions"—at least in the eyes of the negotiators. In this process, the unconditional MFN clause was very important since it provided a mandatory step toward the general and final package. This way of bargaining was inefficient in substance as well as in the actual negotiating because it permitted important and highly protected industries to go untouched and unexposed. The Kennedy round introduced the concept of *linear reduction*. All tariffs would be reduced by, say, 50 percent of their prenegotiation level, and nations would then argue about exceptions to the linear reduction rather than about goods that they felt inclined to offer up on the sacrificial altar. All industries were exposed in principle, and the burden of the proof fell on the protectionist instead of on the reducer of tariffs. Exceptions were to be held to a bare minimum, and any plea for protectionism was exposed to the spotlight of publicity. Nonetheless, the linear reduction was not an inflexible arrangement. It provided a basis from which to start negotiations. It allowed certain industries to be cut by less than 50 percent and others to be cut by more than 50 percent. Furthermore, the time dimension could be introduced by staging cuts over time.

The Trade Act of 1974 continued the process of granting negotiating authority to the executive branch. The U.S. Constitution grants the power to tax to Congress, which is ill equipped to conduct negotiations. Consequently, Congress has delegated the necessary authority to the executive branch, while simultaneously establishing very clear limits to the negotiating authority. The original delegation of negotiating authority was the Trade Agreements Program in 1934. The Trade Expansion Act of 1962 was another in a long series of extensions and renewals of limited negotiating authority. In 1974, yet another of these bills was passed by Congress. This act conferred on the president authority to conduct negotiations with other nations to the extent that tariffs of less than 5 percent ad valorem in 1974 could be eliminated entirely and tariffs in excess of 5 percent could be reduced by 60 perecnt. These reductions would be phased in over a period of years.

Indeed, the Trade Act of 1974 was a very innovative piece of legislation and has several features that are interesting in their own right.[14] First, the Trade Act passed despite opposition from the AFL-CIO. This was

[14]In addition to the clauses mentioned in the text, the Trade Act contained measures for granting MFN status to the USSR, but this crumbled in the face of requirements imposed by Congress about the treatment of Jews within the USSR and their freedom to emigrate. The act also contained authority to institute a system of preferential tariffs for developing nations (see Chapter 10).

the first time that the weight of labor's voice was against tariff reductions and, in accordance with Walter's observation of the weakness of the linkages from group pressure to legislative action, labor did not succeed.[15] Partly, this failure was due to the international climate, which was focused on the forthcoming Tokyo round of negotiations and, from the standpoint of political policy, precluded the United States from being pictured as the scapegoat blocking tariff negotiations. Partly, too, labor's failure was due to the fact that labor leaders did not feel comfortable in their role of opposition and, therefore, did not carry it through with full force and conviction. Second, the act incorporates congressional oversight of actions by the executive branch. Congress sent observers to the negotiations to keep itself informed of the bargaining stance of the United States. This innovation is due to the fact that NTBs were to be a primary focus of negotiation in the Tokyo round, and the delegation of the power to control cannot be controlled as precisely as can tariff-negotiating authority.[16] Congress reserved for itself veto power over NTB reductions since each concession of an NTB had to receive final congressional approval.

THE TOKYO ROUND

The Tokyo round of multilateral negotiations began officially in 1973 and came to a formal conclusion in 1979. The final negotiations, indeed all of them, took place in a world that was less congenial to concessions than previous rounds. The breakdown of the Bretton Woods system, the first energy shock, and all of the related adjustment strains had given rise to widespread inflation and unemployment. The tasks that this round of negotiations had set itself were in many ways intrinsically more difficult than those of its predecessors. It was to have emphasized NTBs and agriculture for both temperate and tropical crops as well as continuing the emphasis on reducing tariff rates levied on imports of manufactured goods. In particular, the third world felt that the negotiations were a failure as far as the proposal to accord them "special and differential" treatment was concerned. Attempts to reduce barriers to imports of tropical agricultural goods by the developed world were not successful. The complex system of reducing NTBs was, at best, a mixed blessing for the developing countries.[17]

The Tokyo round can be counted a success insofar as tariff reductions on manufactured goods among developed nations are concerned. The formula adopted gave an average cut in existing rates of duty of about 40 percent (before exceptions). The United States excluded highly sensi-

---

[15]But see the political argument for trade adjustment assistance in Chapter 9.

[16]This derives partly from the greater difficulty in quantifying NTBs.

[17]See Peter J. Ginman, Thomas A. Pugel, and Ingo Walter, "Mixed Blessings for the Third World in Codes on Non-tariff Measures," *World Economy*, 3 (1980), 217–234.

tive industries such as textiles and apparel covered under the Multifibre Arrangement and nonrubber footwear but did manage to achieve a percentage cut on dutiable manufactures of 31 percent of the existing tariff rate. Given the climate under which these negotiations took place, this was no mean achievement.[18] A good start was made on the reduction of NTBs among the developed nations through a series of codes of behavior that nations sign and obey. Although the language in some of these is necessarily less than precise and binding, such notorious NTBs as government procurement, customs valuation and licensing, and standards (health, safety, environmental protection, technology, packaging and labeling, etc.) are all to be regulated by codes.

But in the process of becoming much more minutely concerned with the detail of trade negotiations, Congress, almost inevitably, had to yield to pressure from protection-minded industries. Textiles, apparel, steel, and sugar all managed to obtain concessions during the passage of the Trade Act of 1974 or during the ongoing negotiations.

What of the future? As Chapter 9 shows, there are serious problems facing the developed world in its acceptance of imports of manufactured goods from developing nations. The stricture that progress toward freer trade can only be made in an atmosphere of prosperity and growth suggests that multilateral trade negotiations are unlikely to make much progress during the next decade. The problems of relocating displaced workers will be too severe for great initiatives in that field. The great progress was made when the developed world was achieving rates of employment that exceeded anything known in history; at best, the medium-run prognosis is for higher rates of unemployment with particular pressures on low-skilled workers. This suggests that governments will be responding to political imperatives (employment) rather than taking economic initiatives (multilateral trade negotiations).[19]

SUMMARY

The processes by which tariffs and NTBs are instituted and bargained down is overcast by a thick mantle of uncertainty. The formation of a national stance on trade policies depends on the philosophy of the government, domestic political pressures, and the international climate. In 1985, the Reagan administration, fearful that a lack of commitment to continued reductions in barriers to trade would allow domestic pressures for protection to gain a dominant position, managed to convince the GATT to

---

[18]Baldwin, *The Multilateral Trade Negotiations*, pp. 26–29.
[19]See Robert Gilpin, *U.S. Power and the Multinational Corporation: The Political Economy of Foreign Direct Investment* (New York: Basic Books, 1975), ch. 1, for a discussion of the qualifications that political considerations impose on economic solutions.

stage a new round of multilateral tariff negotiations. The prospects for and difficulties facing these talks are brilliantly analyzed and presented in *Trade Talks*.[20] This confusing arena for the politics of protectionism suggests that a simple model based on economic and political strengths, though indicative of likely trends, will not be a reliable modeling tool. During the thirty-five years after World War II, great progress was made along the road toward free trade. This progress coincided with an original very high level of protection (a hangover from the Depression) and a period of great prosperity and economic growth. These conditions gave every indication of having run out of steam in the early 1980s, and this would suggest that the scope for large further gains toward free trade is small. One bright feature on the horizon is the potential falling apart of OPEC and the prospects of significantly lower oil prices. Under these circumstances, good economic policy could restore a happier bargaining climate.

The obstacles to further gains toward liberalization are those imposed by the social costs of adjustment of arthritic economies to new international conditions ("economic sclerosis" is an often-heard phrase in Europe). Adjustment involves uprooting workers out of one industry and retraining (and relocating) them for another. Attention must now be focused on reducing those costs that are likely to generate the political pressure for protection. (Chapter 9 addresses the question of appropriate adjustment policies.) If the social costs of adjustment can be maintained at tolerable levels, there is no a priori reason why continued gains toward trade liberalization cannot be made—albeit at a slower pace and probably involving very long phase-in times for new measures.[21]

Bibliography

Aho, C. Michael, and J. D. Aronson. *Trade Talks.* New York: Council on Foreign Relations, 1985.

Baldwin, Robert E. *The Multilateral Trade Negotiations.* Washington, D.C.: American Enterprise Institute, 1979.

Bergsten, C. Fred, and Lawrence B. Krause, eds. *World Politics and International Economics.* Washington, D.C.: Brookings Institution, 1975.

Cline, William R., ed. *Trade Policy in the 1980s.* Cambridge, Mass.: M.I.T. Press, 1983.

Jackson, John H. "GATT Machinery and the Tokyo Round Agreements." In *Trade Policy,* ed. William R. Cline, pp. 159–187.

---

[20]C. Michael Aho and J. D. Aronson, *Trade Talks* (New York: Council on Foreign Relations, 1985).

[21]Compare Baldwin, *The Multilateral Trade Negotiations,* pp. 28–29: "By combining active adjustment assistance policies with less-than-formula cuts and longer staging periods, affected [displaced] workers can be shifted either to higher earning positions or, if necessary, be protected until they voluntarily leave or retire. The preferred approach is to use adjustment assistance policies, but unfortunately our programs in this field are still quite primitive and lack political support from [organized] labor."

Malmgren, Harald B. "Threats to the Multilateral System." In *Trade Policy,*
ed. William R. Cline, pp. 189–201.

Patterson, Gardner. "The European Community as a Threat to the System."
In *Trade Policy,* ed. William R. Cline, pp. 223–242.

Walter, Ingo. "How Trade Policy Is Made: A Politico-economic Decision System,"
The United States and International Markets, ed. Robert G. Hawkins and Ingo
Walter, pp. 23–34. Lexington, Mass.: Lexington Books, 1972.

Questions

1. Why are consumers usually at a disadvantage in the pull and tug of political
decisions on protection? Does this matter?
2. Free trade benefits the haves at the expense of the have-nots. Is this true?
3. Organized labor should oppose free trade. Why?
4. Summarize the positions of the main economic bodies on the most recent
set of hearings on delegation of tax authority to the White House.
5. The GATT is moribund. Comment.
6. Since the major problem in international trade today revolves around the
European Economic Community's Common Agricultural Program (see Chapter 11) and since the GATT does not cover international trade in agricultural
goods, a further round of multilateral negotiations is a waste of time and
effort. Comment.

Crisis in Trade Policy

INGO WALTER

The United States is at a turning point. With mounting pressures to maintain decaying industries and jobs, there could be a major shift away from a 40-year trend of liberal trade policies. Economics and politics are at war to determine future decision-making on patterns of trade and production among the world's community of nations. Yet, every trade policy direction—even free trade—open to the U.S. and other industrial nations carries with it a complex, long-term, and sometimes ambiguous pattern of costs and benefits.

News item: The Ford Motor Company, one of the most internationally integrated of all U.S. multinationals, is a major beneficiary of government-negotiated protection against low-priced, fuel-efficient, and high-quality Japanese automobiles. Ford pleads protection on grounds of maintaining solvency.

News item: President Reagan refuses to renew barriers imposed a few years ago on sales of Taiwanese and South Korean shoes in the United States. This is not only a reversal of earlier policy, but it also comes, paradoxically, just a few weeks after the Administration completed the auto negotiations with Japan.

News item: Italy and Great Britain restrict imports of synthetic fibers from the U.S. They claim controls on natural gas in the U.S. have tended to depress production costs to manufacturers in this country.

News item: The steel industry threatens to sue European suppliers unless the government increases trigger prices, below which imported steel may not be sold in the U.S.

News item: After months of wrangling, Japan finally opens Nippon Telephone and Telegraph to competitive bids by U.S. suppliers of telecommunications equipment. A few months later, it imposes se-

Reproduced with permission from *NYU Business*, 1 (Fall 1981–Winter 1982), 17–20.

vere restrictions on aluminum imports from the U.S., which had been highly competitive because of lower American electric power costs.

News item: Representative Breaux of Louisiana is promised lower sugar imports in return for his vote on the Reagan tax program.

News item: Japan concentrates efforts to export expensive, sophisticated products to Western markets and redoubles marketing efforts in developing countries. With a $2 billion trade surplus expected in 1982, Japan begins to feel a renewal of protectionist pressures in foreign markets and embarks on an ambitious import-incentive scheme, mainly concentrating on industrial raw materials.

Events like these can mean the life or death of entire industries, or at least affect large numbers of jobs, and the hardships of the unemployed can obscure the theoretical workings of liberal trade. Viewed industry by industry, it is often difficult to remember that the U.S. has had an overriding commitment to liberal trade since the end of the Second World War. Yet, regardless of political party or economic philosophy, every president since Franklin Roosevelt has favored trade liberalization, standing firm against recurring protectionist pressures on Capitol Hill. Even the creation of a regional free-trade zone by the European Economic Community—the Common Market—during the 1950s and '60s, the loss of U.S. international market shares in the '70s, and, lately, the immense competitive challenge of Japan and the newly industrializing nations of the Third World have failed to shake a basic faith in the wisdom, and justice, of the free enterprise system that is still held by most people in this country.

CORNERSTONES OF LIBERAL TRADE

The cornerstones of the liberal trade ethic traditionally have been efficiency, growth, equity, and reciprocity. Liberal trade reflects the economic philosophy that the free interplay of market forces, on both domestic and global levels, will ensure maximum efficiency and growth. If the most competitive suppliers have free access to markets, then only the fittest will survive. Consequently, productive assets—capital, natural resources, and labor—will be allocated to those industries that obtain the highest returns in the most efficient utilization of those assets and, therefore, can afford to pay the highest prices for them. The result for nations is a far higher level of real income than would be attained without liberal access to international markets.

Exports permit a country to obtain the maximum economic benefit from its high-growth economic sectors by securing access to foreign markets. Imports, in turn, drive in to "weed out" decaying domestic sectors, thereby permitting capital, natural resources, and labor to be released and reabsorbed into the healthy sectors. This view recognizes that growth is an uneven process, with individual products, industries, and sectors constantly emerging (usually from technological advances), driving to maturity, and then possibly decaying after a more or less prolonged period of slow growth. In the U.S. today, this process could be illustrated by developments in robotics and genetic engineering; aircraft and semiconductors; and footwear and clothing, respectively.

Internationally, as each country exports those goods and services in which it has a global competitive edge and imports the rest, world income and output gain commensurately. Anything that interferes with this constant "churning" between healthy and unhealthy sectors of national economies necessarily retards growth. Clearly, barriers thrown up against import competition have this effect.

At the same time that liberal trade promotes maximum efficiency and growth, however, there may be free-market situations that could reasonably be considered unfair. For example, even as a nation's economy as a whole gains from liberal trade, some workers employed by firms besieged by imports will lose their jobs (and stockholders their investments) when those firms go under. It can be argued that society has a moral obligation to those adversely affected by the dynamics of liberal trade. Even if the displaced workers were compensated by providing assistance to help them enter new jobs in other sectors, the total of such once-and-for-all costs, if correctly administered, would generally be smaller than the cost to society of losing the broader benefits from liberal trade.

In addition to maintaining equity, liberal-trade nations must be willing to grant foreign suppliers access to their domestic markets. This ensures that international trade is reciprocal and, therefore, considered to be fair. Government subsidies to industry, predatory dumping, discriminatory government procurement, and a variety of other, often clandestine, practices distort the trade picture. Moreover, unilateral moves toward protectionism by one country can lead to retaliation and, in the extreme case, a trade war.

PRESSURES FOR PROTECTION

Despite a long record of successful American intellectual leadership and diplomatic initiative in support of liberal international market competition, there have been from time to time noteworthy setbacks involving specific industries. In the 1950s, for example, cheap cotton garments from Asia that were flooding U.S. and Western European markets began to severely damage import-competing firms. The U.S. textile industry was, as it generally is today, a classic case of a senile industry. It is highly labor-intensive, regionally concentrated, low-skill, and a major employer of minorities. Import growth, therefore, was slowed to tolerable rates by negotiating voluntary export restraints (VERs) with major suppliers such as Japan and Hong Kong. By 1962, these arrangements had become firmly set under the Long Term Arrangement on Cotton Textiles (LTA). During the 1960s and early '70s, heavy imports of synthetic garments led to a similar spate of VERs initiated by the U.S. and Western European countries. Ultimately, a body of trading rules known as the Multifibre Arrangement (MFA) evolved and today governs world textile trade. Political considerations necessitated an agreement whereby an entire sector is subject to intergovernmental market-sharing.

In recent years, comparable sectoral troubles in Western Europe and the United States have hit shipbuilding, steel, consumer electrical equipment, footwear, automobiles, and a variety of other industrial goods. Especially in the ultra-sensitive agricultural sector, highly competitive exporters such as the U.S., Argentina, New Zealand, and Denmark periodically confront virtually impenetrable barriers to market access for specific products.

In these cases, economic considerations have been replaced by political considerations in determining patterns of international trade and production, with huge costs being passed on to the consumer and greatly reduced efficiency in resources allocation.

The argument is often made that trade barriers are necessary in order to permit beleaguered industries to modernize, streamline operations, and reestablish their international competitiveness. But this rarely happens. Instead, trade restrictions serve to redistribute income from consumers to producers, reinforce inefficiency, and actually impede adjustment. Recent VERs on imports into the U.S. of nonleather footwear from South Korea and Taiwan apparently did not in the least stimulate competitiveness in the embattled industry and, with the resultant increased prices of both foreign and domestic products, cost American consumers $22,000 for each U.S. job saved. The cost of protection in the steel and auto industries, where union-backed workers have already achieved 40 to 75 percent higher earnings than comparably skilled jobs in other industries, makes the footwear figures look minuscule.

As is true of most older industrial countries, the U.S. has failed to design and implement a workable approach to adjusting to international competitive shifts. Government policies have encouraged resources in uncompetitive industries to remain in place, instead of promoting redeployment of resources to young, growing sectors. Import restrictions, direct and indirect subsidies to industry, absorption of the operating losses of government-owned enterprises abroad, government-supported export credits, and tax breaks are some of the regularly employed measures that prevent markets and trade patterns from working effectively.

IN DEFENSE OF PROTECTION

There are indeed some legitimate arguments for protection. For example, several sectors that are critical to national defense depend on the production of steel, so it may be imperative to ensure the survival of the steel industry at reasonable levels of size. In such a case, the cost of the subsidies or income losses should properly be added to the defense budget.

A gradual redeployment of resources out of decaying industries may prove less costly to society than the abrupt, shock-like declines of sectors. Here, temporary self-destructing subsidies or import restraints may well be justified in the national interest. It may also be that an infant industry needs temporary shielding from imports until it is commercially viable and internationally competitive. Or, given the winds of global competitive change, an industry that lacks competitiveness today may regain it tomorrow, as exchange rates change or other factors evolve. And, if an industry has huge sunk costs, why destroy it only to have to rebuild it later?

In addition to matters of national defense and simple economics, there is another rationale for protectionism. Most Americans are aware that the U.S. is suffering from a social cancer—a vast, and expanding, economic underclass that is the product of many factors, among them decades of racial and ethnic discrimination, social dislocation, an unchecked influx of illegal aliens, poor assimilation of recent immigrants, failures of the educational establishment and the criminal justice system, periodic macro-economic setbacks, and rapid structural and regional economic shifts.

Second-, third-, and fourth-generation welfare families exist in hopelessness and despair. Headlines reveal an explosion of crime against persons and property. Many Americans scan ahead and behind as they walk down city streets at night on the way to a home or apartment with a sophisticated alarm system and triple-lock doors. Urban blight, the likes of which exists nowhere else in the developed world, affects many U.S. cities. The social infrastructure, including urban mass transportation, court and prison systems, police and fire protection, and public schools, is under severe strain. Skyrocketing security costs face business and industry. Taken together, these seemingly intractable problems amount to a national disgrace.

Yet, comprehensive government programs, ranging from the massive Great Society efforts of the 1960s, minimum wage legislation, and CETA jobs to increased welfare allowances, food stamps, and school busing have not produced promising solutions—and in some cases may have made the problems worse.

The underclass stuck at the bottom of the pit needs more than a program which tosses down food and water and hauls out selected individuals, one by one, with tugs on a lifeline. What *is* needed is a simple "ladder"—

the provision of a significant number of low-skill, low-pay, non-dead-end jobs that teach and reward individual effort, accountability, responsibility, productivity, and persistence. This is what has always made the American system tick, and is the only conceivable long-term remedy for a national economic illness of this sort. Such escape-ladder jobs may well exist in the senile, internationally uncompetitive industries besieged by import competition. While it is a certainty that protection of such industries will lower economic efficiency and real incomes at the national level and, perhaps, even retard the nation's overall rate of economic growth, protective barriers applied for escape-ladder reasons may lead to social ends that justify the undeniably high costs involved.

It should also be noted, however, that escape-ladder protection would be unlikely to approach its full potential without parallel government actions with respect to improved training, a reduced minimum wage, and greater tax incentives. Many industries might legitimately qualify for protection on escape-ladder grounds, but only a few could be chosen. And, there will come a future time, when either the costs will begin to exceed the benefits or the country will no longer need or want escape-ladder protection as a tool of social policy.

THE FREE-MARKET BENCHMARK

Departures from liberal trade may well be defensible under a variety of conditions, but the costs need to be clearly identified and justified in terms of the benefits achieved. Economists would argue that there are few cases where impediments to free trade can clearly be shown to be in the national interest. Suppose, however, that free-market competitive conditions were left alone to function without any public or private interference. How would world production and trade patterns evolve? Who would trade what, with whom, and at what price? How would the costs and returns of that evolution—for processors, manufacturers, distributors, consumers, banks, shareholders, workers, and other participants in the economic game—be allocated?

Would healthy industries, in fact, prosper and sick ones die? Would the poor countries of the world inch their way toward industrialization and development? Would multinational companies continue to perform competitively? In what ways would their strategic planning have to accommodate international market developments? With potentially dramatic shifts in international trade patterns, who would gain? Who would lose?

The answers to these questions can yield a solution that could be used as a reference point, a free-market benchmark. Then, if a government proposed to "adjust" the benchmark in some fashion, for whatever purpose, it would have to make a strong case for the predicted socio-economic benefits of that adjustment exceeding socio-economic costs.

THE OUTLOOK

There are undoubtedly plenty of trouble spots that will keep the trade policy pot boiling vigorously for the foreseeable future. Little progress has been made in freeing up agricultural trade. At the conclusion in 1979 of the Tokyo Round of trade negotiations, the effort to define a code of conduct governing safeguards, which are measures to prevent surges of imports from inundating domestic industries and causing politically unacceptable damage, had failed. Growing social welfare movements in some older industrial countries have increased political pressure for the establishment of such safeguards. Anarchy in this area could well lead to a sector-by-sector spread of permanent levels of protection and intergovernmental market-sharing.

After 35 years of discussions, there are still no agreed-upon rules on foreign direct investment and the treatment of multinational enterprises. Given the political realities, the best to be expected is a non-binding, voluntary code of conduct. And, finally, the whole area of international trade in services—banking, consulting, accounting, tourism, advertising, data transmission, and transport—remains to be tackled.

But despite bitter political fighting, self-centered pleading, regionalism, factionalism, and logrolling that are part of the trade policy formation process in the U.S. and elsewhere, the outlook remains basically optimistic. One reason is that a free-market spirit is deeply ingrained in the American character. Industries that seek to mask a weak managerial track record by calling for protection or subsidies are also inviting a rescuing government to play a perfectly justified role in its management, thereby making a mockery of free enterprise.

Another reason for optimism is that tariffs today are at an all-time low, and falling, as a result of the Tokyo Round of trade negotiations. Non-tariff trade barriers such as licensing procedures, discriminatory government procurement, subsidies, restrictive customs procedures, and the use of technical standards to impede imports are now subject for the first time to agreed-upon codes of conduct, complete with complaint and dispute-settlement procedures. The developing countries, once forced to sit on the sidelines in global trade discussions, have won preferential, often tariff-free, access to industrial countries' markets for a broad range of products. They have not received all they asked for, but many are nevertheless rapidly emerging as serious competitors to the established industrial giants.

Finally, the shadow of the 1930s is never far away. Many dangers still lurk in the shadows: subsidy wars, information-transfer bans, retaliation, and the idea, even among some leaders of industry, that free trade is obsolete. Any of these could spark a retaliatory spiral of painful costs and consequences. It is this realization, coupled with a knowledge of the self-righting attributes of free markets and the debilitating fiscal burdens of ignoring them, that gives cause for optimism that continued long-term progress will be made toward a liberal international economic order.

In the end, the U.S. and its partners cannot afford *not* to pursue a policy of liberal world trade.

9

Adjustment and Problem Industries

The message of Chapter 6 was that free trade is beneficial for the allocative efficiency of international production, but there is little hope that the world's politicians could ever accept such a policy without reservation. There are simply too many domestic pressures. Even President Reagan, who, of all recent presidents, has the most devout commitment to market forces, has needed to protect domestic industry from time to time.

The argument for free trade is based on the economic theories considered in Chapters 3 and 4 and, as such, is set in a stationary, nonchanging world. It is possible that protection may have some merit when the cause of the need for protection is dynamic (involves change over time). Free trade generates maximum static gains from trade, but the argument for free trade neglects the costs of adaptation. These costs are essentially short-run and are the basis for the concept of senile-industry protection. The costs of adaptation or *adjustment* (defined as the release of factors from a declining industry and their reemployment in another expanding industry) are the unemployment of factors of production as well as the loss of industry-specific human capital and physical capital. It is possible that intervention in the adjustment process (protection) might be warranted if unrestrained market forces would dislocate the economy too drastically so that adjustment costs would be lowered by reducing the rate of adjustment. Intervention would slow down the rate of change imposed on the economy and might provide special support to displaced workers in their efforts to relocate.

This chapter address three real-world problems:

1. What does the United States government do to ease the costs of adjustment?
2. What about big industries which have become noncompetitive, such as steel and automobiles?
3. What to do about the surge of labor-intensive goods from the newly industrializing countries (NICs) and other developing countries?

POLICIES TO FACILITATE ADJUSTMENT

In a context of adaptation to change, it is useful to divide policies into those that are "positive" and help the national economy to adjust and those that simply slow the pace of change and are, therefore, adjustment-retarding. A recent report on the Organization for Economic Cooperation and Development (OECD) has argued that some form of intervention may be desirable and conceives of "industrial policies" and "employment and manpower" policies. Industrial policies may be described as senile-industry protective measures or phaseout protection for industries that are very badly hurt by foreign competition. Employment and manpower policies are positive in that they attempt to accommodate change by providing training facilities for displaced workers, provide assistance in regional and job mobility, and identify particularly hard-hit groups of workers and generate job-creation programs targeted for such groups.[1] (As in any interventionist policy, the argument for intervention must be qualified by the degree to which effective policies can be devised; many advocates of free trade and laissez-faire argue that government does not know enough to interfere constructively.)

In the United States, adjustment-retarding policies are more easily recognizable than positive programs. Import relief can be obtained by petitioning the International Trade Commission for relief (protection). The commission hears arguments by both sides and recommends a policy to the president, who ultimately institutes a policy. The president must consider the effect of protection on the economy, while the ITC must only consider the problem in terms of the industry. There is no necessary correlation between the commission's recommendation and the president's action. Import relief can be granted to an industry when an article is being imported into the United States in such increased quantities as to be a cause of substantial injury to the home industry. The industry must establish that the import pressure is not "its own fault" and can then receive protection for a period of eight years. This process is clearly adjustment-retarding.

---

[1]OECD, *The Case for Positive Adjustment Policies: A Compendium of OECD Documents* (Paris, 1979), p. 6.

Trade adjustment assistance (TAA) is designed to help trade-impacted firms, industries, communities, and workers. A firm that can establish that it has been harmed by foreign competition can apply for technical and financial assistance. Technical assistance consists of management and marketing consultancy services provided by the federal government. Financial assistance provides loans and loan guarantees with maximums of $1 and $3 million respectively. The program is, therefore, a small-business program. TAA also provides payments to workers displaced by foreign imports, but the main part of the program is merely an extension of unemployment benefits beyond the period enjoyed by domestic workers. The rate of compensation is also somewhat higher.

The rationale for the TAA program comprises three strands, two economic and one political. The first economic argument derives from equity considerations. It is presumed that workers laid off because of international events have greater difficulty in finding alternate employment or suffer larger reductions in income than so-called domestic workers. In fact, there seems to be no substantial difference between the two groups.[2] The second economic argument is based on efficiency—that layoffs in trade-impacted industries will cause more congestion in labor markets (by region, by skill level, and even nationally) and will lead to longer periods of unemployment. The duration of unemployment of trade-impacted workers has been shown to be positively related to the national level of unemployment (national labor market congestion), but the same study was not sufficiently refined to identify regional or skill-level congestion.[3]

The third strand of TAA is political. It argues that the Trade Expansion Acts of 1962 and 1974 could not have passed Congress without some commitment to reimburse those displaced as a result of multilateral trade negotiations: "The political argument [for government intervention in the adjustment process] is that certain interest groups have sufficient political power to block or delay socially beneficial change unless they are generously compensated and otherwise assisted."[4] Certainly the introduction of payments to workers was important in reducing the opposition to trade negotiations by the labor movement as well as reducing pressures within the labor movement for the organization to take a stronger position against negotiations. In addition, the existence of the TAA program was also likely to have reduced any latent public sympathy for protectionist positions. It may be inferred that the existence of TAA also defused some of the enmity to the surge of imports into the United States in

[2]C. Michael Aho and T. O. Bayard, "Costs and Benefits of Trade Adjustment Assistance," in *Structure and Evolution of Recent U.S. Trade Policy,* ed. R. E. Baldwin and A. O. Krueger (Chicago: University of Chicago Press, 1984).

[3]D. O. Parsons, "Unemployment, the Allocation of Labor, and Optimal Government Intervention," *American Economic Review,* 70 (September 1980), 631–635.

[4]Aho and Bayard, "Costs and Benefits."

the late 1970s from the newly-industrializing countries (Brazil, Hong Kong, Korea, Mexico, Singapore, and Taiwan).

If workers are to lose their jobs because of changing patterns of international trade and competitiveness, the process of adjustment will be aided by positive measures to enhance worker mobility and retraining. But the ability of the economy to absorb displaced workers is very sensitive to the prosperity of the overall economy. When substantial unemployment exists, it is difficult to persuade a worker that a new industry has to be found and still more difficult to identify expanding industries. The TAA program allows an extra twenty-six weeks of benefits (after the standard fifty-two weeks) for workers undergoing training programs, but very few availed themselves of this option between 1975 and 1979. During these years, nearly 500,000 people received compensation, but only 17,500 took advantage of the retraining features. TAA is, therefore, mainly adjustment-retarding. In an attempt to improve the positive or adjustment-promoting effects of TAA, the comptroller general of the United States has argued for income maintenance benefits (in excess of standard unemployment compensation) to be tied to retraining or relocation.[5] The other major positive program is the Comprehensive Employment and Training Act (CETA), which has had bad publicity and is targeted at unskilled, young workers without substantial work experience.

Originally scheduled to end in the fall of 1983, it was extended for two years. It was a program that helped small firms improve their efficiency to compete with foreign goods and eased the hardships facing laid-off workers. In this sense, it was largely adjustment-retarding. Even financial and technical assistance would merely delay collapse if the root cause of the problem was different factor prices in the foreign country. Payments to workers eased hardship but also delayed realization of the need to relocate in a new industry. There is at least one well-informed opinion that sees the existence of a TAA program (oriented strongly toward positive measures) to be an important feature of the U.S. economy in the coming years.[6]

SURVIVAL PROBLEMS OF THE U.S. STEEL AND AUTOMOTIVE INDUSTRIES

In the United States in the late 1970s and early 1980s, both the steel and the automotive industries were subjected to crunching competition from abroad to the extent that their survival was placed in doubt. Western Europe had a similar experience. Japan was the premier exporter in

[5]*Restricting Trade Act Benefits to Import-affected Who Cannot Find a Job Would Save Millions,* Report to Congress by the Comptroller General of the United States (Washington, D.C.: U.S. Government Printing Office for the U.S. General Accounting Office, 1980).

[6]J. David Richardson, "Worker Adjustment to U.S. International Trade: Programs and Prospects," in *Trade Policy in the 1980s,* ed. William R. Cline, pp. 393–418 (Cambridge, Mass.: M.I.T. Press, 1983).

both industries, but Brazil and Mexico were also suppliers of steel to the United States and Europe, and some European firms managed to sell steel in the United States. Given the importance of these industries as sources of employment and as components of the defense industry, the question is what, if anything, the governments should do to protect the industries.

Both industries in the United States are highly concentrated, and both determine wage rates effectively on an industrywide basis with a single union so that the union acts as a monopolist confronting a monopsonist. Neither industry has enjoyed adequate rates of return on capital. In 1958, the rate of return on equity and after taxes of the U.S. steel industry fell below that of "all U.S. manufacturing" and exceeded the aggregate rate only once between 1965 and 1985. Concentration in the steel industry has not resulted in exorbitant profit rates.[7] In fact, the president of National Steel Corporation has argued that the industry is "capital-starved" because there is no way in which the firms can raise additional capital because of their unsatisfactory rate of return on equity (an average of 8 percent for the years 1970–1978). Nor has the automotive industry fared much better. In 1981, Ford and General Motors recorded the largest losses ever recorded by U.S. corporations, and Chrysler had to be rescued by the U.S. government and a spectacular chief executive, Lee Iacocca.

The first task is to diagnose the causes of the loss of competitiveness; then it is possible to consider potential remedies. For the steel industry, the problem is one of steady deterioration in relative costs. Dollar costs of hot-rolled steel sheet were virtually equal in Japan and the United States at $66 per short ton in 1958. The U.S. industry was cost-competitive by virtue of transportation costs, and steel was a "domestic good." By 1976, Japanese costs were $121 and U.S. costs $175 for the same product.[8] The source of this decline in competitiveness can be traced to three variables: productivity gains; wage rate increases, and raw material costs (particularly the cost of iron ore). Between 1970 and 1976, the cost of labor in the Japanese industry grew from $1.69 to $5.25 (by $3.56 per hour, or an increase of 211 percent). Over the same period, U.S. wage rates increased from $6.10 to $12.14 (by $6.04 per hour, or an increase of just under 100 percent). During a period of weakness in the yen in 1979, the absolute difference in hourly rates reached $7.00 per hour.[9] Table 9-1 shows these cost changes and the emergence of Japan's cost advantage. Table 9-2 shows that the wage rate in the U.S. steel industry has not been adversely affected by the inroads of imports. Wage rates in the steel industry relative to wages in "all manufacturing" have in-

[7]Robert W. Crandall, *The U.S. Steel Industry in Recurrent Crisis: Policy Options in a Competitive World* (Washington, D.C.: Brookings Institution, 1981), p. 29.

[8]Crandall, *The U.S. Steel Industry*, pp. 171–172.

[9]In mid-1982, high interest rates in the United States had raised the dollar to 245 yen or weakened the yen to about 16 percent below what one Japanese economist considered a reasonable exchange rate in terms of the Japanese trade balance.

Table 9-1
Changes in Input Costs in Japanese and U.S. Steel (in current dollars)

	Labor (man-hour)		Iron Ore (net ton)		Coal (net ton)		Oil (net ton)		Steel* (short ton)	
	Japan	USA	Japan	USA	Japan	USA	Japan	USA	Japan	USA
1956	0.43	3.35	16.7	9.6	22.1	9.9	18.1	18.5	75.0	60.7
1961	0.58	4.36	12.9	11.8	15.5	9.8	15.2	17.7	58.5	70.0
1966	0.91	4.93	11.9	11.7	14.4	9.8	11.9	16.6	54.4	70.0
1971	1.98	6.67	10.5	14.1	19.4	15.3	15.2	26.3	61.0	86.6
1976	5.25	12.14	15.8	27.6	53.6	56.0	64.5	62.5	121.1	175.0

Note: Changes in price combine two effects, changes in the costs of inputs in local currencies and changes in the rate of exchange between the U.S. dollar and the yen. The yen strengthened against the dollar in 1971 and trended upward against the dollar throughout most of the 1970s. Inflation hit both countries in response to the oil-price shock in 1973. Unit labor costs affect costs. These costs vary with changes in absolute labor costs and labor productivity. Japanese labor productivity increased much more than U.S. labor productivity.

The steady increase in the cost of iron ore to the U.S. industry can be explained by the steady depletion of the main U.S. domestic deposit in Minnesota (the Mesabi range).

* Hot-rolled sheet.

Source: Data from Robert W. Crandall, *The U.S. Steel Industry in Recurrent Crisis: Policy Options in a Competitive World* (Washington, D.C.: Brookings Institution, 1981), pp. 169–170.

Table 9-2
LABOR COSTS IN STEEL AND IMPORT PENETRATION

	Nominal Average Hourly Earnings ($)	Real Average Hourly Earnings (1967 dollars)	Imports as a Percent of Domestic Output	Average Hourly Earnings Relative to "All Manufacturing"
1961	3.20	3.57	3.3	1.38
1962	3.29	3.63	4.2	1.38
1963	3.36	3.66	5.0	1.37
1964	3.41	3.67	5.0	1.35
1965	3.46	3.66	7.9	1.33
1966	3.58	3.68	8.1	1.32
1967	3.62	3.62	9.0	1.28
1968	3.82	3.67	13.7	1.27
1969	4.09	3.72	9.9	1.26
1970	4.22	3.63	10.2	1.26
1971	4.57	3.77	15.2	1.28
1972	5.15	4.11	13.3	1.35
1973	5.56	4.18	10.0	1.37
1974	6.38	4.32	11.0	1.45
1975	7.11	4.40	10.3	1.48
1976	7.86	4.61	11.2	1.51
1977	8.67	4.78	15.4	1.54
1978	9.70	4.97	15.4	1.57
1979	10.77	4.95	13.69	1.61
1980	11.84	4.79	14.76	1.63
1981	13.11	4.81	17.36	1.64
1982	13.96	4.83	21.8	1.64

Sources: U.S. Bureau of Labor Statistics; American Iron and Steel Institute; and Robert W. Crandall, *The U.S. Steel Industry in Recurrent Crisis: Policy Options in a Competitive World* (Washington, D.C.: Brookings Institution, 1981).

creased in the face of substantial increases in the share of the U.S. market gained by imports. This suggests that monopoly benefits are being gained by members of the United Steelworkers with the seniority needed to remain employed.

The steel industry in Western Europe comprised old industries and subsidized new capacity, with the result that steel capacity in Western Europe exceeded demand. Steel capacity in the developing world has also increased substantially to the point that world capacity is excessive. These problems aggravate the difficulties faced by steel firms with outdated equipment and high labor costs (Belgium, the United Kingdom, and the United States, among others). This problem is being met, to some degree, in Western Europe and the United States as worn-out steel capacity is being abandoned—often at the insistence of governments unwilling to continue to subsidize the output. In fact, some governments are making the continuation of support to the industry conditional on scrapping inefficient plants.[10]

Similar problems have affected the automotive industry in the United States. Table 9-3 shows the ratio of compensation in the U.S. and Japanese automotive industries to the average wage in all manufacturing in the two countries as well as the ratio of car imports to registrations in the United States. At a minimum, the wage rates in the U.S. industry did not offset the inherent weaknesses of that industry. These included a severe comparative cost disadvantage in small cars, which were demanded by U.S. drivers after the rapid increase in the cost of gasoline during the 1970s. There was also a design disadvantage and a complete lack of competitiveness in terms of product reliability. However, the disadvantages did not show themselves instantaneously: People only change cars when the one they have wears out. Table 9-4 provides striking evidence of the lesser reliability of U.S.-made automobiles.[11] In early 1980, the industry appealed to the International Trade Commission, but the commission did not recommend trade relief (protection). Despite this, the Reagan administration negotiated so-called voluntary export restraints (VERs) that limited Japanese car exports to the United States to 1.68 million cars per year. In 1983, the VER was extended for two more years but was allowed to lapse in April 1985. The Japanese industry then announced that it would allow exports to the United States to increase to 2.3 million cars, and the Reagan administration promptly argued that that figure was more than market forces would allow. The whole

[10]For a description of the problem of the steel industry, see Ingo Walter, "Protection of Industries in Trouble: The Case of Iron and Steel," *World Economy,* 2 (May 1979), 155–187; and Victoria Curzon Price, "Alternatives to Delayed Structural Adjustment in 'Workshop Europe,'" *World Economy,* 3 (September 1980), 205–216. Also see "Manifestly, It's a Crisis," *Economist,* 4 (October 1980), 52.

[11]Similar data are reported in Robert W. Crandall, "Import Quotas and the Automobile Industry: The Costs of Protectionism," *Brookings Review,* 2 (Summer 1984), 8–16.

Table 9-3

COMPENSATION IN THE UNITED STATES AND JAPAN AND IMPORT SHARES OF THE U.S. AUTOMOBILE MARKET

| | United States | | | Japan | | | Imports as a Percentage of Registrations (%) |
	Motor Vehicles ($)	All Manufacturing ($)	Ratio	Motor Vehicles ($)	All Manufacturing ($)	Ratio	
1975	9.44	6.35	1.49	3.56	3.05	1.17	18.2
1976	10.27	6.93	1.48	4.02	3.30	1.22	14.8
1977	11.45	7.59	1.51	4.82	4.03	1.20	18.3
1978	12.67	8.30	1.52	6.85	5.54	1.24	17.8
1979	13.68	9.07	1.51	6.90	5.49	1.26	22.7
1980	16.29	9.89	1.65	6.89	5.61	1.23	28.2
1981	17.28	10.95	1.58	7.65	6.18	1.24	28.8
1982	18.66	11.68	1.60	7.18	5.70	1.26	29.3
1983	19.02	12.31	1.55	7.91	6.24	1.27	27.5

Note: Although the effect of the rate of exchange on absolute compensation is visible, the ratio of automotive compensation to average manufacturing compensation shows how pay scales in the automotive industry responded to competitive pressures.

Sources: Compensation data (wages plus fringe benefits) from U.S. Bureau of Labor Statistics. Import and registration data from *Automotive News*, April 27, 1983.

Table 9-4

FREQUENCY OF AUTOMOBILE REPAIR IN THE UNITED STATES,
BY NATIONAL ORIGIN

Key: 5= much better than average, 4 = better than average, 3 = average, 2 =
worse than average, 1 = much worse than average.

Country of Origin	Model Years 1972–1975*		Model Years 1974–1979†	
	Raw Score‡	Average Score	Raw Score‡	Average Score
Japan§	153/38	4.03	365/86	4.24
Germany	161/46	3.50	204/62	3.29
United States	642/244	2.63	1193/434	2.75
Sweden	27/11	2.45	45/15	3.00

* Assessed by questionnaire in 1976.
† Assessed by questionnaire in 1980.
‡ The raw score denotes the total number of points earned and the number of models reported. Only data for the category "overall record" were used.
§ The improvement in Japanese reliability is due to the improvement in Toyota cars from 3.94 to 4.70. Excluding Toyota, the Japanese average score declined slightly from 4.10 to 4.03.

Sources: Consumers Union, *Consumer Reports: The 1977 Buying Guide Issue* (Mount Vernon, N.Y. 1976), pp. 375–383; and Consumers Union, *Consumer Reports Buying Guide Issue, 1981* (Mount Vernon, N.Y., 1980), pp. 378–398.

problem of Japanese exports to the United States has been confounded by the arrant overvaluation of the dollar (considered in Chapter 15).

Neither industry is likely to be able to survive without some form of protection. Workers in the United Steelworkers and in the United Auto Workers will lose high-paying jobs even if they find alternative employment. The steel industry is in the worse position of the two because it has run down its old equipment and does not have the financial strength to raise capital to install new equipment. The automotive industry is in a far better position in the long run in the sense that the firms may be able to regain their traditional market shares if they are given breathing space during which they can set their houses in order. Given that both industries might survive with *temporary* government help, they can be described as "embattled." The government has two traditional alternatives: to provide protection in the form of a tariff or quota or to allow the market system to work out its own solution. Both courses of action involve risk. If a tariff or a quota is given, there can be no assurance that the industry will reduce its costs (particularly the premium wage costs), so the imposition of protection merely postpones the problem if it does not aggravate it, for under protection competitiveness could deteriorate further. Reliance on market forces runs the risk of having the domestic industry collapse. The collapse of an industry is not a negligible event because the sheer size of efficient production units in the two industries could preclude the reemergence of the U.S. industry even if the United States regained a (small) comparative advantage. The third option is to recognize the transitory nature of the loss of competitiveness by the industry and to offer protection for a finite period of time on the condition that some of the source of noncompetitiveness in the embattled industry would be eliminated in return for the award of protection.

The industries have, of course, asked for straightforward protection. The U.S. steel industry has accused foreign firms of dumping surplus steel in U.S. markets and other foreign industries of receiving subsidies from their governments. In 1978, the ingenuity of economists produced a cumbersome mechanism (the "trigger-price mechanism," which determined import prices below which dumping must be deemed to be taking place).[12] The mechanism was discontinued in 1981, but complaints about foreign dumping continued. It is difficult to identify dumped steel when governments have a strong ownership position in many steel industries, and it is also difficult to engender much sympathy for the steel industry when very high wage rates paid to steelworkers seem to be a major contributor to the lack of competitiveness of the U.S. industry. In Europe, the steel industry has gone further than to ask for straightforward protection and has tried to cartelize the industry by achieving what Walter calls "sectoral protection." This is an arrangement reached among producers in various countries with the tacit or overt approval of their bewildered and beleaguered governments to set limits (quotas) on imports and to divide the domestic market among existing plants. Such an agreement excludes the interests of steel users and handicaps "downstream industries" as well as preempted exporters. Such an arrangement will help sustain uncompetitive industries and plants and any surplus income enjoyed by unions or managers in the protected industry. Sectoral protection does not include any mandatory reduction in protection over time.

Straightforward protection does not encourage the home industry to increase its cost competitiveness by increasing productivity or by reducing any surplus paid to factors of production; it merely preserves the status quo. A hands-off or ideological commitment to free trade runs the risk of having a number of firms in the industry go bankrupt. Implicit in the free trade argument in Chapter 6 was the idea that if the country had a comparative advantage in an industry and lost such an advantage temporarily, a new industry would replace the old one. In reality, as noted, scale economies and size considerations are likely to preclude such an outcome when the firms would be starting from the base of a zero share of the market. Unfortunately, there cannot be any guarantee that foreign industries will not collude once the American industry has been decimated by foreign competition. Imagine, in terms of the automotive industry, the scenario in which General Motors, Ford and Chrysler have all gone bankrupt: Nissan, Toyota, Honda, and Mazda could collude

---

[12]For a description of the trigger-price mechanism, see Walter, "Protection of Industries in Trouble," pp. 165–171.

to maintain high prices and profit margins in the American market. An equally discouraging scenario is if Ford and Chrysler went bankrupt, the terms of trade would shift against the United States (the yen would strengthen against the dollar), and General Motors would be left in a substantial monopoly position unaffected by significant foreign competition.[13]

Neither straightforward protection nor a hands-off free trade policy is ideal when an industry is temporarily troubled by foreign competition. Consider the option of *conditional, temporary protection* (while bearing in mind the difficulty in distinguishing between an industry that can be saved and one that is destined to lose out to foreign industry in the absence of permanent protection). An industry can be given temporary protection in order to preserve a reasonable market share that reestablishes its competitiveness. This does not necessarily imply that the embattled industry will completely regain its original market share when the industry has regained the ability to compete with foreign firms, merely that a substantial amount of the domestic market will be held by the home country's industry. The government must offer protection only on condition that the inefficiencies leading to the (temporary) loss of comparative advantage be eliminated by reforms within the industry.

As noted, the first and very difficult problem is to identify an industry that is merely embattled and not senile. Of course, in industries with national defense considerations, the nation may be faced with offering permanent protection of one form or another, but if it chooses to do so, it should impose conditions on the operation of the industry similar to those imposed on embattled industries.[14] Conditional protection is instituted when management and labor agree to take steps to reduce costs in the home industry (or to improve product quality) in return for their temporary protection from foreign competition. Note that all of the three major parties in an industry—management, labor, and stockholders—gain from protection. If the industry is in serious trouble, objections from stockholders to conditional protection are likely to be small. The protection will last for a maximum of five years and can be expected to take the form of an import quota whose magnitude will vary (inversely) with the severity of the commitments undertaken by labor and management.[15] Labor and salaried workers recognize that their rates of pay exceed those compatible with the viability of the industry, given the marketing effectiveness of management, the stock of capital goods

[13]See Chapter 5 for the effect of foreign competition on the strength of a domestic monopoly.

[14]Unfortunately, the national defense argument is usually couched in terms of straightforward protection. This does not make any difference if (and only if) the industry is perfectly competitive and no factor of production enjoys a quasi-rent or surplus.

[15]The actual commercial-policy device used can vary. A quota has the advantage of relative simplicity. A subsidy per unit of output produced may very well be a superior mechanism since subsidies can be limited to plants and firms deemed embattled while senile plants and firms are excluded.

actually in use, and the cost of foreign goods. In return for protection, labor and salaried workers (including management) agree to gradual decreases in their real (inflation-adjusted) wage rates. It will probably be easier to achieve such an undertaking in an inflationary environment in which nominal wage rates remain constant in money terms. Reductions in nominal or real wage rates could be made smaller when productivity-enhancing changes in working rules and conditions are agreed to or when the mix between take-home pay and fringe benefits is changed.

Management salaries will also be scheduled for reduction in real terms by (at least) the same percentage as the reduction in wage rates of the work force. Salaries may also be safeguarded in the same way as wages. No bonuses will be awarded to management, and steps must be taken to ensure that any promotional increases are legitimate. Dividends to stockholders are prohibited, and if the corporation is a conglomerate, the profits of the embattled firms must be plowed back into the relevant industry and may not be diverted to more profitable sectors of the conglomerate. Profits will be used for upgrading equipment rather than for increasing capacity.

The fundamental idea behind "conditional assistance" is to create a mix of policies that gives the industry time to adjust to the new conditions. In this sense, the concept resembles the aid given to firms under TAA. Conditional protection provides a combination of measures that can be varied by industry to prevent the institution of protection from leading to lower efficiency (in the sense of cost minimization).[16] Conditional assistance is also able to avoid contributing to the longevity of outmoded and inefficient plants that might be able to survive under (overly protective) straightforward, unconditional protection.

There are, clearly, many serious problems to be reckoned with in instituting conditional protection. The process could degenerate like the trigger-price mechanism into a bureaucratic nightmare. There is the question of relations with trading partners. When, as in Western Europe, the embattled industries are publicly owned, there are implications of political responsibility. Finally, there is the question of how such measures could be allowed for under the GATT.

Despite the obstacles that face the institution of conditional protection, such a system has clear advantages over the options of straightforward protection or simple free trade. Frequently, industries are embattled because they are, in Leibenstein's terms, X-inefficient—their costs are simply not minimized because of inertia or some other impediment to full efficiency. These inefficiencies can probably only be removed by a joint determination on the part of all groups involved in the industry to

---

[16]This is Harvey Leibenstein's "X-inefficiency" (Chapter 7). Leibenstein argues that tariffs merely encourage such inefficiency so that, in terms of Figure 7-1, when the tariff is instituted the domestic supply curve shifts up as a result of increased wage rates and profits or reduced productivity. See Leibenstein, "X-Efficiency: From Concept to Theory," *Challenge,* September-October 1979, pp. 13–22.

cooperate in improving industry efficiency.[17] The market system would ultimately produce crisis conditions that would bring the groups together, but by that time the industry may have ceased to be embattled and may have become senile. By imposing conditional protection, the government could serve as a catalyst in bringing the groups together and launching reductions in costs. Certainly, there will be great difficulty in getting labor to accept unilateral reductions in pay unless other groups are also faced with cutbacks.

Another difficulty faces the introduction of "conditional protection." Parliaments and other legislatures have not been exposed to analyses of the degree of sophistication that warrants temporary protection. Most arguments that they hear involve special pleading for permanent protection for a senile or embattled industry or arguments for free trade that posit an eternity of gains from trade and neglect costs of adjustment. But the idea of increasingly sophisticated protective devices requires increased sophistication and determination on the part of the policymakers. They must be prepared and able to terminate protection for both senile and embattled industries. Dyed-in-the-wool free traders argue that the political system does not allow for termination and that all temporary protection will be effectively permanent. This is a valid criticism of all arguments for "slowing the speed of adjustment" protection. Policymakers must be exposed to the more subtle arguments that temporary protection involves if policy is to be made on a rational basis.

The problem is severe. If pressures from imports become sufficiently strong and the ability of the importing economy to adjust without incurring substantial social costs is limited, there will be widespread support for protectionism. The danger is that under such conditions, the tendency toward ever freer trade that has characterized the world since World War II will be reversed, and gains that have already been adapted to will be reversed. The likely cause of such a change in general policy toward international trade is that the economies of the leading nations will be subjected to pressures to adjust at rates that will impose severe adjustment costs—long-term unemployment of displaced workers. Much of this pressure may derive from increases in manufacturing capacity in developing nations, from labor-saving technological pressures such as robotization in the developed world and from inadequate positive adjustment policies. As Walter has pointed out, free trade is an ideal, but it will not be achieved if the governments of the world ignore costs of

---

[17] In this context, the decision of the United Steelworkers to refuse to forgo wage freezes and curbs on cost-of-living raises is discouraging; see William Serin, "Steel Union Vetoes Industry Proposal on Replacing Pact," *New York Times,* July 31, 1982, pp. 1 and 12. This behavior contrasts sharply with the creative approach (or feeling of vulnerability) of the United Auto Workers, which did negotiate substantial give-backs with Chrysler and Ford in 1982 and, in this way, did allow the price differential between U.S. cars and imports to be narrowed. Unfortunately, it would take a very courageous government to discipline the USW by reducing tariffs and protective measures in the face of the union's insistence on the preservation of quasi-rents (at least for those who continue to be employed).

adjustment or allow their economies to petrify into the existing industrial mix.[18] Europe, particularly, seems to be afflicted by so-called economic sclerosis, a hardening of the joints and an inherent inability to adjust to new conditions.

The problems facing the industrial nations in an era when developing, labor-surplus countries can quickly increase their ability to export sophisticated manufactured goods—as evidenced by the success of Brazil, Hong Kong, Korea, Mexico, Singapore, and Taiwan—could prove to be very severe. A simple ideological faith in free trade and the static equilibrium of trade theory may not be enough. The system may be "dynamically unstable" in the sense that once the impetus toward freer trade is vanquished by political pressures arising from the costs of adjustment, the pressures for protectionism will feed on themselves, and barriers to trade will be erected even among the developed, industrialized nations. Conditional protection is one possible answer to the problem.

APPAREL AND FOOTWEAR: SPECIAL PROBLEMS?

In June 1982, the Research Department of the International Ladies Garment Workers Union announced that unemployment in the garment industry had reached 18.1 percent of the work force when the national average was 9.1 percent. Between 1970 and 1980, employment in the footwear industry fell by 60,000 jobs (see Table 9-5). The question is, Should the government actively concern itself with these phenomena, or are they just supportive evidence of what Walter refers to as the "weeding out of decaying domestic sectors"? The free trade argument would allow the industries to die in the face of cheaper imports from abroad—both industries use low-skilled labor intensively and are clear examples of industries in which the United States has a comparative disadvantage.

The only viable argument for preserving these industries through some sort of protection must then lie either in a senile-industry, phaseout protection framework or must rely on the nonapplicability of some of the assumptions of the free trade model. Certainly there is little validity in the argument that the United States can conserve these industries simply by making them more efficient and giving them subsidized loans under TAA programs. Subsidized loans will make the industry more capital-intensive and will generate displacement of workers in much the same way as import growth.

The free trade argument, as presented in Chapter 6, relies on all of the assumptions built into the Ricardian and H-O theories of international

[18]See the supplement following Chapter 8.

Table 9-5

EFFECTS OF IMPORTS ON THE U.S. NONRUBBER FOOTWEAR INDUSTRY

Year	Domestic Capacity (millions of pairs)	Domestic Production (millions of pairs)	Imports (millions of pairs)	Imports as a Percent of Apparent Home Consumption	Employment (thousands)	Cumulative Factory Closings
1970	738.6	562.3	241.6	30.1	212.7	55
1976	556.5	422.5	370.0	47.0	164.2	227
1977	550.5	418.4	368.1*	47.1	156.9	239
1978	556.8	418.9	373.5*	47.6	158.4	229
1979	517.7	398.9	404.6*	50.9	148.9	258
1980	515.7	398.9	365.7*	49.5	143.6	274
1981	489.7	372.0	375.6*	51.0	146.4	293
1982	474.1	359.1	479.7	57.8	135.1	316
1983	466.6	339.2	581.9	63.7	127.4	340
1984	428.9	301.4	725.9	71.3	116.1	424
1985	406.2	266.0	843.1	76.6	104.7	473

*The industry was granted import relief by the Carter administration in mid-1977, in the form of quotas placed on imports from Taiwan and South Korea. These restrictions proved to have small value as Taiwanese and Korean exports were rerouted through Hong Kong (until a requirement that a certificate of origin be furnished for all imports) and because other suppliers from developing countries were ready to fill any void caused by restrictions placed on Taiwan and Korea.

Source: Footwear Industries of America.

trade. One of these assumptions may be particularly important in context, that of full employment at a subsistence wage (although the fact that the wage should exceed or equal some imprecise concept of a subsistence wage is implicit). In other words, can full employment be reached simply by aggregate demand policies? Is it possible that low-skilled labor, such as is predominantly employed in apparel and shoes, is being displaced from employment so quickly by imports and by labor-saving machinery that full employment in the Keynesian sense is no longer compatible with free trade and the going minimum wage? The whole principle of adjustment assumes that there is a job available for the willing worker if the macroeconomy is functioning correctly. Will jobs in other industries open up for low-skilled workers at or above the minimum wage rate? If the answer to the question is no, should the U.S. Congress reduce the minimum wage to something nearer physical subsistence, or should it subsidize workers earning the minimum wage rate? It is quite possible that the number of jobs available at the minimum wage will be drastically reduced by imports from countries where the labor is cheap and where the cost of food and shelter are cheaper in dollar terms than in the industrialized world. In such countries, concepts of subsistence are also lower, and safety considerations carry less weight.[19]

Note that in context, the multifactor version of the H-O theory is useful here. Larger imports will lead to increased exports by the industrialized nations. These exports will use highly skilled labor and technology intensively so that increased imports will lead to a reduction in the total demand for low-skilled labor. There are two facets to the problem: the speed at which low-skilled labor is displaced and the absolute availability of jobs for low-skilled workers. The speed of displacement is a problem of congestion in the labor markets, and adjustment will be more difficult (and the pressures for protection higher), the greater the overall unemployment rate and the more low-skilled workers displaced each month or each year by the combination of imports and labor-saving machinery (which will tend to displace low-skilled workers predominantly). Absolute job availability is a more complicated question: The magnitude of the problem depends on the number of workers displaced, the degree to which they and society can upgrade their skills, and the willingness of displaced workers to perform more menial tasks for which there is a large latent demand.[20]

The problem is that the hard-core unemployed will, almost inevitably, comprise people with the lowest skill levels, and they will be the most

---

[19]Professor John Culbertson of the University of Wisconsin is very pessimistic about the ability of the United States to maintain what he sees as an acceptable economic system if U.S. markets are opened to foreign suppliers with no effective safety standards, no child labor laws, and very low wages; see his *International Trade and the Future of the West* (Madison, Wisc.: 21st Century Press, 1984).

[20]There is the sobering thought that displaced workers may find crime more profitable or attractive than menial and "inferior" jobs.

difficult to upgrade. Consider an industry that employs low-skilled workers intensively and is declining because of its lack of price competitiveness with exports from developing countries. Apparel and shoes would both be good examples. Workers in both industries may be quite highly skilled in their particular occupations, but these occupations are industry-specific, and they are low-skilled in terms of skills transferable to another industry. There will be fewer jobs available for them in the high-tech export industries, and the jobs available will require a higher skill level. The question of the effect of increased capacity for exports by developing countries and the employability of low-skilled labor can best be explained by a "ladder" of compartmentalized job markets segregated by skill level. Table 9-6 depicts such a national job market with and without protection of apparel imports. When apparel imports are restricted, there is a short-run excess supply of labor in the two lowest grades and a shortage of labor in the highest grade. When imports of apparel are allowed to take place without impediment, the demand for skilled workers increases as high-tech exports grow, but the excess supply of low-skilled workers is aggravated by the disemployment of workers from the apparel industry. If the U.S. market were to be thrown open to unimpeded competition from low-wage countries, probably only fashion-related (high-style) garments that require a close liaison between the fashion center and the producers would remain viable in the United States. Workers unemployed at level 6 may choose to take lower-wage jobs at level 7 and will oust

Table 9-6
COMPARTMENTALIZED LABOR MARKETS

Skill Level	Discrimination against Apparel Imports	No Discrimination against Apparel Imports
1. Scientists, engineers, and technicians	S	SS
2. Other professionals	S	S
3. Managers	B	B
4. Machinists, etc.	B	S
5. Other skilled workers	B	S
6. Semiskilled production workers	B	E
7. Low-skilled clerical	E	SE
8. Low-skilled nonclerical workers	SE	VSE

Key: SS = severe shortage, S = shortage, B = balance, E = excess, SE = severe excess, VSE = very severe excess.

Note: Managers are assumed to be equally important in all industries.

As noted in the text, this is an analysis of the impact effect of increased imports of low-skill-intensive imports. The imbalances can be cured by worker upgrading, by bumping (in levels 6 and 7), and by the substitution of labor for capital (in levels 6, 7, and 8) in response to changes in the relative prices of capital and labor.

people from level 7 jobs by virtue of their higher skills. If the displaced level 7 workers do not find employment at their old wage, they may choose to compete at the eighth level and oust workers qualified at that level. This is the mechanism through which the unemployed will comprise largely the very low-skilled workers. Workers can increase their skill attainments by further training and education. They will be tempted to do so if they feel they have the innate intelligence to achieve the higher level (a question of confidence), if they can afford to do so, and if they see the rewards as exceeding the personal and monetary costs. The process can be expensive since it may involve payment for training received as well as the loss of income during the period of training. In the absence of corporate or government programs to upgrade workers (positive adjustment policies), relatively few workers can be expected to increase their skill level. However, the overall skill level of the work force may indeed increase as younger workers seek greater levels of skill prior to entering the work force and older unskilled or low-skilled workers retire early.

This prospect, discouraging as it is, is made even worse if domestic industries (and even exporters) are substituting capital for labor at levels 6, 7, and 8. The process of automation or robotization encourages the substitution of capital for labor at the lower end of the skill spectrum. It is easier to design a machine to replace an unskilled worker performing a relatively automatic or repetitive task than to replace a creative thinker (such as a production engineer) or a supervisor. Of course, the processes of automation and robotization will generate other jobs, and some of these will use relatively low-skilled labor. Nevertheless, and on balance, larger imports of low-skill labor-intensive goods from developing nations with huge population surpluses paid subsistence wages will inevitably create an excess supply of low-skilled workers in the importing nations.

If wage rates, particularly those for low-skilled labor, fall relative to the cost of capital in the developed (importing) country, there may be some reverse substitution of labor for capital. Even then, the prospect is not very cheerful. If level 8 workers earn only subsistence income, their wage rates cannot fall. If imports of clothing come from countries like India, China, the Philippines, and Sri Lanka with their chronic surpluses of low-skilled labor (or labor that can be quickly and cheaply trained to perform at that level), wage rates are unlikely to increase. A free trade market tends to integrate the labor markets in different countries, and such action would expose workers in Europe and North America to the Malthusian problems of high levels of population and high rates of population growth that still exist in the third world. Hong Kong and Singapore are now both experiencing incipient shortages of labor; they are discouraging the establishment of highly labor-intensive industries and are seeking to upgrade their industries by the level of labor skills used. But these are relatively small economic units.

If the concept of full employment is not to be idle political rhetoric nor merely a convenient target for an economic model, developed nations may have to countenance having a certain number of low-skilled jobs available for workers who cannot rise to the skill levels that industry naturally demands. Many workers are incapable of increasing their skill level. For some workers this may be a straightforward problem of inherited intelligence, for others the absence of basic and necessary learning skills. Many people have been raised in a cultural and familial environment in which schooling and skill acquisition are deemphasized. Then, too, as workers grow older, they tend to find skill enhancement more difficult. It may be that the very workers most likely to be unemployed will be those who will find upgrading more difficult if the constraints on upgrading apply preeminently to those at the bottom of the skill ladder. If the domestic-goods sector does not supply the necessary number of low-skilled jobs, the sector's capacity to use low-skilled labor must be artificially stimulated through some positive program (perhaps a subsidy of wage rates for workers earning within some percentage of the minimum wage or the subsistence wage) or protection against imports of all goods that use relatively large proportions of low-skilled labor must be instituted. Or the country must reconcile itself to the existence of a reserve army of low-skilled unemployed for many years.

Apparel Imports

Imports of clothing into the industrialized countries from the developing nations are controlled by the Multifibre Arrangement (MFA).[21] Imports of clothing into the United States, calculated as a percentage of GNP, increased from 0.04 percent in 1968 to 0.1 percent in 1973 and to 0.19 percent in 1978. But the American industry has managed to survive thanks largely to the MFA, which proliferates voluntary export restraints, orderly marketing arrangements, and straightforward quotas. Between 1971 and 1978, output in the clothing industry in the United States actually increased in constant dollars, but this increase was accompanied by a 6.9 percent decrease in the number of production workers and an 8.7 percent decrease in the number of hours worked. Part of the industry's success in surviving may have been due to the use of low-skilled cheap foreign labor under the "offshore assembly provisions" of the U.S. Tariff Schedule. This is an example of what will be termed "production sharing" in Part VI. The production of any finished good requires several processes, some of which can use more low-skilled labor than others. If a firm can perform the high-skilled work in the United States, it can send the components to, say, Haiti, where the components can be stitched together to make a finished garment. Obviously, the saving in cost of performing

---

[21]For a discussion of MFA, see Gerard Curzon et al., *MFA Forever?* (London: Trade Policy Research Centre, 1981).

the activities in Haiti must exceed the costs of transportation and any duties levied. Items 806.3 and 807 of the U.S. Tariff Schedule allow imports of goods made with "production sharing" to pay duty only on the "value added" abroad. (The U.S.-made components come back into the country free of duty.) In 1971, the value of apparel imports under this provision was $69.5 million, or 4.6 percent of the value of domestic output. In 1978, $418.9 million of imports amounted to 7.8 percent of production.

An excellent study of enterprise adaptation to foreign competition has indicated the importance of integration of domestic and foreign operations.[22] Of five firms classified as "growing," three used foreign sourcing successfully: One had a subsidiary in the Dominican Republic; a second used foreign subcontractors for "bottom of the line" products and as a source for some of its standard products; and the third used foreign producers to fill gaps in its product line. All five firms classified as "growing" had emphasized the more highly styled part of the clothing industry in which more (skilled) finishing work was required, and delivery times were shorter and often more crucial than price.

Undoubtedly, foreign suppliers of clothing, particularly firms located in developing nations such as Korea and Taiwan, could (with or without foreign direct investment in manufacturing subsidiaries by U.S. clothing firms) adequately supply most of the needs of the United States for apparel at much lower prices than American consumers are currently paying. The question that is unanswered is whether or not the displaced workers could find alternative employment. There is little point in displacing a gainfully employed worker if that worker will merely be a burden to the economy (through unemployment).[23] One fairly straightforward conclusion is that it seems somewhat inefficient to subsidize the use of capital to make an apparel firm able to compete with foreign competition. The subsidized capital will displace some low-skilled workers and will not benefit the consumer. Only those who remain employed in the industry (and the stockholders and managers) will benefit. It seems unlikely that this is a productive route for a nation to pursue. Such a policy might result from a less than clear understanding of the problem—thinking of the need to protect low-skill-intensive industries because of phaseout reasons or because of political pressures from firms, regions, and communities that rely heavily on these industries. For example, no politician from North Carolina who expects to be reelected can fail to advocate protection of the tobacco growers and the apparel industry.

Yet there is a real problem of adjustment. In this context, we can do no better than to quote a remark made in a television program dealing

---

[22]José de la Torre et al., "Corporate Adjustments and Import Competition in the U.S. Apparel Industry," *Journal of International Business Studies*, 8 (1977), 5–22.
[23]See footnote 10 in Chapter 7.

with the problems of employment in the apparel industry in four countries: England and Belgium, where the industries would disappear without protection; Hong Kong, where export markets were being throttled by MFA; and Sri Lanka, which has hopes of using some of its chronically unemployed population by exporting clothing. A production manager in a clothing factory in Manchester, England, asks:

> What industry would you suggest these people are retrained to go into? Mention half a dozen expanding industries to me in this country at the moment. What are we supposed to do—all become astronauts? All become scientists? There are people in this factory who are very happy with the work they're doing, working in an environment that suits them. They are not cut out to be academics, they are not cut out to be astronauts, they are not cut out to be technologists.[24]

One does not need to be an expert on the cost of living in England to know that a worker there could not subsist on the wage being paid to a clothing worker in Sri Lanka:

> Hema lives in Sri Lanka. . . . Her $5 weekly salary is just under the average industrial wage in Sri Lanka. She lives in a small house outside Colombo. To get to the factory, she has to get up at four in the morning, walk part of the way to work, catch a bus. She rarely returns before eight in the evening. One-sixth of her salary goes on her bus fare alone. She supports a family of nine. Here a small amount of money goes a long way. Her meager pay makes all the difference to her family's standard of living.[25]

If the problem seems to demand the wisdom of Solomon (and maybe a bit more), it does. However much one may sympathize with the need for additional jobs in Sri Lanka, where the official rate of unemployment has hovered around 24 percent for years, one can also understand the attitude of the American worker toward free trade:

> The AFL-CIO has heard the explanations for trade policy come full circle since World War II. As U.S. seamen watched the shipping industry decline and their jobs go to foreign flags, they were told that the U.S. is not a service nation but a manufacturing nation and that exports of manufactures create jobs. However, in the three postwar decades, various types of manufactures went into deficit: textiles, steel, shoes, autos, electronics and some kinds of machinery. Each time exports of a higher technology product was given as

---

[24]Quoted in *The Shirt Off Your Back* (Boston: WGBH Educational Foundation, 1979), pp. 18–19.
[25]Ibid., p. 6.

the "answer." But the lost steel plants in Pennsylvania, autos in New Jersey, railroad parts in California, shoes and machinery in Missouri, and electronics, glass, rubber and aluminum nationwide left expensive scars. Increasingly, huge imports of parts were a major factor even in aircraft and computer sales. So the dollar sign on export sales no longer always added up to jobs.[26]

This speaker represents unionized labor and the older industries, the onetime aristocracy of workers, but the AFL-CIO often speaks on behalf of all workers in the United States.

The question is, Can the United States reattain satisfactory employment levels if its need for low-skilled workers is drastically reduced by automation and imported low-skill labor-intensive goods and there exist no strong positive programs to upgrade the skills of the labor force?

SUMMARY

This chapter has approached three aspects of the difficulties relating to an unswerving obedience to the doctrine of free trade. The first aspect shows the way in which the United States does or does not try to take positive steps to assist the economy to adjust to changed conditions, whether they originate at home or abroad. The record is not encouraging, and the simple reliance of the Reagan administration on the effectiveness of market forces seems misplaced. The United States has never had great success in peacetime in upgrading workers except in periods of severe labor shortage. There would seem to be a large role for government in the creation of efficient positive programs. But the emphasis of trade policy is not toward positive programs but toward adjustment-retarding steps designed to keep threatened industries alive and even, with straightforward protection, to obviate any adjustment in the face of changed circumstances.

The problem of what to do about embattled industries is also a tricky one. There is the understandable attitude of the consumer: "Why should I pay more for a U.S.-built car when the Japanese worker will work to supply it to me for less?" It will take political courage to invoke and enforce conditional assistance, and members of Congress have not been exposed to arguments of the necessary sophistication.

The problem of low-skilled workers is still more difficult. To limit imports of low-skilled labor-intensive goods from developing countries is to risk alienating that bloc of countries economically and politically. To allow free trade to eliminate labor-intensive industries within the United

---

[26]Statement of Lane Kirkland, president of the AFL-CIO, on U.S. trade policy before the Subcommittee on International Trade of the Committee on Finance, U.S. Senate, July 13, 1981.

States, including standard production and assembly jobs in many industries, is to expose the American worker to competitive pressure from the surplus populations of Asia, Africa, and Latin America.

These problems are likely to continue to afflict the U.S. economy for the foreseeable future. They are not just transitory phenomena, likely to evaporate with a temporary set of conditions in world markets. They represent the natural extension of the picture painted by Lane Kirkland in the last quotation.

Bibliography

Aho, C. Michael, and T. O. Bayard. "Costs and Benefits of Trade Adjustment Assistance," in ed. R. E. Baldwin and A. O. Krueger. *Structure and Evolution of Recent U.S. Trade Policy,* Chicago: University of Chicago Press, 1984.

Crandall, Robert W. *The U.S. Steel Industry in Recurrent Crisis: Policy Options in a Competitive World.* Washington: Brookings Institution, 1981.

──────. "Import Quotas and the Automobile Industry: The Costs of Protectionism." *Brookings Review,* 2 (Summer 1984), 8–16.

Gray, H. Peter. "Domestic Efficiency, International Efficiency and Gains from Trade." *Weltwirtschaftliches Archiv,* vol. 21 (1985), 460–470.

──────. *Free Trade or Protection? A Pragamatic Analysis.* New York: St. Martin's Press, 1985.

Michalski, Wolfgang. "The Need for Positive Adjustment Policies in the 1980s." *Intereconomics,* vol. 18 (1983), 42–48.

Pearson, Charles, and Gerry Salembier. *Trade Employment and Adjustment.* Montreal: Institute for Research on Public Policy, 1983.)

Questions

1. The problem with conditional protection is that managers can receive deferred pay through stock options and equity owners receive deferred returns as the stock of the embattled corporation appreciates. How can labor share in the renewed prosperity of the industry?
2. The big problem with all interventionist economic policy is that the government may be too late and has little information on which to base good decisions. This is the strongest argument for free trade. Comment
3. What happens to Warren, Ohio, and Pittsburgh, Pennsylvania, if the steel industry folds? What happens to Detroit if the automobile industry collapses?
4. The need for some kind of TAA is greatest when imports are increasing quickly and when there is high domestic unemployment. Explain. But TAA should be positive, or else it gives displaced workers no incentive to seek alternative careers. Comment.
5. The International Trade Commission is simply a means of legitimizing protection. Comment.
6. Why bother about the free trade argument? Protect inefficient industries and avoid change. Comment.
7. According to Crandall, the VER on Japanese car exports caused Japanese cars to increase by almost $1,000 each in 1981–1982, and dealers were able

to charge premium prices in 1983, so the United States paid Japanese producers about \$2 billion per year in price enhancements. Crandall points out that a tariff would have been preferable to a VER. Why?

8. Because of the reduced severity of Japanese competition, automobile prices paid to U.S. makers increased by approximately \$800 in 1983, and this constituted simply higher profit for the industry. This higher markup was necessary if the industry was to regain its competitiveness because it needed to invest heavily in new machinery. Comment.

U.S. Agriculture:
The International Dimension

MARK DRABENSTOTT[1]

U.S. agriculture is passing through troubled times. While the general economy has enjoyed three years of strong expansion, the farm sector has had a much more turbulent passage. Financial problems of considerable magnitude are spread broadly across the sector—from increased farm liquidations, to restructured agribusinesses, to rising farm bank failures. Following the benevolent decade of the 1970s, U.S. agriculture finds itself adjusting to a harsh new market reality.

An important part of agriculture's current adjustment has resulted from U.S. integration into a world market for food and fiber over the past 15 years. That process has proved to be a two-edged sword. Throughout the 1970s, when market conditions were favorable to exports, U.S. agriculture enjoyed a decade of prosperity unparalleled in modern times. But in the 1980s, the United States has learned that declining exports can bring financial hardship and severe adjustments.

The international dimension is a key factor in U.S. agriculture's current financial stress. This article reviews the recent performance of U.S. farm exports, highlighting some causes of deterioration in the 1980s. It then outlines the dimensions of U.S. farm financial stress, considers the international dimension of current farm problems, and explores the critical role international developments will play in restoring farm economic health.

[1]Mark Drabenstott is a research officer and economist at the Federal Reserve Bank of Kansas City. This article is based on a speech before the Federal Reserve System Committee on International Economic Analysis held at the Federal Reserve Bank of Kansas City on October 18, 1985.

212

RECENT FARM EXPORT
PERFORMANCE

Farm exports were a dream come true in the 1970s. For decades the United States had suffered from chronic oversupply. That condition prompted the farm legislation of the 1930s, which tried to cut back on production and prop up prices. But in the early 1970s, many forces combined to spark a boom in farm exports that, in retrospect, created a halcyon decade for U.S. agriculture.

The export boom was dramatic. In 1970, the value of farm exports totaled $7 billion. That doubled in 1973, the year of the first big Soviet wheat sale. By 1980, the value of farm exports had increased to $41 billion. Export volume reached 162 million metric tons by 1980, compared with only 64 million in 1970. The rapid expansion was fueled mostly by strong economic growth abroad, readily available world credit, opening of trade with centrally planned economies, and a relatively weak U.S. dollar.

Third World countries became important buyers of U.S. farm products. Relatively rapid economic growth and a tide of developed country credit allowed many developing countries to move up the food ladder. For the decade of the 1970s, the real gross domestic product of all developing countries grew at an average annual rate of 5.2 percent, compared with only 3.0 percent in industrial countries. U.S. farmers supplied a large part of the growing world food trade. By the early 1980s, almost half of U.S. farm exports were destined for developing countries, compared with only 30 percent in 1970.

The export boom had profound effects on U.S. agriculture. The excess capacity problem was pronounced dead by many. A farmland boom was ignited, and with rapid inflation and regulated financial markets, many farmers discovered financial leverage. Marginal lands were brought into production, creating soil erosion problems in many parts of the country. Agribusinesses geared up for what was considered a never-ending growth market. Farm income was the highest it had been in the postwar period.

Producers of major crops grew dependent on export markets. For example, in 1984, U.S. farmers exported 55 percent of the wheat they produced, 25 percent of the corn, 32 percent of the soybeans, and 48 percent of the cotton. Thus, about one out of every three acres in this country goes to the export market.

Macroeconomists discovered the significant contribution agriculture could make to U.S. balance of payments. In the 1950s and 1960s, agriculture's net contribution to the current account was meager, usually less than a few billion dollars. But by 1981, the agricultural trade balance reached a peak of almost $27 billion.

The farm export boom ended in 1982. The boom had been waning for three or four years, propped up by large loans to Third World buyers. But in 1982, the value of farm exports declined, and the decline has not stopped since. Obviously, farm exports remain very important. But the decline has had profound implications, not the least of which is that agriculture now contributes to the current account less than half what it did in 1981.

Many forces combined to reduce U.S. agricultural exports in the 1980s. The global recession that began in 1981 left many Third World countries with financial problems that most have not overcome. A strong dollar has kept U.S. producers at a significant price disadvantage. Trade barriers remain a problem to entry into foreign markets. Export subsidies by other exporters still are a target for venting farmers' frustration. And export competition is much keener today than when the boom began.

Declining farm exports have had numerous negative effects on the farm sector. Net farm income peaked at $32 billion in 1979, and while the expensive Payment In Kind (PIK) program boosted 1984's result, real farm income has been low throughout the 1980s. Soft exports have been a primary cause. With slumping foreign demand, U.S. grain surpluses have grown larger and crop prices have moved lower. Agribusinesses have felt the effect of declining farm exports in both lower sales of farm equipment and reduced grain shipments. Grain companies, for example, are currently using only about 40 percent of peak export capacity.

The prolonged decline in farm exports is a major cause of agriculture's bleak outlook for 1986. Farm exports have weakened markedly in 1985. The value of U.S. agricultural exports is expected to total $32 billion, 15 percent below 1984 and more than a fourth less than the 1981 peak. World crop supplies remain large, competitors are anxious to market their stocks, and world demand is weak. As a result of the export decline, and due to a record U.S. harvest in 1985, U.S. grain stocks are rapidly approaching the large levels of 1982 that spawned the PIK program. Depressed crop prices will contribute significantly to an anticipated 30 percent reduction in 1985 net farm income. And the persistence of huge stocks and low prices will keep farm income low in 1986.

DIMENSIONS OF FINANCIAL STRESS

The decline in export markets is one major cause of the problems now facing U.S. agriculture. Deregulation of financial markets and a return to lower inflation are the other major causes. Not unlike the debt problem of less developed countries, U.S. agriculture is adjusting to new market realities with an extremely heavy debt burden accumulated when expectations were much brighter and real interest rates much lower.

U.S. agriculture suffers from a serious debt service problem. As a sector, agriculture still carries a low debt-asset ratio—about 21 percent. But the problem is one of distribution—too much debt in too few hands. And the relationship between debt and income has become a crushing one. In the last 15 years, net farm income has not changed a great deal, while farm debt has quadrupled. The result has been a debt-income ratio that suggests one dollar of farm income must now support nearly ten dollars of debt.

Farm financial stress is concentrated among the nation's heavily leveraged commercial farmers—farms with annual sales greater than $40,000. About 129,000 farms—20 percent of the 634,000 commercial farms—have a debt-asset ratio greater than 40 percent and a negative cash flow.[2] Together, these farms owe $46 billion to all farm lenders. If the farm economy does not improve in the next few years, many farmers in this category will have great difficulty servicing their debt.

The most serious debt service problems are found on farms with a negative cash flow and a debt-asset ratio greater than 70 percent. These farms number about 54,000—9 percent of all commercial farms. These farms likely are in danger of failing in the next year or two. They owe about $23 billion to all commercial lenders, or put in perspective, an amount equal to one-third of all U.S. commercial bank loans to Argentina, Brazil, and Mexico. Thus, we see a farm debt problem of significant dimensions. A substantial portion of farm assets must move from weak to stronger hands.

Financial stress has been exacerbated by the sharp decline in farmland values. Farm asset values have declined more in the 1980s than any time since the Great Depression. For the nation, farmland values peaked in 1982 and have declined 18 percent since then. Declines have been even steeper in many parts of the country. Land values in some areas have fallen more than 50 percent. In the Tenth Federal Reserve District, land values are nearly 45 percent below their 1981 peak. And the pace of asset value decline quickened over the last 18 months. District land values fell 22 percent between October 1984 and October 1985.

The decline in values has added to the financial strain of farmers who borrowed against rising collateral values in the 1970s. As land values have continued to decline, more and more borrowers find themselves unable to service existing obligations without restructuring their debts or selling their assets. Either is increasingly difficult in a declining market. For lenders, the deterioration in the credit quality of farm borrowers has led to higher loan losses and mounting numbers of past due and nonperforming loans.

Commercial banks have witnessed a substantial increase in their farm loan losses. Agricultural banks had much smaller loan losses than nonagricultural banks during the 1970s. But the tables have turned. Agricul-

---

[2]U.S. Department of Agriculture, *Financial Characteristics of U.S. Farms, January 1985*, Agriculture Information Bulletin No. 495.

tural bank loan losses are more than four times what they were in 1980. And the rate of failure among agricultural banks has risen sharply. In 1983, only 7 of 44 bank closings in the United States were agricultural banks. In 1984, that increased to 25 out of 79. And thus far in 1985, 48 out of 95 bank failures have been agricultural banks.

The cooperative Farm Credit System (FCS) is under even greater pressure since all its loans are agricultural. The system already has reported a loss of $426 million in the first nine months of 1985 on its $74 billion farm loan portfolio. And the system will almost certainly record its first annual loss in 1985. Surprisingly, the system's problems have only recently had any sharp impact on Wall Street. The yield spread on FCS bonds over Treasury securities widened noticeably only after the governor of the Farm Credit Administration in September announced a need for public assistance. Since that time, the spread has widened to around 80 to 100 basis points, well above the normal 15 to 30 basis points.

FARM SOLUTIONS: THE INTERNATIONAL DIMENSION

Solutions to agriculture's fundamental problems will not come easily. Because agriculture is no longer a domestic industry, farm policy cannot solve farm problems. Macroeconomic forces and international trade and economic forces also will be critical to restoring farm economic health.

International trade is a critical dimension of agriculture's current adjustment. Agriculture, along with the rest of the economy, has become more dependent on trade. And the opening of the U.S. economy to international trade carries with it two substantial implications for agriculture.

The first is that U.S. macroeconomic policy, through its international effects, has become much more important to agriculture. The combination of U.S. fiscal and monetary policy has direct effects on U.S. interest rates and the exchange value of the dollar. And U.S. interest rates influence world interest rate levels. In the 1980s, agriculture has learned that it is greatly affected when U.S. economic policies keep real interest rates high and thereby contribute to slower economic growth in trading partner developing countries.

The second implication for agriculture is the competitiveness that is brought by a more open economy. The world food market has become keenly competitive since the U.S. export boom began. Many countries—such as Argentina, Australia, Canada, and the European Community—now vie for market share along with the United States in the stagnant world food market.

U.S. agriculture, therefore, must be extremely price competitive, which requires trimming costs. For producers, this has meant a secular decline in farmland values, the major part of crop production costs. Cost reduction is exactly as international trade theory demands. When a country is exposed to a world market, input prices must move toward a common equilibrium across borders. For agribusinesses, greater competition has meant restructuring the industry to eliminate excess capacity. Thus, the past few years have witnessed the merger and acquisition of some hallmarks in the agribusiness world—International Harvester, Allis Chalmers, and Far-Mar-Co, for example.

A more open economy, then, is a critical cause of U.S. agriculture's current adjustment. U.S. agriculture cannot ignore international competitive pressures, nor should an agricultural policy be implemented that impairs the United States' competitive position in a global food market. Moreover, agriculture has a great stake in U.S. economic and international policies that foster economic growth abroad.

International factors can contribute to an improved farm economy in two fundamental ways. The first is obvious—a weaker dollar. A weaker dollar would be of considerable help in boosting farm exports. But a weaker dollar by itself is no panacea for U.S. farm exports.

Agriculture would also benefit greatly from lower federal budget deficits and the attendant lowering of real interest rates. Direct benefits would include reduced agricultural production costs and an early halt to declines in farm asset values. But the indirect benefits would be even greater. In addition to further possible declines in the U.S. dollar, lower interest rates would help lower interest rates worldwide. That would facilitate business investment abroad, especially in developing countries where capital formation is key to their economic vitality.

Stronger income growth in the Third World is the second international factor of critical importance to U.S. agriculture. While U.S. producers like to complain about subsidized production by other countries, the reality is that unless world food demand grows, the United States and other exporters will simply engage in a costly battle over market share. Growth in world food trade is a vital prerequisite for U.S. agriculture's return to economic and financial health. And the economic performance of middle-income and developing countries will be the linchpin to any expansion in trade. While agricultural development is crucial in many recipient countries, their own food production gains are unlikely to be great enough to meet the increases in food demand brought about by rising incomes.

Improved economic performance in these countries will depend on two developments. The first is continued strength in U.S. and western economies to allow Third World countries to generate foreign exchange. And the second is renewed emphasis on economic development assistance to those countries. It is essential that such assistance be targeted to countries where funds could materially improve economic performance and that assistance be long term in character.

CONCLUSIONS

The international dimension has been a fundamental force in U.S. agriculture for the past 15 years. In the 1970s, a farm export boom brought prosperity, encouraged investment, and nurtured lofty expectations. But in the 1980s, declining world trade and reduced U.S. farm exports ushered in great financial stress for U.S. agriculture. Despite the vagaries of competing in a world food market, the painful lessons of recent years suggest that increasing farm exports will be a key part of restoring farm prosperity. Until that growth returns, agriculture's passage through the current period of adjustment promises to remain turbulent. [Table 9-A shows exports for fiscal 1985.]

Table 9-A
U.S. AGRICULTURAL EXPORTS, FISCAL YEAR 1985

Commodity	Value (millions of dollars)
Wheat and products	4,526
Feed grains and products	6,867
Soybeans	3,876
Cotton seed and products	14
Flaxseed (linseed) products	5
Peanuts and peanut oil	216
Rice	677
Cotton, ex linters	1,945
Tobacco	1,587
Fruits	1,200
Vegetables	946
Dairy products	413
Meat and products	906
Hides and skins	1,324
Poultry products	257
Lard and tallow	560
Other	5,306
Total exports (agricultural)	31,187
Total cash receipts from farm marketings	142,000–144,000
Exports as a percent of cash receipts	22%

Source: Data from U.S. Department of Agriculture.

10

Trade Problems of Developing Countries

The theory of international trade and the analysis of commercial policy given in the preceding chapters have emphasized the economics of industrialized, developed nations in which a large industrial sector makes (or used to make) full employment a feasible macroeconomic policy. Developing countries have substantially different economic characteristics and goals. They have large surplus populations that are illiterate and exist either in a traditional, rural sector of near-subsistence incomes or as an underclass in urban ghettos.[1] Most developing countries place the goal of economic development far ahead of personal freedoms, especially the freedom to enjoy the efficiencies of the international market system. In other words, governments in developing countries are prepared to place stringent restrictions and controls on the use of foreign exchange (dollars).

Traditionally, developing countries have been suppliers of primary commodities (minerals and some tropical agricultural products) to the industrialized world. Now some are supplying manufactured goods of varying degrees of quality and sophistication.

The term *developing countries* covers a wide range of economic perfor-

---

[1]The difference between the surplus population in the industrialized countries (discussed in Chapter 9) and the surplus population in developing countries is one of degree. In many developing countries, as much as half the population is either unemployed or underemployed. These unwanted and underutilized people are to a large extent the result of huge rates of population growth caused by rapid declines in death rates and barely reduced birth rates following the introduction of public health measures since World War II. It is this huge stock of excess population in developing countries that will cause the problems considered earlier.

219

mance. It includes, paradoxically, the oil-rich economies with very high per capita income. It includes countries such as Tanzania (termed "least developed" by the United Nations), which has few resources and still less industry. Between these extremes are countries that are making economic progress and others that locked into a world in which little change and growth is taking place.

Since 1970, six countries have emerged as so-called newly industrializing countries (NICs), and these countries have come close to eliminating their surplus population, though they have not yet reached the automaticity of economic growth that characterizes rich countries. The NICs (which include two noncountries, Hong Kong and Taiwan, and one city-state, Singapore, as well as Korea, Brazil, and Mexico) have developed and have been able to export manufactured goods of high quality to the industrialized world. Recently Brazil and Mexico have retrogressed significantly because of the problems associated with servicing their huge external debt (see Chapter 18). Other nations have been making good progress toward development and are exporting manufactured goods in substantial quantities. These countries might be called "near-NICs," and they will shortly be in a position to achieve the high economic growth rates that have characterized the true NICs in recent years.

This broad and heterogeneous group of countries (sometimes referred to as the "Third World" or the "South") are important in their own right, and they are important in international trade. These countries are vital to the prosperity of the industrialized world as suppliers of primary products such as bauxite, copper, and other minerals as well as providing markets for advanced, technologically intensive goods. Some countries in the developing world are also important as buyers of temperate agricultural products such as wheat. Finally, they are good markets for licensing technology developed in the North. Their prosperity and progress contribute to the political stability and smooth functioning of the international economy.

One general characteristic of developing countries is that their need for foreign exchange to buy goods from the developed world usually exceeds the amount they can earn by exporting to these countries. (For a while the oil-rich countries were exceptions to this rule, but even important oil producers such as Indonesia, Nigeria, and Venezuela as well as Mexico are now drastically short of foreign exchange.) For this reason, the developing South seeks to enlarge the range of goods that it exports to the industrialized North. It seeks to provide manufactured goods as well as primary products. But this change in exporting strategy has changed the relationship of North-South international trade from one in which the two blocs trade what were essentially noncompetitive imports of all three kinds to one in which the developing countries export manufactures to the North. Now the North is faced with the problem of adjustment to accommodate these new sources of supply (mainly, but not exclusively, the NICs), and resistance to such change has grown in the North quite recently. This unwillingness of the North to accommodate free entry of manufactures from the South has caused economic strains to exist between the two blocs. The South feels that the industrialized world should be able to absorb its exports freely without erecting barriers to such trade. This state of affairs would conform to the free trade rhetoric practiced by so many representative of the industrialized world, particularly when they discuss the trading policies of developing countries. But the North cannot escape its own internal political pressures. At present, such pressures to restrict imports and to keep out goods from developing countries are strong. The problem is aggravated by the ability of multinational corporations to transfer technology to the developing world. This transferred technology allows the NICs and the near-NICs and some sleeping giants such as China to supply quality manufactured products to the North. MNCs can unite the technology of the industrialized world with the cheap and plentiful (but low-skilled) labor of the developing countries. In countries in which such labor can easily be trained for production-level tasks, the potential for exports from the developing bloc is enormous. Northern economies, particularly the labor force in the manufacturing sector, face substantial adjustment as they have to reallocate factors of production from declining labor-intensive industries to expanding, high-technology industries if the open trading system is not to be discarded.

COMPARATIVE ADVANTAGE OF DEVELOPING NATIONS

The representative developing country is endowed with large amounts of labor per unit of land and physical capital. The labor available is frequently unskilled in terms of the needs of a modern industrial sector because of ineffective educational systems. Much of this potentially surplus labor is employed, often with a very low marginal product, in a subsistence sector of traditional agriculture. Thus in the absence of natural resources, developing nations will have a comparative advantage in the production of goods that use low-skilled labor very intensively. Such labor will be cheap. Unfortunately, the products of such a factor mix are usually crude and unacceptable to more sophisticated nations, and therefore such a country (such as Tanzania) has very little foreign exchange available with which to purchase imports of machinery, food, and pharmaceuticals.

Some developing nations do have important deposits of natural resources, or their climate has allowed them to develop an expertise in the production of a certain (and important) tropical agricultural crop. Copper deposits in Chile and Zaire, tin in Bolivia, cocoa beans in Ghana, and coffee in Brazil are obvious examples. Some developing countries have oil deposits that have been bountiful sources of foreign exchange from 1974 until recently. Even so, countries that do not export manufactured goods, unless they have very rich deposits of a very expensive mineral, are limited in the amount of foreign exchange they can obtain. Usually, exports of this kind are very sensitive to the prosperity of the industrialized world because they are income-elastic and price-inelastic. In Northern recessions, the availability of foreign exchange is severely curtailed.

Foreign exchange scarcity, relative to the demand for it, is typical of most developing nations. The main reason for this scarcity is the need for modern (high-technology) machinery, produced only in the industrialized world, for the major goal of economic development. To develop a manufacturing sector, developing countries need to import machinery that cannot be made at home because of the lack of the requisite technology (and human capital). Sometimes the technology is not available because it is proprietary in Northern countries, but usually the equipment to make the sophisticated machinery is not available in the developing country or the production unit enjoys large economies of scale so that small-volume production is impossible. In addition, developing countries frequently rely on the industrialized world for supplies of agricultural products and drugs. The important thing to notice here is that their agriculture is as backward as their manufacturing sector because of the lack of technological know-how. Recently, the "green revolution" has enabled many developing countries to make tremendous strides in agricultural productivity, and reliance on the wheat-producing countries of the world has declined. This urgent need for foreign exchange for "priority purposes" is the basic cause of restricted use of foreign exchange in most developing countries. People are not allowed to use their earnings to acquire foreign-made consumer goods or for tourism. Frequently, it is difficult for students to get an allowance of foreign exchange for study abroad, despite the urgent need for trained people in developing countries.[2]

Another reason for imposing controls on the availability of foreign exchange is the existence of a rich aristocracy, which could be tempted to convert its local currency for (scarce) foreign exchange for frivolous tourism or to transfer its wealth to a country with greater political stability.

The final claim on foreign exchange is the currently very important question of servicing foreign debt. To supplement the foreign exchange made available by exports, many developing countries borrow foreign exchange in order to be able to increase their rate of investment (capital

---

[2]One of the problems of students' being trained abroad is that once they have acquired the foreign qualifications, they are often unwilling to return home to work in less affluent conditions.

formation). Such acquisitions are usually confined to export industries or the manufacturing sector. Usually, the borrowing has taken place in the form of buying bonds issued in a developed country, and as the bonds mature, their face value must be repaid in addition to the interest on the outstanding indebtedness. *Debt service* is the name given to the amount of foreign exchange needed to meet the scheduled interest payments and the scheduled paying off of existing debt. Because the costs of failing to service debt properly are severe, countries allocate priority to this use of foreign exchange once essential imports have been bought. Another related drain on foreign exchange earnings is the need for MNCs that have established production units in the country to be allowed to send reasonable profits and royalty payments to the parent company. These investments substitute for bond indebtedness in the sense that they bring up-to-date machinery and technology to the country and, like bond indebtedness, impose a foreign exchange cost.

On occasion, a country will be unable to service its debt. Brazil, Mexico, and other Latin American countries have had to have their debt payments rescheduled (see Chapter 18) and to meet the renegotiated conditions have had to cut drastically their rate of growth and their volume of imports. The disruption to a developing economy is tremendous (see the supplement following Chapter 18), and the cost in terms of human misery is also tremendous.

One of the major problems facing a representative developing country is that foreign exchange earnings from basic exports tend to have demand schedules that are price-inelastic and very sensitive to recessions in the North. The price inelasticity of demand for the primary export suggests that there is a maximum volume of foreign exchange that can be earned. This harsh reality forces developing countries to choose between trying to economize on the need for imports by producing substitute goods at home and trying to develop price-elastic exports of manufactured goods to supplement earnings from basic commodities. The economizing and inward-looking approach was very popular in Latin America and involves tariff protection for infant industries. The policy that emphasizes the export of manufactured goods is known as "export-led growth" and has been very successful for the four Asian NICs (the "Four Little Dragons"). For the success of this policy, the exchange rate has to be set at a realistic level, and foreign competition must be allowed to work its efficiency-generating effect. The market, not planners, knows best which industry has a comparative advantage and growth potential. In Latin America, the tendency was for the developing country's economy to be sheltered from foreign competition, and this sheltering did not promote the efficiency of the industries being protected. It also distorted relative prices in the country, with the result that foreign exchange was not valued properly and export industries were handicapped.

The availability of foreign exchange when a country has to rely on

Figure 10-1
AVAILABILITY OF FOR-
EIGN EXCHANGE

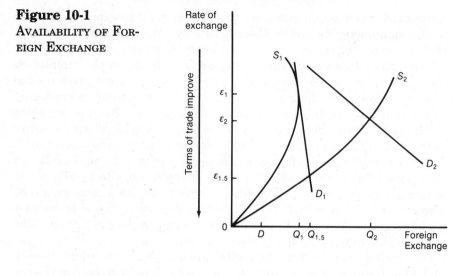

primary-product exports and when it has manufactured exports can be shown as in Figure 10-1. The terms of trade, measured vertically, are represented by the exchange rate, ϵ (the number of units of domestic currency needed to buy one unit of foreign exchange). An increase in ϵ implies a depreciation of the national currency and a deterioration of the terms of trade. The quantity of foreign exchange is measured horizontally. The supply of foreign exchange shows the amount that will be earned according to the market price of the export. The curve S_1 shows the country's dilemma when it relies exclusively on a basic export with price-inelastic demand: There is a maximum amount of foreign exchange that can be acquired when foreign elasticity is equal to 1: Q_1. By rationing the uses to which foreign exchange can be put, the government can foster a demand curve, D_1. Imports plus debt service are severely limited (to Q_1). If debt service amounts to D, imports are restricted to DQ_1. Only noncompetitive imports will be allowed. If a recession in the industrialized countries shifts the curve S_1 to the left and even less foreign exchange is available from imports, the country may be forced to meet its needs by additional borrowing or, in extreme circumstances, by defaulting on its debt service. If noncompetitive imports of machinery play an integral part in the investment pattern in the developing country, the limit on the amount of such imports may severely damage the developmental process.[3]

Contrast this somber position with the opportunities available to a developing country that has the ability to sell price-elastic manufactured

[3]Ronald I. McKinnon, "Foreign Exchange Constraints in Economic Development and Efficient Aid Allocation," *Economic Journal,* 74 (June 1964), 388–409.

goods in Northern markets. The supply curve of foreign exchange now becomes flatter and does not bend back on itself. There is no maximum amount of foreign exchange that can be earned on S_2, but to earn more requires a deterioration in the terms of trade (S_2 slopes upward). In comparison with the original, highly constrained demand curve for foreign exchange, the terms of trade have improved, to $\epsilon_{1.5}$, and the value of imports has increased to $Q_{1.5}$. At the intersection of S_2 and D_1, the value of an additional import may exceed the cost of supplying the export needed to acquire it, and the severity of the controls can be eased to D_2. Under these conditions, the net barter terms of trade have deteriorated to ϵ_2 but the value of imports has increased to Q_2.

Two things should be noted. First, it is essential that the developing country be able to manufacture goods of a quality (and reliability) that will appeal to users in the industrialized countries. This ability will affect the position of S_2. Second, any release of the level of constraint put on the availability of foreign exchange is likely to contribute to the efficiency of the export industries in particular since these industries will become more efficient in design and quality as they sell to foreigners and reap the profits for reinvestment. In addition, the reduced level of constraint on the availability of foreign exchange will make the home economy more efficient in its domestic industries because the level of government regulation and distortion will be reduced. (This feature is the key determinant of the success of export-led growth, which has been much closer to Adam Smith's idea of pure laissez-faire than to a controlled or planned economy.)

The important feature of export-led growth is the degree to which the developing country can supply goods that prove acceptable to customers in industrialized countries. Good design and high quality are important. In this context, *quality* must imply reliability as well as finish. Quality control is important. Workers must be able to produce goods that meet the specifications of their foreign customers, who have different cultural values. In this the MNC may prove to be an important ally of the developing economy. The greater the amount of competition among the economies seeking to achieve export-led growth, the steeper will be S_2 in Figure 10-1.

As long as international trade between the North and the South consisted predominantly of an exchange of noncompetitive goods, the gains from trade were enormous for both sides. The South made huge gains from trade as it acquired machinery and technology that it could not produce itself in exchange for providing goods that were in plentiful supply. The industrialized countries required the basic commodities for continued economic growth, and many of the tropical products were highly valued—coffee, tea, bananas, and cacao (which is the basis of chocolate). Had the developed countries had to rely on their own supply of mineral deposits, they would have been using very low grade deposits at great expense.

The rapid growth of manufactured exports by the NICs has benefited consumers in the developed world but has inflicted serious costs on workers in the labor-intensive import substitute industries. These workers have been displaced. The per-unit gain from imports was reduced for developed countries, but for nations in the forefront of the supply of manufactured goods of high quality, rapid growth was possible. These nations were able to reinvest the profits in industries known to be efficient and successful and to train workers from traditional sectors so that something approaching full employment has been reached in the four Asian NICs.

THE NEWLY INDUSTRIALIZING COUNTRIES

The successes of the four Asian NICs and of Brazil and Mexico until their recent debt-service crises are a clear example of the benefits that derive from being able to ease the constraint on the use of foreign exchange. The NICs were able to generate large increases in the value of manufactured exports and in this way allow imported goods to be used wherever they were likely to prove beneficial.

Table 10-1 shows the ratio of manufactured imports from the NICs to the gross national product of the receiving developed countries. Because of the rampant inflation that took place during the 1970s, money values are relatively meaningless. However, increases in the ratio of imports to GNP shows how imports from the NICs have grown because both the numerator and the denominator are more or less equally affected by inflation. As GNP grew in the importing country, imports from the NICs had to grow at an even faster rate if the ratio were to increase. The table provides data for ten countries and includes four near-NICs or would-be NICs in addition to the six countries already identified as NICs. The rate of growth of imports into the United States has exceeded that into any other country, suggesting that the adjustment problem will have been greatest in the United States.

Table 10-2 shows the rate of growth of GNP per capita and of GNP for a cross section of developing countries. The success of Korea, Singapore, and Taiwan is obvious. Each has successfully pursued the strategy of export-led growth, and each has a culture that lends itself to industrialization. Brazil and Mexico have done well until quite recently, and their recent problems do not show in the data. These two countries have the disadvantage of high population growth rates and a huge excess supply of labor. The Ivory Coast was very successful in the 1960s but seems to have lost its impetus. The original success of the Ivory Coast could have

Table 10-1
IMPORTS OF MANUFACTURERS FROM THIRD WORLD EXPORTERS, 1968–1982
(IN PERCENT OF GNP IN THE IMPORTING COUNTRY)

	Total OECD	Canada	France	Japan	Sweden	United Kingdom	United States	West Germany
1968	0.200	0.189	0.040	0.125	0.224	0.300	0.179	0.171
1970	0.217 (1969)	0.209	0.057	0.271	0.269	0.372	0.265	0.264
1972	0.243 (1971)	0.349	0.094	0.178	0.366	0.477	0.379	0.345
1974	0.473	0.431	0.155	0.468	0.516	0.659	0.575	0.450
1976	0.546	0.561	0.198	0.438	0.524	0.708	0.645	0.646
1978	0.623	0.562	0.231	0.359	0.507	0.744	0.882	0.636
1980	0.694	0.614	0.342	0.434	0.648	0.723	0.954	0.804
1982	0.650	0.661	0.459	0.456	0.713	0.933	1.128	0.893

Note: The exporters are Brazil, Hong Kong, India, Korea, Malaysia, Mexico, Philippines, Singapore, Taiwan, and Yugoslavia.

Sources: Organization for Economic Cooperation and Development and International Monetary Fund.

Table 10-2

RATES OF GROWTH OF PER CAPITA GNP,
1960–1981 (PERCENT PER ANNUM REAL GROWTH)

Country	Rate	Country	Rate
Argentina	1.9	Korea (South)*	6.9
Brazil*	5.1	Malaysia	4.3
El Salvador	1.5	Mexico*†	3.8
Hong Kong*	6.9	Nicaragua	0.6
Israel	3.8	Philippines	2.8
Ivory Coast	2.3	Singapore*	7.4
Jamaica	0.8	Taiwan*‡	6.6
Kenya	2.9	Yugoslavia*	5.0

* NIC.

† Mexico's rate of economic growth is much higher than the relatively low number given here, which is attributable in part to Mexico's relatively high rate of population growth (3.3 percent per year, 1960–1970, and 3.0 percent, 1970–1982) compared with Korea (2.6 and 1.7), Singapore (2.3 and 1.5), and Brazil (2.8 and 2.4). To get growth rates of GNP, simply add the rate of population gowth to the rate of growth of per capita GNP.

‡ 1960–1978, when the People's Republic was admitted to the United Nations and Taiwan was forced to withdraw.

Source: World Bank.

been attributed to a rationality of the economic system (a heavy reliance on the market system), and it enjoyed the special benefits accorded ex-colonies of member nations of the European Economic Community (see Chapter 11).

Release of the constraint of a severe shortage of foreign exchange by aggressive exporting strategies and reliance on the system of markets to identify industries in which the NIC has a comparative advantage have proved valuable aids to economic development, although one should never disparage the supreme importance of internal activities and policies. However, export-led growth faces a severe problem if it is to be a pattern for development of the next wave of developing countries seeking to reach a point at which they can gainfully employ the total work force. This wave would include the Mediterranean countries of Greece, Portugal, Spain, Tunisia, and Turkey as well as such Asian countries as Indonesia, Malaysia, and the Philippines. But if these countries are to grow through a surge of exports, the industrialized nations must buy more and more goods embodying low-skilled and production-level labor intensively. This process will impose serious costs of adjustment on the industrialized world as countries have increasing difficulty in absorbing the displaced workers. As was noted earlier, this pressure is more likely to cause barriers to be imposed against imports than a passive acceptance of the social costs of adjustment. To keep their volume of exports, the NICs will be keeping their prices low and trying to prevent the entry of exports of the second-wave countries from establishing themselves in industrialized countries. As Figure 10-1 shows, the principle of export-led growth implies that the supply schedule of foreign exchange (foreign demand for the countries' exports) is price-elastic so that there is no real limit to exports of manufactures. Implicitly, the country can choose the combination of foreign exchange and terms of trade that best fits its own particular needs. If the demand of the industrialized bloc becomes price-inelastic at some given quantity of imports (developing countries' exports), fierce competition will take place among members of the bloc. This competition will force the supply schedule of foreign exchange for each country upward and will worsen the terms of trade for the group of developing countries and, presumably, for each individual country.

For developing countries, it is important that the industrialized world permit ever increasing amounts of world trade. The South can be expected to spend all it earns, so the reason for Northern reluctance must be the costs of adjustment—the problem of absorbing displaced, low-skilled workers. The secret of a healthy climate for economic development is the ability to continue the growth of the volume of international trade between the developing countries and the industrialized nations. This growth will be concentrated in price-elastic manufactures (in the absence of impediments to those imports). The developing world formed a political wing under the aegis of the United Nations—the U.N. Conference on Trade and Development (UNCTAD)—which provides a platform for the views of the developing countries. The organization has a research arm and periodically draws together spokespeople from both the North and the South. This is the major forum for North-South dialogue, where the problems of Northern contributions to and handicaps of Southern economic development are discussed.

UNCTAD: NORTHERN COMMERCIAL POLICY AND SOUTHERN HOPES

According to the theory of international trade, both parties gain from such trade, so the resistance by industrialized countries against freedom to export from the South is, at first blush, illogical. The need of the North for a prosperous developing South is self-evident. The apparent contradiction between controls over imports and the need and rhetoric for development in the South confuses and irritates the representatives of the developing world at UNCTAD conferences when spokespeople for the two blocs confront each other.

The major proposal for improving the climate for economic development in the international system was developed in the UNCTAD secretariat and ratified in the second UNCTAD conference in New Delhi in 1968. These proposals came to be known as the "new international economic order." Many of the proposals concerned the establishment of funds to stabilize the cyclical variation in the world prices of basic commodities such as rubber and sugar. There was also a proposal for providing the developing nations with preferential access to the markets for manufactures in the industrialized nations. This was the Generalized System of Preferences (GSP). It is the only major step taken by the Northern bloc to promote North-South trade with a view to helping the developing nations increase their exports of manufactured goods and ease their foreign exchange constraints.

The GSP gives developing countries a lower tariff rate in Northern markets than is levied on imports from other developed countries. The rationale for this policy was that the poorer nations should be given every chance to develop economically. Unfortunately, the developed nations inaugurated the policy with numerous restrictions, including the total exclusion of goods in which the developing countries might reasonably have been expected to have a major comparative cost advantage (and therefore potential for a large increase in exports). The GSP was defined by industrial nations in terms of *industrial goods,* and this was defined to exclude all goods processed from agricultural or fishery products. This measure excluded many potentially important exports, because a reduction in the tariff rates levied on these goods could have had quite an important effect on the effective rate of protection. All the developed nations excluded footwear, apparel, textiles, leather-based products, and petroleum-based products from the GSP. The net result of these exclusions is that only 12 percent of the 1970 value of exports to the North are in fact given preferential treatment.[4]

Of all the goods that have been subjected to controls by the North, apparel is the prime example. In 1962, the Kennedy administration took the lead in arranging a long-term agreement covering imports of cotton textiles and apparel. This arrangement was designed to limit the quantity of imports in order to slow down the rate of erosion of domestic production. This was expanded to cover synthetic fibers as well as cotton in the Multifibre Arrangement of 1974. In its original version, the MFA set quotas on imports from individual countries as well as quotas on individual products. In principle, the quotas would be increased each year so that the MFA could be seen as a system of controlled reliance on comparative advantage, an elaborate system of phaseout protection for a senile industry. In practice, the growth of imports from major developing suppliers has been severely restricted through bilateral agreements. These bilateral agreements are frequently unilateral decisions; when the importing country cannot negotiate an agreement, it imposes a quota unilater-

---

[4]Complete data are given in Peter J. Ginman and Tracy Murray, "The Generalized System of Preferences: A Review and Appraisal," in *The New International Order: Confrontation or Cooperation between North and South,* ed., K. P. Sauvant and H. Hasenpflug (Boulder, Colo.: Westview Press, 1977).

ally. (Such quotas have often proved useless if some suppliers are not limited because goods can be channeled through the noncontrolled country or subsidiaries of MNCs can be established there.) When the renegotiation of the MFA comes due every five years or so, there is often talk of limiting the growth of imports to the growth of the market in the importing country and in this way freezing the market *share* accorded to the developing world. This would rigidify the MFA far beyond what can be justified and would allow actual expansion of the (severely disadvantaged) domestic industry. An excellent analysis of the MFA has suggested that the phaseout be structured into the agreement,[5] but this prescription tends to be easily adopted but difficult to enforce when the ultimate liberalization of imports takes hold.

The industrialized world has formally closed off free imports of the good or product group in which the developing world can hope to achieve its major export gains. Other labor-intensive goods have been excluded from the GSP and subjected to quotas: footwear, steel imports, and goods made from local tropical products. These actions sit uncomfortably with the rhetoric of Northern spokespersons on the virtues of free trade— particularly when the developing countries themselves are being urged to open their markets to goods in which the industrial bloc has a comparative advantage.

If the adjustment to free North-South trade can be effected without chronic unemployment of low-skilled workers in the North and temporarily severe dislocations caused by the speed of adjustment, free trade is obviously in the best interest of the industrialized countries as well as of the third world. Certainly consumers would benefit substantially.

It is arguable that the root of the problem lies in the failure of the industrialized world to pay serious attention to the means of promoting adjustment. Not only would such analysis allow the benefits from international trade to be reaped more quickly and with less cost, but emphasis of the key role of adjustment would also make the North-South dialogue more constructive. If Northern spokespersons were to stop giving lip service to the desirability of an open trading system (while condoning the placement of limits on imports of labor-intensive products), there would be a greater understanding of the Northern situation by Southern spokespersons. Just as Northern rhetoric relies on polished oratory and abstract economic analysis, so do Southern speeches and attitudes assume too much (though some of the blame for this can be laid on the shoulders of the North). Southern spokespersons seem to see Northern governments as fully empowered to do what the governments see as being morally appropriate. The South could be interpreted as viewing the North as a monolith motivated by greed and capable of governmental cooperation in its search for ways to keep the South from achieving economic

[5]Gerard Curzon et al., *MFA Forever?* (London: Trade Policy Research Centre, 1981).

development.[6] This shows a lamentable ignorance of the constraints that democratic governments endure in terms of their responsibilities to the electorate if the incumbent politicians wish to stay in power (which they may be expected to want). One Southern spokesperson, commenting on the lack of accomplishment at the Belgrade conference, complained that the "developed countries have shown a lack of political will, inflexibility, and a protection of selfish interests."

Until the oil crisis of 1973, the attitude of the Northern bloc toward economic development in the South was much more benign. In the 1970s, the developed countries were concerned primarily with keeping their own inflation in bounds and adjusting to the new, much higher price of oil. The global terms of trade had shifted against oil-importing nations, and voters in the developed North were too concerned with their own problems to take steps that would increase the amount of adjustment required in order to facilitate economic development by the developing countries that had no oil. Now that the price of oil is trending downward again in response to the world glut, it may be that the Northern countries will be able to take further development-promoting measures to help the South. This is why it is important that the North-South dialogue remain open.

The problem of severe adjustment costs in the North still remains. It is important that politicians in the North recognize that measures that facilitate adjustment will benefit not only their own economies but also the aspirations of the developing world.

One of the major difficulties that faces Northern policymakers is that they have been educated to think about extreme positions. Either they obey political pressures, which conceive of protection as being offered to a threatened industry forever, or they perceive some long-run efficient state in the global economy without impediments to international trade. The political pressures are immediate and national, the long-run equilibrium is cast in a global context, and the share of benefits accruing to any particular nation is not known. Much more thinking is needed about reconciling the two concerns so that Northern countries can more easily accept the needed adjustment and Southern nations may continue to strive for economic development.

FOREIGN AID

Foreign aid is essentially the provision of money (or goods) to the governments of developing countries in order to help in the process of economic development. Aid can be thought of as a gift or as a loan with no debt service; technically, it is referred to as a "unilateral transfer."

---

[6]This interpretation is refuted by the intricacies and disputes involved in North-South trade reported carefully in William R. Cline, ed., *Trade Policy in the 1980s* (Washington, D.C.: Institute for International Economics, 1983).

The purpose of aid is simultaneously to allow recipients to ease their foreign exchange constraints and to add to their rate of capital accumulation. The most successful case of foreign aid on record is the Marshall Plan, whereby the United States made huge contributions to the economic recovery of European nations following World War II. Aid payments to the developing world have had less spectacular results because the conditions in these countries are quite different from those prevailing in Europe in the late 1940s. Europe had the skilled work force needed for fast growth as well as the infrastructure and institutions; what was needed was additional funds for capital accumulation and dollars with which to buy (temporarily) noncompetitive goods from the United States. In contrast, developing countries have to undergo a social as well as an economic transformation in the course of development, and aid, while useful, is not supplying the only missing ingredient.

Aid is never politically popular in the rich countries. Conservatives argue that money received as a gift is often not used efficiently (especially if it is to be spent by governments) and that nations would be much less prone to wasting dollars if the funds were earned by corporations through exports (with a positive opportunity cost). They argue for "trade, not aid" and for free entry for Southern goods into Northern markets. In contrast, liberals have no problem with the transfer of resources from the rich to the deserving poor countries, but they fear that aid will entrench the power of right-wing dictators. Liberals would tend to restrict aid to democratic, perhaps even socialist, regimes in developing nations. (There is an almost exact analogy within the United States: Liberal members of Congress do not want federal grants to be made freely to southern states, in which they fear discrimination still exists, and they seek to ensure that any such transfers will be tied to discrimination-reducing activities.) Finally, there is always the problem of seeming to put the welfare of the foreign poor ahead of that of the domestic poor.

In practice, aid is seldom given in a pure form. Donors require that it be spent on goods produced in the donor's country (so-called tied aid), or aid is given in the form of surplus food. Frequently, aid is given in the form of defense materiel. There are many cases on record of aid being misappropriated or misused by dishonest or ineffectual governments. Fortunately, one institution has contributed to the transfer of resources from the North to the South on subsidized terms. This is the World Bank, originally developed at the Bretton Woods Conference as the International Bank for Reconstruction and Development (IBRD; see Chapter 17). The World Bank makes loans for projects that meet its own experts' criteria for a positive contribution to economic development. The bank finances only the foreign exchange component of major products and has been an important source of foreign exchange and expert advice for developing countries since World War II.

Currently, the World Bank comprises the original IBRD, the International Development Association (IDA), and the International Finance

Corporation (IFC). IBRD floats bond issues in the markets of developed countries and uses the proceeds to finance development projects in the Third World. It is a conservatively run business, and it makes a profit. Its main contributions are the transfer of funds and the expertise it provides. Recipients of these funds are countries that have made some progress along the road to economic development and are creditworthy. IDA, the concessional finance affiliate, extends credit to the poorest and least developed countries of the world at less than market rates of interest (for fifty years at 0 percent interest) and is, in effect, a channel for pure aid. The projects financed are subjected to equally strict appraisal and supervision as those funded by IBRD. IFC deals with the private sector and can take an equity position in ventures.

Given the successful record of the World Bank, it might prove to be a very useful pipeline for increases in aid to be made to the developing world. Certainly, its value as a source of foreign exchange and expertise would prove useful to individual countries. If aid were to be used as a substitute for opening up the markets of the North because of the excessive costs of adjustment likely to be incurred, this aid could be channeled through the World Bank.[7]

SUMMARY

Members of the Third World face a different set of problems from those faced in the industrialized nations, and international trade theory has been developed primarily in terms of industrialized nations. The argument for free trade and freedom of capital mobility are less dominant in countries in which long-term concern with economic development (including both growth and structural and cultural adaptation) is the foremost consideration.

The developing countries find themselves in an inconsistent position. They want (and need) the privilege of imposing impediments in the way of nonessential imports from the industrialized countries at the same time that they need to urge the North to allow their exports to enter into Northern markets freely. They even seek, and have been granted for some goods, preferential access into Northern markets. In general terms, the industrialized nations have agreed that developing countries

---

[7]It was asserted that the North benefits substantially from political stability in the Third World. In a speech before the Council on Foreign Relations in New York on September 23, 1982, the president of the World Bank made this point in the following way: ". . . . The very rapid rise in military spending has crowded out development assistance programs such as IDA. And is it unreasonable to assert that an increase of a few hundred million dollars in U.S. contributions to IDA would do more for international security than a similar amount added to the U.S. military budget, which already runs into the hundreds of *billions* of dollars?"

cannot be treated as equals and tolerate the existence of impediments to imports. But this tolerance does not stop Northern spokespersons from speaking in glowing terms of the benefits of free trade in forcing economic rationality on the developing country.

The world has seen spectacular successes in the past quarter of a century. Hong Kong, Korea, Taiwan, and Singapore have all developed to the point that they are effectively fully employed. Brazil and Mexico also made great achievements prior to the collapse of the Mexican peso and the debt crisis. While the collapse of the Mexican peso was undoubtedly due to extremely bad economic policies under President Lopez Portillo, the world financial crisis was as much due to bad economic policies in the North as to Southern mistakes.

The development of UNCTAD as a political forum for confrontation between the bloc of developing countries and the North and the creation of a special research organization to address the problems of North-South economic relations have contributed to the development process by instituting the GSP. Unfortunately, the developing countries' initiatives were coming into focus at exactly the time that the North experienced the very adverse shock of a quadrupling of energy prices. Concerned with adjustment to that crisis and domestic inflation, the industrialized economies were unable to give appropriate attention to the welfare of the Third World. Further, it could be argued that it was the inability of interventionist policies to solve the problems of the oil crisis and inflation that led to the election of conservative regimes in France, Germany, the United Kingdom, and the United States. These governments favored heavy reliance on the market system and were philosophically opposed to a constructive role for Northern governments in the development process. The result of this chain of events has been a strained North-South dialogue in recent years.

The successes have been achieved largely by export-led growth. This policy imposes severe strains of adjustment on the industrialized countries, and these strains have recently begun to give rise to vociferous and widespread protectionist sentiment. Protection widely applied would throttle the success of export-led growth for succeeding generations of developing countries. The basic problem facing the developing world today is the unpopularity of economic aid, even when that aid is distributed through such a demanding channel as the World Bank, and the widespread protectionist sentiment. The World Bank has suffered because the Reagan administration, caught in a financial bind, is unwilling to contribute more capital funds and to subscribe in greater amounts to the IDA. Protectionism has become a strong political force because the developed countries are finding adjustment to ever increasing amounts of labor-intensive imports a very costly proposition. This problem testifies to the failure of policymakers to develop a coherent policy toward "adjustment facilitation."

Bibliography

Baldwin, R. E., and T. Murray. "MFN Tariff Reductions and LDC Benefits under the GSP." *Economic Journal,* 87 (1977), 30–46.

J. Bhagwati. "Rethinking Global Negotiations." In *Power, Passions, and Purpose,* ed. J. Bhagwati and J. G. Ruggie, pp. 21–32. Cambridge, Mass.: M.I.T. Press, 1984.

Curzon, Gerard, et al. *MFA Forever?* London: World Policy Trade Centre, 1981.

Friedman, Milton. "Foreign Economic Aid: Means and Objectives." *Yale Review,* 47 (1958), 500–516.

Gray, H. Peter. "North-South Trade: An Impasse in Policy Formulation." *European Journal of Political Economy,* 1 (1985), 325–341.

Kreinen, M. E., and J. M. Finger. "A Critical Survey of the New International Economic Order." *Journal of World Trade Law,* vol. 10 (1976), 493–512.

McFadzean, Lord, of Kelvinside. *Global Strategy for Growth.* London: Trade Policy Research Centre, 1981.

McKinnon, Ronald I. "Foreign Exchange Constraints on Economic Development and Efficient Aid Allocation." *Economic Journal,* 74 (1964), 388–409.

Murray, Tracy. "How Helpful Is the Generalized System of Preferences to the Developing Countries?" *Economic Journal,* 83 (1983), 449–455.

Tangri, Shanti S., and H. Peter Gray, eds. *Capital Accumulation and Economic Development.* Boston: Heath, 1967.

Questions and Problems

Problems
1. Report on the population of India, Brazil, Mexico, and Japan at five-year intervals from 1950 through 1980.
2. Calculate the data in Table 10-1 for 1984. In the Standard Industrial Trade Classification, manufactured goods are defined as SITC categories 5, 6 (less 67 and 68), 7, and 8.

Questions
1. In approving the GSP, the GATT argued that discrimination in favor of developing countries was legitimate because "unequals should not be treated equally." Argue the case for or against allowing developing countries preferential access to U.S. markets.
2. The brain drain should not be allowed, and students from developing countries should be forced to return home. Argue the case for or against this assertion.
3. Aid is necessary if industrialized countries are to limit their imports of labor-intensive goods *and* avoid alienating developing nations. Assess this argument.
4. Examine the growth of exports and of domestic manufacturing output for a near-NIC (Greece, Hungary, Malaysia, or the Philippines).

11

Economic Integration

If free trade is "good but unattainable," there may be some advantage to the creation of free trade within a group of countries. This is the germ of the idea underlying *economic integration*. There were two major movements toward economic integration in Western Europe in the late 1950s and early 1960s. The European Economic Community (EEC) was a great success, engendering high rates of economic growth and large increases in intra-area trade. The European Free Trade Area was less integrated and was less successful. Since the serious global recession of the mid-1970s, the EEC has lost its dynamism and is showing signs of internal strain. The EEC has also enlarged its membership significantly in recent years. Starting with six countries, the Community admitted Denmark, Eire, and Great Britain in the mid-1970s and has since admitted Greece, Spain, and Portugal. The admission of the Southern European countries is bound to change the character of the community somewhat since these countries are significantly less affluent than the first nine members. This suggests that adjustment to the entry of those countries will impose greater strains on the existing members.

Europe is not the only place where integration has taken place. The United States imposed economic integration on its states. Latin America has seen several attempts at economic integration, including the Central American Common Market, the Latin American Free Trade Area, and the Andean Pact. There is one important difference between the experience of the United States and other attempts at integration. Modern movements toward integration combine existing nation-states with national identities. In the United States, the national framework never allowed the original colonies or incoming states to be economically independent.[1]

It would be wrong to view the formation of the EEC as a purely economic phenomenon. Much of the motivation for the integration of the six original members was political. The idea was that it would be more difficult for countries to declare war on each other when their economies were interdependent because their economies would not be able to support a major war effort standing alone. The second reason was that the West wanted to assure prosperity in Western Europe in order to weaken the appeal of Russian communism in those countries. The United States was a strong supporter of the formation of the EEC, even though it was generally recognized in Washington that the U.S. economy would be somewhat weakened by the integration of the European economies. This was a clear example of political values taking precedence over narrow economic considerations.

Integration is not a clearly defined concept in the sense that there exist many levels of integration. The key feature of integration is different treatment for members of the group and for outsiders.

FORMS OF ECONOMIC INTEGRATION

The various forms of economic integration can be considered in sequence starting with the least restrictive set of arrangements. The first and loosest form of association is a *preferential tariff agreement,* which provides that imports from a group of selected nations will be subject to lower import duties than similar goods imported from other nations (outsiders). The most celebrated example of this type of organization is the British Commonwealth Preference Scheme, which was effectively limited to members of the British Empire and affiliated nation-states. Commonwealth Preference was inaugurated when the British departed from free trade in 1932 and tariffs were raised against outsider nations. As a consequence, the member nations tended to trade reciprocally among the group. Since the group included a wide range of economies—tropical, subtropical, temperate, land-intensive, manufacturing, primary-producing, rich, and poor—the membership was almost self-sufficient. Therefore, there was an additional advantage in that the problems of financing international trade were much easier among the membership than in the wider group of world nations. First, if Britain increased its imports from one country, that country was likely to spend all the revenue increases within the

---

[1]Texans will point out that their state was independent for a time, but it was never economically viable as a country.

Commonwealth and probably within Britain. Thus a change in the value of imports tended to generate offsetting exports and thus to achieve a rough balance in trade. Second, the pound sterling was the currency in which intra-Commonwealth trade was conducted, and all banking was conducted through London. Thus nations in temporary deficit could easily borrow through London from another member of the group since both used the same currency. Essentially, balance-of-payments constraints were reduced by this degree of integration. However, the integration had the obvious cost, which applies to all forms of integration, that accompanies increased interaction among economies: Business cycles were quickly transmitted through the whole system in much the same way that they are transmitted within a single nation.[2]

The second form of organization is a *free trade area*. Under this arrangement, nations agree to maintain zero tariffs with respect to other members of the free trade area (on certain types of goods) and to apply their own individual tariff structures vis-à-vis outsiders. Clearly, this form of organization is relatively loose. Like all other types of integration, it emphasizes discrimination between insiders and outsiders. When the EEC was formed, Great Britain, in one of its more fateful decisions, decided to stay out because of the clash between EEC requirements and Commonwealth Preference requirements. (It is also possible that Britain, in a fit of arrogance, thought that the EEC would not succeed without its participation.) In opposition to the EEC, Britain took the lead in forming the European Free Trade Association (EFTA). This group (Austria, Denmark, Great Britain, Norway, Portugal, Sweden, and Switzerland) agreed to zero tariffs on manufactures among themselves but excluded trade in agricultural goods from the agreement. This group was more loosely knit than the EEC and, probably because of this, provided no grounds for a surge of investment among the membership. The EFTA gradually lost strength, and three members have deserted it to join the EEC.

The third form is a *customs union* in which members agree to free trade within the group *and* a common or standard commercial policy against outsiders. The most famous example of this is the *Zollverein*, formed in Germany in 1834, which was an important precondition to Bismarck's unification of Germany in 1870.

A *common market* involves the elimination of impediments to international trade among members, a common external tariff, *and* allowance for the free flow of factors of production among members. This description fits the EEC most aptly. The free mobility of labor requires the integration of retirement benefits (old-age pensions), unemployment benefits, and a harmonization of labor laws. The mobility of capital requires consistent

---

[2]This relationship was sometimes burdensome for the peripheral members of the Commonwealth. See John M. Letiche, "Dependent Monetary Systems and Economic Development: The Case of Sterling East Africa," in *Economic Development and Planning*, ed. Willy Sellekaerts (London: Macmillan, 1974).

laws regarding property rights and benefits from stable rates of exchange among the currencies of member nations.

The final form is a full *economic union*. The classic example of this is the United States, in which fifty states are joined together in a full political and economic union with a single currency and single central bank. Except for the excesses of political oratory from time to time, no one any longer thinks of individual states as being in any way sovereign. This state of integration requires more than the harmonization of policies by the individual national governments. It implies the existence of a powerful supranational government (the federal government, in terms of the United States) to deal with economic and international matters. The vestiges of the United States' being an economic union can be found in the fact that the federal government has no jurisdiction over commerce within the individual states but only over commerce between states.

DEVELOPMENT OF THE EEC

The success of the EEC in its early years can be used to illustrate how the economic benefits of integration have been achieved.

The Treaty of Rome was signed on January 1, 1958, formally inaugurating the EEC.[3] The signatories recognized insightfully that shifting to a common external set of tariffs from a series of national tariffs would require a period of adjustment, so they instituted phaseout processes; the actual establishment of zero internal tariffs and a common external tariff would be achieved only after ten years or so. The adjustment process was complicated by the fact that the external tariff involved a lowering of external rates for high-tariff nations such as France and a raising of rates for Germany. The effect of the common external tariff was being experienced at the same time that internal tariffs were being reduced to zero.

The gains from the formation of the Common Market resembled quite closely the gains that are attributed to the establishment of free trade. First, there was the increase in the size of the market for individual firms. The market was no longer bounded by the borders of an individual nation-state. It encompassed six relatively affluent nation-states, making the EEC the second-largest single market for goods in the world. There have been gains from economic efficiency caused by the reallocation of production according to the national factor endowments. These gains would be reinforced by any economies of scale that the larger market would enable individual firms to achieve. These economies of scale might be the direct result of making feasible the purchase of advanced machinery suitable only to larger production units, which, in turn, create the ability

---

[3]The original members were Belgium, France, Italy, Luxembourg, the Netherlands, and West Germany.

to have longer production runs on individual items and to allow labor and machinery to specialize more in certain aspects of production. Economies of scale can also be gained in the important areas of inventories, transportation, and marketing or distribution. As long as full or high employment is attained, the economies give rise to increased productivity of factors and, therefore, to increased real income.

A second source of gains resulted from the impetus to economic growth that the enlargement of market size permits. More growth means the availability of more potential economies of scale and even more efficient allocation of resources. Greater growth also means a younger average age for machinery, and, therefore, a greater proportion of the capital stock will have modern technological achievements incorporated into it. Moreover, growth breeds its own success since it engenders expectations of further growth and leads to the installation of ever more modern capital goods. Nor should the role of MNCs be omitted. The increased size and the affluence of the integrated market in the six countries attracted American MNCs to continental Europe. These companies transferred a great deal of saving and large amounts of proprietary technology to the EEC economy.

Third, there was the gain from increased competition and, through the enlargement of the market, the reduction in strength of any erstwhile national monopolies or oligopolies. Such a change is always likely to give rise to increases in internal efficiency in member firms as they confront competition from firms in other member states. One of the returns to monopoly is an "easy life" for executives and workers, and this ease will be eroded.

All of these growth impetuses derived from the reduction to barriers to trade among member nations. The one area in which the EEC has not been a force for efficiency in resource allocation is agriculture, in which a very restrictive cartel-like agreement among the member nations exists.[4] The effects of the EEC were not limited to Europe, and ex-colonies were given "associate member" status and preferential treatment. This opened up the European market to some African nations (and the number of associated members increased sharply with British entry); now, under the Lomé Convention, the associate members include parts of the Caribbean and the Pacific as well as Africa. This preferential treatment overwhelmed the benefits from the Generalized System of Preferences accorded to developing nations by the EEC to the point that the EEC's GSP was of negligible consequence for developing countries located in Asia and Latin America.

The EEC had lost its first burst of vitality by the time the oil crisis

[4]For a study of the agricultural arrangement and indeed for all aspects of the EEC in its formative years, see Lawrence B. Krause, *European Economic Integration and the United States* (Washington, D.C.: Brookings Institution, 1968).

hit in the mid-1970s. The benefits from integration had been achieved, and more benefits were available only if the member nations could agree to achieving full economic union with a common currency (and central bank) and a common set of taxes. Such a move seems unlikely. There is too much resistance from nationalists and from bureaucrats who see their power and job safety at risk. The admission of new entrants could give short spurts of vitality to the Community, but as the new entrants become more and more "semideveloped," the adjustment costs within the EEC can be expected to be more painful, especially for low-skilled workers.

The success of the EEC came from its dynamism. One interesting question is whether or not a part of its initial success came from an improvement in the net barter terms of trade. Nations that were hurt by the integration process were those that had exported temperate agricultural products to the six member nations. Here the United States suffered most because it was the main supplier of wheat and animal feed grains to Europe. The Common Agricultural Policy of the EEC imposed a tariff on imports of agricultural goods that would raise the cost of imports to the (inflated) prices fixed by the Community. Further, the proceeds of the tariff were to be available to subsidize the exports of any surplus production within the EEC. The diversion of demand for manufactured goods to member countries (as a result of the preferential internal tariffs) was felt most heavily by the members of the EFTA. Sales of manufactured goods by the United States were mainly technological noncompetitive imports.

Formal analysis of the benefits and costs of the formation of the EEC are usually conducted in a static analytic framework and therefore neglect the benefits attributable to the dynamic impetus. Did the formation of the EEC add to the efficiency of the global economy by creating an area of free trade? In formal terms, the question is whether the reduction of the internal tariffs created more trade among members (promoting efficient resource allocation) than it diverted from outsiders to less efficient internal producers. If trade creation within the EEC exceeded trade diversion from more efficient producers to members receiving preferential tariff treatment, the formation of the EEC did contribute to global efficiency (see the supplement following this chapter for a discussion of trade creation and trade diversion). There would be great difficulties of measurement because it would be necessary to examine the rearrangement of trade in the nonmember nations as well as within the EEC. Similarly, such analysis neglects the higher growth rate and the increase in sheer efficiency due to greater competition. On balance, even in simple economic terms, the EEC must be counted as a success by virtue of its contribution to economic growth as well as to international trade. The one area in which the EEC has been clearly destructive of the efficiency of global resource allocation is agriculture. But agriculture has always been a special-interest group in all nations, and there is no nation whose agricultural policy is so open that it can cast stones at the EEC with a clear conscience.

TWO-WAY TRADE IN MANUFACTURES

At the end of Chapter 4, reference was made to S. B. Linder's observation that far more international trade took place between pairs of rich, developed countries with quite similar factor endowments than between the two blocs of nations with very disparate factor endowments. This observation posed a serious qualification to the factor-proportions theory of international trade, which would suggest negligible trade between nations with similar endowments. This kind of international trade is most prevalent within the EEC. Note that this kind of trade involves the simultaneous exporting and importing of the "same" good—another feature that contradicts the factor-proportions theory, which would say that a nation has either a comparative advantage or a comparative disadvantage in a good and will therefore either export it or import it but not both. A detailed study of the composition of international trade shows that although the prevalence of two-way trade (simultaneous exporting and importing) does decrease as the data are disaggregated, substantial amounts of two-way trade continue even at the finest level of disaggregation.[5] Two-way trade (or intraindustry trade) generates gains from trade in the breadth of choice of goods available to consumers and in the degree of competition that exists in individual industries as well as in the standard way of improving the global allocation of resources. Goods that are simultaneously exported and imported can be close substitutes in consumption (VWs and Chevettes) or different versions of the same product (standard and heat-resistant roller bearings). The first are "differentiated" goods, meaning that they have features or characteristics that distinguish them from each other, including reliability and performance characteristics. The second type of goods are "closely related" goods, which are exchanged internationally usually because of the existence of proprietary knowledge applying to different versions owned by firms in different countries.

International trade takes place in a good when the difference in costs of production in two countries exceeds the monetary value of the impediments placed in the way of such trade. These impediments include both the costs of transporting the goods internationally and the cost of tariffs and the cost equivalents of NTBs. The smaller the costs of transportation and the lower the values of tariffs and NTBs, the more likely is trade in a good to take place between pairs of nations with similar resource

---

[5]See Herbert Giersch, ed., *Intra-industry Trade* (Tübingen, Germany: J. C. B. Mohr, 1979), pp. 87–110.

endowments. The EEC, with its zero internal tariffs and close proximity of one nation to other members, is the ideal place for this kind of trade to take place. Trade of this kind also exists between Canada and the United States in automobiles.

Differentiated Goods

Differentiated goods require a sales and marketing force. People have to be informed of the distinguishing characteristics and of warranty and backup services through advertising and other sales promotional activities. People buy these goods because they are convinced that the package of features of the good purchased is sufficiently superior to that of the rival goods to make up for any premium charged (or vice versa). The more similar the goods, the flatter the demand curve facing a particular good. This is the fundamental difference between trade in *standardized goods,* in which each firm faces a perfectly flat demand curve, and trade in *differentiated goods,* in which each firm faces some trade-off between price charged and number of units sold.[6] If there is some leeway with respect to price, there is also some leeway with respect to markup or per-unit profit. Markup may be thought of as the difference between the variable costs of production and the selling price; this margin must at least cover overhead costs and selling expenses. The more distinctive the features of the good (including the appeal of brand name, reliability, and performance aspects), the steeper the demand curve facing the individual firm and the more leeway in pricing policy.

Figure 11-1 shows the demand for a differentiated good in a foreign market. Price p_1 is the landed price of the good in the foreign country after payment of tariffs and other duties and after an allowance has been made for selling costs. The slight downward slope in the curve SS shows the economies of scale available in marketing and promotional activities. The volume Q_{min} shows the minimum quantity that warrants the establishment of a marketing organization. The good is strongly differentiated and has a fairly steeply sloped demand curve. Provided that the demand curve lies above the curve SS at quantity Q_{min}, the product can be sold in the foreign market. The maximum price chargeable is p_2, at which only Q_{min} units would be sold. The manufacturer must make a decision about markup (what price to charge), and that will determine the quantity sold. The schedules in Figure 11-1 are based on existing conditions of supply (and sales effort) by foreign suppliers and other exporters to the market. The curve SS is determined by costs of production in the exporting country, so a strengthening of the exporter's currency will shift the curve SS upward. Increased sales effort by foreign

[6]See Campbell R. McConnell, *Economics,* 8th ed. (New York: McGraw-Hill, 1981), pp. 522 and 569 and accompanying text.

Figure 11-1

FOREIGN DEMAND FOR A
DIFFERENTIATED GOOD

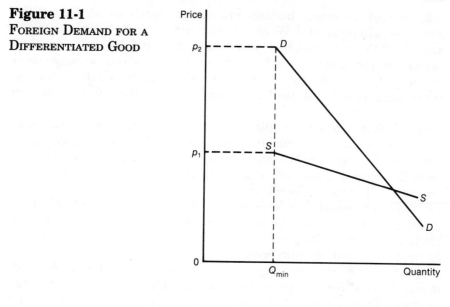

firms will shift the demand curve downward. A similar curve faces foreign
manufacturers in the exporter's home market. It is now possible to see
how intraindustry trade or two-way trade will take place.

Let Figure 11-1 show the demand in Country A for the product of a
firm in Country B. Exports can clearly take place from B to A because
p_2 is greater than p_1. Two-way trade will exist if the firm located in
Country A faces a similar set of conditions in Country B (that is, if p_2
exceeds p_1 in B). If p_2 is greater than p_1, a positive export price range
(EPR) exists. Two-way trade will take place if firms in both countries
face a positive EPR in the other's market. Several factors are likely to
contribute to the likelihood that firms in both countries will face positive
EPRS, and all of these factors are most likely to be met in a situation
like the EEC in which impediments to trade are minimal and in which
the per capita incomes of people in different countries are more or less
equal.

1. The more differentiated the good from the rest of competing members of the same group of products, the steeper will be the slope of the
demand curve. Therefore, for any given set of conditions, the higher
will be the relevant p_2's be. The higher the p_2's in both countries, the
greater can any disparity in p_1's be without either EPR being eliminated.

2. The more similar the real per capita incomes of residents in the
two nations, the more likely are the demand curves to be about the
same height. The closer the values of the two individual p_2's, the more
likely are both EPRs to be positive.

3. If real per capita incomes are approximately equal, factor costs are likely to be equal also. Wages will be much the same in both countries, and so will the costs of skilled labor and capital (all measured in domestic currencies and made compatible through the use of the exchange rate). In addition, the technology available in both countries and the skill levels of the workers will also tend to be similar. All of these factors interact to reinforce one another: The closer the per capita incomes, the more likely are factor costs to be quite similar and the structures of the economies in terms of the availability of skilled workers and equipment to resemble one another. The more these factors reflect one another, the more likely is a similarity of per capita incomes. If real per capita incomes are similar, the costs of production of a standardized manufactured good will tend to be equal: The base number that underlies the SS schedules in the two diagrams will be equivalent, and the p_1's will also be more likely to be equal. The greater the similarity of the p_1's, the lower can be the p_2's compatible with positive EPRs in both countries.

4. If proprietary technology is widespread in the industry concerned, it may be expected to add to the degree of differentiation of individual products. The more industrialized the country, the higher the probability of widespread use of proprietary technology, and the steeper the demand curves will be.

5. In the absence of tariffs and with low-cost transportation available for relatively short distances, the smaller the difference between the p_1's and the variable costs of production, the lower will be the p_1's, and the more likely the existence of two positive EPRS.

Intraindustry trade in which a similar good is simultaneously exported and imported by a country can be attributed to international trade in differentiated goods. The more distinctive the goods produced, the more likely is intraindustry trade to take place. Of course, the existence of different per capita incomes or substantial barriers to trade will result in either one-way trade or no trade at all. Even then, intraindustry trade can take place if the goods concerned are highly distinctive. Under such conditions, intraindustry trade is quantitatively unimportant.

It will be useful to provide some sense of magnitude. The index used to measure the amount of intraindustry trade flows measures the difference between exports and imports as a percent of the total value of exports *plus* imports. If the value of exports equals the value of imports, the index will be zero; if there is no intraindustry trade, the index will have a value equal to 1. Automobiles (SITC 732.1) were traded between West Germany and Italy in 1973 with an index value of 0.08, between West Germany and France with an index value of 0.19, and between West Germany and Belgium with an index value of 0.18.[7] It may be

---

[7]See Giersch, *Intra-industry Trade*, p. 101. The index is named after Professor Béla Balassa, who developed this straightforward measure.

useful to spell out the implications of an index of, say, 0.25: Of 200 units traded, one country would export 125 units and the second country would export 75 units. This state of affairs is clearly quite different from that conjured up by the straightforward factor-proportions theory of international trade.

When the differentiated goods are consumer durables, there exists the phenomenon known as "afterbusiness." Even Rolls-Royces need repair on occasion, and an American owner of a Rolls-Royce will have to import the parts needed from England. Afterbusiness is the supply of replacement parts needed to maintain the existing stock of products sold abroad. Intraindustry trade could continue in afterbusiness long after it had ended in the consumer durable itself.

There is an obvious tendency for the index of intraindustry trade to get smaller as the data base becomes more aggregative. Such a blanket aggregation as "trade in manufactures" would almost inevitably show large amounts of two-way trade, and much of this might be consistent with the factor-proportions theory. However, even when international trade data are broken down as finely as possible, significant amounts of intraindustry trade remain.

Closely Related Goods

The second source of two-way trade is specialization in a certain "subspecies" of a product by firms in different countries. As an example of this possibility, consider the antifriction bearing industry. The United States imports the standard bearings, which can be produced on a large scale in almost any industrial country, but exports bearings that require special features such as heat resistance or rust resistance to the point that the United States is a net exporter of bearings. Two-way trade can exist as a result of this kind of specialization. There are two probable sources of this pattern of international trade in "closely related" goods: scale economies and proprietary technology. Both sources will require relatively low impediments to international trade lest the advantages of scale production be overwhelmed and the proprietary knowledge transferred to the potential importer by licensing or by establishing a foreign manufacturing unit in the potentially importing country.

Figure 11-2 shows the two mechanisms. There is nothing to suggest that the two explanations will not go hand in hand. The larger the scale of output, the more likely is the producer to develop specialist proprietary knowledge in the design and manufacture of the good. Figure 11-2 shows the market in Country D for a particular subspecies of a product. Country C has a large market for this subspecies, and a firm in Country C is therefore able to achieve economies of scale unavailable to a firm in Country D. The market in Country C is shown in the left panel and in Country D in the right panel. The producer in Country D cannot fully

Figure 11-2
ECONOMIES OF SCALE

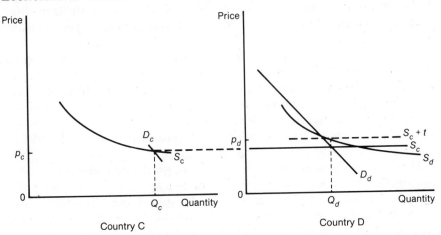

Country C   Country D

exploit the advantages of large-scale production available.[8] The producer in Country C has a cost advantage by virtue of its large home market and the exploitation there of economies of scale. Alternatively, the firm in Country C may have some technological lead in the design and manufacture of the subspecies that allows it to raise factor productivity. Two-way trade will take place when Country D has a lower per capita income and can produce the standardized good more cheaply. If the cost of impediments to international trade push S_c above S_d at the level of demand in Country D, technology licensing or foreign direct investment will take place. The greater the disparity between factor prices in Countries C and D, the more likely is the special subspecies to be manufactured in Country D in addition to the standardized versions. Two-way trade still requires some similarity of per capita income, but this kind of two-way trade is less dependent on "close similarity" than is two-way trade in differentiated goods.

Two-way international trade exists mainly in manufactured goods in such industries as chemicals, pharmaceuticals, specialist food products, and engineering goods. Trade in differentiated goods, particularly those featured in afterbusiness, can take place in goods that are used by manufacturers in the importing country. This kind of trade is particularly likely to exist when multinational corporations are involved in producing final goods in foreign countries. In terms of Figure 11-2, an MNC from Country C could have a plant in Country D and use parts produced in

[8]If the producer in Country D were able to develop the firm to reach full-scale production, it would have a cost advantage in the good and would export to Country C. This derives from the assumed cost advantage in the standardized subspecies and recalls the argument for infant-industry protection.

Country C, where it has economies of scale or because it requires a particular specification. Similarly, an MNC Country D producing in Country C will export in the same way. The Ford Motor Company, for example, is likely to engage in this type of activity because it has integrated its global production to a very high degree and ships parts among plants on a regular basis.

SUMMARY

Economic integration has one signal success to its credit: the EEC. However, the loss of the first burst of vitality and the severe shocks of the oil price increases in the 1970s seem to have robbed the EEC of its dynamism. Even the addition of new members seems to have had but relatively mild expansionary effects. Much more of the time of politicians is now taken up with negotiating the future of the EEC and with the allocation of the costs of running the operations.

The EEC has been protective only in agriculture, but its special agreements with the ex-colonies and the entry of Greece, Spain, and Portugal also suggest that the EEC will be less well able to offer a market to developing countries in Asia and in Latin America. The entry of the semideveloped Mediterranean countries will impose severe adjustment strains on the original six and the three northern newcomers as cheap labor from Spain and Portugal can combine with British, French, and German capital to further weaken the welfare of workers in the northern tier of members. The possible severity of the strains of adjustment may mean that Europe will be inward-looking for the next decade.

The role of increased international trade within the EEC has probably played a large role in its early success as gains were registered in terms of the breadth of choice available to consumers, the reallocation of resources in line with comparative advantage, and the greater degree of competition. Much of the increase in international trade was in two-way trade, which cannot be explained by the orthodox factor-proportions explanation.

It does not follow automatically that the success of the EEC is a philosopher's stone for economic growth. This applies particularly to associations of developing nations that create areas of integration without much all-around contribution to economic development. The process of economic integration may be useful in development, but there is no evidence that it plays more than a facilitating role.

Bibliography

Balassa, Béla. "Tariff Reductions and Trade in Manufactures among the Industrialized Countries." *American Economic Review,* 56 (1966), 466–473.

Giersch, Herbert. *On the Economics of Intra-industry Trade.* Tübingen, Germany: J. C. B. Mohr, 1979.

Gray, H. Peter. "The Theory of International Trade among Industrialized Nations." *Weltwirtschaftliches Archiv,* 116 (1980), 447–470.

Jensen, Finn B., and Ingo Walter. *The Common Market: Integration in Europe.* Philadelphia: Lippincott, 1965.

Krause, Lawrence B. *European Economic Integration and the United States.* Washington, D.C.: Brookings Institution, 1968.

Linder, S. B. *An Essay on Trade and Transformation.* New York: Wiley, 1961.

Questions and Problem

Problem

Describe and explain how intraindustry trade has grown in a specific industry since the formation of the EEC between two of the following countries: Belgium, France, Germany, Italy, the Netherlands, the United Kingdom.

Questions

1. Can intraindustry trade be explained by the factor-proportions theory of international trade? If not, what can explain the phenomenon?
2. Why would one expect greater intraindustry trade between members of the European Economic Community than between the United States and one of the EEC's member countries?
3. Why is intraindustry trade unlikely to take place between a poor (developing) country and an industrialized country?
4. Early in 1986, the Reagan administration accused the EEC of being the world's biggest offender against free trade. The root of the problem was the Common Agricultural Policy of the EEC and the entry of Spain and Portugal. Is this an accurate criticism? (Check newspapers and see Lawrence B. Krause, *European Economic Integration and the United States* (Washington, D.C.: Brookings Institution, 1968).
5. U.S. support of the EEC in the 1950s was based on politics rather than on economics. Why?

Trade Creation and Trade Diversion

The essence of economic integration is discrimination between "insiders" and "outsiders." Integrated communities offer preferential treatment to international trade with insiders. Thus the act of integration could switch trading patterns in two ways:

1. Integration could cause a market to be supplied by an insider with a comparative advantage in the good concerned at the expense of an "inefficient" domestic firm. This is *trade creation*.
2. Integration can also cause the supply of a good to be switched from a country that in a free trade world would have a comparative advantage to an insider that is less suitably endowed. This is *trade diversion*.

If the process of integration sets zero internal tariffs and positive tariffs against imports from outside, both types of changes in trading patterns are likely to ensue. Lowering internal tariffs will generate trade creation as firms that had existed as a result of their previous tariff protection are replaced by foreign suppliers. Trade creation has a positive effect on global efficiency. In contrast, the simultaneous lowering of an internal tariff (to zero) and the raising of an external tariff could cause trade diversion, as the most efficient outsider may not have a competitive advantage big enough to overcome the tariff difference. Trade diversion has a negative effect on global efficiency. Economic integration is deemed to have a beneficial effect only if the amount of trade creation exceeds the amount of trade diversion.

INTERNATIONAL PAYMENTS

The monetary phenomena connected with international payments underlie all international transactions. Of all the factors that distinguish the international economy from a simple autarkic system, the fact that two national currencies are inevitably involved is paramount. The price between those two currencies (the rate of exchange) is the bridge by which production costs of a good in one country are converted into the cost to the user in another country. The ultimate salability of the good in the foreign market depends, then, on the two sets of local prices and the rate of exchange between the two currencies. This same reasoning underlies transactions in assets.

Each nation must somehow live within its own cash flow. This makes a nation no different from a family. The reckoning of the cash flow–expenditure balance is the problem of balance-of-payments accounting and how balance-of-payments imbalances are met by borrowing or running down "bank accounts" or by changing the conditions in the international marketplace so that the nation will live within its revenues. Such decisions do not get made without political input from policymakers and by those likely to be unfavorably affected by the procedures.

12

Foreign Exchange Rates and Markets

The rate of exchange is the price of the currency of one country measured in terms of the currency of a second country. The rate of exchange between the U.S. dollar and the (West German) deutsche mark (DM or D-mark) can be and is expressed in two ways: as the number of cents (dollars) per D-mark and the number of D-marks per dollar.

$$DM\ 1.0 = US\ \$0.4348$$
$$US\ \$1.0 = DM\ \ 2.3000$$

Either is correct. The two prices are necessarily reciprocals, saying the same thing in different ways. The important thing to note at this stage is that when a currency weakens, the numerical value of its exchange rate can go up or down depending on which way the rate of exchange is expressed. Thus a 10 percent decline of the dollar in terms of the D-mark could shift the exchange rate down from 2.3000 to 2.0700 or up from 0.4348 to 0.4783. The *Wall Street Journal* reports rates of exchange of all important currencies against the dollar in both ways. Dealers in foreign exchange markets who transact business in foreign exchange many times each hour have agreed-on conventions as to how individual rates are quoted. Most currencies are quoted as the number of units of foreign currency per dollar (DM 2.3000), but the British pound is quoted in dollars per pound. These conventions become second nature to dealers.[1]

---

[1]The supplement following this chapter develops the "nuts and bolts" of foreign exchange trading. The chapter proper emphasizes concepts.

Foreign exchange rates are determined in foreign exchange markets. Unlike the New York Stock Exchange or London's Covent Garden fruit market, the foreign exchange market does not have a single, centralized physical location. Rather the foreign market consists of a network of telex and telephone systems among the foreign exchange departments of large banks in financial centers all over the world. In fact, the foreign exchange market does not close on working days because of time differences: Tokyo opens before San Francisco closes, and London and Hong Kong are "joined" by Bahrein. Because of the importance of the European markets, major New York banks have "early shifts" of foreign exchange traders on duty in their trading rooms. The senior bank officer in charge of foreign exchange is always on call lest some financial crisis occur somewhere in the world and sudden shifts in exchange rates become likely.[2]

Commercial banks are the main dealers in foreign exchange markets, but there do exist brokers who serve as links between pairs of banks. Banks (dealers) cannot maintain a completely balanced or covered position in every currency at every moment. On occasion, they will deliberately take a "position" in a foreign currency. When a foreign currency is expected to weaken, a bank can "go short"—deliberately allowing its liabilities denominated in that currency to exceed its assets—and vice versa. Most banks limit their maximum positions, and these rules can only be overridden by the bank's senior foreign exchange officer. Banks do seek to make a profit in foreign exchange dealings as well as to provide a service to their depositors and their correspondent banks by handling their foreign exchange needs.[3]

The foreign exchange rate is a very important factor in international economic dealings—perhaps the single most important variable—because although it is determined by the totality of international transactions, it is the one variable that links all of the transactions. Americans are usually not as aware of or as sensitive to the simple mechanics and the underlying importance of changes in the rate of exchange as people in smaller countries. Europeans, Canadians, and Japanese are all much more conscious of exchange rate phenomena than the average American. This sensitivity is attributable largely to the greater importance of international trade and investment in smaller countries. A background knowledge of exchange rate determination is useful in its own right as a prerequisite to working familiarity with international economic relationships that modern life demands.

---

[2] For an excellent description of the New York forieign exchange market and trading practices, see Roger M. Kubarych, *Foreign Exchange Markets in the United States* (New York: Federal Reserve Bank of New York, 1978).

[3] Ian Giddy, "Moral Hazard and Central Bank Rescues in an International Context," *The Financial Review*, 15, (1980), 50–56.

THE SPOT RATE OF EXCHANGE

In principle, the foreign exchange market is like any other market: Price fluctuates to equalize supply and demand. In the foreign exchange-market, what matters is the demand and supply of one currency in terms of one other currency. The price that clears the market is known as the *spot rate of exchange* because it is a price reached on transactions consummated "on the spot," even though in practice the actual exchange of currencies takes place two business days later but at the agreed-on price. In other words. reference to the foreign exchange market automatically refers to the market for spot or current transactions. In reality, there exists a whole series of foreign exchange markets between pairs of currencies and a corresponding series of foreign exchange rates. Exchange rates for April 1 in 1982 and 1985 are shown in Table 12-1. In practical terms, there exists one huge foreign exchange market in which transactions are made between pairs of currencies, and the different exchange rates are made mutually consistent by three-cornered arbitrage (to be explained shortly). Usually transactions made in the New York market will involve U.S. dollars. Similarly, London will be dominated by transactions in which the pound sterling is involved, but many transactions involving

Table 12-1

SPOT RATES OF EXCHANGE AGAINST THE U.S. DOLLAR, APRIL 1, 1982, AND APRIL 1, 1985

Country (Currency Unit)	Cents Per Unit of Foreign Currency, 1982	Cents per Unit of Foreign Currency, 1985	Foreign Units Per Dollar, 1985
Belgium (Franc)	2.21	1.6	62.49
Brazil (Cruzeiro)	0.68	0.02342	4270.00
Canada (dollar)	81.57	73.18	1.367
France (franc)	16.01	10.55	9.48
Great Britain (pound)	178.75	122.5	0.8163
Italy (lira)	0.0759	0.05051	1980.00
Japan (yen)	0.4071	0.3964	252.52
Mexico (peso)	2.19	0.4082	245.00
Netherlands (guilder)	37.53	28.54	3.50
Sweden (krona)	16.87	11.10	9.01
Switzerland (franc)	51.60	38.05	2.628
30-day forward	52.12	38.17	2.620
90-day forward	52.97	38.49	2.598
West Germany (mark)	41.67	32.20	3.106
30-day forward	41.88	32.27	3.099
90-day forward	42.31	32.47	3.080

Note the impressive strengthening of the dollar over the three-year period. For consideration of one strong contributing factor, see Chapter 15.

dollars and some third currency will also be made there because of the great importance of the dollar in international finance.

Participants (or actors) in the foreign exchange market are dealers. Individuals and commercial firms cannot trade directly in this market. Dealers are mainly foreign exchange departments of large commercial banks (often multinational banks). Dealers make most of their transactions to satisfy the needs of their clients—commercial firms and individuals who have to make payments denominated in foreign currency or who have come into possession of foreign currency. These customers include multinational corporations, exporters, importers, tourists, investors, and government departments. They also include private speculators.[4] Not all transactions reach the foreign exchange market: A bank may have two customers whose needs can be offset against each other's. Banks can and do speculate on their own account by deliberately taking a long (assets denominated in the currency exceed liabilities) or short position in a currency in the expectation that the currency will strengthen or weaken, respectively.

Consider the market for deutsche marks in terms of dollars. The price or exchange rate is set in terms of the number of D-marks needed to purchase one U.S. dollar. An increase in the numerical exchange rate, then, denotes a strengthening of the dollar and a weakening of the D-mark. The market is shown in Figure 12-1, which is a variant of Figure 2-1 in Chapter 2. The two schedules show the demand and supply of dollars in terms of the rate of exchange only (all other factors are held constant). For simplicity, assume that the sole source of demand and supply for foreign exchange derives from the needs of exporters and importers in both countries. As the D-mark gets weaker (an upward movement), German importers will need fewer dollars because the more expensive prices of U.S. exports will reduce the demand for them, and U.S. exports to Germany will decline. By the same token, the cheapening of German goods to U.S. customers that follows from the cheaper D-mark will increase the supply of dollars (for D-marks) furnished by U.S. importers. (Prices of goods traded internationally are determined by costs of production in local currency multiplied by the exchange rate, meaning that German goods need to be considered in dollars if they are to compete with American goods in the United States, and American goods need to have their prices seen in D-marks if they are to be compared with locally made goods.)[5] As drawn, the equilibrium, market-clearing rate of exchange is 2.30 (US $1.0 = DM 2.30).

---

[4]A speculator can be defined as anyone taking a position in foreign exchange in anticipation of making a profit.

[5]Thus a good costing $10.00 will be sold in Germany for DM 23 when the exchange rate is 2.30 and for DM 25 when the exchange rate is 2.50. A good costing DM 75 will sell in the United States for $32.60 when the rate of exchange is 2.30 and for $30.00 when the exchange rate is 2.50. In this simple arithmetic example, transportation costs and duties are assumed to be zero.

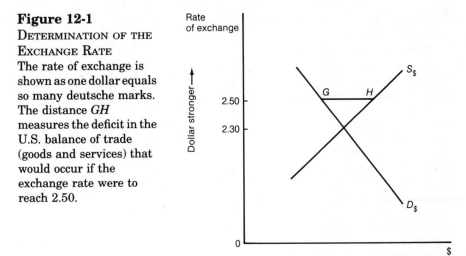

Figure 12-1

DETERMINATION OF THE
EXCHANGE RATE
The rate of exchange is
shown as one dollar equals
so many deutsche marks.
The distance *GH*
measures the deficit in the
U.S. balance of trade
(goods and services) that
would occur if the
exchange rate were to
reach 2.50.

But demand and supply curves can shift when the underlying forces change. There are several possible reasons for such shifts, some of which are very important. Retaining the assumption that the demand and supply schedules relate only to international trade in goods, imagine what will happen when the United States goes into a recession and the German economy continues at its existing rate of employment or capacity utilization (a cyclical disturbance). American demand for German goods will decline at all prices: The supply curve of dollars ($S_\$$) will shift to the left, and the exchange rate will increase (the dollar will strengthen). Alternatively, there could be a real disturbance: a change of tastes in the United States in favor of home goods and against German goods— Detroit improves the quality of its cars, for example. In that event, the supply of dollars would again diminish, and the dollar would strengthen. Finally, consider what would happen if the United States suffered from a burst of inflation unmatched in Germany (a price-level disturbance). The prices of American goods would increase in the United States, so German goods at the old exchange rate would become relatively cheaper and American goods would become less attractive abroad at the old rate of exchange. The demand for dollars would shift leftward (reduced German demand for U.S. goods) *and* the supply of dollars would shift rightward (increased demand for German goods in the United States). The dollar would weaken. These three changes can be seen as representing three important kinds of "disturbances" in the international economic system: a *cyclical* disturbance, a *real* or fundamental disturbance, and a *price-level* disturbance. These distinctions will be seen to be important.

The assumption that the only source of demand and supply for foreign exchange is international trade can now be released. Other demands are shown as relatively insensitive to the rate of exchange, but they

Figure 12-2

DETERMINATION OF THE
EXCHANGE RATE WITH
CAPITAL FLOWS
Capital inflows into the
United States are shown
by K, the horizontal
difference between the
demand for dollars for
goods and services, D_{G+S},
and the total demand for
dollars, D_T. Similarly, the
demand of Americans to
acquire foreign assets is
shown by K', indicating
the difference between the
supply of dollars for goods
and services (import
demand) and the total
supply of dollars.

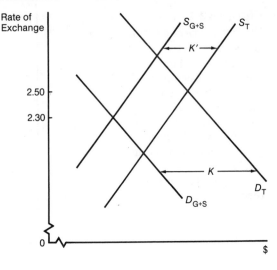

No distinction is made between short-term and long-term capital flows in this figure.

The net inflow of capital into the United States ($K > K'$) strengthens the dollar from 2.30 (which balances trade in goods and services) to 2.50.

may react quite sensitively to other economic variables. This equilibrium is shown in Figure 12-2. The curves are additive; that is, the transactions in capital (investments and short-term money market assets) are added to those induced by international trade. The equilibrium rate is the one that clears the whole market, shown as 2.50 D-marks, indicating a stronger dollar than would exist purely under international trade and, importantly, that the United States will have a deficit in international trade.[6]

The determination of the spot rate of exchange depends on the demand for imports and the supply of exports, the level of income, the demand for foreign financial assets, and the demand for direct investment (in real assets) in both countries. Transactions that are more sensitive to changes in the rate of exchange (international trade in goods and services) will tend to adjust to the other flows.

How do all the submarkets for individual pairs of currencies relate? They relate because the market will enforce consistent "cross rates." Consider three (imaginary) exchange rates among the dollar, the pound, and the mark at some moment in time: $1.00 = DM 2.30 and $1.50 = £1.00. The appropriate cross rate must be £1.00 = DM 3.45. These three rates would be internally consistent. If spontaneous transactions jarred

[6]See Chapter 5.

the DM/$ rate to 2.40, profitable three-way arbitrage would be possible. A foreign exchange trader, spotting the internal inconsistency in the three rates, would quickly to buy the currency that was relatively cheap. The dealer would buy DM 2.4 million with $1 million and would immediately convert the marks into pounds at DM 3.45 per pound (buying £695,652) and convert the pounds back into dollars (acquiring $1,043,478 at an exchange rate of 1.50). The dealer will have made a profit of $43,478 (less transactions costs and the cost of three phone calls) in the space of a couple of minutes. In practice, three-way arbitrage takes place on very narrow discrepancies (which is why exchange rates are always quoted to four decimal places in practice; see the supplement following this chapter). What is important is that this kind of arbitrage will eliminate the discrepancy that makes it profitable and make sure that consistent cross rates are enforced. The purchase of marks with dollars will strengthen the mark against the dollar, the purchases of pounds with marks will strengthen the pound against the mark, and the purchase of dollars with pounds will strengthen the dollar against the pound. The final set of rates might be as follows:

Before Arbitrage	After Arbitrage
$1.00 = DM 2.40	$1.00 = DM 2.35
DM 3.35 = £1.00	DM 3.40 = £1.00
£1.00 = $1.50	£1.00 = $1.447

The after-arbitrage rates do not permit further profit for even the smallest of transaction costs. The act of arbitrage will continue for as long as the potential for profit exists, and except for the possibility that a contract will not be honored, the profit is achieved without risk. Therefore, the activities of profit-seeking arbitrageurs (dealers) will enforce consistent cross rates and will in this way integrate all the individual submarkets in operation into the larger foreign exchange market.

One of the "disturbances" considered was the effect of different rates of inflation in two countries. The currency of the faster-inflating country was seen to weaken (depreciate). The question to be answered is, What is the relationship between the difference in the rates of inflation and the rate of change in the exchange rate? A difference in the rates of inflation experienced by the two countries is only one factor affecting the exchange rate among many. For simplicity, the discussion here assumes that such real factors as tastes and supply capabilities (factor endowments) and cyclical factors such as the degree of boom or recession stay constant; the only source of change in the exchange rate is the difference in the rates of inflation in the two countries. The answer to the question is to be found in the relative purchasing power parity theorem, developed by a Swede, Gustav Cassel, at about the end of World

War I.[7] It closely reflects the price-specie-flow theorem of David Hume, which is more than 150 years older. The theorem says that if one nation experiences inflation at a faster rate than its trading partner, the first country's currency will weaken at the same rate as the difference in the rates of inflation. This can be seen more clearly if one country (the United States) is assumed to inflate while the second country (the Federal Republic of Germany) has constant prices in its currency (deutsche marks). Again let us assume no transactions in assets, so that trade in goods is the sole determinant of the rate of exchange, and the terms of trade are fixed. In monetary terms, the terms of trade, which are determined by such real forces as supply capabilities and tastes, can be represented by the degree of price competitiveness of the industries in the two countries. Call this ratio C^*. The ratio is written as follows:

$$C^* = \left(\frac{p_f}{p_d}\right)\left(\frac{1}{\epsilon}\right) \tag{1}$$

where p_f indicates the level of prices in Germany in index number form and p_d indicates the level of prices in the United States. The rate of exchange is denoted by ϵ and is measured in terms of the number of deutsche marks per dollar. It is intuitively correct to define the competitive ratio (C) so that the numerical value of the ratio increases when the price competitiveness of a country's industry increases. This fact requires that the exchange rate (expressed as deutsche marks per dollar) get larger when the dollar weakens and that the exchange rate enter in the somewhat awkward form of a reciprocal ($1/\epsilon$).

When inflation hits the United States, the value of p_d increases and U.S. industry becomes less price-competitive. C declines, but the required competitiveness (C^*) remain unchanged. If p_d increases from 100 to 105, there are two ways in which C can regain its original numerical value (C^*): Either p_f can increase by 5 percent, or $1/\epsilon$ can increase by 5 percent. If p_f is fixed because the German economy does not inflate, ϵ must decrease from 2.30 to 2.185 (in terms of Figure 12-1) for equilibrium to be reestablished in the foreign exchange market.[8]

In plain prose, the relative purchasing power parity theorem states that inflation will not change the cost of a bundle of goods in New York in terms of a similar bundle in Frankfurt, Germany. Suppose that on January 2, 1986, $100 would buy a certain bundle of goods in New York and that if the dollars had been converted to deutsche marks at the going rate of exchange, they would have bought a specific (but not neces-

---

[7]The idea that price levels determine the flows in the foreign exchange market recalls Hume's payments-adjustment mechanism: See Chapter 2.

[8]The reason the price-specie-flow mechanism does not work is that the German authorities have repressed the inflation by macroeconomic policies (tight money) and the U.S. authorities have not.

sarily equal) bundle in Frankfurt on the same day.[9] If, during 1986, the two countries suffer from unequal rates of inflation and cyclical and real conditions do not change, the experiment could be repeated on January 2, 1987. Purchase the original bundle in New York for a larger number of dollars, convert those dollars to marks, and the marks will buy exactly the same bundle of goods in Frankfurt on January 2, 1987, as was bought one year earlier.

Exchange Rate Intervention

It has been assumed to this point that the market for foreign exchange (unlike the markets for wheat, butter, and other agricultural commodities) is allowed to find its own level without government interference. Government policies toward foreign exchange markets vary quite considerably, and three main sets of conditions can be identified as being practiced by the major economic powers: a clean float, a dirty float, and fixed parities.

A *clean float* is a system of foreign exchange markets in which the (dirty) hands of the government do not intervene. Governments may engage in foreign exchange transactions for their own normal purposes, since governments do buy imports and earn foreign exchange. A clean float has the advantage that the economic forces that prevail indicate the (true) rate of exchange. In other words, the spot rate that clears the foreign exchange market under a clean float is a freely determined rate. But it can fluctuate around the true equilibrium rate quite substantially. If foreign exchange traders see the same information and believe that a currency is about to weaken, they will tend to take a short position in that currency. This factor tends to weaken the currency in question as the dealers conduct net sales (depressing the price). Thus heartened by the confirmation of their expectations, the dealers sell more and drive the price down still further. Optimism can force an increase in a currency's price to too high a level in exactly the same way. The problem is that dealers, though acting independently, think in the same way, see the same facts, and read the same data. They will therefore tend to act in the same way and consequently push currencies below or above their "true" value. The spot rate under a clean float is simply the price that clears the foreign exchange market; it is not necessarily the "true" price or the price that will balance payments for the countries concerned.

Volatility of this kind will tend to discourage exports and imports and to eliminate the consequent gains from international trade. Exporters and importers need to know what price they will actually pay for the goods they buy. Too much volatility in an exchange rate—whether caused by dealer behavior or by real phenomena—will impede international trade

---

[9]Note that the two bundles in New York and Frankfurt are not identical. Some goods are not traded internationally (e.g., housing), and only traded goods will have world-determined prices.

and reduce the efficiency of the global economic system. For this reason, nations may adopt a dirty float.

A *dirty float* exists when governments (usually central banks) deliberately intervene in foreign exchange markets to prevent the exchange rate from fluctuating too greatly. The hands of the government dirty the system, and the resulting market-clearing price may or may not be the one that would be reached by underlying economic forces. Presumably, a dirty float will reduce the fluctuation of the exchange rate, but if the interventions are correctly performed, the exchange rate will be allowed to follow its true underlying trend. The problem here, of course, is that the government's operators do not know exactly what that trend is, and by intervening, they tend to smother the signaling system (the market) on which estimates of the trend would be most effectively based.

Fixed parities exist when governments agree to fix the exchange rate of their individual currencies at preagreed prices. This is dominant governmental intervention. It is the kind of arrangement that existed in the nineteenth century under the gold standard when the parity between two currencies was fixed by the amount and fineness of gold in the national currency unit. This provided an arbitrary parity, and nations could change their exchange rate only by devaluing their currency's gold value. This gives rise to the distinction between devaluation and depreciation. Both expressions imply a weakening of a currency in the foreign exchange market, but *devaluation* implies a reduction in the currency's gold content and takes place under a fixed-parity system, whereas *depreciation* means a loss of value against other currencies without any ultimate benchmark value. In theory, if two nations devalued their currencies simultaneously and by the same amount, devaluation could take place without any depreciation!

From 1946 to 1971, the world's financial system lived under a so-called dollar standard when the values of all currencies were expressed in terms of dollars (and through that in terms of gold at $35 per fine ounce). Under the Bretton Woods system, exchange rates tended to be preserved by national governments until there was no avoiding devaluation. Thus changes in exchange rates came infrequently, but when they came, they were very large. For example, in 1949, the pound was devalued against the dollar by about one-third (from $4.20 to $2.80).

If a government wishes to enforce a price in a marketplace, it can only do so by being willing to supply whatever amounts of the underlying good the market chooses to require at that price. Alternatively, if the predetermined price is higher than the equilibrium price, the government must stand willing to buy all that the private sector wishes to supply at the predetermined price. Agricultural price fixing usually involves a higher-than-equilibrium price being agreed to by the government for internal political reasons. Then farmers will produce the goods in question and force the government to buy them. The governments have to have lots of storage capacity if the price is wildly excessive, but governments usually only have to provide domestic or local currency, which they can obtain fairly easily. When the commodity in question is foreign exchange, the problem is different. It is considered unlawful and antisocial for one government to print notes in another country's currency—it is, in fact, simple forgery. Therefore, if a government wishes to maintain the price of its currency in terms of foreign exchange at a higher-than-equilibrium price, it must stand ready to supply foreign exchange in order to buy up excess supplies of its own currency. Figure 12-1 shows that at the rate of exchange of 2.50, there is an excess supply of dollars of *GH*. Every year, the government must provide foreign exchange in the amount of 2.50 × *GH* if it is to preserve the price at 2.50. Now a government, indeed a country, has finite amounts of foreign reserves or gold, deposits denominated in foreign exchange, and the ability to borrow foreign exchange. Ultimately, unless the equilibrium price shifts, the government will be unable to maintain the price of 2.50—no one can buy forever out of a limited amount of reserves. This was the reason the Bretton Woods system ultimately collapsed (see Chapter 17).

The world's financial arrangements allow all three methods to be used at the same time by different nations. The European nations are trying to maintain a set of fixed rates among themselves but allow the "collection of currencies" to fluctuate against non-European currencies such as the dollar and the yen. This system has periods of difficulty as member nations are forced to devalue their currency periodically. The Canadians and the Japanese are quite prepared to intervene in foreign exchange markets (a dirty float), while the United States during the first Reagan administration maintained a clean float. In September 1985, the United States switched to a dirty float because of the arrant overvaluation of the dollar (See Chapter 15). Most developing countries impose currency controls on their residents so that they are renouncing the idea of a free foreign exchange market entirely and tend to maintain an exchange rate fixed in terms of some major currency.[10]

The spot rate is determined by the demand for and supply of a particular currency in the foreign exchange market. Spot rates are kept consistent with each other by three-cornered arbitrage so that the whole network of exchange rates is simultaneously determined. Governments interfere with transactions in in their own currencies to differing degrees, but the developed countries of the world accept the principle of free access to foreign exchange markets and, therefore, to exchange rates determined by supply and demand. Exchange rates change over time as the underlying conditions change: A cyclical change causing a recession in one country will tend to strengthen that country's exchange rate temporarily; a real change embodying changed tastes or productive capacity will cause a

---

[10]With consequent periodic large devaluations—witness the history of the Mexican peso in recent years.

permanent change in the rate; differential rates of inflation will be matched by matching (offsetting) changes in the exchange rate. Changes in the net flows of capital will also affect the spot rates by strengthening the currency of the country receiving the capital inflow.[11] One problem with capital flows is that, to the extent that they are reversible, they impart instability to the exchange rate since what flows in in one month or year may flow out in the following year and impart an opposite effect on the spot rate. This is the importance of the distinction between long-term capital and short-term capital on the presumption that long-term capital is not reversible while short-term capital is likely to flow in and flow out again. This distinction is developed in Chapter 13.

FORWARD MARKETS IN FOREIGN EXCHANGE

Importers and exporters necessarily take positions in foreign exchange when they undertake to buy or supply goods whose price is denominated in foreign exchange. In this way, they expose themselves to the risk of loss due to fluctuation in the foreign exchange rate between the time the contract is entered into and the time payment is made. If a firm can avoid this risk by "pairing itself off" with another firm that has an equal and opposite risk, uncertainty can be avoided.[12] If uncertainty can be avoided, people will be more willing to enter into contracts with foreigners, and the international trade mechanism will work that much more efficiently as an allocative mechanism. One of the ways in which a firm can avoid foreign exchange risk is by entering into a forward contract for foreign exchange. Forward markets are simply markets that allow transactions to be agreed to in the present for culmination at some specified future date. For example, a forward contract in foreign exchange entered into on January 1 for ninety days in the future will set a price (exchange rate) to which both parties agree on January 1 at which the two currencies will be exchanged on April 1. An importer will make such a contract with a bank, but the bank is merely serving as an intermediary for another commercial firm that has an opposite risk (or is taking a speculative position).

A firm is exposed to risk in foreign exchange for two distinct reasons. The firm may have received a shipment of goods (whose invoice is denominated in a foreign currency) and may be entitled to a period of grace before payment is due. If the firm has ninety days' credit on the shipment,

---

[11]The importance of capital flows in determining the spot rate is developed in William H. Branson, "Asset Market Equilibrium, the Exchange Rate and the Balance of Payments," in *Readings in Money, National Income and Stabilization Policy,* 4th ed., Ronald L. Teigen, pp. 436–439. (Homewood, Ill.: Irwin, 1978).

[12]Note that when two units of a multinational corporation trade with each other, there is no foreign exchange risk for the multinational as a unit.

that period of grace is tantamount to an interest-free loan for ninety days for the face amount of the invoice. (If the shipment is invoiced at DM 230,000 and the local interest rate on commercial loans is 10 percent per annum, the credit would be worth $2,500, 230,000 × 0.4348 × 0.10 × 0.25, where the four numbers are the face amount, the exchange rate, the annual interest rate, and the fraction of the year for which the loan is outstanding.) To enjoy that advantage, the importer is "short" in deutsche marks: There is a liability (the invoice) with no offsetting asset in the same currency. The advantage could be eradicated (and more) if the dollar weakens during the ninety-day period. Only if the importer feels sure that the dollar is not going to weaken substantially during the ninety days will the correct action be to remain exposed in marks and to bear the risk. There are three other options: The importer can feel that the dollar will depreciate by more than the 2.5 percent break-even margin during the course of the ninety days, in which event the importer may pay cash (converting at the spot rate) and renounce the credit; a second option is to buy marks ninety days forward even if the forward rate is less attractive than the spot rate (but the forward premium on the mark is less than the break-even 2.5 percent); a third option is to borrow money in dollars from the local bank, convert those dollars into marks at the spot rate, and invest the marks in German commercial paper to mature when the invoice is due.

Only if the importer can be sure that the period of credit is a benefit will the payment be postponed for the ninety days. The most practical way of looking at the cost of a forward contract (in comparison with converting at the spot rate and renouncing the credit) is as an insurance policy against a weakening of the dollar. (Of course, it is always possible that the dollar will strengthen during the ninety-day period, in which case the importer is in the position of a man who took out term insurance on his life and did not die.) By taking out a forward contract, the importer knows exactly what the goods will cost him in his own currency and can make rational pricing decisions on the basis of that information.

The second way in which a firm is exposed to foreign exchange risk involves the delay between signing an order and actual delivery. This problem can be very severe in purchases of complex equipment that is made to order and might require a year or more for manufacture. The purchaser is exposed to foreign exchange risk if the contract is denominated in foreign exchange. There is always uncertainty in such orders, and normally firms make an attempt to reduce the risk by tying the final price to changes in the cost of raw materials and to changes in the cost of labor. Taking out forward cover eliminates exchange rate risk if the period of cover is equal to the delivery time; if the delivery time exceeds the maximum length of a forward contract (one year in major currencies), the exchange rate risk is only reduced and not eliminated. Consider an Italian firm purchasing a machine from an American engineering firm with the delivery scheduled for six months in the future. The Italian firm can compute the cost of the machine in lire at the time the order is placed but has no reliable information as to the dollar-lira rate six months hence and therefore has no reliable idea of the cost of the machine in lira when it is delivered. A contract buying dollars 180 days forward will give the Italian firm a certain price. Of course, the exchange rate could move favorably to the lira in the six months and the Italians will have paid dearly for the privilege of knowing the future lira price of the machine (the "insurance premium" *plus* the favorable effect of the appreciation of the lira). If the exchange rate moves unfavorably to the lira by more than the cost of forward cover, the firm has made a tangible benefit from the forward contract as well as having firm knowledge about the future cost of the machine. Because commercial firms are not experts in foreign exchange forecasting, they will normally tend to avoid being exposed in foreign exchange.

Of the four options, standing exposed and renouncing the period of credit by paying cash are the extremes. The option of forward cover must be weighed against the option of buying the foreign exchange now and investing abroad to avert the foreign exchange risk. This latter procedure is called a "money market hedge."[13] In normal circumstances, when the spot and forward foreign exchange markets are integrating efficiently, there will be no appreciable difference in the cost of a forward contract and a money market hedge. Therefore, most commercial firms (MNCs excepted, perhaps) will rely on forward contracts as a means of insuring against their foreign exchange risk.[14]

THE SPOT-FORWARD DIFFERENTIAL

How do the spot and forward markets interact, and how is the cost of a forward contract determined? The crucial mechanism here is the willingness of the commercial banks who are dealers in foreign exchange to conduct *interest-rate arbitrage*.

Assume there is only one future market (ninety days) and that the spot rate (ϵ_s) is 2.3 ($1.00 = DM 2.30). Let the forward rate (ϵ_f) be 2.323 so that the dollar is at a forward premium (is stronger forward than spot). The cost of forward cover in D-marks is as follows:

---

[13]See David K. Eiteman and Arthur I. Stonehill, *Multinational Business Finance*, 3rd ed., (Reading, Mass.: Addison-Wesley, 1982), pp. 205–211. Note that a money market hedge can last as long as the delivery time. For other ways of hedging, see the supplement following this chapter.

[14]Multinational corporations are big enough to have their own banking connections in many countries and their own staff of experts on foreign exchange trading. They will tend to have regional financial centers. By coordinating the foreign exchange exposures of their many subsidiaries, it is possible for MNCs to judge the risk situation better and to reduce transaction costs in obtaining the insurance protection through use of their own facilities.

$$\frac{\epsilon_f - \epsilon_s}{\epsilon_s} \times 4 \qquad\qquad (2)$$

so

$$\frac{2.323 - 2.300}{2.300} \times 4 = 4\% \text{ (annual rate)}$$

To take a position in D-marks and to cover that position in the forward market costs 4 percent per annum.

Suppose that the interest rate paid on good-quality, short-term financial instruments in Germany is 12 percent per annum and that paid in the United States is 6 percent per annum. An American banker will immediately perceive that there is a larger profit to be made by investing in Germany than in the United States—a difference of 6 percent per annum.[15] American bankers will immediately sell assets yielding 6 percent in the United States, convert the funds into D-marks, and invest in German short-term financial instruments. In the process, the American bankers will find themselves exposed (long) in marks and vulnerable to any decline in the value of the mark in terms of the U.S. dollar. The appeal of the higher interest rates in Germany is reduced. However, the bankers can find a solution in forward cover. They can simultaneously sell dollars for marks in the spot market, invest in Germany to earn the 6 percent per annum more available there than in the United States, and avoid exposure in marks by taking out a forward contract at an annualized cost of 4 percent. There is a net gain of 2 percent per annum that follows from investing in Germany. The difference in the rates of interest exceeds the cost of insurance against depreciation of the mark. The more professional term for the act of insurance is *hedging,* so the 4 percent cost is usually referred to as a *hedging premium.*

Such a situation cannot last indefinitely; it will "self-destruct." The American bankers cannot buy marks in the spot market and buy dollars in the forward market without affecting the rates of exchange in both markets. The simple process of buying marks spot will tend to push up the value of the mark, causing ϵ_s to fall to 2.2250. At the same time, the surge of purchases of dollars in the forward market will strengthen the dollar there and push the value of ϵ_f to 2.2584. The cost of hedging is now

$$\frac{2.2584 - 2.2250}{2.2250} \times 4 = 6\%$$

There is now no further incentive for American bankers to sell assets in the United States and to invest the funds in Germany because the

[15]The numbers are, of course, much exaggerated.

cost of forward cover exactly equals the difference in the interest rates. Only if a bank is willing to expose itself in marks is investing in German short-term instruments worthwhile.

To this point there has been a tacit assumption that the short-term rates of interest in the two countries are not affected by capital flows. The greater size of national money markets relative to foreign exchange markets suggests that the greater part of the adjustment will take place in the cost of forward cover (the spot-forward differential); similarly, central banks may offset (wholly or partially) the inflow and outflow of capital by open market operations. In practice, there is likely to be some small adjustment in the difference between the two domestic rates of interest so that the hedging premium (cost of forward cover) will not reach the original difference in the two interest rates. The full expression for ninety-day interest-rate parity is then

$$i_f - i_d = \frac{\epsilon_f - \epsilon_s}{\epsilon_s} \times 4 \qquad (3)$$

where i_f and i_d represent short-term foreign and domestic interest rates, respectively.

Empirical research on the relationship confirms it quite strongly. However, the relationship cannot be exact because of the existence of transactions costs and because of the number of short-term interest rates available in any well-developed national financial market. This behavior does not rule out the possibility of some uncovered investments taking place, but to the extent that such investments work against the relationship expressed in equation (3), they merely create the opportunity for more *covered-interest arbitrage.*

Covered-interest arbitrage is the pattern of behavior that validates equation (3). Banks will buy foreign money market instruments as long as they provide a means of increasing the rate of return on assets compatible with the absence of exposure in foreign exchange. Arbitrage, by definition, involves the simultaneous purchase and sale of an asset for profit or, in modern terminology, a locked-in profit. Three-cornered arbitrage can be thought of as arbitraging over space, interest arbitrage as arbitraging over time. Under interest arbitrage, the bank has a balanced position in each currency at the time that the asset matures. The explanation was given in terms of American bankers taking advantage of the profit opportunity, but it is also possible for German bankers to do so. Unless the Germans are multinational banks with dollar liabilities (deposits) or easy access to borrowing dollars, they will be at something of a disadvantage, since they will have to borrow dollars from a bank located in the United States, and this transaction may add enough to costs to eliminate the profit opportunity. Small banks are at a similar disadvantage, but since small banks are not likely to be foreign exchange dealers, they are unlikely to be aware of the fleeting opportunities for covered-interest arbitrage anyhow.

The interest-parity theorem—equation (3)—is useful because it shows that when the foreign exchange markets are in equilibrium, there will be no advantage in choosing a money market hedge over forward cover. The two options will cost the same. Both options rely fundamentally on the difference in interest rates at home and abroad, and both mechanisms will weaken the spot rate for dollars relative to the forward rate.[16]

The foreign exchange markets have evolved a simplified arrangement to facilitate covered-interest arbitrage. This is a situation in which two banks swap dollars for marks. A bank seeking to balance its foreign exchange position may wish to acquire dollars spot and buy marks forward, and a second bank may wish to indulge in covered-interest arbitrage. Rather than go through two transactions each, one in the spot market and the other in the forward market, the two banks will agree to swap currencies over time for a fee (the swap rate). The swap rate is simply the forward spot hedging rate and is equal to the difference in interest rates. The bank borrowing the currency with the higher interest rate will pay the fee. The exchange of currencies is reversed automatically at the end of the period. By this process, transactions costs are reduced.[17]

THE MECHANICS OF SPECULATION

Speculation makes a profit by buying something cheaply and selling it later at a higher price. It is risky because the price of the asset purchased may not go up. One can speculate in practically anything that is traded in an efficient market. In many markets, including the market for foreign exchange, one can speculate both ways: One can buy in the expectation of a price rise or one can sell what one does not own in the hope of a price decrease (the sale being consummated with a purchase made later at a lower price).

Speculation in foreign exchange involves deliberately taking an uncovered position in a foreign currency (short or long) in the expectation of a price change. A speculator might buy Japanese yen with dollars in the expectation that the yen will strengthen (appreciate) against the dollar; alternatively, a speculator might sell lire without any compensating asset denominated in lire, in the hope that the lira will weaken against the dollar (the speculator's home currency). Speculative profits are made if the speculator has guessed correctly; speculative losses follow from a wrong guess.

There are costs to speculation, so the change in the exchange rate

[16]See Eiteman and Stonehill, *Multinational Business Finance*, pp. 205–211.
[17] See Kubarych, *Foreign Exchange Markets in the United States*, pp. 10–12.

must not only be in the direction forecast but must also be sufficiently big that the speculative gain exceeds the costs involved. The fee paid to foreign exchange dealers is an obvious cost, but the cost of the fee per dollar converted decreases quickly with the size of the transaction. Speculators must therefore speculate with large amounts of money to reduce average currency conversion costs, and this nearly always involves the use of borrowed funds. Consider a speculator with $10,000 who expects the lira to fall against the dollar. The speculator can use his $10,000 as security for a loan in Italy of $100,000 worth of lire, the proceeds are invested in the United States at the dollar rate of interest. If the lira weakens by 10 percent, the loan can be paid off with $90,000 (converted into lire at the new exchange rate), and the speculator has made a profit of $10,000 less costs. If costs are zero, the rate of return on invested (exposed) capital is 100 percent.[18]

But costs are not zero. The speculator must pay the interest on the loan but has also earned some interest from investing the dollars in the U.S. market. Almost always, the costs of borrowing a weak currency exceed the rate of interest that can be earned on a currency expected to strengthen. The speculator will endure costs from carrying the short position as well as from conversion fees. The profit can be expressed as follows:

$$\pi = \frac{\epsilon_t - \epsilon_o}{\epsilon_o} - \frac{CF}{\$100,000} - (i_\mathrm{I} - i_\mathrm{US})\left(\frac{t}{360}\right) \tag{4}$$

where π is the profit per dollar invested, CF represents conversion fees; and i_I and i_US are the Italian and U.S. rates of interest. The subscript o indicates the original rate of exchange, and t denotes the rate of exchange at time t (calculated on a 360-day year). In the last factor, t denotes how long the position was held. Let i_I be 16 percent per annum and i_US be 10 percent per annum. Let the lira weaken by 4 percent[19] and conversion fees amount to $200, or 0.2 percent. The speculator makes a profit when the weakening of the lira comes about one month after the speculative position has been taken. The 4 percent profit (per dollar) is reduced by 0.2 percent for conversion fees and 0.5 percent net interest cost. The speculator makes a profit of 3.3 percent on $100,000, or $3,300—a better than 30 percent profit on own funds invested ($10,000) in a month. That is the happy outcome for the speculator. Now look at the gloomy side. Suppose the lira only weakens by 1 percent after nine months. The net receipts from the venture are $1,000—the loan is repaid with $99,000. The costs are $200 for conversion and net interest costs of 4.5 percent

[18]The example neglects some arithmetic niceties. The speculator's own capital is assumed to remain invested in dollars in the United States and becomes involved in the computation only if it is needed to help repay the loan—in a loss situation.

[19]If ϵ_o is 1,600 lire per dollar, ϵ_t is 1,664.

($4,500). The speculator only retrieves $5,300 out of his committed security of $10,000. There is a still worse scenario if the lira actually strengthens!

When the foreign exchange market is operating under a clean float, the speculator must "outguess" the market. When governments intervene, the speculator must consider not only market forces and market expectations but also governmental reactions. When exchange rates were ostensibly fixed under the Bretton Woods system, it became apparent from time to time that a currency was severely overvalued and that good economic policy require that it be devalued. But monetary authorities were (and are) often more concerned with taming speculators than with good economic policy (not to mention the fact that incumbent politicians tend to lose face in the event of a large devaluation),[20] and frequently the authorities tried to outwit the speculators. In 1966, the pound sterling was badly overvalued as a result of inflation in Great Britain, but the official exchange rate was maintained because an election was due shortly. The British authorities supported the pound by borrowing foreign exchange and using the proceeds to buy sterling in the foreign exchange market. Many speculators were badly burned by borrowing pounds at very high interest rates when the Labour government did not allow the pound to devalue after the election. The speculators had all of the (high) carrying costs of the short position (in sterling) and no profit to show. The pound was eventually devalued in November 1967, by just over 14 percent.

RECENT BEHAVIOR OF EXCHANGE RATES

The era of fixed rates of exchange came to an end in early 1973 (see Chapter 17). Since then, rates of exchange have been allowed to fluctuate relatively freely (with the exception of the rates among the currencies of the members of the EEC). Let us examine the recent behavior of the exchange rates of four important currencies—the U.S. dollar, the Japanese yen, the deutsche mark, and the pound sterling—for the years 1976–1985. This period witnessed the second oil shock, severe monetary tightening in the United States in fall 1980 in response to excessively low rates of interest in the United States prior to that time, and the softening of oil prices in 1983–1985. It is possible to identify the causes of the longer-lasting fluctuations in exchange rates.

All transactions in foreign exchange markets, spot and forward, are conducted in what are called "nominal" rates of exchange. In contrast,

[20]Not only is a devaluation in some sense a blow to national pride, but, in addition, it involves an adverse shift in the terms of trade, increasing the cost of imported goods and generating inflation. The larger is the ratio of imports to GNP, the larger the inflationary impetus.

economists are interested (as well) in what the rates of exchange look like after the nominal rates have been adjusted for differing rates of inflation in the two countries. These rates, called "real" rates of exchange, are the nearest measure available of the terms of trade. Of course, the real rates of exchange are computed at actual levels of employment and in the presence of capital movements so that the correspondence between the abstract concept developed in Part II and the numbers presented in Table 12-3 is only approximate. There is the additional problem that available measures of inflation are imperfect for this purpose, which should emphasize only inflation in tradable goods.

Selected nominal rates are given in Table 12-2. From a comparison of the rates in the two tables, it would be possible to compute a measure of the relative rates of inflation in different countries (price-level disturbances). Measurement error apart, all other changes must be due to cyclical or real disturbances. Nominal rates of exchange are important (Table 12-2) because they are the rates at which transactions are carried out at the particular time. In the turbulent periods following the breakdown of the system of fixed rates and the oil-price shocks of 1974 and

Table 12-2
NOMINAL EXCHANGE RATES

		Yen per Dollar	Deutsche Marks per Dollar	Pounds Sterling per Dollar
1976		296.38	2.52	0.554
1977		267.79	2.32	0.573
1978		208.42	2.01	0.521
1979		218.18	1.83	0.471
1980		225.68	1.82	0.430
1981		220.63	2.26	0.494
1982		249.06	2.43	0.572
1983		237.55	2.55	0.660
1984	March	225.27	2.60	0.687
	June	233.57	2.74	0.726
	September	245.46	3.03	0.796
	December	247.96	3.10	0.843
1985	March	257.92	3.30	0.889
	June	248.84	3.06	0.781
	September	236.53	2.84	0.733
	December	202.79	2.51	0.692
1986	March	178.69	2.28	0.681

Source: *Federal Reserve Bulletin,* various issues.

Note: Data for 1976–1983 are annual averages.
Data for 1984–1986 are monthly averages.

The dollar's strength reached a short-term peak in February 1985, when it exchanged for 260 yen; 3.3 marks and 0.915 pounds. The surge in the strength of the dollar in late 1984 and early 1985 was mainly seen in terms of the European currencies. The rapid weakening of the dollar after the official intervention, which began in September 1985, is easily visible. See also Table 12-3.

1979, inflation affected the industrialized democracies unequally, so much of the variation in nominal rates in the 1970s could be attributed to price-level disturbances.[21] But there were real effects as well. Japan's dependence on imported oil meant that the yen weakened substantially in real terms in the second half of 1979, but the Japanese took prompt remedial steps (including recession) that allowed the yen to strengthen again quite quickly. The strength of sterling in the early 1980s was due to a combination of the development of North Sea oil and the very tight monetary policy of Prime Minister Margaret Thatcher's first years in office. Tight money led to high interest rates, which attracted foreign funds to London and strengthened the pound.[22] When the level of interest rates in Britain was allowed to recede, the pound weakened.

The nominal rates given in Table 12-2 are necessarily bilateral. International transactions take place in a multicountry world, and the actions of the individual countries affect exchange rates directly through the two countries concerned and indirectly through their effects on transactions with third countries. The rates given in Table 12-3 are *real effective rates*. The rates are given in index number form and reflect events in fourteen countries. Each exchange rate is deflated into a real rate, and the importance of the real rate is weighted by the importance of international trade with the country concerned. Thus in Table 12-3, the strength of the dollar is shown in index number form (1980–1982 = 100), and the dollar gets stronger as the number increases. But this number reflects changes in the real rates of exchange with all fourteen countries included in the computations. The data in Table 12-3 are as close as economists can come to a measure of a nation's multilateral terms of trade. There are of course problems in computing the number, since the inflation index chosen cannot be completely correct and because trade patterns change over time. One final caveat is in order: There are no grounds for supposing that the base years (1980–1982) saw a "correct" set of exchange rates, and the numbers only show strength and weakness relative to the base period. Recall that a strong currency means that the terms of trade have moved in favor of the country in question but that its industries will tend to find themselves squeezed by foreign competition. It is immediately apparent that, as the competitiveness ratio indicates, real rates are the necessary guide for the pressures on an industry.

There are other influences on the currencies identified in Table 12-3, but the three nondollar currencies can be considered as forming a bloc that moves contrary to the dollar. When the dollar is weak, the other three currencies will be relatively strong, and vice versa.

---

[21]For an analysis of the interrelation among oil prices, food prices, and inflation, see H. Peter Gray, "Oil-Push Inflation: A Broader Examination," *Banca Nazionale del Lavoro Quarterly Review* March 1981, pp. 49–67.

[22]This effect was very similar to that achieved by the Reagan administration in the United States in 1982–1985; see Chapter 15.

Table 12-3

REAL EFFECTIVE EXCHANGE RATES (1980–1982 = 100)

	United States	Japan	West Germany	United Kingdom
1976 June	94.8	97.8	104.1	68.9
December	95.5	98.2	106.8	67.8
1977 June	94.2	102.5	105.1	73.7
December	91.7	109.7	106.7	77.2
1978 June	89.5	118.3	105.2	75.5
December	87.4	119.3	107.2	77.6
1979 June	88.6	105.9	106.5	86.0
December	88.9	95.3	107.9	88.3
1980 June	87.2	107.5	104.8	98.2
December	91.9	110.6	98.8	105.4
1981 June	103.6	104.1	96.4	103.2
December	101.5	103.3	97.9	98.1
1982 June	110.6	91.3	99.5	99.0
December	111.9	94.2	100.7	95.0
1983 March	110.6	96.3	99.0	89.2
June	112.7	96.8	99.5	95.2
September	114.1	94.8	99.5	95.4
December	115.4	98.5	100.7	93.0
1984 March	111.9	99.9	98.5	90.6
June	116.3	97.7	97.0	89.6
September	121.6	96.7	95.1	88.5
December	124.2	95.6	94.9	85.2
1985 March	129.6	94.0	94.0	86.5
June	124.7	93.1	94.2	93.9
September	117.9	95.5	96.1	95.9
December	111.9	92.9	97.9	93.1
1986 March	101.7	116.4	98.9	90.8

Source: Morgan Guaranty, *World Financial Markets,* various issues.

Note that the pound was very strong (because of Prime Minister Thatcher's economic policies) in 1980–1982, the base period. It weakened in late 1985 because of the weakness in the price of oil. For an explanation of the construction of the indexes, see source.

The dollar began to strengthen in the second half of 1980, when tight money was instituted with Draconian ferocity by the Federal Reserve System and the nominal short-term interest rate rose from 8.126 percent in July to 15.661 percent (per annum) in December.[23] Since that time, a combination of budget deficits on the part of the Reagan administration and monetary restraint have caused the dollar to strengthen further. This strength of the dollar has imposed great pressure on the multinational corporations, which have to repatriate foreign profits that are now earned in very cheap currencies, and has hurt exporting and import-competing industries in the United States. Note the dramatic change in the competitiveness of U.S. industries vis-à-vis their Japanese counter-

[23]These are rates on new U.S. Treasury Bills. (U.S. Treasury data).

parts between December 1980, and December 1984. The dollar has strengthened by more than one third at the same time that the Japanese yen was weakening by about 15 percent. Of course, some of this movement is attributable to the inverse relationships of the data in Table 12-3, but not all of it can be explained in this way. (Ask Chrysler!) In late 1984 and early 1985, a speculative surge seems to have developed, particularly involving movement out of European currencies into the American dollar. This speculative surge brought about a combined intervention by European central banks to sell dollars in early March 1985. The immediate success of the intervention was not apparent, but European currencies strengthened shortly after in response to some relatively mild instability in the U.S. financial system (a large savings and loan association in Ohio had to close its doors, and a government securities dealer failed). It is possible that the intervention had the effect of unsettling the confidence of some of the speculators, causing small events to have disproportionately large repercussions. As a general rule, the farther a market price is away from some range considered "normal," the more taut are the nerves of the people in the market. The governmental intervention may have made it clear to speculators that the existing price was excessive and contributed to their subsequent actions in this way.

The yen weakened steadily and drastically from the onset of tight money in the United States in late 1980, and this weakness contributed to the large bilateral trade surplus that Japan enjoyed with the United States. One of the major contributors to this weakness has been the large federal deficit in the United States which forced up interest rates and attracted the very large Japanese savings.[24] (The Japanese save roughly three times as much of their disposable income as Americans.) The weakness of the yen started to be reversed in September 1985, when the monetary authorities of the five leading commercial nations agreed that something had to be done to weaken the excessively strong dollar. Since then the yen has soared in value and the Japanese economy has gone into a mini-recession (despite the benefits of large decreases in the world price of oil at this time).

The D-mark was relatively strong until the second half of 1980, and since that time, its strength seems to derive mainly from the presence or absence of a flow of funds to New York. In fact, the European economy as a whole was in a protracted recession, emerging only in 1985. The Europeans simultaneously benefit from the high rate of the dollar in that it allowed them to generate current account surpluses, with resulting expansionary effects, but the high rates of interest in the United States attracted funds and kept European interest rates higher than was desirable from a macroeconomic point of view. These strains were the topic of discussion at several economic summits.

[24]See Chapter 15.

The strength of the pound in the second half of the 1970s was mainly attributable to the development of North Sea oil, with a salutory effect on the British balance of payments (but with negative effects on British manufacturing). At the same time, Britain became a full member of the EEC and exposed its market for manufactures to competition from the economies of the other members of the Community. The election of Margaret Thatcher resulted in a stringent dose of monetary restraint, which, in turn, pushed short-term interest rates to very high levels. The consequent inflow of funds strengthened sterling. With the passage of time, British monetary policy eased and the pound weakened as a result of the decline in British interest rates and, in 1983–1985, the fall-off in oil revenues. The weakness in the pound as well as in other European currencies in terms of the dollar (and in real terms) led to a significant increase in expenditures in Europe by American tourists in 1984 and 1985. One major British department store was advertising in the *New York Times* that a visitor could make such a "profit" on the extreme strength of the dollar that the cost of the journey would be repaid! The pound strengthened with the other European currencies after September 1985.

SUMMARY

Foreign exchange markets are of supreme importance in international economics because the actual rates serve as the bridge by which costs and prices in two countries can be compared. The markets are highly efficient in the sense that transaction costs are relatively small, and the existence of forward markets provides a very good way in which exposures can be hedged.

Unfortunately, foreign exchange markets do not always clear at the "right price," and as a result, some instability is introduced into national economies. Frequently, the source of the "inappropriate rate" is a macroeconomic problem in one of the countries involved. The high rates of interest in the United States that follow from the huge federal deficit lead to an overvalued dollar, to the detriment of many corporations (see Chapter 15). So-called incorrect rates can also be caused by speculation in favor of a currency. The harm done by an incorrect level of a currency (an overvalued or undervalued rate for a protracted period) probably has greater significance than an erratic or fluctuating rate on a day-to-day basis. The latter impedes international trade and investment by increasing the accompanying uncertainty; the former can weaken an industry—in extreme cases driving firms into bankruptcy.

Exchange rate movements are probably the single most important aspect of international economic relationships relative to domestic relationships.

Bibliography

Grabbe, J. Orlin. *International Financial Markets.* New York: Elsevier, 1986.

Kubarych, Roger M. *Foreign Exchange Markets in the United States.* New York: Federal Reserve Bank of New York, 1978.

Levi, Maurice. *International Finance.* New York: McGraw-Hill, 1983.

Poniachek, H. A. "International Financial Markets." In *Handbook of International Business,* ed. Ingo Walter and Tracy Murray, ch. 18. New York: Wiley, 1982.

Wihlborg, Clas G. "Forecasting Exchange Rates." In *Handbook of International Business,* ed. Ingo Walter and Tracy Murray, ch. 17. New York: Wiley, 1982.

Questions and Problem

Questions

1. Why can a government more easily support the price of wheat at a price higher than equilibrium than it can support its exchange rate?
2. If a central bank wants to strengthen its currency, should it buy or sell foreign exchange in the foreign exchange market? Give reasons.
3. How does arbitrage promote efficiency?
4. Why does arbitrage "self-destruct"?
5. The relative purchasing power parity theorem explains how nominal rates adjust when there is a price-level disturbance. Show how this involves a changing nominal rate of exchange and a constant real rate.
6. There is no such thing as a "clean float." Explain why this statement is true in a purist, long-run sense.
7. Why will banks seek arbitrage profits when interest parity does not hold? How would they do so if the spot and forward rates of the dollar against the deutsche mark were the same and interest rates were higher in Frankfurt than in New York?
8. Speculating is a great way to get a large amount of money. Comment.
9. Why did the dollar weaken after September 1985? For background, read the financial press for September 1985 through March 1986. Also see the "Treasury and Federal Reserve Foreign Exchange Operations" reports in the *Federal Reserve Bank of New York Quarterly Review.*
10. Select a currency other than the yen, mark, or pound and write a brief account of its recent performance in foreign exchange markets, explaining any major trends or gyrations.

Problem

(This problem can be varied to encompass as much work as needed and can become a brief term project.)

Pick a country and a currency. Compile the main balance-of-payments entries for the last ten years (as Table A). Then record (as Table B) the nominal rate of exchange of that country's currency with the U.S. dollar (use *International Financial Statistics or the Federal Reserve Bulletin* as your source). Then compute and record (as Table C) the real rate of exchange of the selected country's currency against the U.S. dollar using quarterly data for six years. A worksheet model

Table C

REAL RATE OF EXCHANGE

Period	Nominal Rate	Index (_____ = 100)	Local Inflation (_____ = 100)	U.S. Inflation (_____ = 100)	Relative Inflation Index	Real Rate of Exchange (_____ = 100)
1980 (1)						
(2)						
(3)						
(4)						
1981 (1)						
etc.						

is provided. (Be sure you understand how to deflate nominal values by use of index numbers.)

Be sure to list sources and explain the choice of deflator used.

The trick is that the way in which the "relative inflation index" is applied to the index of the nominal rate depends on the way in which the actual nominal rate is reported. Here there is no substitute for common sense. Assume that the foreign country is West Germany. If the exchange rate is quoted as 2.30, the formula is

$$R = N\left(\frac{\text{US inflation}}{\text{WG inflation}}\right)$$

(An increase in N will be expected by purchasing power parity if Germany inflates faster than the United States, but if purchasing power parity holds, R is constant.)

Graph the nominal and real rates (in index form) for your period.

Finally, provide a brief explanation of any major changes in either the nominal or the real rate during the period. This requires looking at the history of the chosen country. A good reference is *The Economist*. Local information can often be obtained from consulates and from central bank publications.

Mechanics of Trading in Foreign Exchange

THOMAS A. FETHERSTON

Appalachian State University

The foreign exchange (FX) market results (currency prices) are part of the truncated financial news presented in the morning and evening newscasts in the United States. The twice-daily offering newscasts in the United States. The twice-daily offering of foreign exchange prices as opposed to the single postmortem for stock, bond, and commodity trading performances is indicative that trading in currencies is different from trading in most other financial assets. Whether a U.S. resident is on the East or West Coast, trading in foreign exchange continues at the end of the normal business day in the respective time zones. When the trading day closes in Los Angeles, trading activity in the currency market shifts with the sun to Asia and continues around the globe until it again reaches the East Coast (see Table 12-A). Even a novice can discern that the foreign exchange market is global and is in operation twenty-four hours a day.

The tumultuous period following the breakup of the fixed exchange rate system in 1973 had brought home to Americans the importance of the value of one currency in terms of another. We have grown to understand the inflationary effects of a declining currency, the increased purchasing power of a rising currency, and the relationship between the so-called overpriced dollar and the disruption to some of our export and import industries.

The twenty-four-hour foreign exchange market requires constant surveillance. The intensity of interest in monitoring the market depends on the nature of the market participant. The players in the market can be dichotomized into two general types, either passive or aggressive. The aggressive participant is trying to accomplish goals in the market itself, whereas the passive participant is using the foreign exchange market to achieve some other goal. The market is dominated by aggressive participants, who, when trading with each other, are playing a zero-

281

Table 12-A
FOREIGN EXCHANGE DEALING HOURS ACROSS THE GLOBE

Greenwich Mean Time	City	Opens or Closes
0000 (midnight)	San Francisco	Closes
0000	Hong Kong*	Opens
0430	Bahrain	Opens
0700	Tokyo	Closes
0730	Frankfurt	Opens
0830	London	Opens
0930	Hong Kong	Closes
1000	Bahrain	Closes
1300	New York	Opens
1600	Frankfurt	Closes
1600	San Francisco	Opens
1630	London	Closes
2130	New York	Closes
2300	Tokyo	Opens

*Singapore is also an important foreign exchange market. It opens and closes one hour later than Hong Kong.

sum game—for every gain there is an offsetting loss. The institutions in this category are the major commercial and merchant banks of the world as well as many second- and third-tier financial institutions.[1] Also in that group are the central banks of countries attempting to achieve some sterilization of monetary flows or political goals and who are willing to do so at the risk of losing precious international reserves. The passive actors attempt to use the foreign exchange market in the classic "hedge" (insurance) sense. The hedgers attempt to prevent loss or consolidate gains in other economic activities that involve foreign exchange exposure.

The two basic kinds of currency (foreign exchange) exposure flowing from international commerce are transaction and translation exposure. *Transaction exposure* arises when contracts for delivery of future goods and services to foreign firms generate revenues denominated in a currency different from that used to produce the goods or services (and similarly for purchases from abroad when the invoice is denominated in foreign currency). Any change in the value of the foreign currency can produce losses or gains in the conduct of normal commerce. *Translation exposure* comes about when a multinational corporation consolidates the financial statements of its foreign subsidiaries with the parent corporation's financial statements. Any changes in the exchange rate between the two currencies can produce gains or losses that are not related to "normal" business activity. The current accounting ruling (Financial Accounting Standards

[1]The major foreign exchange dealers are primarily U.S. commercial banks. The list of top ten dealers in 1984 was headed by Citibank and featured only two non-U.S. banks, Royal Bank of Canada and Barclays Bank (British). Those ten dealers account for 34 percent of the estimated market volume, according to "The Traders Whose Customers Love Them," *Euromoney,* May 1984, pp. 203–205.

Board No. 52) allows gains and losses from translation to be run through an adjustment account and explained in a footnote on the consolidated statement rather than being incorporated as gains or losses on the quarterly income statement. The net gains and losses must be recognized upon the sale or dissolution of the subsidiary. Translation exposure, although less important than transaction exposure, can still require hedging.

The normal consideration of the foreign exchange market, which comprises only a spot and a forward market, is not complete. There exists a swap market that allows for the simultaneous purchase and sale of a currency in one transaction. The spot market allows for execution of price today with settlement two business days later. The forward market allows a trader to arrange a price today for settlement on some future date. The future dates are multiple periods of thirty days (30, 90, 180 days, up to several years). The shorter maturities are common, and the longer-dated ones are rare. The level of activity is far greater in the spot market than in the forward market, by a wide margin. The size of the gross turnover of currencies dwarfs the level of international trade that necessitates foreign currency demand. The estimate of daily trading in the market of $150 billion indicates that annual global foreign exchange trading may approach $38 trillion.[2] Other estimates have placed the foreign exchange trading volume at even higher levels. Whatever the correct trading volume is, it is far in excess of the need for foreign exchange that the $98.8 billion global current account deficit in 1985 and its requisite financing would necessitate.[3]

In addition to the normal subsets of the foreign exchange market are the new vehicles in foreign exchange that allow for hedging and speculation in various currencies. The currency futures of the International Money Market (IMM) of the Chicago Mercantile Exchange offer standardized contracts and expiration dates that allow individuals and smaller institutional players access to the foreign exchange game. Another innovation of the post–Bretton Woods era is the introduction of listed and non-listed currency options. The purchaser of an option has the right either to call (buy) or to put (sell) a standardized amount of a currency to the writer of the option at a stated price. The currency option is a boon to both hedgers and speculators. For the hedger, it offers the opportunity to buy insurance against adverse currency shifts causing losses in the course of international trade. The currency hedger in the forward market and in the futures market protects himself from losses by locking in a rate but at the same time gives up any potential for gain if the currency moves in his favor. The option contract is asymmetric in that it offers

[2]"Foreign Exchange Market: Round the World on $150 Billion a Day," *The Economist*, November 30, 1985, p. 83.

[3]"World Economic Outlook 1986," *International Monetary Fund*, p. 212. Note that this figure is a statistical discrepancy since the global current account must be zero.

the purchaser insurance but at the same time does not prevent the holder of the option from profiting if the hedged currency moves in the hedger's favor.

The options and futures markets are parallel markets to the global foreign exchange dealer market in a manner similar to the relationship between the domestic dollar market and the offshore Eurodollar market. They have unique features that allow for their existence but are mere appendages of more dominant elements. In the FX case, the futures and options markets allow the dealers to lay off positions with the general public. The aggressive players speculate in these markets and at the same time provide liquidity for those seeking a hedge by taking a net short or long position (at a price) to meet the net demand for hedges.

SPOT MARKET

The actual purchase and sale of foreign exchange sometimes causes confusion for the layman. Part of the confusion comes from the unique terms of the foreign exchange market. The value of a currency is so many units of another currency or the reciprocal of that value expressed as so many units of one currency per unit of the other currency. From an American perspective, the rate would be expressed in dollars per unit of the foreign currency. The reciprocal of that expression, European or foreign terms, would be so many units of the foreign currency per dollar. The first relationship is often referred to as direct and the second indirect. Both expressions of value are correct, but in the dealer market the indirect expression (units of foreign currency per dollar) dominates. The British pound is one exception in that it is still expressed as so many units of foreign currency per pound (for example, $1.2500 = £1). The expressions of currency values presented in the daily financial press view the currencies in both ways. The dollars-per-mark or marks-per-dollar values for a given date may be DM 2.2500 and $0.4444, respectively. Those rates are expressed to four decimal places, each 10,000th of a unit being referred to as a "point." The need for such accuracy is troublesome to individuals who find it difficult to think beyond 44 cents per D-mark in the example. The four-decimal-place (number of points) convention bespeaks the need for accuracy on sizable transactions where, in the jargon of the foreign exchange traders, "one dollar" is shorthand for $1 million. In addition, foreign exchange traders in the pursuit of profits book numerous transactions with meager profit rates that can only be expressed in three or four decimal places. The convention also appears to be a function of the competitive nature of the dealer market.

The rates presented daily by the financial press and the other media seem to indicate that the currency can be bought and sold at the single stated value. The rate shown, however, does not represent buy and sell interests; it is a composite of the bid and offer spread of the dealer market in the respective currency. The composite DM 2.2500 is short for a bid of DM 2.2495 per dollar and an offer of a dollar at DM 2.2505. The spread between the bid and offer in this example is 10 points, and the composite expression is just a simple average of the two prices. The price of the currency depends on which role one is playing in the market—customer or dealer. The following example defines the roles that can be played for a given foreign exchange quote.

Indirect	Bid	Asked
Dealer	DM 2.2495 Buy dollars Sell DMs	DM 2.2505 Sell dollars Buy DMs
Customer	Sell dollars Buy DMs	Buy dollars Sell DMs

Direct	Bid	Asked
Dealer	$0.4443/DM ($1 = DM 2.2505) Buy DMs Sell dollars	$0.4445/DM ($1 = DM 2.2495) Sell DMs Buy dollars
Customer	Sell DMs Buy dollars	Buy DMs Sell dollars

The dealer and customer roles can be reversed when dealers are giving quotes to each other. The ability of the customer to buy at the bid side of the market and sell at the offer side is an illusion created by the fact that the other side of the transaction has currency value. In our sample direct quotation, the item being bought and sold is the mark. In the indirect quote, the asset being bought and sold is the dollar. Following that convention, one can see that the dealer is always trying to buy at the lower bid side and sell at the higher offer side of the market. The customer would be quoted a currency by the dealer either from a foreign exchange trader personally or through a sales representative of the foreign exchange dealer who acts as a liaison between the trader and the customer. The sales liaison profiles the type of customer asking for the quote, thus indicating to the trader the degree of competition required to effect a trade. Some customers, firms who are less active or less sophisticated than others, end up seeing wider spreads and thus incur higher foreign exchange transaction costs.

The dealers can and often do quote and deal with each other without the use of a broker intermediary; but for reasons of secrecy or efficiency, they resort to using the well-developed foreign exchange broker network, which helps in matching opposite interests. The brokers working for a small commission discreetly explore their contacts to match buyers and sellers. They take no position in the market and are thus deemed to be disinterested parties. The nature of their reward system would draw them to servicing the most active dealer accounts first with quotes and information on market activity.

SWAP MARKET

The swap market, as stated earlier, exists between the spot and outright forward market. It offers the opportunity to effect a buy or a sale in the spot market and an offsetting sale or buy at some forward date. The swap rate between two currencies is driven by the relationship between interest rates on like interest-earning instruments for the respective countries. Traders who wish to invest in a foreign short-term-interest instrument denominated in FX can find the cost of a "round-trip ticket" in that currency. The difference in value of the spot and forward contract is a function of interest parity theory:

$$\left(\frac{\text{Forward} - \text{Spot}}{\text{Spot}}\right)\left(\frac{12}{n}\right) = i_{\text{US}} - i_{\text{F}}$$

where n is the number of months in the forward contract, i_{US} is the U.S. interest rate, and i_{E} is the interest rate in the foreign country.

This formula will never be exact due to various risk factors, the impediment of transaction costs, and the lack of perfect interest instrument substitutes. Even accepting the lack of mathematical exactness, it does underline the importance of the relationship in explaining short-term foreign exchange changes in response to interest-rate shifts. The level of global communications is such that any divergence from the equilibrium position would stimulate flows to bring the currency relationship back to equilibrium. If interest rates on British short-term treasury issues were 2 percent greater than U.S. Treasury issues of the same maturity, the forward premium on the dollar for the same maturity would approximate 2 percent. The effect of an increase in interest rates in Britain would tend to affect the four variables in the interest parity relationship. Assume an increase in the margin between short-term rates for the British T-bills over U.S. T-bills from 2 percent to 4 percent due to contractionary monetary measures of the Bank of England. An incipient increase in U.K. rates will set off the following market movements in an attempt to achieve a new equilibrium. There will be an exit from U.S. T-bills at the margin, forcing rates up slightly, and an increase in the demand for pounds (supply of dollars) spot, causing the pound to rise (dollar to fall). At the same time, there will be an increase in the demand for U.K. T-bills, resulting in a slight fall in the U.K. T-bill rate. Arbitrageurs who are trying to gain a riskless yield pickup will sell the proceeds from the maturing U.K. interest vehicle forward, which adds to the demand for dollars (supply of pounds), increasing (decreasing) the value of the dollar (pound) forward. This process will continue until the interest differential and discount (premium) on the pound (dollar) achieve the new equilibrium level.

The swap market is an integral element in the ongoing process of attempting to equilibrate interest parity. The dealer market has a unique way of quoting swap rates. The following represent the dealer quote for the spot and 30-, 90-, and 180-day rates given as one quote:

Indirect	DM 2.2495–2.2505, 47/37, 110/100, 220/200
Direct	$0.4443–0.4445, 8/10, 20/22, 40/44

The market convention is to truncate the complete forward rate quote into a shorthand to save time, which is a scarce commodity in a rapid-fire trading environment. The convention is to subtract (add) the "trailer rates" 47/37, 110/100, 210/200 (8/10, 20/22, 40/44) from (to) the outright spot rate if the left-hand term is greater (less) than the right-hand term. From the quotes given, subtraction is in order in the indirect case and addition in the direct case, indicating that the dollar (D-mark) is selling at a forward discount (premium).

The full rates on the example are as follows:

	Indirect	Direct
Spot	DM 2.2495–2.2505	$0.4443–0.4445
30 days	DM 2.2448–2.2468	$0.4451–0.4455
90 days	DM 2.2385–2.2405	$0.4463–0.4467
180 days	DM 2.2275–2.2305	$0.4483–0.4485

The spread between the bid and offered quote is a function of the dealer risk reward system. The further into the future, the greater the uncertainty for the dealer making the market quote. There is also more activity in the spot market than in the swap or in the outright forward market. Facing more uncertainty, the dealer will attempt to increase his return and in so doing widen the spread between bid and asked. The second relationship is tied to the target rate of return per trade and overall profitability. More activity in the market allows the dealer to make less per trade and still be profitable, whereas less activity would have the dealer attempting to achieve greater profitability per trade.

FORWARD MARKET

The forward market allows passive and aggressive participants in the foreign exchange market to hedge and speculate without having to use any precious capital. The market procedure does not require any margin (funds set aside) against the settlement of the contract in the future.

Having no safety margin to protect his position from a customer's reneging on contracts that have, from the customer's perspective, gone awry, the dealer limits forward-transaction trading to customers of the highest credit category. Individuals, even wealthy ones, are not allowed to participate in this market. The lack of individual participation in this market was one of the important factors in the origination of the IMM currency futures contracts and other currency futures offerings that are open to all hedgers and speculators. The futures contracts do require margin, however, and are for standardized contract sizes and settlement dates.

The outright forward market in the past has had a limited maturity schedule, for even the major currencies of the world. The vast majority of the transactions are of money market duration, with contracts measured in years being the exception. The introduction of currency swaps and medium-term financing in different currencies, an innovation of foreign exchange capital market instrument engineering, could assist in assuring a wider, deeper forward market with longer maturities.

Here are some sample outright rates:

	Direct ($/£)	Indirect (¥/$)
Spot	$1.5405–1.5415	¥ 163.1005–163.1005
30 days	$1.5305–1.5325	¥ 163.0950–163.1000
90 days	$1.5200–1.5250	¥ 162.9990–163.0060
180 days	$1.5100–1.5175	¥ 162.5550–162.5700

The forward quotes indicate that in terms of dollars, the pound (dollar) is selling at a forward discount (premium). The quotes in terms of yen indicate that the yen (dollar) is selling at a forward premium (discount). The pound costs fewer dollars forward and the dollar costs fewer yen forward; both are therefore at a premium. The inverse relationship implies that more pounds and dollars would be required to buy dollars and yen, and therefore they are discounted in the direct and indirect quotes. The forward rates are, as noted earlier, a function of interest differentials between the respective countries.

CROSS RATES

The dollars-per-pound and yen-per-dollar rates can be used to determine the yen-per-pound cross rate. Cross rates are used to determine the value of respective currencies when they are not traded or quoted against each other. The cross rates can be computed in either of the two following ways (the offer spot rates are used for pedagogic purposes):

Multiplying   Dollars/pound × yen/dollar = yen/pound Rate
$1.5415 × ¥ 163.1005 = 251.4194 yen/pound

Dividing $$\frac{\text{Dollars/pound}}{\text{Dollars/yen}} = \text{yen/pound}$$

(The dollars-per-yen rate is the reciprocal of the yen-per-dollar rate.)

$$\frac{\$1.5415}{\$.00613} = 251.4194 \text{ yen/pound}$$

The division procedure should be used to find the cross rate when one is quoting two currencies in terms of the same third currency. Use multiplication to find the cross rate when the third currency is quoted directly and indirectly against the two other currencies.

CURRENCY FUTURES

The fact that the forward market had entry participation requirements that prevented many speculators or hedgers from profiting or protecting themselves in that market created a need for instruments that would offer the same or similar opportunities. The first of these instruments offered in the United States was the currency future of the IMM. Since 1976, currency contracts in British pounds, Canadian dollars, West German deutsche marks, Japanese yen, Mexican pesos, Swiss francs, Dutch guilders, and French francs have been offered. These contracts are denominated in set amounts of currencies (e.g., 25,000 pounds, 100,000 Canadian dollars, 125,000 deutsche marks, 125,000 guilders). The contracts call for delivery of the set amount of currencies at maturity dates on the third Wednesday of March, June, September, and December. The purchaser (who receives the FX at maturity) or seller (who delivers the foreign exchange at maturity) of a contract must deposit the margin set by the IMM. The minimum initial margin requirement of $2,200 per contract is often exceeded by individual brokerage firms. The IMM market is an open outcry market as opposed to the negotiated foreign exchange dealer market. The customer using the IMM pays commissions to a broker rather than the dealer markup. The trading ceiling and floor in the foreign exchange forward market are unlimited, but day-to-day trading limits in the IMM are typically $750 for the D-mark and $1,250 for the British pound. The limit rule does not apply to the contract of nearest expiration, which can move without limits. The trading hours are 7:30 A.M. to 1:30 A.M. Chicago time. The pricing of the contracts is in dollars per unit of currency of that contract (e.g. $0.4445/DM). The clearing corporation of the exchange keeps a daily tally of gains and losses. The holders of contracts that profited from the day's trading activity are debited by the amount of the gain and the losers are credited. If the losing position falls below minimum maintenance margin, it must receive the required new funds to meet minimum margin or the account will be closed out and all losses realized. Most contracts are closed out at expiration by a purchase (sale) offset to the original transaction, which is counter to the norm of the FX forward market of settlement of currency against currency.

CURRENCY OPTION MARKET

The currency option in the United States was first offered by the Philadelphia Exchange. The option expiration dates are May, June, and September for the put and call options. A put option gives the purchaser the right to sell a currency at the stated striking price for a given period of time. The call option gives the purchaser the right to purchase a stated amount of foreign exchange at a set price for a given time. The standardized options fill the needs of either the less affluent hedger of the speculator in foreign exchange. The options currently offered on the Philadelphia Exchange are in British pounds, Canadian dollars, West German deutsche marks, French francs, Japanese yen, and Swiss francs. The writers of the currency puts and calls can be hedgers and speculators of comparable size or participants from the dealer network.

The presentation of the various aspects of the foreign exchange market sets the stage to show the mechanics of hedging or speculating in foreign currencies. The following analysis ignores the spot market because we are assuming that we are hedging some future liability or asset exposure in a foreign currency or are attempting to profit from some expected change in currency values that the market has not already discounted. To keep everything consistent, the following is in dollars per unit of foreign currency, and our hedge or speculative position size is £1 million. The time frame of our examination is ninety days forward for both hedge and speculative examples. The currency used in all our examples is the British pound, which can be hedged or speculated against using the forward market and the other instruments described.

Hedging Scenario

Assumption: Customer owes £1 million worth of dollars in ninety days.

SELECTION 1 Buy sterling forward ninety days. No matter what the spot rate is in ninety days, settlement is known with certainty today.

SELECTION 2 Buy the twenty sterling futures contracts necessary at £50,000 per contract expiring close to but beyond the date for the needed funds. If the pound falls in value relative to the dollar, the loss in the futures contract is offset by the gain due to the lower dollar cost of pounds in the future. If the pound rises in value, the futures contract will increase in value, offsetting the higher cost of pounds in the future.

SELECTION 3   The purchase of eighty calls on the pound at £12,500 per call at a date and striking price nearest the ninetieth day will offer a hedge and a potential for gain. If the pound increases in value, the call will also appreciate and provide an offset to the increased value of the liability. However, if the pound falls in value, the loss can only be the cost of the option, which could be less than the decline in the pound. A decline in the pound in excess of the cost of the call options lowers the dollar cost of pounds and is in effect a profit. (This is the asymmetry referred to earlier.)

Speculation Scenario

The market speculator, guided by divination, forecasting model, or the gut feeling, believes that some commodity is going to fall or rise in value in excess of the current expectations of the market. Consistent with the hedge example, the spot market is ignored. The unit of speculation is £1 million, and the speculator's expectations are that the pound will decline against the dollar more than the foreign exchange market then currently estimates in the next ninety days.

SELECTION 1   The speculator can sell the pound forward ninety days, and if it declines in excess of market expectations, he will buy it back at a lower price in terms of dollars. The profit comes as a result of selling high and buying low. Whichever way the pound trades, however, the speculator has an open position in the pound that must be closed out by delivery of pounds at settlement or by purchase of an offset forward contract in pounds.

SELECTION 2   The same conditions must prevail with respect to speculator expectations and market expectations. The speculator would sell eight pound futures contracts. If the speculator's expectations prevail, the contact will be closed out at a price lower than the sale, resulting in a profit. Again, however, if the pound rises in value, the pound futures contract will appreciate and must be closed out by an offsetting purchase at a loss.

SELECTION 3   The asymmetry of the currency option in the hedge case also comes into play in the speculation example. The speculator with the same expectations can sell twenty pound puts at a striking price and expiration date that is conducive to maximizing profits from fulfilled expectations. If the pound falls in value and meets speculator expectations, then profits will flow. However, if the pound appreciates, the value of the put option will fall, but the loss is not open-ended. The put value can decline to zero and no further liability is incurred. In the forward and futures contracts, the liability for being wrong is open-ended.

CONCLUSION

The placid period of the Bretton Woods currency arrangement, with just a few dramatic currency realignments per decade, has been replaced by a frenetic market where changes between currency values can shift by as much as 2 percent in a day. As a result of or concurrent with world economic integration, we have evolved a global financial market and with it a need to develop an understanding for a subject area that most Americans have in the past eschewed.

Bibliography

Bell, Steven, and Brian Kettel. *Foreign Exchange Handbook*. Westport, Conn.: Quorum Books, 1983.

Brown, Brendan. *The Forward Market in Foreign Exchange*. New York: St. Martin's Press, 1983.

Chalupa, Karel. "Foreign Currency Futures: Reducing Foreign Exchange Risk." *Economic Perspectives,* Federal Reserve Bank of Chicago, Winter 1982, pp. 3–11.

Gendreu, Brian. "New Markets in Foreign Currency Options." *Business Reviews,* Federal Reserve Bank of Philadelphia, July 1984.

Kettel, Brian. *The Finance of International Business*. London: Graham & Trotman, 1979.

Riehl, Heinz, and Rita M. Rodriguez. *Foreign Exchange and Money Markets*. New York: McGraw-Hill, 1983.

Rothstein, Nancy A. *The Handbook of Financial Futures*. New York: McGraw-Hill, 1983.

Walker, Townsend. *A Guide for Using the Foreign Exchange Market*. New York: Wiley, 1981.

Walmsley, Julian. *The Foreign Exchange Handbook: A User's Guide*. New York: Wiley, 1983.

13

Balance-of-Payments Accounting

Nations need to have some awareness of their international cash transactions and their international cash reserve position in much the same way that an individual needs to have an awareness of his or her bank balance. Like individuals, nations operate under a cash flow constraint: the expenditures must not exceed income plus cash on hand plus borrowings. Also, because it is a cumbersome process to change the spending patterns of a nation, nations need to have some idea of their future commitments to and expected revenues from foreigners so that no unforseen cash squeeze will develop without warning. The international accounts provide the data needed to assess the current (and future) international cash positions. The international accounts try to measure the flow of transactions over a specified period of time (usually a year). The accounts show whether a nation has been spending more than it has been generating as a result of its current earnings and whether any discrepancy between expenditures and receipts is getting larger or smaller over time. The crux of the problem is that a nation cannot print international or foreign money (it may only print its own), so that a national cash position must be seen in terms of available foreign exchange.

Because the matter at hand is a question of the availability of cash, it is crucial to distinguish between current transactions (income and expenditure mainly from exports and imports) and capital transactions (investments and borrowings). A nation, like an individual, can always meet a temporary deficit or cash shortage by borrowing—provided that there are willing lenders. But if the temporary shortage becomes permanent, willing lenders will ultimately disappear, and the nation (like the individual) will have to alter the pattern of expenditures in order to bring them into line with receipts.

When the unit is a nation, the crucial factor is where an individual or firm generates its money: It is a question of residence, not citizenship. The United States will incur an international expenditure (debit) when a person who works in New York City (earning dollars) buys a bottle of French wine or goes to Paris for a vacation. That person could be an American citizen by birth or a French citizen working for a French bank. It could even be a French firm with assets denominated in dollars repatriating those dollars to its head office in Paris because it wants to declare an extra dividend for shareholders. Because the national accounts subsume the actions of millions of economic units, the transactions with foreigners need to be collected and summarized so that the economic authorities can identify any serious cash flow shortage that may come about in the future. In an emergency, the authorities could choose to borrow from abroad, but such borrowing can provide only a temporary easing of the problem.

For a nation to curtail the expenditures of its residents with foreigners (in foreign exchange) is a slow process. When an individual is faced with a cash flow crisis, the individual can, as many students know only too well, quickly adjust expenditure patterns by "doing without." A reduction in expenditures (and living standards) is brought about directly and effectively, and the cash flow problem is solved (at some discomfort). Rather than cut down on living standards, the individual may be able to work longer hours or to get a second job (usually at a lower wage rate) so that revenues are increased. In contrast, a nation is a complex collection of firms, individuals, and families, and a foreign exchange problem (a shortage of cash) ensues when the aggregate of economic units is spending more than it is taking in—when home-country residents are spending more with foreigners than foreigners are spending in the home country. Usually, this process may be thought of as expenditures on current items (exports and imports), but it can also consist of the acquisition of foreign assets (foreign investment). Under these conditions, the task of the authorities is to get home-country people to spend less with foreigners and to entice foreigners to spend more in the home country. To do this, the governmental authorities must resort to macroeconomic measures affecting the economic activities of the aggregate economy. These are the familiar tools of monetary and fiscal policy—now instituted to prevent a foreign exchange crisis and not necessarily to promote full employment in the short run. Indeed, macroeconomic tools may be used to create local unemployment in the short run in order to prevent more serious unemployment, such as might result from a foreign exchange crisis, later. The severe implications of what can happen to a national economy's performance when a foreign exchange crisis comes about are apparent from the data on the Mexican economy contained in the supplement following this chapter.

Just as the authorities need GNP accounts to be able to analyze the performance of the economy and the actual or potential need for domestic policy action, so too they need data on international transactions. The international accounts (balance-of-payments accounts) provide these data.

Because of the slow speed of reaction of a national economy, it is fairly clear that balance-of-payments policies should be instigated before matters reach the critical stage. Because economic policy has its limitations in that it cannot impose arrantly severe measures without causing a major disruption in the domestic economy, it is important that danger signals be observed quickly and remedial policies instigated quickly. Putting off remedial policies will almost inevitably involve going (more deeply) into debt to foreigners, and when the crisis ultimately comes, there are not only the basic problem but the effects of the debt to be taken care of as well. Borrowing is a valid solution to a deficit only when some "natural event" will turn the tide back in favor of the debtor nation and allow it to replenish its reserves.

Carrying the analogy of the individual one stage further, there is a need for a nation to have some awareness of whether or not the nation is living or spending beyond its income. Just as an individual can spend at a faster rate than income allows (by drawing down bank balances or borrowing), so, too, a nation can import more than it exports. In so doing, it will run down its international reserves or borrow from foreigners. In international terms, it is reducing its international net worth (assets owed by foreigners to residents less residents' debts to foreigners) and is living beyond its international income. The process cannot continue indefinitely, and some change in the pattern of expenditures must be made when the nation runs out of additional sources of loans.[1]

This analogy of living beyond the nation's international income must be qualified. A nation may deliberately have a deficit on current transactions in order to augment the rate of domestic capital formation. Under such circumstances, a nation is spending beyond its international income but is not consuming beyond its income. As long as the capital formation can be financed, there is no problem. The problem occurs when the foreign exchange needed to service foreign debt exceeds the available foreign exchange earned by exporting goods. Then the nation faces a financial crisis in the international sector, and this will quickly be transmitted to the home economy. Similarly, a nation may be exporting more than it imports, generating a positive balance on current international transactions, but may be acquiring foreign assets (investing abroad) at a still

---

[1]This is the problem invoked by the huge deficits on current transactions invoked by the economic policies of the Reagan administration (see Chapter 15).

faster rate so that it is still running an overall deficit. This can be compared to an individual who earns $300 per week, spends $250 on consumption (a surplus on current transactions) but buys stocks at the rate of $100 per week. In most cases, cash flow deficits involve living beyond one's income—either as an individual or a nation—but in certain circumstances it may be necessary to qualify the equating of a cash deficit and living beyond income when asset acquisition is taking place. But if the rate of investment is to be maintained in the face of a cash flow problem, the standard of living (consumption) must be reduced.

The set of international accounts of a nation should, then, cover every transaction involving the nation's currency and foreign exchange. The accounts also need to distinguish different kinds of transactions so that the authorities can identify any changes by kind of transaction. The accounts must pay particular attention to the distinction between current transactions (buying and selling goods that are used up) and capital transactions (buying assets and incurring debt). Interest earned on assets and paid on debt constitutes a current transaction, and changes in the asset position (international net worth) will feed back on next year's current balance.

Be aware that our focus in this chapter is on the way in which U.S. accounts are compiled. Other nations have slightly different systems of accounting, and any work on another nation's balance of payments must be preceded by an examination of that nation's accounting procedures.

INTERNATIONAL ACCOUNTS

The international accounts comprise many subaccounts, which are treated sequentially.

Balance of Merchandise

The most important (biggest) single entry in a set of international accounts is, nearly always, the value of exports and imports. The merchandise balance is the value of exports minus the value of imports. The importance of this subbalance is due to its sheer size, the speed with which it is generated, and its comparative accuracy. It also has direct implications for the level of domestic aggregate demand.

Data on the value of merchandise imports and exports were the first kind of international financial data compiled on a regular basis. In the early economic history of nation-states, import duties were an important source of government revenue, and, therefore, records were kept of the volume of imports and the kinds of goods imported. The other important source of revenues for the government was excise taxes, which necessitated the keeping of a record of certain kinds of imports. Concern that the nation exported more than it imported meant that records were kept on exports as well. However, despite the apparent simplicity of keeping records of the value of exports and imports, particularly in the modern age, the data are not perfectly reliable. The sheer volume of transactions almost necessarily generates omissions or double counting.[2]

The balance on merchandise trade is published first because it is collected by a small number of government agencies and organizations. The data are available immediately at the end of the time period under consideration and need only to be assembled and reported. Consequently, the first estimate of the merchandise balance is published within about a month of the end of the period covered.

However, the merchandise balance as a single number can cover a multitude of complexities. Table 13-1 gives a breakdown of exports and imports by class of goods. Changes in the totals or in the net balance hide quite considerable variation in the volume of trade in different categories.

Exports use factors of production. Therefore, any increase in the volume of exports adds to the demand for domestic factors of production. The most usual measure of demand for factors is the unemployment rate (for labor) simply because of its important consequences for social welfare. By the same token, imports compete with domestically produced goods for spenders' money and do not use domestic factors of production. Imports reduce the demand for domestic factors of production. Composition of the categories of goods aside, an increase in net exports of merchandise will add to aggregate demand, thereby increasing the level of employment. Note that the statement is much more accurately put as a change in the net balance on merchandise trade. It is difficult to substantiate whether any given trade balance increases or decreases employment compared with a no-trade situation.

The size of merchandise trade relative to other items in the international accounts can be seen in Table 13-2. The importance of merchandise transactions in that table is exaggerated somewhat by the common practice of netting out certain kinds of transactions. Even so, exports and imports in 1980 were each in excess of $200 billion. The next largest individual item was net portfolio investment, which amounted to $29 billion.

Balance on Services

Merchandise is tangible; services are not. In the United Kingdom, this category of trade is called *invisibles*. The services account includes a large number of different types of transactions: tourist expenditures,

[2]See *The Balance of Payments Statistics of the United States: A Review and Appraisal,* Report of the Review Committee for Balance of Payments Statistics to the Bureau of the Budget (Washington, D.C., 1965), ch. 2.

Table 13-1
U.S. Merchandise Trade (in Millions of Dollars)

	1960	1970	1973	1974	1976	1978	1980	1982	1984
Exports									
Agricultural	4,860	7,353	17,978	22,410	23,380	29,466	41,300	37,012	38,145
Capital goods (excl. autos)	5,511	14,366	21,811	30,366	38,726	46,500	74,100	72,678	72,484
Automotive	1,266	3,652†	6,878†	8,625†	12,100†	15,600	17,300	15,914	20,869
Consumer goods	1,396	2,717	4,791	6,382	8,003	10,400	16,700	14,307	13,411
Total*	19,651	42,662	71,379	98,268	98,268	136,900	215,700	212,275	218,744
Imports									
Food	3,286	6,158	9,128	10,585	11,585	15,400	18,100	17,118	21,345
(Cocoa, coffee, and sugar)	(1,657)	(2,089)	(2,707)	(4,069)	(4,144)	(5,118)	(6,255)	(3,917)	(4,859)
Raw materials	7,887	15,117	28,211	54,686	64,725	84,800	134,500	108,202	122,582
(Fuels and lubricants)	(1,580)	(3,063)	(8,967)	(27,489)	(37,079)	(42,906)	(83,789)	(66,365)	(62,259)
Capital goods (excl. autos)	562	3,782	8,132	9,544	11,061	19,200	30,300	38,153	60,757
Automotive	633	5,955†	10,319†	12,078†	16,364	24,200	22,100	34,304	56,789
Consumer goods	1,901	7,551	13,218	14,786	18,436	28,900	34,400	39,658	61,299
Total*	15,072	40,049	70,424	103,673	123,917	172,500	245,400	243,941	330,514

*Details do not add to total.
†The Canadian–United States automotive agreement was instituted in 1964.

Source: U.S. Department of Commerce.

The imports of fuel and lubricants increase sharply in 1974 and 1980 in response to the two dramatic increases in the world oil price in 1974 and 1979. Note that 1982 was a recessionary year and 1984 an expansionary year.

Table 13-2
U.S. BALANCE OF PAYMENTS, 1972–1984 (IN MILLIONS OF DOLLARS)

Transaction or Balance	1972	1976	1978	1980	1982	1984
Current Transactions						
Exports of merchandise	+ 49,381	+ 114,745	+ 142,054	+ 223,966	+ 211,217	+ 219,916
Imports of merchandise	– 55,797	– 124,051	– 175,813	– 249,308	– 247,606	– 334,023
Balance of trade	– 6,416	– 9,306	– 33,759	– 25,342	– 36,385	– 114,107
Services (net)	– 3,717	+ 2,713	+ 3,657	+ 3,359	+ 5,907	– 948
Investment income (net)	+ 8,192	+ 15,975	+ 20,899	+ 32,762	+ 27,304	+ 19,109
Other transfers	– 3,854	– 4,998	– 5,055	– 7,056	– 8,034	– 11,413
Balance on current account	– 5,795	+ 4,384	– 14,259	+ 3,723	– 11,211	– 107,358
Capital Transactions						
U.S. government (excl. official reserves)	– 1,568	– 4,213	– 4,644	– 5,165	– 5,732	– 5,516
U.S. direct investment	– 8,063	– 12,468	– 16,345	– 18,546	– 3,008	– 4,503
(reinvested profits)	(– 4,533)	(– 7,872)	(– 11,469)	(– 16,998)	(– 5,323)	(N.A.)
Foreign direct investment	+ 977	+ 3,962	+ 7,897	+ 10,854	+ 10,390	+ 22,514
(reinvested profits)	(+ 597)	(+ 1,750)	(+ 2,583)	(+ 6,190)	(– 164)	(N.A.)
Private portfolio investments (net)*	+ 4,864	– 17,221	– 18,027	– 28,995	– 35,548	+ 64,537
Balance on capital account	– 3,790	– 29,976	– 31,119	– 41,852	– 27,882	+ 77,032
Economist's balance	– 9,585	– 25,592	– 45,378	– 38,129	– 39,093	– 30,326
Balancing Items						
Increase in official foreign reserve assets	+ 10,705	+ 17,945	+ 33,293	+ 15,492	+ 2,668	+ 2,971
Change in U.S. official reserves	+ 32	– 2,530	+ 732	– 8,155	– 4,965	– 3,131
Allocation of SDRs†	+ 710	—	—	+ 1,152	—	—
Statistical discrepancy‡	– 1,862	+ 10,177	+ 11,354	+ 29,640	+ 41,390	+ 30,486
Accountant's balance	0	0	0	0	0	0

+ indicates a receipt and – a payment by a U.S. resident. N.A. = not available. * Includes both short-term and long-term assets. † See Chapter 17. ‡A balancing item. **Source:** *Survey of Current Business,* various issues.

transportation, dividend-and-interest payments and receipts, and royalties from licensing arrangements as well as miscellaneous services such as the earnings from the rental to foreigners of movies and TV films and the expenses incurred abroad in the manufacture of movies, the net balance on postal and telegraph services, the expenditures in the United States of foreign workers and employees of foreign governments and international institutions, and the expenditures of the embassies and institutions.

The volume of trade in services is important.[3] In 1974, exports and imports of services were almost 40 percent of the sum of merchandise exports and imports. Before the recent very large increase in the prices of energy and food, the ratio was higher, amounting to 48 percent of commodity trade. (See Table 13-3.)

Trade in most services contributes to (exports) or detracts from (imports) the level of aggregate demand in the nation in exactly the same way that merchandise trade does. But there are important exceptions. Payments and receipts of dividends, interest payments, royalties, and some fees do not involve the use of factors of production in the period in which the payment is made or the credit is received. Therefore, it is not possible to regard the sum of the balance on merchandise and the balance on services as representing net additions to or subtractions from the demand for factors in a nation.

Tourism is extremely important in the international accounts of some countries. Spain and some of the Caribbean islands derive as much as half their total current earnings of foreign currency from the sale of tourism services. Tourism is a traditional deficit item in the accounts of rich countries. It is quite income-elastic and is also elastic to the rate of exchange and, on the basis of imperfect evidence, the level of transportation costs. In addition, tourism activities involve the transportation of the tourists. As with all transportation, that for tourists enters into the international accounts only if a foreign carrier is used, in which case the tourist imports transportation from a foreign resident. If the tourist travels by the national airline of the country of residence, the transportation is a domestic transaction! As a general rule, the tourism transportation balance has the same sign as the tourism balance.

Transportation, whether tourism or merchandise, is a complex item in international trade. As a general rule, the more affluent the nation, the less likely it is to have a comparative advantage in transportation, particularly merchant shipping. However, the transportation activity is so closely allied to national feelings of patriotism that most nations have an international airline and a merchant fleet to show the flag. The act of transportation involves the use of foreign services, such as landing

---

[3]The Reagan administration has recently put great emphasis on attempting to reduce the level of impediments to international trade in services.

fees for aircraft and docking fees for ships along with related port services. The identification of national carriers with national pride and a desire to "show the flag" has led many nations to subsidize their airlines and their merchant fleets. In developed nations, the merchant fleet is often given a subsidy because it is unable to compete in the freedom of the international oceans where tariffs and other protective devices cannot operate. This policy is usually justified by appeal to the national defense argument.[4] Developing countries tend to maintain international airlines that are a net balance-of-payments drain in order to enhance the national image.

"Fees and royalties from affiliated foreigners" refers to payments made by subsidiary corporations to their parents for management services, or for the use of patented know-how. These are entered separately, partly because they identify a transaction that results from direct foreign investment and multinational corporations and partly because they are made at prices not disciplined by the market.

"Income from investments" comprises three kinds of payment flows: dividends paid to parent corporations by subsidiaries, interest earned on portfolio investments by firms and individuals, and interest paid on government loans. This flow varies with the size of foreign investments (assets) and with the rate of return earned on those assets. The growth in investment income (net) in the United States balance of payments is impressive (Table 13-2). It identifies a steady increase in net assets owned abroad, but the growth probably depends more directly on the inflation of profits after the oil shock in 1974 and the accompanying very high interest rates. Investment income is traditionally included with "services" in the balance-of-payments accounts, but it is identified separately in Table 13-2 because of its importance and because it does not contribute as strongly to the demand for labor at home as exports of factor-using services.

Provided that the balance on investment income does not vary greatly from year to year, a change in the balance on goods and services can be used to indicate any change in the contribution of the foreign sector to aggregate demand in the home country and, therefore, to employment.

The treatment of reinvested profits of foreign subsidiary corporations of MNCs deserves special mention. When a foreign subsidiary makes a profit, it normally sends some back to the parent and retains the rest for reinvestment locally, in much the same manner as domestic corporations. Obviously, such retained profits contribute to the home country's international net worth and, therefore, should be entered as a credit in current transactions. However, the fact that they do not pass through the foreign exchange market must also be recognized. Accounting practice is to include them as a credit in current transactions and to enter them

[4]See Chapter 7.

Table 13-3
U.S. International Trade in Services, 1970*–1984 (Millions of Dollars)

	1970	1974	1977	1980	1982	1984
Credits (Exports)						
Travel	2,331	4,032	6,150	10,090	11,293	11,386
Passenger fares	544	1,104	1,366	2,582	2,979	3,023
Other transportation	3,113	5,697	7,264	11,430	12,437	13,799
Fees and royalties from affiliated foreigners	1,758	3,070	3,883	5,695	5,572	6,530
Fees and royalties from unaffiliated foreigners	573	751	923	1,170	1,567	1,585
Government:						
Defense agencies	1,501	3,379	7,351	8,231	12,097	10,086
Miscellaneous	332	419	557	362	440	624
Film rentals	240	326	442	463	(not reported separately)	
Miscellaneous	1,054	1,995	3,364	4,744	6,576	7,463
Receipts from U.S. Income abroad						
Direct investments*	8,169	19,157	19,673	36,842	22,888	23,078
Other private assets	2,671	7,356	10,881	36,522	57,127	59,301
U.S. government assets	912	1,074	1,625	2,572	4,131	5,230
Total credits	23,205	48,360	63,479	120,703	137,107	142,105
Debits (Imports)						
Travel	3,980	5,980	7,451	10,397	− 12,394	− 16,008
Passenger fares	1,215	2,095	2,748	3,607	− 4,722	− 6,508
Other transportation	2,843	5,942	7,874	10,896	− 11,638	− 14,666
Fees and royalties from affiliated foreigners	111	160	243	515	− 42	− 187

Fees and royalties from unaffiliated foreigners	144	186	196	254	295	329
Government:						
Defense agencies	4,855	5,032	5,823	10,746	− 11,913	− 11,851
Miscellaneous	725	967	1,358	1,769	− 2,296	− 2,133
Private miscellaneous services	827	1,262	2,190	3,222	− 3,700	− 3,762
Payments on investments						
Direct investments†	875	1,331	2,834	9,336	− 4,844	− 10,188
Other private assets	3,617	6,491	5,841	21,326	− 33,769	− 38,543
U.S. government assets	1,024	4,262	5,542	12,512	− 18,229	− 19,769
Total debits	20,186	33,708	42,100	84,580	− 103,896	− 123,944
Net balance	+ 3,019	+ 14,652	+ 21,379	+ 36,123	+ 33,211	+ 18,161

Several things are worth noticing in this table. Note the decrease in the deficit on travel as the dollar weakened until 1980 and the increase in 1984 when the dollar was strong. The travel balance with Western Europe changed even more since it was the dollar's weakening against European currencies that was most noticeable in the 1970s and the consequent growth of European tourism in the United States.

The government (defense agencies) receipts are (inappropriately) transfers of armaments under military grants and construction activities. Expenditures comprise expenditures by U.S. personnel stationed overseas, the hiring of foreign personnel, and (inappropriately) purchases of equipment and supplies.

Receipts from investments show remarkable growth. The growth is important because it identifies one of the benefits to the parent country of having had its own multinationals invest abroad. Receipts from direct investment are the profits sent home. The phenomenal growth in receipts over the decade indicates both the growth of investments and the inflation of prices. As we shall see in Chapters 14 and 15, some of the direct investments of U.S. multinationals have been financed with portfolio investments in the United States and by government borrowing to finance balance-of-payments deficits. The growth of returns on portfolio and government investments also indicates the substantial elevation in world interest rates between 1977 and 1980.

The inclusion of profits retained abroad in the current account is somewhat spurious since these funds do *not* go through the foreign exchange markets. Balance-of-payments accounts allow for this by putting an offsetting item in direct investments. Their inclusion is, however, quite correct in the sense that the current balance measures the change in the international net worth of a country.

Sources: Data from Anthony J. DiLullo, "Service Transactions in the U.S. International Accounts, 1970–80," Survey of Current Business, 61 (November 1981), 29–46, and other official sources.

*Includes profits retained abroad.
†Includes profits retained in the United States.

simultaneously as direct investment debits (capital outflows); in other words, the accounts pretend that the profits were repatriated and then immediately reinvested. The amount of reinvested profits can be subtracted from the amount of direct investment to determine actually how much money flowed out in a year for the acquisition of new assets. In recent years, this has become relatively small, and in 1979, disinvestment took place as more capital was repatriated than invested.

"Unilateral transfers" comprises foreign aid, personal gifts to friends and relatives abroad, personal and institutional private charitable donations, and similar transactions. When unilateral transfers are added to the balance on goods and services, we obtain the *balance on current account* (see Table 13-2). This number is used to measure net foreign investment in the national income accounts and provides the best available estimate of the potential net acquisition of international assets earned by the nation during the period.

Long-term Capital Account

The long-term capital account includes three types of transactions: government loans, private portfolio capital movements, and private direct investment. Any outflow of capital involves the purchase of a foreign asset and, therefore, requires that domestic currency be changed into foreign currency for the purchase. A foreign investment or capital outflow is a debit in the balance of payments, but the debit occurs only if an asset is purchased from a foreign resident. Thus there is no need for the asset to be foreign. The purchase of a U.S. government bond by an American resident from a foreign resident is just as much a capital export as if the bond represented the debt of some foreign government.

Government loans, net of repayments and long-term foreign borrowing by the government, are self-explanatory. Ordinarily, they represent, for developed nations at least, a way in which foreign aid can be provided to developing countries. This kind of loan usually involves a much longer term than a commercial loan and often carries a rate of interest that is well below the appropriate market rate. Two other kinds of loans are worth mentioning. One that is of diminishing importance is the type of loan made from the United States to war-torn nations after World War II. Although these loans carried market rates of interest, their real value has been eroded by inflation in the United States (the loans were denominated in U.S. dollars) and have, through repayment, been significantly reduced in volume. The final category of loans relates to medium- and long-term borrowings made by the United States to support the dollar in the foriegn exchange market during the last years of the Bretton Woods era (see Chapter 17). Government loans are normally entered as a net figure showing the change in the net claims position of the government vis-à-vis foreign governments—new extensions less repayments and borrowings. A Treasury bill that is sold in New York in the routine way and is bought by a foreigner is not a part of government foreign investment in the normal sense and would be included as a credit on private portfolio capital.

Private portfolio investment comprises simultaneous inflows and outflows and consists of purchases of both debt and equities—debentures, bonds, preferred stock, or common stock.

Direct international investment identifies the flow of money sent abroad by multinational corporations to acquire real, productive assets in a foreign country. Examples of this might be when Volkswagen builds a manufacturing plant in Pennsylvania or when Du Pont builds and operates a petrochemical plant in Indonesia. The reasons for foreign direct investment are considered in Part VI.

Short-term Capital

Short-term capital movements measure the inflows and outflows of funds that are invested in very short-term financial instruments such as Treasury bills and money market instruments like commercial paper and negotiable certificates of deposit. These funds can be very volatile, moving from one financial center to another in search of higher interest rates and returning whence they came as soon as interest rates warrant. These features make them extremely difficult to measure reliably and make them unreliable sources of foreign exchange because the flows are so easily reversed. In the current presentation of the U.S. balance of payments short-term and long-term funds are not distinguished, on the grounds that even volatile funds can be lodged in long-term bonds and the maturity of the financial instrument is no guide to the permanence of the flow of foreign exchange.

"Statistical discrepancy" (previously called "errors and omissions") is a balancing or "fudge factor" that acknowledges gaps in the underlying data and generates the accountant's requirement that debits must equal credits. The size of the discrepancy has become huge in recent years. Large amounts of the discrepancy can probably be attributed to unrecorded capital flows (mainly short-term), but the fruits of illegal transactions probably also have an important role to play. Payment for drug shipments may account for large amounts of discrepancy, as may laundering of profits from drug transactions and other illegal operations.

DEFINITIONS OF BALANCE

What do economists (balance-of-payments analysts) mean by a deficit? Accountants, of course, require that debits equal credits, and they therefore insist on a zero overall balance. Economists, however, would like to be able to identify transactions undertaken for their own sake (because the price is right) and to separate them from transactions made as a result of an attempt by government to eliminate a deficit, the logic here being that transactions undertaken for their own sake are those that indicate any tendency to overspend. The economist identifies the acts of official bodies, usually central banks, as being intended to offset any imbalance in private transactions and, at least with fixed exchange rates, to measure the support needed to maintain the currency at its par value in the foreign exchange market. This sum measures any excessive expenditures and identifies any trends in expenditures. For analysis, certain subbalances are also useful. They are presented in the following simple schematic chart.

	Net Receipts (surplus)	Net Payments (deficit)
Balance on goods and services	11	
Balance on transfers	9	
Balance on current account	20	
Balance on capital account		32
Economist's balance		12
Official financing	12	
Accountant's balance	0	0

Every transaction entered above the economist's balance is considered to be undertaken for its own sake. Any transaction below the economist's balance is considered to be some official action designed to support the exchange rate or to prevent its weakening too greatly and is considered "compensatory."

In arriving at a working definition of payments balance or imbalance, it is a good idea to recall the purpose of the compilation of the international accounts. The authorities wish to be able to identify changes in their international reserve position (their cash position), trends that seem to be likely to endanger that position by using up reserves, or changes in total foreign assets, liquid and illiquid. But it is difficult in a world of floating exchange rates to know how much of a trend to attribute to changes in exchange rates and how much to changes in liquid asset positions. Certainly, a country experiencing inflation would probably want to allow for the effect of purchasing power parity on the rate of exchange before attributing much of an underlying real trend to changes in the rate of exchange. But the reason that nations try to identify forces operating in the international markets is that nations would find sudden disruptions of their international trading position very hard to accommodate without disrupting their domestic economies (that is, without causing a severe recession or possibly a drastic inflationary surge). National economic authorities would want to soften the impact of any severe disruption in international markets on their home economies. They would need foreign exchange reserves to accomplish this purpose by intervening in the foreign exchange market. Alternatively, they do not want to be supporting their own currency and run out of reserves suddenly so that a sudden shift in the terms of trade would be forced on the home economy.[5] However much nations pay homage to the concept of a clean float, everyone knows that a clean float will be tolerated for only as long as the foreign exchange market works smoothly and accommodates changed circumstances without violent fluctuations in the exchange rate.

Using our schematic chart, it is possible to identify the country's balance-of-payments situation. The nation is exporting more goods and services than it is importing. It has a positive balance on goods and services, and its earnings on earlier foreign investments (direct, government, and portfolio) exceed its unilateral transfers (foreign aid, etc.). It has a positive balance on current account, indicating that it is generating more money abroad on the basis of current transactions than it is using. It is therefore acquiring claims against foreigners and is increasing its international net worth by 20 units of foreign exchange per year. These 20 units of foreign exchange are a form of saving and could be used to acquire more gold (the international money par excellence), to increase the nation's stock of foreign exchange held in foreign banks or foreign money-market instruments, or to acquire foreign assets. In practice, the residents have chosen to acquire foreign assets (direct, government, and portfolio combined) at the rate of 32 units per year. The current balance (the enabling amount) is less than the desires of residents to acquire foreign assets. The nation must raise the additional 12 units to make up the difference. Under a system of fixed rates of exchange, the authorities would borrow from foreign central banks or run down their stocks of gold or foreign exchange reserves. But the authorities could try to finance the deficit by raising the domestic rate of interest and encouraging foreigners to invest in the country; the inflow of funds will finance the deficit of 12 units. In the schematic chart, the authorities have chosen to supply the 12 units out of reserves rather than to let interest rates rise and possibly damage the performance of the home economy. Under a system of flexible rates (clean or dirty), the authorities would be more passive and would allow the nation's currency to weaken. This would tend (if properly reinforced by other measures) to increase the rate of international saving (the current balance) by making exports cheaper (and more competitive) abroad and imports less attractive at home.

The economist measures the balance of payments as the amount by which the authorities have "shored up" the exchange rate. This balance is sometimes known as the "official settlements balance." In reality, this balance is the difference between the country's ability to save vis-à-vis

---

[5]Supporting an exchange rate at something above (stronger than) its true value means that the nation is experiencing terms of trade that are more favorable than the true state of affairs. If the support of the exchange rate is withdrawn, the country undergoes a sudden change in its *perceived* terms of trade, with all of the need to readjust its standard of living and its output mix. This problem is discussed in Chapter 14.

foreigners by having a positive current balance and the desires of its residents to acquire foreign assets net. The balance can therefore be seen as the difference between saving and investment. (Of course, both can be negative, in which case the balance would be the sum of the two.) International saving is accomplished by going without the other imports that the nation could have had to match its exports (plus transfers). International investment *net* is the disposition of saving. (The analogy to an individual is quite close.) If international investment is larger than the (separately determined) international saving, there is a deficit. The government provides the additional funds needed to generate balance by drawing down its international reserves.

Ideally, the international accounts would distinguish between permanent transactions and reversible transactions. Permanent transactions comprise current transactions and the acquisition of illiquid assets.[6] Reversible transactions include such flows as short-term interest-sensitive capital flows. Then portfolio capital movements could be included as accommodating or compensatory items, and the economist's balance would involve only permanent transactions—the current account and direct and government investment.

There is one final and important point to be made. The balance on current account (international saving) is the most amenable to policy tools available to the authorities. This means that there will be a tendency for the authorities to make international saving adjust to international investment. It is the balance on current account that will change in response to policy directives simply because (except for the ability to manipulate interest rates to attract temporary flows of short-term capital) the flow of international investment is not easily controlled or influenced. Multinational corporations indulge in direct investment in accordance with quite long run perceptions of profit, and government loans are more sensitive to political than economic variables.

BALANCE-OF-PAYMENTS ACCOUNTING UNDER FLEXIBLE RATES

The balance-of-payments techniques described in this chapter and the concept of balance evolved under regimes of fixed rates of exchange. The gold standard, which reigned from the Battle of Waterloo to the beginning of the First World War, and the Bretton Woods system, which prevailed from 1946 to 1971, were both fixed-rate systems. Between the two world wars, nations tried to maintain a fixed-rate system, but it was washed away by the worldwide depression, and the international financial system was not working smoothly. Under fixed-rate systems,

[6]Of course, not even direct investment is inevitably permanent. Multinationals do sell off "mistakes."

governments guarantee that the exchange rate of their currency will not deviate greatly from the agreed-on par value (set in terms of gold). As noted earlier, the problem of interpreting a deficit or surplus becomes much more difficult when rates of exchange change during the course of the period under analysis. For example, the United Kingdom devalued the pound sterling by 12.5 percent on November 17, 1967. Clearly, British annual balance-of-payments data for that year do not reflect the need for further changes in the exchange rate in 1968: The devaluation probably had no effect at all during the last six weeks of the year because a new rate of exchange (with all its implications) takes some time to exert an effect. One authoritative study reported, "There is a significant price responsiveness, but adjustment lags run to years and not quarters."[7]

But balances do have meaning under flexible rates. The current balance indicates the change in the international net worth of the country—the degree to which the flow of international saving has made possible an acquisition of foreign assets (net) or the redemption of debts. Changes in the rate of exchange during the course of a year will have affected (to some small degree at least) the rate of saving accomplished in individual months, but the end-of-the-year figure is a fact. The net balance on capital flows indicates the degree to which the nation's residents have acquired foreign assets and, in detailed data, the degree to which this investment has been divided among direct investments, profit retention abroad, government loans, and portfolio transactions. Changes in the rates of exchange during the course of the year will affect the year-end value of the assets if nothing else, but the end-of-the-year number shows the amount of assets acquired or divested (net). The economist's balance measures the reduction in the nation's international reserves. The balances still retain quite precise meanings for the national balance sheet.

SUMMARY

Balance-of-payments accounting is necessary if the authorities are to make intelligent policy decisions affecting the nation's ability to transact business with foreigners and to safeguard the domestic economy against serious upheaval. Intelligent policy does not necessarily demand intervention; it may involve reliance on the efficiency of the foreign exchange market to determine what the (real) rate of exchange should be. The authorities should sit passively by and accept the verdict of market forces. This was the original announced policy of the Reagan administration. With sublime faith in a noninterventionist stance, the Reagan administration allowed market pressures to push the dollar to a position of great

---

[7]Rudiger Dornbusch and Paul Krugman, "Flexible Exchange Rates in the Short Run," *Brookings Papers on Economic Activity,* 3 (1976), p. 566.

strength (see Chapter 15). Speculative forces caused serious fluctuations in the foreign exchange market (particularly in the first three months of 1985). In September 1985, the Reagan administration encouraged intervention in the foreign exchange market by the Federal Reserve System and foreign central banks, and a dirty float was reinstituted. This policy was reinforced at the Tokyo economic summit in May 1986.

It is useful for a nation to have some measure of the degree to which its industries are or are not retaining their price competitiveness (as indicated by the current account balance) and for the developed world to recognize the need for a current surplus if funds are to be transferred to the developing countries. But above all, nations need to have the power and the information necessary to prevent crisis or panic in the foreign exchange market by intervention.

The Mexican Experience

Mexico's recent economic experiences provide a case study of the costs that can be inflicted on an economy when it neglects its balance of payments and finances international deficits. Mexico went from prosperity and rapid economic development to stagnation and depression. Mistaken international economic policy was an important contributory cause. The problems were aggravated by the policies of the developed world in 1980 and by the monetary policy of the United States in particular.

In the second half of the 1970s, Mexico's economic outlook was excellent. A fast-growing industrial sector was contributing to economic development, and oil reserves in the Gulf of Mexico were discovered and harnessed. Mexico still had the very serious problems of high rates of population growth, widespread disguised unemployment, and a laggard educational system. Oil exports began to be substantial in 1978 and 1979. They might have been expected to provide enough foreign exchange to allow Mexico to develop economically without the usual critical shortage of foreign exchange (see Chapter 10). The Mexican government then proceeded to ignore its balance of payments and the competitiveness of the Mexican economy by fixing the value of the peso in terms of the U.S. dollar from 1972 through 1981, with one major devaluation of the peso in 1976–1977. Developing nations are prone to inflation at faster rates than developed countries, and the Mexican economy was no exception. Fixing the peso in terms of the dollar meant that the peso's purchasing power in foreign markets increased steadily.

The nominal rates of exchange in pesos per dollar and the real rate of exchange in index-number form are given in Table 13-A. The peso strengthened in real terms by about 21 percent between January 1972 and December 1975, despite the fact that oil revenues had not yet begun. The 1976–1977 devaluation of the peso restored the real value of the peso to a 12 percent depreciation in December 1976 (relative to January 1972). This probably put the real rate in the neighborhood of the correct value at that time. But the same mistake was made again, and the real value of the peso appreciated by about 33 percent between December

Table 13-A

MEXICO'S BALANCE-OF-PAYMENTS CRISIS

	Nominal Rate of Exchange (P/$)	Real Rate of Exchange (Jan. 1972 = 100)	Rate of Economic Growth (%)	Current Account Balance (billions of dollars)
1972 (January)	12.50	100.00	—	—
1972	12.50	98.34	7.27	−0.92
1973	12.50	88.20	7.60	−1.42
1974	12.50	81.94	5.90	−2.87
1975	12.50	78.88	4.07	−4.04
1976	19.95	112.24	2.12	−3.41
1977	22.74	104.46	3.26	−1.85
1978	22.72	98.00	10.89	−3.17
1979	22.80	92.96	9.16	−5.46
1980	23.26	82.02	8.30	−8.16
1981	26.23	78.34	16.93	−13.90
1982	96.48	150.48	−0.05	−6.22
1983	143.80	128.79	−4.66	5.33
1984	192.56	118.90	3.47	3.97
1985	371.70	158.14	2.69	n.a.

Notes: Rate-of-exchange data are the average for the month of December. Growth data are computed as the percent change in inflation-adjusted gross domestic product. The real rate is also reported in pesos per dollar; a decrease in the number implies a strengthening of the peso (improved terms of trade for Mexico). On July 23, 1986, the peso was quoted at 631 to the dollar. (*n.a.* = *not available.*)

Source: International Monetary Fund, *International Financial Statistics,* various editions.

1976, and December 1981. Although foreign exchange earnings from oil revenues were increasing during this period, the current balance was always negative, and the interest burden of foreign debt was growing steadily.

In fall 1980, the nominal and real rates of interest on dollar-denominated loans increased (see Table 15-1 in Chapter 15). The interest burden increased spectacularly, and financing from abroad, needed to balance the current deficit, became more costly and harder to obtain. Mexico found itself in a financial crisis (together with many other Latin American countries). Mexico had suddenly to restrain its imports and increase its exports to earn foreign exchange to pay interest on its foreign debt and to pay off maturing debt. Mexico had to make imports less attractive by making them more expensive: This involved a devaluation of the peso against the dollar in both nominal and real terms. It also required a cutback in the amount of spending by Mexican firms and individuals. The cutback in expenditures can be seen by the change in the growth rates beginning in 1982. The nominal value of the peso was cut almost in half in February 1982 and again in August of the same year. The exchange rate actions had to be reinforced by tight monetary policy. The results were spectacular: The growth rate plummeted from 16.93

percent in 1981 to −4.66 percent in 1983. At the same time, the current balance (international saving) reversed itself from a deficit of $5.75 billion in 1982 to a surplus of $5.21 billion in 1983.

The real value of the peso had become ridiculously high—to the point that Mexicans found visiting the United States cheaper than vacationing in Mexico (in complete contradiction of the theory of comparative advantage!). Mexicans who were financially aware and able to acquire dollars with pesos did so as a straightforward speculation against the peso (which would have been richly rewarded) or to buy nonfinancial assets (such as land) in the United States.

The social costs have been enormous. Even though world events were unlikely to have allowed Mexico to continue its successful development without interruption, the costs of neglect of the balance of payments and the appropriate exchange rate caused a crisis of stagnation instead of what might otherwise have been merely a short interruption. The growth process has been completely stopped. Domestic inflation is out of hand and the tenure of the government, once the most entrenched political party in the democratic world, is now subject to some doubt. Consumer prices doubled in Mexico in 1983. Industrial production declined by 8.8 percent in 1983 alone. There are no reliable data on unemployment rates but unemployment has increased tremendously since the onset of the crisis.

If this state of affairs were not bad enough, two more serious mishaps have made the task of adjustment even more difficult: A huge earthquake hit the Mexico City area in 1985 and, in 1986, the world price of oil fell spectacularly. The earthquake played havoc with one of Mexico's major exports (tourism) and the decrease in the price of oil cut the value of oil exports in half.

14

Mechanics of Balance-of-Payments Adjustment

Because a nation that is spending in excess of its foreign exchange earnings must face the possibility of eliminating that excess, it is important that nations understand the means of eliminating a deficit. The fact that the existence of a deficit for one country implies a surplus for another country (since the world is a closed system) is not relevant: The pressure on a surplus nation to eliminate a surplus is far less than the pressures on a deficit nation close to exhausting its international reserves. Mechanics are discussed in this chapter; policy questions are considered in Chapter 15.

The deficit elimination process is considered first under a system of so-called adjustable pegs. This is the exchange rate regime that prevailed from 1946 until 1971 and is the most convenient way for presenting the mechanics of the problem. Under a system of adjustable pegs, the existing exchange rate is supported by the authorities until such time as they choose to change the official value of their currency. An exchange rate change is therefore a deliberate policy action. In our discussion, we will assume that there is no deficit (or surplus) on capital transactions, so that the problem of deficit elimination may be examined purely in terms of the current account (positive or negative international saving). Both assumptions will be dropped when we discuss the system of flexible rates and the existence (and changes in the rate) of international investment. It is worth noting here that unless a country is prepared to impose quite drastic measures to control capital flows, it is usually more efficient to have the current account do virtually all of the needed adjustment:

International saving adjusts to satisfy the rate of international investment.[1]

It is self-evident that a nation does not have to balance its payments monthly or even yearly. In practice, there are three ways in which a nation can deal with a deficit: It can finance the deficit by running down international reserves or by borrowing; it can suppress the deficit by taking some steps that will eliminate the deficit but will also involve renunciation of another economic target (such as full employment); or it can *adjust* the mix of output and the rate of use of goods so that the deficit is eliminated. Financing merely postpones any action and, implicitly, waits for some favorable event to take place (or countenances another policy later). Suppression deliberately renounces a domestic economic target and either countenances a reemergence of the deficit when the suppressive measure is released in response to domestic political pressures or awaits the same favorable event that financing foresees. Adjustment will ordinarily involve three identifiable actions, each of which will cause the economy to consume fewer goods and services. First, the deficit represents additional supplies of (foreign-made) goods for use in the home country, and these will be renounced. Second, the country will undergo an unfavorable shift in the terms of trade (real rate of exchange), with the result that there will be less temptation to buy foreign-made goods and foreigners will have a greater incentive to buy home-country exports. Third, a country adjusting to eliminate a deficit will often have financed its deficit for some years previously, so elimination of the deficit must also involve rebuilding international reserves and running a surplus (to pay off loans and to acquire new reserves). All three actions involve a reduction in the country's general standard of living.

THE ABSORPTION APPROACH

Because a zero balance on capital transactions is assumed, the economist's balance is equal to the balance on current account.

The absorption theory relies on two basic definitions of income (Y) for the output of goods and services and of absorption (A) for the consumption of goods and services.

$$Y = C_d + I_d + G_d + X \qquad (1)$$
$$A = C_d + I_d + G_d + M \qquad (2)$$
$$Y - A = X - M \qquad (3)$$

[1]The inflow of liquid capital into the United States in the early 1980s resulted in an overvalued dollar because saving adjusts to investment almost automatically under flexible rates of exchange; see Chapter 15.

where C, I, G, X, and M stand, respectively, for the money value of consumption, investment, government expenditures on goods and services, exports, and imports. The subscript d denotes value added domestically. Y, then, measures the total value of output and A the total value of goods used up. From equation (3) it is apparent that a current account deficit ($X < M$) derives from a nation using up more goods than it is producing. The deficit is attributable to an excess of goods used up over goods produced, and the equivalence between a deficit and an "excessive" standard of living is self-evident. If we assume that the deficit is used to supply additional consumption in a developed country and additional public goods financed by the government, the deficit must be eliminated by reducing these two categories of expenditure.[2]

The absorption theory makes three behavioral assumptions. One is a spending relationship, and two specify relationships between patterns of expenditure and the relative price competitiveness of the nation's primary and industrial output. Using

$$C = \left(\frac{P_f}{P_d}\right)\left(\frac{1}{\epsilon}\right)$$

as a measure of the relative price competitiveness of the home country and its foreign trading partners, the three relationships are as follows:

$$\frac{\Delta M}{\Delta Y} > 0 \tag{4}$$

$$\frac{\Delta M}{\Delta C} < 0 \tag{5}$$

$$\frac{\Delta X}{\Delta C} > 0 \tag{6}$$

where Δ indicates a small change in value. C, described in the preceding paragraph, is a measure of the terms of trade or, more properly, the (inverse of the) real rate of exchange. Relationship (4) is the marginal propensity to import and is positive. As the country's competitiveness increases (as foreign goods become relatively more expensive), the value of imports decreases and the value of exports increases (with income levels held constant).

If a nation has a deficit, it is because it is spending too much on foreign goods and not selling enough to foreigners. To reduce spending on foreign goods, the authorities will tighten macropolicies and reduce the level of aggregate demand in the home country. The value of imports is reduced because the marginal propensity to import is positive. In the United

[2]Campbell R. McConnell, *Economics*, 8th ed. (New York: McGraw-Hill, 1981) describes public or social goods on pp. 93–97.

States and other industrialized countries, imports consist of both finished consumer goods and semifinished goods as well as primary materials. A reduction in final output reduces home output and usage as well as imports of finished goods, and the reduction in home output causes reductions in the use of foreign-supplied inputs. Unlike its cousin, the familiar marginal propensity to consume, the marginal propensity to import is not linear. It increases in value as national income approaches capacity as more and more sectors have to rely on imports to meet additional demand placed on the home economy. This means that there is no useful way of defining a multiplier for international trade, except, possibly, for the depths of a depression, where the propensity may be almost linear.

If a nation is spending too much with foreigners and decides to eliminate the current deficit by tightening macroeconomic policies, it will cause unemployment as a "side efffect." This side-effect is inevitable because when macroeconomic policies are tightened, aggregate demand is reduced for domestic output as well as for imports. To this point, the national standard of living will have been reduced by inflicting upon the unemployed a much lower standard of living and leaving the standard of living of the employed virtually untouched. So it is not likely that a nation will tolerate a permanently depressed economy as a cost of maintaining balanced payments, and the unemployed will object too, since they are carrying an undue burden. This policy could be reflected in national elections, although it is surprising that both Great Britain and the United States (under the Thatcher and Reagan administrations) should have been so tolerant of levels of unemployment that had not been equaled since the Great Depression. But whatever the political state of affairs, it is inefficient to have unemployed resources standing idle.

A deliberately induced recession will reduce imports and cure a deficit because the recession will affect M but will leave X pretty much unaffected (although some diminution of X may result because of the effect on global aggregate demand of the home nation's recession). The recession involves a renunciation of the home nation's high-employment macroeconomic target. If balanced current account can be achieved only by a recession, it is obvious that the nation's competitiveness is not "right." An increase in competitiveness will increase X *and* decrease M and will make the current balance positive at the existing (subtarget) level of employment. An increase in competitiveness will make everyone feel the effects of the current-account deficit as imported and exported goods both become more expensive for those who remain employed. No longer are the unemployed the only sufferers. Further, an increase in $(X - M)$ will increase the demand for labor at home, will tend to expand domestic employment, and will increase output (Y). If $\Delta M / \Delta Y$ is positive, an increase in Y generates an increase in M and reduces the new-found current surplus. But the mechanism has begun to take shape. The combination of the two measures of deliberately cutting back output in the face of a current deficit (and creating unemployment) and of changing the competitiveness of the nation's output in international markets and at home by increasing C (which will increase employment) can work on both the employment target and the balance-of-payments target simultaneously. The joint application of these two policy measures is the essence of the absorption approach. The two measures are called, respectively, *expenditure reductions* and *expenditure switches*.

Expenditure reductions reduce the standard of living or the rate of absorption to that allowed by the earnings of foreign exchange. In the process, the cutback on spending frees up resources to be employed in the production of goods for foreigners (exports) and for the substitution of goods for imports. Resources are needed in these industries once an expenditure switch has been instituted by, for example, a devaluation of the nation's currency. A devaluation increases the value of the competitive ratio and enhances the competitiveness of the nation's exports in foreign markets and the nation's import substitutes in home markets. Nothing suggests that the correct combination of these two measures is immediately apparent. Essentially, the argument calls for groping toward the correct combination by observing the gradually changing current deficit and unemployment rates.

Expenditure reductions are straightforward macroeconomic measures. Expenditure switches are more varied. A devaluation, a change in the announced exchange rate, is an expenditure switch, and it affects the relative costs of all internationally traded goods in home and foreign markets by an approximately equal percentage. Other expenditure switches have narrower effects. A tariff or NTB on imports affects only the home market in the particular goods. A subsidy on exports affects the competitiveness only in foreign markets (if not offset by foreign governments). In 1966, the British government was faced with a very large and serious balance-of-payments deficit. A newly elected government wished to avoid a devaluation and, as a substitute, imposed a 15 percent ad valorem tariff on all imports of manufactured goods. This measure was unpopular with Britain's trading partners, but it was carefully thought out to impede the importation of goods that British industry could produce (competitive imports). Britain planned to get as big an effect on M as possible by its selective duty.[3] The policy was a failure, and the inevitable devaluation took place in November 1967.

Devaluation is the expenditure switch par excellence. It affects all internationally traded goods equally (at least initially). But it is remotely possible that a devaluation will not constitute an effective expenditure switch. The problem has occupied economists for a long time and may have a certain relevance even now for developing countries with one predominant export. The effect of a devaluation (an increase in C) will work on the current balance by increasing revenues and decreasing expen-

---

[3] For details, see *The Economist*, December 3, 1966, pp. 1045–1046.

ditures with foreigners. The effect of what amounts to a change of price on revenues is intimately connected with the elasticity of demand. Suppose that foreign demand for the home country's exports were perfectly inelastic. Cutting the price of exports would result in a decrease in export earnings. Similarly, if import demand is also completely inelastic, there will be no substitution of domestic goods for imports and therefore no reduction in expenditures on imports. For a devaluation to be an effective expenditure switch, it requires that the demand for imports and the foreign demand for exports have certain minimum price elasticities. The crucial measurement, called the Marshall-Lerner condition, is that the sum of the two elasticities exceed unity.[4] In practical terms for industrialized countries such as Japan, members of the EEC, and the United States and Canada, which have large amounts of trade in price-sensitive manufactured goods that could easily be produced domestically, there is no reasonable doubt that the Marshall-Lerner criterion is met. If it were not met, the country with the deficit would confront the rather ridiculous situation that when it lost competitiveness by domestic inflation, it would generate a current surplus at the going exchange rate. There is an argument that one of the problems of the oil-price shocks in 1974 and 1978–1979 was that the oil exporters were importing as much as their economies would allow (and therefore their demand for imports was price-inelastic), and the demand for oil by the industrialized nations was also inelastic in the short and medium run. Thus the oil-price shocks did create a period of chronic imbalance of payments between the oil-importing and the oil-exporting countries that had to be met by oil exporters' lending money to oil importers (acquiring assets in oil-importing countries) to avoid drastic disruptions for balance-of-payments reasons. The medium through which the loans were effected was the Eurodollar market (see Chapter 18).

Figure 14-1 presents a diagrammatic explanation of the absorption approach. Competitiveness is measured vertically, and the values of Y and A are measured horizontally (in foreign exchange). The line AA shows the amount of absorption or domestic aggregate demand—equation (2)—at which the value of exports will equal the value of imports. The values C^* and Y^* show the values of C and $Y (= A)$ at which the current account is balanced. Any combination of Y and C to the left of AA indicates a payments surplus, as shown in relationship (4). To the right of line AA, the country must run a deficit because the demand for imports exceeds the value of exports that can be made at the given level of competitiveness. The twin economic goals of current-account balance and full employment will only be reached when $A = A^* = Y^*$ and $C = C^*$. Consider first the point A_1 at the same height as C^*: This is a rare case in which the current deficit is due entirely to excess aggregate demand (A exceeds

---

[4] A detailed explanation of the Marshall-Lerner condition is given in the supplement following this chapter.

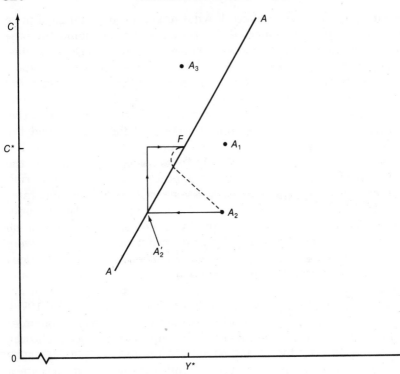

Figure 14-1
THE ABSORPTION APPROACH TO THE BALANCE OF PAYMENTS
Y^* denotes full-employment national output at a competitiveness equal to C^*.
The larger the marginal propensity to import, the steeper will be the slope of
line AA through point F.

full-employment income), and the deficit can be eliminated simply by
reducing the amount of domestic expenditure (an expenditure reduction)
without requiring any expenditure switch. Of course, in practice it would
be virtually impossible to have excessive aggregate demand and to avoid
demand-pull inflation and inducing a decrease in competitiveness. As
aggregate demand is reduced, export industries find the capacity to cater
more to export orders, and imports are reduced. Point A_2 represents
the most common form of a deficit when the country is absorbing goods
and services at a rate in excess of full-employment income and its international competitiveness is too low. This could follow from a burst of inflation
at home when the inflation reduced the actual value of C (with the fixed
rate of exchange), or it could result from an adverse real disturbance
when the required competitiveness had shifted (this will be discussed
in greater detail later in this chapter). Mechanically, the first thing to
do is to institute expenditure reduction until the deficit has been eliminated. This would bring the economy to point A_2', which would be a

position of less than full employment because it lies to the left of Y^*. When the expenditure reduction brought about a fall in the demand for imports, it also resulted in less aggregate demand for domestic goods. A numerical example may make the inevitability of unemployment at point A_2' more clearly apparent. At A_2, let A = 1,025, full-capacity Y = 1,000, M = 125, and X = 100. The marginal propensity to import is 10 percent. To bring X and M into equality, A must be reduced by 250 ($1/0.1 \times 25$), reducing A to 800, at which value it will equal domestic output (Y). Full-employment Y is 1,000. From A_2', an expenditure switch will increase competitiveness, increase X, make home goods more attractive relative to imports, and increase output in import substitute industries. As the deficit is reduced, the familiar multiplier relationship will take hold and add further to domestic aggregate demand until full employment is reached. This sequence is shown in Figure 14-1 by the three solid lines. In practice, the macroeconomic authorities wishing to adjust would follow the dotted line and grope their way toward point F by small, sequential expenditure reductions and small switches.

It is always possible that competitiveness will exceed C^* and that exports will inevitably exceed imports when full employment is reached. Point A_3 shows a position of full employment and excessive competitiveness. If demand-pull inflation is to be avoided, the country must run a current surplus and transfer the international saving to would-be borrowers through international financial markets or through foreign direct investment. To expand aggregate demand to the point at which current balance would be obtained would force the country into a demand-pull inflationary condition. If the country is willing to endure a lower standard of living than is permitted (actual competitiveness greater than C^*), the country can acquire foreign assets; if not, it must upvalue its currency (revalue the currency) and reduce its competitiveness. Given that international saving must adjust to the flow of international investment, the analysis of point A_3 allows us to anticipate the conclusion to this chapter: When the residents of a nation, including the country's multinational corporations, decide to acquire assets abroad, the country must reduce its rate of absorption to permit the generation of the needed current surplus (international saving) and must also improve its competitiveness to make such a surplus possible without inflicting unemployment on the domestic economy.

THE MONETARY APPROACH TO THE BALANCE OF PAYMENTS

Before considering the modern monetary approach, it is useful to examine in detail how the classic gold standard would work to cure a balance-of-payments deficit. The analysis is simply a development of Hume's mechanism (Chapter 5).

Gold standards involved fixed rates of exchange by virtue of the gold content of the national currency units. If a nation's merchants found themselves selling more to a country than was bought from it, they were assumed to take payment in terms of gold. Because gold was the basis for the home money supply (as well as "international money"), a deficit in the balance of payments (balance on current account) automatically implied a reduction in the money supply in the deficit nation. Assuming no capital movements, the decrease in the home money supply would force up the rate of interest, and this, in turn, would bring about a recession. As long as the country was running a current deficit, gold would continue to flow out, and "monetary policy" would be inexorably and automatically tightened. As long as there was a deficit on current account, the recession was reinforced. Of course, the recession helped to reduce the value of imports (though analysts of the gold standard do not use the concept of a marginal propensity to import and usually do not consider the process by which balanced payments are restored). In terms of Figure 14-1, the analysis is equivalent to point A_2. Competitiveness must be increased, but rates of exchange are fixed. The increase in competitiveness must be brought about by a decrease in the price level in the home country. Depending on the degree to which reductions in wages and prices are resisted, the system must work cumbersomely, since it induces a recession in order to force down domestic prices. Of course, the foreign nations may inflate as a result of their inflow of gold, and this will reduce the amount of recession in the home (deficit) country. Only when price levels have declined sufficiently for $X - M$ to become positive will the country be able to expand out of the recession.[5] Then, as in the absorption theory, the nation gropes its way toward the point of internal-external balance at which both targets are met. The important thing about the gold standard was its automaticity, its reliance on the automatic tie between the domestic money supply and the balance on current account (or the balance of payments). Note (this point will be developed further) that the gold standard relies on an expenditure reduction induced through monetary tightness and then, by an absolute lowering of input prices, on an expenditure switch.

What is important in the gold standard is that the authorities "obey the rules of the game." This means that the central bank does not break the link between the balance of payments and the money supply. Gold (money) must leave the country of a deficit nation and must not be replaced by paper money. The mechanism must be allowed to work its inevitable and inexorable, even ponderous, cure. Fairly obviously, the gold standard will eradicate a payments deficit more quickly, the more willing local workers are to accept a reduction in pay and the more quickly prices fall. In a modern economy, it is arguable that the gold standard would

---

[5]The gold standard tacitly assumed that the Marshall-Lerner condition was met.

be a socially intolerable mechanism because of the unemployment that the eradication of a deficit would require given current resistance to wage decreases. Of course, unions might learn that some decrease in *real* wages was inevitable if the country had a deficit from living beyond its income, but so far, most people seem to have faith that the political mechanism can be used to prevent a decline in real wages.[6] If governments do offset the decrease in the money supply (and attendant expenditure reductions) when a nation has a payments deficit, ultimately the situation must right itself by some favorable real disturbance, or the country is heading for a balance-of-payments crisis.

The monetary approach to balance-of-payments theory is a modern version of the gold standard involving control over the money supply by deliberate policy rather than through gold flows that leave no active role for the central bank. Like many economic theories, it simplifies the real world to the point that it can be accused of oversimplification.

The monetary approach assumes that the behavior of an economy can be explained in terms of its supply and demand for money balances. Every household and firm has a certain requirement for money balances (depending on income and the price level and rate of interest). If the supply of money exceeds the sum of all the individual demand, excess money exists, and households and firms will try to adjust to rid themselves of excessive holdings of money. In the process, they will substitute other assets for money by buying real or financial assets, and they will buy more goods. Thus excessive money in an economy will lead to attempts to buy more financial assets, thereby driving up their price and lowering their yield or rate of interest, and to attempts to buy more goods, which, given full employment and maximum output, will lead to an increase in the general price level. The price increases in goods and assets will continue until the excess money is absorbed into demanded money balances (that is, until money supply equals money demand). This essentially domestic mechanism can be internationalized. Starting from a position of full equilibrium—full employment, saving equal to investment, exports equal to imports, capital account balance, and the demand for money equal to the stock of money supplied—let the central bank in the home nation suddenly inject too much money into the economy (excessive growth in the money supply). People and firms will tend to increase their spending and to acquire more financial (nonmoney) assets. Because of the full-employment assumption, the need for additional goods can be met only by additional imports, and because purchases of domestic financial assets will force down their yields, people will seek out foreign assets. Excessive monetary growth in the home country will lead to a deficit on both the capital and the current account. This deficit will siphon off some of the

---

[6] Sometimes this miracle is to be accomplished through protection, including, presumably, a terms-of-trade or optimum tariff. Other than that, there is a touching faith on the part of the electorate in the ability of politicians to offset real shocks.

excess money, and a self-corrective mechanism is begun. It follows from this theory that a deficit on the balance of payments must be caused by excessive monetary creation in the deficit country.[7]

The monetary approach recognizes all foreign investment in short-term assets as spontaneous, implying that the only cause of a deficit is cash flows from one central bank to another. In this way, a deficit automatically affects the money supply in both countries.

One of the important features of the monetary approach is that a deficit is self-curing. Starting, once again, from full equilibrium, let the authorities in the home nation allow the money supply to grow more quickly than real underlying economic growth warrants. The immediate effect is to push up the prices of domestically made goods and domestic assets. However, both markets are extremely sensitive to price, and foreign goods and assets are perfect substitutes for domestic goods and assets. The extra money immediately spills over onto imports and foreign assets. The deficits on current and capital accounts drain some of the excess money out of the system. If not all of the extra money has been drained away, and the mechanism is not instantaneous, there will be an ongoing movement in the next period, resulting in another pair of deficits and further draining of excess money out of the system. When all of the excessive money has been drained out of the system, balance is restored to the international accounts, and the deficit has cured itself. All that is required to eliminate a payments deficit is a reduction in (the rate of growth of) the home supply of money, and this can be accomplished either by the automatic mechanism or by counteraction (negative monetary growth) by the central bank.

As with the gold standard, the emphasis is on the equilibrium conditions of money balance. The adjustment mechanism is not as fully detailed as the conditions that generate the equilibrium conditions. Also as with the gold standard, when one nation suddenly develops a new gold mine, the increase in the money supply in one country will cause some total inflation in the world economy as its money supply is increased with a finite total output.

The reverse holds. A failure to increase the domestic money supply by an amount sufficient to finance full-employment growth will generate a surplus in the balance of payments as foreigners buy more home-country goods and assets, supplying the money-short economy with money from abroad. This surplus is also self-curing: As soon as the surplus on current and capital accounts have generated an inflow of sufficient money, the money conditions are back in balance, and there exists no reason for an imbalance in the international accounts.

Note that the demand for imports is so sensitive to the price of home-

---

[7]The monetary approach does not pay attention to the likelihood of real disturbances. An adverse real disturbance could require the monetary authorities to reduce the money supply; in this sense, a deficit is due to a failure to destroy sufficient money.

country goods that the smallest increase in home-country price levels leads to a large increase in imports.[8] The same high sensitivity to relative yields exists in the demand for foreign assets. Here the assumption is made that differences in risk have already been accounted for by the differences in yield, so a small change in the yield of home-country assets will lead to a large-scale acquisition of foreign assets. The two kinds of assets are highly substitutable.

The monetary approach adds some useful perspective to the absorption approach. The monetary approach emphasizes the similarity between a devaluation and a reduction in the national money supply and, through this, shows how devaluations can be nullified by failure to control the money supply growth. A devaluation lowers the prices of home goods in foreign currency and therefore reduces the purchasing power of the stock of money of the home currency in foreign exchange. In international terms, a devaluation reduces the stock of money. It may also lead to a reduction in the price level of home goods measured in foreign exchange, as would a reduction in the domestic money supply with the exchange rate held constant. Of course, the value of the competitiveness ratio would change because of changes in different components, but the result would be the same. It follows, then, that a devaluation could be nullified by expansionary monetary policy. There are many examples of such nullifications in practice, and the monetarists do well to emphasize this relationship. The approach also emphasizes the cash flow character of balance-of-payments concerns. The whole problem is one of financing expenditures, and if the expenditures are financed by spontaneous foreign borrowing, no deficit exists by either measure. Unfortunately, the monetarist approach does neglect differences in the subaccounts, which means that the approach would not pick up the danger signals in a case of crisis caused by overborrowing and a sudden loss of lender confidence. The monetary theory also ties in excessive monetary creation in one country with upward pressure on world price levels. When the deficit nation is a large country, such as the United States, this can have a global inflationary effect, and the United States would, under these conditions, export some of its inflationary impetus. The excessive rate of monetary growth during the late 1960s did contribute to inflation in Europe as central banks there were unable or unwilling to sterilize the monetary inflow.

The value of the contribution of the monetary approach is impaired by its emphasis on equilibrium conditions and deemphasis of the mechanisms of adjustment to deficits and surpluses. The real world does not usually react with the tidiness that the monetary approach assumes. A second weakness is the failure of the theory to spell out how the deficit will be divided between the current and the capital accounts. This is

---

[8]Although this is not obvious when a deficit occurs, it is obvious when there is a surplus because of inadequate monetary creation. This is also explicit in the literature on the monetary approach.

important because the value of interest and dividend flows is affected by the country's international net worth, and deficits on current account reduce and on capital account increase the country's international net worth. Future payment conditions are, then, affected by the composition of the deficit among the subaccounts.

The monetary approach is, in fact, an updated version of Hume's price-specie-flow mechanism and the full gold standard to which Hume's analysis was closely related. This similarity is emphasized by the assumption of the monetary approach that money flows caused by payments imbalances cannot be offset by central bank action in the surplus countries.

COMMON GROUND OF THE
TWO THEORIES

People who prefer nice tidy solutions tend to be irritated by the existence of two explanations of the same phenomenon and the assurance that both contain "some truth." This section makes the two theories more compatible and shows that a full understanding of the adjustment mechanism derives from features of both arguments. The whole question lies in the assumptions of the two theories and in the relevance of the particular assumptions to the real-world problem.

The first and major point is that both theories rely on the same mechanics. The monetary theory contains expenditure reductions and expenditure switches in exactly the same way as the absorption theory, but it does not call the forces that are invoked by the same names and prefers to think of the reductions and switches being automatically invoked, whereas absorptionists think of them as discretionary interventions by policymakers. Consider the monetary-approach mechanism as explained in absorptionist language. There is a deficit, and the monetary cure is that a reduction in the money supply will automatically generate "tight money," which will force up the rate of interest and reduce the level of employment. This is merely an expenditure reduction. True, the monetary approach emphasizes an expenditure reduction brought about by monetary policy and disregards fiscal policy, but that is the difference. Once expenditure reduction has taken place, there will be slight pressures to increase competitiveness, mostly through downward levels on domestic prices, and coupled with great sensitivity of demand to relative prices, the expenditure switch is both automatic and highly effective. No need to question whether the Marshall-Lerner criterion is met—it is more than met, the sum of the elasticities is very large. Because of this sensitivity, there is no need actively to spell out the role of expenditure switches.

The second important point is that the time horizons of the two theories are quite different. The absorption approach is short-run and resembles so-called Keynesian economics, whereas the monetary approach is long-run. The bone of contention between the two is whether or not a surplus or a deficit could last forever. It is possible, under the absorption approach, for a country to restrict absorption to below-full-employment output and to institute an expenditure switch such that a surplus will be achieved (on current account), and there is nothing in the theory that shows how this surplus will terminate. The monetary approach emphasizes that no one can run a surplus forever and therefore insists on the automaticity of long-run balance. This is where the time horizon of the two theories is able to reconcile an apparent incompatibility. Nothing in the absorption approach argues that a surplus or deficit can or will last forever, merely that it can last for a year or more (short-run framework). A nation with an ongoing deficit must ultimate run out of willing lenders or reserves, and clearly some action must be taken. A nation with an ongoing surplus also faces the same ultimate need to eliminate the surplus. Either the surplus will be eradicated by action by the deficit nation (if one nation runs a surplus, another somewhere must run a deficit, since the world is a closed financial system). Alternatively, a surplus nation may grow tired of accumulating international assets at the expense of its current terms of trade, competitiveness, or standard of living. The surplus nation will eliminate the surplus by appreciating its currency and instituting an expenditure expansion. The absorption approach allows for surpluses and deficits to be seen in terms of economic policy goals, and these goals include the stock of international reserves as well as the more usual goals of full employment and price stability. The third way in which a surplus can be removed is for a real disturbance to take place. When a surplus nation faces an adverse real disturbance, it is likely to choose to allow its surplus to disappear rather than to institute policy action.[9]

The similarity between a devaluation or depreciation and restriction of monetary growth is also a matter of differences in viewpoint. Excessive monetary growth is an expenditure expansion (a negative expenditure reduction). Clearly, the absorption approach allows for a cure for a program of deficit elimination to be undertaken with some fixity of purpose. The process is not instantaneous. One authoritative study by Dornbusch and Krugman suggests that an expenditure switch gains strength slowly and achieves full effectiveness only after 1½ to 2 years.[10] It is important, then, that the expenditure reduction and expenditure switch be kept in force during that period and thereafter. But, as the monetary approach points out, there is the all-too-appealing option of easing up once the big decision has been made: Politicians screw their courage to the sticking point to institute the package of measures needed to eliminate the deficit and then, that done, try to restore their popularity by easing off on the severity of their actions. Frequently, this is done by easing monetary

---

[9]This is a policy consideration and is discussed in Chapter 15.

[10]R. Dornbusch and P. I. Krugman, "Flexible Exchange Rates in the Short Run," *Brookings Papers on Economic Activity,* 3 (1976), 537–575, particularly 560–566. But see Figure 15-5 in the next chapter.

tightness, and the expenditure switch is offset. The absorption approach works in a year-to-year or quarter-to-quarter setting and would identify any policy change in later periods as being an easing of conditions and would allow for it to offset the original actions. The monetary approach is right to emphasize the need for continued restraint.

The absorption approach is a perfectly valid explanation of the way in which balance-of-payments adjustment is brought about. It is a short-run model and therefore must explicitly allow for changes in economic targets or economic policies in the future (particularly during the period in which recent policy measures are taking hold). The actions needed to eliminate a deficit can require an active interventionist government using Keynesian macroeconomic policy measures, or it can assume a passive role in which it deliberately allows market forces to take hold and effect a cure for any imbalance. In the latter scenario, it is important to avoid any policy measures that will interfere with the adjustment process, although, presumably, it would be permissible to allow discretionary policy actions that reinforce the natural workings of the market system. An example would be for the central bank to institute open market sales to reinforce the decline in the money stock brought about by the international deficit. The mechanism must involve a reduction in living standards and rate of economic growth—this is implicit in the idea of expenditure reduction. How the policy measures are instituted—whether actively or passively—is a matter of philosophical and political concern. In either event, what is needed is some combination of expenditure reduction or expenditure switch. In practice, the assumed huge sensitivity of the choice between foreign and home-country goods to their relative prices—an assumption of the monetarist model—is not warranted. The sensitivity of the current account to an expenditure switch is dependent on the importance of the trading partners and on the time frame of analysis. It is, then, unrealistic to assume that the question of the expenditure switch can be left to changes in the absolute price level in one or both countries.

CHANGES IN COMPETITIVENESS

Early in this chapter, a government instituted by an expenditure switch changing the official parity of its national currency in terms of foreign currencies. Under the adjustable-peg system, a government institutes a devaluation by announcing that it will no longer support its currency in foreign exchange markets at the earlier parity of, say, 100 pesos to the dollar but would instead support the currency at 125 pesos to the dollar. This would devalue the currency and lower the price of home goods in foreign markets while raising the price of foreign goods in the home market. This kind of expenditure switch has the big advantage that it does not discriminate among industries or among trading partners. The question is whether there would be a lasting 25 percent increase in competitiveness.

The competitiveness ratio was defined as follows:

$$C = \left(\frac{P_f}{P_d}\right)\left(\frac{1}{\epsilon}\right)$$

with the rate of exchange (ϵ) defined as the number of units of foreign currency bought by a unit of domestic currency. If the country devaluing by 20 percent were, for example, Mexico, it would be necessary to respecify the devaluation from 1 cent to 0.8 cent. The second term in the definition would increase from 1/1 to 1/0.8. Mexican goods become cheaper abroad, and imports become more expensive in Mexico.

Putting the question of the response of the change in competitiveness to a change in the exchange rate another way, it is possible to ask, Will a given percentage change in the nominal exchange rate lead to an equal percentage change in the effective rate of exchange?

There are three reasons why an increase in competitiveness following a devaluation might not be maintained.

1. The devaluation might induce inflation at home. This is a very likely outcome, as many countries rely on imports of consumer goods and of raw materials. Imports of consumer goods will increase the cost of living faced by workers, and if wage rates are indexed to the cost of living or if unions conceive of wage agreements in real (inflation-adjusted) terms, the cost of labor might increase as a result of devaluation. Thus, P_d will increase when firms pass on any increase in labor costs, and an increase in P_d reduces the value of C. Imports of raw materials will also affect the cost of goods produced for the foreign and home markets, and P_d will rise in consequence. Clearly, the more widespread are wage-indexing plans and the more dependent a country is on imported raw materials, the more probable is some offsetting of a devaluation. Wage-indexing plans protect workers against a decrease in the real value of the wage rate and in this way are counterproductive when conditions require a reduction in the national standard of living.

2. Foreign countries may not want the devaluing country to gain a competitive edge. Suppose Mexico to trade in important amounts with the United States, with whom Mexico has a deficit, and with Brazil and Spain, with whom Mexican trade is in balance. If Mexico devalues the peso, Brazil and Spain may choose to devalue their currencies by an equal amount, and the Mexican economy will enjoy no benefit from the devaluation in trade with those two countries. Mexico's trade balance with the United States will improve. Of course, the expenditure reduction will probably also impart a small surplus to Mexican-Brazilian and Mexican-Spanish trade.

3. Finally, the economic authorities may give in to political pressures after the devaluation and make the expenditure reduction less severe. When this happens, the expenditure reduction is weakened, and if the expenditure increase has any effect on domestic wage rates and the prices of goods, the expenditure switch is also weakened.

Any of these processes will reduce the size of an expenditure switch; this phenomenon may be referred to as "slippage." If slippage is expected to occur following a devaluation, the original devaluation must be made that much more severe, so that the net effect of the devaluation (the change in the real rate of exchange) is big enough to eliminate the deficit.

FLEXIBLE RATES OF EXCHANGE

It requires political courage to impose a reduction in living standards or growth rates on a nation, particularly in a democracy where incumbent politicians are likely not to be reelected. For this reason, many nations do not devalue their currencies as quickly as is technically desirable. The way out of this dilemma is to hand over the decision mechanism to the impersonal ways of the market. A system of flexible exchange rates, especially a perfectly clean float, would take the politicians "off the hook."

The advantages of flexible rates are that they introduce an expenditure switch automatically without any long-winded decision process having to be undertaken. What, then, are the disadvantages? Why did the world operate on a set of fixed exchange rates for so long (from 1946 to 1971)?

One of the reasons, the possibility that nations would intervene in foreign exchange markets to allow them to generate a net current surplus in a time of depression, is considered in Chapter 16. It was this experience in the 1930s that led the framers of the Bretton Woods system, which lasted from 1946 to 1971, to rely on a system of adjustable parities for exchange rates.

One of the problems is that speculation in foreign exchange would lead to wide gyrations in nominal rates of exchange, so exporters and importers would not be able to obtain a reliable estimate of the cost of imports or the proceeds from exports. Equally, gyrating prices would not provide good indicators for firms planning to invest in line with comparative advantage.

The advantage of flexible rates is that they eliminate any decision-making delay in instituting expenditure switches. Since 1974, the industrialized nations of the world have been suffering from quite different rates of inflation as oil-price changes impinged upon individual economies and set off varying degrees of induced inflation (as wage rates rose with living costs). Flexible exchange rates in the 1970s and early 1980s were remarkably efficient in maintaining relatively stable effective rates of exchange. They also allow automatic expenditure switches to be made for any real disturbances. The value of a system of flexible exchange rates in a time of uneven national rates of inflation can be illustrated by the experience of Mexico in the late 1970s and early 1980s as described in the supplement following Chapter 13. Mexico chose to fix the value of the peso to the U.S. dollar during the 1970s. When Mexican inflation began seriously to outpace the rate of price increases in the United States, the effective rate of exchange of the peso appreciated (got stronger) and became well in excess of any reasonable exchange rate between the two currencies compatible with balance. Mexico was forced to borrow to finance current deficits and ultimately was subjected to a financial crisis with large devaluations and depreciations of the peso accompanied by stringent expenditure reductions at home and heavy unemployment. A system of flexible rates of exchange will prevent price-level disturbances from inducing serious imbalances in the international accounts.

However efficient a system of flexible rates may be in countering incipient price-level disturbances, they can lull the authorities into a false sense of security when real disturbances take place. The key here is the nonautomaticity of expenditure reductions. When a price-level disturbance takes place, there is no underlying change in real conditions or the terms of trade and, therefore, no need for an expenditure reduction. This situation is handled almost perfectly by a system of flexible rates. When a real disturbance takes place, a deficit nation needs to undergo an expenditure reduction to make the restoration of balanced payments possible. If the authorities have mentally allotted the whole question of balance-of-payments policies to the flexible exchange rate system, they will not be cognizant of the need to institute an expenditure reduction ahead of time—ultimately, if the needed increase in exports causes demand-pull inflation, the expenditure reduction would, presumably, be instituted, but this is a cumbersome procedure.

ADJUSTMENT MECHANICS AND DISTURBANCES

In this discussion we make the assumption that the flow of international saving (the current balance) will adjust to the flow of international investment. All adjustment will be made through the balance on current account. A deficit requires an increase in international saving. There are three kinds of disturbance: a real disturbance, involving a change in one of the underlying demand-supply configurations in the world; a price-level

Figure 14-2

ADJUSTMENT TO DISTURBANCES AND FOREIGN INVESTMENT

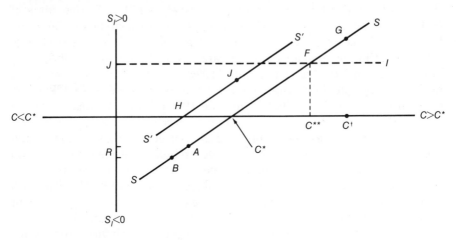

disturbance, involving only different rates of inflation at home and abroad; and a cyclical disturbance, caused by the onset of recession in one or more countries.

Figure 14-2 shows the flow of international saving as determined by the value of the competitiveness ratio. The line SS slopes upward, showing that the Marshall-Lerner condition is satisfied (the steeper the slope, the greater the sum of the elasticities of demand). SS is drawn for a given set of conditions in a fully employed world. There is only one complexity in this construct: SS has the expenditure reduction built into it. In other words, a movement from point A to point B assumes a concomitant expenditure reduction of an amount equal to the vertical distance between A and B. This assures that the resources needed to supply the additional net exports are available. The vertical distance between A and B is identified by R in Figure 14-2. As drawn, the country must have competitiveness equal to C^* to achieve a balanced current account at full employment.

A real disturbance will cause a change in the position of the line SS. Suppose foreigners suddenly want less of the country's exports—an adverse disturbance. The country will have to reduce the prices of its goods and increase the price of imports if it is to reestablish a balanced current account. (This procedure is essentially the analysis required with offer curves in Chapter 3.) Because this is an adverse disturbance, competitiveness must increase. The line SS will have shifted to the right, there will be a new value for C^*, and real per capita income in the country will have decreased. A favorable real disturbance will shift SS to the left. A price-level disturbance causes a movement along the curve—it changes the existing value of C. Under a system of fixed rates of exchange, inflation in the home country unmatched by inflation abroad will reduce the nation's competitiveness, and the value of competitiveness will decrease from C^* to H. With competitiveness H and full employment being maintained, the country will run a current deficit equal to HA. Recognizing that the country's currency has become overvalued, the authorities will devalue the currency and return the competitiveness to C^*. A cyclical disturbance drops the assumption of full employment. If the home country has a spontaneous recession, its demand for imports will be reduced, and the line SS will shift to the left to $S'S'$. The currency *could* appreciate to reduce the actual competitiveness and maintain a balanced current account, or the competitiveness could be left at C^* and the country would run a current surplus of C^*J. The important point is that real disturbances bring about a shift of the schedule and price level disturbances involve a movement along the line SS.

Now let there be a deficit on capital account brought about by foreign direct investment by the country's multinational corporations. Let this deficit be indicated by the line II. This line is drawn parallel to the horizontal axis so that the flow of direct investment abroad by MNCs is considered independent of the prevailing competitiveness. This is something of a simplification. In fact, MNCs are more likely to invest abroad when the home currency is relatively strong and they expect that the strength is no transitory event. Then foreign sources of supply are more likely to be cheaper than home production, and the line II may therefore be expected to have a negative slope.[11] Starting from point C^*, a nation experiencing a sudden surge of outward investment at the rate shown by the line II will have to institute expenditure reductions to release the resources needed to generate a current surplus equal to FC^{**}. This expenditure reduction is subsumed in the line SS when competitiveness is increased to C^{**}. Then the nation will have reasserted balance in its international transactions: The current account will show a surplus of FC^{**}, and the capital account will show a corresponding deficit. The nation will have reduced its absorption by FC^{**} and in the process allowed its terms of trade to deteriorate by the devaluation or depreciation of the currency required to increase the competitive ratio.

Were the country's rate of foreign investment to increase further— say to a rate of $GC^\dagger$—a further expenditure reduction and devaluation would be required to generate the needed larger flow of international saving. The fact that the new, larger outflow on capital account requires a change in the competitiveness ratio and a corresponding expenditure reduction means that an increase in the rate of capital outflow has the same effect on the economy in the short run as an adverse real disturbance.

In a tranquil world without real disturbances, the task of the authorities is simply to ensure against a price-level disturbance brought about by

---

[11]MNCs invest abroad for a wide variety of reasons. The relative cheapness of foreign manufacture will therefore impart only a small downward slope.

creeping inflation at home. Flexible rates of exchange will take care of this problem. In an era of real disturbances, the authorities must try to identify the direction of the disturbance (favorable or adverse) and attempt to assist the economy to adjust to the new situation. This means instituting an expenditure reduction when needed and making sure that short-term capital movements do not impede the system of flexible exchange rates from giving the appropriate expenditure switch.

SUMMARY

Balance-of-payments adjustment requires the redistribution of resources toward export and import-competing industries because the elimination of a deficit needs greater supplies of exports and less reliance on imports of goods that can be made at home. It is in the current account that most of the adjustment takes place, and the elimination of a deficit involves a reduction in the quantity of output left over from international trade for domestic absorption. Deficit elimination therefore involves a reduction in the nation's standard of living or in its rate of economic growth. These measures are likely to be politically unpopular.

The mechanism of deficit reduction can be divided into two separate parts: the actual reduction in the rate of absorption caused by monetary restraint or by fiscal tightening and the expenditure switch required to make foreigners want to buy more home-country goods and home-country residents to substitute home goods for foreign-made goods wherever possible. The usual means of instituting an expenditure switch is to allow the value of the country's currency to decline in foreign exchange markets, either through devaluation in a world of fixed rates or through depreciation under a system of flexible rates. There are other ways of limiting the attractiveness of foreign goods—tariffs and quotas, for example—but such means discriminate among industries and among trading partners. Discrimination induces political antagonism and possible counteraction.

The expenditure reduction and switch measures must be left in place if a deficit is to be removed. They cannot be allowed to weaken in the face of domestic political pressures. This need for protracted restraint is made more apparent by the insistence of the theorists who launched the monetary approach to the balance of payments. Their concern that an increase in the domestic money supply will offset a devaluation lays stress on the need for the authorities to hold both sets of measures in place. However, the magnitude of the expenditure switch can be eroded by the firms' passing on to their customers the increased costs of foreign inputs (made more expensive by the currency devaluation). This process, referred to as "slippage," implies that the percent change in competitiveness will be less than the percent devaluation of the home currency.

Much of the analysis implies a disturbance that creates a deficit, the curing of the deficit, and a return to balanced international accounts. In the real world, disturbances can follow hard upon each other. It is necessary to distinguish, whenever possible, between real and price-level disturbances because the appropriate policies will differ. It is also necessary to distinguish between temporary and permanent (or quasi-permanent) disturbances. Temporary disturbances will reverse themselves later, provoking little need for any adjustment in the home economy. Price-level disturbances are caused by different rates of inflation in different countries and need only a remedial change in competitiveness to reestablish balanced payments—no expenditure reduction is required. All of these complications suggest that continued surveillance of the international accounts is necessary, and the issue cannot usefully be left to a system of flexible rates of exchange, no matter how efficient such a system may seem.

Bibliography

Bergstrand, Jeffrey H. "Is Exchange Rate Volatility 'Excessive'?" *New England Economic Review,* (September-October 1983), 5–9.

Dornbusch, R., and P. I. Krugman. "Flexible Exchange Rates in the Short Run." *Brookings Papers on Economic Activity,* 3 (1976), 537–575.

Johnson, Harry G., "Why Devaluations Often Appear to Fail." *Eastern Economic Journal,* Vol. 1 (October 1974), 231–238.

Kemp, Donald S. "A Monetary View of the Balance of Payments." *Federal Reserve Bank of St. Louis Monthly Review,* April 1975, pp. 14–23.

Murphy, J. Carter. "Reflections on the Exchange Rate System." *American Economic Review,* 75 (May 1985), 68–73.

Whitman, Marina. "Global Monetarism and the Monetary Approach to the Balance of Payments." *Brookings Papers on Economic Activity,* 3 (1975), 491–536.

Questions

1. Why is a current deficit usually associated with "living beyond one's income"?
2. For a devaluation to constitute an effective expenditure switch, the currency's effective or real exchange rate must weaken. Explain.
3. Distinguish among suppressing, financing, and adjusting to a disturbance.
4. A nation living beyond its full-employment income must cut absorption if it is to eliminate a current deficit. Explain.
5. The monetary theory is really nothing more than an up-to-date version of gold-standard economics. Show this to be true.
6. Why is a system of flexible rates most suited to a world in which price-level disturbances predominate?
7. An increase in the deficit on capital account requires that absorption be reduced on two counts. Explain.
8. $Y = 10,250$, $X = 1,000$, and $M = 750$. What is the value of A? What must

the balance be on capital account if payments are to be balanced? What is the cost to the country of maintaining this balance-of-payments position? What is the balance on current account of all of the remaining countries in the world?

9. The sum of the elasticities is 2, so a 10 percent devaluation (without slippage) will generate a 20 percent increase in the current balance. $X = 1,000$, $M = 1,000$, $Y = 10,000$, and $A = 10,000$. The deficit on capital account is 500. By how much must the country devalue its currency if there is no slippage? What should the expenditure reduction be?

10. Under the gold standard, prices change by half as much as the change in the gold stock. If the sum of the elasticities equals 1, how much gold must leave the country before payments balance is restored?

The Marshall-Lerner Criterion

A devaluation must, if it is to achieve its objective, reduce the deficit (or increase the surplus) on current account. It must increase revenues, decrease expenditures, or do both. A devaluation is merely a means of reducing the cost of exports to foreigners and increasing the cost of imports to home-country buyers. The idea is to substitute the use of home-country goods for foreign-made goods at home and abroad.

A price cut does not always generate an increase in revenues, nor does a price increase provoke a reduction in expenditures. The elasticity of demand for the product is crucial here.[1] It is therefore not surprising that the Marshall-Lerner criterion for a successful devaluation (an increase in international saving) hinges on the elasticities of demand for exports and imports. In this simplified treatment, we ignore the possibility that supply schedules will be less than perfectly elastic, and we also ignore the income effect that results from a change in the terms of trade.[2] The purpose is to show, in commonsense terms, why a devaluation will have no effect if the sum of the two elasticities of demand is equal to unity.

There is one tricky aspect even in a simplified presentation. When assessing the effect of a change in revenues consequent upon a devaluation, it is necessary to specify the currency in which the results are being reported—home currency, which is devalued, or foreign currency. Suppose a country devalues its currency (the dollar): This will make exports cheaper in terms of foreign currency (the mark) but it will not change the price of imports in marks. Alternatively, a devaluation of the dollar will leave the price of exports unchanged in dollars, but imports will be more expensive in dollar terms. Our computations will be conducted

---

[1] See McConnell, *Economics*, pp. 453–458.
[2] The exposition would be made more complex if import expenditures were assumed originally to exceed export revenues (a current deficit); therefore, they are assumed to be equal. To move from a deficit to a surplus, this condition must be met; alternatively, the problem could be seen in terms of moving from zero to positive international saving to offset international investment.

in marks because that is the currency that does not change its value and is therefore a better measure of monetary flows.

Case 1. Elasticity of demand for exports (η_x) = 1; elasticity of demand for imports (η_m) = 0. The dollar is devalued by 10 percent.

Export revenues do not change. Exports drop 10 percent in price but increase in volume by 10 percent. Import expenditures do not change. The price of imports in marks does not change. People in the home country might be tempted to substitute now cheaper home goods for imports because the price of imports will have gone up in dollars. But because in this example η_m = 0, there is no tendency to substitute home goods for imports, and the quantity of imports purchased will be unchanged.[3] If revenues and expenditures both remain unchanged, the current account remains unchanged.

Case 2. η_x = 0 and η_m = 0. The dollar is devalued by 10 percent.

This devaluation will cut the cost of exports in marks by 10 percent but will not lead to any increase in the quantity sold. Revenues in marks will decrease by 10 percent. There will be no change in expenditures on imports (see case 1). The Marshall-Lerner criterion is not satisfied, and the flow of international saving decreases.

Case 3. η_x = 1 and η_m = 1. The dollar is devalued by 10 percent.

The devaluation of the dollar leads to constant revenues in marks (see case 1). The demand for imports is price-sensitive. As a result of the increase in price of imports in dollars, home-produced goods are now relatively cheaper, and substitution takes place. Expenditures on imports are constant in dollars and, therefore, decline by 10 percent in marks. The current account has increased by 10 percent of the value of imports (= the value of exports by assumption). The Marshall-Lerner criterion is satisfied, and the flow of international saving has increased.

The greater the sum of the elasticities, the smaller the percentage devaluation needed to eliminate a deficit of a given size. Put another way, the Marshall-Lerner formula tells us (if it could be computed) how much of a shift in the terms of trade is necessary to eliminate a deficit of a given size.

As in the theory of balance-of-payments adjustment, no attention is paid to the fact that exports and imports comprise many categories of goods. Some goods could be quite price-sensitive and others perfectly price-inelastic. Encompassing all types of imports of exports in a single composite glosses over some problems. However, it raises an interesting policy question. If the sum of the elasticities is quite low (say, 2), this implies a fairly large shift in the terms of trade to get rid of the deficit on current account. How much better it would be for the deficit country if the country were allowed to devalue only for transactions involving

---

[3] Home-produced goods are cheaper because the price of imports has increased in dollars. The perfectly inelastic demand for imports means that home goods will not be substituted for imports that are absolute necessities.

goods with highly elastic demand. Such discriminatory procedures bring out strenuous complaints from trading-partner nations. Countries have been known to use tariffs on imports with high elasticities of demand to this effect.

When the United Kingdom devalued sterling by 33 percent in 1949, the British government suggested to the Scotch whisky distillers that they retain their price in dollars (that is, increase the sterling price of exports by 33 percent). This action was based on the presumption that the demand for Scotch whisky was inelastic. Of course, the government was encouraging the distillers to act as a monopoly industry, and the distillers were happy to oblige.

15

Balance-of-Payments Policymaking

The economic authorities of a nation need to be concerned with the adequacy of their foreign exchange reserves (their balance of payments) for several reasons. These reasons vary according to the economic status of the nation. *Developing countries* require a steady inflow of noncompetitive imports if growth and development are to take place smoothly. A sudden shortage of foreign exchange will require a change in policy that will probably invoke a recession as well as restrict the availability of imports. Once a growth impetus is lost, it may be difficult to regain the momentum. This problem is common in Latin American countries in recent years. *Industrial countries* need to be sure that they are not forced by a shortage of reserves to take drastic deflationary actions and to inflict on their economies the need for major shifts of resources from one industry to another (with all of the attendant social costs). Finally, the *reserve-currency country* (the United States) is the country whose national currency forms the basic medium of exchange and store of value for international transactions. Because other countries tend to hold reserves in this currency, the reserve-currency nation can more easily finance balance-of-payments deficits and can finance them for longer than most other nations. A key-currency nation has life too easy and tends to delay corrective action for longer than is in its own best interests; for example, the United States has never borrowed from the International Monetary Fund and in this way given an official body the right to supervise its economic policies.[1] In 1971, the United States came close to causing

---

[1] The International Monetary Fund is described in Chapter 17. For now it can be considered an international bank for central banks experiencing balance-of-payments difficulties.

a financial crisis of major proportions because it had too long neglected its balance-of-payments deficits—that is, it had conducted its economic policies without paying more than superficial attention to their balance-of-payments effects.

For a nation to face a crisis in its international payments implies a large adjustment involving the transfer of factors of production from one sector to another. As was seen in Chapter 9, this is not a simple task, nor is it devoid of social costs. Moreover, the larger the deficit and the greater the shortage of reserves, the more drastic the expenditure reduction is likely to be. This suggests a serious recession with all of the attendant social costs. Reserves allow nations to eliminate any deficit more slowly, with shallower recessions and less disruption of factor markets during the course of adjustment. If a nation carries its deficit to the point that it is down to minimal international reserves, the expenditure reduction will have to be severe and immediate, and the expenditure switch must match the reduction in severity. But expenditure switches are slow-acting, so the greater the deficit and the greater the need to restore reserve balance through international saving (current surpluses), the longer the recession must endure. There is thus a strong argument in favor of early action and gradual adjustment in response to disturbances that adversely affect the balance of payments.

The problem is, of course, that the balance of payments tells the analyst only that something is wrong. It is up to the analyst to diagnose the cause of the deficit and, given the level and availability of international reserves, to recommend how quickly adjustment should be instituted, how, and with what severity. In a financial crisis, the analyst has no room for maneuver because the option of tempering the rate of improvement in the current account by partially financing the deficit through reduction in the reserve balances is lost.

Because the world is a "closed economy," there is a surplus for every deficit (statistical discrepancies aside). The problem is that a country may enjoy having a surplus and therefore not "play its part" in the elimination of a deficit. No pressure exists to require a country with a positive balance of payments to eliminate that surplus. It is merely piling up more and more international reserves, and it can invest these reserves, at interest, in a foreign central bank. The desirability of a surplus derives from the element of insurance that it provides against some future unfavorable shock or disturbance. Armed with a surplus, a country can experience an adverse shock without having to engage in the politically unpopular routine of expenditure reduction and expenditure switch. The adverse disturbance will make the surplus disappear, but that is all. Of course, a nation can ultimately acquire too much in international reserves and allow its citizens to enjoy the better terms of trade and greater absorption that an elimination of a surplus will allow. What this means is that a deficit nation will have to institute an expenditure reduction, but it is unlikely that a corresponding surplus nation will ease its task by instituting expenditure expansions. Of course, the competitiveness change (expenditure switch) does affect both countries, but that is less direct and much slower to work. In contrast, the deficit nation must move quickly to eliminate the deficit, if only because a protracted deficit (and running down of the international reserve position) could lead to more serious problems in the future. Once a nation's reserves are exhausted, the deficit must be eliminated at once almost irrespective of the social cost involved.

Disturbances do not originate only in foreign countries. Domestic policies can neglect the need for balance-of-payments discipline and lead to deficits. Most frequently, these domestic policies cause or allow the domestic price level to increase more quickly than that of its neighbors and, by so doing, to instigate a price-level disturbance.

Whatever the cause of the deficit, if the conditions remain unchecked for long, the remedy will be painful: a reduction in the rate of absorption and concomitant expenditure switch. Such steps tend to be unpopular with home-country electorates. Politicians have a tendency to want to postpone adjustment measures until after the next election. In the United States, with major elections scheduled for every other November, there is seldom any time when balance-of-payments policies can be instituted without some concern for their political repercussions.

This chapter considers balance-of-payments policymaking for industrialized countries (including reserve-currency countries). First it examines the sensitivity of policies to the kind of disturbances that may give rise to a deficit. It considers the advantages of flexible exchange rates as a setting in which international economics is conducted and assesses the choice between the elimination of deficits by means of the current account as opposed to the possibility of imposing controls over capital outflows. Then it analyzes the severe problems in international payments that characterize the economic policies of President Reagan. The huge current deficits that the United States has experienced in the mid-1980s are very likely to require a severe adjustment within the following decade.

PRINCIPLES OF BALANCE-OF-PAYMENTS POLICYMAKING

If an efficient automatic system of balance-of-payments adjustment existed, policymaking would be unnecessary. It is with this beautiful idea in mind that, from time to time, people rhapsodize over the gold standard. In fact, the automaticity and efficiency of the gold standard (in terms of striking a balance between the effectiveness of the adjustment process and the minimizing of social costs) is not very well documented (see Chapter 16). The gold standard is a regime of fixed rates of exchange par excellence, and like the monetary approach to the balance of payments, the gold standard assumed that the expenditure reduction process was tied in to the automatic mechanism in addition to changes in competitiveness.

Hume's payments adjustment mechanism (Chapter 2) is the essence of an automatic adjustment to eliminate a deficit under a gold standard. Prices in the deficit country are lowered as gold leaves the country, and the money supply is reduced. Presumably, prices are increased in the foreign country as the gold inflow there increases the money supply. Competitiveness changes, and an expenditure switch is inaugurated. At the same time (though this aspect is not stressed by Hume), the deficit nation will be pushed into a recession. What is difficult to conceive in this modern age is how the absolute level of domestic prices will be lowered. Given the components of the competitive ratio,[2] the rate of exchange is fixed, and the only source of a change in competitiveness is a change in the ratio of price levels, and this requires a reduction in the absolute level of prices and wages in the deficit nation. In modern times, resistance to reductions in money wages and to changes in real wages is substantial, and wage rates yield only slowly to the inexorable pressures of recession and unemployment.

A system of flexible exchange rates, in contrast, will find a nation adjusting its competitiveness quite quickly as the rate of exchange responds to pressures in the foreign exchange market, and changes in absolute price levels in the two countries are relatively small. As noted in Chapter 14, there is always the risk of slippage, and this could be said to have been very important during the 1970s as prices of manufactured goods tended to rise in step with oil prices. However, a devaluation will inevitably raise the cost of imported inputs in domestic currency and provide an inflationary impetus that must be overcome if substantial slippage is to be avoided.

Implicit in what has been presented is that the current account, the rate of international saving, will adjust to the capital account. This argument was also made in Figure 12-1, in which current transactions were shown as being sensitive to changes in competitiveness (the real rate of exchange) and capital transactions were not. The same assumption is built into Figure 14-2. None of this suggests that capital transactions are completely immune to changes in the real rate of exchange, but the current account (and the rate of absorption in the deficit country) is the main means by which the deficit is eliminated, and in Keynesian economics, policy measures such as monetary and fiscal policy work on the rate of absorption. For these reasons, balance-of-payments adjustments will normally take effect through manipulation of the current account.

There have been efforts to eliminate payments deficits by controlling

$$^2C = \left(\frac{P_f}{P_d}\right)\left(\frac{1}{\epsilon}\right)$$

capital outflows (attracting capital inflows through interest-rate policy would be merely an example of financing a deficit). Many countries impose controls over capital exports in attempts to prevent the rich from fleeing a weak national currency, but these are more or less permanent measures and unrelated to balance-of-payments deficits. The United States has always endorsed a policy of freedom of capital movements with the exception of a short period between 1968 and 1974, but the lesson is that capital tends to be a very flexible thing and the net of controls must be drawn very tightly indeed if it is to have much effect.

The U.S. experience with capital controls began when the dollar was having difficulty maintaining its official value under a fixed-rate system. The first problem was one of a large drain of financial capital as foreign firms floated bond issues in New York because interest rates there were much lower than in Europe (and because the costs of flotation were also lower). In 1963, the United States attempted to equalize the interest costs in New York and Europe by imposing an *interest equalization tax,* which taxed interest earned from foreigners at a premium rate. Thus it became no cheaper for a Norwegian to borrow in New York than in Europe because the two-percentage-point difference in yields (200 basis points) was countered by the tax levied on foreign interest, so American lenders would want the same rate of return on Norwegian bonds as Europeans. (The idea was that the tax would preclude the need to raise interest rates in the United States during a recession and at the same time help the balance-of-payments position). In 1965, President Johnson imposed so-called voluntary limits on direct investment abroad—effectively on the largest 500 firms in the United States. These controls were not very effective and became mandatory in 1968 when the United States was suffering from the inflationary strain of the Vietnam War (and associated heavy expenditures in foreign exchange in the Pacific). The United States was suffering from a real and a price-level shock simultaneously. Devaluation of the dollar was ruled out by the existing international financial arrangements (see Chapter 17), and the wartime demands led to high expenditures that could not be offset by higher domestic taxation because of the unpopularity of the war.

The controls were directed at large nonfinancial corporations that were supposed to increase the net balance on their individual transactions. Profits from foreign investments were to be repatriated at a minimum rate, and there were limits on the export of capital, based on the firms' historical record. Investment in European countries was permitted only at the rate of 35 percent of the firm's rate in preceding years. The program was less restrictive for investment in developing countries, where financial transfers were more likely to result in increased exports of U.S.-made machinery. The Foreign Direct Investment Program did contribute to the cash flow position of the United States, but only temporarily. The most interesting feature of the program was that it had very little apparent effect on the rate of acquisition of foreign assets by the large U.S. corporations. Except for 1968, when uncertainty about the meaning of the regulations may have affected corporate planning, firms continued to acquire foreign assets at the same or a higher rate as in the mid-1960s.[3] What changed was the contribution of funds transferred from the United States. The large multinational corporations simply financed more of their acquisitions abroad in local capital markets in Europe and paid higher rates of interest. When the program's effectiveness weakened in 1973 (before being finally terminated in 1974), the MNCs promptly paid off their high-interest foreign indebtedness with funds from the United States. But by then the dollar had been devalued, and the system of fixed exchange rates had collapsed under the strain.

Nowadays, with international financial markets much more closely interwoven than in the 1960s, capital controls would not work unless accompanied by regulations of remarkable severity and burdensomeness.

Given the existing freedom of capital movements and the difficulties in impeding the freedom of movement of capital (of residents), there seems to be little alternative to having the current account (and the domestic economy) accommodate the desired pattern of capital flows. The problem with this scenario is that, to the extent that capital flows are more variable than current account transactions, there may be a tendency for nations to institute balance-of-payments policies for a temporary situation (a reversible disturbance) and, a couple of years later when the pattern has changed back, to have to institute reverse policies. Since balance-of-payments measures involve the reallocation of resources from one industry to another—usually from or to domestic goods industries to or from export and import-competing industries—policymaking that reverses itself after a couple of years will inflict unnecessary costs on the economy. This problem of reversible disturbances and of unnecessary policy changes is not caused only by changes in the pattern of capital flows. An example of a current-account reversible disturbance (or shock) would be a crop failure in a food-importing country due to a very unusual set of climatic conditions (India in a year when the monsoon does not function as usual would be the standard example). The same conditions would not be expected to recur the following year, and it would be costly to institute expenditure switches in one year only to have to reverse them the next. The signals to the producer sectors of the economy would be misleading. Running down the nation's stock of food and its stock of liquid international reserves (financing the deficit) would be the more appropriate policy action when a disturbance was known (or thought) to be self-reversing. Unfortunately, the balance-of-payments analyst can only observe historical data and would need a crystal ball to see whether

---

[3] It is arguable (in contradiction to the argument just made) that the increase in the rate of foreign direct investment was partly due to the steady decline in U.S. competitiveness as the dollar became more and more overvalued (through the price-level disturbance).

an existing deficit can be left to cure itself. The crop failure case is relatively easy (if only because a permanent climate change would be a terrible prospect), but it is less easy to diagnose the appropriate response to a sudden outflow of capital. Should the analyst allow the foreign exchange markets to impose an expenditure switch on the economy (with the need for a concomitant expenditure reduction), or should the authorities support their currency in the foreign exchange market by deliberately financing the spontaneous deficit? Balance-of-payments policy, then, depends on the available level of reserves (to finance a deficit over a protracted period), the kind of disturbance that gives rise to the deficit (self-reversing or not, and real, price-level, or cyclical), and the size of the deficit. In other words, balance-of-payments policy must take a medium-term or a long-term view of the problem.

When faced with a deficit, the authorities have three options: to finance the deficit by using up cash reserves, to suppress the deficit by making it go away by sacrificing some other dimension of economic performance, and adjusting to eliminate the deficit by altering the rate of absorption and the competitiveness. Clearly, these three options can be intermingled so that a country might deliberately choose to adjust to a new set of conditions slowly (following a real disturbance) so that the rate of adjustment was bearable. Such a policy would necessarily require financing the deficit temporarily until the full adjustment was made. Similarly, an economy might have a severer than necessary expenditure reduction inflicted on it to reduce the deficit (the marginal propensity to import is positive) so that the slow-working adjustment mechanism could take hold when no loss of reserves is possible.

One thing that a government should not do intentionally is postpone instituting a policy of adjustment (financing a deficit) without good grounds for thinking that the disturbance is self-reversing. Too often, particularly under fixed rates of exchange, governments have allowed domestic inflation to reduce the economy's competitiveness and not allowed the nominal exchange rate to change sufficiently. This is a price-level disturbance and is corrected, virtually automatically, by a system of flexible rates of exchange (such as the world now employs). In terms of Figure 15-1 (a variation on Figure 14-2), a loss of competitiveness would cause a movement leftward and downward along the line SS to register a current deficit. Flexible exchange rates would keep the effective rate of exchange (the national competitiveness) approximately constant. Under fixed rates, the nation might choose to suppress the deficit by causing a recession and shifting the line SS upward. As a general rule, flexible exchange rates are particularly suited to a world in which price-level disturbances are the major cause of changes in international competitiveness. Given the different experiences with respect to inflation in the industrialized world in the aftermath of the oil-price shocks, it was remarkably fortunate that the world had a system of flexible rates in force

Figure 15-1

COMPETITIVENESS AND BALANCE OF PAYMENTS

Recall that the line SS has the needed expenditure absorption built into it as C varies.

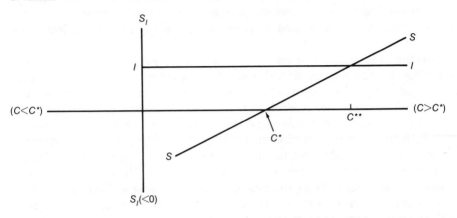

at that time. Nor can there be any realistic consideration of a return to a system of fixed rates of exchange (which some people advocate from time to time) until different propensities to inflate have been eradicated.

The weakness of a system of flexible rates of exchange emerges when there is a self-reversing real disturbance, since a clean float would inflict on an economy a double shift in competitiveness and would in the process send confusing signals to business firms. If the balance-of-payments policies are sufficiently sophisticated and policymakers can foresee the future correctly enough to diagnose a self-reversing real disturbance, the correct course of action is to finance the deficit and to support the currency in the foreign exchange markets, providing essential constant competitiveness.

A real disturbance shifts the line SS. An unfavorable disturbance shifts it to the right, denoting the existence of a deficit at the going value of $C*$. If the real disturbance is foreseen as likely to last for a long time, the correct procedure is to institute expenditure reduction and expenditure switching policies so that the deficit is eliminated. If the disturbance is severe, it may be desirable to finance the deficit in part to allow the adjustment process to take place relatively slowly.

The temptation to suppress a deficit is always great. Under a system of fixed rates, the suppression eliminates any need to support the currency in the foreign exchange markets. But these are the devices that effectively allow the policymakers to postpone any attempt to solve the basic problem. Examples are numerous; the behavior of Mexico in the late 1970s, the United Kingdom in the mid-1960s, and the United States in the late 1960s are quite clear-cut. The means by which nations can suppress a deficit are many. The most important are forcing the economy into a

348   INTERNATIONAL PAYMENTS

recession, putting restrictions on imports, imposing controls on capital exports, and artificially pumping up the rate of interest to attract an inflow of capital. The last policy could be considered to be financing the deficit by attracting foreign money into the nation's financial markets as opposed to running down the nation's international reserves.

Forcing an economy into a recession shifts the line SS upward and has the side effect of making sure that any export industries that are working at capacity will have the resources needed to supply and even pursue foreign orders. But the practice sacrifices the domestic goal of high or full employment without introducing the needed expenditure switch. The (more slowly working) expenditure switch should be instituted with the expenditure reduction if the disturbance is seen as long-lasting.

Putting restrictions on imports will, presumably, promote the demand for home goods and lessen the demand for imports. It is a kind of selective expenditure switch. It has the disadvantage that the country's trading partners will not tolerate the procedure for very long without threatening to retaliate against the country's exports. Such a reaction would undo the positive aspects from the balance-of-payments standpoint and echo the retaliatory tariff scenario considered in Chapter 7. This policy can be instituted for a short period when accompanied by an expenditure reduction, but it can only be effective when reinforced with other measures. It will probably, eventually, need to be replaced by a devaluation or depreciation of the national currency.

Controlling capital outflows is not very effective, particularly in the modern setting of highly integrated financial markets and when multinational corporations have money balances in several countries.

Raising the domestic rate of interest will attract foreign deposits into the home-country financial system and in this way strengthen the home-country's currency or finance a current deficit. The problem with this policy is that it tends to cause a recession at the same time (thereby reducing the potential size of the deficit). It does have the problem that raising the rate of interest paid on deposits in a debtor nation will, when the debts are defined in the debtor's currency, raise the cost of interest payments on the debt. If a nation has no debts and chooses to raise its rate of interest, the cost of "borrowed funds" will be the new higher rate of interest. When a country is deeply in debt, the additional interest cost ascribable to the new borrowed funds could be exorbitant. Consider a country with existing indebtedness (in terms of time deposits by foreigners) of 10,000 carrying an interest cost of 7½ percent. The interest cost of the indebtedness is 750. Now let the rate of interest paid be forced up to 8¼ percent (a 10 percent increase). The cost of the old indebtedness is now 825 (when the time deposits have matured and been reinvested). To break even, the increase in the interest rate must attract 75 currency units plus the interest payable on those funds (another 6 units) before there is a positive cash flow. There is yet another problem. Money that moves between countries in response to differences in interest rates is a pool of money—a stock, not a flow. Most of the money that will be attracted will be attracted in the year when interest rates are raised. In the second year (even in the absence of a rate increase abroad), the rate of inflow will fall off. The third year will be even worse. Thus if the deficit is constant over time (excluding the additional interest burden), a nation cannot realistically expect to suppress a deficit in this way for more than a short period. Financing through private markets, like financing of any kind, has a finite life. Ultimately, adjustments must be made if the deficit is to be removed.

The reader will recognize in all of this discussion of balance-of-payments deficits how closely the problems are analogous to the financial problems of individuals. Financing is temporary for countries and individuals. Adjustment is painful for both, and suppressive mechanisms are short-term responses that do not eliminate the basic cause of the cash flow deficit.

For countries, all of these different aspects of deficits have to be considered in a political setting, and the advantages and disadvantages of individual policies must be determined in the light of the expected reaction of the country's residents.

The essence of policymaking is to recognize the fundamental roles of the two adjustment mechanisms, expenditure switches and expenditure reductions, and to recognize as well the value of softening the impact of a disturbance by means of some of the suppressive measures or through financing. Harsh measures must be taken if the change in conditions is permanent, but not all change is permanent, and the possibility of a trade-off between speed of adjustment and the level of international reserves must be countenanced.

This discussion has been couched in the terms used by the absorptionist theory. Obviously, price-level disturbances can be introduced by excessive creation of money. However, the role of money is neither automatic nor instantaneous. Price levels and interest rates do not respond to changes in the supply of money in some precise and mechanical way, although the relationship among the stock of money, the price level, and velocity will make itself felt sooner or later. Any undue expansion of the money supply must, then, sooner or later bring about a price-level disturbance (unless foreign trading partners are inflating at an equal rate). Inflation at home can be tolerated (from a balance-of-payments point of view) only when it accompanies a favorable real disturbance. This may have been the thinking underlying the appreciation of the Mexican peso— that the peso could remain fixed against the U.S. dollar because oil revenues would provide the needed favorable real disturbance. This possible explanation of Mexican financial policy does not condone inflation, and even if oil revenues had not been overestimated, an appreciation of the peso might be preferable to inflation. What was unacceptable was the actual policy of seriously overestimating the future balance-of-payments benefits of oil revenues and, in the process, of allowing the peso to become so seriously overvalued as to encourage imports of luxury items to be financed by government borrowing from abroad.

THE REAGAN DEFICIT ON CURRENT ACCOUNT

Table 15-1 provides the data needed to assess the effect of the economic policies of the Reagan administration on the U.S. current account in the first five years of the administration. The table shows the real rate of interest on short-term assets in the United States, Japan and Germany, the deficit in the federal government's budget in the United States, the real effective rate of exchange of the U.S. dollar against a basket of foreign currencies, and the U.S. balances on goods and services and current account. Anyone doubting the degree of support for the totality of Reagan's policies should recall the size of his victory in November 1984. The negative effect of the economic policies on the current balance was not exploited by the Democratic candidate, but the result of the Reagan policies was to reduce the nation's international net worth by $144 billion in the first term.

The mechanism by which this result was achieved derives from a direct relationship between the size of the federal deficit and the rate of interest, provided that the rate of growth of the money supply is kept low enough to preclude inflation. This mechanism is known as "crowding out" and it is illustrated in Figure 15-2. In a closed economy, the rate of interest (for short-term risk-free instruments such as Treasury bills) is determined by the amount of funds generated by saving and the demand for funds by borrowers. If the central bank is determined to keep monetary growth low enough to avoid inflation and the flow of saving by households is insensitive to the interest rate (this may be a slight simplification), the supply of "loanable funds" is given and is interest-inelastic. On the other hand, the demand for loanable funds depends on the net demand for funds by business, which may be assumed to be sensitive to the rate of interest charged and the borrowing by the federal government, which is interest-insensitive. Of the four components of the interest-rate determination mechanism (household saving, money supply growth, federal borrowing, and business borrowing), only business borrowing is sensitive to the rate of interest, and it must therefore be the balancing item. The cost of borrowing will rise until the supply of loanable funds net of government borrowing is equal to business demand for funds. In Figure 15-2, the supply of loanable funds is measured horizontally, and the interest rate is measured vertically. The supply of loanable funds consisting of household saving and any increase in the supply of money is measured rightward from G and amounts to GN. The federal deficit $(G - T_x)$ amounts to G and is measured leftward from the vertical axis. Subtracting the federal deficit from the supply of loanable funds gives the net supply, N, which is drawn as completely inelastic to the rate of interest. Net business demand for funds, DD', is drawn as interest-sensitive, and the market clears at a percent. If the federal budget had been balanced, the net supply of loanable funds is B, and the rate of interest is b percent. Private investment of the amount NB has been crowded out by government borrowing. Of course, each dollar of reduction in the federal deficit will add less than one dollar to the supply of loanable funds because increased taxes will siphon some funds out of saving or because reductions in government spending will allow some families to save less.

Figure 15-3 shows how the high rate of interest attracts foreign saving once the financial markets of the world are integrated. The only addition to Figure 15-2 is the supply of foreign funds that will flow into the country in response to the high rates of interest there. Foreign inflows of saving are shown as interest-sensitive, and foreign rates are assumed to be approximately equal to b percent. The inflow of foreign saving, FF', adds to the supply of loanable funds available. Foreign flows are interest-sensitive, and the new rate of interest is determined by the intersection of the (unchanged) business demand for funds and the total supply of funds. The new interest rate is c percent, and home-country investment has increased by NK. But the inflow of funds must go through the foreign exchange market and will strengthen the home-country currency. This is shown in Figure 15-4, which shows how the dollar strengthens against the deutsche mark as a result of high dollar interest rates. Now Germany runs a current-account surplus equal to the capital inflow. The appreciation of the dollar (against the mark) has been exactly enough to balance payments with a surplus on capital account (NK) and an equal and offsetting deficit on current account. Net exports of the United States in the amount NK have been crowded out of existence by the federal deficit.

Clearly, nothing is this precise and tidy in the real world, but the underlying mechanism will hold. The data in Table 15-1 support the simple analysis provided—that there is a direct link from the federal deficit to the interest rate and from the interest rate to the rate of exchange and to the deficit on current account. This causal mechanism receives strong support from Figure 15-5. The left-hand panel shows the very close relationship between the size of the federal deficit and the strengthening of the dollar in real terms in the foreign exchange markets. The right-hand panel shows that the current-account deficit closely follows the federal deficit, with a lag of one year. This observed lag is in conformity with the built-in delay between a change in competitiveness and a change in the current balance.

In late 1984 and early 1985, the dollar surged again. Some of this surge can be attributed to sheer speculation by foreign exchange traders and some to the buoyancy of the American economy as a result of the

Table 15-1
THE CURRENT ACCOUNT UNDER THE FIRST REAGAN ADMINISTRATION

Year	Quarter	Real Rates of Interest* (% per annum)			Real Effective Exchange Rate of the U.S. dollar (1980–1982 = 100)	U.S. Federal Deficit† ($ billions)	U.S. Current Balance† ($ millions)
		USA	Germany	Japan			
1979	—†	2.42	5.76	5.60	88.0	27.3	−991
1980	—†	3.80	−3.43	6.81	89.4	73.8	+1,873
1981	1	4.50	10.52	4.79	94.5		
	2	6.47	8.72	6.22	101.2	78.9	+6,339
	3	7.33	8.04	6.08	105.0		
	4	5.02	5.46	4.53	102.2		
1982	1	6.27	5.76	3.95	105.0		
	2	7.65	5.09	4.81	107.5	127.9	−8,061
	3	6.66	2.77	5.78	112.6		
	4	4.47	1.64	6.19	114.2		
1983	1	3.95	1.63	5.83	110.1		
	2	4.27	4.60	5.19	111.1	195.4	−40,790
	3	4.70	3.52	4.90	114.1		
	4	5.30	3.97	5.56	114.4		

1984	1	5.13	2.16	5.65	113.0		
	2	6.55	4.71	5.09	115.1	175.3	−107,858
	3	6.91	5.23	3.93	120.4		
	4	5.45	5.25	4.70	123.3		
1985	1	4.98	3.70	4.43	128.4		
	2	4.48	2.99	5.03	125.3	202.8	−117,664
	3	4.57	2.37	4.08	118.9		
	4	4.66	3.11	2.84	113.0		

* Short-term interest rates are, unfortunately, not exact equivalents. The U.S. rate is effectively an "earning rate" for depositors (ninety-day commercial paper), while the German and Japanese rates are "lending rates" (three-month loans in Frankfurt and the three-month "Gensaki" rate).

† The deficits are shown as annual amounts because to show quarterly data would imply a greater than warranted exactness. Obviously, many factors affect relative real interest rates between home and abroad, and the consequent international capital flows and the federal deficit is merely a single, very important item. Figure 15-3 shows the existence of a one-year lag between changes in real exchange rates and the current balance.

‡ Annual data provided for background.

Sources: Nominal short-term interest rates from OECD, *Main Economic Indicators*, various issues, and the *Federal Reserve Bulletin*, various issues; real effective rates of exchange from Morgan Guaranty, *World Financial Markets*, various issues; federal deficit and current deficit from *Survey of Current Business*, various issues.

Figure 15-2

DOMESTIC CROWDING OUT IN AUTARKY

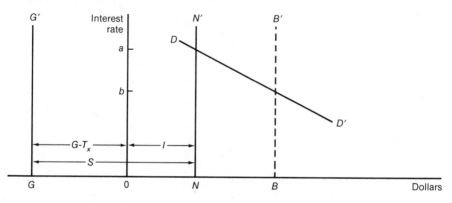

economic stimuli provided by the Reagan administration. In fall 1985, the central banks of the five main countries (France, Germany, Japan, the United Kingdom, and the United States) agreed to intervene in the foreign exchange markets to push down the dollar. This move met with some initial success, particularly against the yen. Whether the weakening of the dollar could have been sustained without an easing of interest rates in the United States was questionable, but the Federal Reserve Board encouraged lower interest rates at the same time that foreign central banks were intervening to weaken the dollar in foreign exchange markets.

The overvaluation of the dollar may seem to be a contradiction in terms. In a world of freely flexible exchange rates, it is difficult to see how a currency could be overvalued, since the foreign exchange market will determine its value. However, it is possible for the foreign exchange

Figure 15-3

DOMESTIC CROWDING OUT WITH INTEGRATED CAPITAL MARKETS

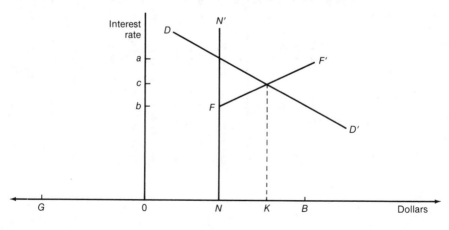

Figure 15-4

INTERNATIONAL
CROWDING OUT
$S_{\$(G\&S)}$ and $D_{\$(G\&S)}$ show
the goods-and-services
schedules. $D_{\$(total)}$ shows
the sum of the German
demand for dollars for
goods and services and
(short-term) financial
assets.

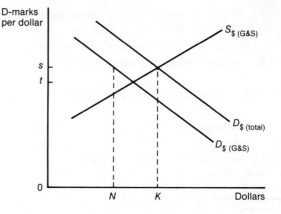

Figure 15-5

FEDERAL DEFICITS, EXCHANGE RATES, AND CURRENT-ACCOUNT DEFICITS
The exchange rates are real exchange rates, and the federal deficits are cyclically
adjusted.

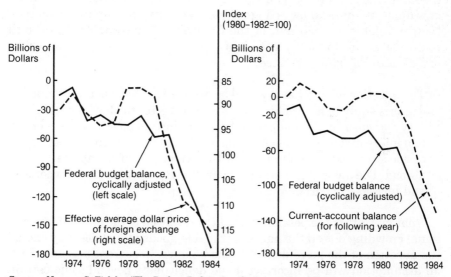

Source: Norman S. Fieleke, "The Budget Deficit: Are the International Consequences Unfavorable?"
New England Economic Review, May-June 1984, pp. 5–10. Data updated by Dr. Fieleke.

markets to allow a currency to strengthen in response to nonsustainable
forces, meaning that the strength of a currency is subject to inevitable
reversal at some unknown time. It is in this sense that the dollar was
overvalued in 1982 through 1985.

The overvaluation of an important currency can have repercussions
in four main areas:

1. Problems for developing countries
2. Effect on domestic industries
3. Misdirection of domestic investment
4. Siphoning off of foreign saving

1. Developing countries suffer to the extent that they have debts defined in dollars. This problem has been particularly important in the 1980s because of the so-called third world debt crisis. Latin American countries in particular have been subjected to balance-of-payments crises because they borrowed too much in the 1970s. Now they must service their debt, pay interest, and repay principle, when interest rates are high and when their customers in the developed world are in recession. To service debt when interest rates are high and the currency of denomination is strong requires a much greater allocation of exports.

2. The combination of flexible exchange rates and a large budget deficit leads to a deficit on current account. This could be called "international crowding out" because the nation's export and import substitute industry are crowded out of markets by the high value of the dollar. At the same time, the inflow of foreign saving that generates the international crowding out does allow a higher rate of domestic capital formation. Martin Feldstein, chairman of the Council of Economic Advisers until mid-1984, seems to consider the loss of international net worth desirable, on balance. Feldstein asserted:

> The question of whether it would be desirable to have a lower valued dollar is equivalent to asking whether it is better to allow the temporary increase in the budget deficit to reduce domestic investment and interest-sensitive consumer spending or to reduce the proportion of goods for export and of goods that compete with imports from abroad. The answer is clear in principle: It is better to reduce exports and increase imports.[4]

What matters is the possibility that the duration of the effect of international crowding out on the nation's tradable-goods industries may exceed the duration of the large deficit on the balance on current account. Such an assumption will be incorrect if the deficit lasts beyond some certain critical length. International crowding out has long-term effects on the tradable-goods industries because of the effects of very low or negative profits at home (and high profit rates abroad).

Given domestic price levels and prices in local currencies, an overly strong currency on the part of one nation increases the costs and prices of goods produced in that country relative to the goods of firms that

[4] Martin Feldstein, *Is the Dollar Overvalued?* Paper presented to the Council on Foreign Relations, New York, April 7, 1983. It raises the question of the temporary nature of the budget deficit and scorns to consider an equally temporary financing of the deficit through monetary policy.

compete in the same markets and are located in different countries. Unless prime costs can be reduced as the home local currency appreciates, internationally competing companies and industries will lose market shares and sales volume, and profit rates and profits will be reduced. The main damage of currency overvaluation is felt in the loss of dynamism in firms confronting foreign competition in home or foreign markets. Profit-seeking corporations are organic entities, and they can be deprived of profits only at some significant cost to their ability to survive in a competitive setting. Reduction in profits is the most serious effect of currency overvaluation.

Firms require infusions of new equipment, new products, new ideas. All of these requirements are met out of reinvested profits, which means that a firm starved of profits becomes less well able to compete. In principle, reduced profits can be offset (in part at least) by reductions in the rate of dividend payout and the rate of reinvestment maintained. This option is rarely exercised by firms, except in extremely severe conditions, because it will adversely affect their costs of equity. A reduction in the flow of reinvested profits results in reduced expenditures on research and development, product innovation, and equipment replacement. The lack of expenditures on R&D in its broadest sense, together with an inability of a firm to maintain the up-to-dateness of its equipment and productive capacity, reduces a firm's ability to compete in markets in the longer run. While firms in countries with overvalued currencies are experiencing penury, their foreign competitors are likely to be enjoying above-average profits as higher prices in their domestic currencies combine with increased rates of capacity utilization and market shares to generate exceptionally high flows of profits. To the extent that dividend increases tend to lag behind profits and that the cost of inputs also lags behind the increase in prices in domestic currency, the firms are blessed with a cornucopia of funds that can be devoted to all activities that are likely to improve the firm's competitiveness in future years. Thus the damage from currency overvaluation is positively related to the duration of the overvaluation and, one may surmise, becomes increasingly severe as the overvaluation continues because of the cumulative nature of the effects of increased or reduced flows of internal reinvestment.

Depressed industries suffer too from the inability to retain good executives and to attract new people. It is axiomatic that in hard times, it is the better people who are able to find other jobs, and the depressed organization is left with those who cannot obtain good employment in other industries. Further, a firm will inevitably lose its share of the domestic market. Such a loss may be difficult to recoup even when the currency has ceased to be overvalued. Foreign firms may have used their high profit rates to establish marketing and distribution organizations that are more firmly founded than would have been possible in the absence of (temporary) currency overvaluation.

3. The misdirection of domestic investment follows inevitably from the bias in relative profit rates experienced by industries that do or do not compete directly with foreign industry. Greater than warranted investments will be made in domestic industries, and when the currency overvaluation is finally terminated, there will be excess capacity in domestic industries and inadequate capacity in tradable-goods industries. This problem is part and parcel of the adjustment costs for reversible or self-reversing disturbances. If, as a result of the long period of overvaluation of the dollar, the nation must run a current surplus in order to repay the accumulated debts, the change in the exchange rate will be much greater and the misdirection of investment will be very important.

4. Siphoning off of foreign saving takes place when foreign funds are attracted to the nation with the overvalued currency. The net result is that other nations must sacrifice their rate of domestic investment to earning a current surplus (international saving rather than domestic saving). There is little evidence to suggest that the total rate of saving abroad will be affected, and, therefore, the two forms of saving are competitive. This leads to stress and strain among trading partners as politicians abroad are unhappy over their low rate of investment (though usually happy over the current-account surplus). In a global recession, foreign nations feel that their saving is financing the growth of the economy with the overvalued currency. In fact, the flow of income in the individual countries is probably roughly equal (because the Keynesian multipliers for investment and net exports are equal); it is in the mysteries of firm and industry dynamics that the damage can be inflicted.

POLICY HARMONIZATION

There is an inevitable tendency to look at balance-of-payments problems from the viewpoint of a single country (or a pair of countries with bilateral imbalances). Another dimension plays an important role in the 1980s, when the world is recovering from two oil-price shocks and a major debt crisis (as well as a downward spiral in oil prices in 1985 and 1986). It is also necessary to look at the world as a whole. Each nation has a balance-of-payments target or series of targets. The world is a closed economy, so the sum of all targets must be zero if the international payments system is to generate no friction. If the sum of all targets is not zero, the sum of all balances will be zero, and the payments system might not work smoothly if nations resist fiercely the discrepancy between what they want to achieve and what they can achieve.

The system works smoothly when the developing countries are willing to accept the surplus saving of the North (the sum of current surpluses of the industrialized countries) and the North is willing to finance those surpluses by long-term investments. Small changes within the two blocs can be made, but major goals are fulfilled. But not every country can expect to run a current surplus, and this may be the root problem of the current international payments system. Given the two oil-price shocks in the 1970s and the debt crisis of 1982, the North first wanted the South to run financial deficits and to buy goods on balance (to run current deficits), and the North was prepared to finance those purchases. Then came the debt crisis; the North suddenly wanted the developing nations to reduce their indebtedness, and the South was forced into a position of wanting to run current surpluses. Now the North had nowhere to ship its surplus saving. The United States ran huge current deficits (albeit unintentionally), but the system remains muddled because nations' domestic and international performance goals are not in synchronization.

The system of flexible exchange rates was supposed to resolve this problem by dragooning nations into having their actual balances conform with the constraint of a global zero, *and,* presumably, national domestic performance would adjust to the international conditions. But if the actual balances achieved are not compatible with the targets of the individual nations, the system does not work efficiently. Countries are always trying to achieve their goals despite the impossibility of doing so: They take policy measures to achieve the goals, and these measures are countered by other countries' policies.

The hope must be that the recent decline in the price of oil and energy will allow the world's financial system to restore itself to some sort of inner compatibility where targets are within an eyelash of being feasible. Then the system will work well. But that requires intrabloc compatibility among the industrialized countries as well as compatibility between North and South.

SUMMARY

Balance-of-payments policymaking requires that economists be able to identify the sources of foreign disturbances and the kind of each disturbance. They must then be able to convince politicians that the recommended course of action is advisable. Balance-of-payments economists must also be able to identify sources of balance-of-payments deficits that are the consequence of domestic policy actions and must generate corrective action. Clearly, this process requires a skill in crystal ball gazing, which is difficult to come by. It also requires a recognition of the fact that the purpose of balance-of-payments policy is to reduce social costs of adjustment. The normal yardstick against which the social costs might be compared would be the free operation of a system of flexible exchange rates. The completely laissez-faire stance of Adam Smith is not always correct, but it does generate adjustment and prevents political considerations from postponing unpleasant measures at some future cost. But the Adam Smith–David Hume mechanism is not always correct. When shocks are self-reversing, a laissez-faire policy inflicts a double dose of adjustment on the economy. When shocks are severe, they may need to be spread out over time.

The United States is the preeminent nation in international trade and finance, and its dollar is the key currency in world financial dealings. In the late 1960s, the United States was so committed to the Bretton Woods system of fixed rates of exchange revolving around the dollar that it nearly caused a crisis of major proportions when the system was finally ended in 1971 (see Chapter 16). In the Reagan administration, international crowding out and the concomitant indebtedness of the U.S. financial system to foreigners may well cause a second crisis before the end of this century. The crisis this time will be more likely to inflict hardship on the U.S. economy than to cause a breakdown in the global financial system, but there is a good argument that neglect of the existing deficit on current account and the continuing inflow (and reinvestment) of foreign funds will require a major adjustment in the U.S. economy when current balance (if not positive international saving) must be regained.

Bibliography

Dunn, Robert M., Jr. *The Many Disappointments of Flexible Exchange Rates,* Essays in International Finance No. 154. Princeton, N.J.: Princeton University Press, 1983.

Johnson, Robert A. "U.S. International Transactions in 1985." *Federal Reserve Bulletin,* 72 (1986), 287–297.

Kindleberger, Charles P. "Assets and Liabilities in International Economics: The Post-war Bankruptcy of Theory and Policy." *Economic Notes* (1982), 47–66.

Questions

1. The secret of successful balance-of-payments policy is not to let imbalances pile up and get worse through suppression. Explain.
2. Capital controls cannot work because bankers will do anything for a buck. Agree or disagree.
3. Capital controls cannot work because money will pour through a sieve. Explain.
4. Update Table 15-1 and Figure 15-5.
5. Compile the current and basic balances for Germany, Japan, the United Kingdom, and the United States.
6. Use the data from question 5 to decide what the current balance of the rest of the world should be and what the basic balance should be.

V

THE INTERNATIONAL
MONETARY SYSTEM

The international monetary system is important because when it works well, it facilitates international economic transactions that are extremely beneficial to the world economy. One way to judge its effectiveness is to consider how its characteristics impede the free flow of goods, services, or capital. Day-to-day fluctuations in exchange rates of significant magnitude have always been considered a symptom of an unsatisfactory international monetary system simply because such fluctuations will increase the uncertainty involved and decrease the volume of transactions. Much more important than the variability of day-to-day rates of exchange is the possibility of a breakdown in the international financial system. The collapse of the international monetary system certainly aggravated the Depression, if, indeed, it was not the primary cause. The world had a near-escape from a breakdown of a similar magnitude in 1982 when the third world debt crisis arose. Self-evidently, the international monetary system is not so well designed that it can be considered foolproof: Its system seems to have a capacity for destabilizing swings after severe shocks, and central bankers have not yet learned to put the importance of the system ahead of the importance of benefits for their national economies until crisis has been reached—although there is much greater cooperation now than in the 1930s.

The international monetary system is a backdrop against which international economic transactions take place. We do not notice its existence until things begin to go wrong, but by the time we notice trouble, the problem may be far advanced, and drastic measures may be necessary.

16

The Gold Standard and the Interwar Years

It is not really possible (and certainly not useful) to examine the existing international monetary system without some awareness of the system's historical evolution. In fact, it could be asserted that to understand the present system, one must know what went wrong with the predecessor system. Almost always, the features of a new system can be traced directly to what went wrong with the old one. The failure of the interwar years (1919–1939), with all of the damage wreaked on the world's economies, derived from a fixation with the gold standard and a lack of understanding of the limits of that system for correcting something that was not functioning properly. The post–World War II system was tailored to eliminate the bad features of the system of the interwar years. The present system can be traced to the breakdown of the post–World War II system, and one may imagine that the next system will evolve to eliminate the flaws in the present system.

The reasons for breakdowns in the world's monetary system are not usually a direct response to an inherent flaw in the system. What usually happens is that the system is exposed to some drastic disturbance and cannot cope with the adjustment that is necessary. Probably, this failure results from a lack of understanding of the appropriate response and also to a lack of international cooperation and coordination. But shocks come in different sizes and shapes. One cannot create a system that will be proof against all shocks unless one can guarantee intelligent foresight and wise policy measures on the part of the constituent national governments. The breakdown of an existing system is most likely to derive from its inability to facilitate a particular type of change.

Ideally, the international financial system should allow nations to reach their economic goals as well as circumstances allow. Usually, a nation's economic goals may be thought of as comprising high employment, a relatively stable price level, and a satisfactory rate of economic growth; the unimpeded flow of goods, services, and capital can be taken as contributing to these goals. However, nations have secondary sets of targets or goals, and these might involve a policy of building up the level of international reserves held by running a surplus on autonomous international transactions. Frequently, a nation will wish to increase its international net worth by running a surplus on current account. There can be no guarantee that these secondary goals will be mutually compatible. In fact, for a nation to want to increase its international net worth, there must be another nation that is willing to run a current deficit. For a nation to be able to increase its international reserves, another nation must (in the absence of the creation of international money of some kind) be willing to reduce its reserves by an equal amount. All nations together cannot run current surpluses because global payments constitute a zero-sum game: Every credit carries a corresponding debit. A second role for the international financial system is to make the disparate desires of nations mutually compatible.

It is instructive to think of the world's financial system as having endured four periods with quite different characteristics. The original (medieval) international financial system was the gold standard. Gold constituted international money. During the hundred years between the defeat of Napoleon (1815) and the outbreak of World War I (1914), a sophisticated version of the gold standard reigned supreme. While it is easier to consider this period to have lasted for a hundred years, Great Britain did not, in fact, go back on to the gold standard until 1821, and the system was beginning to break up as early as 1913. But relative to any other system that has held sway in the modern industrial world, its duration was exceptional. The second period lasted roughly twenty years, from 1919 to 1939 (the outbreak of World War II in Europe). It cannot be said to have been governed by a system, and the best way to describe those twenty years is as a nonsystem. Economic decisions were fundamentally misguided after World War I, and these decisions plunged the world economy into chaos. The period started off with an attempt to reconstitute the gold standard, and when that collapsed, there was a series of frequent devaluations of currencies as each nation sought to achieve a surplus on current account. Period 3 began after World War II, and its main features were agreed to at an international conference held in Bretton Woods, New Hampshire, in 1944. The system is usually referred to as the Bretton Woods regime. It allowed for fixed exchange rates, but these rates could be changed by government decision. It was known as an "adjustable-peg" system because currencies were pegged to the dollar (and through the dollar to gold), but the peg could be changed by devaluation or revaluation. The Bretton Woods system lasted for a quarter of a century, until it broke down in 1971. Since that time, in period 4, the world has been operating under a system of flexible exchange rates of varying degrees of cleanliness. The Reagan administration relied heavily on a clean float on largely philosophical grounds. This reliance was repudiated somewhat in March 1985 and discarded completely in September 1985, when a meeting of the major economic policymakers of the five major countries agreed to intervene in foreign exchange markets to force down the dollar—in effect, the United States renounced the effectiveness of a clean float. To see how successful these interventions were, it is possible to examine the changes in nominal exchange rates between August 1985, and April 1986: the yen strengthened from ¥ 237.46 to ¥ 175.09 and the deutsche mark from DM 2.794 to DM 2.273. In fact, the decline of the dollar against the yen was so rapid and so large that the Japanese government felt compelled in March 1986 to begin to intervene to stabilize the dollar (to prevent its further decline). By August, 1986, the yen had strengthened to less than ¥ 155.

Members of the EEC have set for themselves an internal fixed-rate system (which allows the whole group of currencies to float against the dollar and the yen), but this arrangement has met with imperfect success, especially when individiual nations need to devalue their currencies periodically. Such devaluations may be due to relatively fast inflation (a price-level disturbance) or a change in the terms of trade (a real disturbance).

No system has worked perfectly or will ever do so. One reason is that when the world's economic targets are not mutually compatible, nations try to achieve their own policy targets instead of passively accepting the verdict of the market. Second, politicians tend to avoid deliberate adjustment when such policies would involve (unpopular) expenditure reductions. Practically any system will work if the real disturbances to which the system is exposed are small and if balance-of-payments adjustment steps do not impose hardship on the electorate. To judge the effectiveness of a system, then, it is useful to think in terms of three criteria:

1. How severe were the real shocks to which the system was exposed?
2. What were the social costs of adjustment, and how much political antagonism did these costs raise?
3. To what degree did the political system suppress the real shocks and the consequent need for adjustment?

In terms of these criteria, the gold standard will be found to have received high marks because there were no huge shocks and because no one cared too much, in the nineteenth century, about social costs. The nonsystem between the two world wars was subjected to a huge real shock (the economic aftermath of World War I) whose effects were aggravated by wrong financial and economic policies within and among nations. The Bretton Woods era was marked by a steady change in the underlying conditions (of supply and demand), and these constituted a series of small but cumulatively large real shocks. The key-currency country, the United States, could not adapt and subverted their effects. Ultimately, President Nixon renounced the role of the keystone currency for the U.S. dollar on August 15, 1971; in this way he instituted the fourth period, one of flexible rates. The system of flexible rates has not proved as successful or as effective as some people had hoped. But this may have been caused by an excess of optimism. Since the system incorporated flexible rates of exchange in early 1973, the world has been subjected to a sudden increase in food prices (1973), to oil-price shocks (1974 and 1979), and to a release from the suppressed need for adjustment that the Bretton Woods fixed-rate system had accumulated in its dying years. In so storm-tossed a decade, economists should not be in a hurry to assess the virtues or shortcomings of a system of flexible exchange rates: It may be that flexible rates are not (and cannot be) a cure for major international real disturbances unless they are reinforced by appropriate domestic policies. However, flexible rates do allow the economic system to incorporate a series of small cumulative shocks.

This chapter considers the first two periods—the gold standard and the failure of the interwar system.

THE GOLD STANDARD (1815–1913)

The defeat of Napoleon in 1815 started a century of almost unbroken economic growth in Europe. There was rapid economic growth as Great Britain finished its period of industrialization and settled into a pattern of steady self-sustaining growth and as the continental nations began to industrialize. Further, this was a relatively peaceful century. Only one war of major significance took place (between France and Prussia in 1870), and there were social upheavals, particularly in 1848. The nation on whose currency the gold standard mainly relied, Great Britain, was involved in only two relatively minor wars in the Crimea (against tsarist Russia) and in South Africa disputing ownership of that territory with Dutch settlers. The United States withdrew from the gold standard during the Civil War and "returned to gold" only in 1884.

This period of rapid economic growth made the social costs of adjustment smaller for any given disturbance, as there was always a source of increased living standards and relatively easy alternative employment for displaced workers. The second criterion, then, was less important in this period than in others. So, too, was the third criterion—at least in the country of the so-called key currency, Great Britain. The processes of adjustment and concerns with social costs were simply not allowed to impede the functioning of the corrective (adjustment) mechanism. The Bank of England viewed its responsibility to maintain the gold standard and to allow the domination of market forces as a paramount duty. Its obligation to do so was no more challenged than was the dogma of the Church of England.

The gold-standard mechanism involves two primary features: fixed rates of exchange (irrevocably so) and a link between the balance of payments and the money supply. When a nation ran a deficit, gold left the country. This automatically reduced the domestic money supply, or a reduction was enforced by action of the central bank: The rate of interest rose. This stimulated a recession, unemployment rose, and the price of domestic inputs fell. Since prices followed costs downward, the competitiveness of the nation increased. But it increased through a change in the ratio of the domestic price levels at home and abroad (P_f/P_d).[1] In the surplus nation, the opposite was taking place, and prices were tending upward, stimulated by an inflow of money. As is evident from Figure 15-1, it makes no difference whether the disturbance that causes the deficit is a real disturbance or a price-level disturbance provoked by a burst of self-indulgent inflation; the cure involves an increase in competitiveness.

How well did the gold standard work? This question is often posed in a way that suggests it worked well. This supposition causes people to recommend a return to the gold standard in the twentieth century. First, we have not much of an idea as to how well the gold standard worked. It was an effective vehicle for ensuring balance-of-payments adjustment— no question! A country either adjusted or ran out of gold and withdrew from the gold standard. But we have no data on the social costs imposed by a slavish adherence to an inflexible adjustment mechanism. It is probable that wage rates and, particularly, prices were more flexible then, so the adjustment could take place with less resistance than would currently be experienced.

Probably the key element in the successful international operation of the gold standard as an enforcer of international adjustment was the dominance of London as the single major financial center and the dominance of the pound sterling as the international money par excellence. Sterling was, in today's expression, the key currency; without that currency, the system would not work.[2] For international transactions, there was a single world currency, and other minor currencies were known to be convertible into that currency at fixed rates. This assurance of fixed rates made the international movement of financial capital relatively easy for Europeans. For countries in Latin America and Asia, whose

---

[1] The adjustment mechanism under the gold standard was, simply, Hume's mechanism described in Chapter 2.

[2] In period 3, the U.S. dollar played this role. Nowadays, the dollar is still the primary currency in international finance but not the only currency of importance.

currencies were less reliable and who were likely to "go off gold," international borrowing and international trade were conducted in sterling so that the "peripheral country" bore the risk of any change in the value of its currency. Only "solid" nations were on gold, but everyone joined in the international financial system based on the gold standard, and to be "on gold" was a sign of financial respectability. This is the reason that nations such as the United States, which were forced to renounce the gold standard because of war or civil strife, regarded the reestablishment of the gold standard as such an important postwar goal.

Deliberate support of sterling by the Bank of England during periods of weakness coupled with a very sensitive mechanism enabled the gold standard to survive for almost one hundred years. The most important fundamental point is that England's balance on current account did not weaken throughout the period. The nation ran a steady surplus on current account. This was due more to remittances of interest and dividends than to any innate positive balance of trade. But Britain was in effect the world's banker, and any banker can suffer net withdrawals of deposits. Sometimes foreigners who had money invested in sterling needed it for domestic reasons, and sometimes British banks wanted to lend out more to foreigners than the current surplus could accommodate. Then sterling became weak, and the Bank of England went into action. The bank would raise the rate at which it loaned to British banks (the bank rate). This would have three simultaneous effects: High interest rates would engender a slowing of the British rate of economic growth and even induce a recession so that the demand for imports would fall; foreign short-term deposits would increase because sterling was better than gold because you could earn interest on sterling; and long-term capital outflows proved to be quite interest-sensitive so that when the rate of interest went up, countries postponed borrowing. Bank of England action, then, enhanced international saving by the British, generated financing, and cut down the rate of international investment. As is to be expected from a monetary action, the more immediate and more important impact was on capital-account transactions. Changes in the current account were in the "right direction" but were probably quite small. Not only do changes in relative prices take a long time to take hold, but the gold standard also had a particular feature that was important. Great Britain was the source of much lending, and a great deal of the money loaned came back to the British economy in the form of orders for capital goods. Thus when London was squeezed, the outflow of loans was also squeezed, and the value of British exports decreased. The main force here was the attraction of an inflow of short-term (interest-sensitive) money, which financed the temporary deficit, and the reduction in the outflow of long-term loans had some small effect, as did the recession induced in the British economy.

Great Britain (London) was the source of financing for capital expenditures in the colonies, Latin America, and even the United States. These loans were usually made to finance imports needed for developmental projects (usually noncompetitive imports). When the outflow of loans was interrupted, the demand for exports also fell, usually with some lag. The short-run impact of an increase in bank rate was to attract foreign short-term deposits in British banks and to reduce the rate at which capital flowed out. The current account was fated to suffer a little later on, but by then the period of weakness of sterling was over. Of course, any recession induced at home by the high interest rates would enhance the current account quite quickly by reducing the need for imports. This is the second feature of the gold standard that warrants attention. The rate of interest in England was higher because of the tendency to increase assets held abroad. According to some writers, this process of financing economic growth in faraway places may well have retarded growth in the British hinterland (Ireland, Scotland, and Wales) by starving those areas of capital.

Part and parcel of this kind of system is the need for a complete faith in the effectiveness of the market system by the economic authorities in the key-currency country. The British, as economic leaders of the world, subscribed to this belief. It was part of the intellectual heritage of Adam Smith. The British economy bore the brunt of any adjustment measures that were needed by the world economy. The domestic economy was subordinated mercilessly to the needs of the international financial system. For this reason, the gold standard would probably have been seen as inadequate according to the second criterion. But the accepted orthodoxy viewed this as an appropriate way to operate, and it was this feature that was likely to be the most important factor contributing to the fact that the gold standard lasted so long. As mentioned earlier, during that entire century, the United Kingdom had a current surplus (positive international saving), which was loaned out to foreigners.[3] As the century wore on, the balance on goods and services became steadily less important as a source of international saving, and interest receipts from past loans and investments became more important.

Other nations accepted British financial dominance. When their economies could not meet the stringent conditions of the gold standard (including a complete absence of any controls over capital exports), nations had to withdraw from the gold standard and lost any opportunity to borrow in the London bond market. (The classic example is the renunciation of the gold standard by the United States during the Civil War.)

The mechanism of payments adjustment under the gold standard is fully compatible with the mechanisms presented in Chapter 14. The major distinction was the importance of capital account. The British could afford

---

[3] When the U.S. dollar was the key currency under the Bretton Woods system, there was much concern over the "cost of being world banker" (criterion 2). People had more faith or were less sophisticated in period 1, or, more important, the franchise was not universal in the United Kingdom at that time—voters had to be landowners!

to finance their deficits for short periods because they were able over the long term to restrict their foreign investment to the amount of international saving (current surpluses). What was important was the elasticity of supply of short-term deposits, and this elasticity of supply was very large because everyone had perfect faith that sterling was as good as gold, and since it also paid interest, it was really better than gold.

BETWEEN THE TWO WORLD WARS
(1919–1939)

In addition to its huge cost in human terms, World War I was a large real disturbance *and* a large price-level disturbance. The United Kingdom sold off large amounts of the international assets it had acquired during the first period (and had greatly reduced inflows of interest), while the United States changed from a net debtor before the war to a net creditor after 1918. This change in interest flows was a major real disturbance, but it was reinforced by the development of the U.S. manufacturing sector and the loss of British manufacturing leadership. Britain's economy was "worn out," and the continental countries had been destroyed by the war. Germany was occupied by troops of the victorious allies and was forced by the Treaty of Versailles to pay reparations to France and other countries. The world had also lost the dominance of a single currency and capital market (London). New York was now a rival capital market. All of these things meant that the competitiveness required of nations had changed substantially since before the war, and investors could no longer have unquestioning faith in the strength of sterling, so the elasticity of supply of foreign deposits was reduced. The final point worthy of notice is that the study of economics had little to offer politicians on how to adapt to the new conditions.

Politicians quickly decided to restore the gold standard (it was all they had known and had worked well before the war). However, they faced one fundamental question: At what parity should individual countries return to gold? Here parity means the gold content of the currency, and since the U.S. dollar was the only currency strong enough to accept the gold-standard conditions, the question was really, What rate of exchange should nations institute against the U.S. dollar? Given national price levels, there was, presumably, some value of C that would allow a country to return to the gold standard relatively quickly and to abide by all its rules of complete freedom of capital movements. The problem can be stated quite simply: Given that some rate of competitiveness was necessary for a country to accept the postwar gold standard, should that value of C be achieved by varying ϵ from its prewar value, or should the competitive ratio be established by varying P_f/P_d by forcing down the existing domestic price level? The pound-dollar rate was the most important rate, since it involved the two major currencies, so the key decision was that made by Britain. Before World War I, a pound had been worth $4.86. In a decision that ranks among the most fateful in history, the authorities decided to return to the gold standard at the prewar parity. This required that (relative to U.S. prices) the price level in the United Kingdom be forced down drastically. The price-level reduction in the United Kingdom had to be great enough to cancel out any excess of U.K. wartime inflation over U.S. inflation *and* to allow for the adverse real disturbances that had taken place. The price-level disturbance could have been allowed for by applying the purchasing power parity formula. In 1919, British wholesale prices were three times what they were before the war, whereas in the United States, prices had only doubled. Prices in the United Kingdom had to fall by one-third just to eliminate the price-level disturbance, or the purchasing power parity rule could have been applied and Britain could have established a parity of $3.24.[4] While that parity would have saved the British economy great hardship, it would still have required that British prices decline, but by considerably less.

In attempting to force down the British price level, the authories had to institute very tight money and to cause a deep recession. The export industries were already depressed because of the high level of British prices, and a tight monetary policy created high rates of unemployment. Wages and other prices fell slowly. Britain finally returned to the gold standard in April 1925 but was able to allow the free export and import of gold and silver only by maintaining high interest rates and high unemployment rates. In terms of Figure 15-1 in Chapter 15, British policy was to impose a recession on the economy so that the SS schedule would shift upward. This allowed the needed competitiveness ratio to be achieved by depressing the economy. Of course, actual competitiveness was far less than that required for full employment and "being on gold." It was under these conditions that John Maynard Keynes began to concern himself with the problem of chronic unemployment and with the question of how best the international financial system should operate.

The narrow dollar-pound problem affected the rest of the world and was in turn affected by conditions in other countries. The British depression of the 1920s reduced British demand for imports and caused deflationary conditions to be aggravated in other countries as well, particularly in Commonwealth and European countries. The other serious problem was "reparations." Reparations were monetary payments paid by the losers in a war to the victors—paid ostensibly for the costs of the war inflicted on the victors. The Prussians had imposed reparations on the

---

[4] The data varied substantially from year to year in the gyrations of the immediate postwar experiences. See Leland B. Yeager, *International Monetary Relations* (New York: Harper & Row, 1966), p. 268. This book and Donald Winch, *Economics and Policy* (London: Hodder & Stoughton, 1969) provide excellent reports of this episode.

French after the 1870 war and, since most of that war was fought on French soil, reparations became a kind of "tribute" paid to the victors. In the nineteenth century, France paid its reparations off in full. The French also remembered. They imposed very severe reparations conditions on the Germans under the Treaty of Versailles. But payment was a much more difficult problem in the depressed 1920s than in the buoyant, high-growth era of the second half of the nineteenth century. To pay the victorious allies the prescribed reparations, Germany had to run a current-account surplus (to save internationally). This required a lower standard of living at home and a competitive ratio that would generate the needed current surplus to be devoted to payment. If Germany was to run a surplus, another country had to run a deficit. With high rates of unemployment, none of the nations that were to receive reparations wanted to increase imports.[5] As a result, the German standard of living was reduced, but the Germans were unable to run the necessary current surplus (they could save domestically but could not translate the domestic saving into international saving!). Frequently, the Germans met the required reparations payments by borrowing foreign currency—often from the U.S. government.

Another problem that beset Germany was inflation. In an attempt to meet its own bills, the government printed money and set up a hyperinflation that fed on itself and brought ruination to large numbers of people. Hyperinflation can be defined as a rate of increase in the price level of *50 percent or more per month*. German hyperinflation began in August 1922 and lasted until November 1923.[6] Using the U.S. dollar as a measure of price stability and assuming relative purchasing power parity, it is possible to get some idea of the German experience. In June 1920, a dollar was worth 39 marks. In June 1921, the rate of exchange had risen to 69 marks. In June 1922, the rate of exchange was 317 marks. Then the hyperinflation began! In January 1923, the rate of exchange was 18,000 marks to the dollar, and by June of the same year it had risen to 100,000 marks per dollar. From that time until currency stabilization (reform) took place in late November 1923, the value of the mark sank at an ever increasing rate. During the sixteen months of hyperinflation, prices rose by a multiple of *100 billion*. The inflation rate peaked in October 1923, when it reached 32,400 percent per month. This trauma is important because it left scars in the minds of Germans for many years to come, and as late as the 1970s, the head of the German central bank was relating his recollection of the hyperinflation. The result was that Germany has been a pillar of financial rectitude after World War II, and the fear of inflation was great enough to allow the nation to

---

[5] Keynesian economics, with its analysis of additions to and subtractions from aggregate demand, had not been formulated, but the idea that imports competed with home employment was fully understood.
[6] The inflation began in September 1920 and took almost two years of monetary self-indulgence to work itself up into hyperinflation.

tolerate quite high levels of unemployment rather than risk too easy a monetary policy.

France's wartime inflation was too great to allow it the delusion of returning to the gold standard at the prewar parity. France's postwar experience also witnessed some inflation (the value of a franc sank from 6 cents in 1920 to about 2 cents in 1926). But this weakness of the franc was caused not only by inflation in France but also by an outpouring of francs seeking safety abroad. The result was that when France went back onto gold in 1928 at 4 cents to the franc, the French economy still had a weak enough currency to run a strong surplus. The undervaluation of the franc was responsible for the fact that Ernest Hemingway, Gertrude Stein, and Elliot Paul (among other Americans) chose to live in France and write for American publishers (drawing their incomes in dollars).

All of the sacrifice undergone to restore the gold standard was wasted. The system was never really operative, if only because the United Kingdom's ability to stay on gold hinged on high levels of unemployment. The strains of international financing proved too great, and the United Kingdom went off gold in September 1931. The first crack in the wall was the panic of Credit Anstalt in early 1931 in Vienna.[7] Credit Anstalt was a famous old bank that was larger than the Bank of Austria. However, it had lost its old and traditional base of business when the eastern portions of the Austro-Hungarian empire were split off into independent states by the Treaty of Versailles. Weakened by the slump of 1929 and discredited by having absorbed a weak financial institution, depositors lost faith in the bank and sought to withdraw their money. If Credit Anstalt were forced to close its doors, the Austrian economy would have to leave the gold standard, and financiers sought to shore up the Austrian economy and, in so doing, restore confidence in Credit Anstalt. The obvious economic solution was to combine the German and Austrian economies, but the French, with veto power from the Treaty of Versailles, prohibited such action. France also blocked the extension of an international loan to Credit Anstalt. But the Bank of England extended a loan to the Bank of Austria, which in turn supported Credit Anstalt. The gold standard was preserved! Almost immediately, the German banking system went under strain. The Germans met their need for foreign exchange by having high interest rates and attracting foreign deposits so that when an important commercial bank failed, foreign depositors looked to be ready to withdraw all their deposits, and Germany would have to default. The final link in the chain was the weakness in sterling. The Bank of England had made sizable loans to the Austrian National Bank and the German Reichsbank. Its liquid assets had been substantially reduced, and in the process of shoring up the two central banks, the Bank of England

---

[7] Credit Anstalt exists today as a large, efficient bank. This is not the same institution as existed prior to World War II.

had alienated an important depositor, the French government. In the middle of the period when the Bank of England was under strain, the British government released a report on the state of the national finances that stated that the volume of short-term liabilities of the Bank of England far exceeded its liquid assets. Britain was unable to create enough confidence in sterling to prevent large-scale withdrawals. The rate of unemployment hit 22 percent, and there was a sizable government deficit. There was no answer but to impose controls on international capital movements and prohibit the export of gold. The gold standard had collapsed.

The postwar gold standard never fully absorbed the real disturbance created by World War I. Social costs were imposed in the form of stagnant European economies with widespread unemployment. The result of these conditions led to the accession of the Labour Party in Great Britain. The system was set too great a task—to force prices back to their relative positions prior to World War I. The system broke under the strain.

Not all nations left the gold standard at the same time. The cheapening of the exports of countries that had gone off gold aggravated employment problems in countries that had not gone off gold because leaving the gold standard involved a substantial reduction in the nations' rate of exchange.

The United States was having its own troubles. Starting with the collapse of the stock market in October 1929, the country suffered a rash of bank failures, ending with the bank holiday in 1933. One part of President Roosevelt's economic program was to go off gold in 1934.

What followed was a period of years in which each individual nation sought to cure its own rampant unemployment by running an export surplus. As a result, huge barriers to trade were erected, and nations competed in trying to steal an advantage by devaluing their currencies—to no avail. As has been stated several times, the world economy is a closed system: When one nation runs a current surplus (adding to domestically generated employment), another nation perforce runs a current deficit (subtracting from domestically generated employment). Keynes's call for public works to get the British economy moving again was heeded in the United Kingdom and imitated to some degree in continental Europe, but little was done in the United States to add to aggregate demand. Almost every government, including Keynes's own, was afraid that if it expanded the national economy, it would run a balance-of-payments deficit (the marginal propensity to import is positive) and would run out of money. These governments did not realize that foreign expansion would add to their exports in the same way that home expansion would add to foreign exports, and, indeed, in the atmosphere of competitive devaluations and of a complete absence of international economic cooperation, such fears were not groundless. Because the depression was a global problem, global cooperation and coordinated Keynesian policies were called for. Because of the magnitude of the problem, the expenditures had to be large and sustained. It is a sorry comment on the human race that such universal expenditure on the necessary scale and of the necessary duration could be achieved only by war.

The 1930s saw high tariffs (including the Smoot-Hawley tariff in the United States—see Figure 8-1 in Chapter 8) and the widespread introduction of quotas (particularly on agricultural goods). There were also competitive devaluations of national currencies designed to give tradable-goods industries an advantage in world markets. All of these measures were used to try to generate more employment for one country at the expense of all the other countries in a world in economic disarray. The whole process came to be called "Beggar My Neighbour" after a children's card game, traditional in Britain, that involved trying to triumph at the expense of other players.

The advent of World War II in September 1939 immediately increased levels of employment in combatant and noncombatant nations alike. It was, in a way, exactly what Keynes had called for—large government deficits and relatively easy monetary conditions (though Keynes had had other "public goods" in mind). The war also meant that countries had no hesitation in placing strict controls on capital movements and current international transactions. Moreover, there was a *force majeure* when it came to worrying about the effect of policies on the balance of payments. Everything became subservient to the war effort. The United States sold, largely on credit, great quantities of food, equipment, and munitions prior to entry into the war on December 7, 1941. The civilian population had little to spend their wages on because there were few consumer goods available; money balances were built up, and the level of tariffs and quotas became unimportant since most international trade was conducted by government in basic materials.

SUMMARY

At the beginning of this chapter, it was asserted that each international financial system grew out of the ruins of the old one. Each new system corrected the weaknesses of its predecessor. That assertion can hardly be said to have been substantiated to this point.

The gold standard had no predecessor: It evolved naturally as a fixed-rate system because gold was accepted as the basis for money in all important countries. Circulating coins were made of (almost) pure gold and were "full-bodied," meaning that their gold content had a value (almost) equal to the face value of the coin. Knowledge of the size and purity of a foreign coin enabled an exporter to quote prices in local currency. The exporter could rely on being able to ship gold coins home, melting them down, and selling the gold in payment for his goods. Because there were costs of handling and transportation, it was better to receive home-country money, and the fixed-rate system did contain a small amount of variability. Even so, traders did take foreign coins home and melt them down when the imbalance in monetary flows was such that the flows of debits and credits did not offset each other. This was the mechanism underlying David Hume's mechanism for the automatic equilibrating of international payments. Gold was universally acceptable, and gold coins were, therefore, international money. As such, the circulation of gold coins in everyday commerce promoted international trade.

After World War I, politicians tried to re-create the old system. Unfortunately, they had no idea of the correct parities, and in the key ratio (dollars to pounds) set the weaker currency at a huge premium. The politicians wanted the financial system to coerce the real system (wage rates and competitiveness) into finding its true relation without collapsing. In timeless economic theory, it is usually assumed that a system will reach its equilibrium, so analysis pays little or no attention to the capacity of the politicoeconomic system to stand the strain. In this instance, the financial system was not strong enough for the task.

What replaced the gold standard was a nonsystem. It left to the manipulations of government the task of devaluations and control of the domestic price level, which would establish a "correct" set of competitive ratios. Take the dollar-pound ratio, for example. The planned parity of $4.86 was certainly inappropriate, and by renouncing gold, the nonsystem might have been expected to find the correct ratio by a series of groping policy measures. The problem with the system of flexible rates as it really existed in the 1930s was that the world economy was in complete disarray, with iniquitously high rates of unemployment and excess capacity. In their efforts to escape from the morass, governments introduced high tariffs and quotas that altered the appropriate system of parities. Nothing was right.

However, even in the breakdown of the gold standard, there was some support for the hypothesis that the new system corrected the weaknesses of its predecessor. The devaluations did rid the international financial system of an impractical set of rigid rates of exchange.

There was no incentive to re-create a similar system after World War II. One of the many reasons for the failure of the gold standard was the subordination of good economic policy to the hatreds of the war. The lack of cooperation among the victorious allies was legendary, and the withdrawal of the United States into isolationism did not help matters. In what can only be considered an amazing exercise in foresight, the Western allies got together in 1944 at Bretton Woods, New Hampshire, to devise a new international financial system to be put in place after the war. The intent of every representative at that conference was to avoid the economic catastrophe of the 1930s. John Maynard Keynes, who led the British delegation, was convinced that his theory of macroeconomic policy would cure deep depression, provided that the world's financial system allowed nations to follow his recommendations. But the delegates wanted, in addition, to create a system that would facilitate international trade and investment.

Bibliography

Harrod, Roy. *The Life of Keynes.* London: Macmillan, 1951.

Kindleberger, Charles P. *The World in Depression, 1929–39.* Berkeley: University of California Press, 1973.

Winch, Donald. *Economics and Policy.* London: Hodder & Stoughton, 1969.

Yeager, Leland B. *International Monetary Relations.* New York: Harper & Row, 1966.

Questions

1. The gold standard worked because it subordinated all other economic goals to the question of payments balance. Explain.
2. The gold standard worked because it was a sterling standard and because the Bank of England invented (and played according to) the "rules of the game." Discuss.
3. If winners impose reparations, they should be prepared to accept payment (that is, to run a deficit on goods and services account). Why is this so, and why were the Allies unwilling?
4. "Beggar My Neighbour" merely distributed a given amount of aggregate demand among countries in the world; it did not increase aggregate demand. Explain.
5. Sir Winston Churchill once remarked that the decision to try to "return to gold" at $4.86 was his biggest mistake ever (and he made some lulus). Why was this such a big mistake?
6. According to Yeager (*International Monetary Relations*, p. 262), "7 percent [bank rate] would bring gold from the North Pole." Why would this happen, and why was it vital in the operation of the nineteenth-century gold standard?

17

The Bretton Woods Era and the Current System

This chapter traces the development of the international financial system since World War II. The first twenty-five years were governed by the Bretton Woods system. Since 1973, the system has relied on flexible rates of exchange of varying degrees of cleanliness. Both systems are considered in terms of the criteria developed in the preceding chapter. Both systems support the assertion that the characteristics of a new system can be traced directly to the major weakness of its predecessor system.[1]

THE BRETTON WOODS SYSTEM
(1946–1971)

The economists who assembled at Bretton Woods were concerned to create an international financial system in which countries would be free to follow macroeconomic policies that would enable them to meet their own domestic economic targets (high employment) and prevent international trade and investment from being impeded by tariffs, quotas, and other measures attributable to balance-of-payments problems. The outcome of the conference was a recommendation that three supranational bodies be formed: the International Monetary Fund (IMF or the Fund);

---

[1] It is not surprising that a system needs to be changed because the conditions to which it applies change. The crucial policy question is whether or not the existing system was kept in place too long because politicians and economists did not identify the need for change.

the International Bank for Reconstruction and Development (IBRD), now known as the World Bank; and the International Trade Organization (ITO). The last was never ratified by the necessary governments, and its responsibilities to prevent the use of tariffs for balance-of-payments purposes or for sheer mercantilism was taken over by the GATT (see Chapter 8). The World Bank was designed to extend loans to the developing world. It has proved to be a very constructive force in ensuring that loans are used only on viable projects and that the projects escape the graft that is sometimes found in developing economies.

The fund is responsible for the smooth working of the international system so that balance-of-payments problems will no longer impede the smooth functioning of the global economy.

The Fund was to play two roles: that of umpire and that of banker. The umpire was to make sure that countries undertook the proper corrective actions in the face of a balance-of-payments deficit, and the banker was to loan money to countries so that they could introduce corrective measures gradually without causing a local crisis and so that they need not sacrifice domestic employment policies to short-lived foreign disturbances. In practice, the two roles were combined by the simple expedient of having the Fund's lending contingent upon the condition that the borrowing country accept and institute the recommendations of IMF experts. In fact, the analogy between the Fund and a banker is dangerous. As it was originally constituted, the Fund was more of a credit union than a bank. The Fund could not create money; it could only lend out the deposits of its members.

The IMF's ability to lend money to deficit nations was based on a system of deposit quotas. The size of a nation's quota was determined by its national income and the degree to which its currency was used as a basis for international trade. The United States and the United Kingdom were the major depositors in the Fund in the first stages. With this system of deposit quotas went voting power, so in effect the developed world has always dominated the policies of the Fund. Each nation paid in to the Fund one quarter of its quota in gold and the rest of the quota in its own currency. This process gave the Fund a portfolio of gold and national currencies that could be loaned to deficit nations. The ability of a nation to settle its international debts was not increased until it had borrowed more than 25 percent of its quota, since the first 25 percent was "its own international money." Only when a country had borrowed against its own national currency did the Fund contribute to the nation's foreign exchange resources.

The IMF was empowered to refuse access to its assets by members; this gave the IMF authority in its role of umpire and adviser to deficit nations. The Fund would not have the nerve to refuse a country's demand to borrow back its own money, so a loan of the first quarter of the quota was automatic. The second 25 percent was usually granted without imposing conditions on the borrower, but borrowings beyond that were conditional. The IMF would send a team of experts to the deficit country and advise (coerce) its political leaders to take unpleasant steps to get rid of the deficit that caused the country to borrow. The advice of the Fund was almost always to restrict domestic aggregate demand (to reduce absorption) by means of monetary and fiscal policy. Prior to the global inflation of the 1970s, there was a tendency for most countries to run deficits because they had let expansion proceed too quickly. Straightforward reduction in absorption was an appropriate remedy. Some economists felt that the Fund did not sufficiently encourage devaluation of the currency.

The Bretton Woods system was to be based on fixed rates of exchange because the system of flexible rates that existed in the 1930s was associated with the miseries of that time. Rates were to be fixed by having all nations specify gold parities for their national currencies (thereby establishing exchange rates). These rates could be changed by governments when circumstances warranted, but, except when changing the official parity, nations undertook to maintain their currencies within 2 percent of parity by intervening in the foreign exchange markets. Devaluation of a currency was supposed to take place when the currency was in "fundamental disequilibrium"; the problem was that the Fund never managed to define the term. The ability to devalue a currency (and to change the exchange rate) meant that the original parities were not set in stone, and the Bretton Woods system avoided the fatal flaw of the attempt in the 1920s to return to the gold standard. This idea of devaluation when appropriate but fixed rates at other times was referred to as an "adjustable peg" system.

It is important to see the Fund as it was constituted in its early days because at that time there was only one currency in demand. The United States ended World War II with the only industrial economy that was not in shambles. The United States was to be the source of all the capital goods needed by European nations to rebuild their economies and also received a great deal of money in interest on loans made by it during the war. This situation had a profound influence on the characteristics of the Fund: The American conferees were very much aware that, in its early days, the Fund would have applications to borrow gold and a single currency, the U.S. dollar. Therefore, the U.S. delegation took care to ensure that the total amount of money that could be borrowed would be no more than the United States could afford to lend (and which the U.S. Congress would approve when asked to ratify membership in the IMF).

The system was marked by its pragmatism. While the emphasis was on fixed exchange rates, the Fund accepted a huge realignment of currencies in 1949 when all of the major Western European nations devalued against the dollar by between 20 and 30 percent. A second element of pragmatism was the way in which the reduction in wartime financial controls was to be carried out. It was recognized that a country torn apart by the war could not immediately allow freedom of capital movements. The rule was imposed that any nation was entitled to take the necessary time to reduce its wartime controls, but a bona fide effort to reduce them should be made. Moreover, once a regulation had been eased, it could not be reinstated if a balance-of-payments problem arose. Once the massive devaluations of 1949 had taken place, the world settled into a regime of fixed rates except for devaluations by France (1958 and 1969) and by the United Kingdom (1967).

The Bretton Woods system lasted for twenty-five years. One way to get an understanding of the international financial system is to explain why it lasted so long and why it did not last longer. This system must be seen as revolving around the U.S. dollar in much the same way that the nineteenth-century gold standard relied on sterling. The crux of the problem lies in the behavior of the U.S. dollar against other currencies. Recall that an important feature of the success of the gold standard was that the United Kingdom was able to keep international investment in line with international saving and was able to attract money to London to meet short-run liquidity needs. The United States began the Bretton Woods era with all of the gold in the world and with all of the major nations in debt to it. Every other nation needed imports of capital goods from the United States if its economy was to be rebuilt. In terms of a free trade world with unrestricted capital movements, the dollar was terrifically undervalued in 1946. The undervaluation was held within bounds by the regulations that the European nations imposed on foreign transactions by their firms and citizens. The Bretton Woods era can usefully be subdivided into three periods. In the first period, from 1946 to 1958, the undervaluation of the U.S. dollar was gradually eroded; in the second, from 1958 to 1967, the continuing deficits of the United States were easily financed; and in the third, 1967 to 1971, desperate measures were undertaken to sustain the value of the dollar at $\frac{1}{35}$ of a troy ounce of gold.

The First Period (1946–1958)

The first period began with the market dominance of the two North American countries. Only these two countries were strong enough to ignore the balance-of-payments constraint (the Canadian dollar was at that time more or less fixed in value to the U.S. dollar by virtue of the very large amount of international trade between the two neighbors). All of the European nations were striving to export goods to the United States and Canada so that they might earn more dollars with which to pay for additional imports of food and machinery. This was the period of the dollar shortage. In 1949, as noted, there was a wave of huge devaluations against the two dollars by the European currencies. These devaluations brought the exchange rates back to an area of "reality," and prices began to have some effect on transactions. The dollar was still undervalued, but by less, and the undervaluation was mitigated by the controls over spending in North America that the Europeans kept in force. As the Europeans rebuilt their economies, their need for imports from the United States grew smaller (they were able to supply a wider range of their own needs), and their abilities to export goods to the United States improved. In terms of the analysis of Chapter 14, the growth effects were such as to constitute a favorable shift in $C*$ (to the left) for Europe. The SS schedule of the United States shifted downward (in terms of Figure 15-1) gradually through time as European recovery proceeded. The gap between the actual value of C (determined by price levels and the exchange rate) and the value of $C*$ narrowed steadily. Some of the beneficial effects of the European recovery were devoted not to decreasing $C*$ but to eliminating the holdover of wartime controls on the freedom of international transactions. In technical terms, there was a suppressed disequilibrium, and the suppressive regulations were allowed to evaporate as the need for them diminished.

It is convenient to think of C and $C*$ taking on the same values on January 1, 1958, the day on which the European Economic Community came into being, although any estimate will be approximate at best. It was in 1958 that the change in conditions took place. Prior to 1958, the United States, with remarkable enlightenment, tried to encourage spending on imports and encouraged foreign investments in order to promote European recovery. In 1958, the Eisenhower administration felt that the time for such measures was past and that it would seek balanced international accounts. Unfortunately, it soon found itself running surprisingly large, unintentional deficits. There were two reasons for this change. The formation of the EEC and its counterpart organization, the European Free Trade Area, led to discrimination in favor of intrabloc trade and away from U.S. exports. This effect would have increased the value of $C*$ for the United States (an adverse shift in the terms of trade). Fortunately for the United States, the great success of the EEC and its high rate of growth brought about an equal and opposite effect so that the terms-of-trade effect on $C*$ was quite small. The really strong impact of the EEC was felt in the capital account. The EEC was a large market second only in prosperity and buying power to the United States, and it attracted large amounts of foreign direct investment by U.S. multinational corporations. The deficit on capital account (reason 2) shifted $C**$ to the right for the United States, requiring an increase in competitiveness.[2] This surge of foreign direct investment had two secondary effects:

---

[2] Successful MNC subsidiaries would make a positive contribution to the U.S. balance of payments in the long run when the cumulative flow of repatriated profits (and other dollar remittances) exceeded the outflow of capital.

The foreign direct investment did generate a demand for U.S. exports because the foreign subsidiaries used machinery with which managers were familiar and, in some cases, U.S.-made parts; and second, the MNCs transferred technology to Europe and substantially reduced the technological lead of the United States economy.

The Second Period (1958–1967)

The second period was characterized by U.S. deficits (and therefore an overvaluation of the U.S. dollar), which were easily financed. The surplus dollars in the foreign exchange market at the existing parities were absorbed by foreign central banks and private corporations, who redeposited these dollars in American financial markets. After the period of stringency, Japan and the European nations, as well as many individual corporations, were only too pleased to build up their dollar reserves to a level that gave them greater degrees of safety against temporary disturbances.

The United States was running an unusual kind of balance-of-payments deficit in this period. The current account balance was positive, indicating positive international saving, but this flow of saving was inadequate to finance the very large amount of international investment undertaken by MNCs. There was no need for concern on the part of the United States about its international net worth, but there were indications that when the easily available financing ran dry, there would be a problem in supporting the parity of the dollar. It was during the second period that the United States tried to stanch the outflow of capital. In 1963, the interest equalization tax was imposed. This measure was designed to reduce the quantity of bond issues made in New York by foreign corporations. These flotations were made in New York because U.S. interest rates were lower than European rates, and to the extent that these bonds were bought by Americans, they amounted to (portfolio) foreign investment. Under interest equalization, a tax was levied on new issues of foreign bonds (and purchases of foreign stocks) according to the maturity of the instrument. This tax effectively raised the cost of borrowing in New York. In 1965, MNCs were asked to reduce the balance-of-payments drain that their investments generated. Originally, this set of capital controls was voluntary, and it discriminated in the severity of its restrictions according to the characteristics of the host country. Developed countries with small imports from the United States were more severely discriminated against than developing nations with high marginal propensities to import. Multinationals were asked to control their net drain on the balance of payments by maximizing their exports of goods and services plus profit repatriation less foreign investment. In 1968, the voluntary program was made mandatory.

The Third Period (1967–1971)

Once foreign nations had increased their dollar reserves to the desired level, financing the ongoing U.S. deficit was markedly less easy, and balance-of-payments policies began to bite on the U.S. economy. The third period of the Bretton Woods era was marked by increasingly frantic U.S. efforts to maintain the value of the dollar in the face of endemic deficits. There was an ingrained belief that the Bretton Woods system of fixed parities had to be maintained and that the system could not withstand a devaluation of the dollar.[3] The problems of policy were aggravated by the Johnson administration's commitment to an unpopular war in Vietnam. The Vietnam War pushed the U.S. economy into something approaching demand-pull inflation (the unemployment rate for white males over 20 years of age bottomed out at 2.1 percent in 1969). The fiscal measures designed to reduce the demand for consumer goods (a surcharge on individual income taxes) seemed to have had the effect of reducing the flow of household saving rather than reducing consumption. Not only did the Vietnam War induce a price-level disturbance by generating a high rate of capacity utilization (the inflation rate in the United States—as measured by the consumer price index—rose from an average of 1.6 percent per annum in 1963–1965 to an average of 5.5 percent per annum in the years 1968–1970), but it also generated a large increase in the demand for imports. The increase in the demand for imports was partly due to the price-level disturbance but was also due to the large amount of foreign expenditures incurred by the war effort. These included expenditures in Southeast Asia by military and nonmilitary personnel and the costs of supplying the war effort and of repairing and maintaining ships and equipment, mainly in Japan and Korea.

The effort to restrict the balance-of-payments drain attributable to foreign direct investment by MNCs met with partial success. Except for the first year of the mandatory capital controls, when the meaning and details of the regulations were not fully understood, the Foreign Direct Investment Program (FDIP) did not seem seriously to reduce the rate of acquisition of foreign assets by MNCs. But FDIP did increase substantially the amount of asset acquisition that was financed by funds borrowed in foreign capital markets.[4] The program was successful in reducing the rate of outflow of funds from the United States, but when the regulations were eased substantially in 1973 (and finally terminated in 1974), much of the foreign indebtedness incurred in the late 1960s was paid off with funds borrowed in the United States at lower rates of interest.

---

[3] This proved to be fallacious. It was a serious error because the actual and inevitable devaluation was delayed for a very long time, and during the process, the balance-of-payments situation of the United States deteriorated further. Only when the system seemed likely to break under its own weight did President Nixon devalue the U.S. dollar on August 15, 1971.

[4] For details, see H. Peter Gray, *International Trade, Investment and Payments* (Boston: Houghton Mifflin, 1979), pp. 523–525.

European nations and Japan were urged (some would say pressured) to reinvest their surpluses in the United States in the belief that their failure to do so would bring the Bretton Woods era to an end. The specter of another period like the 1930s was always there to haunt noncompliers. It became ever clearer that the dollar was substantially overvalued, and foreign depositors lost faith in the dollar as a home for international reserves. The system was terminated in 1971 because the U.S. current account ceased to be in surplus, foreign goods were weakening the levels of employment in the United States, and no other course seemed available.[5] President Nixon simply announced that the United States would no longer sell gold at $35 per fine ounce. The key currency had cracked under the strain. Immediately a major effort was made by the ten largest countries to set a new set of parities, reflecting, in effect, a devaluation of the dollar. This effort bore fruit in the Smithsonian Agreement of December 1971 (discussed later in this chapter).

The crux of the problem was the exchange rate of the dollar against all other currencies. Unlike the United Kingdom in the nineteenth century, the United States did not run balanced payments over the long run; instead it loaned out more than it was saving internationally on a continuing basis. The exchange rates among the other countries were more or less in order and were of less importance to the survival of the Bretton Woods system. But because the U.S. dollar was the reference point around which all other rates of exchange resolved, the dollar could not be reduced in value without major surgery. The only way out seemed to be to set *all* rates free to fluctuate in line with market forces. This was the mentality in Washington during the first Nixon administration.

During the third period, the need for more international liquidity was also a matter of concern for economists. Robert Triffin saw the problem as serious well before anyone else, and his efforts made a direct contribution to its solution. Triffin argued that as the volume and value of international transactions (trade and investment) grew, nations would need increased amounts of international reserves. Because the dollar was as good as gold (and maybe even a little better) until the late 1970s, the United States was able to supply the world with the additional liquidity it needed by the simple expedient of running deficits. This was a planned mechanism in the Eisenhower administration before 1958, but the deficits of the 1960s also served the same purpose. Triffin knew full well that the United States could not run deficits forever and that this source of international liquidity would ultimately dry up. There were three possible solutions:

[5] See Lawrence B. Krause, *Sequel to Bretton Woods* (Washington, D.C.: Brookings Institution, 1971), ch. 1.

1. an all-around increase in the price of gold,
2. instituting flexible rates of exchange to reduce the need for reserves, and
3. authorizing the IMF to create international money.

   1. Raising the price of gold meant mainly increasing the value of the amount of gold in existence. There might be some increase in supply, but this was expected to be relatively small. The objections to such a system were that it would have an uneven effect, giving additional international liquidity to countries that possessed gold in their international reserves, and that it would provide a large boost to gold-producing economies such as Russia and South Africa. The objections were fairly obvious, and many people were unwilling to aid a nation whose socioeconomic system was based on racial division, although many economists pointed out that raising the price of gold would benefit black gold miners in South Africa as well as the South African nation as a whole. In practice, this scheme was adopted when gold prices were set free to follow market forces and Americans were allowed to hold gold.

   2. Triffin argued that flexible rates were undesirable because the foreign exchange markets would be dominated by speculators and the rates would vary excessively from day to day and week to week. In practice, this has not been a characteristic of the market, although long-run overvaluations of currencies have proved to be a serious problem.

   3. The creation of additional international money by the IMF was the scheme proposed by Triffin and the one ultimately adopted. In 1967, the governors of the IMF (mainly national politicians) approved the creation of *special drawing rights,* or SDRs. When the governors of the IMF perceived a shortage of international reserves worldwide (as distinct from a shortage in a single country or group of countries), they could issue a line of credit to each member nation. The term *SDR* has two meanings. The special drawing right was a line of credit established within the Fund that could be used only in settlement of international debts by member governments. These rights or lines of credit were denominated in a unit of account called an SDR, originally set equal to a U.S. dollar. The mechanism worked in the following way. If the world was perceived to lack international liquidity or money, the Fund would issue special drawing rights to each of its members according to their quotas. Thus each nation's international reserves would be increased at the stroke of a pen. But these dollars or SDRs could be used only on the books of the IMF. A deficit of the United States, say, with Germany would be settled by transferring the requisite amount of money from the United States' SDR account to the German account. Each country pays interest on the difference between the number of SDRs cumulatively allocated to its account and the number in that account and earns interest when the number of SDRs in the account exceeds the cumulative allocation.

The interest rate is an average of Treasury bill rates (or near-equivalents) in a group of major industrial nations. The value of the SDR is now different from a dollar, having more or less maintained the value of the original dollar. It is now fixed as a mixture of the values of the five major world currencies (dollar, franc, mark, pound, and yen). Use of SDRs is not free, and accumulation brings a reward.

THE CURRENT SYSTEM (1973–   )

From the moment that President Nixon stopped the convertibility of the dollar into gold at the price of $35 per troy ounce of gold, there was an interregnum until early 1973, when rates were set free to float.

Nixon's action to terminate the Bretton Woods system also involved a series of domestic measures including wage and price controls and a 10 percent surcharge on many imports. But the August 15, 1971, declaration set the stage for some serious bargaining as to the future of the international monetary system. This bargaining culminated in December 1972 with the Smithsonian Agreement, which set a new alignment of *fixed* rates of exchange, reflecting devaluation of the dollar against the yen (16.88 percent), the mark (13.58 percent), the French franc (8.57 percent), and the pound sterling (8.57 percent) as well as against other currencies. Only the Canadian dollar did not strengthen against the U.S. dollar. The new rates did not stop the deficit, which grew substantially during 1971. The ingrained effects of a dollar overvalued for more than ten years could not be quickly eliminated simply by changing exchange rates. At best, the new parities were guesses at the appropriate but unknown set of C^{**}. Such changes in competitiveness, even if not eroded by slippage, take a long time to catch hold.[6] It seems sensible to suppose that the larger the change in competitiveness needed, the longer will it take for nations to adjust to the new conditions and for new exchange rates to take hold. Buyers have to be made aware of new relative prices, orders have to work their way back into the productive sectors of the national economies, and capacity changes in individual economies have to be brought about as the mix of goods produced must change.

When the new rates did not solve the imbalance, all currencies were set free to float in early 1973. This practical step was ultimately confirmed by the Jamaica Agreement signed in Kingston, Jamaica, in January 1976 and incorporated into the Articles of Agreement of the IMF in April of the same year. Almost immediately, the international financial system was subjected to an onslaught of large real disturbances. World food prices rose sharply in 1973 as Russia and India had very bad harvests.

[6] R. Dornbusch and P. I. Krugman, "Flexible Exchange Rates in the Short Run," *Brookings Papers on Economic Activity,* 3 (1976), 560–566, suggests it can take as much as two years for a devaluation to become fully effective.

The Organization of Petroleum Exporting Countries (OPEC) managed to increase the price of oil by a factor of 4 in early 1974. These shocks resulted in quite severe price-level disturbances as different nations reacted to the shocks in different ways.[7]

The interesting question is whether the new system of flexible exchange rates would have allowed the countries of the world to work themselves out of the severe imbalances that existed at the time of the collapse of the Bretton Woods system. The answer is probably yes, but this must be a guess because the sudden onslaught of real shocks did not allow the system of flexible rates to address that problem for a few years. Almost as soon as flexible rates were instituted, they were burdened both with the task of eliminating the imbalance that remained from having kept with the Bretton Woods system for too long and with adjusting to changes in the world price of many major commodities. It is certainly unreasonable to say that the system of flexible exchange rates has not worked well; the system was subjected to major shocks, and it may have been a success simply by preventing a breakdown or crisis.

In one sense, flexible rates were inevitable in 1973. To have set a new system of fixed-rate parities would have implied a knowledge of the correct values of C^{**} for each of the major trading nations. Given the national price levels, only a system of flexible rates would allow the international financial system to grope its way toward the appropriate set of rates. Not all the economists in the world would have been able to compute the values of the C^{**}.

In fact, the system of flexible rates was showing signs, toward the end of 1978, of having reestablished a position of approximate compatibility. Inflation rates were slowing, and payments imbalances were decreasing. Then the second oil-price shock hit. This shock was larger than the first in terms of the increase of the price of oil in dollars but smaller relatively (a smaller percentage increase). Once again, oil importers suffered serious deficits on current account, but this time the industrialized world was forced to recognize the need for a positive real rate of interest to be paid. The Federal Reserve Board in the United States tightened money drastically in fall 1979, and interest rates shot up. A global recession ensued. Nations that had borrowed to finance their oil import bills (and their current deficits after the first oil shock) now found themselves with huge interest payments just at the time when the global recession had made their ability to export much weaker. This problem pushed the world's financial system very near to a global crisis, and the system came close to being reorganized yet again. Fortunately, concerted efforts by the IMF and the central banks of the industrialized nations together with a remarkable degree of self-discipline by the debtor nations prevented the collapse of some major banks and of the financial

[7] See H. Peter Gray, "Oil-Push Inflation: A Broader Examination," *Banca Nazionale del Lavoro Quarterly Review,* March 1981, pp. 49–67.

system. The danger was always that a default on major loans that private banks had extended to the oil-importing nations (and to Mexico) would force the banks to close. When a major bank closes, there can be a severe domino effect as depositors withdraw money from other banks perceived to be near default, pushing them over the brink, and banks follow each other into bankruptcy.

In theory, the existing system should last forever. There is no innate rigidity built into the system because exchange rates are free to vary according to market forces and additional liquidity can always be created by the Fund in the form of SDRs. But no system is foolproof. No system can withstand incorrect policies on the part of major governments and important banks (a financial system built on fractional reserves is always potentially vulnerable). The new system can prevail if countries administer sensible balance-of-payments policies. Deficits must engender adjustment; the system cannot survive major nations financing deficits in the hope that something favorable will occur.

The new system has still not managed to give surplus nations an incentive (or a need) to take expansionary corrective action, and the burden of adjustment still falls on the deficit nations. There must be some practical understanding that, at a minimum, surplus nations must not prevent adjustment by deficit nations. Politicians still need to delay expenditure reductions. It was this problem that brought the world near to crisis in 1971: The United States had subordinated its balance-of-payments policies to the overriding needs of the Vietnam War and to the belief that the Bretton Woods system could not survive a devaluation of the dollar (that is, that crisis would follow immediately from the devaluation of the dollar). In the 1970s, it was commercial bankers and oil-importing governments that pushed the system near to crisis. With hindsight, bankers extended far too much credit to oil-importing nations and allowed these nations to adjust to the oil shock much too slowly. The Jamaica system has survived this crisis, and both bankers and central bankers have learned from the experience.

SUMMARY

It was asserted that international financial systems should be judged in terms of three criteria: the size of the real shocks, the social costs the shocks were likely to raise, and the degree to which the shocks were suppressed. How well did the Bretton Woods system and the Jamaica system succeed? Recall that the design of an international monetary system is to allow the world economy to achieve gains that can be generated by international trade and investment without introducing destabilizing (or upsetting) effects on national economies. In other words, the international financial system should not be a source of disturbances but should allow the system to adjust slowly and efficiently by providing a dampening effect (rather than an aggravating one).

The Bretton Woods system was subjected to relatively mild shocks, which were stabilizing in the early years of the system (that is, they tended to redress a suppressed imbalance). Over time, the mild shocks continued, and they mounted up. Over twenty-five years, their cumulative effect was substantial. The three major changes were the recoveries of the European and Japanese economies, the formation of the EEC and the accompanying transfer of technology; and the Vitenam War. The essence of the problem was that the key-currency nation was not strong enough or disciplined enough to play its role (of maintaining balanced payments and, preferably, basic balance over a period of years). In this, it did not match the performance of sterling in the nineteenth century. The dollar did not generate enough international saving to finance its international investment and had to run down its stocks of financial assets. Running down stocks must eventually lead to depletion of those stocks. It is probably fair to say the social costs of adjustment would have been quite small had they been allowed to happen as conditions changed (after 1958, when the dollar became overvalued). But under the existing belief that the exchange rate of the dollar had to be maintained, the adjustment could only have been accomplished by inducing a recession of some severity, and American politicians were not prepared to accept the social and political costs of such measures. Only when the main focus of economic policy became the financing of the Vietnam War was the balance-of-payments problem suppressed for domestic political reasons, but that involved the elimination of the positive international saving that had marked the United States' international accounts since the end of World War II.

Whatever the motives, the actual breakdown left the world in an extreme position. The dollar was seriously overvalued, and the United States was deeply indebted to foreigners. Moreover, those debts were mainly lodged in liquid assets that could be quickly withdrawn. Such a sudden withdrawal would have forced the American economy into a very severe recession as the dollar weakened substantially and a changed mix of output was required. That a crisis was avoided was testimony to the great improvement in international cooperation on financial matters since World War II.

The current system has an entirely different history. Starting from a position of great imbalance and with the debtor nation not having the option of imposing controls over international transactions such as those possessed by the European nations after World War II, the system was immediately afflicted by major shocks. It absorbed the first wave of shocks without a hint of crisis or panic (see Chapter 18). The industrialized nations all suffered from inflation in the aftermath of the first oil shock, and flexible rates of exchange allowed the price-level disturbances to be absorbed relatively easily. One important plus that the Jamaica system enjoyed was the fact that the oil shock and the increase in agricultural prices in 1973 both helped the United States relative to Japan and West Germany.

Most analysts would argue that the world was very fortunate that a system of flexible rates had been introduced before the onset of the first oil-price shock. It seems extremely unlikely that a fixed-rate system could have successfully sustained the strains. However, there is a counter-opinion.[8] The argument is made that a set of fixed exchange rates would have imposed greater discipline on countries and would have limited their ability to permit domestic inflation as a part of the response to the oil-price shock. Salaries and wages did tend to keep pace with increases in the cost of living in most industrialized countries, and the inflationary impact was accommodated rather than countered. In the absence of the power to depreciate their currencies, national governments would have had to impose severe monetary restraints. Presumably, this would have brought about severe recessions. The different rates of inflation in different industrialized countries could be seen as suggesting that policymakers chose the inflation-or-unemployment trade-off that best fit their countries' social and political setting. A system of fixed rates would have imposed greater social costs of adjustment. The community of nations had just about adjusted to the 1973 oil-price shock only to have another one imposed in 1979 when the Shah's regime collapsed in Iran.

After the global recession of the early 1980s, the price of oil began to subside. This is yet another, albeit gradual, disturbance to which the system of flexible exchange rates should be able to adjust. Future problems are much more likely to revolve around a rapid decline in the value of the U.S. dollar as foreigners repatriate their money and U.S. banks come under strain from a net deposit withdrawal or from a recurrence of the third-world debt crisis. The current system has been subjected to major external shocks ever since its inception. It has come perilously close to crisis when the third-world debt problem arose. Some easing of the adjustment strain was allowed to show itself in different rates of inflation in different countries, but the amount of suppression has not been extreme. The domestic political costs have been high for some politicians who found that their arsenal of policies did not allow them to ignore world events, and continental European nations have tended lately to vote out the incumbent government on principle—presumably because the economy has been performing so badly and because unemployment rates there have been so high.

[8] Hendrik Houthakker, "The International Agenda," *Eastern Economic Journal,* 11 (January–March 1985), 64–70.

Bibliography

Gardner, Richard. *Sterling-Dollar Diplomacy,* 2nd ed. New York: McGraw-Hill, 1969.

Harrod, Roy. *The Life of Keynes.* London: Macmillan, 1951.

Krause, Lawrence B. *Sequel to Bretton Woods.* Washington, D.C.: Brookings Institution, 1971.

Machlup, Fritz. *Remaking the International Monetary System.* Baltimore: Johns Hopkins Press, 1968.

Tew, Brian. *International Monetary Co-operation, 1945–56.* London: Hutchinson University Library, 1958.

Triffin, Robert. *Gold and the Dollar Crisis.* New Haven, Conn.: Yale University Press, 1961.

Questions

1. How did a virtually fixed rate-of-exchange system last for twenty-five years?
2. Why did the Bretton Woods system last for only twenty-five years?
3. How did the IMF increase the global supply of reserves?
4. Would fixed exchange rates have worked after 1973? Support your answer.
5. Trace the sudden shift in real and nominal exchange rates in the United States from 1978 through 1982. Use quarterly data, and take your choice of inflation indexes.
6. Using the *Treasury Bulletin* as a first source, what was the change in U.S. liquid international reserves (at the disposal of the government)? Use annual data from 1952 through 1973.
7. Why are SDRs important in the scheme of the global economy?

18

Current International Financial Problems

At the Bretton Woods Conference in 1944, the participants set as one of the key targets for the postwar international financial system the free international mobility of capital. In other words, controls over the sending of money to foreign countries, widely instituted during the Depression and solidified during the war, were to be dispensed with as quickly as economic conditions permitted. The intent was to allow capital to move among nations to the point at which it would provide the greatest contribution to global output and would earn the highest expected rate of return. In all probability, the participants at Bretton Woods envisaged most of these (liberated) capital movements taking the form of long-term loans from the developed North to the capital-short South (the developing nations). This would mirror the experience of the world during its period of rapid economic development and growth in the nineteenth century. Of course, most, though not all, of the transfers that took place during the nineteenth century were between a colonial power and its colonies. The breakdown of the colonial system and the speed at which it would occur after World War II were not apparent in 1944. Nor did the participants foresee the role of foreign *direct* investment by multinational corporations as being as important as it turned out to be (see Part VI).

By the mid-1980s, the international financial system had achieved much more than the participants at Bretton Woods would have thought possible. Instead of national capital (long-term) and money (short-term) markets in national capitals being loosely linked by sluggish equilibrating capital movements, the huge modern advances in communications technology have effectively integrated the national markets into a single global set of financial markets. Currencies flow among countries in response to very small changes in relative financial conditions in one center or the other. Thus an announcement or a change in policy in Washington, New York, London, or Frankfurt will have an almost instantaneous effect on the financial conditions in all of the major financial markets in the world.[1] In addition to the technological advances in communications, two developments contributed to the merging of financial markets: the emergence and growth of the Eurodollar market and the spread of foreign direct investment by multinationals and the concomitant spread of multinational commercial banks.

The commercial banks, operating in the Euromarkets, undoubtedly contributed to the world debt crisis of 1982. They loaned too much money to countries that could not service their foreign (hard-currency) debts. The borrowing countries used the borrowed funds to pay for imports of energy at the very high prices that followed the oil-price shocks of 1973 and 1979, and they also "needed" the money for capital formation and economic development. Much of this borrowing was based on short-term loans; if the loans could not be refinanced (new loans made to replace old ones), this meant high debt service.[2] In 1981, interest rates on hard currency shot up sharply, but inflation rates did not increase, so the real rates of interest increased sharply too. The debt service burdens rose astronomically as old loans at "low" rates of interest had to be refinanced at "high" rates of interest. Many countries could not meet their financial commitments. Commercial banks in the industrialized countries were faced with the prospect of having huge amounts of loans becoming, at best, illiquid assets. This threatened their own domestic solvency and could (in the absence of strong support from their own central banks) have caused major banking crises within national economies. Such is the kind of debt crisis that spreads from the internationalization of world financial markets back into national monetary systems.

EUROMARKETS AND MULTINATIONAL BANKING

Like so many features of the current international financial system, the Eurocurrency markets find their roots in the monetary conditions that existed in the aftermath of World War II. At that time, the U.S. dollar was the world's major currency. Effectively all international trade was paid for by the transfer of dollars from one bank account to another, and central banks held their international reserves in dollars. The dollar

---

[1] The flow of foreign exchange into the United States that contributes to the "overvaluation" of the U.S. dollar would be far smaller in the absence of this very high degree of integration among the world's national financial centers.

[2] "Debt service" is the amount of interest payments and scheduled repayment of principal due in a year. It is usually expressed as a percentage of export earnings.

is substantially less dominant in the 1980s, but it is still the world's most important single currency for international transactions. In the 1950s, governments, banks, and corporations that conducted large amounts of international trade and payments frequently preferred to hold any temporary balances in dollars than to convert them to other currencies that might devalue against the dollar at any time. If the funds were to be spent in the near future, holding them in dollars also averted the costs of conversion into home currency and back again into dollars. This policy was followed despite the fact that weaker currencies normally yielded higher rates of interest.

This pattern of behavior was reinforced by an institutional feature of European banking. Commercial banks in Europe are allowed to operate as unregulated banks for all transactions with foreigners and in foreign currencies. The most important regulation that escaped was the cost of holding reserve requirements (which earned no interest) against deposits. Thus a French bank could accept a deposit in German marks or Swiss francs or in dollars without paying some proportion of that deposit into the central bank. Banks kept two sets of books—one for domestic transactions with local customers in home currency and one for international business. An institutional feature of the U.S. banking system was also a major contributor to the emergence of the Eurodollar market. The rate of interest that could be paid by U.S. banks on time deposits was regulated at below its free market level by Regulation Q of the Federal Reserve System. Thus, in the United States, the spread between borrowing and lending rates for U.S. banks was higher than was needed for banks to make a reasonable profit.

These three roots were drawn together by an act of the USSR. The Russians had acquired a sum of dollars by selling some goods to the West. They wanted both to keep these funds in dollars and to avoid depositing them in a New York bank where they feared the funds might be expropriated (or frozen) in a time of cold war strains. The solution was to find a non-U.S. bank that would accept a deposit in dollars. The Russians asked the French bank that handled most of their free-world business to do this for them; the bank obliged. The bank quickly found that there was a potential loan demand for dollars that it could meet by accepting deposits in dollars. This loan demand would pay interest rates high enough to cover the cost of the deposits and administrative costs. Operations in dollars were therefore profitable, and the bank sought out more dollar deposits. The bank's cable address was "Eurobank," and the term *Eurodollars* was born.

In the early years of the market, the dollar was effectively the only currency used in this way. As other currencies became stronger (particularly the mark and the Swiss franc), the Eurodollar market became the Eurocurrency market. The headquarters of the market is London, but "offshore banking offices" exist in the Bahamas and the Cayman Islands, and there is a similar Asian dollar market in Singapore and Hong Kong. Recently, banking regulations in the United States have been changed to allow American banks the privilege of making international dealings (in the European fashion) from their American headquarters.[3]

The Eurodollar market grew quickly because it was able to pay higher rates on time deposits than were available in New York (because of Regulation Q) and could still lend more cheaply than New York–based banks because it was not afflicted with reserve requirements on deposits and other costs of regulation. The original depositors were firms that had sold goods for dollars, and the major borrowers were firms and governments that needed short-term financing to pay for goods purchased from abroad. As long as Regulation Q kept banks' costs of deposits in the United States below the free market price, there was little difficulty in getting deposits, and American banks were in the habit of accommodating their customers by routing their surplus cash into the banks' European subsidiaries as Eurodollar deposits. Another source of cost saving enjoyed by Eurobanks was the wholesale nature of the business. Only large transactions were handled. Originally, the minimum transaction was $1 million, but this has now fallen to $250,000. Dealing only in very large transactions with clients whose credit ratings were impeccable kept the administrative costs very low and gave the Eurobanks a further competitive edge over competitors operating in national markets.

The Eurodollar market established itself in the period in which Regulation Q held sway in the United States. By the time Regulation Q was abolished, the market had established itself, and it could continue to operate profitably on a narrower markup of loan rates over deposit rates than competitors based in the national markets (and afflicted with the costs of regulation).

At the same time that the Eurodollar market was growing, multinational banking grew. Banks established foreign subsidiaries for two reasons. First, American banks wanted to continue to serve their multinational corporate clients as they opened subsidiary firms in Europe in the 1960s and later. American banks enjoyed a competitive advantage over European banks in serving the MNC subsidiaries because they knew and understood the firm's operations "at home." They did not want foreign banks acquiring this detailed knowledge of their clients' needs. Second, U.S. banks were not able to conduct "offshore banking" or Eurodollar business from their head offices because U.S. banking law did not offer the same flexibility as that enjoyed by European banks (including banks in the United Kingdom). The U.S. banks certainly did not want to be nonplayers in the Eurodollar market—it was too profitable![4]

---

[3] See K. Alec Chrystal, "International Banking Facilities," *Federal Reserve Bank of St. Louis Review,* April 1984, pp. 5–11, for a description of these developments.

[4] European banks became multinational later, as their national MNCs grew. They also established themselves in New York in order to have a good source of entry into the dollar deposit market: They needed to be able to borrow dollars at competitive rates in the event of a financial crisis.

In addition to the benefits that derived from proximity to their clients' foreign subsidiaries and entry into the Eurodollar market, U.S. banks also enjoyed the advantages that accrue to a firm having branches or subsidiaries in many countries. Information is gained more cheaply, more accurately, and more promptly when a firm has its own sources in foreign countries. There are also gains from diversification of operations into different national economies in much the same way that an investor can reduce risks and increase profits by holding a variety (portfolio) of stocks instead of placing all of the assets in a single type of investment. The presence of American banks in Europe markedly increased the number of large banks that could become serious participants in the Eurodollar market and therefore facilitated the very high rates of growth of that market.[5]

Eurobanks are always under pressure to find funds to match their loan demand without having to push the rates charged on loans above the rates available in the national market. Furthermore, if the market is not to shrink, the Eurobanks must always be able to pay slightly higher rates on deposits than national markets are paying. Both of these pressures exist within the context of maintaining enough of a markup of loan rates over deposit rates to cover administrative costs and to make an adequate return on invested capital. These pressures led to innovations in loan-making in 1973. First Eurobanks started to make loans to the governments of developing countries (a hitherto untapped source of demand), and they devised a system whereby these loans could be made jointly (syndicated) so that the face amount of a single loan could be increased substantially. Because rates of interest on deposits were capable of substantial variation, Eurobanks also introduced a means whereby they could lend long-term but could insure themselves against having to pay more for deposits than the borrower was paying for the loan. Loans were made for a period of years at a rate of interest that was fixed relative to a key deposit rate (the rate at which Eurobanks offered to lend money to each other). Thus a borrower might take out a ten-year loan at a rate of interest of 1½ percent above the base rate, and the loan rate would be recalculated at six-month intervals. The amount charged over the base rate would consist of a standard premium to cover administrative costs and profit plus an allowance for risk.

In 1974, the Euromarket provided a great service to the world by serving as the means through which the huge balance-of-payments deficits that followed on the oil-price shock could be taken care of. Average deposits in the Euromarkets grew by $45 billion in a single year.

The fourfold increase in the price of oil in 1974 followed the embargo of shipments to the developed nations by Arab oil producers. This increase

---

[5] Data on the size of the Eurodollar market are notoriously unreliable, but rates of growth should be accurately indicated. In 1968, the total value of deposits was $25 billion; in 1972, $91 billion; and in 1975, $205 billion.

in the price of a noncompetitive import required huge adjustments by all oil-importing countries. Because life-styles cannot be changed overnight, adjustment takes time, and sudden balance-of-payments shocks had to be financed. The oil exporters were unable to increase their spending on imports as quickly as their revenues grew and had to find a place to lodge their funds. The Euromarkets were the place chosen. The market had the advantage of being beyond the scope of national financial regulators, and therefore deposits there would be less easily interfered with by governments smarting under the new higher price of oil. It was to the Euromarkets (still at that time predominantly a Eurodollar market) that nations with balance-of-payments deficits sought financing. The net flow of funds from oil importers to oil exporters went smoothly via the Euromarkets as oil exporters used the markets as a means of lending deficit nations the funds with which to pay their debts. Interest rates remained fairly low, and given the inflation in the industrialized countries, the inflation-adjusted (or "real") cost of borrowing was very low indeed. In 1975, the real rate of interest in the United States (and therefore approximately the rate in the Eurodollar market) was −2.81 percent per annum (a nominal rate of 6.33 percent on prime commercial paper less an inflation rate of 9.14 percent—measured as the percentage annual change in the consumer price index). In 1979, pressure was brought to bear on the Federal Reserve System to increase the real rate of interest paid on dollar-denominated dollars. The nominal rate increased sharply and peaked at 20.32 percent in the third quarter of 1981. The real rate peaked at 7.65 in the second quarter of 1982 (see Table 15-1 in Chapter 15). The very low, even negative real rate in the years following the oil-price shocks can be attributed to the very easy, accommodating monetary policies of the Ford and Carter administrations.

It is now disarmingly simple to see how the developing, oil-importing countries could be trapped into borrowing excessively. Adjustment to the new, much higher price of oil would damage the growth impetus and inflict severe social costs. The interest costs of borrowing (not adjusting) were seductively low when measured by the real rate of interest charged on dollar-denominated loans. The Eurobanks were willing, even eager to lend money at the "base rate plus." All of the industrialized countries seemed to be financing their increases in oil payments in the Euromarkets. Someone should have seen the trouble ahead. The whole process was simply too easy and too painless for what amounted to a major adverse shift in the terms of trade.

As explained earlier, debt service is the amount of foreign exchange needed by a country to pay the interest and principal due on its international indebtedness in any particular year. Because the main, if not the only, source of foreign exchange for a developing country is its earnings from exports, debt service is usually computed as a percentage of export earnings. The burden of debt service is measured by the opportunity cost (the benefits from alternative uses) of the foreign exchange devoted to debt service.

The capability to service debt is the ratio of debt-service payments to export revenues. This number can be reduced if refinancing of principal coming due is easily obtained.[6] If additional indebtedness is seen as being required for the continuation of economic growth and development (see Chapter 10), the task of acquiring both the additional loans and new loans to refinance old maturing debt is more severe. The value of the ratio can be increased in two ways: by increasing the amount required for debt service and by a reduction in the value of exports. A third possibility is reducing imports, but that usually implies either the sacrifice of the rate of growth or the standard of living or the existence of nonessential imports. (There are always nonessential imports, but they become increasingly difficult to stamp out.) Under stress, "nonessential imports" can be redefined!

When Volcker suddenly tightened money in the United States, nominal interest rates rose worldwide (because of the degree of financial integration). Because, after a period of tight money, recession set in and price increases became smaller, the real rate of interest increased much more quickly and by a larger percentage than the nominal rate of interest. The nominal and real interest rates charged on Euromarket borrowings by developing countries quickly reflected the new higher costs of funds, and this substantially increased their debt-service ratios. At the same time, the tight monetary policy of the United States and, to a lesser degree, of the rest of the industrialized world caused a recession in the industrialized world. This reduced the volume and value of exports from developing countries. Both effects of tight money served to increase the ratio of debt service as well as the burden of debt service. This combination of effects caused the debt crisis (although Mexico had its own self-induced problems in addition to the global effects).

THE DEBT CRISIS

In the scenario of a global recession and reduced markets for exports from developing countries and of a large overhang of debt and debt service, it was inevitable that debtor nations should face serious economic problems. The growth of the debt-service ratio from 1977 to 1982 (and beyond) is shown in Table 18-1. The faster growth of the debt-service ratio than of the debt ratio is attributable to the rapid increase in nominal interest rates in the developed world. There is no absolute number that serves as a danger signal, but lenders seem to have been unaware of

---

[6] Repaying principal involves an improvement in the international asset position (international net worth) and therefore involves a surplus on current account. Refinancing leaves the amount of indebtedness unchanged.

Table 18-1

DEBT-SERVICE AND DEBT RATIOS OF COUNTRIES WITH RECENT DEBT-SERVICING
PROBLEMS*

	1977	1979	1981	(%) 1982	1983	1984	1985
Debt-service ratio†	22.3	30.2	33.8	41.6	36.2	36.6	38.2
Debt ratio‡	171.7	178.1	194.5	246.0	268.1	256.8	245.8

* Defined as countries that incurred external payments arrears during the period 1981–1983 or rescheduled
their debt during the period 1981–mid-1984.
† Includes only total interest payments and scheduled repayments on long-term debt. (Tacitly assumes
that short-term debt can be rolled over.)
‡ Long-term and short-term debt.

Source: International Monetary Fund, *World Economic Outlook, April 1985* (Washington, D.C., 1985),
pp. 261, 266.

any danger signals prior to the actual cries for rescheduling. The debt-
service ratio of some countries is given in Table 18-2.

If a bank loses money on a bad loan, this is a matter of no great
consequence except to the loan officer who made the loan and the bank's
management and stockholders. The bank will presumably have its own
capital against which such a loss can be charged, and the bank is still
able to operate legitimately as a depositary institution. An epidemic of
large bad loans becomes serious when the bank becomes insolvent and
must close its doors. Under these circumstances, the depositors lose the
liquidity of their deposits temporarily (including any deposits by other
banks), and some large depositors may incur losses. If the closure of a
single bank starts a domino effect and causes other banks to close either
because they incur losses or loans or because depositors start a "run on
the bank," a crisis develops.

A bank must close its doors when it cannot meet depositors' legitimate
demands or when it has exhausted its capital reserves.[7] A bank closure
puts a large strain on the solvency of other banks, particularly large
banks in which many depositors are exposed beyond the limits of deposit
insurance. Widespread, cumulative bank failures institute a financial
crisis of the magnitude that can lead to a depression. It is important,
therefore, for the central banks to be aware of the policies that need to
be followed to preserve the solvency of their own banking systems and
to have agreed-on rules of conduct where international banks are concerned.

The exposure of fourteen major U.S. banks—including Citibank, Bank
of America, and Chase Manhattan—to potentially defaulting loans in
five Latin American countries exceeded the value of the banks' capital

[7] On this matter and others related to the debt crisis, see an extremely valuable paper by John G.
Heimann, "The Effects of Political, Economic and Institutional Developments on International Banks,"
Journal of Banking and Finance, 7 (1983), 615–622.

Table 18-2

DEBT OWED BY CERTAIN DEVELOPING AND EASTERN
EUROPEAN COUNTRIES, JUNE 1982*

Country	Debt ($ billions)	Debt-Service Ratio†	Debt Service Disrupted
Mexico‡	64.4	58.5	Yes
Brazil	55.3	87.1	Yes
Venezuela‡	27.2	26.7	Yes
Argentina	25.3	102.9	Yes
South Korea	20.0	21.1	No
Poland	13.8	N.A.	Yes
Chile	11.8	60.4	Yes
Yugoslavia	10.0	30.3	Yes

* Debt owed to commercial banks of industrialized countries.
† Excludes maturing short-term principal but includes interest on short-term debt. This assumes that short-term debt can be refinanced without difficulty.
‡ Oil exporter.

Source: William R. Cline, *International Debt and the Stability of the World Economy* (Cambridge, Mass.: M.I.T. Press for the Institute for International Economics, 1983), p. 35.

at the end of 1982.[8] Had all of the loans been declared worthless by the bank examiners, there can be no doubt that the United States would have faced a major financial crisis. Clearly, the governments of the nations in which creditor banks were headquartered had a large stake in seeing that the debtor nations continued to "perform" on their debt so that the banks' capital base would not be completely eroded. The answer was to reschedule the debt so that the amount of debt service was within the capacity of the debtor nations.

The key problem here is that the debtors were sovereign nations. As such, they cannot go bankrupt in the traditional sense of the word, which applies to privately owned or incorporated business enterprises. Moreover, when a sovereign government cannot meet its debt-service requirements, the creditor cannot lay hands on the property of the debtor as a means of salvaging some part of the outstanding loan. This is the question of "country risk" in lending to sovereign governments. (In addition to the possibility that the country cannot meet its obligations, there is also the possibility that it will not do so.)

Self-evidently, the banks loaned too much to some sovereign borrowers; the proof is that the borrowers could not meet their commitments. This raises questions as to how the banks could have been so inept. In fact, lending to sovereign governments requires even greater expertise and savoir-faire than lending to large commercial borrowers. One writer sug-

[8] See William R. Cline, *International Debt and the Stability of the World Economy* (Cambridge, Mass.: M.I.T. Press for the Institute for International Economics, 1983), table 6, p. 34.

gested that the lender should be a "Renaissance person": "exceedingly intelligent, a holder of doctorates from respectable institutions in economics, political science, sociology, psychology, and perhaps a few other fields as well, totally objective, with a great deal of common sense."[9] But bankers also made loans with too little information, and not even Renaissance persons can operate effectively if they lack vital data.

Heimann identifies the following key points that we have learned from the crisis:

1. There was too much financing and not enough adjustment by the borrowing economies (though this may have been due, in part, to the very low real rates of interest and the easy access to credit).
2. There was too much lending by commercial banks and not enough by the IMF and other multilateral agencies (implying some slowing of the speed to adjustment to so large a shock was warranted).
3. Banks loaned too much on short term.
4. There was a shortage of accurate information.
5. There is no adequate mechanism to force sovereign borrowers to meet their financial commitments.
6. Lenders should have been more skeptical in their assessments of borrowers' ability to repay and more conservative in forecasting financial and economic trends.[10]

One explanation of the problem is that bankers, in addition to lacking adequate information, focused on the wrong pattern of lending. As long as each borrower's success or failure is deemed to depend on random factors peculiar to the borrower, making many loans (or taking part in many syndicates) reduces the overall risk of the loan portfolio. If borrowers are charged a reasonable risk premium over the base rate plus markup, the bank can afford to have some losses and will still receive an adequate rate of return. The problem arises when all loans go sour at the same time—that is, when the likelihood that one borrower will fail is codetermined with (correlated with) the likelihood that another borrower will fail. Banks can make loans to large numbers of sovereign countries, and if the reason for possible loan default is the ineptness of national economic policy, the risks will not be positively correlated. But if the loans are made to a group of countries that all depend for their ability to service their debt on the prosperity of the industrialized world, lending to sovereign developing countries implies that the likelihood that one borrower will "fail" is, in reality, codetermined with the likelihood that other, similar borrowers will fail. Thus the recession induced by the sudden increase in real rates of interest that started in 1979 turned

[9] Ingo Walter, "Country Risk, Portfolio Decisions, and Regulation in International Bank Lending," *Journal of Banking and Finance*, 5, (1981), 85.
[10] Heimann, "Effects."

ostensibly unrelated loans into correlated loans. What banks had perceived to be a diversified portfolio of loans was, in fact, not diversified because all the borrowers depended for their ability to service their debt on export sales to the industrialized countries. When these countries went into a deep recession in 1982 (after two years of very slow growth), the markets were not available. When the base Eurodollar rate rose (on annual averages) from 8.8 percent in 1978 to 12.1 percent in 1979, to 14.2 percent in 1980, and to 16.8 percent in 1981, the interest cost of debt rose spectacularly.

It is probably also true to say that bank lending officers had little idea of the amount of borrowing that was being done.

The crisis arose because debtor countries borrowed too much and adjusted (to reduce the need for energy imports) too little. Had interest rates risen steadily and gradually with the cost of oil, there would have been a greater incentive for the debtor countries to economize on all imports (including oil). Unfortunately, the level of interest rates was kept very low by the monetary authorities in the United States and other developed countries as they sought to have their own economies accommodate the surge in oil prices as easily as possible. When the second oil-price shock hit the global economy in 1979–1980 and inflation increased sharply, easy money with low real rates of interest could no longer exist. Inflation in the United States, which had declined to 5.8 percent in 1977, increased to 9.6 percent per annum in 1981.[11] It is arguable, but not subject to proof, that the easy, accommodating monetary policy following the 1973–1974 oil-price shock was working quite effectively. The rate of inflation in the industrialized countries was declining, but relatively little had been done to reduce either reliance on imported oil or demand for oil. In other words, the financial crisis of the early 1980s would not have occurred in the absence of the second oil-price shock. Unfortunately, the developing countries, which could least well afford to finance the oil-induced balance-of-payments deficit, did not undertake adjustment measures quickly enough or seriously enough.

Banks have little option but to accommodate demands for debt rescheduling because they do not want the borrower officially to default on the loan (in which event their assets would become officially nonperforming and subject to severe markdowns in value by bank examiners—with the possibility of deposit withdrawals and the threat of insolvency that accompanies large losses). Rescheduling does, however, need more than the commercial banks themselves, and the IMF has played a key role in the negotiations for debt rescheduling. Only the IMF has the power to impose drastic expenditure reductions on sovereign governments because it can impose conditions on its lending.

---

[11] International Monetary Fund, *World Economic Outlook, April 1985* (Washington, D.C., 1985), p. 212.

The banks are hostage to their own past errors. There is an old adage that argues that when a man owes a bank $1,000, the bank "owns" him, but when a man owes the bank $1 million, he "owns" the bank. Banks cannot do anything but help the debtor to recover financially. Banks cannot foreclose on sovereign borrowers. The idea of the bank as hostage applies equally to a large commercial borrower who is in danger of bankruptcy if it is believed that the firm can escape bankruptcy with more resources and more time.

Mexico is a special case. Mexico is the largest third-world debtor (only Brazil comes close; see Table 18-2), but the country is also an oil exporter. "Oil is Mexico's curse and its salvation" was the opening line of a 1985 review of Mexico's economic outlook.[12] Mexico's new-found oil was the reason for the mistaken economic policies of President Lopez Portillo (see the supplement following Chapter 13), who believed that oil would allow Mexico to ignore the effect of domestic inflation on its real exchange rate. Mexican oil reserves also blinded bank lending officers to the danger of default. And Mexico is a special case because the falling price of oil, while it will reduce nominal interest rates, will also reduce Mexico's earnings. There is resentment that the oil, which was to have taken the lead in generating economic development in Mexico, now seems to be earmarked for debt service and repayment while the country languishes in serious recession.

The amount of debt outstanding is still tremendous. The problem has been significantly eased by debt rescheduling, but plenty of cause for concern still remains. However, the financial community has, at a minimum, bought time with which it is able to set its plans should the debtor nations "walk away from their debt." The one threat that makes walking away from the debt unattractive is the probable exclusion of the nation from major capital markets for the foreseeable future.

THE 1985 INITIATIVE

The orthodox description for balance-of-payments deficits is for the International Monetary Fund to make credit available on the condition that the deficit nation take measures to reduce the deficit. The official term for such action is *conditional assistance*. This policy has been pursued by the IMF in the debt crisis. All the debtor nations have tightened their economic belts and instituted measures that were bound to induce a domestic recession. As growth stops and unemployment skyrockets, the volume and value of imports will decrease and the current account will improve. In the context of the debt crisis, the decrease in imports would leave funds available for debt service. International saving will

---

[12] Youssef Ibrahim, "Mexico Suffers Greatly as Oil Prices Decline but Debt Lingers On," *Wall Street Journal*, October 9, 1985, p. 1.

increase and become positive, so that not only will interest payments be met but indebtedness can be reduced. This set of policies would continue until such time as the debt had declined to manageable proportions. These policies imply that exports will not be substantially reduced, although the loss of exports by the creditor nations does have a downward effect on GNP in those nations.

These policies have obvious costs. In economic terms, they increase unemployment; in social terms, they invoke widespread misery and want in the debtor nations and threaten political stability. In the past, economic failures have led developing countries to lose faith in the democratic form of government and to suffer the institution of so-called strong or autocratic governments of the extreme right or the extreme left. At the same time, there is the international political effect of a tendency on the part of the population of the debtor nation to blame the creditor country for their misery, to the detriment of good international relations.

The orthodox prescription has been given the full support of the U.S. government until late in 1985. At the annual meetings of the IMF and the World Bank in Seoul, the Reagan administration proposed a new initiative that stands the orthodoxy on its head. This represents an important change of heart on the part of an essentially conservative administration. The new initiative argues that the debt crisis can best be solved through economic growth in the debtor countries. The World Bank is to make large loans (to be cofinanced by commercial banks) that will allow the debtor nations to resume their precrisis rate of capital formation. If the projects financed by long-term loans under the auspices of the bank are designed to have a large effect on the capacity to export or the need for imports, the existing debt can be repaid on its (new) schedule, and the *relative* burden of the debt will be diminished. Such a policy certainly seems to augur a more humanitarian approach to the solution of the debt crisis (for which the debtor nations cannot be held completely responsible), and it may offer a better long-run hope of a full cure than the belt-tightening measures invoked by the IMF.

The unwillingness of the debtor nations to endure the austerity imposed by orthodoxy may have been the catalyst that led to the new initiative. It is possible that the Reagan administration feared the political implications and repercussions of the austerity. Fidel Castro was urging the debtor countries openly to declare default on their existing debt and, in so doing, struck a popular and sympathetic frequency in Latin America. The president of Peru announced that his country's debt service would be limited to 10 percent of export earnings.

The new initiative involves a smaller role for the IMF and a larger one for the World Bank. The World Bank will make large loans that are to be supported by the governments of the developed world and cofinanced by private banks. These loans will reintroduce economic growth; by directing the growth toward projects that save foreign exchange, the

same debt-service burden will constitute a smaller part of national income
and of foreign exchange earnings. The principle is that a growing country
will be able to increase both its total saving and its international saving
(both measured in dollars). There will be a period before the growth
effects take hold, and the needs of the debtor nations for financing during
that period will be made available.

The success of the new strategy rests on two premises. Both conditions
will not be met automatically.

1. It is assumed that creditor banks will increase their loans to the
debtor nations either by rescheduling the debt for longer maturities or
by adding, quasi-automatically, any shortfall of interest directly to the
outstanding indebtedness. This assumption will not be willingly accepted
by commercial banks. The main international banks already have more
doubtful loans on their books than they can justify either to their shareholders or to the Federal Deposit Insurance Corporation and the bank
examiners. The so-called regional banks outside of the main money centers
became involved in the lending to developing countries rather passively
by accepting the invitations of the major banks to take part in syndicated
loans. (Once bitten, twice shy!)

The U.S. government has significant leverage on these banks, and
the cooperation of these banks can probably be relied on (after much
grumbling). In fact, there is no reason why the creditor banks should
escape totally from the mistakes of overlending to the debtor nations. As
one official spokesperson described the problem: "There is plenty of blame
to be shared by central banks, commercial banks, and debtor governments." Even so, it may be necessary for governments to underwrite a
guarantee for any such loans—possibly through the World Bank.

2. It must be possible for debtor nations to increase their earnings
of foreign exchange by increasing their exports to those nations whose
currencies can be used to pay debt service (in practice, the industrialized
countries). Given the current depth of protectionist sentiment in the
industrialized countries, this requirement will not be met automatically.
In the United States, the Reagan administration faces severe opposition
to the continuation of a free trade stance when many surplus nations
are seen to be protecting their own markets. In the U.S. Congress in
1985, many protectionist bills were introduced, among them one proposing
that quotas be instituted on imports from countries that were running
overall surpluses on their current accounts. The Reagan administration
sought to fight this protectionist surge by taking the lead in the inauguration of a new round of multilateral trade negotiations under the auspices
of the GATT (see Chapter 8).

What of the new initiative? Certainly, it represents an improvement
over the Draconian belt-tightening measures of orthodoxy. Curing past
policy errors by invoking deep recessions is not likely to enhance the

Third World's willingness to accept free enterprise economic policies (despite their proven efficacy relative to the more severe kinds of planning used in communist countries). If democracy and free enterprise or mixed economic systems are at all related, anything that denigrates the free enterprise system will also inhibit democratic regimes in the Third World.

The new initiatives will have one positive effect that may not be immediately apparent. It is very probable that the emphasis on economic growth and the gradual reduction in external indebtedness will lead the flow of direct investment in the debtor countries to resume. These flows carry with them not only capital and technology but also foreign linkages to potential export markets.

If the existing, relatively liberal international trading system cannot be maintained, the debt crisis requires that any protective legislation be discriminatory. The type of discrimination (by global and bilateral current-account balances) included in the congressional bill just described is the kind of protection that will permit the resolution of the debt crisis to be promoted at the same time that home industry is afforded some relief. The problem of the debt crisis indicates the need for financing to be made available to the debt-ridden countries if the industrialized world does choose to slow the rate at which it accepts labor-intensive imports.

The new initiative has many positive features. It will allow the debtor countries to regain some dynamism in their economies and makes specific recommendations as to the financing of the external debt service during the years before the growth takes effect. The emphasis is explicitly on greater reliance on private enterprise (in keeping with President Reagan's well known economic values), and in the context of many of the debtor countries, this emphasis is not misplaced. Where nationalized industries are political necessities, it is desirable that they be made to operate more as private profit-seeking corporations and that politicians keep their hands off the operating procedures except insofar as they represent the shareholders and punish nonperforming executives.

The debt crisis is not amenable to quick or easy resolution. Nor is it clear that the original belt-tightening measures were capable of resolving the crisis at all. They were more likely to invoke political crisis in Latin America. The new initiative does offer some hope. It may not be enough and may need to be supplemented by some unilateral transfers (aid). There seems, a priori, no reason why this should not involve some role for the creditor banks.

SUMMARY

The development of the Eurodollar market and the expansion of commercial banks from essentially national into international financial systems have contributed to the integration of the world's capital market. This integrated capital market, and the Eurodollar market in particular, was a valuable mechanism in allowing the world to finance the huge increase in import bills caused by the oil-price shocks. Unfortunately, it was all too easy for both developed and developing countries to finance their deficits, and very little was done to reduce the dependence on high-priced oil. The second oil-price shock precipitated a crisis when the United States invoked highly restrictive monetary policy and threw the world into a deep recession. The sudden increase in interest rates and in debt service coupled with a recession in their major markets caused the major borrowers to be unable to service their outstanding debt. The great danger of the debt crisis was the possibility that by making major commercial banks insolvent, it would trigger a financial crisis reminiscent of the early 1930s. By careful cooperation among the IMF, the creditor banks and their governments, and the debtor countries, the crisis was eased temporarily. During this period, the world's central banks came to agreements regarding their conduct to prevent a global financial crisis in the event of stark default by the large debtor nations. The social costs of the belt-tightening policies invoked by the IMF have strained the political stability of democratic governments in many debtor nations. Possibly because of the political implications, the Reagan administration proposed a new approach to the problem that would reduce the social costs in debtor countries but faces two serious impediments: the need to enlist the aid of creditor banks to increase their exposure to debtor countries and the protectionist sentiment that was widespread in the industrialized world. To the extent that the price of oil is trending downward and will trigger a steady reduction in nominal interest rates, the difficulties facing the new initiative will be eased.

Bibliography

Cline, William R. *International Debt and the Stability of the World Economy.* Cambridge, Mass.: M.I.T. Press for the Institute for International Economics, 1983.

Gray, Jean M., and Gray, H. Peter. "The Multinational Bank: A Financial MNC?" *Journal of Banking and Finance,* 5 (1981), 33–63.

Heimann, John G. "The Effect of Political, Economic and Institutional Development on International Banks." *Journal of Banking and Finance,* 7 (1983), 615–622.

Khoury, Sarkis J. "Sovereign Debt: A Critical Look at the Causes and the Nature of the Problem." *South Carolina Essays in International Business,* 5 (July 1985).

Walter, Ingo. "Country Risk, Portfolio Decisions, and Regulation in International Bank Lending." *Journal of Banking and Finance,* 5 (1981), 77–92.

Questions and Problems

Questions

1. Why was the existence of the Eurodollar market important in 1974 and 1975?

2. How can the Eurodollar market pay more on deposits *and* lend for less than New York banks?
3. Describe the new initiative of the Reagan administration. What are its positive features?
4. How can developing-country debt cause serious disruption in American financial markets?
5. Will the developing countries ever be out of debt? If not, what level of debt should they aim for?
6. Why would banks lend to sovereign borrowers when they have so little claim on assets?

Problems

1. Examine the data on a major U.S. bank to ascertain:
   a. Its capital
   b. Its exposure to loans in developing countries
   c. Its exposure to loans to the five major Latin American debtors: Brazil, Mexico, Chile, Argentina, and Venezuela
   (Annual Reports of the bank and its report to the Securities and Exchange Commission are good sources.)
2. Trace the expansion of a major U.S. bank to discover the time path of its expansion into foreign countries. For the last twenty years, at five-year intervals, list the number of branches, the number of countries in which the bank has subsidiaries or branches, and the amount of deposits.
3. What are the current deposit rates and loan rates in the Eurodollar market? (See *Euromoney*.)
4. Examine Mexico's balance of payments over the past five years to see how much indebtedness has been reduced. Also examine the rate of change in gross national or gross domestic product. (This problem can be applied to all major debtor countries.)

Mexico's Stop-and-Go Road to Economic Prosperity

JOSEPH G. KVASNICKA

In mid-July [1985], after several months of growing problems in the country's international economic relations, the Mexican government announced a series of measures designed to arrest the deepening crisis. The measures included a devaluation of the peso, substantial reduction in government expenditures, and a tightening of import restrictions. It is expected that the measures will gradually improve the country's balance-of-payments position, reduce its inflation, and thus relieve the growing concerns about its financial integrity among its international creditors, to whom Mexico owes close to $100 billion.

However, while placating the international financial community, and thereby assuring Mexico of a continuous flow of desperately needed foreign credits, the measures may be expected to have a profound impact on Mexico's domestic conditions, slowing its economic growth, and further increasing its already high unemployment. The measures thus represent yet another delicate balancing act between domestic and international economic considerations on the politically treacherous road to recovery from the economic crisis that hit Mexico in mid-1982.

THE ROAD TO CRISIS Mexico's current financial and economic problems are the culumination of developments that began several years ago, following the discovery of vast oil resources in 1977. With a vision of untold riches, the Mexican government embarked on free-spending policies aimed at rapid economic development, and at accelerating the rise in the country's overall standard of living. Year after year, expenditures exceeded revenues, and the government's budget showed a continually larger deficit. The financing requirements of the government's deficit added to the already booming demand for the country's meager supply of domestic capital resources. Interest rates, the "price" of credit, began to rise rapidly.

To moderate the increase and thus to keep the expansion going, the Central Bank accelerated its monetization of the government's debt, i.e., purchasing government securities issued to finance the debt by newly created money. The bank's claims on the government rose from 17 billion pesos in 1970, to 134 billion in 1976, and to 2.1 trillion in 1982.

In addition to "printing press" financing of its deficit, the government turned to foreign sources. A growing portion of the deficit was financed by borrowing abroad. The public foreign debt rose from about $8 billion in 1974, to over $60 billion by early 1982. Private borrowing abroad by Mexican banks, businesses, and individuals also rose sharply over the period. By 1982, the total private foreign debt outstanding exceeded $20 billion.

The necessary byproduct of the free-spending ways was rising inflation. During the 1960s, prices were rising at only 3½ percent annually, but in the 1970s, the annual rate increased to 20 percent; by 1981, inflation was running at close to 30 percent. The rising inflation began to sap Mexico's economic vitality, particularly as the government failed to take it into consideration in formulation of its policies with respect to the exchange rate of the peso. For six years, through February 1982, the Mexican government kept the exchange rate of the peso fixed despite the widening differential between Mexican and world prices. As a result, Mexican products became "overpriced" on the world markets, while foreign products became relatively cheap in Mexico. This discouraged exports and encouraged imports. Between 1977 and 1981, Mexico's merchandise imports grew by 45 percent per annum, while non-oil exports increased hardly at all. As a result, Mexico's trade account continued to deteriorate despite rising oil revenues.

The onset of worldwide recession in 1981, combined with substantial weakening of oil prices and rising interest rates, provided the final blow. Declining oil revenue and soaring interest payments on Mexico's huge international debt led to a sharp deterioration in the country's balance-of-payments position. The country was not generating enough foreign revenues to finance its international debt. In a belated effort to correct the growing deficit, the government devalued the peso from 26.5 to 46 to the dollar in February 1982. . . . However, the devaluation was perceived by the market as being insufficient, and the anticipation of further devaluation triggered a flight of speculative capital. By August 1982, the Mexican authorities were faced with dwindling foreign exchange earnings, depleted international reserves, and a huge amount of maturing international debt. In this crisis atmosphere, the peso was "set afloat" . . . in a last ditch effort to stop further deterioration. But the action came too late. The government was unable to meet its scheduled foreign debt payments and had to turn to the international community for financial help to avert a default on its commitments.

STARTING ON THE ROAD TO RECOVERY To shore up the situation, and to help with immediate financial needs, the central banks of several industrial countries (including the United States) extended a $1.85 billion loan to the Mexican government, and the U.S. government provided an additional $1 billion in advance payments for Mexican crude oil. At the same time, the Mexican government approached the IMF with a request for a loan, and began to negotiate an orderly postponement and restructuring of its debt payments to foreign creditors.

In order to qualify for a loan from the IMF, the government had to commit itself to an "austerity program." The primary emphasis of the program was on drastic cuts in public spending as a means of reducing the country's inflation. Reluctantly, but with political courage and determination, the government embarked on a belt-tightening program. Large numbers of construction projects for new housing, roads, and ports were stopped, and public subsidies on food, fuel, and rents for the poor were terminated or drastically reduced. The austerity measures, combined with a worldwide slowdown in economic activities, plunged the Mexican economy into a deep recession. After growing at over 8 percent annually between 1978 and 1981], Mexico's real GNP declined by one-half percent in 1982, and by 4.7 percent in 1983. Unemployment soared, and Mexico's standard of living declined dramatically.

Painful as they were domestically, the drastic measures, with some help from developments abroad, produced internationally desirable results. With the depressed domestic conditions reducing the demand for imports, and the pickup of activities in the United States boosting the demand for Mexico's exports, the trade deficit disappeared. In 1983, Mexico recorded a $13 billion surplus in its international trade. As a result, the country's international reserves, virtually depleted in 1982, were replenished and reached a comfortable level of over $7 billion by late 1984. In 1984, improvements continued. Inflation declined, from 100 per-

Figure 18-A
MEXICO'S EXTERNAL
DEBT (in billions of
dollars)

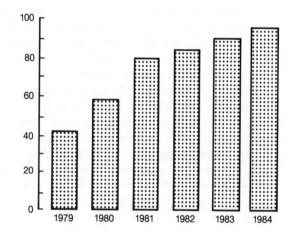

cent in 1982, to 81 percent in 1983, to 65 percent in 1984. Economic activity bounced back from a decline in 1982 and 1983, to a strong 5 percent growth in 1984. The country's domestic standard of living began to rise again.

The improving conditions set the stage for a successful completion of debt rescheduling negotiations with the creditor banks. Encouraged by Mexico's progress on both the domestic and international economic fronts, the banks became more receptive to granting concessions. In September 1984, an agreement in principle was reached between the government and 530 foreign banks concerning rescheduling of payments for some $49 billion of public foreign debt. Interest rates charged by banks were reduced, and the repayment period stretched out to ease the repayment burden. In the view of many observers, Mexico became a shining example of how the international debt crisis, plaguing so many other developing countries in Latin America and elsewhere, can be resolved.

SOME SETBACKS Mexico's spectacular road to recovery began to turn slippery in 1985, underscoring the delicate balance between growth, inflation, and the country's international accounts. The emerging problems were reminiscent of the sequence of events that had plunged Mexico into crisis in 1982. With the resumption of growth, inflation began to accelerate, and the country's trade account to deteriorate. During the first half of 1985, imports increased 40 percent under the impetus of the advancing domestic economy, while non-oil exports were down 15 percent. With total exports down and imports up, Mexico's trade surplus dropped from $7.5 billion during the first half of 1984, to $3.9 billion during the same period in 1985. A deficit loomed as a distinct possibility in the near future.

The trade account problems were again being exacerbated by the government's administration of its exchange rate system.[1] Since 1982, the government has been following a policy of daily adjustment in the official peso/dollar exchange rates. However, the approaching election (to be held in early July) apparently made the government reluctant to match the devaluation to the accelerating inflation, because it feared political discontent caused by a cut in the electorate's standard of living. The result was an increasingly over-valued peso that was encouraging imports and discouraging non-oil exports. The over-valuation also opened a gap be-

---

[1] Mexico's two-tiered exchange rate system was established in August 1982 as part of the measures to deal with the debt crisis. It consists of so called Free Rate and a Controlled Rate. The Free Rate is applied to "non-essential" international transactions (such as the tourist expenditures), and has been set daily to reflect free market forces of supply and demand. The Controlled Rate is applied to government-authorized international transactions, including payments of interest and principal on foreign debt contracted before August 1982, and to payments for imports of essential materials and parts needed to maintain economic activities. Exporters are also required to convert all proceeds of their foreign sales into pesos at this rate. About 85 percent of Mexico's international transactions are being financed at this rate.

tween the officially maintained exchange rate and the "black market" (essentially a free market-determined) rate, [which] led to a resumption of capital flight from Mexico.

Finally, the continued weakening of the world oil prices added to Mexico's growing problems by cutting into government revenues. Nearly 45 percent of total government revenue is derived from oil exports. With oil income down, the budget deficit again began to rise, jeopardizing the achievement of the IMF-imposed goal of deficit reduction. This raised doubts about the continuation of IMF's financial support, and thus threatened the flow of new international credits needed for the day-to-day functioning of the Mexican economy.

MID-COURSE CORRECTIONS Dealing with these potentially threatening developments implied some domestic economic sacrifices. However, faced with mid-year elections, the government appeared to hesitate. Only after the election did the government act. Between July 10 and July 20, it announced a series of measures which included:

—Establishing a free float for the previously government-administered "free exchange rate."
—16.7 percent devaluation of the official "controlled rate" and the establishment of "regulated" float effective August 5.
—Elimination of import permits for goods amounting to about 37 percent of the country's total imports, and a substitution of a sliding tariff scale ranging from 0 percent to 50 percent in proportion to the "value added" to the imported product.
—Reduction in government expenditures by $410 million in 1985 (out of a budget of $51 billion), and a "much greater," as yet unspecified reduction, in 1986.

The steps taken by the government may certainly be viewed as "proper" from the viewpoint of Mexico's international obligations. The devaluation of the official rate will discourage imports and encourage exports, leading to an improvement in the country's trade account. A larger trade surplus will, of course, mean larger foreign exchange earnings; this will improve Mexico's capacity to make payments on its foreign debt. The floating of the "free rate" will further strengthen this impact. In addition, the floating will eliminate the frequent disparity between the free rate and the black market "super-free rate" and thus, hopefully, eliminate the arbitrage and frequent capital flights that have been draining Mexico's international reserves. The measures affecting imports will streamline the country's import restraint system, and will also contribute to the improvements in the trade account by retarding imports. Finally, the cutbacks in government expenditures will improve the government's budgetary position, and thus satisfy a condition for continued financial support by the International Monetary Fund.

There is, however, the "other side" to the measures—their domestic impact. The anticipated improvement in the trade account will be actually achieved through a reduction in the international purchasing power of the Mexican consumers—effectively a reduction in their standard of living. Similarly, the cutbacks in government expenditures will mean the release from government employment of an estimated 50,000 workers. Many of these will undoubtedly add to the already very high number of unemployed in Mexico, further aggravating the social climate in the country.

And so, it appears that once more, Mexico's tightrope balancing act—in which the government has been trying to satisfy, on one hand, the immediate economic aspirations of its people (on whose support it depends for its continued political existence), and on the other, the demands of the international financial community (on whose financial resources it depends for Mexico's long-term growth and prosperity)—is leaning toward sacrificing the domestic over the international goals. Hopefully, the balancing maneuvers taken by the government recently will again succeed in correcting the deteriorating international trends without seriously aggravating the socio-political climate in Mexico. A growing number of observers are, however, skeptical. They feel that the stop-and-go pendulum of Mexico's economic policies—and of other debtor countries that have been following essentially the same road—has attached to it a ratcheted wheel that tightens the nation's social fabric one more notch at each swing; inevitably a breaking point will be reached, with possibly far-reaching social and political consequences.

It is this growing danger that underscores the urgency for the development of a more broadly based approach to the solution of the international debt problem. While it may be true that many of the problems confronting Mexico—as well as other debtor nations—today are at least in part the outcome of economic policy lapses of their governments during the eu-

Figure 18-B
MEXICO'S REAL GNP
(% change)

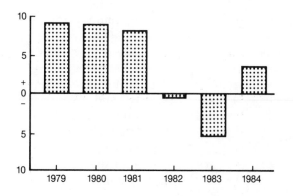

phoric Seventies, many observers believe that at least some of the blame must be shared by the creditor banks worldwide for their lack of prudence and foresight in their "free-lending" sprees of the past decade. They too, the observers feel, must now be ready to assume a greater burden in easing the looming socio-political crisis in debtor nations. And finally, the governments of the major industrial countries, who cannot but be vitally interested in the ultimate political outcome of the evolving events, must stand ready to extend a helping hand where necessary. Only such a broadly based, tripartite approach, many observers believe, will lead to the ultimate resolution of the debt crisis in Mexico.

MULTINATIONAL CORPORATIONS

Multinational corporations are a new form of economic organization that has developed very quickly in the last quarter century. These corporations, which possess the managerial techniques to integrate production and sales on a global scale, have effectively transformed the way in which goods and services are exchanged among nations. They are not the only cause of the huge increase in interdependence in the world, but they are probably the single main cause.

There has been great discussion of their mechanics and of their effect: To what do they owe their ability to produce and sell globally? Are they beneficial for the national economies? In fact, they comprise such a wide range of types of firms and industries and are located in so many countries of widely differing characteristics that a simple answer is not possible.

19

Internationally Mobile Factors of Production: The Multinational Corporation

To this point, this book has adopted David Ricardo's assumption that factors of production can move freely within nations but cannot move between nations. This is a sensible simplification for two reasons. First, it is certainly easier for factors to move internally than internationally, and there can be severe impediments to the international movement of factors. Second, the theory of international trade is much more comprehensible with the assumption of international immobility of factors of production, and the effect of internationally mobile factors can be more sensibly treated as an appendage to the theory developed in earlier chapters. Nonetheless, it is self-evident that factors of production have and do move internationally. During the colonial eras, large amounts of capital (loans) were made from the metropolitan country to its colonies. Since World War II, the heritage of the colonial era is the freedom of movement of people from erstwhile colonies to the erstwhile mother country; consequently, Great Britain has many workers from India, Pakistan, Africa, and the Caribbean and France many from northern and central Africa.

In this modern era, the multinational corporation has become extremely important in facilitating the international movement of factors of production. This type of international factor migration is different from the more general movement of labor and capital and implies *operating control* over the factors in the foreign country.

THE INTERNATIONAL MOVEMENT OF
GENERAL FACTORS OF PRODUCTION

This section is concerned with those factors of production that move from one nation to another at their own volition (without any part being played by an MNC). This kind of factor movement can be seen as responding to expected economic gains in excess of any perceived costs (economic or noneconomic). The section considers the problem first in terms of people (labor), then in terms of capital, and finally in terms of skilled workers (human capital).

It is obvious that workers have moved in the past and are still doing so today. During the seventeenth and eighteenth centuries, black Africans were brought to the Western Hemisphere by force to work in the labor-intensive industries of sugar production in the Caribbean and cotton in the southern United States. In the nineteenth century, thousands of Europeans came through Ellis Island in New York in search of a better life in the United States. Nowadays, relatively unskilled workers move from Tunisia and Algeria to France, from India and Jamaica to Great Britain, from Pakistan and Jordan to Saudi Arabia. The EEC has proved a magnet for workers from Mediterranean countries such as Greece, Spain, and Yugoslavia, but this movement has slowed since the onset of the recession of the 1980s. In the United States, there are many immigrants (legal and illegal) from Mexico and the Caribbean islands (Jamaica, Haiti).

The best way to understand the process of migration is as one instigated by hopes of economic betterment (sometimes conceived of in terms of the welfare of the children rather than the adult migrants). The disparity between the actual standard of living and the hoped-for one represents the motivation. Against this gain, there are costs and impediments. There is the anguish of leaving home and family and the uncertainty of the reception in the foreign country. Language barriers may exist, but if friends are already in the country of in-migration, information about job opportunities (and even financial help) can be provided. The costs of physically moving long distances are an obvious impediment, especially if the migrant is poor. Frequently nations put controls on in-migration of (low-skilled) workers.[1] Barriers to migration resemble barriers to the movement of goods. Usually, countries impose quotas on in-migrants, sometimes outright prohibitions. The pull and tug of the political process is also much the same as for tariffs. Workers in developed nations recognize the potential damage that in-migrants may do to their wage rates and bargaining power and generally oppose freedom of in-migrants.

Capital also moves internationally. When a rich country (or a resident

---

[1] The process is frequently different for skilled workers whose migration is desired by the country of in-migration and discouraged by the country of out-migration. This will be discussed in detail shortly.

of one) acquires an asset in a foreign country, such as a bond, the asset becomes part of the portfolio of assets, and the process is called *portfolio investment*. The presumption is that the investor does not have operating control over the use to which the funds will be put. This type of investment can be effected by means of the purchase of a bond, the acquisition of a bank loan, or of shares in a foreign corporation. The whole process is to be distinguished from the acquisition of assets abroad by an MNC (which has operating control): This latter process is called *foreign direct investment*.

People will lend to foreigners rather than domestic borrowers because they expect to get a higher return on their investment. Just as the motivation for labor to move internationally is a higher rate of return, so too it is with capital. Generally, capital flows from rich (capital-plentiful) countries to poor countries. The rate of return on capital will tend to be higher in capital-scarce countries, and it pays developing (poorer) nations to borrow because this allows them to increase their rate of capital formation (as well as to acquire noncompetitive goods from abroad). The additional capital formation will yield a sufficient return to service the debt (pay the interest and amortize the principal) out of the net value added by the investment. Of course, there are other risks involved, which means that the difference between the rate of interest (or return) available at home and the rate of interest earned abroad is not all extra return. There is the risk of war or of financial collapse abroad, or, if the loan is made to a foreign government, it may simply refuse to pay.

A loan from abroad allows a country to run a deficit on its current balance of payments—to import more than it exports. The additional imports can be used for capital formation. When the interest and principal are being paid and repaid, the debtor country must earn foreign exchange by the sale of exports for these purposes as well as for imports.

The process of international factor migration fits in easily with the factor-proportions theory of international trade. International trade tended to equalize the relative rates of return to factors of production as the capital-scarce country imported goods that embodied large amounts of capital and eased the shortage of that factor; similarly, capital-rich countries tend to import goods with a large content of labor (labor-intensive goods). Trade had the effect of easing the shortage of the scarce factor and reducing its relative share of national income. The international migration of factors of production accomplishes much the same effect. In-migration of labor makes labor relatively more plentiful and tends to reduce the wage rate; similarly, foreign investment makes capital less scarce abroad (and more scarce at home), causing the rate of return on capital to be lowered abroad and boosted at home. This effect of migration can be seen in terms of Figure 19-1, which shows how the movement of labor between two nations tends to equalize the wage. The total labor force in the two countries is measured along the horizontal axis (XY).

The schedule MPL_I measured from the left-hand vertical axis shows the marginal productivity of labor in Country I. Because Country I is relatively rich, the curve has a higher intercept than the MPL_{II} curve, which is drawn "leftward" from the right-hand vertical axis. The wage in each country is determined by the intersection of the individual country's supply of labor and the appropriate MPL schedule (W_I and W_{II}). The work force in Country I is XO and in II, OY. Labor in Country II has an incentive to migrate to Country I in search of higher wages, and as workers migrate, OS shifts to the right to identify the new division of the total labor force. Given that there are some "natural" impediments, migration will not carry on until A, when wages would be equal in both countries, but will stop short of that at $O'S'$, where the wage in Country I has fallen (to W_I') and the wage in Country II has risen to W_{II}'. (Note that because the two MPL schedules have not shifted, capital is deemed not to have relocated between the two countries.)

Consider what migration of both capital and labor means for the simple factor-proportions (H-O) theory of international trade. Migration of the plentiful factor to the other country tends to reduce the difference in relative factor endowments and to reduce the difference in the returns earned by both factors in the two countries. This can be seen by reference to Figure 4-2 in Chapter 4. In that figure, Country I is capital-rich and has a production possibility curve that denotes a comparative advantage in autarky in the capital-intensive good (good A). Country II has an autarkic comparative advantage in good B. Now let labor migrate from Country II to Country I in search of the higher wage rate available there and capital migrate from Country I to Country II in search of higher rates of return. Country I's comparative advantage in good A will diminish as its production possibility curve becomes more symmetrical or circular; similarly, Country II's production possibility curve will change shape, losing length and gaining height (reducing its comparative advantage in good B). In the absence of impediments to factor movements, the process would continue until relative factor intensities (and relative rates of return) were identical in both countries, and in terms of the simple H-O model, *no international trade would take place.*[2] The production possibility curves would be identical, and with the (assumed) identity of tastes, relative prices would be equal in autarky.

In fact, there are barriers to the international migration of factors of production, so even in a simple two-factor model, trade would never be totally eliminated. Probably, some minimum improvement in the standard of living is needed before people will emigrate, and that fact, reinforced by the probable existence of quotas on in-migration, will prevent wage rates from ever becoming equal. Capital loaned abroad must always incur

[2] The simple H-O model implies simply two homogeneous factors. The existence of immobile natural resources will ensure that some trade will always take place (in noncompetitive goods).

Figure 19-1

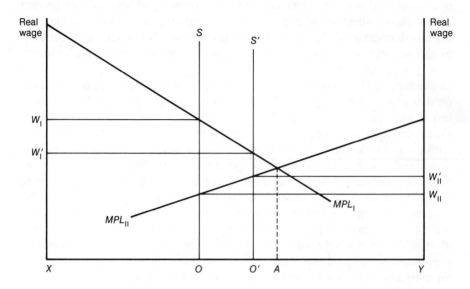

WAGE DIFFERENCES AND THE MIGRATION OF LABOR

risks, so rates of interest can never be exactly the same in both countries. But the bigger the barriers to trade in goods and services, the greater the incentive for international migration (and vice versa). (For capital movements, this becomes more apparent for multinational corporations, which tend to establish foreign subsidiaries when the local—which is to say, foreign—market is protected by tariffs and quotas.)

Now let us complicate the analysis slightly by introducing the other three factors of production in order to see how they affect the conclusion that factor migration will substitute for international trade. In the first place, land cannot move internationally (the spoils of war excepted). Absolutely noncompetitive imports will not be eliminated by factor migration (nor gap fillers when the source of their noncompetitiveness is a specific type of land). Human capital can move. Skilled workers can migrate and will do so if the difference in the standard of living warrants. Skilled workers are more likely to have knowledge of foreign job opportunities and are, proportionately, more likely to move than sheer unskilled labor. Technology can also move internationally. Usually, technology is transferred by means of investment by an MNC, but it can move by means of a simple leasing of a patent in return for payment of royalties. If technology moves (in either way), technological noncompetitive imports can be eliminated.

The movement of human capital has received a great deal of attention in developing nations, where there is a tendency to argue that the loss of skilled workers is a greater impediment to economic development than the benefits that accrue from having students receive professional training in advanced countries. This is the so-called *brain drain*. To send a student to a developed country for professional (or university) training is a benefit to the developing country *if* the student returns home and applies the acquired knowledge in the home country. But many students stay on in the country of education and never return home. This is understandable. Frequently, the standard of living to which they can aspire is higher in the advanced country, and they have already satisfied its professional qualifications. Not only does the developing country lose a skilled worker, but it also loses an intelligent and educated citizen, and if one believes that intelligence is inherited, the developing country is also tending to suffer a reduction in the intelligence of its citizenry (however imperfectly measured) over time.[3] The whole question of the brain drain is a very difficult problem. Some people argue that students who stay abroad should be taxed in some way for the benefit of their country of origin, but the problems of enforcement are likely to prove overwhelming. Most developing nations insist on repayment of any support given during the period of study in the developed country. Some developed countries recognize the problem and prohibit students from abroad from having employment for more than one or two postdegree years, but there are always loopholes. A cynic might even think that for every regulation there is a corresponding loophole, if the individual can only find it.

Skilled workers also move among the developed nations. This movement hardly constitutes a brain drain of serious proportions since the shortage of human capital is much smaller in developed countries. The most frequent type of migration of skilled workers comes in response to wide salary differences in a particular profession. Many medical doctors in the United States have received their training abroad. Often the source of the gain for the immigrating medical doctors is a difference in the costs of medical education in the United States and abroad. In Great Britain, where medical training was paid for by the government (including a living allowance for the student), the gain to migration was substantial and increased with the level of qualifications of the medical practitioner.[4] Since that study was performed, Great Britain has imposed exit taxes on emigrating medical doctors who have not served in the British health system for a given number of years.

Other types of factor movement can also generate payments: Leased technological know-how involves payment of a royalty to the owner of the technology. The problem is more complex when people have moved. Then it becomes necessary to distinguish between temporary movements and permanent movements. People working abroad on a temporary basis (Yugoslav, Turkish, and Greek workers in Germany, for example) usually

---

[3] There is considerable disagreement over the degree to which genetic and environmental factors determine intelligence. This is the key to the movie *Trading Places* (very funny!).

[4] Samuel Levy, *Some Aspects of the International Migration of Human Capital: The Case of British Physicians*, doctoral dissertation (Detroit: Wayne State University, 1969).

try to save as much money as they can and often send money home to families who have not accompanied them. Thus the in-migration of labor involves an outpayment of foreign exchange. For some recipient nations, this can be very important. There are severe difficulties in measurement because many workers try to avoid declaring their wealth, but in Pakistan in 1983 remittances from workers abroad (mostly in the Persian Gulf) exceeded the total value of Pakistani merchandise exports by $200 million. Workers who migrate to stay and whose families move with them seldom send much money home.

To sum up, factors of production do move internationally in response to economic incentives and are impeded by both natural and artificial barriers. To the extent that the factors move, they tend to reduce the basis for trade in competitive goods and in technological noncompetitive imports. But factors seldom move to the degree necessary to affect seriously the pattern and flow of international trade as it was explained in Chapters 4 and 5. In one way, the migration of factors does not have an important or potentially important effect in terms of the foreign exchange it generates for the source countries. Frequently, as in the case of Pakistan and some of the eastern Mediterranean and Adriatic nations (Greece, Turkey, and Yugoslavia), the foreign exchange earned by workers abroad would be very difficult to replace by increased sale of exports.

THE MULTINATIONAL CORPORATION

A multinational corporation (MNC) exists when several (at least three) production units are owned *and* controlled by a single management and are located in different countries. This definition excludes corporations that produce in one country and control only marketing and distribution subsidiaries in other countries, but such firms are rare. Normally, corporations with production plants in different countries will also have some marketing and distribution subsidiaries as well. The essence of an MNC is *control*. Clearly, if the parent corporation owns 100 percent of the equity of the subsidiary, it has control, but when the share of the equity is reduced below 50 percent, the issue of control becomes less clear-cut. This factor becomes important when some host governments, particularly in developing countries, require that foreign subsidiaries be owned to at least 51 percent by their nationals (the MNC's stake is limited to 49 percent or less). Almost invariably, the multinational retains operating control—usually through separate agreements that manage to divorce control from outright ownership.[5] One of the features of the surge of multinational development since the mid-1950s has been the great techno-

---

[5] See R. Hal Mason, "A Comment on Professor Kojima's 'Japanese Type versus American Type' of Technology Transfer," *Hitotsubashi Journal of Economics*, 20 (February 1980), 42–52. These might be managerial agreements whereby the subsidiary purchases managerial services from the parent or supply contracts granting the parent a monopoly on the supply of technically advanced goods.

logical advance in communications technology and in management technology, both of which allow parent companies to exercise more and better control over a family of subsidiary units. It is not possible to set a benchmark of equity ownership at which control exists. Most long-established U.S. MNCs have control by virtue of dominating equity holdings. In contrast, the modern tendency is for more "joint ventures" in which local firms and the multinational each own roughly half of the equity. This new pattern is very typical of Japanese foreign direct investment (where "direct" means involvement in control of operations) and to a lesser degree of new U.S. MNCs. For the purposes of reporting data on MNCs, the U.S. Department of Commerce uses the following definition: all foreign business organizations in which a U.S. entity owns an interest of 10 percent or more and/or those in which 50 percent or more of the voting stock is owned by U.S. residents even though no single U.S. group owns as much as 10 percent.

How important are MNCs? According to the data in Table 19-1, they owned assets in countries other than their home or source country in 1976 in the amount of $287.2 billion. The revenues (but not the value added) of multinationals surpass the GNP of many small or less developed countries. Table 19-1 shows the growth of foreign assets held by the MNCs of different countries. What is immediately apparent is the domi-

Table 19-1

STOCK OF DIRECT INVESTMENT BY MAJOR COUNTRY OF ORIGIN

Country of Origin	Value ($ billion)		Share (% of total)	
	1967	1976	1967	1976
United States	56.6	137.2	53.8	47.6
United Kingdom	17.5	32.1	16.6	11.2
West Germany	3.0	19.9	2.8	6.9
Japan*	1.5	19.4	1.4	6.7
Switzerland	5.0	18.6	4.8	6.5
France	6.0	11.9	5.7	4.1
Canada	3.7	11.1	3.5	3.9
Netherlands	2.2	9.8	2.1	3.4
Sweden	1.7	5.0	1.6	1.7
Belgium and Luxembourg	2.0	3.6	1.9	1.2
Italy	2.1	2.9	2.0	1.0
Subtotal	101.3	270.4	96.2	94.2
All other	4.0	16.8	3.8	5.8
Total	105.3	287.2	100.0	100.0

* Fiscal year beginning April 1 of year indicated; all others are year-end figures.

Source: Data from U.N. Economic and Social Council, *Transnational Corporations in World Development,* Commission on Transnational Corporations, 4th Session, E/C 10/38, table III-32.

nance of the developed or industrialized countries as countries of origin, particularly of the United States and the United Kingdom in 1967. Since then, the share of these two countries has been eroded by the multinationalization and growth of large corporations from other important manufacturing countries, particulary West Germany and Japan. Much of the ownership of these foreign assets of different nationalities is concentrated in relatively few MNCs: About 300 corporations accounted for 70 percent of U.S. foreign direct investment, and 82 firms accounted for 70 percent of West Germany's stock of direct investment abroad. Unfortunately, these numbers are dated but the trend for greater rates of growth of foreign direct investment by German and Japanese countries continues and the share of U.S. corporations continues to decline (see Table 20-1 in Chapter 20).

Table 19-2 shows the stock of foreign direct investment by host country or bloc of countries. Note that the major hosts are also the developed nations that provide most of the important MNCs. Developed nations acted as hosts to 74 percent of the stock of foreign direct investment at the end of 1975. Developing nations are not maintaining their earlier share for three reasons. Probably the most important is the extremely rapid growth of foreign direct investment within the bloc of developed nations (almost $78 billion in the four-year period 1972–1975). Some

Table 19-2

STOCK OF DIRECT FOREIGN INVESTMENT BY MAJOR HOST COUNTRIES

Host Country	Value ($ billion)		Share (%)	
	1967	1975	1967	1975
Developed Market Economies	105.0	259.0	69	74
Canada	18.9	38.9	18	15
United States	9.5	28.5	9	11
United Kingdom	8.4	23.3	8	9
West Germany	3.1	15.5	3	6
Developing Countries	32.8	68.2	31	26
OPEC Nations	9.1	15.6	9	6
Venezuela	3.5	4.0	3	2
Tax havens*	2.3	8.9	2	3
Others	21.4	43.7	20	17
Brazil	3.7	9.1	4	4
Mexico	1.8	4.8	2	2
India	1.3	2.4	1	1
Malaysia	0.7	2.3	0.7	1

* Bahamas, Barbados, Bermuda, Cayman Islands, Netherland Antilles, and Panama.

Source: Data from USESC, *Transnational Corporations*, tables III-33, III-47.

friction between firms and governments has resulted in MNCs' being less willing to invest in developing countries where the risk of government overthrow is seen as substantial and where the attitude of the host is not hospitable. In contrast, many developing countries are actually seeking out foreign direct investment (under prespecified conditions), particularly when the subsidiary is designed to service export markets. This love-hate relationship will continue to influence patterns of foreign direct investment, especially the pattern between industrialized countries on the one hand and developing countries on the other.

Not only are MNCs important in determining flows of international investment, but they also play a large role in the patterns of commodity trade among nations. Standard international trade theory of the type developed in Part II tacitly assumes that an exporter and an importer have no interlocking financial relationship other than any ongoing commercial one. Transactions are assumed to take place "at arm's length." In fact, trade between MNC subsidiaries and the parent and among related MNC subsidiaries is quantitatively important. This is understandable because control over successive different stages of production represents an important cost saving for multinationals. Trade in commodities between the United States and other countries consisted of 48.4 percent of trade conducted among so-called related parties. The trade, intrafirm trade, includes trade between U.S. parents and foreign subsidiaries as well as U.S. subsidiaries and foreign parents. Broken down by type of good, the importance of international trade at less than arm's length in 1977 was as follows: petroleum, 59.4 percent; other raw materials, 23.5 percent; semifinished manufactured goods, 37.6 percent; and finished manufactured goods, 53.6 percent. Within the class of manufactured goods, transportation equipment (mostly automobiles and motorbikes and parts) was by far the most important: 84.7 percent of goods in this category imported from developed countries was from related parties.[6] This type of international trade includes both finished goods (Mazdas and Mercedeses) as well as replacement parts and parts for use in the assembly plants of the Big Three U.S. automakers. The role of distribution networks in this relationship is important: General Motors imports cars from its foreign subsidiaries for sale through its network of dealers, and Japanese manufacturers (Nissan and Toyota) have set up marketing and distribution subsidiaries in the United States and sell their exports to them.

The benefits of intrafirm trade derive partly from straightforward economies that become available when a vertical production process is carried out under a single management control (so-called internalization efficiencies, which will be discussed shortly) and "production sharing." Production

[6] G. K. Helleiner and Real Lavergne, "Intra-firm Trade and Industrial Exports to the United States," *Oxford Bulletin of Economics and Statistics*, 41 (November 1979), 298.

sharing allows a firm to allocate the various manufacturing processes to factories in countries where production costs are lowest. In its simplest form, this process is likely to involve a U.S. corporation's producing complex parts in the United States, where highly sophisticated capital and workers are more easily available, and shipping those parts to a plant in Mexico or a Caribbean country, where they are assembled by workers whose low wages reflect the plentiful endowment of low-skilled labor. Frequently, the act of assembly also incorporates simple parts made in the host country as well as the assembly of complex components. Of course, the savings from running two separate organizations must exceed any costs of transportation, any duties that must be paid, and any additional costs of administration. Management authority Peter F. Drucker suggests that production sharing will be the major source of MNC growth in manufacturing activity in the rest of this century.[7] This process is aided and abetted by Sections 806.3 and 807 of the U.S. Tariff Code, which allow imports of finished goods in subsidiary factories to be taxed on the basis of value added abroad rather than on the basis of total value.

It is appropriate here to develop the theme of the advantages that MNCs derive from intrafirm trade. MNCs can allocate production among production units in different nations more effectively than this can be achieved by long-term contractual arrangements, and MNCs also enjoy the advantage of better communications among their own units than among people working for different firms. The spread of MNCs has increased the knowledge of executives about the costs of inputs in different parts of the world, and firms are more willing to transfer technology to a foreign subsidiary than to an arm's-length foreign firm. In this way, the existence of MNCs improves the international transfer of technology. The reverse of this coin is that factors of production in the home country are exposed to foreign competition more directly. The big threat to the bargaining power of the United Auto Workers is the threat of foreign manufacturing by General Motors and Ford, and this threat reinforces the competitive effects of imports from Japan.

Intrafirm trade is particularly important in linking foreign manufacturing (using low-cost labor) with marketing and distribution systems in the industrialized country. This makes possible the manufacture in developing countries of goods that need established warranty and service-support systems: Independent manufacturers in developing countries would be severely handicapped in the provision of this kind of marketing and distribution network (especially in competition with preexisting organizations from home-country giants and the large Japanese firms).[8]

---

[7] "The Rise of Production Sharing," *Wall Street Journal,* March 15, 1977, p. 17.

[8] The Korean automotive industry has had good success in Canada since 1984 and has now begun to penetrate the U.S. market.

THE MULTINATIONAL CORPORATION
AS A FIRM

To serve a foreign market, a corporation has a choice between exporting or building a foreign subsidiary from which the foreign market will be supplied "locally." But a subsidiary in a foreign country operates in an alien environment and will therefore tend to compete at a disadvantage with equally endowed local (indigenous) firms. This situation can be visualized in terms of the average variable, marginal, and fixed costs of a foreign subsidiary all being slightly higher than those of the equivalent indigenous firm. This is the cost of being foreign and the fundamental question concerning the development of multinational enterprise (here we use the term *enterprise* as the generic term and refer to MNCs as the individual entities). To overcome this cost disadvantage, the foreign subsidiary of an MNC must have an offsetting advantage—either cost reduction or some design feature that enhances the selling price. Clearly, no such advantage could accrue to an individual firm under conditions of perfect competition when all firms are, so to speak, created equal. MNCs can flourish only in a world in which there exist some imperfections in a product or a factor market. This condition seems to imply something "antisocial" about MNCs because they must have some monopolistic or oligopolistic advantage in some market.[9] What follows is an explanation of the way in which MNCs overcome the fundamental disadvantage they face. The explanation is more than a narrow market-imperfection approach and has been called "eclectic" by its originator in the sense that the theory draws on a wide variety of explanations of the development of the MNC.[10]

The eclectic theory is most easily understood by working through Table 19-3. The theory distinguishes three groups of influences that affect the ability or the desire of a firm to become an MNC. First, ownership advantages are the attributes enjoyed by large firms that enable them to lower their costs of operation in foreign countries relative to those of indigenous firms. Internalization advantages are sources of increased efficiency that accrue to having a single managerial control over operations in several countries. Finally, location-specific factors identify the features of different economies that affect the best way of supplying a foreign market, given existing ownership and internalization advantages.

The important feature of an MNC is its ability to transfer production-related factors of production internationally: It is therefore able to combine its privately owned firm-specific advantages with locally available factors

---

[9] This is the theory of MNCs that derives from Stephen S. Hymer, *The International Operations of National Firms: A Study of Direct Investment* (Cambridge, Mass.: M.I.T. Press, 1976).

[10] The most detailed explanation of the eclectic theory is given in John H. Dunning, "Explaining Changing Patterns of International Production: In Defence of the Eclectic Theory," *Oxford Bulletin of Economics and Statistics*, 41 (November 1979), 269–278.

Table 19-3
THE ECLECTIC THEORY OF INTERNATIONAL PRODUCTION

Stage 1: Ownership Advantages
Specific attributes belonging to individual corporations. They derive mainly from size and
established position and include any monopoly power that the MNC may enjoy.
Proprietary technological know-how
R&D capacity
Reservoir of experienced workers and managers with industry-specific human capital
Trademarks and known brand names

Stage 2: Internalization Advantages
Advantages that accrue to large firms able to accomplish goals more cheaply within the
single firm than can be accomplished in a market setting among separate corporations.
Ability to take advantage of internal economies of production
Ability to take advantage of production sharing (a special, international version of internal
economies of production, leading to intrafirm trade)
Economies of scale in overhead operations (marketing, finance, purchasing)
Economies from a broader market position
Avoidance of costs of negotiating contracts

Stage 3: Location-specific Factors
Factors that favor production either at home or abroad. (They constitute the C and N
variables in Figure 19-2.)
Prices of internationally immobile inputs
Differences in quality of infrastructure (public; educational; commercial and legal)
Transportation costs
Tariffs and NTBs (including discrimination by foreign governments against foreign subsid-
iaries)
Economies of marketing when production is located near the market
Difficulties of "foreignness" (sometimes called "psychic distance" between the home and
host countries)

Source: Adapted (freely and with permission) from John H. Dunning, "Explaining Changing Patterns
of International Production: In Defence of the Eclectic Theory," *Oxford Bulletin of Economics and
Statistics,* 41 (November 1979), table 2.

of production in a foreign country. Many of the advantages that MNCs
are able to transfer abroad derive from sheer size and possession of an
established position in the industry in question. MNCs are predominantly,
though not exclusively, large corporations with a stock of privately owned
technology (usually protected by patents), a reservoir of managerial and
professional talent with expertise in the industry, and the virtual assurance that ongoing research and development (R&D) at home can provide
continuing injections of proprietary know-how for any foreign subsidiary
in need. Size probably also affects the conditions under which the MNC
can raise capital and loans, and an established firm is likely to possess
a globally known brand name or trademark. All of these ownership advantages reflect market imperfections that favor the MNC. The example of
cheaper access to capital is a clear case of a marketing imperfection.

The possession of privately owned technological know-how also gives the MNC an advantage, but the social implications of this are not negative. Presumably, the firm invested its own funds in the necessary R&D, and this knowledge is as much the fruit of investment as a machine. Having an available team of experts is simply an advantage of being big and established in the industry. The last two advantages are efficiency-promoting advantages and, contrary to the market imperfections theory, suggest that the existence of MNCs has a positive effect on world economic efficiency. But whatever their implications for efficiency, these advantages exist. They are the basic means by which an MNC can overcome the costs and disadvantages of being foreign.

These disadvantages include factors other than the simple elevation of cost curves because MNC managers do not fully understand how the local economy operates. The disadvantages may include discrimination against foreign subsidiaries by the local government (particularly when governments purchase large amounts of goods) and the risks of nationalization or expropriation by the host government. The latter risk, like the possibility that the freedom to repatriate profits or capital will be interfered with, is most prevalent in developing countries in which balance-of-payments problems may arise and in which governments are prone to violent shifts in philosophy. These factors are likely to encourage a potential MNC to lease its technology to a foreign firm and to enter into managerial and supply contracts with such a firm rather than to expose its own capital to the political risk. In technical terms, the question is whether the firm can externalize its ownership advantages by working through the market with an arm's-length firm or whether it can fully reap the value of its technology only if it *internalizes* the technology transfer by bypassing the market and setting up a foreign subsidiary in the foreign country. If foreign investment is considered more beneficial than leasing the technology to a foreign firm, the firm has shown the existence of an *internalization advantage.*

There are three important forms of internalization: economies of vertical integration, economies of intrafirm trade, and economies in using technology in a foreign country.[11] The secret of the problem is that for the MNC to reap a reward on its expenditures on R&D, the firm must be able to keep its technology secret (otherwise everyone knows and there is no commercial advantage in having developed the technology *and* no incentive to keep investing in R&D). Foreign firms that lease technology are just not as protective of the secret as employees of the firm that owns it. There are also severe problems in making the market work in the transfer of technology. The owning firm knows what the technology is and must convince the lessor of its value without revealing so much of

[11] The authoritative paper on this subject is by Stephen P. Magee, "Information and Multinational Corporations: An Appropriability Theory of Foreign Direct Investment," in *The New International Economic Order,* ed. J. Bhagwati (Cambridge, Mass.: M.I.T. Press, 1977), pp. 317–340.

the secret that the lessor can guess the rest! Technology also requires a great deal of haggling and is expensive in terms of legal costs and managerial time because each piece of technology is unique and there exists no organized market for the product.[12] Given these inadequacies of the market (high costs, uncertain prices, risk of leakage to competitors), the incentive to internalize the transfer of technology by establishing a foreign subsidiary is not surprising.

The fact that a piece of technology is rented to a subsidiary does not preclude payment of a rental fee by the subsidiary to the parent. In addition to the obvious desirability of such a fee for cost accounting, royalty payments serve two other purposes: First, if the subsidiary is not wholly owned by the parent (if it is a joint venture), the royalty payment assures the parent of an appropriate revenue for the technology. Second, royalty payments for the use of proprietary technology are legitimately expensed and are therefore not taxed in the host country.[13]

The final determinant of how to serve a foreign market depends on locational factors. If the foreign market can be supplied more profitably from the home plant (because the home country has a comparative advantage in the good), no foreign subsidiary will be created. Clearly, the attributes of the home country and the importing country will be crucial in determining the relative profitability.

Whether or not locational factors (country attributes) favor the establishment of a foreign subsidiary can be analyzed in terms of Figure 19-2, which illustrates the fact that the costs of a foreign subsidiary (relative to the costs of production in the home country) are a composite of mobile ownership-specific advantages and immobile factors of production such as land and labor. An MNC has a production unit in the home country or source country, and it can export to a foreign market if its costs are less than those of indigenous firms in the foreign market by an amount sufficient to overcome impediments to trade (tariffs and transportation costs). The cost advantage of producing in the home country can be divided into two components: the cost advantage derived from the use of immobile factors of production (C) and the cost savings from the use of the firm's own proprietary technology (T). Simple comparative advantage (as taught in Part II) exists when $T + C$ exceeds zero. When the sum of T and C exceeds the per-unit cost of impediments to trade (N), the foreign market can be supplied with exports. When the sum of savings attributable to the transfer of technology to a subsidiary and the impediments to trade exceed the source country's comparative advantage (C), foreign direct investment becomes feasible. If the foreign or host country has a comparative advantage in the production of the good, C is negative. In fact, the

---

[12] For a good overview of the role of technology in foreign direct investment, see R. E. Caves, *Multinational Enterprise and Economic Analysis* (Cambridge: Cambridge University Press, 1982), pp. 200–207.

[13] Royalty fees are frequently treated more leniently by foreign exchange regulations in developing countries and can therefore be repatriated to the parent more easily than simple profits.

Figure 19-2

EXPORT OR INVEST ABROAD?

All quantities in the diagram represent a cost or a cost saving in cents per unit of output.

C is the difference in cents per unit of output of nonproprietary inputs into the production process. In a world of identical technology, as was assumed in Chapters 3 and 4, C represents the difference in costs of production at home or abroad and is therefore an indicator of comparative advantage. C is positive when the home or source country produces things more cheaply.

T is the saving (cost reduction) in cents per unit deriving from the ownership by the MNC of proprietary know-how or technology.

N is the cost per unit of transportation, tariffs, etc.

D is the disadvantage of being foreign. Obviously, it is very difficult to measure this in cents per unit, and the disadvantage may be eroded with time.

I is the savings achieved as a result of internalization efficiencies.

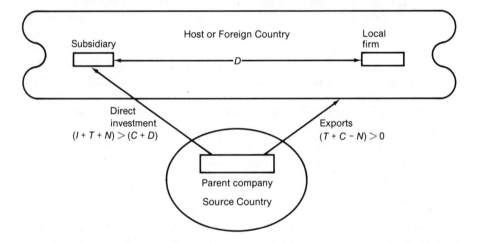

criterion for establishing a competitive foreign subsidiary must allow for the disadvantage of being foreign (in cents per unit of output, D) and the efficiency gains from internalization advantages. Thus a foreign subsidiary can be successfully established when $I + T + N > C + D$ while exporting can be accomplished when $C + T > N$.

This simple analytic framework already makes several real-world influences apparent. A government wishing to protect its home industry by raising tariffs is also encouraging foreign direct investment since an increase in N will encourage this. The greater the disadvantage of being foreign, D, the less likely is a corporation to invest in the host or foreign country. Thus high political risk or severe antipathy for foreigners is likely to discourage foreign investment. The more important the role of technology in determining production costs, the more likely is a foreign subsidiary to be viable in the foreign country (and the more likely is the foreign government to increase N to attract that investment). This simple framework does not allow for economies of scale and tacitly assumes that production units in both countries would achieve maximum scale economies. This assumption is not necessarily valid, and the effects of different scale economies can be incorporated in the variable C in which a large unit in the home or source country generates greater scale economies than a small-scale foreign subsidiary. (Boeing is an obvious example.)

The cost savings from technology transfer are shown as being available to the foreign subsidiary without cost. This is a simplification, since one cannot set up a foreign unit and adapt a process to local conditions without some cost. Nor is there any reason to suppose that the two criteria are mutually exclusive. The board of directors has a choice, and more subtle variables will enter into the decision. One example is provided by the petrochemical industry. An American MNC had an established export market in Europe but found that it had reached a limit to its sales because foreign customers were not prepared to rely on a foreign and distant source as a number one or number two supplier of an important ingredient in their production processes. In consequence, the MNC opened in Europe a manufacturing subsidiary that could make a wide range of products locally.[14]

The electic theory is a useful general introduction to the theory of the MNC insofar as its determinants are concerned. The analysis is positive, not normative. Indeed, it is extremely difficult to make normative statements about MNCs because of the wide range of activities that the organizational form comprises. (This is the subject matter of the two following chapters.)

The next task is to put a little flesh on the bones of the items in Table 19-3. Four activities can be distinguished:

1. The realization of internalization efficiencies (in addition to those related to international technology transfer and to production sharing)
2. The exploitation in foreign countries of owned technology
3. The establishment of a presence in a foreign oligopoly
4. The preservation of an existing, profitable operation

1. Internalization advantages or efficiencies derive from the substitution of internal organization for the costs of using the price mechanism provided by a system of markets. The existence of sales forces and purchasing offices in nearly all firms is evidence that the use of the market as a signaling device is not costless. For many activities, the market is a remarkably efficient way of signaling need and scarcity or surplus, particularly when transactions are numerous and frequent and the goods transac-

---

[14] See H. Peter Gray and Ingo Walter, "Investment-related Trade Distortions in Petrochemicals," *Journal of World Trade Law*, 17 (July–August 1983), 283–308.

ted are quite standardized. On occasion, as with the transfer of technology, these conditions are not met, and the market may be more expensive than the use of judgment by managers (internal decision making).

In addition to such advantages, firms may derive actual cost reductions and efficiency gains by having managerial control over several stages of production at once. This process is known as *vertical integration*. An example would be for Ford Motor Company to integrate backward to parts production and back again to the production of steel, paint, and glass. This was the pattern adopted by Henry Ford when the Ford Motor Company established itself as one of the major corporations in the world. The vertical integration allowed the corporation to reduce the uncertainties of scheduling and the related costs of higher inventories, it enabled the firm to specialize in the production and development of the kinds of primary materials needed by the automotive industry, and it enabled better communication as to what was possible between the metallurgists and the automotive engineers. It is this improvement in communication that makes production sharing preferable to supplying a marketing and distribution organization in the home country by long-term contracts with an indigenous firm in a labor-surplus country.[15] Not only are production efficiencies achieved in ongoing operations, but also a common managerial control can facilitate integrative planning between two production units involved in successive stages of production so that production costs can be further reduced. Kindleberger cites the inefficiency that derived from the inability of the British coal and railway industries to take advantage of the economies of scale inherent in larger coal cars because the larger coal cars would have required simultaneous and coordinated investment in new equipment by both industries.[16]

Except for the costs of doing business in a foreign country and of impediments to international trade, the efficiencies of vertical integration are indifferent to national boundaries. The usual way for vertical integration to involve international direct investment is through the acquisition of basic sources of raw materials. To the extent that a raw material is industry-specific and internationally immobile (and is therefore a noncompetitive import), international investment is mandatory if the corporation is to acquire direct control over a source of its supply. Frequently, the MNC can also bring new extractive technology with it. Production sharing, which makes use of differences in relative factor costs, also becomes feasible with vertical integration.

2.　When a firm possesses a piece of proprietary know-how (technology), it seeks to generate as large a return as possible on it. When the use of the technology in a foreign market requires foreign investment, the firm

[15] The economies of vertical integration were first identified in a classic article by R. H. Coase, "The Nature of the Firm," *Economica*, 4 (1937), 386–405. These economies increase world efficiency.

[16] C. P. Kindleberger, *American Business Abroad* (New Haven, Conn.: Yale University Press, 1969), pp. 19–22.

will establish a subsidiary in that market and make the same product abroad. This practice of making the same thing in different markets is known as *horizontal integration* and is a direct consequence of the ease with which technology can be transferred within a firm. This phenomenon has already been considered in terms of the shortcomings of markets as means of allowing the owner of an intangible, knowledge-based asset to obtain a reasonable return on investment, but some kinds of technology cannot be patented and cannot, therefore, be revealed to strangers and still command a price. It is necessary to distinguish between *product technology,* which includes patented know-how and usually relates either to a new product or to a new machine, and *process technology,* which is know-how obtained through experience in the production of a certain good and cannot be patented. Process technology can be used to generate a return in a foreign country only by establishing a production unit there. The process technology might include ways of production or might simply involve a spin-off in a foreign country of knowledge generated in the home country. Frequently, such technology requires that it be exploited by the firm's own engineers, who have hands-on experience. The greater ease with which an MNC can relocate skilled persons is important in the exploitation of process technology.

In stage 3 of the product cycle, see Chapter 4 above, the development of a foreign production unit is an example of horizontal integration. Later, when production of the good ceases in the originating or source country, the combination of foreign production and home-country marketing and distribution is vertical integration.

3. If there exists a foreign oligopoly (with accompanying high rates of profit), foreign firms with knowledge in the industry will be tempted to "join the club." To establish a firm in an oligopolistic market can be expensive; the operation requires very heavy expenditures on brand identification and sales promotion and possible large losses in the early years of local production. Probably only an MNC that is well established abroad will have the size, resources, and technological ownership advantages necessary to force itself into such a market. Existing members of the oligopoly may be expected to make the costs of entry into the market very high indeed and may even sacrifice their own profit rates temporarily, going so far as to sell at a loss, to inflict a very heavy burden on the would-be entrant. A small firm starting from scratch would quickly succumb. The foreign MNC has a much greater ability to withstand such fierce competitive action: It has financial resources abroad, it has technology and a brand name of its own, and it has the marketing know-how. Another advantage is that it can use any excess capacity in the local production unit to supply its other operations. Usually, entry into an oligopoly by an MNC involves buying out a small firm on the fringe of the oligopoly or a low-caste member of the club that has some minimum productive capacity and a minimum market share.

4. Safeguarding an existing profitable situation is another reason a firm might invest abroad. Reference has already been made to the establishment of a petrochemical subsidiary in Europe in order to enhance the profitability of the local marketing organization. This is the standard case. A firm has a local marketing and distribution subsidiary, coupled, perhaps, with a very small production base. The comparative advantage (C) that allowed the MNC to supply exports competitively has evaporated due to a real disturbance: If the marketing and distribution subsidiary is to be maintained, foreign direct investment is required. The profitability of the marketing and distribution organization will be sufficient to warrant any loss that the manufacturing operation may incur. This is one of the most important single reasons for foreign direct investment, though, frequently, firms may anticipate the loss of comparative advantage so that the investment is made prior to the actual loss of competitiveness in exports. A second possibility is that the market abroad has grown to the point that full economies of scale can be achieved. According to one study, the actual decision-making process leading to foreign investment rests more on market strategy and decisions than on any other single factor.[17] But this reason may not be only defensive, because local production capacity is frequently a positive feature in brand acceptance in consumer goods. This reasoning is likely to be particularly relevant in direct investment among the industrialized nations.

One scenario could lead to defensive investment in natural resources. If a vital natural resource is controlled, it becomes inaccessible to actual or potential competitors. In this way, for example, aluminum companies might seek to acquire control over bauxite deposits.

Why Do Firms Go Multinational?

The volume of assets owned by multinationals has increased tremendously since the late 1950s. Much of this increase in assets has come from takeovers of foreign firms, and not all of it is the product of saving and investment in the traditional sense. Undoubtedly, and despite some glamorous failures, the organizational form has been a success.

All of the reasons listed in Table 19-3 contribute in some degree to the growth of MNC operations, but the most important factors are likely to be ones that offer some competitive advantage to MNCs over one-nation firms. The spread of a stock of technology owned largely by American companies in the early 1960s was transferred to Europe (particularly after the formation of the EEC). The reluctance of firms to license their proprietary technology has played an important role, and the complex interrelationship that includes vertical economies, production sharing,

---

[17] Judd Polk et al., *U.S. Production Abroad and the Balance of Payments: A Survey of Corporate Investment Experience* (New York: National Industrial Conference Board, 1966), p. 63.

and foreign production for home-country marketing and distribution organizations has undoubtedly played a major role, particularly in the establishment of manufacturing plants in labor-surplus countries.

One important feature of the growth of MNCs that is not immediately obvious is the amount of direct foreign investment that takes place within the developed world and, in particular, within the same industry. Cross investment is taking place as European pharmaceutical corporations invest in North America and as North American firms establish and expand their facilities in Europe. This is intraindustry investment and resembles intraindustry trade considered in Chapter 11. Most of this kind of investment can be explained by the large amount of product-specific technology in many high-tech industries, especially chemicals and pharmaceuticals. Thus a company with a patent on a drug or a particular chemical may find that impediments to trade require it to locate in the foreign market. This has become more likely in recent years, as relative factor costs have grown more similar in the industrialized countries (in other words, in Figure 19-2, C approaches zero). This kind of direct foreign investment frequently relates in pharmaceuticals to local laws concerning drug production. While these laws could be seen as an NTB, they are accidental rather than pure. The other major development has been an increased willingness on the part of certain developing countries that have been successful in stimulating economic growth to allow new investments to take place within their borders.

SUMMARY

Despite Ricardo's assumption, factors of production do move internationally, and this movement sometimes plays a role in reducing cost disparities in competitive and differentiated goods. When the factor of production transferred is technology (or related human capital in the form of engineers), the mobility of factors of production can displace trade in noncompetitive goods as well. The purpose of factor migration is nearly always economic, so that the migrant factor will generate a higher total return. For people, this means prospective income in excess of personal costs, and for capital, a higher rate of return after due allowance for any increase in risk. There exist barriers to factor migration in much the same way that there exist barriers to trade; their purpose is to protect the welfare of the groups that would be harmed by the admission of the foreign factors.

MNCs have the power to move a group of factors internationally, and this ability provides the MNC with a competitive advantage over a new foreign firm. The MNC can move physical and financial capital together with skilled workers and technology. The MNC provides a package of mobile factors that can be united with locally available factors to produce at the least available cost. This ability to move a group of interrelated factors together is the important dynamic attribute of the MNC, and it is able to move such a group more cheaply and more quickly than a single-nation firm. The MNC can move the group more cheaply because it can use skilled workers already on its payroll and can guarantee these workers that their pension fund rights and their chances for further promotion within the organization will be enhanced by the tour of duty abroad. Foreign firms cannot attract the technology and the skilled workers as cheaply: Workers will not be willing to leave an ongoing relationship with a good employer except for a remarkable package of benefits, and arranging a lease for technology is a slow process. The MNC, with its network of subsidiaries, is in a position to learn of profitable investment opportunities in its industries very quickly. The movement of a package of resources, combined with operating control (either directly through a wholly owned subsidiary or jointly with another firm in a joint venture), allows the firm to achieve some efficiency gains that both allow it to compete with local firms and must have some beneficial effect on world production.

Bibliography

Caves, Richard E. "International Corporations: The Industrial Economics of Foreign Investment." *Economica,* 38 (February 1971), 1–27.

———. *Multinational Enterprise and Economic Activity* (Cambridge: Cambridge University Press, 1982).

Dunning, John H. "Explaining Changing Patterns of International Production: In Defence of the Eclectic Theory." *Oxford Bulletin of Economics and Statistics,* 41 (November 1979), 269–278.

Hood, Neil, and Stephen Young. *The Economics of Multinational Enterprise.* White Plains, N.Y.: Longman, 1979.

Kindleberger, Charles P. *The International Corporation.* Cambridge, Mass.: M.I.T. Press, 1970.

Vernon, Raymond E. and Louis T. Wells, Jr. *Manager in the International Economy,* 3rd ed. Englewood Cliffs, N.J.: Prentice-Hall, 1976.

Questions

1. Why does labor migrate?
2. Why does the United States not put greater effort into restricting the flow of illegal immigrants?
3. Why would an American investor (say, a bank) lend money to foreigners?
4. The "brain drain" is beneficial to countries like the United States that admit many well-trained foreign students. Argue one side of the argument.
5. In a simple H-O theory, factor migration substitutes for international trade completely if tariffs exist: Why is this theorem farfetched?
6. The eclectic theory says that only big firms invest abroad and become MNCs,

yet there are many examples of quite small firms with foreign operations. Solve this paradox.

7. The existence of imperfect competition is at the root of all foreign direct investment. Imperfect competition means a suboptimal allocation of economic resources, and, therefore, MNCs must exist to the detriment of the efficiency of the global economy. Comment.

8. For manufacturing industries, it is very difficult to conceive of foreign direct investment that does not involve proprietary process or product technology. Show this to be true even when the proprietary technology is *not* the main motivating force.

20

National Benefits and Costs

Multinational corporations cannot transfer technology or redirect flows of national saving without generating repercussions on the other parts of the two economies involved. It is useful to consider the benefits to be derived from the process of foreign direct investment for people in the home (parent) country and in the host country. Self-evidently, the process is believed to be beneficial for the MNC, although many corporations have regretted making some of their investments after the event. What is of concern here is the benefit to the nation-state. Costs in this context must exceed the narrow realm of economic variables and must include such elusive concepts as the impairment of economic independence and political sovereignty.

EFFECTS OF FOREIGN DIRECT INVESTMENT ON THE HOME-COUNTRY ECONOMY

In addition to the political repercussions, the effect of foreign direct investment (FDI) on the source or home country can be seen as having three broad economic effects: It impinges on the balance of payments, on the rate of accumulation of domestic wealth, and on the problem of employment.

Balance-of-Payments Effects

When a nation's MNCs acquire foreign assets, there is an outflow of capital, and to avoid diminution of the country's international liquid reserves, it is necessary to run a corresponding surplus on current account. In the terms developed in Part V, the nation must generate the international saving needed to finance the international investment by the MNCs. There is, then, a short-term drain on the parent nation's balance of payments, which requires a reduction in the rate of domestic absorption and some shift in the terms of trade. The MNC must buy enough of the host country's currency to purchase land there, to build a factory, and to equip that factory; some of the money may be borrowed from the host country's banks, but some must flow from the parent country. If the firm already has a subsidiary in the host country, the funds may be partly met by profits retained abroad. In practice, the reduction in absorption may not need to be very significant. If the MNC reduces investment that would otherwise have taken place at home, the reduction in absorption needed to finance the outflow of funds is almost automatically taken care of. Of course, some adverse shift in the terms of trade will be needed to allow the country to run the necessary surplus on current account. Clearly, this is a short-run cost imposed on the rest of the society by the MNC.

In return, the MNC will ultimately earn profits on its foreign investment, which will generate return flows of foreign exchange as these profits are repatriated. The terms of trade facing the parent nation can be expected, ultimately, to turn in its favor. Indeed, international receipts that can be attributed to past foreign direct investment by U.S. multinationals amounted to $30 billion in 1984 (after adjusting for earnings in the United States by foreign MNCs in the amount of $11.5 billion, the net figure was $18.5 billion).[1] When the amount of foreign exchange generated by MNCs exceeds the amount that MNCs are currently investing, the MNCs are exerting a favorable effect on the country's cash flow, and this will turn the terms of trade in favor of consumers in the parent country.[2] In 1984, foreign direct investment by U.S. MNCs amounted to $6 billion. Foreign direct investments *into* the United States amounted to $21 billion, so the net FDI was negative.

Table 20-1 shows how U.S. foreign direct investment has been funded for the thirty-five years 1950–1984. Changes in U.S liquid reserves are the balancing item, but even allowing for some inaccuracies in the data, it is obvious that the United States incurred a great deal of financial

---

[1] These figures include earnings on royalties and management fees from foreign affiliates.

[2] There is an accounting problem here. Much of the acquisition of foreign assets by U.S. MNCs was financed by inflows of funds on portfolio account, and the interest on that debt should be entered as an offsetting flow.

Table 20-1

SOURCES OF FUNDING FOR U.S. FOREIGN DIRECT INVESTMENT, 1950–1984

| | (Millions of Dollars) | | | |
Years	International Saving*	Portfolio Investment (−=Inflow)	Changes in Liquid Reserves	Foreign Direct Investment*
1950–54	−1,411	+1,785	−10,102	6,906
1955–59	+7,278	+6,297	−12,083	13,064
1960–64	+23,002	+16,380	−9,064	15,686
1965–69	+17,145	+2,831	−12,001	26,315
1970–74	+4,367	−56,654	+27,661	33,360
1975–79	−4,107	−58,695	−23,410	77,998
1980–84	−143,109	−119,330	−59,742	35,963
Totals	−96,835	−207,386	−98,741	209,292

* Includes retained profits.

Portfolio acquisitions are shown as a plus. The Table is based on the relationship that monies used to acquire real assets abroad (foreign direct investment) in excess of the balance on current account (international saving) must equal the spontaneous net inflow of financial funds plus the reduction in the Government's international reserves. An inflow of financial funds has a minus sign and includes all inflows including direct investment in the United States. Portfolio flows only include private-sector transactions for U.S. residents.

debt in order for MNCs to acquire foreign assets. Much of this financing took place in the first term of the Reagan administration. The net benefit to the economy of the foreign direct investment is substantially less than a straightforward inspection of the return flows from foreign subsidiaries would reveal (if only because U.S. residents pay interest on financial assets owned by foreign residents).

If the rate of dividend payout is held constant over time (at less than 100 percent), the absolute value of dividends will rise as the value of foreign assets grows as a result of profit reinvestment. The nation will ultimately benefit from foreign direct investment. It will also benefit if foreign direct investment yields a higher rate of return than the forgone domestic investment. Recall that the return on foreign investment should exceed the available rate of return at home after discounting for risk. But that is *ex ante* estimation, and it does not always follow that it holds in practice. MNCs have made serious mistakes, and these mistakes may be compounded by changes in political conditions that could not possibly have been foreseen. Two things suggest that foreign direct investment is probably not beneficial to the nation in terms of the rate of return: the problem of after-tax yield and the problem of the underlying asset. When a corporation compares investment at home and investment abroad, it is comparing an after-tax return in both cases. But some people argue that the national concern is with a before-tax return for home investments in comparison with an after-tax return on foreign investments. The idea is that when a firm pays taxes on a home investment, it pays taxes to the home government, and therefore the national interest is best reckoned by before-tax yields on home investments. In contrast, a firm investing abroad will repatriate (at best) all of its profits *after* payment of foreign taxes. The firm is indifferent as to who receives the taxes, but national welfare is not: Payments to the home government are to be counted as a benefit from the investment, whereas payments to a foreign government are not.[3] The second consideration that biases the analysis in favor of investment at home is the argument that if a foreign investment goes bankrupt, the home country has nothing; the firm has lost its investment, and the country has lost along with it. However, when a home-country investment goes bankrupt, the firm may lose its investment, but the real assets still exist, and if they are not completely industry-specific and firm-specific, they have value.

The crux of the question of benefit is intergenerational. In the long run, given reasonable investment successes, the home country will benefit from foreign investment. However, one generation may lose (through reduced absorption and less favorable terms of trade) while international assets are being acquired (international investment is positive). Ultimately, the net flow will be inward (flows of foreign investment will be less than the return flow of dividends); then absorption will be greater than full-employment domestic income, and the terms of trade will be more favorable. People who live and die during a period of net foreign investment do not benefit (at least according to this simple rule of thumb), whereas those who live during periods of disinvestment or very slow growth of assets abroad will benefit from past investments.

To the extent that foreign direct investment promotes greater global economic efficiency and spurs faster foreign growth and enhanced demand for the exports of the home country, foreign direct investment may have indirect beneficial effects before a net inflow begins.

Rates of Home Investment

When a nation's MNCs acquire foreign assets, they transfer funds overseas and must consequently reduce the volume of funds available to finance home investment in capital formation. This process could come about as a result of a deliberate reduction in domestic investment by the MNC transferring funds abroad, or it could result from changes in the cost and availability of credit in financial and capital markets (as the outflow of funds raises the interest rate). When exchange rates are

---

[3] This simple argument needs to be qualified by the fact that the government renders services for some of the taxes it receives. If support services, such as road and sewer building, are paid for by taxes, it does not matter to which government the funds are paid. What does matter is the amount of funds paid for national social goals such as education support and income distribution measures.

flexible, the outflow on capital account (net) will dominate the current account, and resources will be devoted to foreign investment instead of domestic investment. Does this matter? Foreign investment matched by international saving increases the total value of the assets of the country in just the same way as domestic capital formation. Saving is the sum of domestic saving and foreign saving, and it is saving that increases net worth. The answer, then, as in so much of economics, is "it depends." If a reduction in the rate of capital formation means that the capital stock in some industries does not get modernized at some appropriate speed (because the rate of capital renewal is slowed down), this can damage the competitiveness of an industry. Similarly, a lower rate of capital formation at home can slow the development of new industries that may have very large growth potential.

The most important effect, and the one most likely to generate political repercussions, will be the effect of foreign direct investment on employment patterns.

Employment Effects

In the United States, the AFL-CIO argues for restraint on the freedoms of American corporations to invest abroad on the grounds that production jobs are displaced at home. Indeed, the AFL-CIO sees the fact that U.S. MNCs do not pay corporate tax on foreign profits until those profits are repatriated to the parent corporation as a privilege that should be abolished. (The official name for this privilege is "tax deferral"). In 1972, the AFL-CIO had two of its supporters introduce a bill in Congress that would have made foreign direct investment less appealing (including the elimination of the deferral privilege). The bill did not pass, and since then the political power of the AFL-CIO has waned.[4]

Three questions must be answered: Does the existence of MNCs reduce the number of jobs available domestically? Is the skill mix affected by the existence of MNCs? Are individual regions or classes of workers badly affected? Researching these problems calls for a deal of good judgment, and the only reliable study is now somewhat dated.[5]

LEVEL-OF-EMPLOYMENT EFFECTS   Any question about the impact of foreign investment presents serious measurement problems. In a strict sense, the problems are insoluble since the researcher can only observe what has happened. To measure the effect of MNCs really requires a comparison of what happened when foreign investment took place and what happened when it did not. The latter is almost always unreproducible

---

[4] For details on this, the Burke-Hartke bill, see Neil Hood and Stephen Young, *The Economics of Multinational Enterprise* (White Plains, N.Y.: Longman, 1979), pp. 302–306.

[5] Robert G. Hawkins, "Jobs, Skills, and U.S. Multinationals," in U.S. Congress, House, Committee on International Relations, Subcommittee on International Economic Policy, *Hearings*, February 5, 1976.

and can only be estimated. As one economist put it, to discover this kind of truth, you need to run the world over twice—once with and once without foreign investment. Probably, the most thorough attempt to measure the effect of MNCs on jobs available in the parent country finds that the process of direct investment has, to some degree, *increased* the number of jobs available. That MNCs have closed plants in the United States and laid off workers is not disputed. What is questionable is whether the production cutbacks actually result in a net reduction of jobs in the United States. The ambiguity results from the fact that foreign production by an MNC has four possible effects on U.S. production and jobs; these may be positive or negative according to the context in which the production cutbacks are made.

1. The output of a foreign subsidiary may displace U.S. exports to host-country or third-country markets.
2. The output of foreign affiliates may be exported back to the United States to serve the U.S. market.
3. The existence of a foreign subsidiary serving the foreign market more closely may stimulate U.S. sales of intermediate and other goods not produced by the subsidiary.
4. The mere existence of foreign operations carries the need for more legal, administrative, and managerial workers. It may also permit, to the chagrin of host governments, a larger research effort to be built up in the parent country.

The question, then involves the number of jobs that will be lost to the U.S. labor force through effects 1 and 2 and the number that will be gained through effects 3 and 4. The negative effects will all be felt by production workers (hence AFL-CIO hostility to MNCs), whereas effect 3 may involve high-skilled technical workers to some degree and effect 4 will create jobs for so-called white-collar workers. The potential for an induced change in the skill mix is apparent.

The most crucial question in determining how many production jobs are lost to foreign production by MNC subsidiaries is whether the markets in the host countries were and could have continued to be served by exports from the home country. If changes in the competitiveness of home-based production units—due to changes in U.S. competitiveness, for example—were to make exporting no longer feasible, supplying foreign markets by local production does *not* displace home-country jobs. Similarly, if foreign sources could have preempted domestic production, as, for example, in black-and-white TV sets in the 1960s,[6] supplying home

---

[6] For a detailed description of the havoc wreaked on employment in a vulnerable industry, see the testimony to the U.S. Congress by Paul Jennings, the president of the International Union of Electrical, Radio and Machine Workers to the Joint Economic Committee, July 27, 1970, reprinted in H. Peter Gray, *The Economics of Business Investment Abroad* (London: Macmillan, 1972), pp. 201–204.

markets from foreign subsidiaries does not cause the displacement of U.S. workers, since they would have been displaced in any event. It is in interpreting the evidence as to whether or not the home-country production unit would have lost its competitiveness in any event that good judgment is required.

Hawkins's study found that MNCs in manufacturing enterprises provided $3.7 billion more sales in 1970 than in 1966. This production boost translates into just over a quarter of a million jobs *net*. The jobs are heavily concentrated in the following industries: drugs, cosmetics, and soap; office machinery; other electrical equipment; and other manufacturing. The industries suffering losses of jobs were industrial and other chemicals; lumber, wood, and furniture; and textiles and apparel. The study suggests that foreign investment does not have a *net* adverse effect on U.S. employment and that when the U.S. market was supplied from a foreign manufacturing subsidiary, the motivation for foreign investment was to preserve the MNC's market share in the United States rather than to discipline the union. In other words, the motivation for foreign investment was defensive.

SKILL-MIX EFFECTS   The impact of foreign investment has been unequal by skill class, as might be inferred from the four different types of effects listed earlier. Hawkins's study computed the skill requirements in expanding and declining industries from U.S. census data. This figure was then applied to the change in employment in the different industries to obtain an estimate of the total effect. When the average compensation per worker was used as the single most indicative measure of skill composition, it was clear that expanding industries ($8,080 per worker) tended to employ more skilled workers than the declining industries ($7,367 per worker). Expanding industries use professional, technical, managerial, clerical, and administrative workers to a greater degree than industry in general. Declining industries tended to have greater utilization rates of artisans, operatives, and laborers. This result confirms what might be expected: The U.S. comparative advantage lies in its use of skilled workers, and thus foreign subsidiaries will naturally tend to displace lower-skilled jobs.

Localized Effects

When an industry is damaged severely by the loss of its markets, either through a surge of imports or as a result of a rapid shift of production to overseas subsidiaries, the home economy will find the task of absorbing the displaced workers more difficult. Workers of similar skills and skill levels will be made available, and, perhaps even more problematic, unemployment will be concentrated in a single geographic locale and could bring about a depressed region. Detroit and southeastern Michigan when the car industry is in the doldrums is an obvious example. When Chrysler

Corporation was in danger of going bankrupt, one of the arguments made in support of the guarantee of its loans by the federal government was that Chrysler's bankruptcy would entail the bankruptcy of the city of Detroit.

Some economists believe that MNCs use the possibility of relocating productive capacity to foreign countries with cheap and amenable labor as a means of punishing aggressive unions. Undoubtedly, the decision to move abroad is not independent of the wage rate in the home country (and the wage rate for an equal skill level abroad). Whether the motivation to move abroad is one of cost reduction or simple spite, the movement of capital and technology is a means of improving the competitive efficiency of the global economy. In this sense, freedom to invest abroad is very close to the free trade argument. But the net effect of direct foreign investment by U.S. MNCs has not been to reduce the number of jobs available but to reduce the number of production-level (blue-collar) jobs available. Antagonism toward MNCs by organized labor is quite rational. The official AFL-CIO recommendation is to argue for the creation abroad of "fair labor standards" and to eliminate preferential tariff treatment for goods assembled abroad containing parts supplied by the home country. But the AFL-CIO also seeks, with a less substantiated argument, a straightforward reduction of imports from all sources, including foreign subsidiaries.

The final concern for the parent nation is the limitation that the existence of foreign subsidiaries places on the freedom to form international political policy. Often, foreign subsidiaries, particularly in developing nations, are viewed as constituting a sort of neocolonialism, with the consequence that any irritation that occurs between parent and host nations can be enlarged into an issue embracing the existence of foreign subsidiaries. The essence of the problem is the fact that the host country can always discriminate against or expropriate the subsidiary. Thus the government of the parent country cannot do anything but allow itself to be interested in the welfare of the foreign subsidiaries of its corporations and then is accused of conducting foreign policy to keep the world safe for MNCs. However, the host government is always tempted to use its sovereignty over MNCs as a trump card in a complex, multifaceted, political game that has its origins in some issue that is completely unconnected with multinational business. Finally, the host-country government is vulnerable to criticism by its own opposition for alleged favorable treatment of MNC subsidiaries. In some countries, identification of big business with MNCs and a feeling of hatred toward big business make foreign subsidiaries a natural political target in the host country.

Conclusion

Foreign direct investment has several beneficial aspects. It allows the free flow of resources internationally, making resource allocation more efficient; it promotes the degree of competition in many markets (including labor markets where the fear of having production shift abroad may weaken a labor monopoly); and it spreads proprietary know-how and managerial processes around the world, boosting global efficiency. In addition, FDI by corporations of rich countries serves as a vehicle for the transfer of resources to poorer nations.

From the narrower point of view of identifiable benefit and cost, the argument may appear to be less strong. The balance-of-payments benefit may take a long time to become positive. Payment of foreign taxes, a matter of some indifference to the MNC, may severely reduce the national benefit from investments abroad. The loss of all physical capital as well as financial capital in the event of a mistake and the prospect of costs of dislocation when the outward surge is too fast suggest that the nation as a whole benefits but little. Add to this the political cost, and one may well wonder where the benefit is to be found. But this negative assessment neglects two important qualifications. First, most foreign investments are a reaction to a change in competitiveness (a real disturbance), so to hamper the outflow would involve a weakening of home-country firms rather than a strengthening of the national economy. Second, controls over foreign direct investment have never proved very effective. The options of the authorities would be limited to relatively indirect and cumbersome methods such as control over inward trade flows and discriminatory taxes.

COSTS AND BENEFITS OF A DEVELOPED HOST COUNTRY

Many of the problems that result from massively unequal flows of FDI, from industrialized to developing countries, for example, are not of great concern in industrialized countries.[7] Nowadays, sufficient investment takes place among countries in the industrialized world that modern flows between Europe and North America are more or less balanced. (Investment in Japan is still far smaller than investment by Japanese MNCs, and this is a matter of some concern for politicians and economists concerned with the continuance of good relations between European and North American countries and Japan.) The United States is now the host country with the largest amount of foreign direct investment (but not, of course, the country with the largest amount per capita).[8]

If FDI is more or less balanced in terms of current flows if not in

---

[7] Rich nonindustrialized countries, such as Canada and Australia, do have problems with dominance of foreign ownership in their manufacturing sectors.

[8] For studies of foreign direct investment in the United States, see H. Peter Gray, ed., *Uncle Sam as Host* (Greenwich, Conn.: JAI Press, 1986).

terms of stocks of foreign-owned real assets, questions of political leverage and erosion of sovereignty become less significant. The benefits of foreign direct investment are three: the introduction of new proprietary technology in the host economy, the willingness of entering MNCs to locate in backward areas of the host economy, and the ability of the entrant MNC to reduce the degree of imperfection in a host-country goods market.

New proprietary technology can be introduced to the host economy by MNCs, but much of this technology is likely to be involved in a two-way flow. A foreign pharmaceutical MNC might invest in the host country at the same time that one of the host's MNCs invests abroad on the basis of its technological know-how. The stock of technology used in both countries is increased as a result of FDI. It might be possible that in a free trade world, some of this FDI would not be needed, but frequently with high-technology products, some of the barriers to trade are natural (e.g., high transportation costs because of special characteristics of the product such as the instability of a chemical compound) or accidental NTBs (see Chapter 7) designed to ensure quality control rather than to protect the competing domestic firms. Frequently, countries have imposed tariffs and other barriers to trade on technological noncompetitive imports (see Chapter 5) in order to encourage local manufacture of the good in question. Though this behavior pattern is more typical of developing countries, it can be used by industrialized countries that seek the introduction of a particular technology in their economy.

Governments in most countries exert some control over incoming FDI. The process of licensing the establishment of a foreign corporation can be used to promote the host country's regional economic policy. Nearly all nations have regions that are relatively depressed and have higher than average unemployment rates. The problems of regions such as these can be eased by the establishment of new industries. Foreign investments are, frequently, new projects (as opposed to takeovers of existing local firms), and these are susceptible to what might be called "locational nudging" by the licensing authority. In the United States, competition among the individual states, usually consisting of tax remissions and subsidized loans, will take the place of locational nudging by the licensing authority. The more intense the need or desire for a plant, the greater will be the subsidy offered by a particular state or region. This attribute of inward FDI is particularly important given that inward FDI tends to be concentrated in fast-growth industries.

The final benefit of FDI is its effect on the degree of competition that will prevail in a product market in the host country. In the process of forcing entry into a particularly profitable (oligopolistic) market, an MNC will necessarily generate lower prices and benefit consumers. This potential benefit must assume that the market is protected against foreign competition by barriers to international trade of some kind. The problematic aspect of this potential benefit is its duration. The benefit may last only as long as the MNC is forcing its way into the market and could end when a new equilibrium oligopoly is established.

Industrialized hosts can experience costs of inward FDI through some diminution of national sovereignty. Canada is a classic example of a country that has so much inward FDI that its manufacturing sector and much of its extractive sector are more than half owned by foreign MNCs. This is particularly exasperating when the MNCs control the rate and mix of output of their subsidiaries, with the result that the MNC's global interest rather than Canada's national interest is the criterion for decision making. A second way in which national sovereignty can be seen as being impaired is through the problem of "extraterritoriality." This problem arises when the laws and interests of the home or parent country are exercised over the MNC's subsidiary. Although antitrust laws can be extended beyond the boundaries of the home country, the most common source of major extraterritorial conflict is the question of differences in political allegiance. Thus the home-country government will attempt to prevent the subsidiary from selling goods to a third country that has friendly relations with the host but not with the home country. The sale of trucks to Communist China by the Canadian subsidiary of a U.S. automotive corporation is a classic example. Canada had good relations with China (as the United States does now) and was incensed when production by factories on Canadian territory was vetoed by a foreign government. A similar fracas arose when a subsidiary located in Argentina received an order from Cuba.

One final cost possibly experienced by an industrialized host is that research and development expenditures may be curtailed in the host country and centralized in the home country. To the extent that economies of scale and local concentration (agglomeration) are available, this move makes economic sense, but no country likes to see the rate of expenditure on R&D reduced. Host countries are particularly sensitive to this kind of diversion.

COSTS AND BENEFITS FOR A
DEVELOPING HOST COUNTRY

This is a subject on which there is endless debate within international bodies and within developing countries. The level of the debate has been raised since the disaster in Bhopal, India, in December 1984, when almost two thousand people were killed by the escape of poison gas from a subsidiary of a U.S. MNC (owned approximately 49 percent by Indian stockholders). This problem is sufficiently important and topical to warrant separate treatment in the supplement following this chapter. The conclusion of that supplement is that industries that are capable of generating disasters (beyond the confines of company grounds) need special consideration by both the host government and the parent MNC.

A nation in the course of developing (very few low-income stagnant nations become host countries) is necessarily underendowed with capital and technology and needs to be able to earn foreign exchange to acquire them. In consequence, the argument in favor of allowing inward foreign investment rests on the ability of inward FDI to provide those three dimensions. There is also the possibility of some serendipity whereby, through so-called spread effects, the MNC subsidiary enhances the human capital of the host and spreads technology into indigenous host-country firms.

The ideal inward investment would transfer hard currency to the host country in order to purchase land and to build a factory and would equip the factory with machinery that is sufficiently advanced that it allows good-quality products to be made with local workers who will have been trained up to use the machinery. The factory will purchase semimanufactured goods (intermediate goods) from local factories and by insisting on tighter tolerances will upgrade the technical standards in these local firms. Finally, the firm will sell some of its product to foreigners so that payment to the parent company for the use of technology and the repatriated profits (a balance-of-payments debit) will be more than offset by balance-of-payments credits (exports).

Probably no foreign subsidiary is ideal. An obvious problem for the host government is that if it wants, for political reasons, to encourage joint ownership with indigenous firms, the MNC will transfer less money into the country. A common complaint in developing host countries is that the foreign subsidiary uses a technology that is "inappropriate" (too advanced to allow maximum use of local workers or to have its need supplied by local firms). The result of this is a subsidiary that operates in an enclave, apart from the local economy. Nor do foreign subsidiaries often make positive contributions to the host's balance of payments (after the initial inflow of capital). Often, they buy parts from abroad (a balance-of-payments debit); send royalties, interest payments, and profits out of the country; and concentrate their sales on the domestic market.

Governments can try to make sure that foreign subsidiaries do make a positive contribution to the host's balance of payments by requiring minimum quantities of exports. A second way is to offer the foreign subsidiary special tax breaks if it will export virtually all of its product. The host creates an export zone, which is designed for firms (mainly foreign but not exclusively so) that will export all of their output (except substandard goods). Many MNCs seeking to serve their own home market are attracted to such zones because they charge no import duties on imported raw materials, firms are not handicapped by the red tape imposed on normal foreign subsidiaries, and profit taxes are low. Subsidiaries in export zones use local services and pay taxes for them and use members of the local labor force who are taxed on their earnings and who live outside the export zone. Export zones are being established in India and China, and all of Singapore is practically an export zone.

If the benefits, potential or actual, are straightforward, the costs are not. Foremost among the costs is a feeling of a lack of sovereignty, that is, domination of the manufacturing sector by foreign subsidiaries. When most of the advanced manufacturing forms are foreign-owned and foreign-controlled, there is a feeling that they control the progress of the national economy. Countries that were colonies until the end of World War II or have histories of economic domination by foreigners are particularly sensitive to the presence of overwhelming amounts of manufacturing capacity controlled from abroad. It is this fear, sometimes referred to by radical opponents of MNCs as "neocolonialism," that leads host governments to insist on having locals, possibly the government, own at least 50 percent of the equity. Such joint ventures are becoming increasingly common. In practice, this may be something of an illusion, as MNCs often set up several contracts that separate their control from the actual equity participation.[9]

A second possible cost is that the MNC may not contribute enough to the host economy to warrant its presence. This is likely to manifest itself in terms of an inadequate balance-of-payments contribution or in terms of "inappropriate technology" and the lack of any spread of positive benefits into the economy. Fairly self-evidently, a narrow accounting concept would show that a foreign subsidiary designed to serve the local market is unlikely to have a positive balance-of-payments effect and will show nothing but debits as payment is made for imported intermediate goods and for repatriated profits and royalties. This approach is a bit naive because it fails to take into account the foreign exchange saving engendered by local value added to what would otherwise be noncompetitive imports. If the subsidiary makes goods that cannot be manufactured locally without the MNC's presence, there is a foreign exchange saving that can easily be overlooked. The second possibility is that the MNC subsidiary adds little to the gross domestic product (gross national product less payments for royalties and repatriated profits) because the operation is too technologically sophisticated to use local factors of production. This is a serious problem facing developing host countries. Many insist on complete reliance on local workers and managers within a period of years (indigenization of the labor force); as is apparent from the Bhopal incident, this policy cannot be pursued without discrimination and without risk.

Another possibility is that the host government will have given too

---

[9] See footnote 5 in Chapter 19.

much away to attract the investment in the first place. A clear example of such behavior can be seen in the contracts given by many Caribbean governments to foreign hotels. Extractive industries, which rely on the exploitation of local raw materials, are also likely to be unpopular in developing countries. One reason for this is that they divert any surplus away from the host nation, which, understandably, feels that any pure economic rent deriving from natural resources should belong to the host economy.

Once a foreign subsidiary establishes itself in the local market, the likelihood that an indigenous firm will be able to establish itself in that market is significantly reduced. In other words, if the Ford Motor Company establishes a car production unit and sales network in a country such as Brazil, it will be very difficult for a local entrepreneur, starting from scratch, to establish a competitive indigenous firm. Probably the only firms that could compete with Ford under such circumstances would be other MNCs. This idea can be expanded to suggest that foreign MNCs retard the development of local entrepreneurs. In fact, this does not seem a very important cost because MNCs will not dominate the whole economy and will leave to the local business sector those sectors in which foreignness is a substantial handicap. In fact, Ford might play a constructive role in the scenario if Ford creates a dealership network and trains local managerial and technical personnel in the individual dealerships.

SUMMARY

The role of the MNC in transferring technology to other countries is a very great benefit to the functioning of the world economy. Local economies can improve the range of products they manufacture and can adopt foreign managerial skills. It is very difficult to overestimate the contribution that MNCs make to the world economy and to the ability of developing economies to enlarge their modern sectors. The role of the MNC is also to improve the efficiency of the world economy in that their activities will reduce the ability of economic groups to dominate local markets and to command some premium in their rate of return as a result of imperfect competition.

None of this comes without cost. The essence of the MNC is the establishment in a foreign country of a unit of production that is controlled from abroad. The political strains are obvious. Even if MNCs were always to be well behaved, which they are not, there would be grounds for conflict between the interests of the MNC and the interest of the host government.[10] Moreover, there are difficulties in establishing working

[10] For a report of the more flagrant antisocial acts of MNCs, see Hood and Young, *The Economics of Multinational Enterprise*, pp. 348–352.

relations between a host government in a developing country and the high-technology management of an MNC: Because the two interested parties do not communicate well with each other, problems can arise.

The costs to the home country depend on the degree to which FDI is a consequence rather than a cause of a real disturbance. Even when foreign investment is not merely a spiteful move to discipline the local labor force, there are potentially severe costs of adjustment in the home country. Nor is it clear, unless a person takes a very, very long view, that a steady outpouring of foreign direct investment is beneficial to the home economy in terms of a straightforward return on investment. The problem with trying to assess the costs of an outflow of foreign direct investment is that no one knows what would have happened in the absence of that outflow.

When developed economies are the hosts, there seems to be little argument against allowing free movement of capital and technology. The market system and the system of governmental controls both work well to ensure that no foreign subsidiary will be able to make huge, unwarranted profits. Instead, both countries gain from two-way investment as proprietary technology is made available. There is some concern in developed, natural-resource-rich countries such as Canada that the foreign corporations will dominate large parts of the economy, but much of the foreign investment in Canada was the result of the imposition of tariffs designed to protect Canadian industry against the economies of scale available in larger markets. These tariffs had the effect of encouraging FDI.

For developing economies, the problems are severe. Politicians have an intense interest in promoting economic development, and the advent of a foreign subsidiary is likely to promote the sought-after development. Unfortunately, many host governments lack the needed sophistication to identify both the benefits and the costs and in some cases are too naive to bargain with the high-powered managers of MNCs. The potential role of MNCs in economic development is huge, but, as is discussed in Chapter 21, MNCs can create problems for the world economy as well as for developing hosts.

Bibliography

Gray, H. Peter. *The Economics of Business Investment Abroad.* London: Macmillan, 1972.

_____, **and Ingo Walter.** "Investment-related Trade Distortions in Petrochemicals." *Journal of World Trade Law,* 17 (July-August 1983), 283–307. This paper argues the existence of a surplus deriving from foreign investment in developing countries.

Hood, Neil, and Steven Young. *The Economics of Multinational Enterprise.* White Plains, N.Y.: Longman, 1979.

Kindleberger, Charles P. *Multinational Excursions.* Cambridge, Mass.: M.I.T. Press, 1984. Ch. 2 deals with the problem of the relative sizes required by economic and political units for maximum "efficiency."

Kojima, K. "A Macroeconomic Approach to Foreign Direct Investment." *Hitotsubashi Journal of Economics,* 16 (1973), 1–12.

Vernon, Raymond. "The Product Cycle Hypothesis in a New International Environment." *Oxford Bulletin of Economics and Statistics,* 41 (November 1979), 255–268.

Questions

1. FDI will almost inevitably involve balance-of-payments debits for the home country. How will the funds for these debits be raised? Does it matter to the welfare of the home economy how they are raised?
2. The big problem with FDI from the point of view of the home country is the reduction in the level of employment of production workers. Given the idea of balanced current account, how can this come about? Is it serious?
3. If both parent and host are developed countries, it is almost impossible for FDI not to be beneficial. Comment.
4. Developing countries face serious problems, but they will, presumably, benefit from inflows of "ideal-type" FDI. Explain the benefits that are likely to accrue.
5. Not all FDI is "ideal." What problems can FDI bring to a government that is not alert to the dangers?
6. The Bhopal disaster suggests that the elimination of technological noncompetitive imports by local manufacture is not always reasonable. Cultural factors and indigenization can clash with necessary technology. Comment.

Disaster in Bhopal

In December 1984, a subsidiary of an American MNC (owned 51 percent by Union Carbide) accidentally released a cloud of poisonous gas over the city of Bhopal, India. Just under two thousand people were killed, and ten times that number were harmed.[1] This was clearly a severe cost of having that particular investment in India. The disaster can be attributed to failures by the government of India and by Union Carbide and its subsidiary, Union Carbide India Ltd. (UCIL), and to a lack of communication between the two parties to the extent that no one confronted the problem of the incompatibility of the Indian government's insistence on the use of local labor and UCIL's inability to devise safety procedures for so volatile a chemical using only low-skilled labor to supplement the few engineers.

Two things need to be made clear. First, disasters happen in developed as well as developing countries. The technology of disaster control devices is lagging behind the technology of production. The near-disaster in the nuclear power plant at Three Mile Island, Pennsylvania, is evidence of the problems that exist even in a technologically sophisticated country. The Chernobyl disaster in the USSR in April 1986 seems to have had very similar causes to the Bhopal disaster: Safety procedures were inadequate.

Second, the problem in India was a management control problem, not an example of callous profit seeking on the part of the MNC. The costs of the disaster (defined as having significant harmful effects beyond the confines of the plant) and the attendant costs in corporate image are greater than any cost saving that could have been achieved by cutting corners.

The root problem seems to have been a failure of communication between the corporate subsidiary and the government of India. The latter insisted on the use of disaster-avoidance (safety) technology that allowed

[1] For the basic details of the disaster, see the series of four articles in the *New York Times* on December 12, 1984, and January 30 and 31 and February 3, 1985. Broad coverage of the disaster and its repercussions was given in a special issue of *Chemical and Engineering News*, 63 (February 11, 1985).

for the use of the maximum number of people with minimum technological skills. The corporation seemed to acquiesce in this set of controls and did not insist on the use of a technologically advanced prevention system. In the equivalent plant in West Virginia, the disaster avoidance system is highly automated; in India, people with scant training watch gauges. Cultural problems seem to enter into the question of safety controls. A willingness to undergo frequent disaster simulations seems to be lacking in countries in which the capacity of chemical plants for disaster is only imperfectly appreciated. In Bhopal, many of the workers could not read the danger signs, and there seems to have been a general lack of understanding of the potential of the problem. There was, however, a lack of interest on the part of the parent company (Union Carbide) in the operation in Bhopal. Gladwin and Walter attribute this lack of interest to what they call "control dilution."[2] The regulations and requirements of the host government had left Union Carbide with no control over the operation of the plant; they therefore abdicated responsibility for it *in their own minds* (whether or not they could abdicate legal responsibility is another matter). Safety inspection teams from the United States visited the site very infrequently, and the local personnel were not kept up-to-date on information affecting the efficiency of safety measures. Add to this a rudimentary (to the point of being ineffectual) system of inspections by the local government, and the disaster was inevitable.

The implications of the disaster for the operation of highly dangerous and technologically sophisticated plants in developing countries are clear. First, some assessment must be made of the operation's potential for disaster using up-to-date technology. If the host government wishes not to use the up-to-date disaster avoidance technology, it must reassess the potential for disaster. The question of the desirability of a plant and the appropriateness of the technology applies jointly to the production technology and the disaster avoidance technology. If the net benefits are insufficient, the investment should not be approved. A similar minimum standard should be set by the MNC. If it deems the combination of local regulations and disaster potential excessive, it should not invest in the foreign production unit. Both criteria require some estimate of the likelihood of disaster and its potential harm—both informed guesses.

There is a more pressing problem in determining what steps, if any, should be taken in existing plants. All MNCs and all host governments should assess the likelihood of disaster and the magnitude of that disaster. If the likelihood and magnitude combined are excessive, either the local host government should allow the introduction of high-technology control devices and insist on the operators' (indigenous or foreign) being appropriately trained, or the MNC should divest itself of the operation. It is

[2] Thomas M. Gladwin and Ingo Walter, "Bhopal and the Multinational," *Wall Street Journal,* January 16, 1985.

essential that the responsibility for disaster, if any, be clearly delineated ahead of time. Only then will the responsible party have the incentive to ensure that the controls be instituted to reduce the likelihood of disaster to some (low) socially acceptable level.

The essential problem in Bhopal was that a technology was introduced to a society that was not prepared for it. The industrialized countries in the West have been gradually made aware of technologies of greater sophistication and danger for more than two hundred years. Given the speed-up in technology development, disaster controls have not always kept pace with the potential for disaster. In developing countries, the technology is being introduced at a much more rapid pace, and society may not be able to adapt sufficiently quickly. This possibility suggests that industries susceptible to disaster be subject to a different and more intensive review when their establishment in a developing country is being considered. The usual criteria were developed for textile factories and manufacturing concerns; chemical and pharmaceutical plants may need to be considered quite separately.

21

The Problem of Multinational Corporations

The multinational corporate form of organization achieved stupendous growth during the third quarter of the twentieth century. This growth, rather than any novel quality, caused the MNC to move to center stage in the arena of world politics and to give rise to books such as Servan-Schreiber's *American Challenge*.[1] If multinational operations are more efficient (that is, if they can produce and sell goods more cheaply than uninational firms), they will flourish. Their promise is efficiency, but they bring with them a set of related problems in corporate governmental relations and complicate the problems of world economic policy. This chapter is concerned with an assessment of these problems, with how governments might deal with them, and with how MNCs might adapt their behavioral patterns to minimize the potential frictions.

A word of caution is in order at the outset. Many people have strong feelings about the social implications of MNCs, regarding them either as the ultimate form of exploitative big business and inherently evil or as the savior of the world's economic problems, constructively transferring resources from one nation to another according to the needs of global society. In any study of human organizations and activity, extremes can be found. The study of MNCs is no different. Some MNCs are ruthless exploiters of natural resources of developing countries and are prepared to go to any length to safeguard their investment—up to and including sponsoring revolution. At one period in its history, the United Fruit Com-

[1] Jean-Jacques Servan-Schreiber, *The American Challenge* (New York: Avon Books, 1969). This book is not anti-American.

461

pany personified this type of behavior. More recently, the company has seen the wisdom of cooperating with the desires and needs of host countries.[2] Some MNCs are generally beneficial as a side effect of their own search for profit and efficiency, operating in the same way that the invisible hand works to promote economic gains. The subject profits from a skeptical approach with an open mind. Instead of looking for the divinity or the devil incarnate, the student of MNC behavior does well to think in terms of social costs and social benefits, being careful to define these concepts in advance. It is also very advisable to avoid blanket condemnations or blanket praise. As was implicit in Chapter 20, the nature of the host nation's economy plays a decisive role in determining whether the MNC will be generally beneficial or is capable of harming the host. By the same token, the type of subsidiary—manufacturing or extractive—will have different repercussions on welfare in different nations.

BENEFITS AND COSTS OF MULTINATIONAL CORPORATIONS

The multinational corporate form of organization has many positive features that benefit global society.

1. It is an effective and efficient vehicle for the international mobility of capital and contributes to an increase in the average productivity of a given stock of capital.
2. It is an effective and efficient vehicle for the international transfer of technology and human capital. In this process, MNCs increase the productivity of both factors of production *and* their indigenous cooperating factors in the host country.
3. MNCs achieve economies of vertical integration and thus improve the efficiency of global industry.
4. Because of their greater awareness of international cost structures and market potential, MNCs probably allow greater gains from international trade to be achieved than could be attained by a simple system of international markets handicapped by imperfect knowledge.
5. By investing in productive facilities (particularly manufacturing facilities) in developing countries, MNCs provide the base for spread effects, which will contribute to the economic development of their hosts.

However, on the negative side, MNCs' interests can conflict with those of the host or parent government, and MNCs are vulnerable to charges

---

[2] See Thomas E. Sutherland, "Foreign Trade and Foreign Policy: An Uneasy Coexistence," *Michigan Business Review*, May 1965, pp. 1–11.

that they use economic power to their own advantage and to the disadvantage of weaker economic units.

1. The benefits of the MNC's efficiency are alleged to accrue to stockholders and executives disproportionately. These benefits are denied to workers and host governments because of the economic power and flexibility of the MNC. This type of indictment of the MNC focuses on income distribution and is accentuated when the benefits and costs of the multinational corporate form are viewed from a national (as distinct from a global) viewpoint. The indictment is one of unfair division between corporation and government, worker and management, and host government and parent government. This problem is not peculiar to the MNC; it is more obvious for an MNC because of the greater number of dimensions. Most of these aspects of costs to national governments have been considered in Chapter 20.[3]

2. MNCs reduce the sovereignty of the host nation. Consequently, they can antagonize host-country nationals and, if MNCs' aims conflict with the short-run economic goals of a host nation, host-country politicians as well.

3. MNCs can use their international flexibility and the mobility of their operations to avoid governmental constraints that are imposed on domestic business, to the detriment of the parent country and the parent country's uninational firms.

4. MNCs can amass economic power to the point that they can form cartels that reduce the level of competition among productive firms and preclude entry into industries. To the extent that they succeed, they can become immune to the attempts of national governments to control them.

THE POTENTIAL FOR CONFLICT IN GENERAL

In any country, the potential exists for a clash between the narrow search for profit on the part of a corporation and the goals of society. In abstract theory, the forces of competition will constrain the private-enterprise sector in the long run so that business will be unable to generate any spare resouces that it may devote to the needs of society that are not identified by market forces. For example, in a perfectly competitive industry, a single firm could not reduce its rate of despoiling the environ-

---

[3] This problem reaches its most serious level in natural-resource extraction industries when the resource earns a pure economic rent. This problem is referred to in detail in Carlos F. Diaz-Alejandro, "North-South Relations: The Economic Component," in *World Politics and International Economics*, ed. C. Fred Bergsten and Lawrence B. Krause (Washington, D.C.: Brookings Institution, 1975), pp. 213–241.

ment (with consequent increases in private costs) without consigning itself to ultimate failure. However, some dimensions of social policy do not conform to the results of market competition: treatment of labor, safety regulations, consumer safety, and environmental protection, to name but a few. In developed economies, these considerations and others (such as the need for competition and accountability) are likely to be achieved by a series of measures that control business activities by imposing equal constraints on all firms to ensure that social standards are met. The emphasis on these types of controls will vary widely among nations. In developed nations with sophisticated government sectors, the controls will be strongly enforced. In developing countries, however, the controls are likely to be ineffectual or nonexistent. There will be considerable differences not only among the constraints from one country to another but also among the potential conflicts between private conduct of the business and social goals. The MNC, therefore, is likely to be faced with the problem of having to operate effectively in a variety of political climates with differing degrees of potential conflict and differing networks of social controls.

The evidence suggests that MNCs may not fully perceive the importance of variation in local conditions in which their subsidiaries operate (see the supplement following Chapter 20). The MNC is not often sensitive to the implications of local differences in business climates. Ingo Walter suggests that the problem of the need for sensitivity to local conditions is left to local managers of subsidiary plants with no general guidance from the parent organization: "Serious effort on social issues confronting the firm tends to be unplanned and reactive in nature, in response to crises that suddenly materialize and have to be dealt with as best they can in an *ad hoc* way."[4] This neglect suggests that relations with local governments are unlikely ever to attain the degree of harmony necessary for the MNC to reap all of the gains from the efficiencies the organizational form makes possible.

The issue is the degree to which MNCs should be concerned with local problems on a preplanned basis and the degree to which they should consciously renounce short-run profit in the interests of conforming with the social goals of the host nation. What is involved is discretionary action on the part of management to help to achieve (or at least not to impede) the attainment of local socioeconomic objectives. This conduct can be called "social responsibility," which Walter has defined in the following way:

> It is the voluntary, or "discretionary," action on the part of managers to help achieve prevailing social objectives in ways *other than* those

---

[4] Ingo Walter, "Social Responsibility and the Future of Multinationals: Guidance without Rules," *Intereconomics*, 5 (1976), 141–145, from which this discussion of social responsibility draws heavily. See also Ingo Walter, "A Guide of Social Responsibility of Multinational Enterprise," in *Social Responsibility and Accountability*, ed. Jules Backman (New York: New York University Press, 1975).

dictated by market forces or imposed upon the firm by public policy. It is the exercise of self-guidance by the firm and those who manage it. And above all, it is the systematic adherence to particular moral and ethical standards by the firm as a cohesive and structured organizational system.[5]

The required degree of exercise of social responsibility depends on the level at which the government effectively constrains business enterprises. Usually, MNCs originate in nations in which business firms are closely regulated by a body of law and a network of professionally staffed institutions.[6] These laws and institutions form a web of social control that, for the most part, strips the need for corporate social responsibility from a business enterprise. When a firm expands into foreign nations and achieves multinational status, some of its subsidiaries are likely to face a much less closely knit web of control—if indeed there is any control at all. In fact, host governments are frequently not able to formulate their requirements of foreign subsidiaries effectively in an evolving and rapidly changing political and economic climate.[7] Host governments' awareness of the need for constraints often results from dissatisfaction with the conduct of a foreign subsidiary. Thus, if the behavioral pattern that is appropriate to the parent nation where the web is strong is carried over to the operation of the affiliates, there is an obvious potential for conflict. It is not possible to operate a subsidiary efficiently when no attention is given to social responsibility. The outcome must be conflict, possibly conflict that feeds on itself over a period of time only to reach a point at which peaceful resolutions and cooperation are no longer feasible. The end result is likely to be harmful to both sides.

Failure on the part of MNCs to understand the variation in the political climate and in the need for social responsibility must impair the efficiency of the organization and reduce the positive benefits that accrue to the global economy from the multinational corporate form of organization. Walter argues for the creation of a technology of social responsibility whereby the headquarters of the MNC not only are made sensitive to nonmarket, social issues as they arise in different nations but also become better able to offer constructive suggestions to subsidiary managers on these issues. The need for such a technology is growing rapidly. This

[5] Walter, "Social Responsibility," 141.

[6] In the United States, there exist the Anti-Trust Division of the Department of Justice; the Food and Drug Administration; the Federal Trade, Power, and Interstate Commerce Commissions; the Environmental Protection Agency; the National Labor Relations Board; and the Securities and Exchange Commission.

[7] See Robert O. Keohane and Van Doorn Ooms, "The Multinational Firm and International Regulation," in *World Politics and International Economics*, pp. 170–171. Be aware, however, that some governments are so well organized that is it possible to devise concession agreements whereby the rights and responsibilities of subsidiaries are negotiated and agreed to prior to the establishment of the subsidiary. See David K. Eiteman and Arthur I. Stonehill, *Multinational Business Finance* (Reading, Mass.: Addison-Wesley, 1982), pp. 310–316. These agreements do not always remain unimpaired.

growth follows from the multiplication of areas in which MNCs operate, the increased number of areas in which governments recognize their responsibilities, and the new or growing international political strains between the developed world and the poor nations.

Since Walter assessed the problem, things have improved. The U.N. Centre on Transnational Corporations was able to report that about 150 MNCs now had corporate guidelines for managers. They were described by the center as follows:

> Good [corporate] citizenship requires a sensitivity to local and national social and economic conditions and that the company's business should be to the mutual benefit of the investor and the [host] country. Although this subject is normally dealt with in general terms, it is sometimes treated in a specific and detailed manner, covering such areas as reinvestment of profits, national employment and local purchasing, the sharing of knowhow, ideas and technology with host countries, the use of currency transactions for speculation and so on.[8]

Although there may be a considerable gap between published statements of intent and actual conduct, sets of guidelines must have a socially beneficial effect on the conduct of managers and the mental set of directors.

Organizational Forms

The need for recognition of the exercise of social responsibility rests on the assumption that MNCs achieve maximum efficiency only when they integrate the operations of many separate production and marketing facilities. It also assumes that the interlocking of operations may contravene a local socioeconomic goal or sensitivity. What Walter's argument assumes, with some empirical support, is that the network of organizations is controlled from the center by executives who are attuned to operations in the parent country. It is useful to think of this method of operation as the one that is least well developed among the three possible forms of organizational structure. The identification of these three organizational forms, which differ in the way in which executives think about the corporation's goals and activities, has been made by Perlmutter.[9] The mental attitudes can be characterized as ethnocentric (home-country-oriented), polycentric (host-country-oriented), and geocentric (world-oriented).

---

[8] U.N. Centre on Transnational Corporations, "Corporate Guidelines," *CTC Reporter,* September 1978, pp. 16, 32. For an attempt to concoct a set of "rules of social responsibility," see "Guidelines for Multinational Enterprises" in *International Investment and Multinational Enterprise* (Paris: OECD, 1976), pp. 5, 11–17.

[9] Howard V. Perlmutter, "The Tortuous Evolution of the Multinational Corporation," *Columbia Journal of World Business,* January-February 1969, pp. 9–18, from which this section draws heavily.

An *ethnocentric* attitude reflects a belief in the greater efficiency of the people from the parent company. There may be a suspicion that complex organizations are beyond the capabilities of local personnel in foreign subsidiaries and that home-country practices can be transferred to any host country (to the presumed benefit of the host country). It follows that an ethnocentric MNC will tend to use parent-country nationals in positions of responsibility to a greater degree than is objectively desirable because it considers parent-country nationals to be the only suitable candidates for top executive ranks in the parent corporation. Parent-country nationals who have served in foreign subsidiaries and seem to have become tainted by a sense of social responsibility may not be eligible. Such a picture is necessarily extreme but is not unknown. Biases of this nature do exist, although they may be less common than they were in the 1950s, when the surge of new managerial techniques in the United States made the MNC a more viable form of organization.

A *polycentric* attitude accords so much respect to the host-country culture that it allows or encourages each subsidiary to operate as a quasi-independent firm.[10] The parent merely requires a measure of control over financial outlays and a satisfactory rate of return on its investment. Note that a polycentric MNC will also tend to reserve top executive ranks for parent-country nationals. However, the motivation is different, stemming from a conviction that each person should specialize in and remain in the country of upbringing. A polycentric MNC is highly sensitive to issues of social responsibility and maintains a very low profile in political matters simply because it deemphasizes its foreignness. The independence of operations in polycentrism can severely restrict the ability of the MNC to achieve economies of vertical integration, and it is possible that this form of organization is applicable mainly to horizontally integrated MNCs.

The ultimate form of organization and attitude is *geocentrism*. A geocentric MNC is almost truly global, and the nationality of the parent country does not dominate. Top executives derive from many countries. Operations of different subsidiaries are enmeshed to the degree that individual national sensitivities allow. Social responsibility is built into the system of thinking at all executive levels.

Different attitudes tend to manifest themselves in different divisions of MNCs. The R&D component tends to be more geocentric than other divisions, finance is ethnocentric, and marketing, as might be expected, is polycentric. The costs of ethnocentrism are unnecessary frictions with host governments, a lack of feedback of ideas from subsidiaries to the parent corporation, a high rate of executive turnover in the subsidiaries, and, possibly, an inferior ability to obtain executive talent in the subsidiaries. These last three costs derive from the awareness of subsidiary execu-

---

[10] Union Carbide's plant in Bhopal, India, was so polycentric as to be independent; see the supplement following Chapter 20.

tives that their potential is limited by ideological constraints within the organization. Geocentrism is likely to develop a top-heavy central bureaucracy at headquarters as a result of the high degree of centralization. Polycentrism sacrifices potential internal economies of organization.

In the light of Perlmutter's three categories, Walter's plea for social responsibility amounts to an argument for increased geocentrism.

THE POTENTIAL FOR CONFLICT: SPECIFIC PROBLEMS

There is no question about the fact that MNCs tend to encroach on the political sovereignty and independence of the host nation. The sovereignty issue is at the heart of the concern for policies of social responsibility on the part of subsidiary managers. Nation-states, mindful, perhaps, of the colonialism of the nineteenth and early twentieth centuries, desire political independence. This desire, often fierce, is at odds with a world in which economic forces are constantly driving nations (rich and poor) toward interdependence (see Chapter 1). Technology is evolving so that nations' interdependence is growing. The way in which MNCs contribute to this economic interdependence causes the host governments to have the most serious misgivings about the multinational corporate form of business and leads them to question the advisability of allowing an MNC entry into the nation, even though they recognize the positive economic benefits that might accrue. This concern found its most articulate expression in Servan-Schreiber's treatise, which called for Europe to guard against the Americanization of its industrial sectors. The Americanization was seen as a cultural revolution that was transmitted through the MNCs (and the managerial techniques accompanying their development) and that contributed to the loss of European personality. European ways of doing things would be eradicated by transatlantic techniques and modes of behavior adopted in a drive to acquire affluence at any (cultural) cost. However, developed nations have achieved some semblance of accommodation with MNCs. This accommodation derives in part from the two-way flow of direct investment as well as from an overt recognition of the benefits of MNCs and of modern managerial techniques.[11] Nevertheless, the impairment of sovereignty is still a serious problem facing developing countries. These nations fear that they have escaped old-fashioned colonialism only to endure a new kind in which powerful MNCs will usurp their newly found independence. The developing countries face a contradiction in their economic and political aspirations: Growth comes more easily with MNCs, and independence is sacrificed. However, the

---

[11] Canada is an exception, and this is due to the large amount of foreign direct investment in raw materials and to the dominance of foreign investment in manufacturing.

problem for developing countries is not the simple one of admit or not admit. No country except Burma, whose economic growth record is not exemplary enough to serve as a model for other nations, has ever shunned foreign economic involvements entirely. The question facing the developing country is "not Should we throw the rascals out? but rather a more prosaic one: What further constraints can we devise to minimize the costs imposed on us by these (foreign) firms and to maximize our rewards from their activities?"[12]

It is obvious from the attitude expressing the central core of host-country policy that host countries are unlikely to see the unrestrained workings of the market as the best solution. FDI should be allowed on a discriminating basis, and it should not impair the host country's self-image nor its plans for economic development.

Many of the problems that derive from the clash of interests have already been considered as costs in Chapter 20. They include such things as extraterritorial pressure, the inhibition of the development of indigenous entrepreneurs, the possibility of political instability as MNCs' behavior causes xenophobia, and the possibility that local tastes will be changed to no national purpose (if Coca-Cola establishes a demand for its products by advertising campaigns and ousts local soft-drink producers, for example).

Another factor affecting the idea that the country's economy can be administered by the local government is the practice of MNCs to use different plants in different countries to produce one or two parts for assembly in a third country. This practice of sharing and integrating production allows the MNC to achieve some of the cost savings of vertical integration. Such a pattern of allocation of production is central to the growing trend toward economic interdependence. This process puts the local economy in the position of being a simple cog in a machine, and the government faces the possibility that the MNC will omit its subsidiary from the worldwide production network at any time. To an economist, this means simply that the individual plants have to maintain their efficiency in international terms, and the process contributes to raising global output. To the host, it is an invasion of the sense of independence.

There is no suggestion that MNCs would be irresponsible in their allocation of production among subsidiaries of different nationalities, but it does create competition among developing countries to subsidize local operations. In this way, the MNC is exploiting the weakness of the developing economies. Such subsidies might take the form of tax breaks, subsidized training programs for local workers (although this has enduring benefits), or subsidized loans in local currency.

An MNC will hinder economic development if it earns a pure economic rent on its extractive operations and does not allow the host economy

---

[12] Keohane and Ooms, "The Multinational Firm," pp. 170–171.

to benefit from the rent earned by local deposits of natural resources. This possibility is much less likely in the modern era, when host governments are becoming far more sophisticated in their understanding of the implications of MNC operations. For example, an export duty will allow the host economy to capture much of any economic rent that exports of minerals might otherwise generate for the MNC.

The effects of cascading tariffs in the home country could be expected to induce an MNC to export raw materials from the host country in crude (unprocessed) form. The possibility of an export duty could be used to offset the cascading effect of tariffs in the home country by reducing the export tax rate as the raw material is processed further.

Three aspects of MNC opeations may require intergovernmental cooperation to curtail worldwide activities that are socially damaging. The first is the possibility that large MNCs might collude to form a global cartel. This would have the same implications as a series of national monopolies. In some minerals, such as petroleum, producer nations have set up a cartel, slightly different from the usual concept of a cartel because it comprises government-owned corporations. What matters is whether the MNCs will find antisocial behavior of this type sufficiently rewarding and whether intergovernmental cooperation will be strong enough to discipline any such arrangement.[13]

Although the main appeal of MNCs is that they improve the allocation of global resources, they do take advantages of so-called tax havens. Tax havens are a means of escaping payment of taxes within the law and can best be described in terms of U.S. tax regulations. U.S. MNCs are allowed to defer payment of the taxes due on the profits of their foreign subsidiaries until the profits are actually remitted to the parent corporation (and foreign taxes paid are entered as a credit against U.S. taxes). Some countries, notably the Netherlands Antilles, allow foreign firms to establish foreign subsidiaries there without any payment of tax on the profits of those subsidiaries. Thus it becomes possible for an MNC to send profits to the tax haven instead of leaving them in the host country or repatriating them to the parent, and in this way the MNC avoids payment of taxes to Uncle Sam. The subsidiary can then make a profit by lending the funds to the parent company or some subsidiary at a market rate of interest and avoiding taxes altogether on the profits made. Another means of escaping taxes is through "manipulative transfer pricing." When an MNC transfers goods from one unit to another, it has to set a price for the goods sold in order that the selling subsidiary can compute its profit and the buying subsidiary its costs. If tax rates in the two countries are unequal, a manipulating MNC might arrange for all of the profit generated by the manufacture of the goods to be

---

[13] This problem is treated in Charles P. Kindleberger, *Multinational Excursions* (Cambridge, Mass.: M.I.T. Press, 1984), ch. 16 (written with Paul M. Goldberg).

attributed to the low-tax location. For example, if Country A has a tax rate on profits of 60 percent and the home country has a tax rate on profits of 40 percent, a sale of $1 million worth of parts from the subsidiary in Country A to the parent corporation made at the price that would hold for an unrelated firm might yield the subsidiary a profit of $50,000. Of that $50,000, only $20,000 would accrue to the MNC. However, if the goods were sold to the parent for the sum of $950,000, the subsidiary would make no profit and pay no tax to the government in Country A. The parent could cost the items at $1 million, and the profit of $50,000 would have been transferred to the parent at a saving of $10,000. Host governments are now much more sophisticated in identifying devices such as these and do not hesitate to tax the subsidiary appropriately. Another advantage of manipulative transfer pricing exists when the host country has foreign exchange controls that govern the repatriation of profits. Manipulative transfer pricing will help ease that constraint.

The final point at issue is the possibility that an MNC will invest abroad in order to escape from stringent environmental controls at home. If the host government places a higher value on additional income and a lower value on the cleanliness of its environment, the FDI is beneficial. Presumably, the existence of a tax on polluting activities reflects the scarcity of pollution assimilation capacity. If that is scarce in a rich country and plentiful in a poor country, the transfer of dirt-producing activites to a country where the benefit-cost ratio is much higher is a constructive act. The problem exists when the host is unaware of the damage that is likely to be done by the pollution activities and therefore imposes no tax out of ignorance rather than preference.

FOREIGN DIRECT INVESTMENT AND THE THEORY OF INTERNATIONAL TRADE

The essence of the efficiency gains of MNCS is the combination of internationally immobile factors of production (unskilled labor and land) with internationally mobile factors of production under the control of a large corporation. The theory developed in the first part of Chapter 5 provides a big step forward in understanding FDI. The emphasis on noncompetitive imports and differentiated goods identifies the two kinds of goods that are likely to lead to foreign direct investment. Explicit recognition of the role of the internationally mobile factors of production (physical and financial capital, human capital, and proprietary technology) provides insight into the way an MNC can achieve a competitive advantage even though it is operating in an alien country. The explicit introduction of transportation costs and barriers to trade (such as tariffs) indicates the reason that some MNCs will be forced to locate production facilities abroad. Simple H-O theory is not an adequate basis for understanding FDI.

But the so-called pragmatic theory needs supplementing by recognition of the importance of internalization economies and the trade-off between political risk of exposure and higher profit rates. International trade theory will only describe the role of what Dunning has called "location-specific factors" (see Table 19-3 in Chapter 19). Economies of internalization must also be capable of being separated into three kinds: straightforward vertically integrated economies of production, gains from integration of foreign production and home-country marketing and distribution activities, and gains from internalizing the use of proprietary technology within the same corporate entity.

If the pragmatic theory is to be seen in terms of money costs, there is the very important question of how MNCs will cost the factors of production that they transfer abroad. Capital will be set at the cost of capital plus some return for risk. Technological know-how might be priced at the price at which it would be leased to a trustworthy foreign corporation. Skilled workers would have to be costed at their opportunity cost to the corporation (at home) plus any special inducements needed to persuade the technicians to relocate. These might include special cost-of-living allowances and, if spouses and children were to accompany the technicians, the cost of schooling in private schools. Skilled technicians are also likely to need special insurance against increased risk, including both political uprising and terrorism as well as exposure to exotic diseases to which the technician has no immunity.

MNCs contribute to the spread of technology and know-how and increase global efficiency. MNCs make possible a combination of factors that could not otherwise be brought together. They also improve the efficiency of commercial intelligence. The traditional or H-O theory of international trade is set in long-run equilibrium and assumes that all business persons know the prices of goods and the cost of factors in all countries.[14] In practice, this is simply not true; business executives' knowledge of foreign countries can be quite limited. Tests have shown that people have "mental maps" that show an awareness of nearby phenomena in considerable detail (particularly in the industries and areas of direct concern to the individual). As the distance from the home base increases, the detailed knowledge is quickly reduced. A business person in New York has little knowledge of prices and conditions in Malaysia or Indonesia. But executives in MNCs have "home points" wherever the MNC has a subsidiary, and for an executive in a firm which subsidiaries in Bombay and São Paulo, information about conditions in India and Brazil will be much more precise. In addition, executives employed by MNCs

---

[14] The pragmatic theory, with its short-term focus, is less constrained, but any improvement in commercial intelligence is entirely extraneous to the theory.

have access to reliable information quite quickly from local managers. Under the umbrella of MNCs, international trade may in practice approach the idealized conditions subsumed in the traditional theory.

SUMMARY

The multinational corporate organizational form attempts to operate in a realm above simple nationalism. In some senses, this is socially beneficial because such actions will increase the efficiency of the global economy. In practice, the earth is fragmented into nation-states that seek to further their own narrower interests rather than the efficiency of the global economy. Contact between MNCs operating at the supranational level and national governments can cause friction and miscommunication. The sets of concerns can be antagonistic. The friction may be reduced by greater experience and greater awareness, but the potential adversary position will never be completely reconciled. It is important, therefore, that both host governments and MNC personnel work to increase their understanding of the other's point of view.

Bibliography

Bergsten, C. Fred, and Lawrence B. Krause, eds. *World Politics and International Economics*. Washington, D.C.: Brookings Institution, 1975.

Keohane, Robert O., and Van Doorn Ooms. "The Multinational Firm and International Regulation." in Bergsten and Krause, pp. 169–209.

Kindleberger, Charles P. *Multinational Excursions*. Cambridge, Mass.: M.I.T. Press, 1984.

Walter, Ingo. "A Guide to Social Responsibility of Multinational Enterprise." In *Social Responsibility and Accounting,* ed. Jules Backman. New York: New York University Press, 1975.

Questions

1. The whole problem of MNCs lies either in excessive economic power or in political domination of small countries. Comment.
2. If MNCs can switch production plans around on a global scale without concern for local conditions, they become a great political power in any single developing country. Explain.
3. Control over MNCs is unlikely because the MNCs are relying on market forces *and* because governments cannot allow their "corporate citizens" to be judged supranationally. Comment.
4. The best way for a developing country to control MNCs is to develop the capability to do so to its own advantage. World measures are unlikely to be effective. Explain.
5. How might a developing country control an MNC to ensure that it does not have any adverse effect on the local economy?

22

CONCLUSION

Interdependencies and the Future

This book has examined the many aspects of international economic involvement separately and sequentially. The analysis has been mainly "static," meaning that the analysis takes conditions as given and unchanging, and the evolution toward equilbrium and the constancy of that equilibrium position were assumed. It is the purpose of this chapter to integrate the separate aspects and to provide some awareness of how the analysis provided can be of use to practitioners in the real and inconstant world.

In economics, everything depends on everything else, so any change in any aspect of a problem will exert some effect on the ultimate (equilibrium) solution. In international economics, the likelihood of change is even greater than for a national economy. Change can take place in any country in the world and in the relationships between pairs of countries. Obviously, what matters is the magnitude of the change and the "closeness" of the change to the country in question. For example, anyone analyzing the United States' economy would be much more concerned with a small (externally oriented) change in a major trading partner such as Canada than with a large internal switch in policy in India or the USSR.

The international economic involvement of a country depends on five factors:

1. How different resource endowments lead to international trade and to gains from trade
2. The effects of commercial policies at home and abroad
3. The role of real exchange rates
4. Patterns of capital transfers and debt service (financial transfers)
5. The effects of multinational corporations (MNCs) on resource endowments and financial flows

All five forces are exerted in a setting provided by the existing international monetary system.

Figure 22-1 identifies the major interactions among the seven components of the global economic system. The solid lines indicate primary causal relationships, the dashed lines, relatively minor or feedback effects. As drawn, the pattern of trade is the major outcome of the various interactions, but the amount and direction of financial transfers (capital flows and debt service) can also be seen as an outcome of the existing system and such historical factors as the amount of earlier borrowing. The international financial system is shown as affecting the real rate of exchange

Figure 22-1
ECONOMIC INTERDEPENDENCIES

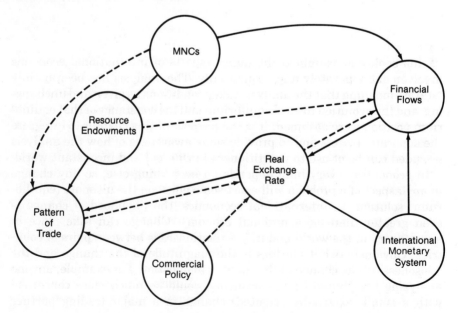

and the pattern of financial transfers. The role of the system on the real exchange rate is direct in the sense that international financial conditions and agreements limit the degree to which the real rate of exchange is allowed to respond to spontaneous economic events. Similarly, the international financial system affects the freedom of capital flows and in this way affects the rate of exchange indirectly. As the causal relationships in the figure show, the effects of the financial sectors (on the right-hand side) affect patterns of international trade mainly through their impact on the real rate of exchange.

The factors that concern the exchange of goods and services do react on the real rate of exchange, and MNCs also form a link between the financial sectors and the patterns of international trade in goods and services.

The figure does not permit any assessment of cyclical patterns of response to changes in the level of investment and unemployment. Much of the effect of the international monetary system on the real exchange rate is to be found in the degree to which the exchange rate is allowed to flex in response to economic conditions. The role of the international financial system is, then, deeply involved with short-run adjustment processes and balance-of-payments policies.

Change can take place in any of the sectors identified in the figure. The effects of any such change will take considerable periods of time to work themselves out fully. In the absence of any intervening change or disturbance, a good approach to the analysis of the global system under change is to assume that the economic system is essentially stable and that it will approach the new equilibrium gradually and steadily. The trick in policy formulation and in understanding the behavior of the economic system is to identify the new, ultimate equilbrium that is consonant with the new conditions and policies. Given the intricacies of the relationships (especially the multicountry dimensions), identification of the new equilibrium is not an easy undertaking, but the *direction* of change can usually be worked out with a fair degree of assurance. As the system approaches its new equilibrium, the analyst will have an ever more accurate concept of the ultimate equilibrium position.

The adjustment process is usually and reasonably considered to occur at a natural speed that is positively related to the "distance" between reality and the ultimate equilibrium. Thus a large shock or disturbance will bring about substantial dislocation and rapid adjustment at first, but the speed of adaptation to the new conditions will diminish with the passage of time. One of the goals of economic policy may be to slow down the dislocationary effect in the early stages of the adjustment process.

A system that is characterized by infrequent and minor disturbances and allows equilibrium to be approached quite closely before any new disturbance takes place can be called "tranquil." Such systems are easily analyzed, and policy usually consists merely of considering the desirable rate of change. When disturbances of substantial size follow hard upon each other so that the new equilibrium is shifted even before the system has begun to approach it at all closely, the system can be called "turbulent." In recent years, the global economic system has become turbulent. The Bretton Woods era ended with a bang as its abandonment released suppressed disturbances, and since the early 1970s the world has been bouncing from one disturbance to another. The oil-price shocks are the most obvious sources of disruption to an established economic order, but they were reinforced by the transfer of technology and capital to developing countries by MNCs and by the emergence of the NICs and the concomitant fast increase in the ability of the Third World to displace domestic production of labor-intensive goods in the industrialized countries. This combination generated a countervailing surge of protectionist sentiment in the industrialized North. The recent and still ongoing debt crisis together with the huge U.S. current deficit and the Japanese current surplus have compounded the problems facing international policymakers since the early 1970s.

Such conditions imply the need for a short-run approach to both analysis and policy formulation in turbulent times. This in turn requires an explicit recognition of the direction of change of the terms of trade in the absence of any policy measures taken to suppress the turbulence. If the speed of change is to be slowed, the financial implications of such a policy must be worked out and accommodated.

In a period of pronounced turbulence such as the world has recently undergone, it may not be possible to place a simple reliance on the ability of the system to reach the new long-run equilibrium unaided. Thought must be given to the short-run steps needed to facilitate the passage of adjustment. The long-term benefits are still desirable, and most of them are still available. These are the traditional gains from free trade and from freedom for capital movements. The potential availability of the maximum gains from the international sector must not be allowed to blind policymakers to the question of short-run adaptation (or vice versa).

In turbulent times, policymaking and analysis involve a certain amount of groping for a solution. If the world is not tidy, it is not reasonable to expect the policy solution to be tidy.

What of the future? One cannot foresee future tranquillity or turbulence. But the existence of strain in future economic international relations is almost certain. The turbulence of recent years leaves a great deal of adjustment still to be accomplished if the world is ever to achieve a satisfactory level of simple allocative efficiency. The potential for chronic unemployment, the hangover of the debt crisis, and North-South antagonism are all problems that will not disappear overnight.

Ideally, the system would return to a tranquil state, and the governments of the world would cooperate to eliminate the existing barriers to a liberal international trading system in much the same way as was done after World War II. This seems unlikely. There are far fewer admitted barriers in place, and these have become less transparent and are more deeply embedded in the fabric of the world's economy. Voters are less tolerant. The world does not have the same potential for economic growth with which to ease the pains of economic adaptation. Most important is a straightforward conflict between economic and political reality. It is fairly self-evident that the growth of MNCs and the integration of financial markets are, together with the existence of economies of scale and production sharing, pressing the world into a more unified economic system. At the same time, nationalist feelings are tending to favor smaller political units and less reliance on the global economy. The conflict between political desires and economic reality may be difficult to avoid. Certainly, it is unlikely to generate a world of simple tranquillity.

The world is going to continue to present interesting and difficult problems for the student of the international economy. Easy answers will probably tend to be as spurious in the future as they have been in the past. Markets will not solve the complexities, but only a courageous or foolhardy economist or political economist would think that all can be solved through intelligent foresight and policymaking.

Index